...ULTANTS

...h J. Bernabe
...tudies Consultant
...range Public Schools
...range, New Jersey

...Barnett
...tudies Consultant
...Texas

...ker Gibson
...te Professor of Political Science
...University
...tonio, Texas

Peter Janovsky
Dodge Vocational School
New York City, New York

Arthur L. Miller
Social Studies Consultant
Clayton Public Schools
Ballwin, Missouri

Gary Cole
Social Studies Consultant
Parkway Public Schools
Chesterfield, Missouri

CO

Ke
Soc
We
We

Ma
Soc
Wi

L.
Ass
Tri
San

Cit

CIVICS

Citizens and Society

Second Edition

Allan Kownslar
Terry Smart

Webster Division
McGraw-Hill Book Company
New York · St. Louis · Dallas · San Francisco
Auckland · Bogotá · Hamburg · Johannesburg
London · Madrid · Mexico · Montreal · New Delhi
Panama · Paris · São Paulo · Singapore
Sydney · Tokyo · Toronto

Allan O. Kownslar and Terry L. Smart are nationally known social-studies-curriculum specialists. **Allan O. Kownslar** received his undergraduate degree from Trinity University, San Antonio, Texas, and his doctorate from Carnegie-Mellon University, Pittsburgh, Pennsylvania. He taught social studies for fifteen years in public schools in San Antonio, Amherst, Massachusetts, and Pittsburgh. Since that time, Dr. Kownslar has authored or coauthored eleven social-studies programs and has written numerous articles on the teaching of social studies. He is currently on the faculty of Trinity University. **Terry L. Smart** received his undergraduate degree from Indiana University and his doctorate degree from the University of Kansas. He began his teaching career in the Houston, Texas, public schools and has served as a social-studies-curriculum consultant and specialist. Dr. Smart is the author of *Fundamentals of the American Free-Enterprise System,* a text for secondary schools, and he has written and produced several educational-television programs. He is currently on the faculty of Trinity University.

Acknowledgments for permission to reprint copyrighted materials appear on pages 564–566

Editorial Development: Bob Nirkind
Editing and Styling: Mary Ann Jones
Design Supervisor: Valerie Scarpa
Production Supervisor: Judith Tisdale

Photo Research: Ilene Cherna

Library of Congress Cataloging in Publication Data

Kownslar, Allan O.
    Civics: citizens and society.

    Includes index.
    Summary: A textbook discussing the rights and duties of citizenship within the political, legal, and economic systems of the United States.
    1. Civics—Juvenile literature. 2. United States—Politics and government—Juvenile literature. [1. Civics. 2. Citizenship. 3. United States—Politics and government] I. Smart, Terry L. II. Title.
JK274.K693 1983   320.473   81-20924
ISBN 0-07-035433-2   AACR2

1 2 3 4 5 6 7 8 9 10 VHVH 91 90 89 88 87 86 85 84 83 82

Contents

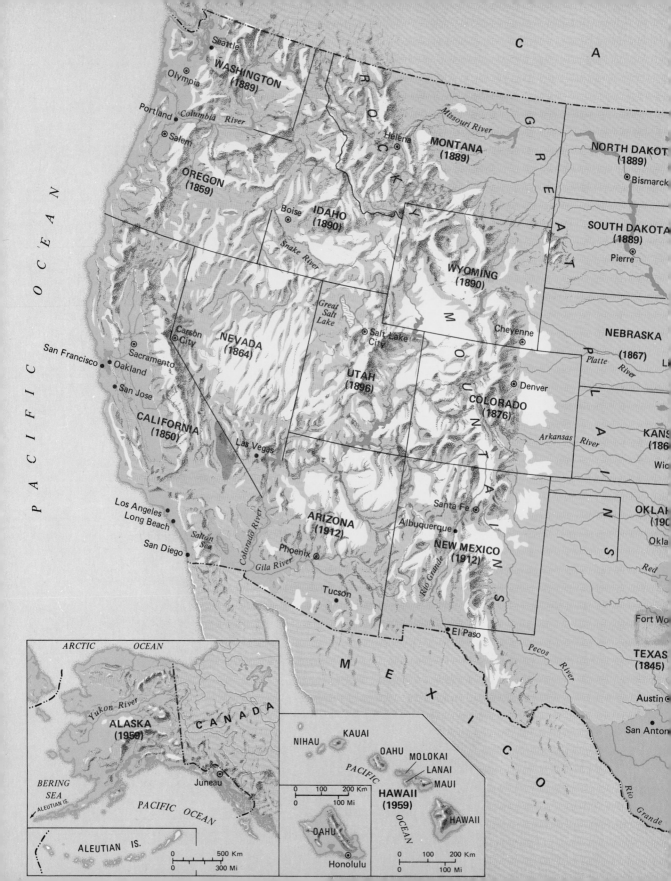

C A

WASHINGTON
(1889)

Seattle

Olympia

Portland
Columbia River

Salem

OREGON
(1859)

Helena

MONTANA
(1889)

Missouri River

NORTH DAKOT
(1889)

Bismarck

Boise

IDAHO
(1890)

Snake River

SOUTH DAKOTA
(1889)

Pierre

WYOMING
(1890)

Great
Salt
Lake

NEVADA
(1864)

Carson
City

San Francisco

Oakland

Sacramento

San Jose

CALIFORNIA
(1850)

Salt Lake
City

UTAH
(1896)

Cheyenne

NEBRASKA
(1867)

Platte River

Denver

COLORADO
(1876)

KANS
(186

Wic

Arkansas River

Las Vegas

Los Angeles
Long Beach

San Diego

*Salton
Sea*

Colorado River

Phoenix

ARIZONA
(1912)

Gila River

Tucson

Santa Fe

Albuquerque

NEW MEXICO
(1912)

Rio Grande

OKLAH
(190

Okla

Red

Fort Wo

El Paso

TEXAS
(1845)

Pecos River

M   E   X   I   C   O

Austin

San Anton

Rio Grande

PACIFIC OCEAN

ROCKY

GREAT

MOUNTAINS

PLAINS

ARCTIC OCEAN

Yukon River

ALASKA
(1959)

CANADA

Juneau

BERING
SEA

ALEUTIAN IS.

PACIFIC OCEAN

ALEUTIAN   IS.

0   500 Km

0   300 Mi

NIHAU

KAUAI

OAHU

MOLOKAI

LANAI

MAUI

PACIFIC

OCEAN

HAWAII
(1959)

OAHU

Honolulu

HAWAII

0   100   200 Km

0   100 Mi

0   100   200 Km

0   100 Mi

CANADA

Lake of the Woods

Lake Superior

St. Lawrence River

Ottawa

VERMONT (1791)

MAINE (1820)

Augusta

MINNESOTA (1858)

Minneapolis • St. Paul

WISCONSIN (1848)

Lake Huron

MICHIGAN (1837)

Lake Ontario

Montpelier

Portland

NEW HAMPSHIRE (1788)

Concord

Lake Michigan

Madison

Milwaukee

Lansing

Rochester

Albany

Boston

MASSACHUSETTS (1788)

Providence

RHODE ISLAND (1790)

IOWA (1846)

Chicago

Detroit

Buffalo

Lake Erie

Cleveland

Hartford

CONNECTICUT (1788)

Des Moines

Mississippi River

ILLINOIS (1818)

Toledo

Akron

OHIO (1803)

PENNSYLVANIA (1787)

Newark

New York

NEW JERSEY (1789)

Trenton

INDIANA (1816)

Columbus

Pittsburgh

Harrisburg

Philadelphia

Springfield

Indianapolis

Cincinnati

Baltimore

Dover

DELAWARE (1787)

WEST VIRGINIA (1863)

Annapolis

Washington, D.C.

MARYLAND (1788)

Missouri River

Kansas City

Jefferson City

St. Louis

Louisville

Frankfort

Ohio River

KENTUCKY (1792)

Charleston

VIRGINIA (1788)

Richmond

Norfolk

MISSOURI (1821)

Nashville

North Carolina (1789)

Raleigh

APPALACHIAN

TENNESSEE (1796)

Charlotte

ARKANSAS (1836)

Memphis

Columbia

SOUTH CAROLINA (1788)

Little Rock

Birmingham

Atlanta

Mississippi River

MISSISSIPPI (1817)

ALABAMA (1819)

GEORGIA (1788)

LOUISIANA (1812)

Jackson

Montgomery

Sabine R.

Baton Rouge

New Orleans

Tallahassee

Jacksonville

FLORIDA (1845)

Tampa

Lake Okeechobee

GULF OF MEXICO

Miami

ATLANTIC OCEAN

THE UNITED STATES

—··—··— International Boundary

———— State Boundary

———— Original Thirteen States

(1787) Year of Admission to Union

✵ National Capital

⊙ State Capital

0   100   200   300   400   500 Km

0   100   200   300 Mi

LIST OF MAPS, CHARTS, AND GRAPHS

Let's say you are walking along a street and you come to a traffic light. The light is red. What do you do?

You may think this is a silly question. Everyone knows that a red light means "stop." If the light is red, you wait until it changes to green. Then you go ahead.

But how do you know the meaning of the colors? If the light turns green and you cross the street, how can you be sure that cars will wait for you?

Traffic lights are so much a part of our everyday lives that we do not have to ask such questions. We know that stopping for red lights and proceeding on green lights is one of the rules of daily life.

Behind such everyday acts there are other questions: How are our rules made? How are they enforced? What part do we have in making and enforcing our rules? The answers to questions such as these are the concern of the first unit of this book. You will read about how people live together in groups. You will see how people learn the customs of their groups. You will learn how people make rules for themselves—in short, how people govern themselves. In particular, you will learn how we came to govern ourselves as we do.

unit

1

Learning about Citizenship

Chapter 1 People and Society

The most important thing to remember in studying civics is very simple. It is so simple that we sometimes forget it. We are surrounded by other people. We depend upon others and they depend upon us. Even when we try to set ourselves apart, we must take others into account.

Let's say, for example, that you like to be alone. You plan a hike by yourself into the mountains near your home. Your goal is very personal—to be alone, away from others. Yet your ability to do this depends on what other people do or have done. Is there any wilderness near you? Other people may have built farms or vacation homes near the trail. If there is wilderness, can you get to it? The wilderness may be owned by a timber company that has put up a fence to keep people out. Even if you are allowed in the area, will too many others have been there before you? The land may be a state or national park. The hiking trails may be overcrowded, ripped up by trail bikes, and littered with candy wrappers. If so, the area is hardly a wilderness anymore.

We are involved with other people, whether we want to be or not. What we do—even alone—is affected by other people. From the day we are born, other people touch our lives in almost everything we do.

It is not just other people who affect us. We affect them as well. Think of that hike in the wilderness. If you take a radio with you, you may spoil someone else's peace and quiet. If you leave litter, you will spoil the natural beauty of the area. You may have other effects as well.

You may buy hiking boots because you go hiking so often. You may buy a backpack to carry clothes and other gear. By buying these things, you and other hikers help to support businesses. You help make jobs for boot makers, tent stitchers, salespeople, and many others. You will probably take food on your trip. Did you buy it or grow it yourself? Even if you grew it yourself, you probably bought seeds or fertilizer from someone else. That helped make more jobs for others.

We live in a complex modern country. Many jobs are specialized. Every time we buy something, we are aware of how much we depend on others and how much they depend on us. But even in countries with fewer modern businesses and industries, people depend on other people. Even if a family grows almost all of its own food on a plot of land, it is still not independent. The rules of the place where the family lives decide whether or not the family farms the land on shares, or rents it, or owns it. These rules have been worked out by many people, often over many centuries.

This chapter will look at some of the ways in which people are connected to each other. In the first half of the chapter, you will look at how people all over the world live together. In the second half, you will look at one country—the United States. Who are the people of the United States? Where do they live? What do they have in common? How do they differ?

Words to Know

society —— the largest group of people who share a common way of life

culture —— the way of life shared by a society

values —— a group's beliefs about what is right or proper

norms —— the rules of behavior of a society or a group

role —— a special behavior expected from someone in a given position

subculture —— the way of life of a group within a larger society

socialization —— the day-by-day process by which a person learns the skills, values, and norms of a society or a group

peers —— one's equals in a society

adolescence —— the period between childhood and adulthood—in our society, roughly the same as the teenage years

The People Connection

People live together in groups. This "people connection" shapes our lives from our first day to our last. Human groups come in many sizes. Each of us is part of many groups. We are born into a family, and that family is part of a group of other families called a *community*. The community may be a city or a neighborhood. That community, in turn, is part of a still larger community—for example, a state or a nation. There are still other groups that overlap with these. You belong to a group made up of all the students in your school. You belong to a group called *teenagers*. You belong to a group made up of others of your sex. You are part of a group made up of others of the same race or national background. You belong to a group made up of others whose family incomes are like yours. You may also be a member of formal groups, such as religious organizations or clubs.

Groups help to distinguish us from other people. Groups can also help to unite us with others. Other students in your class may be a different sex from you, may speak with a different accent, or may be more or less serious about learning. Yet they have something in common with you. You are all part of one group that unites you over and above all your differences. You are all part of the same society—the society made up of all the people living in the United States.

Living in Societies

A society is the largest group of people who share a common way of life. This does

Teenagers are both a group and a part of a larger group—the group is people their own age, and the larger group is the community in which they live.

not mean that all the people in a society live in exactly the same way. It does mean that they do generally agree on some things. For example, the people of the United States share a government. They share a belief in freedom and equality. They share a system of laws. They share a number of habits and ways of doing things. The people of China make up a different society. They have a system of government which is different than ours. They share different outlooks and ways of doing things.

Societies do not always have the same boundaries as nations. There may be more than one society in a nation. For example, the people living in the Sudan in Africa do not share a single society. Arab Moslems there live one way, and blacks who are not

Moslems live another way. There is little common feeling among them. Although the two groups share a common country, they do not share a way of life. They are two different societies.

Societies and Cultures The glue that holds a society together is the common way of life shared by people within the society. This way of life is made up of many things—beliefs held in common, knowledge shared in common, objects known to all, and common ways of doing things. Together, these things make up the **culture** of a society.

Do not confuse this use of the word *culture* with another meaning of the term. "Culture," to many people, means Mozart, Shakespeare, and museums. Culture as a way of life is a much broader term. The beat of rock music is part of our culture. The cheering at a football game is part of our culture. The skyscrapers of Chicago and the barns of Pennsylvania are also part of our culture. They make up the "American way of life." All those who share that way of life belong to the same society.

Features Common to All Societies

Each society has its own way of life that sets it apart from other societies. But all societies do share some features. Indeed, some patterns are seen over and over in different societies. Each society must face the same problems, even though the *answers* to those problems will differ from one society to the next. The patterns of relationships are the same in all societies. Now we will discuss four features common to all societies:

Exchange Let's say that Lisa Rodriguez owns a lawnmower. She takes it from house to house and offers to mow people's lawns. She sets a price, depending on the size of the lawn and the time it takes to mow it. Lisa's business involves an exchange. She offers a service. In return, she asks for a payment. An exchange occurs when one person or group assists another and each side gains something.

Lisa's lawnmowing is an exchange that involves money. Some exchanges involve other things. Perhaps Lisa mows the lawn of an elderly neighbor for free because she knows he cannot pay her. She gets no money or goods as a reward. She does get an emotional reward—the satisfaction of having performed a good deed. Or Lisa may wave to another neighbor every time she sees her. The neighbor smiles and waves back. In this case, an exchange is taking place that involves no goods. There are only emotional rewards. It is still an exchange. Such exchanges help bind together the society in which Lisa and her neighbors live.

Cooperation Let's say that Sally and Jim Brady and some of their friends like to play tennis. There are no courts near their home, but on the corner there is an empty lot. The lot is covered with weeds and littered with broken bottles. After getting permission from the owner of the lot, the young people pitch in to clean it up. They level it off, plant grass, and put up a tennis court. Now they have a place to play, thanks to their cooperation.

Many acts in our society are the result of cooperation. Sometimes the cooperation is given freely, as in our example. At other

FEATURES COMMON TO ALL SOCIETIES

Exchange   Cooperation   Competition   Conflict

Whether they take place on a football field, in school, or at home, cooperation and competition are features of life common to all societies.

times cooperation may be ordered by someone in command. For example, a teacher may divide a class into four parts and direct each group to work together on preparing a report.

Those who cooperate do so in order to share in a reward or a benefit. In our first example, the reward was a place to play tennis. In the second example, the rewards were increased knowledge and good grades on their report card.

Competition The reverse of cooperation is competition. When two or more people or groups compete, they each try to get complete control of a reward or a benefit. For example, the tennis players cooperated to set up a court, but when they play tennis, they compete. Only one player or one pair of players can win each match. The teacher in our example set up a network of cooperation. But the teacher might also have each of the four classroom groups compete against the others by telling the groups that the best report would win a

prize. The result would be competition among the four groups.

Like cooperation, competition follows certain rules. Those rules are set by each society in its own way. For example, in a country such as the United States, many companies compete in making and selling the same product—automobiles. But they compete according to rules set down by the society. Certain practices are not allowed. An automobile company that breaks the rules is punished.

Conflict Competition is carried on for limited goals. It is fairly easy to control. Conflict disrupts. It spills beyond limited goals. It is more hostile.

Let's consider an example. A soccer match shows competition. It is played according to clear rules. The goal is a limited one: scoring more points than the other team. If a riot between fans of the two teams breaks out during the match, that is an example of conflict. There are no rules. The fans on each side may use fists, feet, chains, clubs. Their goal is to overpower the other side's fans, to "teach them a lesson."

An extreme example of conflict is war. War is an attempt by one nation to overpower another nation, to destroy or defeat it.

Each society makes rules for settling conflicts. Without such rules, societies would break apart. There are many different ways of settling conflicts. Take the soccer riot, for instance. In one society, unarmed police might form a human chain and push the rioters off the field. In another, police with clubs might swing into action. In still another, armed troops might fire into the crowd.

Values and Norms

We said earlier that each society has a common way of life, or culture. The answers that society has to the problems of exchange, cooperation, competition, and conflict are part of its culture. But the culture is more than this. It includes a set of beliefs about what is right, or proper. These beliefs make up the culture's **values.**

Our society believes that it is right for people to own property. To use someone's property without permission is to commit a crime. Other societies feel that property belongs to the society as a whole. In such societies, a person who claimed he or she was the single owner of a piece of land would not be acting properly.

Which is more important, progress or tradition? Our society favors progress. Labor-saving inventions are welcomed, even though they may put some people out of work. In some other societies, progress is frowned upon. Old ways of doing things are the best. Inventions that would change ways of doing things would be rejected.

Should everyone be treated equally? Our society says "yes." For example, the Constitution says that all persons should have "equal protection under the laws."

Yet, in the past, who was more likely to get a traffic ticket, a business executive in a limousine or a teenager in a "souped-up" sports car? Who was more likely to get a high-paying job, a man or a woman, a white or a black? Unfair treatment on the basis of class, race, and sex existed side-by-side with the belief in equality for all.

Of course, our society is not the only one that has clashes between values and practices. No society lives up to *all* of its values all of the time any more than one person always lives up to his or her values. The values are important because they serve as a guide for the society.

Values are the principles by which a society lives. The society translates values into rules of behavior called **norms.** These norms tell people how they should act. They also give people an idea of how they can expect others to act. Those who follow the norms are considered "normal" and are accepted by the society. Those who do not follow the norms are avoided.

Some norms deal with the "do's and don'ts" of social relationships. For example, when introduced to another person we do shake hands. We do wear shoes to a formal dinner. We do address an elderly woman differently from a young girl. We do not stir tea with our fingers. This sort of norm is based upon customs and habits. A person will not be arrested for going barefoot to a fancy banquet. But people will frown or think the person is rude. Usually that is enough to make a group member obey a norm.

Some norms do have greater force behind them. For example, it is a social norm that people should obey traffic signals. It is also a law—that is, a norm that is enforced by the government. If a person does not obey traffic signals, that person may be punished by the courts.

The norms mentioned above apply to everyone in the society. Some norms, though, apply only to certain persons who

Native Americans are one of many subcultures—groups with their own values and norms—found within our society.

fill certain **roles.** A role is a special behavior expected from someone in a given position. For example, as a student you have one role. Your teacher has a different role. The rules that govern you are different from the rules that govern the teacher. Likewise, the host at a party is expected to act differently from a guest. In these cases, the norms or rules are different for different people.

So far we have been talking about values and norms that are shared by a whole society. But there are groups within societies. These groups share most of the values and norms of the whole society. They also have some values and norms of their own. We use the term **subculture** to describe the way of life of such a group.

Many people speak of a teenage subculture. When teenagers get together, they often seem to have their own rules of behavior. For example, teenagers have a vocabulary that puzzles many adults.

Many other subcultures can also be found in the United States. They may be shared by groups of people who have the same job (jazz musicians, physicians), racial or national groups (blacks, Italian Americans, Chicanos), and even groups of people from the same area (Appalachia, the West). In a society as large as that of the United States, it is not surprising to find many norms and values in many different subcultures.

Socialization

How do people learn the values and norms of their society? They are not born knowing them. The newborn baby is helpless and must entirely depend on others. This new member of society must learn all the skills, values, and norms that he or she needs to have to live in that society. All this day-to-day learning prepares a person to take his or her place in society. We call this process **socialization.**

Discovery of Self The first step in socialization is the discovery of self. The newborn baby has no way of knowing that the world is divided into "self" and "others." The baby learns this slowly. The baby cries when it feels hunger or when it is wet. Then it finds that it can make this sound of crying stop and start. It notices that crying brings attention. Someone comes to see what the crying is about. That someone is an "other."

As the child grows, it develops an image, or picture, of itself. There is a physical self, made up of fingers that wiggle and feet that kick. There is also a social self, the image the child forms as a result of dealings with others. By noticing which actions are approved by others and which are disapproved, the child slowly learns the values and norms of the society.

Agents of Socialization

Many people and groups play major roles in socialization. It is these "others" that we look to for our social reflection.

The Family The family plays the first part in socialization. Even before a baby learns to talk, it forms a self-image based upon how its family reacts to it. Do people like me? Can I trust people? Am I good? Children learn the answers to these questions by what their families *do,* not by what they *say.*

Our society offers a wide range of child-rearing practices. Some parents expect strict obedience from their children. If a child misbehaves, they scold or punish the child. Other parents are freer with their children. If a child misbehaves, they explain why such behavior is unacceptable. They

The school, from kindergarten through college, is the formal agent used by society to socialize young people.

To be accepted by one's peers is an important part in an adolescent's socialization. This process occurs not only in the classroom, but also on the playing field.

do not threaten or scold the child. Still other parents are quite permissive. They rarely correct a child, even for behavior that annoys or harms someone.

Strictness and permissiveness are part of a family's efforts to socialize a child. Much socialization, though, is unplanned. The child watches its parents in their everyday actions. How does a man act? How does a woman act? Does a parent say one thing and then do another? When, if ever, is it all right to tell a lie? When is it all right to get angry? When should anger be hidden? This learning goes on all the time. Slowly, the child learns what society expects of it, and what it can expect from society.

Peers and Play Groups As children grow older, they begin to have more contact with other children their own age. The toddler plays in a sandbox with another toddler from down the street. The first grader goes to school with other first graders. These are the child's **peers,** or equals. They are another important group in the child's socialization. To be accepted by society, a person must be accepted by his or her peers.

The toddler has to learn to play with others of the same age. One early lesson is when to hold tight to a toy and when to share it. The child learns about fighting and about following the rules. The lessons grow more complex as the child grows up.

At times, conflicts arise between family and peers. "Mom wants me to wear my hair short, but all the other kids wear theirs long." "Dad says I'm too young to date, but Sam and Mary and Jim and Florence go out on dates all the time." These conflicts create pressure on the individual. Each person must learn to balance the pressures of the different agents of socialization.

The family plays the first major role in the long process of socialization. Strictness and permissiveness play an active part in the family's efforts to socialize a child, and the result often determines the child's outlook on life.

The School The formal agent that society uses to socialize young people is the school. The school passes on knowledge that will help the child to take part in society. But facts are only a small part of what a school teaches. The school also teaches values: patriotism, good citizenship, morality. It also gives students first-hand practice in dealing with a large organization. Thus, schools teach skills that will help a person deal with other organizations in society—an employer, for example, or the government.

Not all the teaching that goes on in schools is done by the teachers. Peer groups also play a part in school. Students may learn one lesson in a classroom and another in the hallways. Once again, each person must choose between conflicting values.

Adolescence

Societies mark a special time during which an individual passes from childhood to adulthood. In some societies, a person's passage to adulthood takes place rather early. Special ceremonies may mark the passage to adulthood. The person is then a member of the adult world. In our society, the passage is drawn out over several years. We call this time **adolescence.** Our society does not need adolescents in the work force. They have time to learn how to be adults.

During adolescence, the peer group takes on special importance. We need to be accepted by others of our own age. Sometimes we may have to choose between peer groups. We look to the chosen peer group to see how we should act and what we should think. There is a great deal of pressure to do what the group does. There are other pressures too. Each of us must learn to be our own person at the same time that we are seeking to be accepted by others.

By the time they reach adulthood, most people know the values and norms of the society as a whole. They know what is acceptable and what is not acceptable.

They are also part of a peer group to which they look for approval and support. Perhaps they also share a subculture. In any case, they probably have a picture of themselves and their place in society. Socialization continues, though, as long as a person lives. One learns new roles and new values as one grows older. The roles of parent and employee bring with them new values. Later, one learns that society expects different things from older people. As long as life goes on, so does socialization.

REVIEW
---

1. What is a society?
2. What is the difference between a value and a norm?
3. List three examples of subcultures in the United States.
4. Name three agents of socialization.
5. Why is adolescence an important period in a person's socialization?

Words to Know

urban area —— an area with at least one town of 2,500 or more
suburb —— an urban area that is near a large city and largely dependent upon the city for jobs and services
rural area —— an area with a town population of fewer than 2,500
alien —— someone who lives in a country but is not a citizen
naturalization —— the process by which an alien becomes a citizen
ethnic group —— a group of people who have a common race, religion, or national origin
minority —— a group within a society that differs in important ways—appearance, subculture, values—from most members of that society and is therefore considered to be "different"

prejudice —— an emotional belief that members of a certain group are unequal, a prejudgment
discrimination —— the act of treating a person or a group differently from other people

The United States— A Complicated Society

Our society is as complicated as it is huge. It is made up of 226 million people, from the rocky coast of Maine, across the dry plains of the Dakotas, to the mountainous West, snowy Alaska, and balmy Hawaii. The nation's population today is fifty-eight times what it was when George Washington became our first president. This society includes professors and sharecroppers, Jews and Protestants, bookies and bankers, priests and peapickers. All members of the society share a common culture. But because the society is so huge, it contains people with many different subcultures, values, and norms.

Where the People Live

Some subcultures are defined by the places where people live. People in large cities have their own set of values and way of living that are not shared by other people in the United States. Likewise, people in rural areas have *their* own sets of values and norms.

Urban Areas Three out of four people in the United States live in **urban areas.** These are areas with at least one town with a population of 2,500 or more. In larger cities, people live close together. They often come from many different backgrounds. They perform many different jobs. Many of their contacts are with strangers

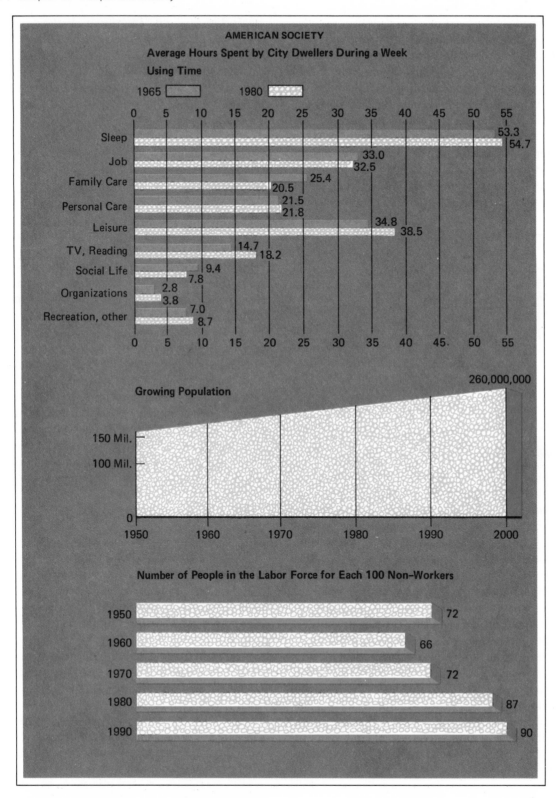

AMERICAN SOCIETY

Average Hours Spent by City Dwellers During a Week Using Time

1965 ☐   1980 ▦

Category	1965	1980
Sleep	53.3	54.7
Job	33.0	32.5
Family Care	25.4	20.5
Personal Care	21.5	21.8
Leisure	34.8	38.5
TV, Reading	14.7	18.2
Social Life	9.4	7.8
Organizations	2.8	3.8
Recreation, other	7.0	8.7

Growing Population

260,000,000

150 Mil.
100 Mil.
0

1950   1960   1970   1980   1990   2000

Number of People in the Labor Force for Each 100 Non-Workers

Year	Number
1950	72
1960	66
1970	72
1980	87
1990	90

and other people they do not know well. Urban people often depend on formal methods to enforce social norms—police action, for example.

Suburbs A suburb is an urban area that is near a large city and largely depends upon the city for jobs and services. Suburbs share many features of large cities. Yet in some ways they are more like rural areas. For example, people are not packed as closely together in suburbs as they are in cities. A suburb is more likely to have one major ethnic or economic group. People are more likely to know their neighbors personally. They recognize the people they see on the street. But people in the suburbs depend on the police to enforce social norms, especially when the suburb is near a large city.

Rural Areas One out of four people in the United States lives in a **rural area**— a place of fewer than 2,500. Their lives are very different from the lives of citydwellers. Homes are more spread out—perhaps scattered across the countryside, perhaps side-by-side in towns or villages. People tend to have similar backgrounds. They have about the same income. The range of jobs is more limited. People know most of their neighbors, or at least know something about them. Social norms are often enforced informally. The risk of gossip helps people behave by the norms. An unruly child can often be handled by parents rather than by the police.

Population Shifts At one time, almost everyone in the United States lived in rural areas. As the nation grew, people moved into cities. The cities grew. Now another trend is taking place. People have been moving out of the large cities into the suburbs. Since 1960, the population of many large cities has declined. The areas around cities—called metropolitan areas—continue to grow.

Another change has also been taking place. When the United States was founded in 1776, most people lived along the Eastern seaboard. This is no longer true. The population has spread across the entire continent—from the Atlantic Ocean to the Pacific Ocean—and the population is still spreading. A census is taken every 10 years to find out where people live. The last census showed that people had been moving away from the Northeast and into the South and the West. Among the fastest-growing states were Arizona, Texas, California, and Oklahoma.

Who the People Are

Some of the subcultures within United States society are based on national origin or race. These groups may have special ways of dressing, cooking, speaking, or raising children. These groups add to the richness of United States society.

Natives and Immigrants As a country, the United States is a little over 200 years old. Settlers from Europe lived in this land for hundreds of years before the nation was formed. But still other people lived here for thousands of years before the settlers came from Europe. These Native Americans were the people who met Columbus in 1492. He mistakenly called them Indians. The meeting was quickly followed by mistreatment by the Europeans. This mistreatment continued as settlers and pioneers, moving west, forced Native Americans off their land.

The Native Americans are today only a small part of the population of their own homeland. The last census counted some 1,362,000. Most of them live on lands set aside for them by law or treaty. Today they are among the poorest United States citizens, with high death rates and low levels of education. In recent years, however, Native American groups have been fighting for and winning their rights. They stress group pride and demand better treatment from their society.

A person who immigrates to the United States from a foreign country may become a citizen by meeting certain requirements. These requirements including passing a test on the United States Constitution. The last step in the process is taking an oath of allegiance to the United States.

There are other Americans who are called natives. A native United States citizen is a person who was born on United States soil or who was born abroad to a parent or parents who are United States citizens. About 96 percent of the people in the United States are native citizens. The remaining 4 percent (about 9 million people) were born as citizens of another country. They came to the United States as immigrants.

About half of the immigrants in the United States have become United States citizens. Those people who are not citizens are known as **aliens.** Aliens who wish to become citizens must live here at least 5 years. They must also meet certain requirements set down by United States law. For example, they must know how to read and write. If they meet all the requirements, they may become United States citizens through the process of **naturalization.** The final step in this process is taking an oath of allegiance to the United States.

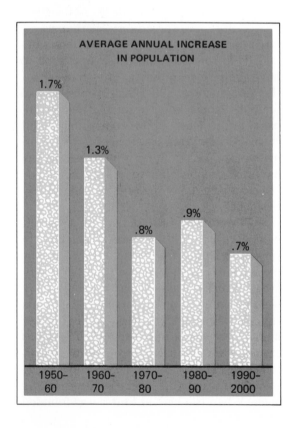

AVERAGE ANNUAL INCREASE IN POPULATION

1.7% 1950–60
1.3% 1960–70
.8% 1970–80
.9% 1980–90
.7% 1990–2000

At one time, immigration was a major source of new Americans. The years from the 1840s to the 1920s were times of high immigration. Many cities swelled with immigrants. The newcomers often lived in slums and worked for low wages in factories. Many had to face poor treatment by native citizens. The immigrants kept many of their old ways, and so added an international touch to many cities. Their influence can still be seen in areas such as New York's Chinatown and Little Italy.

Whites and Nonwhites Seven out of eight people in the United States are white. The backgrounds of these people vary widely. They include both native citizens and immigrants. There are people whose ancestors came from English-speaking and non-English-speaking countries. There are Protestants, Roman Catholics, Jews, and members of many other religions.

About one out of eight people in the United States are nonwhites. The largest part of these (11.7 percent) are black. Other racial groups include Native Americans and Asian Americans.

Blacks Blacks are the largest racial minority in the United States. There are some 26 million blacks. Most of these people are descended from Africans who were brought here as slaves. Although slavery was abolished in 1865, its aftereffects still haunt the nation. Only since the 1950s have large numbers of blacks entered the mainstream of United States society. Legal barriers to equality are fewer today, but many social barriers remain. Racism continues to interfere with black/white relations in many parts of the nation. Often, the demands of black people for full equality come up against the resistance of whites.

In recent decades, many blacks moved out of the rural South into industrial cities to look for good jobs. But some blacks are now returning to the South. They are seeking their roots in what was once the heartland of slavery. A black pride movement has emphasized the strengths of their ways of life.

Ethnic Groups White people in the United States have had a renewed pride in their own backgrounds in recent years. This pride has centered on **ethnic groups**— groups of people who have a common race, religion, or national background. White ethnic groups include Italian Americans, Polish Americans, Irish Americans, Spanish Americans, Jews, German Americans, Scandinavian Americans, and many others. Each group is descended from immigrants. Some of these immigrants may have come to America in colonial days. Others arrived more recently.

The feeling of ethnic solidarity is stronger among some white ethnic groups than among others. Some people may pay little attention to their own ethnic back-

A renewed pride in one's racial, religious, or national background is now a common feature of ethnic groups.

Parades are a favorite way for ethnic groups—such as the Chinese in this picture—to get together and exhibit their ancestral heritage.

ground. They prefer to think of themselves as plain United States citizens. But others feel themselves to be rooted in a particular ethnic past. They draw strength from old traditions. They enjoy the customs that give their group its special place in this country. The largest white ethnic groups are British Americans (32.7 million), German Americans (28.3 million), Irish Americans (18.2 million), Spanish Americans (14.6 million), and Italian Americans (9.7 million).

Spanish Americans Spanish-speaking Americans from many countries make up a large minority. There are over 5 million Mexican Americans, or Chicanos, mostly in the Southwest. Over 1.5 million Puerto Ricans live along the east coast, mostly in New York City. Puerto Rico, an island in the Caribbean, is a part of the United States. Its residents are United States citizens by birth. In addition, many people from other Latin-American countries have come to the United States.

Asian Americans Over 3 million Asian Americans live in the United States. About 700,000 of them are of Japanese ancestry and 806,027 of Chinese ancestry. Most Asian Americans live along the west coast and in Hawaii. There are also many Asian Americans in New York City and Chicago.

REVIEW
---

1. In which type of community do the largest percentage of people in the United States live, urban areas or rural areas?
2. What does an immigrant have to do to become a United States citizen?
3. Which of the following ethnic groups are white and which are nonwhite: Irish Americans, Jews, Spanish Americans, Japanese Americans, Scandinavian Americans?
4. Where do most Asian Americans live?
5. What, if anything, do you think should be done to help various groups that have suffered from prejudice and discrimination during the course of the history of the United States?

Norwegian Americans are one of many ethnic groups who enjoy dressing in the native costumes of their homeland and displaying their national pride.

Prejudice and Discrimination

United States society contains many groups known as minorities. Some, such as blacks and Orientals, are racial minorities. Some, such as Italian Americans and Jews, are ethnic minorities. A **minority** is a group that differs in obvious ways—appearance, subculture, values—from the majority of members of a society.

Minorities are often targets for prejudice and discrimination. **Prejudice** is an emotional belief that members of a certain group are unequal. Prejudice is based on feelings. It is not based on facts. A person who is prejudiced deals with people as "typical" members of a group rather than as individuals.

Discrimination is the act of treating a person or a group differently from other people. If a restaurant owner serves meals to all people except blacks and Chicanos, then the owner is discriminating against blacks and Chicanos. If a club refuses to accept members with Italian-sounding names, it is discriminating against people of Italian origin.

Prejudice and discrimination are found all over the world. They are both serious problems in the United States. We speak about the evils of prejudice. We have passed laws forbidding some types of discrimination—such as a restaurant owner's refusing to serve a member of a minority group. But prejudice remains. Laws against discrimination are sometimes poorly enforced.

The United States takes pride in its image as a "melting pot" of different racial and ethnic groups and as a source of refuge for immigrants. But we have not yet succeeded in working out conflicts among the groups that make up our diverse society.

How the United States Works

Why People Work

People work because they have to. They work to survive. At one time, the relationship between work and survival was much closer. In prehistoric times, every person was needed to provide food and shelter. People lived in small groups then. Such groups could support only a few people who were too sick or too old to work. There was not enough to go around unless everyone produced.

Now, with the aid of machines, people are able to produce much more than they need for themselves. We can now support many people who are ill or unable to work. In fact, we may have to. There are now more people than there are jobs.

Throughout this book, the "How the United States Works" sections will focus on some jobs that keep our country running. Some of these jobs are high-paying. Others pay less well. The amount of training needed for these jobs varies too. Some require special training. Some require high school diplomas. Others are open only to college graduates.

In spite of their many differences, these jobs do share one common factor: They are all a part of the huge, complex machine that is the United States. They each play a role in helping the society run smoothly.

Reading About . . .

People and Places

The place where people live often shapes their lives. In this country, most people live in urban areas. There are different ways of life in any urban area. The following short readings look at several sides of urban life:

As you read, think about the following:

- What do the people in these readings have in common?
- What sets the people apart from each other?

Apartment House
by Gerald Raftery

A filing-cabinet of human lives
Where people swarm like bees in
  tunneled hives,
Each to his own cell in the towered
  comb,
Identical and cramped—we call it home.

Commuter
by E. B. White

Commuter—one who spends his life
In riding to and from his wife;
A man who shaves and takes a train
And then rides back to shave again.

People
by Lois Lenski

Tall people, short people
Thin people, fat,
Lady so dainty
Wearing a hat,
Straight people, dumpy people
Men dressed in brown;
Baby in a buggy—
These make a town.

chapter
Review

Fact Review

1. Exchange, cooperation, competition, and conflict are common to all societies. For each of the following, tell which feature is represented:

a. One person stands on another's back to reach apples in a tree.
b. One child trades marbles for another child's jacks.
c. Violence breaks out in a labor dispute.

d. A runner receives a blue ribbon for winning a race.
2. Subcultures often have values and norms that are not shared by the rest of a society. Name a value or a norm of the teenage subculture that is not shared by the rest of the United States society.
3. Give examples of unplanned socialization in the family and in school.
4. How might the subculture of people in large cities differ from that of people in rural areas? Give two examples.
5. Into what sections of the United States are most people moving?
6. Which of the following groups makes up the largest ethnic minority in the United States today: blacks, Indians, Italian Americans, or British Americans?
7. Which do you think is the greater problem, prejudice or discrimination? Explain.
8. Do you think that the goal of abolishing all discrimination is possible? Explain.

Developing Your Vocabulary

1. Explain the difference between the words in the following pairs:
   a. society and culture
   b. norms and laws
   c. racial minorities and ethnic minorities
   d. prejudice and discrimination
2. In what way is a subculture like a culture? In what way is it different?

Developing Your Reading Skills

Read the following paragraph and then answer the questions that follow:

Many groups within United States society have their own subculture that sets them apart from other people. Sometimes a special way of talking is part of a subculture. For example, teenagers and jazz musicians each have their own slang that many other people do not understand. Sometimes a subculture involves special ways of cooking. There are Jewish, Italian American, and Japanese American food specialties. Subcultures may also involve distinct beliefs, such as the Amish belief that people should live simply.

1. Which of the following do you think is the main idea, or point, of this paragraph?
   a. Teenagers, jazz musicians, and the Amish all have their own subcultures.
   b. Special foods are a part of many subcultures.
   c. Many subcultures can be found in the United States.
   d. A subculture is made up of special ways of speaking, cooking, and believing.
2. Why did you select either *a, b, c,* or *d* above?

Developing Your Writing Skills— Forming and Supporting an Opinion

In this chapter, you have seen certain features of United States society. The people of our nation share a common culture that we call "the American way of life." But there are also many separate subcultures within our society, each with its own set of values and norms. Now consider the following questions:

Forming an opinion
1. In what ways do these various subcultures contribute to United States society?
2. In what ways do they cause problems?

Supporting an opinion
After thinking about these questions, write your thoughts down in paragraph form on a separate sheet of paper. Begin your paragraph with the *topic sentence* given. It tells what the paragraph is about. Choose one of the two versions of the topic sentence. Then continue your paragraph with evidence or arguments that support your topic sentence.

Your topic sentence
Your supporting evidence or arguments
I think the United States would be better off if it had (many/no) separate subcultures. _____
_____
_____
_____

YOUR GOVERNMENT & ITS HISTORY

The American People—Past and Present

In this chapter, you have examined some of the characteristics of the American people, past and present. Many individuals have written about our people. One such writer was J. Hector St. John de Crevecoeur (krev KOER). He was a Frenchman who came to this country before the American Revolution in 1776. De Crevecoeur traveled some in the colonies and, for a time, lived on a farm in New York before returning to France in 1790.

While de Crevecoeur lived in America, he wrote about its people. His writings were published in 1782 as *Letters from an American Farmer*. In his book, he had this to say:

The visitor to America has arrived on a new continent. A modern society offers itself to his view, different from what he had seen before. It is not composed, as in Europe, of great lords who possess everything and of a herd of people who have nothing. Here are no very rich or royal families, no courts, no kings, no bishops, no invisible power giving to a few a very visible one; no great manufacturers employing thousands, no great luxuries. The rich and the poor are not so far removed from each other here as they are in Europe. With the exception of a few towns, we are all workers of the earth. . . . We are a people of farmers, scattered over an immense territory. . . . We are all filled with the spirit of work . . . because each person works for himself. If a visitor travels through our rural areas, he sees not the hostile castle and the haughty mansion, contrasted with the clay-built hut and the miserable cabin, where people dwell in terrible poverty. . . . The meaning of our log houses is a dry and comfortable dwelling. Lawyer and merchant are the fairest titles our towns give. . . . We have no princes for whom we toil, starve, and bleed. We are the most perfect society in the world. Here man is free as he should be. . . . In this great American land, the poor of Europe have by some means met together. Formerly, they were not numbered in any lists of their country, except in those of the poor. Here they rank as citizens. . . .

Americans are the western pilgrims, who are carrying along with them that great mass of arts, sciences, energy, and love of work that began long ago in the east. . . . The Americans were once scattered all over Europe. Here, they are incorporated into one of the finest systems of population that has ever appeared. The American should, therefore, love this country much better than that in which either he or his forefathers were born. Here, the rewards of his work follow with equal steps the progress of his labor. . . . The American is a new man who acts on new principles; he must, therefore, consider new ideas, and form new opinions. This is an American.

According to the 1790 census, the Americans de Crevecoeur wrote about numbered 3,929,000. By 1860, that population had grown to 31,513,000. In 1860, Americans who lived in urban areas numbered 6,216,518, and 25,226,803 lived in rural areas. Most living in rural areas made a living by farming.

By 1980, the population of the United States had increased to 226,504,825. Most people were living in urban areas, and fewer than 5 percent farmed for a living.

The increase in population from 1790 to 1980 was due to several factors. First, there was a rising birthrate in America. Second, as the United States expanded in territory, the people already living in those territories became Americans. Third, immigration brought many new people to this country. It is estimated that about 250,000 immigrants came to live in the United States between 1790 and 1820.

Since 1607, when some of the first Europeans reached what became the English colonies, over 50 million people have migrated to the United States. This is the largest migration of people in all recorded history. It has also provided us with one of the most diverse populations of any country in the world.

President John F. Kennedy wrote about the importance of immigration to America in *A Nation of Immigrants:*

One way of indicating the importance of immigration to America is to point out that every American who ever lived, with the exception of one group, was either an immigrant himself or a descendant of immigrants.

The exception? Will Rogers, part Cherokee Indian, said that his ancestors were at the dock to meet the *Mayflower.* And anthropologists believe that the Indians themselves were immigrants from another continent who displaced the original Americans—the Aborigines.

In just over 350 years, a nation . . . has grown up, populated almost entirely by persons who either came from other lands or whose forefathers came from other lands.

1. Who was J. Hector St. John de Crevecoeur? Describe four impressions that early Americans made on him.

2. In what two ways did the population of the United States change between 1790 and 1980?

3. What are three reasons for the growth of the population of the United States?

4. What did President John F. Kennedy say about immigration to America?

5. How would you describe the past and present population of the United States?

SKILLS Developing your basic civic education skills

(comprehending, reading, and writing)

Understanding What You Read

Paragraph 1 The population of the United States has increased over the years. We know this because, by law, the United States government must take a census, or "head count," every 10 years. In 1970, the population of the United States was 203,302,031 persons. In 1980, 10 years later, the population had increased to 226,504,825. These totals can be compared to the census of 1790. At that time, the population of the United States was 3,929,000.

Paragraph 2 Population figures from 1970 to 1980 do not show that every city, town, or area in the United States increased in population. Some areas gained many more people than others. Some areas lost population. This can be seen in the listings and bar graphs on these pages.

Paragraph 3 A more in-depth analysis of the 1980 census is seen in reports prepared by the staffs of *The Washington Post, The New York Times,* and the Associated Press. Their reports showed the following comparisons regarding the population of the United States (based on information from the U.S. Census Bureau). The number of United States households increased 27 percent from 1970 to 1980. There were 63.4 million households in 1970 and 80.4 million in 1980. The average num-

CHANGES IN THE POPULATIONS OF SOME AMERICAN CITIES		
	Population 1980	Percent change since 1970
Phoenix	765,000	+31.0
Houston	1,594,000	+29.2
San Diego	876,000	+25.5
San Antonio	785,000	+20.0
Tulsa	361,000	+ 9.3
Dallas	904,000	+ 7.1
Los Angeles	2,967,000	+ 5.5
St. Louis	453,000	− 27.2
Cleveland	574,000	− 23.6
Detroit	1,203,000	− 20.5
Philadelphia	1,688,000	− 13.4
Baltimore	787,000	− 13.0
Boston	563,000	− 12.0
Chicago	3,005,000	− 10.8
New York	7,071,000	− 10.4

SOURCE: U.S. Census Bureau

ber of people in households declined from 3.11 in 1970 to 2.75 in 1980. California, the most populous state (23.1 million people), had the most households (8.6 million). New York and Texas were next in total population and households. Utah had the largest average number of people per household (3.20). Hawaii was next (3.15). The District of Columbia had the smallest number of people per house-

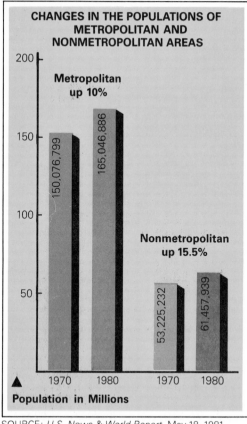

CHANGES IN THE POPULATIONS OF METROPOLITAN AND NONMETROPOLITAN AREAS

Metropolitan up 10%

Nonmetropolitan up 15.5%

150,076,799
165,046,886
53,225,232
61,457,939

1970　1980　　1970　1980

Population in Millions

SOURCE: *U.S. News & World Report,* May 18, 1981.

hold (2.39). Florida had the next smallest (2.55).

Paragraph 4　The census data also showed some interesting statistics about the ages of Americans. In 1980, 25.5 million people in the United States were over 65 years of age. This was a 28-percent increase over 1970. In 1980, 51 million people were under the age of 15. In 1970, there were 58 million people under the age of 15.

Paragraph 5　The average age of Americans had changed as well. In 1980, the average age was 30. In 1970, it was 28. In 1980, Florida had the highest average age at 34.7 years; Utah had the lowest at 24.2. In the Northeast, the average age was 31.8. In the Middle West, it was 29.6. In the South, it was 29.7. And in the West, it was 29.3. Average ages by racial or ethnic groups in 1980 were as follows: whites—31.3; blacks—24.9; American Indians, Eskimos, and Aleutian Islanders—23; Asians—28.6; Spanish-Americans, or Hispanics—23.2.

POPULATION DISTRIBUTION IN THE UNITED STATES				
Section of Country	Population		Share of Total U.S. Population	
	1970	1980	1970	1980
Northeast	49,061,000	49,137,000	24.1%	21.7%
Midwest	56,590,000	58,854,000	27.8%	26.0%
South	62,813,000	75,349,000	30.9%	33.3%
West	34,838,000	43,165,000	17.1%	19.1%
Growth of Suburbs, Nonmetropolitan Areas				
Suburbs	83,336,000	98,352,000	41.0%	43.4%
Nonmetropolitan areas	53,225,000	61,458,000	26.2%	27.1%
Decline of Cities				
All central cities	66,741,000	66,695,000	32.8%	29.4%
20 largest central cities of the North	22,814,000	19,991,000	11.2%	8.8%

SOURCE: U.S. Census Bureau

Paragraph 6 Figures released by the U.S. Census Bureau show even more details about the two largest racial minority groups in our country, blacks and Spanish-Americans. Blacks in 1980 numbered 26,488,218, or 11.7 percent of the total population. This is up from 11.1 percent in 1970. Spanish-Americans numbered 14,605,883, or 6.4 percent of the 1980 total population. This is up from 4.5 percent in 1970. Census officials stressed, however, that the Hispanic totals are misleading. This is because many Hispanics listed themselves as white or some other racial designation. People were classified as being of Hispanic origin only if they listed themselves that way on the 1980 census form. During the 1970 census, those who designated themselves as Mexican, Cuban, or any other Hispanic group were classified as white.

1. What was the population of the United States in 1970? In 1980? In 1790?

2. Which cities gained in population from 1970 to 1980? Which cities lost population during that 10-year period?

3. By what percentage did metropolitan areas increase from 1970 to 1980? By what percentage did nonmetropolitan areas increase during that 10-year period?

4. Which section of the country had the greatest percentage of population in 1970? Which section of the country had the greatest percentage of population in 1980?

5. List three statistics concerning each of the following as they relate to the 1980 census.

   a. households
   b. the ages of the population
   c. the median age of the population

d. two largest racial minority groups

Reading for the Main Idea

The *main idea* of a reading is the most important point an author wants to make or stress. The main idea of a paragraph is usually found in its first sentence. The remaining sentences in the paragraph back up the statement made in the first sentence with supporting information. For example, review the first paragraph in the section you just read. The main idea of that paragraph is this: "The population of the United States has increased over the years." In the rest of the paragraph, the author shows that the population of the United States had increased from 3,929,000 in 1790 to 226,504,825 by 1980.

6. Which one of the following is the main idea in the second paragraph?
   a. Phoenix and Houston had large increases in population from 1970 to 1980.
   b. Not all areas in the United States increased in population from 1970 to 1980, but many did.
   c. Metropolitan areas increased 10 percent in population from 1970 to 1980.

7. Tell why you selected either *a*, *b*, or *c* in question 6.

8. Which one of the following is the main idea in the third paragraph?
   a. A comparison of census information for 1970 and 1980 reveals no changes among the American population.
   b. The median age of Americans was 30 in 1980 and 28 in 1970.
   c. A comparison of census informa-

tion for 1970 and 1980 reveals many changes among the American population.

9. Tell why you selected either *a, b,* or *c* in question 8.

Applying What You Comprehend

By correctly answering questions 1–5, you showed that you *comprehended,* or understood, the information presented in this account. Comprehending what you read, hear, or see is among the more basic levels of learning. It does not mean that you have done anything with the information or that you have evaluated its worth. It only means that you understand what has been presented. You must first comprehend what has been written, said, or shown about a topic before you can apply or evaluate it effectively.

When you thought about the main ideas of the paragraphs of the reading and answered questions 6–9, you were *applying* some of what you had comprehended. You also did this if you completed the Chapter Review on pages 32–33. When you apply what you have learned, you take the meaning of a main idea and use it to connect to something else. For example, you made some comparisons of racial attitudes, past and present. That was applying what you had learned. In doing this, you moved up a step in the ladder of learning. But keep in mind that however far you move up that ladder, you must still comprehend the information before you can apply it.

10. What is another word that means *to comprehend?*

11. What is meant by applying what you comprehend? Give an example.

Developing Your Writing Skills

If you completed the Chapter Review on pages 32–33, you read about how to form paragraphs and topic sentences. A *paragraph* is a division of a written composition that expresses one point. It may be part of a larger idea, but it is complete in itself. A paragraph usually consists of several sentences.

The *topic sentence* is the first sentence of a paragraph. The topic sentence tells what the paragraph will be about.

In a paragraph of more than one sentence, all the sentences that follow the topic sentence contain information, ideas, and opinions that back up the topic sentence. In a sense, the topic sentence of a paragraph is a conclusion about an idea or thought. The rest of the sentences in the paragraph then serve as supporting evidence.

12. Express an opinion in paragraph form on the subject of the 1980 U.S. census. Your paragraph might begin with the following topic sentence: "The 1980 U.S. census revealed many things about the population." The remainder of the paragraph would include supporting facts or ideas.

Special Note: As you read this book, you will continue to develop your skills of comprehension, application, reading, and writing. Thus, from time to time, you may wish to review pages 36–39.

2 Living with Laws

Sometimes people grow tired of having to obey the law. "Why are there so many laws?" they ask. "Do we really need laws?" Stop and think for a minute about what our lives might be like if all laws were suddenly dropped. A typical day might go like this:

You bounce eargerly out of bed. No more laws! You feel free. You head for a friend's home, looking forward to a great day with nothing to hold you back.

At the corner you dart across the street, ignoring the traffic light. Brakes screech. Drivers curse. You skip down the street, laughing. You never did like to wait for that light to change anyway. Now no one can make you wait. You think of all the things you can do with no laws to prevent you.

Your daydreams are interrupted by a car speeding along the sidewalk. The driver, too, is feeling free. You jump back just in time. "Why don't the police catch that guy?" you wonder. Then you remember—without laws there are no police.

A sack of garbage splatters down beside you. You wipe the stains from your shoes. There is no use reporting the person who dropped it.

Down the block, a man is piling chairs and tables on the sidewalk. An elderly couple is pleading with him. They are tenants who are being thrown out of their apartment. The man keeps bringing out furniture. "Get out!" he tells the couple. "I don't have to get any court order. You

can forget about your rent deposit too. I'm keeping it. Just try to stop me."

You hear a radio blaring from an open window. An announcer is reporting the news. A mob is rampaging through the streets downtown. They are breaking windows and taking whatever they want. Nothing is illegal, so everything is permitted.

On the corner, you see a heavyset man grabbing a wallet from a small, thin man. You remember something you once read about laws and government. Without laws, it said, the stronger people would rule the weaker people. "Am I as strong as I think I am?" you wonder.

A picture like this one has always troubled those who study societies. Most such students believe that societies would quickly fall apart without laws. There must be rules, they say, so people will know what is expected of them. There must be someone to make and enforce the rules.

There is a word for a society without laws—without a system to make laws. The word is **anarchy.** As far as we know, no large-scale human society has ever lived in anarchy. From the very beginning, human beings living together seem to have set up rules of behavior. They may not have used words such as *law* and *government*. But they had rules, and someone enforced them.

In this chapter, you will look at the reasons for having laws. You will also study the way the United States' system of laws has developed.

I. Why societies need laws
  A. Definition of laws
    1. Laws should be just.
    2. Laws should be enforceable.
  B. Reasons laws are needed
    1. To settle disputes
    2. To discourage wrongdoers
    3. To guide the running of society
    4. To protect individual and group rights
    5. To limit the abuse of rights by the powerful
II. Laws through the ages
  A. Earliest laws
    1. Code of Hammurabi
    2. The Ten Commandments
    3. Greek laws
      a. The laws of Draco
      b. The laws of Solon
    4. Roman laws
      a. Laws of the Twelve Tables
      b. Code of Justinian
  B. The Middle Ages
  C. England
    1. Common law
    2. Precedent
  D. Modern law: Two great traditions

Words to Know

anarchy —— a condition in which society has no laws nor government to make laws

law —— a binding rule of society that has been set up by the customs of the people and backed up by some kind of force

civil law —— the law dealing with disputes between private parties or between private parties and the government

criminal law —— law dealing with acts seen as harmful to a society

administrative law —— law dealing with how the government is to be organized and what powers each part of the government will have

civil rights —— the basic rights of an individual

Why Societies Need Laws

Societies need laws to help people live together peacefully. That has been the belief of most thinkers through the ages. Without laws, people would have no rights except those they could enforce themselves. This means that few people would have rights.

A Definition of Laws

What do we mean by the word *laws*? In Chapter 1, we saw that a law is one kind of norm, or rule. Some norms are backed only by public opinion. Laws are different. They are norms that are backed by organized force. In our society, that force is in the hands of the government and its officials—the police and the courts.

Who makes the laws? That depends on the particular society and law we are talking about. Some laws begin as customs. Slowly, the customs become more and more important. People begin to think of the customs as needed for the society's well-being. They begin to punish those who do not follow the customs. In this way, the customs turn into laws. Some laws begin as rules that are set up by some kind of ruling power. That power may be a tribal chief, a king or a queen, a group of people, individuals, or an elected body. It may also be a judge or group of judges in a court. These rules are laws because someone says they are and because someone—the chief, the courts, or the police—is prepared to back them up.

To sum up, then, **laws** are the binding rules of society that have been set up by the customs of the people or by some kind of ruling power.

This definition of laws does not say anything about good or bad laws. Any rule, no matter how evil, can become a law if it can be made binding on a people. Most of

WHY LAWS ARE NEEDED

To Settle Disputes

To Discourage Wrongdoers

To Guide the Running of Society

Bill of Rights

To Protect Individual and Group Rights

To Limit Abuse of Rights by the Powerful

Laws can be either bad—such as the law allowing slavery—or good—such as the law banning it.

us can think of some bad laws from former times. In the United States, for example, there were once laws that allowed one person to own another as a slave. Other laws punished people for helping slaves to escape. These laws were set up by the ruling power. They were binding, and they were enforced.

Today, most people would agree that these laws were evil. Some people thought so even when they were in effect. For example, some whites broke the law and helped slaves to escape. Most people, though, obeyed the law even if they thought it was wrong. The laws were set up and enforced by the government. Anyone who broke the law risked punishment.

Laws Should Be Just. Most people would agree that laws should not be evil. Most people would say that laws should be fair. The laws should reflect the highest values of a society.

Laws sometimes fail because they are ignored. During prohibition, people broke the law continually and built stills in order to make their own liquor.

What *should be* is not always what *is*, however. Laws are not always seen as being fair and just. In any society, laws are sometimes passed that some people believe to be unjust. People do not always agree on values. They do not always agree on what is just and what is unjust.

In the United States, there are accepted ways for people to change laws that they think are unjust. You will study many ways to bring about changes in the laws in later chapters. But what if efforts for change do not work? What if an unjust law stays on the books? Should you, as an individual, obey an unjust law? Or should you break the law and face the punishment? This is a question that has bothered people for centuries. It is a hard question, and people disagree about the answer. It is also a hard question for the ruling powers: If large numbers of people think that a law is unjust and refuse to obey it, how can it be enforced?

Laws Should Be Enforceable. There have been many laws that failed because people just ignored them.

This shows us that laws must be enforceable in order to be effective. An unpopular law may be impossible to enforce. Lawmakers must take this into account. They must ask themselves: Is this law just? Can it be enforced?

People ignore laws when they no longer make sense. Early in this century, horses and cows were frightened by that new invention, the automobile. Some towns in the United States had laws saying that a person carrying a flag or lantern should always walk in front of an automobile. This would warn the owners of animals that an automobile was coming. As automobiles became a part of the country's way of life, such laws seemed silly. People paid no attention to them.

Sometimes laws try to change the way people act. In 1917, a law went into effect in the United States that said people could not make, transport, or sell alcoholic beverages. This law angered many people. Many people broke the law and made their own beverages or bought them illegally. In the end, the law was taken off the books.

Reasons Laws Are Needed

Of all the hundreds and thousands of laws that are passed every year in the United States, very few raise the kinds of questions we have been discussing. Most laws are routine. Most can be enforced. These laws are obeyed by most people. The reason is that most laws meet one of five main needs. Let us take a look at those five needs:

Laws Are Needed to Settle Disputes. Tim and Tom are neighbors. Their homes are side by side on a tree-lined street. One of the trees shading the streets is in Tom's front yard, near the fence separating Tom's yard from Tim's. In a thunderstorm, a limb is torn from the tree. It falls across the fence in Tim's driveway and on Tim's car. Tim asks Tom to pay for fixing the car's dented roof. Tom refuses. What happens next?

If there were no laws, it is hard to say what would happen next. Tim might "take the law into his own hands," as the saying goes. But laws are written for just such problems. Laws set down basic ways of settling disputes. When a dispute arises, a judge or a jury can apply the law to the specific case.

In our complex society, there are many types of disputes. There are disputes between people. There are disputes between people and businesses. There are disputes between people and government. There are also disputes between businesses and government.

All the laws that help settle such disputes belong to a class of law called **civil law**. Civil law deals with disputes between private parties or between private parties and the government. It helps to determine the rights and duties of each party in a dispute.

Laws Are Needed to Discourage Wrongdoers. Mary lived in a large apartment building in a big city. One day, she was waiting alone for the elevator. A group of girls suddenly appeared and demanded her money. Mary fought back. The girls hit her with a club, took her purse, and ran away. Mary was badly injured. A neighbor who saw the girls running away called the police. The police caught the girls, who were still carrying Mary's purse. They were put on trial and later sent to jail.

The law lists a number of acts that are considered harmful to society. These acts are called *crimes*. In most cases, deliberately injuring a person is a crime. Stealing is also a crime. The girls in the above case were tried for these crimes. The law gives guidelines for deciding whether a person has, in fact, committed a crime. For example, the law would help to determine whether all the girls were responsible for the injury, or only the girl who actually hit Mary.

Not all crimes are equally serious. Some crimes—like driving too fast or spitting on a public sidewalk—are much less serious than others. These are usually called violations, rather than crimes. The wrongdoer may merely be fined, or given a warning.

Laws about crimes tell people what behavior is not acceptable. Such laws warn people that if they take certain actions, they will be punished. The idea is to prevent people from doing the wrong thing. The class of law that deals with crime is called **criminal law.**

Laws Are Needed to Guide the Running of Society. During the 1970s, people in the United States became aware of what was called the "energy crisis." Oil-producing nations stopped selling oil to the

When people's needs are not met, such as during the "energy crisis" of the 1970s, administrative laws are passed to organize solutions to the problem.

United States. The country could not produce enough oil. Long lines of cars formed at gas stations. Fuel prices rose sharply. Even after oil shipments started up again, things did not return to normal.

Most people agreed that more could be done to help meet the nation's fuel needs. In 1977, the government passed a law that set up an organization to handle energy problems. The law stated what the job of the new organization would be. The new organization would help plan oil production and the use of fuel. The law also stated how the new organization would be run.

There are many laws of this sort. They are known as **administrative laws.** They help to spell out how government should be organized. They state what powers belong to the different parts of government.

Laws Are Needed to Protect the Rights of People and Groups. Ira had a taste for good food. At college, he rarely ate in the student cafeteria. He saved his money and went out to eat as often as he could. Steak with mushroom sauce and fresh lobster were his favorites. When the school

year ended, Ira returned to his home town. He wanted to take his parents out for a nice meal. They went to the best restaurant in town, but they were turned away at the door. "We don't serve your kind here," the restaurant manager said. Ira was mad. He knew that what the manager had done was wrong.

Ira was mad because his rights had been violated. A *right* is something that is owed to a person. United States society believes that people have natural rights that cannot be taken away. Freedom to think what you want is one natural right. Freedom to be treated fairly without regard to the color of your skin or national origin is another right. These rights that belong to members of our society are sometimes known as **civil rights.**

United States society has laws to protect these rights. Some civil rights laws are also criminal laws. They make it a crime to deprive someone of his or her rights. For example, the restaurant manager mentioned above had to pay a fine because he broke a criminal law. Civil rights laws may

Unlike the past, today's laws guarantee us the freedom to work where and for whom we please.

Agents of the state keep careful watch on acts which, though legal, can lead to abuse of other's rights.

also be part of civil law—the law that covers disputes. The law may allow Ira to sue the restaurant for violating his rights. If Ira wins the suit, the restaurant might have to pay him money.

Laws Are Needed to Limit the Abuse of Rights by the Powerful. Molly worked in a factory in a small town. She did not have much choice. It was the only place nearby where she could work. The factory owners knew this, so they paid low wages. "Take it or leave it," they said. Finally, Molly and the other workers decided to form a labor union. The union would fight for better wages. When the factory owners found out what was happening, they fired Molly and several others. But Molly knew there was a law to protect workers who tried to form unions. After lengthy court hearings, Molly was given her job back. The company even had to give her pay for the time she missed at work.

People and organizations that have power sometimes abuse the rights of those who do not have power. Employers may abuse the rights of workers. Labor unions may abuse the rights of their members—or those of nonmembers. Hospitals and doc-

tors may abuse the rights of patients. A polluting factory may abuse everyone's right to clean air and drinkable water. Many laws are designed to prevent such abuse. They control working conditions, union activities, medical rights, and pollution—among countless other things.

Most important, there are laws that protect us against the most powerful institution of all—the government. Governments have life-and-death power over their citizens. That is why people need protection against governments. United States society has chosen to write protections against government into its basic laws. The government must respect the individual's rights to free speech, to freedom of religion, to a free press. It cannot simply step in and take away property. It does not have a free hand to tap telephones or eavesdrop on conversations. It cannot keep a person in jail for long periods of time without a trial. You will study these protections more fully in Chapter 12.

———————— REVIEW ————————

1. Which of the following statements are true of *all* laws?
   a. They are just.
   b. They are backed by organized force.
   c. They are established either by custom or by some kind of authority.
   d. They are enforced.
2. The laws that people ignore are an example of what kind of laws?
   a. unenforceable laws
   b. administrative laws
   c. criminal laws
3. Give two examples of criminal law.
4. Give two examples of civil law.
5. Give an example of a law—not mentioned in this chapter—that you think is unjust. Why do you think it is unjust.

Hammurabi is shown here receiving the laws.

Words to Know

code —— a listing of all laws that are in effect

natural law —— certain fundamental principles of justice that are believed to apply to all people

precedent —— something decided in an earlier court case

common law —— a system based both on laws and on judges' decisions, or precedents

civil-law system —— a system, dating back to the Code of Justinian, that is based upon laws arranged in codes, and in which precedents do not have the force of law

Laws through the Ages

Earliest Laws

No one can say when the first law was made. It is likely, though, that people had laws long before they could read and write. These first laws were part of a society's rules for living. They were passed on by word of mouth from generation to generation.

Code of Hammurabi When people learned to write, they began to make records of their laws. This made it easier to know just what the law was. In the ancient Middle East, writing was not done on paper. Instead, words were chiseled into stones.

This is how we know about one of the earliest lists of laws. It was put together around 1790 B.C. on the orders of Hammurabi, a king of ancient Babylonia, in what is now Iraq. Hammurabi had all the laws of Babylonia listed together. Such a listing is called a **code.** The Code of Hammurabi was chiseled into stone. Today, the code is in a museum in Paris, and the writing is still readable.

The Code of Hammurabi is as hard as the stone it is written on. Robbers will be put to death. Men who strike their fathers will have a hand cut off. A person who causes another to lose an eye will have his or her own eye put out. As harsh as it seems today, the code was written to help judges be fair in their rulings. All judges were to follow the code. The law did not depend on the opinion of one person, but on written rules. That is the way our laws are today: They are assembled in codes.

The Ten Commandments Another code of laws that came from the ancient Middle East is the Ten Commandments. Actually, this is part of a larger code, called the Law of Moses. Moses was a leader of the ancient Hebrews. The code that bears his name sums up the religious rules of the Jewish people. The code also had an effect on the beliefs of Christians and Moslems.

The Ten Commandments are *moral* rules. They are rules for telling what is right from what is wrong. Unlike the Code of Hammurabi, the Ten Commandments do not have a list of punishments. One commandment, for example, states that stealing is wrong. Still another says that telling lies about a neighbor is wrong. Still another says that people should honor their parents. Many of the ideas from the Ten Commandments are found today in United States laws.

Greek Laws The ancient Greeks brought a new idea to lawmaking. Both the Babylonians and the Hebrews had thought of law as God-given. In the Bible, it says that God gave the Ten Commandments to Moses. But the Greeks gave humans a role in lawmaking. To be sure, the Greeks believed in gods and goddesses. They believed that these gods wanted people to obey the law. But they also believed that people could change laws when the need arose.

The Laws of Draco In 621 B.C. a Greek by the name of Draco drew up a code of laws for the city-state of Athens. It was a time of unrest and disorder. The people wanted Draco to write down laws that would help restore prosperity and order.

Draco's laws were harsh, and for good reason: Until his time, Athens had no strong law against murder. If a man's brother was murdered, the man himself had to catch and punish the murderer. Draco provided trials for people accused of murder and many other crimes. He made punishments harsh so that the victims of crime would accept the law and not seek revenge themselves. For example, a thief could be put to death. It did not matter how small an item the thief had stolen. "Those that stole a cabbage or an apple were to suffer even as villians that committed . . . murder," said a Greek writer of a later period. Draco's name has become part of the English language. Today, anything unusually harsh or cruel is called *draconian.*

The Laws of Solon Solon was a young man of about 17 years when Draco's law went into effect in Athens. Some 30 years later, he had become a high official of the Athenian government. Solon wrote a new set of laws to replace Draco's code. It was a much fairer code. For example, Solon's laws applied to all people equally. Draco's laws included two sets of punishments—one set for citizens and another, harsher set for slaves. One out of three Athenians was a slave.

Solon wanted even ordinary people to know the laws. He had the laws posted in a public place. The laws were written on wooden rollers. To read the laws, one turned the rollers. Under Solon's laws, any person could go to a court if he or she thought another person was guilty of a crime. For at least five centuries, Solon's code formed the base of law in Athens. In our language today, the word *solon* means "lawmaker" or "legislator."

Roman Laws: Laws of the Twelve Tables Around this same time, another great civilization was forming farther to the

Solon, a high official of the Athenian government, wrote the first code of laws which was applied to all people—citizens and slaves—equally.

west, in Rome. The Romans not only drew up a code of laws, but they also made schoolchildren memorize them. This was not very difficult. The laws were fairly simple. For the most part, they represented customs that had been followed by Romans for hundreds of years. They were arranged in an easy-to-learn fashion, in twelve tables. This code, called the Laws of the Twelve Tables, was written around 450 B.C. New laws were added from time to time. The Laws of the Twelve Tables remained in effect for centuries.

Rome grew rich and powerful. Its armies conquered lands in Europe, Africa, and Asia. The ideas of Roman law spread as Rome's empire grew. One idea was especially important: The Romans believed that certain principles of justice applied to all people. They called these principles **natural law.** These ideas grew and devel-

oped over the following centuries. They were the seed of the thoughts expressed in the Declaration of Independence.

Code of Justinian In time, the Roman system of laws became very complicated. Some laws applied to all people and some only to the citizens of Rome. Even scholars were no longer able to keep all the laws in their heads. Several Roman leaders tried to put the laws together in a new code, but failed. When part of the Roman Empire collapsed in A.D. 476, the laws were a hopeless jumble. In some cases, two laws gave opposite answers to the same problem.

After Rome's collapse, some parts of its system of laws were carried on by the Eastern Roman Empire, with its capital at Constantinople. The emperor Justinian I ordered his lawyers to draw up a list of the best Roman laws. After 5 years of painstaking labor, the lawyers produced a new code of law. It was called the Code of Justinian, or the "Body of Civil Law." It went into effect in A.D. 533–534.

Even though the Roman Empire is now only a memory, the Code of Justinian continues to influence modern law. It was updated by the French emperor Napoleon in 1804. The laws of many nations are still based upon the Code of Justinian, as changed by Napoleon.

The Code of Justinian was different from our modern laws in several ways. For example, theft was not a crime. It was treated as a dispute between two people. It was up to the victim to sue the thief. If the victim won the suit, the thief might have to repay up to four times the value of the stolen property. In one way, the Code of Justinian was far ahead of the laws of many nations today: It gave both married and unmarried women the right to own property and to make legal agreements.

The Middle Ages

The fall of Rome meant more than the breaking up of an empire. It meant an end to the system of laws that had helped to keep that empire together. New legal systems took the place of Roman law. The Ro-

With the Fall of Rome, European societies organized a new system of rules known as **feudal law.** Under feudal law, society was stratified—divided into layers—with the peasants on the bottom; the lords, for whom the peasants worked, in the middle; and the royal family on the top. Feudal law set guidelines as to what peasant and lord could reasonably expect from one another.

man Catholic Church made Roman law the base of its own legal system, called canon law. As the influence of the Church spread, so did canon law. During the Middle Ages much of Europe became Catholic. Canon law was used not just in religious matters, but in everyday life as well.

Another kind of law was used in Europe from around A.D. 800 to 1300. Societies in Europe at this time were organized in layers. The ordinary people were at the bottom. They lived on land owned by large landowners, or lords. In effect, these lords were the government. They had full power over the people living on their lands. They even had their own armies. In time of war, a number of lords and their armies might fight in the service of the king. The lords were supposed to be loyal to the king, just as the common people were supposed to be loyal to their lords. In fact, the lords held the real power, because they had the soldiers to fight the kings' battles.

The law gave special duties to each level of society. For example, peasants had to work a certain number of days a year on the lord's fields. In return, the lord had to provide protection for his people. This system of law, known as *feudal* law, also put limits on what a lord could demand. In later times, when kings pulled together the separate parts of their kingdoms to form nations, the idea of some limits to power applied to them as well. The idea that kings were under the rule of law was an important one.

England

Although the Romans once ruled what is now England, their system of laws never took hold there. The English put together their own system of laws. It came in part from the European law just mentioned, in part from older laws, and in part from England's own experiences.

Under Henry II, the same rules of law were applied throughout England, thus being known as *common laws.*

Common Law In the early Middle Ages, England's system of law was a jumble. Each lord had his own courts. In some courts, punishments were harsh. In others, they were not. As the English kings slowly gained power, they also took over the courts. Henry II, who ruled England from 1154 to 1189, played a major role. He sent judges around the country to hold court in many places. Wherever they went, these judges applied the same rules of law. These rules became known as the **common law** of England. To this day, we speak of the British system of law as common law. It is the basis of law in most English-speaking countries today, including the United States.

Like earlier systems of law, common law reflected the society in which it developed. In the Middle Ages, English society punished wrongdoers harshly. A thief might be whipped or branded with a hot iron. In other cases, thieves might be fined or put in prison. In the most serious cases, they were put to death. Unlike the Code of Justinian, common law treated theft as a crime and not as a private dispute. On another matter—women's rights—early common law was quite unliberated. It treated unmarried women more or less equal with men. But married women were treated less well. A married women could not make a legal agreement or own property without her husband's consent. If she committed a crime, her husband was responsible. Today's common law is much different. Punishments are far less severe. In most cases, the law treats men and women as equals.

Precedent Common law is sometimes called "judge-made law." It grew out of the decisions of judges over a long time. Common law also takes in many rules made by lawmaking bodies. British laws today are made by the British Parliament. In the United States, laws are made by Congress or by the states. The judges who must apply these laws still rely on **precedent**—the decisions of judges in earlier cases. Many of these precedents played an important part in limiting the powers of government and in protecting the rights of the people.

Modern Law: Two Great Traditions

The law systems of many countries today can be traced back to two great traditions. Some countries, like the United States and Great Britain, follow the **common-law system.** Other countries, including most of Europe, follow the ideas first set down in the Code of Justinian. We call this the **civil-law system** (Do not confuse this use of the term *civil law* with the other use,

which refers to disputes between parties.). Still other countries have blended the two systems together. Japan, for example, follows many common-law ideas about people's rights. At the same time, Japan has a code of laws just like countries with civil law systems.

The common-law system depends much more on precedent than the civil-law system. In the civil-law system, judges must base their decisions on a written law in a law code. They cannot decide a case on precedent alone. The laws in civil-law systems are assembled into organized codes. In common-law systems, codes of law also exist, but they can be changed or added to by the decisions of judges in later cases.

In the United States, the federal government and forty-nine of the states follow a common-law system. One state, Louisiana, does not. Louisiana was founded by French settlers, who brought with them a system of civil law. Louisiana's laws still reflect this system.

REVIEW

1. What was Hammurabi's main contribution to the development of laws?
2. Name two ways in which the laws of Solon were different from the laws of Draco.
3. How does Roman law still influence the legal systems in some countries today?
4. What was special about the English system of common law?
5. Do you think that a judge should have to base every decision on a written law? Or should a judge also be permitted to base decisions on other judges' decisions? Explain.

How the United States Works

Work and Law

In United States society, work is governed by laws. Laws affect how long people work, what they are paid, and the conditions under which they work. To see how important work laws are, just look back to the year 1900. At that time, there were few laws about working conditions. Those were also the days before there were labor unions to offset the power of factory owners. Workers were often at the mercy of their bosses.

In those days, people would work for months and then find that their salary had been cut. If they complained, they were fired. If they became sick, it was just too bad. There were no paid sick days and no health plans.

Some factories at that time were dark, crowded "sweatshops." People in sweatshops worked 12- to 18-hour shifts, 6 days a week for very low wages. Most of the workers were women and children. In those days, women were generally paid half the wages that men were paid for doing exactly the same work. Children were given even less, so naturally, factory owners preferred hiring children. There were no health or safety laws to protect the workers. People fainted from the heat and lack of air. Tuberculosis was a common illness.

It took a tragedy to start getting changes. That tragedy was the Triangle fire. In 1911, the Triangle Building in New York City went up in flames. The building was a firetrap. Still, 145 people would not have died if the sweatshop owner had not locked the doors. He did not want his workers to waste time by going outside to cool off, so he locked them in. During the fire, a number of young women jumped out of the windows and fell seven stories to their deaths. The others died inside.

As a result of this terrible fire, some important safety and health laws were passed. Now there are also laws to prevent child labor and laws to make sure that there is equal pay for equal work. Among other things, there is a limit to the number of hours in the workday and there is a minimum wage, or payment.

Reading About . . .

How Much Law Is Enough? ————————————————

In this chapter, you have seen some of the reasons why societies have laws. How much law does a society need? That is a difficult question. With too many laws, a person's rights and freedoms are limited. With too few laws, a society can become an unsafe place to live. A balance must be reached.

As you read about the log-cabin builder below, think about these points:

● Should O.C. be punished for building a cabin in the same way that cabins have been built for centuries?

● Does the government have a right to make sure that the homes of its citizens are safely built?

O.C. Helton is battling modern-day technology and county officials over a building permit for his log cabin.

O.C. was in the process of building a log cabin for himself and his family of seven—until the county stepped in.

"Log cabins are as old as time. You can't beat 'em for warmth and . . . the ones I've built are a lot more sound than many of the homes I see going up today," said O.C.

However, according to County Building Director William L. Carroll, "We're in a technological age. Log cabins aren't all that common these days. But they are unique now, and we have to make sure they're structurally sound."

O.C. drew up some plans on poster paper and headed for Everett, the county seat, to get a building permit.

"First they told me the plans looked like a bunch of centipede tracks," Helton recalls. "Then they told me I had to get an architect or structural engineer to approve the plans."

Carroll explained that the plans should be drawn to scale in a standard architectural manner and that while regular building plans did not need the approval of an engineer, a log cabin did because it is different.

O.C., who was taught the art of building a log cabin by his father and grandfather, was "put out" that anyone would think that he could not build a sound log cabin, so he began building it without the permit.

He was ordered to stop construction, but he refused. He was then ordered to appear in County Superior Court.

Fact Review

1. In United States society, which of the following might make a law?
   - **a.** a police officer
   - **b.** a king or queen
   - **c.** an elected body
   - **d.** a judge
   - **e.** a soldier
   - **f.** the President
2. Give an example of an unenforceable law.
3. List five reasons why we need laws.
4. Give two examples of how a powerful person or institution might deprive someone of his or her rights.
5. How did the Greek idea of law differ from that of the Babylonians and the Hebrews?
6. Who was the ruler who updated the Code of Justinian?
7. How did feudal law eventually help to restrict the powers of kings?
8. Give an example of a society in which murder was treated as a private dispute. Give an example in which theft was treated as a private dispute.
9. What advantage might there be to treating murder and theft as a civil, rather than a criminal, matter? What disadvantage?

Developing Your Vocabulary

1. Match the words in *a* to *d* with the phrases in (*1*) to (*4*).
   - **a.** law
   - **b.** anarchy
   - **c.** code
   - **d.** precedent
     - (1) A listing of many laws.
     - (2) A binding rule that is made by some authority.
     - (3) Something decided in an earlier court case.
     - (4) All people are free to do as they please.
2. What is the difference between civil law and criminal law?

Developing Your Reading Skills

Read the following paragraph and then answer the questions that follow:

We owe a debt to many earlier peoples for our modern-day system of law. We got the idea of grouping laws into codes from the Babylonians. We inherited many of the moral principles behind our laws from the Hebrews. The idea that laws could reflect people's needs as well as divine will came from the Greeks. The idea of natural law came from the Romans and the basic principles of common law from the English. Without these contributions, our laws today would be poorer.

1. Which of the following do you think is the main idea, or point, of this paragraph?
   - **a.** Our laws would be poorer without moral principles to back them up.
   - **b.** Many earlier peoples contributed to our present system of laws.
   - **c.** The English, more than any other people, helped shape our system of laws.
   - **d.** Our laws are based on natural law.
2. Why did you select either *a, b, c,* or *d* above?

Developing Your Writing Skills— Forming and Supporting an Opinion

In this chapter, you have considered the role of law in United States society and in earlier societies. Now consider the following question:

Forming an opinion Would you prefer to live under a system of coded laws or under anarchy?

Supporting an opinion After thinking it over, write a paragraph that answers the question above. Begin with a topic sentence that sums up your opinion. Then continue with evidence or arguments.

YOUR GOVERNMENT & ITS HISTORY

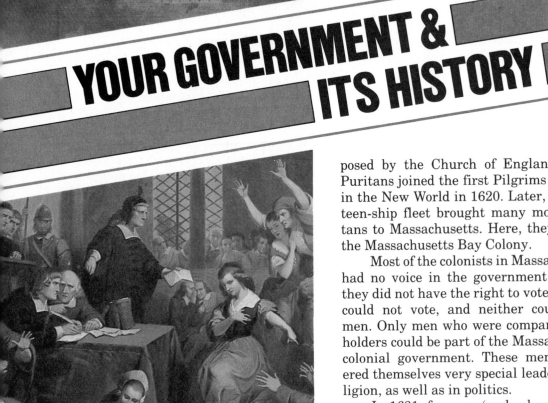

America's First Laws

The first Europeans to settle in the New World often passed laws as strict as those in the Old World. They passed such laws to protect their own way of life or their particular beliefs.

One such group was the Puritans. A religious group from England, the Puritans believed in simple worship. They wanted the Church of England to do away with great ceremonies, colored windows, and religious music. For this, they were op-

posed by the Church of England. Some Puritans joined the first Pilgrims to settle in the New World in 1620. Later, a seventeen-ship fleet brought many more Puritans to Massachusetts. Here, they settled the Massachusetts Bay Colony.

Most of the colonists in Massachusetts had no voice in the government because they did not have the right to vote. Women could not vote, and neither could most men. Only men who were company stockholders could be part of the Massachusetts colonial government. These men considered themselves very special leaders in religion, as well as in politics.

In 1631, freemen (male church members) in each Massachusetts town were given the right to elect representatives to the General Court. The General Court was the legislature, or lawmaking body, of the colony. The Puritan Church was the only church recognized in the colony, and only a select few could become full church members.

Puritan laws condemned all wars that were not for protection. Laws were also set up to punish people for gambling and heavy drinking. These activities were against the Puritans' religious beliefs. Puritan laws did not allow people who lent money to charge interest on those loans. People who showed a lack of respect for God could be put to death. Some Puritan laws even stopped Quakers and Roman Catholics from worshiping in Massachusetts or, in some cases, even from living there. The Puritans felt that other religious groups would contaminate, or stain, their own beliefs.

Greater religious freedom existed in the other English colonies, but they still made laws to protect their interests. Most colonies also allowed more men to take part in government. Maryland, Pennsylvania, and Rhode Island were among the colonies with greater freedoms.

Virginia allowed greater male involvement in its early colonial government, but it denied religious freedom for many. In 1619, Virginia's white, land-owning, adult males elected representatives from each county in the colony to form the House of Burgesses. This was the first representative lawmaking body in America. The colony was ruled by the House of Burgesses, a governor (appointed by the English king), and the governor's special council. The burgesses were mostly rich male planters. They made the laws for the colony. But all laws had to be approved by the governor.

Many of the early laws approved by the House of Burgesses served to protect the way of life of the planters. No male could vote unless he owned at least one house. All religious ceremonies had to be conducted by the Church of England. It is called the Episcopal Church in the United States today. Failure to attend public worship without a good excuse got one a $50 fine. (This was also true in Massachusetts and other Puritan strongholds in America.)

Eventually, protests against some of the strict laws of the Puritans and the Virginia burgesses led to their end or to less enforcement.

New laws were also set up by other Europeans and their descendants who came to America. The Pilgrims were another religious group from England. They obtained a charter, or legal right, from the London Company to settle on the company's land in Virginia. But the Pilgrims' ship, the *Mayflower,* was blown off course. In 1620, it landed near Cape Cod in Massachusetts. Since the Pilgrims had no charter to set up a colony in Massachusetts, they drew up their own agreement. It became known as the Mayflower Compact. This was the first time a group of Europeans had set down in writing a new form of government in the Americas. The Mayflower Compact was an outgrowth of the English concept of self-rule.

Many of the early Americans dared to experiment with the making of laws in a new land. This experiment would later prove valuable as Americans prepared themselves for self-rule.

1.   Who were the Puritans? What kinds of laws did they pass? Why?

2.   What was the Virginia House of Burgesses? What kinds of laws did it pass? Why?

3.   What compact, or agreement, did the Pilgrims prepare? Why was this compact important?

4.   How do you think experimenting with lawmaking can help a people learn more about government or governing?

SKILLS Developing your basic civic education skills

(thinking critically and sequencing cause and effect)

Understanding and Applying What You Read

In this chapter, you learned that the word *anarchy* means a condition in which a society has no laws or government to make laws. Anarchy means the absence of any guiding rules. You also learned that the term *law* means a rule of society set up by the customs of the people and backed by some kind of force. Keep the meanings of these terms in mind as you read the following stories.

Situation 1: Free-for-All

The basketball game between Jefferson and Washington high schools began promptly at 7 P.M. During the jump ball, one of the Jefferson guards held the arms of the Washington center, which allowed a Jefferson forward to get the tip from his own center. As he ran down the court with the ball tucked under one arm, he was tripped by a Washington cheerleader. The cheerleader quickly grabbed the ball and threw it down the center of the court, allowing a Washington player to score.

Before the ball came back into play, two of the referees began a fistfight over who would give the ball to the Jefferson team. At the same time, players from both benches started to shoot one ball after another into the nets, claiming points scored for each basket made. The game continued like this for 2 hours.

Situation 2: The New Settlement—Account from a Diary

December 10: As we crossed the river, we heard our elders speak of freedom, visions that were soon to be realized. No more brutal restrictions. Ours was to be a world right and free.

January 3: Camped along the riverbank, conversation flowed as the fires burned brightly. Talk of our arrival, talk of our dream.

January 16: Today, we arrived at our destination. We are finally here. What a beautiful place. More so than could be imagined.

February 3: Plans for our new community were completed today. Some arguments arose but were quickly settled. A few of the families wanted a location nearer to the riverbank, but were persuaded to remain where they were for the benefit of the community.

May 15: Problems arose again today. Over one-fourth of our settlement left at sunrise, taking more than one-half of the community supplies. But they soon returned and spoke of an attack. All their supplies had been lost, and three members of the party were killed.

June 10: More disagreements after another attack occurred. This time, however, enemy raiders had come all the way into our settlement and killed four of our people.

Our community hunters refused to go too far from the settlement for fear of raiders; therefore, the large meat surplus shrank until a shortage became certain.

July 21: Situation is growing more severe. Farmers of community refused grain to our hunters today. "No meat, no grain," they said. Our hunters replied by withholding what meat they did have from the whole community.

August 5: Tragic situation occurred today as our townspeople, encouraged by our farmers, attacked the hunters and chased them out of the community. Members of the community, fearing starvation, then turned on the farmers and robbed their storage area. No grain was left.

September 4: My family has remained in our small dwelling for the past few days now. Fear runs through the community. We fear not only the constantly attacking raiders but also each other. Our food supplies are running extremely low.

September 20: My father was killed today, trying to steal food from another family. Our situation is hopeless. We have very little to eat. At least we have not seen the raiders for some time.

October 7: The raiders attacked what remained of our settlement today, killing most of those who were left. I was taken captive, along with a few others.

October 20: Today, I await my death. I am the only survivor remaining from our original community. What happened to our search for freedom?

1. In Situation 1, briefly describe what happened. Could just one word describe it? Explain.

2. What did the game seem to lack? Why?

3. In Situation 2, what did this group of people dream of achieving? What happened to them? Why did it happen? How could it have been avoided?

4. What one word might best describe this people's society? Explain.

Using Critical-Thinking Skills

Critical thinking means thinking in a way that involves careful judgment. A major part of critical thinking includes the decision-making process. Decision making is actually a vital part of our everyday life. Consider what happens when you have to decide whether to devote some extra time to preparing for a test at school. First, you recognize a question or problem: Should you spend time studying for a test tomorrow in civics? You must then decide, for example: (1) What might occur if you do not spend time studying for the test? (2) How well do you really know the material to be covered on the test? (3) What might be asked on the test? (4) What is your current grade average? (5) What might happen if you devote time to study? (6) What else could you do instead of studying for the test?

You next form a hypothesis. A *hypothesis* is a starting point for discussion. It is often a basis for an argument or reasoning. It is a statement based on consideration of at least some, often limited, evidence or information. The hypothesis can be used as a basis for further investigation. A hypothesis can be an idea that has not been proven true, a temporary explanation, an educated guess, or a trial idea. A hypothesis is a statement open to proof.

Whatever you decide to do about preparing for the test, your decision is a hypothesis. You check the truth of your hypothesis when you take the test the next day. When you receive the grade for the test, you can determine if your hypothesis was correct. ("I did need to spend that time studying for the test.")

Your answer forms a more definite conclusion, also called a generalization. A *generalization* is a principle, a statement, or an idea based on a careful examination and testing of available information. It is based on more examination and testing of data than is a hypothesis. Based on experience, a generalization about preparation for the civics exam could be: "One should spend considerable time preparing for Ms. Jones's civics test."

If you wish to make a statement about preparation for all your civics exams, you can form a synthesis as your answer. A *synthesis* is the combination of two or more generalizations or ideas into a new one. Consider from past experience the generalizations you might have formed about the preparation time that is required to take the civics tests.

You most probably will have formed a generalization about preparation time required for each test. If you combine all those generalizations into a new one, you will have a synthesis.

Thus, the basic parts of the decision-making process can be summarized as:

STEP 1   recognizing a problem or posing a question

STEP 2   forming a hypothesis in answer to the problem or the question

STEP 3   testing the validity or truthfulness of the hypothesis

STEP 4   forming a more definite conclusion, or generalization, in answer to the problem or question

STEP 5   arriving at a combination of two or more generalizations, or a synthesis

5.   What do you think is the main difference between (a) a hypothesis and a generalization, and (b) a generalization and a synthesis?

6.   Once stated, do you think a hypothesis could always remain unchanged? Explain your answer.

7.   Do you think a generalization could ever be revised or changed? Explain.

8.   Think again about information you examined in Situation 1, the account of the fictitious basketball game between Jefferson and Washington. Which one of the following could best be a problem or question in relation to that story? Tell why.

   a.   what determines the final score of a basketball game

   b.   who is the high scorer

   c.   what happens in a contest without any rules

9. Which one of the following could best be a hypothesis in response to the problem you selected in question 8? Why?

    a. The team with the best athletes usually wins the most games.

    b. Joseph Swift will probably score the most points, as he has done in previous games.

    c. A contest without any rules can result in anarchy.

10. How might you test the validity of the hypothesis you selected in question 9?

11. Review Situation 2, the fictitious diary. What would be a problem or question you might pose in relation to that account?

12. What hypothesis might you form in answer to the problem you posed in question 11? How might you begin to check the truth of your hypothesis?

Determining the Sequence of Events and Cause-and-Effect Relationships

Thinking citizens in our society must also be able to place events in proper sequence and to determine cause-and-effect relationships. *Sequence* means the order in which one thing follows another. A *cause* is something that produces a result or consequence. It can be a person, an event, or a condition responsible for an action or a result. It is often the basis for an action. An *effect* is something brought about by a cause. It is an outcome or a result.

The words *sequence, cause,* and *effect* have specific meaning when applied to the information in Situation 1. The sequence of events noted by the author of Situation 1 would be:

I. The game began at 7 P.M.

II. A state of anarchy began when one of the Jefferson guards held the arms of the Washington center.

III. A free-for-all continued during the remainder of the game.

IV. The game ended just after 9 P.M.

The information as presented in I–IV is sequential. It appears in the order in which it happened.

The term *cause-and-effect* also has specific meaning when applied to the information in Situation 1. The cause-and-effect relationship of information presented in Situation 1 could be diagrammed in the following manner:

Anarchy at the Basketball Game

Causes	Effect
1. players who did not abide by the rules	a complete lack of order or enforcement of any rules basic to playing a basketball game
2. fans who discarded the rules	
3. referees who did not enforce the rules	

13. List in chronological order what you regard as the sequence of major events in the fictitious diary account in Situation 2.

14. How can the term *cause-and-effect* apply to information in Situation 2? Make a diagram like the one above.

15. Do you think there is any value in putting events about a topic in sequence? Why or why not?

16. Do you think there is any value in determining cause-and-effect relationships about a topic? Why or why not?

3 How We Are Governed

The last chapter was about laws. This chapter is about government—the organization that enforces laws.

What do you think of when you hear the word *government*? Do you think of the President and Congress? The police and the courts? State governors and city mayors? Soldiers and tax collectors? All of these are part of our system of government in the United States. Do you think of freedom of speech? Freedom of religion? The right to a fair trial? The right to vote? These are also part of our system of government. Do you think of your responsibility to obey the law? That is another part of our system of government.

People at other times or in other countries—and some people in our own country—might have more negative thoughts about government. Some might think of secret police knocking on the door in the middle of the night or a king shouting, "Off with their heads!" Some people might think of brutal attacks by police or soldiers who are out of control. Others might think of laws that favor the rich and powerful over the poor. These can also be part of government when governments misuse their powers. That is why the people who set up the government of the United States gave us certain safeguards.

One of those safeguards is that the government is based upon laws. Every member of our society—from the President down to the poorest citizen—has the same duty to obey the law. At the same time, each and every member of our society has the same rights under the law.

The more you know about your government, the more it will mean to you. In this chapter, you will read about some of the things that all governments do and some of the types of government other people have known. Then you will see how the United States came to be governed as it is.

I. Jobs and types of government
  A. What all governments do
    1. Supply goods and services
    2. Protect citizens
    3. Pass on values
    4. Encourage people to fill needed roles
  B. Types of government
    1. Rule by one person
    2. Rule by a few people
    3. Rule by many people
II. How the United States is governed
  A. Background to the Constitution
    1. Learning from England
    2. Learning from Independence
  B. The Constitution
    1. The federal system

    2. Separation of powers: checks and balances
    3. Allowing for change
    4. Guaranteeing the rights

Words to Know

government —— an organization set up to make rules for a group of people and to see that the rules are carried out; a power that rules a people

monarchy —— a government in which power is passed down from one member of a family to another

dictatorship —— a government in which one person seizes and holds total power

democracy —— a government in which the people rule themselves

republic —— a democracy in which people choose representatives to run the government for them

parliamentary democracy —— a democracy in which a single group of people makes the laws and carries them out

presidential democracy —— a democracy in which one group makes laws and another carries them out under the leadership of a president

Jobs and Types of Government

A **government** is an organization that is set up to make rules for a group of people and to see that the rules are carried out. Stated another way, a government is a power that rules a people. All the people themselves may hold that power, only a few people may hold it, or even one person may hold it. In the United States, the form of government is based upon the idea that all of the people should share in ruling themselves.

What All Governments Do

Not all governments are alike. Still, all governments do have some things in common. There are four things that all governments try to do.

Supply Goods and Services Governments supply services that people would find hard to supply for themselves. For example, when you mail a letter, the government, which runs the post offices, delivers it for you. This is a service. Governments build roads, water lines, and sewers. They build schools to give their people an education. These are all services.

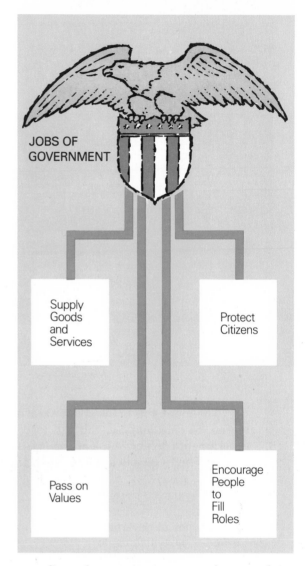

JOBS OF GOVERNMENT

Supply Goods and Services

Protect Citizens

Pass on Values

Encourage People to Fill Roles

Sometimes governments also supply goods. During past wars, the United States government ran factories to make weapons. Today, it generates electricity from giant dams that it has built. In some countries, governments run factories to make goods such as matches and automobiles. In the United States, however, most goods are made by privately-owned businesses.

Protect Citizens Another thing that governments do is supply protection. If you saw a gang beating up a boy in a dark alley, you would call the government—in the

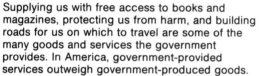

Supplying us with free access to books and magazines, protecting us from harm, and building roads for us on which to travel are some of the many goods and services the government provides. In America, government-provided services outweigh government-produced goods.

form of the police. One job of the police is to protect citizens from each other. If you heard that a foreign army was marching toward the United States, you would expect another part of government—the military forces—to go into action. The job of our military forces is to protect us from other nations. Other parts of our government also supply protection. One part of government works to protect us against unsafe foods. Another protects us from poisons in the air and water. Local governments usually run the fire departments that protect us against fire.

Pass on Values When was the first time you said the Pledge of Allegiance? You may not remember when. But if you have lived in the United States during all your years at school, you have probably said the Pledge so many times that you know it by heart. The Pledge sums up some of the values of our society—a belief in liberty and in

justice. The Pledge is taught in schools, and this helps to pass on these values to United States citizens. Some values that are taught in the schools are related to government—for example, patriotism and a belief in the United States' system of government. Others are general values—for example, a belief in fair play and honesty.

The laws themselves also help to pass on values and norms. As we have seen, laws are norms that are enforced by the government. Laws usually express values as well. A law might require a minimum wage for certain jobs. But the law does more than set a norm that employers must follow. It also shows a value—the belief that people should be paid a salary that is high enough for them to keep up a comfortable standard of living.

Encourage People to Fill Needed Roles Governments often encourage people to do certain things—to take on roles

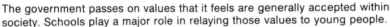
The government passes on values that it feels are generally accepted within society. Schools play a major role in relaying those values to young people.

that will help the society. For example, the United States government gives medals to soliders who act bravely. This is done to encourage other soldiers to be brave. Also, our government encourages people to give money to charities. It does this by giving special tax breaks for some types of gifts. At the same time, governments can also *discourage* certain roles. By passing laws against gambling, for example, a government is trying to discourage people from becoming gamblers.

Types of Government

A person from the United States who goes abroad will discover many new and different things. Languages will be new. A tourist might hear Chinese, Russian, Hindi, Portuguese, or any of the hundreds of languages that are used in the world. The tourist might visit different climates. There are the high, cold mountains of Nepal, the steaming jungles of Brazil, and the green rolling hills of Ireland. The tourist might eat many new types of food—pasta in Italy, couscous in Algeria, or curry in India.

With so many new and different things, the tourist might overlook a very important difference—the governments of the many countries. There are many types of government in the world. The differences in the governments are due to each country's special history. Each country has shaped its government to its special conditions.

Still, there are some common patterns to be found. To make studying governments easier, people often divide them into three types. The types are: (1) rule by one person, (2) rule by a few people, and (3) rule by many people.

Rule by One Person There are several types of government in which one person rules. The most common types today are the monarchy and the dictatorship.

A **monarchy** is a government in which the right to rule is passed down from one member of a family to another. When a ruler dies, another member of the family takes over. The rulers in monarchies have different titles in different countries. Some of these titles are emperor, grand duke, king, queen, shah, and maharajah.

In a **dictatorship,** one person holds the power. Usually, that person seizes power by force. The power to rule is not automatically passed on to a member of the family, though. Usually, a dictator holds

Under a monarchial form of government, the right to rule is passed on from within the family.

unlimited power. The dictator's word is law. There are no safeguards for personal rights and freedoms. Adolf Hitler, in Germany, and Benito Mussolini, in Italy, were two modern dictators.

Rule by a Few Sometimes a small group of people share the power of running a government. The group makes all the decisions. It sets policies for the country to follow. This type of government is very much like a dictatorship. The only difference is the number of people sharing the power.

This form of government is very common in the world today. Sometimes the small group may be members of a political party. For example, the Soviet Union today is ruled by the leaders of the Communist Party. Sometimes the small group may be members of the armed forces who seize power. For example, a group of generals overthrew the government in Chile and took power in 1974.

Rule by Many People When all the people have a say in how the government works, that form of government is called

democracy. Democracy can take different forms.

In a direct democracy, all the people in a community may gather at a meeting to vote on public matters. This only works in small communities. It was practiced in the ancient Greek city-states. It is still practiced today in some New England towns to decide on local matters.

In an indirect, or representative, democracy, the people elect representatives. The representatives carry on the business of running the government and making the laws. This form of government is also known as a **republic.** It was a form of government used for a time in ancient Rome. It is the form of government we use today in the United States.

There are two major types of representative democracy. One is parliamentary democracy. The other is presidential democracy.

In a **parliamentary democracy,** voters elect members to a body called a *parliament*. The parliament has the power to make laws. The parliament usually also has

TYPES OF GOVERNMENT

Rule by a Few People

Rule by Many People

Rule by One Person

the power to act as judge or jury in some matters. Great Britain is the oldest and perhaps the best-known parliamentary democracy.

In a **presidential democracy,** the people elect representatives to a lawmaking body. The people also elect someone—a president—to carry out the laws. The representatives in this kind of government help keep the power of the president under control. The president also serves as a check on the power of the lawmaking body.

In practice, very few governments are purely one form. In Great Britain, for example, there is a monarch—the Queen. But there is also a parliament that handles the business of governing. In France, there is an elected president, but there is also a parliamentary body that makes the laws.

No form of government is automatically good or bad. A monarch can rule wisely and well. A small ruling group can sometimes meet the needs and wants of the people it rules. On the other hand, rule by many people can sometimes be unfair. Those groups of people who have the most votes could sharply limit the rights of the minority.

Still, most people in the United States believe that government by the greatest number of people is the best. A government that is ruled by one person or by a few people can too easily become a government that only fills the needs and wants of a few. Democracies, with all their possible flaws, must try to pay attention to the needs and wants of a greater number of people.

—————— REVIEW ——————

1. Define the word *government.*
2. Match the job of government in the left-hand column with the example in the right-hand column:
   - a. providing goods and services
   - b. protecting citizens
   - c. passing on values and norms
   - d. encouraging people to fill roles

   (1) arresting people who break the law
   (2) passing laws to encourage business investments
   (3) building dams to make electric power
   (4) teaching patriotism in the schools

3. A government in which voters choose people to represent them is a:
   (a) dictatorship.
   (b) monarchy.
   (c) republic.
4. A government in which voters elect one body that makes the laws and carries them out is a:
   (a) presidential democracy.
   (b) a parliamentary democracy.
5. Of all the jobs of government, which *one* do you think is the most important? Why?

Words to Know

unalienable right——a right that can neither be given up nor taken away

constitution——a document that tells how a government is to be organized, and what powers each part of the government is to have

federal government——the central government in a federation; the national government of the United States

reserved powers——powers that are set aside by the Constitution for the states

concurrent powers——powers that are shared by the federal and state governments

separation of powers——the division of government into branches, each with its own powers

executive branch——the part of government that carries out the laws

legislative branch —— the part of government that makes the laws

judicial branch —— the part of government that runs the courts and says what the law means

checks and balances —— part of the separation of powers, in which each branch of government can check, or block, the actions of other branches so that all are in balance

constitutional amendment —— a formal change in the wording of a constitution

How the United States Is Governed

The basic rules of our government today are found in the United States Constitution. The Constitution was written over a period of a few months in Philadelphia in 1787. Yet the ideas written down in the Constitution can be traced far back into history. Some of the ideas go back to the laws of the ancient Middle East. Others come from the ideas of democracy in ancient Greece and Rome. But most of the ideas come from many centuries of the English experience. Before we look more closely at the Constitution, let's look at some of the events that led up to it.

Background to the Constitution

Learning from England Early settlers from England brought to American shores their three-masted ships, their gunpowder, their square-toed shoes, and their political ideas. It is the political ideas that have made the most lasting impact.

One major idea was that government should have limits. The English settlers knew from their past experience that it was dangerous to live under an all-powerful king. They began limiting their king's powers early in history. In 1215, a group of English nobles—wealthy people with special titles—decided to limit the powers of King John. They forced him to sign the *Magna Charta*—"great chart." In it, King John agreed to respect certain rights. One was the right of the nobles to have a say about how much tax they should pay. Another was the right to a trial by jury. At first, these rights applied only to nobles. But the English had started an idea: A ruler's powers could be limited.

A second major idea was that government should represent the people it governed. Again, the idea first applied only to a few people. Nobles and church officials sat on a council to give advice to kings. Then, rich merchants were added to the council. Each merchant on the council represented other merchants. By 1400, the king's council had become known as Parliament. It had the two houses, or parts, that it has today. Slowly, Parliament gained the power to make laws, not just give advice. Many centuries passed before Parliament truly represented everyone. Only within the last 100 years has it come to represent the poor as well as the rich, women as well as men.

A third major idea that came from England was that people are born with certain rights that no government should take away. In part, the idea of these rights can be traced back to the Roman belief in "natural law." But these rights became practice with the English Bill of Rights of 1689.

That bill completed the job of limiting the power of the English kings. The Bill of Rights made it clear that Parliament was more powerful than any king. It also gave certain rights to all English people: the right to trial by jury, the right to petition the government, the right not to have to suffer cruel or unusual punishment for a crime. These and other rights later became part of the United States government.

All these ideas came to America with the English settlers. They became part of

In England, William III and Mary were the first rulers to acknowledge that a monarchy had limited powers over the people it represented.

the heritage of the people of the United States. When, in the 1770s, many settlers became unhappy with British rule, these ideas formed the basis of a new government of their own.

The first step in forming the government of the United States was a war of independence. The fighting began in 1775, when British redcoats clashed with colonial settlers at Lexington and Concord in Massachusetts. The war dragged on for years. But the American colonists were certain of victory. In 1776, their Second Continental Congress summed up the political ideas of the colonists in a bold claim to freedom. The Declaration of Independence listed complaints against British rule. It also laid

down the ideals that the new American citizens and their government would fight for. (You will find the text of the Declaration of Independence on pages 546–548.)

The Declaration of Independence made three important statements. First, it declared that "all men are created equal." That statement was a rallying cry—a call for the people to fight for their independence. It did not describe what things were like. In the early years of the new American nation, full rights belonged only to white males over the age of 21 who owned property. But those who did not have those rights used the rallying cry to stir the consciences of those who did have the rights. In time, "all men" came to mean "all peo-

To win their freedom from the repressive rule of the British, the American colonists had to fight a long, hard war. The first battles were fought at Lexington and Concord in Massachusetts. The minutemen—pictured here in combat—typified the brave American settler who put down the plow to fight for independence.

ple"—whatever their sex, race, or property. Today, groups that feel left out of political life in the United States still use the same cry, trying to awaken the consciences of those people with power.

Second, the Declaration said that governments "derive their just powers from the consent of the governed." In other words, the government gets its power from the people. If the people want to change their government, that is their right. This was a truly revolutionary idea at the time—and it still is.

Third, the Declaration stated that all people "are endowed by their Creator with certain unalienable rights." An **unalienable right** is one that can neither be given up nor taken away. No government, said the Declaration, can take away the rights to "Life, Liberty, and the Pursuit of Happiness." The people of the United States still hold firmly to the idea that these rights are sacred.

Learning from Independence The thirteen colonies that broke away from Great Britain had thirteen separate governments. They were like thirteen independent nations. Since the colonies had just thrown off British rule, they did not want to give up their independence to a strong central government. The colonies also knew that they needed each other, so they chose to set up a loosely knit organization of states. They thought that keeping the central government weak was the best way to protect the rights of the people and the thirteen states.

The Second Continental Congress wrote a **constitution** for this new govern-

The Declaration of Independence made official the ideals for which the new United States government stood.

Fact Block: The United States under the Articles of Confederation

Executive Branch	Legislative Branch	Judicial Branch
none	A one-house lawmaking body called *Congress*, made up of members elected by state legislatures.	none
General Provisions		

1. Each state had one vote in Congress.
2. Congress had no power to tax. States gave the amount of money they wanted to.
3. To carry out many of its duties, Congress had to have the votes of nine out of the thirteen states.
4. Congress could not control trade between the states. Each state could charge a tax on goods coming in from another state.
5. Congress had no way of enforcing its laws. Sometimes states took over the powers that were supposed to belong to Congress—for example, dealing with other nations.
6. Members of Congress were paid by their states. They could be replaced at any time by the state legislatures.
7. No change could be made in the Articles of Confederation without the agreement of all thirteen states.

ment. A constitution is a document that tells how a government is to be organized and what powers the government is to have. This new constitution was called the Articles of Confederation. It was in effect from 1781 to 1789. The following Fact Block lists the main features of the Articles of Confederation.

The Articles of Confederation had one strong point: They formed a new nation— the United States of America. People began to think of themselves as something more than New Yorkers or Virginians. They were now citizens of the United States.

But the Articles were too weak to form the basis of a lasting government. The new nation was poor. Soldiers in rags begged to be paid for their service during the Revolution. People who had loaned money to the struggling government wanted it paid back. Congress had asked the states for money. But the states pinched their pennies. Congress could not even pay interest on the money it had borrowed.

The thing that was the most damaging to the nation was the lack of any way of enforcing the laws. There was no person or group to carry out the laws. There were no national courts—only state courts. If a state did not approve of a law passed by Congress, it just ignored the law. By 1787, many people in the United States were deeply worried about the future of their new nation. Some people wanted to drop the Articles of Confederation and write a completely new constitution. Others wanted to work on the Articles and add a new feature here or there. Most people agreed that something had to be done.

In 1787, Congress called for a meeting of delegates from all the states. They met at Philadelphia from May to September—fifty-five delegates named by all the states, except Rhode Island. It was soon clear that those who wanted to rewrite the constitution outnumbered the others. The United States was to have a brand new constitution. As a result, that Philadelphia meeting is now known as the Constitutional Convention.

The fifty-five delegates—all men, all white, and mostly rich—are famous as the founders of our government. Many were al-ready famous for other deeds. George Washington led the Continental Army against the British. Benjamin Franklin helped arrange peace with Great Britain. James Madison, Edmund Randolph, William Peterson, and Alexander Hamilton had all played important roles in earlier events. Most of the delegates were lawyers with experience in colonial or state government. They were well educated. They knew their history—ancient as well as modern. They had a knowledge of many types of government. This knowledge helped them in the huge task of setting up a new type of government.

Even today, the original documents which formed the framework of our governmental system are on display.

The Constitution

The delegates to the Constitutional Convention created the framework for the United States government as we know it today. They developed a new constitution that had little in common with the Articles of Confederation. By September of 1787, the delegates had completed their task. Then, the document went to the thirteen states for approval. Some states approved at once. Others took years to talk it over. By the summer of 1788, nine of the states had given their approval and the Constitution went into effect. By 1790, all thirteen states had entered the new Union.

In place of a loose confederation, the Constitution created a strong union of states. In place of a weak central government, the Constitution set up a strong central government. The many powers of the government were carefully arranged to safeguard against any misuse. The new Constitution was open to change. Amendments could be added without the approval of all the states. Most important of all, the new Constitution created a workable form of government. The delegates in Philadelphia built the Constitution to last. For almost 200 years, the Constitution has stood the test of time.

Fact Block: The United States under the Constitution

Executive Branch	Legislative Branch	Judicial Branch
President Vice President (Cabinet officers and other appointed officials who assist the President became a part of the executive branch later.)	A two-house lawmaking body called Congress. *Senate* (upper house) Two senators from each state who were chosen by state legislatures. (This changed later to election by popular vote.) (*To please the smaller states*) *House of Representatives* (lower house) One or more representatives from each state depending upon the size of the population. (*To please the larger states.*)	Supreme Court Has power to decide all cases arising under the Constitution and to settle disputes involving two or more states. Lesser federal courts
Compromises Reflected in the Constitution		
1. All money-raising bills had to begin in the House of Representatives. (*To please the larger states*) 2. All slaves were counted as three-fifths of a person for purposes of deciding how many representatives a state had in the House of Representatives. (*To please the southern states*) 3. All slaves were counted as three-fifths of a person for purposes of federal taxing. (*To please the northern states*)	4. Slave trade from abroad was not to be stopped until 1807. (*To please the southern states*) 5. Any treaty with a foreign country had to be approved by a two-thirds vote in the Senate. (*To please the southern states, which feared that treaties might harm southern farmers by interfering with trade with other countries*)	

You will find the complete text of the Constitution on pages 549–563. Now let's look at the outstanding features of this document. First, study the Fact Block that shows how various compromises at the Constitutional Convention helped to shape the new government.

The Federal System The Constitution set up a **federal** government in place of the old government. A federal form of government has two layers of rule. There is a central government for the whole nation. There are also separate governments for each state. Each layer of government has separate and distinct powers. Those powers are given in the constitution, which is "the supreme law of the land."

Like the old government, the new government arose from a union of separate states. But the states were no longer the most powerful part of the government.

They gave up some of their powers to the central, or federal, government. Now the central government was more powerful than any state government.

The delegates at Philadelphia gave the federal government alone the power to answer questions that affected the nation as a whole. One example was trade between the states. A farmer in Connecticut might want to sell butter to an innkeeper in New York. If New York were to put a tax on butter from other states, then trade between the states would be hurt. Such taxes were used by states under the Articles of Confederation. The founders wanted to see that this did not happen again. They gave the federal government alone the power to control and tax trade between the states and trade with foreign nations.

The federal government alone was given the power to make and print money.

Under the system of checks and balances, the President presents his State-of-the-Union address to Congress and all interested parties each year.

State governments had to stop printing their own money. The federal government was also given the power to make treaties with foreign nations. Only the federal government could keep an army and a navy.

But the states kept some powers for themselves. In fact, under the present federal system, the states hold all powers that are not given to the federal government by the Constitution. These are the **reserved powers.** Thus, state governments may build highways, run schools, issue driver's licenses, set a minimum age for leaving school, and control the hours of businesses.

Some powers belong both to the states and to the federal government. These are known as **concurrent powers.** Both the federal and the state governments have the power to tax. Both have the power to pass laws and to set punishments for crimes.

Separation of Powers: Checks and Balances The founders wanted to make sure that the new government would not misuse its powers. From history, they knew that governments and government officials often did misuse powers. Even democratic governments did so. The years under British control had given people a fear of strong government. That was why the first national government, under the Articles of Confederation, was so weak. If the new federal government was to be strong, there must be safeguards. But what kind of safeguards?

Perhaps you have seen an old movie about gold mining. Some prospectors who have been partners for years strike it rich. Now they begin to distrust each other. Will one of them grab the gold and run? They make arrangements so they can watch each

To insure that no government would abuse its powers, our founders instituted a separation of powers dividing government into three branches—the legislative (facing page), the executive (above), and the judicial (below).

other. At night they post a guard, sometimes two guards—one to watch the other.

The founders posted their own guards over the powers of our national government. They divided the government into three branches, or parts. Each branch has part of the powers. But no branch has all the power. Each branch stands guard over the others.

This division of government is known as the **separation of powers.** The three branches are the legislative, the executive, and the judicial. The **legislative branch** is called Congress, which is made up of the Senate and the House of Representatives. Congress has the power to make laws. The **executive branch** is headed by the President. It has the power to carry out laws. The **judicial branch** is headed by the Supreme Court. It has the power to judge the

other two branches. The Court can throw out laws that go against the Constitution. The Court can also order the executive branch to stop any actions that break a law or are forbidden by the Constitution.

Each branch of government can *check,* or block, the actions of the other branches. The three branches are in *balance.* Thus, we speak of our system as one of **checks and balances.**

Here is an example of how the system works. Congress may pass a law, but the President can veto, or cancel, it. Then, Congress may pass the law again—this time by a two-thirds vote—and the President cannot veto it. But the law may still be canceled if the Supreme Court decides that it goes against the Constitution.

Here is another example of checks and balances. The President appoints federal judges. A President's appointments can influence how the Supreme Court rules. But the Senate must approve the President's appointments. It can block any appointments that it does not like. (You will see many other examples of checks and balances in later chapters of this book.)

Allowing for Change The Constitution is a living document. The founders meant it to be so. They knew that it might become necessary to make changes in the Constitution.

The founders did not want it to be too hard to change the Constitution. They remembered the Articles of Confederation. All the states had to approve any change in the Articles. That was a hard task. On the other hand, the founders did not want changes to be too easy—not as easy as changing a law, for example. The Constitution was far more important than individual laws. It was the framework of the government.

The founders of the Constitution wrote into it a way of making changes, or *amendments.* This is described in Article V of the Constitution. Three-fourths of the states must agree to any change. (You will look at this amending process more closely in Chapter 12.)

The Constitution can also change informally to keep up with the times. For example, when the Constitution was written, most people lived on farms. There were very few factories. No one worried much about the problem of children being made to work in factories. The Constitution did not mention child labor and it did not give Congress the power to pass laws about child labor. But it did not forbid Congress from using that power. Later on, child labor *did* become a problem, so Congress passed laws to control it.

Most people agree that the Constitution does allow Congress to control child labor. The reasoning goes like this: Goods produced by children working in factories usually go to other states for sale. The goods are part of interstate commerce. The Constitution *does* give Congress the power to control interstate commerce. Thus, Congress can pass laws to control working conditions in factories.

This example shows an informal change in the Constitution. There has been no change in the actual words of the Constitution. The only change is in the way the Constitution is read or interpreted. Both Congress and the federal courts helped to bring about this new reading of the Constitution. Congress used a new power and the courts upheld the use of that power. (In the case of child labor, many years passed before Congress and the courts agreed on the same reading of the Constitution.)

Guaranteeing Rights The founders put the Constitution together with care. As we have seen, they wanted to guard against any abuse of power by the new federal government. They thought they had built enough safeguards into the Constitution. But many people in the United States did not agree. They insisted that the document needed a listing of rights belonging not to

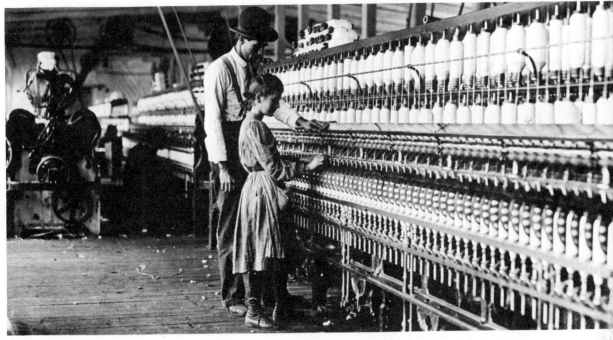

Child labor, once unregulated, is now controlled under Congress's interstate-commerce jurisdiction.

the state or federal government, but to the people.

In 1791, two years after the Constitution went into effect, it was amended to include such a listing. These amendments are known as the Bill of Rights. They include certain freedoms that the federal government must respect. Other rights were added later by other amendments. Today, we consider these rights to be the basis of our freedoms. Many of them can be traced far back in history—to the Magna Charta, the English Bill of Rights, and other documents about which you have read.

These basic rights include freedom of religion, freedom of speech, freedom of the press, and freedom of assembly. We have freedom of petition—the right to tell government officials our opinions. We have a right to fair treatment in the courts—including a right to a speedy trial by jury. We have a right to be secure in our homes, without worrying that police might break

through the door at any moment. If we are accused of a crime, we have a right to be told what that crime is. If we are convicted of a crime, we have a right not to have to undergo cruel or unusual punishment. This is only a brief listing of our constitutional rights. You will read more about them in Chapter 12.

──────── REVIEW ────────

1. Name three major political ideas that we took from the English.

2. In what way has the phrase "all men are created equal" been a rallying cry for people who have been kept from taking full part in United States society?

3. What is the difference between a confederation and a federation?

4. List three weaknesses of the Articles of Confederation.

5. What feature of the Constitution is most important to *you?* Explain.

How the United States Works

Government Jobs

When you think of government workers, elected officeholders are probably the first to come to mind. But elected officials are a very small part of our government's work force. The President alone has a large White House staff. The President also appoints a Cabinet to give him information and advice. Each member of the Cabinet is the head of a huge department. The Department of State, for example, employs foreign diplomats. Each diplomat also has a staff. This staff may include interpreters, secretaries, receptionists, legal aides, cooks, junior diplomats, bodyguards, and others. Most of these people work in foreign countries. In Washington, though, the Department of State hires many other workers. They do everything from answering telephones to advising on international matters.

That is just one department. There is also the Department of Justice, the Department of Health and Human Services, and the Treasury Department, to name a few. Try to imagine all the scientists, aides, engineers, office workers, accountants, social workers, and administrators that are hired. These are only a few of the positions needed to carry out the laws and policies of this country. Without even considering the armed forces, the federal government employs almost 3 million people. The armed forces hire almost 2.5 million more. These people work all over the world. Their jobs range from running a fork lift to playing a bugle.

So far, only federal workers have been mentioned. However, nearly 15 million people work for state and local governments. Most of these people are connected with schools. But not all are teachers. Schools also need librarians, nurses, dieticians, administrators, kitchen workers, maintenance people, and others.

Education is only one service that governments supply. Roads must be built and cared for. Police and fire fighters must be hired. Parks must be maintained.

This list contains only a small number of the jobs needed to run the United States. There are many career possibilities that you have probably never thought about. In the chapters that follow, you will be taking a closer look at some of the jobs that help keep our government and society going.

Reading About . . .

A "Government" Scandal

The success of any form of government depends upon the people who run it. A dictator can make wise decisions. People who live in a democracy can make poor choices. As you read, think about these points:
● In what way do you think the government that was set up by the students in George Muldoon's class is different from the government of the United States?
● What do you think a student who did not like what was happening in Amasudatamalie could have done about it?
● What do you think were the main reasons for the fact that corruption became widespread in Amasudatamalie?

An experiment in self-government by a seventh-grade class has ended in scandal with the teacher, George Muldoon, assuming dictatorial powers over a make-believe government riddled with real corruption.

"I thought . . . we've got another Watergate," said teacher George Muldoon after he took power over the "Amasudatamalie" government in his Mill Valley School class.

Muldoon seized power after a meeting on Friday, when all but four of the twenty-seven students confessed to "crimes" under laws they established when their "country"—known as Amasudatamalie—was formed in January.

Muldoon recalled, "They thought I was too strict. So I said, 'OK, fine, you set up some rules and live by them.'"

The students set up a government like that of the United States.

They printed money—with a picture of a baby on one-dollar bills, a hippie on tens, and a skull on hundreds. Class members had to pay in Amasudatamalie dollars to use the pencil sharpener, books, a wastebasket or a door. Top bidders won the right to operate the "concessions" and reap the revenues from them.

But within weeks, the system began to crumble.

The Department of Beautification—the name chosen for the police force—issued a rash of violation notices for such crimes as sitting on desks and littering in the classroom.

"Some people never got arrested, though," one student observed. "People with money had more power than the president."

Muldoon said that class police eventually fingerprinted the whole class, kept files on them—and me—and began accepting payoffs for not issuing tickets.

The bank was also knee-deep in scandal, with the president using bank funds to pay other students to do her work. They, in turn, stole from the bank.

But the crime that eventually brought Amasudatamalie's downfall was counterfeiting. Muldoon said. The chief culprit admitted Friday that he used a duplicating machine to produce more than three hundred thousand dollars.

His racket bacame so good that he soon "retired" from his job as head of the health department and persuaded six other students to join the ring.

When police said that they would fine the students for loafing around on their desks, one counterfeiter said, "We'd just slip them $100 and tell them to forget it."

Finally, Muldoon pulled a coup.

"I said, 'OK, your country is falling apart. The police are running amok. Your treasury is broke. Now you're going to be run by a dictatorship.' And I took over."

chapter
Review

Fact Review

1. Why is the Magna Charta an important part of the political heritage of the United States?
2. How was Congress, under the Articles of Confederation, different from Congress under the present Constitution?
3. Name three Americans who were delegates to the Constitutional Convention.
4. Why was the national government, under the Constitution, given power to regulate trade between the states?
5. Which of the following powers belong to the federal government, which belong to state governments, and which are shared?
   a. make treaties
   b. keep armies and navies
   c. issue driver's licenses
   d. set taxes
   e. operate schools
   f. make money
   g. pass laws about crimes
   h. regulate trade with other nations
6. Give two examples of checks and balances in the federal government of the United States.
7. From where did the idea come that a government should be representative of the people? Explain.
8. Do you think that citizens of the United States should have the right to change their form of government to a monarchy? To a parliamentary democracy? To a direct democracy? Explain your answer. How did the Declaration of Independence treat the issue of the people's right to change their government?
9. Which of the following statements regarding the Constitution of the United States are true and which are false? Indicate a true statement with a *T* and a false statement with an *F*.
   a. The Constitution is a framework for government.
   b. The Constitution does not allow Congress to pass laws to control working conditions in factories.
   c. The Articles of Confederation were written two years after the Constitution went into effect to include certain freedoms that the federal government must respect.
   d. The writers of the Constitution wrote into it a way of making changes called amendments.
   e. Among our basic rights are freedom of religion, freedom of speech, freedom of assembly, and freedom of the press.
   f. Many of the freedoms guaranteed to all Americans in the Bill of Rights can be traced back to the Magna Charta.

Developing Your Vocabulary

1. Match the words in *a* to *e* with the phrases in *(1)* to *(5)*.
   a. confederation
   b. concurrent
   c. legislative
   d. monarchy
   e. constitution
      (1) the branch of government that makes laws
      (2) a loose organization of states
      (3) shared by federal and state governments
      (4) a document that gives a framework for a government
      (5) a government with a hereditary ruler
2. What is the difference between a parliamentary democracy and a presidential democracy?

Developing Your Reading Skills

Read the following paragraphs and then answer the questions that follow.

The writers of the United States Constitution created a federal form of government. A federal government is one in which a number of states join together to form a union. Each state in that union agrees to give up some of its powers to the federal government. In the United States, our federal government began in 1788.

1. Which one of the following do you think is the main point, or main idea, of the paragraph above?
   a. When a number of states join together in a new political plan, they create a federal government.
   b. The United States government is a federal government.
   c. States must give up some of their powers when they agree to join a federal government.
   d. The federal government of the United States came into existence in 1788.
2. Why did you select either a, b, c, or d in question 1?

The division of the federal govenment into three branches, or parts, was done to make sure that the new government would not misuse its powers. This division was set up by the nation's founders. It has come to be known as the separation of powers. Under the separation of powers, the three branches of government are the legislative branch, the executive branch, and the judicial branch. No one branch of government has all the power. Each branch stands guard over the others.

3. Which one of the following do you think is the main point, or main idea, of the paragraph above?
   a. The three branches of government into which powers are separated are the legislative, the executive, and the judicial branches.
   b. Each branch of government is set up to watch over the others.
   c. The division of the federal government into three branches was established as a safeguard against the misuse of powers.
   d. The division of government is known as the separation of powers.

4. Why did you select either a, b, c, or d in question 3?

Developing Your Writing Skills— Forming and Supporting an Opinion

In this chapter, you have studied about why and how the federal government of the United States came into being. Now consider the following question:

Forming an opinion — Do you believe that any person should ever be above the law? Think of a historical example of someone who was above the law.

Supporting an opinion — After thinking it over, write a paragraph that answers the question above. Begin with a topic sentence that sums up your opinion. Then continue with evidence or arguments to support your opinion.

YOUR GOVERNMENT & ITS HISTORY

Writing the Declaration of Independence

Thomas Jefferson was a man of many talents. In his time, he was known for his abilities as an architect, an inventor, a mathematician, a scientist, a historian, a lawyer, an educator, a farmer, a musician, and a political philosopher. Jefferson is best remembered, though, as the third President of the United States and as the author of the Declaration of Independence.

Jefferson was a member of the Second Virginia Convention in 1775. That group chose him as a delegate to the Second Continental Congress. In the spring of 1776, he was selected to be a member of the committee formed to draw up a declaration of independence.

Thomas Jefferson's role in the writing of the Declaration of Independence was described by writer Clara Ingram Judson in a book entitled *Thomas Jefferson, Champion of the People.*

John Adams of Massachusetts; Roger Sherman, Connecticut; Benjamin Franklin, Pennsylvania; Robert Livingston, New York; and Thomas Jefferson, Virginia, were appointed to serve on the committee to write the Declaration. . . .

"Five is too large a group for the actual work of the writing," Franklin said after they had talked for a time. "I suggest that one man prepare a draft and then we all go at it."

"That man should be Jefferson," John Adams said quickly. "A Virginian is needed for this work. Jefferson has studied and thought more on the matter than any of us." The others approved his feeling. So Jefferson went to his rooms, opened his new writing desk, sharpened a pen, and laid out paper. Then he began to write.

"All men are created equal," he wrote, and paused. Were the people ready for that bold statement? Would they understand that the goal of political equality . . . was quite different from physical, mental, or economic equality, which no government could promise? Colonials had little education, on the average; but he trusted them to understand. One must have faith and make a beginning. He wrote on. . . .

On Friday, the twenty-eighth of June, the declaration was read to the House. On Monday, July first, the earlier Virginia resolution—that the colonies be declared free and independent states— was reopened, debated, and, on the following day, passed.

Then the Declaration of Independence prepared by the committee of five was taken up. For 2 days, members of Congress argued hotly over this phrase and that. Jefferson sat silent. . . . By July fourth, debate had grown bitter. The heat was frightful. Clouds of flies from the . . . stable next door were maddening. Late in the day, the vote was taken; the Declaration was accepted. Jefferson sighed. Some of his favorite sentences had been cut. The most serious loss was the section against slavery. Perhaps people were not ready for all he had hoped to include. But, overall, the changes were minor.

Jefferson left the noise and confusion of the Congress. As he walked on a quite street, phrases from the paper drifted through his mind:

"When in the Course of human events, it becomes necessary for one people to dissolve the political bands which have connected them with another, and to assume among the powers of the earth, the separate and equal station to which the Laws of Nature and Nature's God entitle them, a decent respect to the opinions of mankind requires that they should declare the causes which impel them to the separation.

"We hold these truths to be self-evident, that all men are created equal, that they are endowed by their Creator with certain unalienable Rights, that among these are Life, Liberty, and the pursuit of Happiness—that to secure these rights, Governments are instituted among Men, deriving their just powers from the consent of the government. . . ."

Suddenly, Jefferson was weary. "Perhaps the whole of it is overlong," he thought. "Perhaps those few words are the meat of it, and some day, the king and his power, the colonies and their wrongs, will be forgotten. Today—or so it seemed to be—we have taken a step on the road toward . . . freedom. Perhaps July the fourth, 1776, will be a day to remember. . . ."

1. For what two roles is Thomas Jefferson best remembered?
2. Who were the five members of the committee to draft the Declaration of Independence?
3. Why was Jefferson chosen to write the first draft of the Declaration of Independence?
4. What do you think is the most important point made in the first paragraph of the Declaration of Independence? In the second paragraph?

SKILLS   Developing your basic civic education skills

(types of evidence)

Thinking Further about the Declaration of Independence

In this chapter, you learned that members of the Second Continental Congress approved the Declaration of Independence on July 4, 1776. The full text of the Declaration is on pages 546–548.

Sometimes when we read historical documents, we read them with a respect that outweighs critical evaluation. In other words, because we know what that reading represents, we accept what we read without questioning it. But do we really understand what we are reading? Does the reading really say what it appears to say? Several years ago, Jack Harmon, an employee of the Southwest Research Institute in San Antonio, Texas, wrote an article about the Declaration of Independence. The following is what he had to say about it.

I would like to suggest for each citizen—man, woman, and child—to read and discuss at least a part of the Declaration of Independence.

There are those who will object. Most people see the Declaration of Independence as a scroll done in fancy penmanship and suitable for framing and forgetting. They have never read it or thought about it—let alone discussed it. So why start now?

Just take the first paragraph. Look at it in plain type, unadorned by the fancy scrolls that may have kept you from it before. Read it aloud. It has the ring of freedom in it, a majesty that reaches out from the words themselves.

"When in the Course of human events, it becomes necessary for one people to dissolve the political bands which have connected them with another, and to assume among the powers of the earth, the separate and equal station to which the Laws of Nature and Nature's God entitle them, a decent respect to the opinions of mankind requires that they should declare the causes which impel them to the separation."

Do you believe all that? Have you ever thought about it? How would you go about discussing it? One way you might start is to look at the word *necessary*. How do you know when something must be done? Who tells you?

Think about that phrase "one people." How did the colonists become one people? Didn't they come from different backgrounds? Some were rich; some were poor;

some were white; some were red; some were black. How could the colonists justify calling themselves one people? Are we one people today? Should we be?

This can get you some lively discussion. You may want to dampen the heat of the argument by moving on.

Consider the words "When in the Course of human events, it becomes necessary for one people to dissolve the political bands which have connected them with another, and to assume among the powers of the earth, the separate and equal station . . . ."

Is there any other basis for this necessity? Maybe the phrase "to assume . . . the separate and equal station to which the Laws of Nature and Nature's God entitle them" can offer a clue. Can you name a law of nature? Who passed it? Is it one law that applies to everybody, or is it different for each individual?

The first sentence of the second paragraph should be enough to convince you that the Declaration deals with issues that men and women have been talking about for centuries and that they should be talking about today. Just read it aloud again: "We hold these truths to be self-evident, that all men are created equal, that they are endowed by their Creator with certain unalienable Rights [rights that cannot be given up], that among these are Life, Liberty, and the pursuit of Happiness." Do you know any truths, that is, truths that are true always and true for everybody? How can you be sure they

are true? Are they self-evident, or do you have to be told them?

Now consider these words: ". . . that among these are Life, Liberty, and the pursuit of Happiness." Do you have an unalienable right to pursue your happiness in any fashion that meets your fancy? Can you put yourself above the law? If these words do not mean this, what do they mean?

The discussion could and should go on. These issues certainly were not solved when Jefferson wrote them. They are not solved today. They live or die in your understanding of them and in your actions. They are worth reading and discussing.

1. Of all the questions raised in this article, which three do you regard as the most significant? Tell why you selected these three questions.

2. Do you agree with what Jack Harmon is urging people to do? Why or why not?

Why Have Written Compacts?

You have learned that part of our political tradition calls for the use of written compacts, or agreements. This means that we have adopted the practice of written, witnessed, dated, and recorded agreements between the governed and the representatives they chose to govern. (See pages 72–81.) The Pilgrims were among the first Americans to use such a practice. They wrote the Mayflower Compact of 1620.

Think about what might occur if we did not have a tradition of written government contracts. Begin by picturing an imaginary student council. What if that council had no written constitution? That could mean it had no rules or guidelines to limit the powers of its delegates or officers.

Next, suppose that the student council held a meeting in a nearby park. The meeting might be unknown to the other members of the student body. This could happen because there would be no written constitution saying when the council was to meet, where it was to meet, or whether it had to let the other students know about it.

At this secret meeting, the student council might decide certain things. First, elections of delegates to the student council could be ended. Only the present members of the student council would decide who would become members of their organization. Second, no student who was not a member of the council would be allowed to attend council meetings or to make any recommendations to it. If a student complained about this, the council could simply say that it had violated no rules, since none existed for it to follow. Instead, the council could just make its own rules.

3. What had the imaginary student council in this story decided to do?

4. What could allow this imaginary student council to do those things?

5. Do you think having written compacts with governments is important? Explain?

Who Should Write a Constitution?

You have learned that some Americans called a convention in Philadelphia in 1787. That convention had the task of creating a new form of federal government. A federal government is one in which a number of states join together to form a union. Each state in a federal government agrees to give up some of its powers to a federal government. (See pages 72–81.)

You have also learned that many important Americans attended that convention in Philadelphia. George Washington was there. He, like many others, was a well-to-do farmer and had been a military leader. Many others at the convention were lawyers, and some had served in the colonial governments. All the delegates had some education and were well-read people.

Yet, many people were not allowed to attend the Philadelphia convention. Women, blacks, nonproperty owners, and males under the age of 21 were not invited. State laws forbade any of those people to vote or hold public office. Later, these groups would gain those rights, but that was not the case when the federal constitution was written. Think about the sort of people who would be allowed to attend a convention today. Who would they be?

Imagine that your student body had been asked to write a new constitution for your student council. It could use the old constitution as a guide, but a new one had to be written. Your task would be to help decide what kinds of students should be allowed to write a new constitution. Once written, the new constitution would have to be approved by a majority of the student body.

6. Which students do you think should be allowed to participate in writing a new constitution for your student council?

7. How would the students who were to write the new constitution be selected?

8. If a group is going to write a constitution with a government, what groups or individuals should be allowed to help?

What Is Historical Evidence?

Citizens sometimes have to decide what kinds of evidence to use when they examine a topic. There are two kinds of historical evidence, or sources of information available about the past. The first kind of historical evidence is a *primary,* or *original source.* This is something written or told during an era or an actual object from a certain period of time, such as an Egyptian pyramid, a mummy, or a coin. An excerpt, or direct quote, from the writings of Thomas Jefferson is an original source from the period of the American Revolution. An autobiography is another kind of original source, as are letters, diaries, and cartoons.

The second kind of historical information is the *secondary source.* This is something written or made using the ideas in original sources. A small model of an Egyptian pyramid would be a secondary source. If someone today wanted to write a book about Jefferson, he or she would use, among other things, the writings of Jefferson, which are original sources. The book itself, though, would be a secondary source. The account written by Clara Judson, which appears on pages 86–87, is a secondary source. Other kinds of secondary sources could be write-ups in your local newspaper about past events, interpretations by the authors of this textbook of what happened in the past, or a history of the Pilgrims and the Mayflower Compact.

Most sources fit nicely into one of the two categories of historical evidence. The Declaration of Independence, for example, is an original source. So are all the laws passed by Congress and speeches given by the President of the United States. The census information collected in 1980 also is an original source. But someone's history of our laws or interpretations of the 1980 census figures are secondary sources.

9. Classify each of the following as either an original or a secondary source. Explain your choice.
  a. Pledge of Allegiance
  b. account of students' problems with the Pledge of Allegiance
  c. cartoon about the Pledge of Allegiance

10. Name two other sources you can classify as original. Explain your choices.

11. Name two sources you can classify as secondary. Explain your choices.

12. Do you think there is any value in classifying evidence as either an original or a secondary source? Why or why not?

Special Note: Since all the information in this book is either in the form of original or secondary sources, when classifying these materials, you may wish to review pages 88–91.

UNIT 1 REVIEW

Fact Review

1. Give three examples of values that you believe to be part of United States culture.
2. Name three ways in which differences between city life and rural life might lead to different subcultures.
3. Which of the following are examples of civil laws and which are examples of criminal laws?
   a. a law about who must pay for damages caused by auto accidents
   b. a law to prevent bribery
   c. a law to settle disputes over the value of land taken for highways
   d. a law to settle disputes between neighbors about noise
4. What are two differences between a democracy and a dictatorship?
5. Give three examples of goods and/or services provided by the national government of the United States.
6. Give examples of two compromises that were put into the Constitution to satisfy the larger states. Give examples of three compromises put in to satisfy the Southern states.
7. Give an example of a formal change that has been made in the Constitution. Give an example of an informal change.
8. Do you think that the division of powers between our federal and state governments is about right, or is one of these too powerful? Explain.

Developing Your Vocabulary

1. Match the words in a to e with the phrases in (1) to (5)
   a. socialization   d. government
   b. adolescence   e. amendment
   c. code
      (1) a change in a constitution
      (2) the way we learn the values of our society
      (3) a listing of laws
      (4) the period between childhood and adulthood
      (5) a power that rules a people
2. What do we call the division of government into executive, legislative, and judicial branches?

Developing Your Reading Skills

Read the following passage and then answer the questions that follow:

Human beings live together in groups called societies. Each society has its own culture, or way of life. Each society develops its own values, along with rules for living that reflect those values.

Rules that are especially important to a society are called laws. They are binding rules, because they are enforced by a part of society. If someone breaks a law, he or she may be punished.

All known, large-scale societies have had ways to make laws and to see that they are carried out. The organization that does this is the government.

In the United States, government is based on the idea that all of the people should share in ruling themselves. This idea was behind our war of independence against Great Britain and behind documents such as the Declaration of Independence and the Constitution.

1. Identify the one statement below that is not supported by the reading:
   a. Laws reflect the values of a society.
   b. Anarchy is a common form of government.
   c. The part of society that makes laws is called government.
   d. A desire for self-rule helped lead to our war of independence.
2. According to the reading, all large-scale societies have which three of the following:
   a. culture   c. laws
   b. government   d. subcultures

The writers of the Constitution had written a new plan for government. That plan created three balanced branches, each with its own job. Congress was to be the *legislative branch*. Its job was to make laws.

At first, the Constitution was just a plan on paper. Little by little, the people of the United States learned how to use that plan to build a government. They tinkered with the plan. They added to it. Sometimes they threw out parts that did not seem to work. The government grew, and as it expanded, it became more complicated and harder to understand. The federal government that began as a few pages of paper drawn up during the hot Pennsylvania summer of 1787 has grown into a giant. Today, its laws touch almost every part of our lives. It is Congress that has the job of writing those laws.

Look around you. You will see that the federal government affects your life in many ways. What have you eaten today? Your food probably had to meet standards that were set by laws Congress passed. How did you come to school? If you took a bus, money voted by Congress probably helped to pay for the roads that the bus traveled. If you took a subway, the federal government probably helped pay for the rails that the train followed. Do you watch television? The stations you watch need a license from the federal government. Do you wash your own shirts? Then you have probably seen a label on each shirt telling you how to wash the shirt. That label is there because the federal government ordered it.

These are just a few of the ways that the federal government enters your life. All the things mentioned above show the results of federal laws that have been passed by Congress. Can those laws do everything? Can they enter every part of your life? To answer these questions, this unit will explore the workings of Congress. You will discover what Congress can do and what Congress cannot do. You will also study the way a law is passed, in order to see how the system of checks and balances works in the legislative branch of government.

unit

2

Congress

Chapter 4 The Power and Structure of Congress

In March of 1789, the newly-elected members of the First Congress of the United States began to gather in New York City. Bad weather and muddy roads slowed the arrival of many members. It was April before enough of them had assembled so that they could get down to business.

Those first members of Congress faced many problems. The Constitution gave them an idea of how Congress should be set up. For example, it said that Congress should have two parts: a House of Representatives—or simply the House—and a Senate. The Constitution also described their main job—making laws. But the Constitution did not say much about how Congress should run itself on a daily basis.

So the members of Congress, from their very first meeting, began to make rules for themselves. Members of later Congresses added to these rules or changed them when the rules no longer seemed to work. Some ways of doing things—although they were never made into rules—became customs that members of Congress followed year after year.

Congress has changed a great deal since 1789. In the first place, it has grown. The First Congress began with only fifty-nine representatives and twenty-two senators. Today, there are 435 representatives and 100 senators. In the second place, it has moved. Congress shifted its home from Philadelphia to Washington, D.C., in the year 1800. It moved into the present Capitol Building in 1819. In the third place, Congress has changed its ways. It has swept aside the spittoons and sawdust that were

common in public buildings in the early days of the nation. It has streamlined its practices and brought them up to date. In the House, a member can now vote by putting a special card in one of 40 machines on the House floor and pressing a button. This records the vote electronically on a master computer board. (The Senate, which has fewer members, does not yet use computers.)

Congress now gathers at noon on January 3 of every odd-numbered year. This begins a new **term** of Congress, lasting two years. The term is divided into two sessions, one for each year. Each session and each term are numbered. The members who met in New York in 1789 were beginning the first **session** of the First Congress. The lawmakers who gather in Washington, D.C., in January of 1987 will be starting the first session of the 100th Congress.

The House of Representatives and the Senate remain in session until their members vote to **adjourn,** or end, the session. Once Congress has adjourned, only the President of the United States can call it back into a special session. This is done only in emergencies, such as a threat of war or an economic crisis. At such times, Congress might have to pass laws to deal with the problem. President Harry Truman called the last special session in 1948, to handle economic problems.

Let us now look at the powers of Congress and the way that Congress is organized.

Words to Know

term —— the period during which one set of elected legislators serves; also, the length of time an elected official serves (One term of Congress lasts two sessions, or two years.)

session —— a series of meetings (One session of Congress lasts from January 3 until the session is adjourned.)

adjourn —— end a meeting or a session

delegated powers —— the powers of Congress that are listed in the Constitution

implied powers —— the powers of Congress not listed in the Constitution but needed in order to put into effect the delegated powers

elastic clause —— the statement in the Constitution, that gives Congress its implied powers (It allows the power of Congress to expand to meet new problems.)

impeach —— formally accuse a government official of a serious crime

The Powers of Congress

Lawmaking Powers

Congress is the legislative branch of the federal government. This means that its main job is to make laws. Article I, Section 1 of the Constitution gives the range of Congress's powers. It says: "All legislative [lawmaking] powers . . . granted [in this document] shall be vested in a Congress of the United States . . . ."

Through its power to make laws, Congress plays a vital role in our everyday lives. Laws do much more than tell us what we can and cannot do. Through its laws, the government builds canals and gives out hot breakfasts to schoolchildren. It gives out loans for building houses. It does a million things that affect us every day.

But Congress cannot make laws about everything. It must follow the Constitution. Two sections of Article I of the Constitution spell out just what Congress can and cannot do. Section 8 gives the "do's." Section 9 gives the "don't's." Some other powers are found elsewhere in the Constitution. These powers are described in the following Fact Block. Look them over.

Reasons for Balancing Powers Why did the writers of the Constitution allow Congress to do some things and keep it from doing others? Remember that the writers had lived under two very different governments. They felt that one, the government of England, had been too strong and that the other, the Articles of Confederation, had been too weak. In the Constitution, they tried to strike a careful balance. They wanted to create a government that was neither too strong nor too weak.

We can see how this balance works if we consider the subject of money. Money is needed for a government to do its jobs. But

Fact Block: What the Constitution Says

Powers of Congress

1. Congress can set federal taxes. Section 8 mentions *duties*—taxes on goods brought into the country—and *excises*—taxes on goods made in this country. There are also other kinds of taxes, including the federal income tax (allowed by the Sixteenth Amendment).
2. Congress can spend money for the country's defense and for the general welfare of the people.
3. Congress can borrow money and pay the federal government's debts.
4. Congress can make laws about trade among people of different states and about trade between the United States and other countries.
5. Congress can make laws about how a person may become a citizen of the United States.
6. Congress can made laws about *bankruptcy* (not being able to pay what one owes).
7. Congress can print or coin money and say how much it is worth.
8. Congress can set up standards for weighing and measuring.
9. Congress can make laws to punish *counterfeiters*—people who make fake money, stamps, or government bonds.
10. Congress can set up post offices.
11. Congress can have roads built.
12. Congress can give people *patents* (rights to make, use, and sell inventions) and *copyrights* (rights to control the publication or sale of literary, musical, dramatic, or artistic works).
13. Congress can set up courts that are lower than the Supreme Court.
14. Congress can make laws to punish crimes committed on United States ships on the high seas and crimes against international law.
15. Congress can declare war.
16. Congress can organize the armed forces, make rules for them, and pay for them. But Congress cannot pay for armies for more than two years at a time. This restriction does not apply to the Navy.
17. Congress can make laws to help set up state militia, or National Guard, units. Congress can also call on the militia to enforce the country's laws, to put down rebellions against the government, and to stop any invasion of the country by enemies.
18. Congress can make laws for the District of Columbia.
19. Congress can admit new states to the Union.
20. Congress can make laws to carry out the powers listed above and to put into effect all powers granted to the federal government by the Constitution and its amendments.

What Congress Cannot Do

1. Except in times of rebellion or invasion, Congress cannot take away from a person in prison the right to demand a *writ of habeas corpus.* This is a court order that requires a prisoner to be brought before a court. The court then decides if there are grounds for continuing to hold the prisoner for trial.
2. Congress cannot pass *bills of attainder.* These are laws that punish people for crimes without first giving them a trial.
3. Congress cannot pass *ex post facto laws.* These are laws that punish a person for doing something that was not against the law when the person did it.
4. Congress cannot tax exports—goods that are shipped out of the country.
5. Congress cannot make laws about trade that favor one state over another.
6. Congress cannot take any money from the federal treasury without passing a law to do so.
7. Congress cannot give anyone a title of nobility, such as *king, queen, lord, noble, prince, or princess.*
8. Congress cannot pass any law that violates the Bill of Rights or any other part of the Constitution.
9. Congress cannot pass laws on matters not covered by the Constitution. The Constitution declares that if a power is not granted to the United States, it is reserved for the states or for the people.

Due to its powers of taxation, the government is able to implement many much-needed programs.

the Articles of Confederation had been too weak. They did not give the national government the power to tax and raise money. This meant that the national government could not pay its bills unless the states freely gave their money to it. The national government was allowed to raise an army, but it had no money to pay the soldiers. When they put together the new Constitution, the writers gave the national government the power to collect its own taxes.

The writers also put checks on these powers, however. Congress had to pass a law before any money could be spent for a certain purpose. Congress also had to tell the people how much money was coming in and how it was being spent, so that the people would know where their money was going. If the people did not like the way their money was spent, they could complain to their representatives or senators.

Implied Powers Besides trying to balance weakness and strength, the writers also tried to allow for change. Look back to the powers listed in the first part of the Fact Block. These powers are given to Congress by the Constitution. They are known as *delegated powers.* Nowhere among them

does it say that Congress has the power to spend money for breakfasts for schoolchildren. Yet Congress does just that. Is Congress going against the Constitution?

The answer is "No." The writers of the Constitution knew that they could not list each and every thing that the government could do. Instead, they wrote Article I, Section 8, Clause 18 of the Constitution. This says that Congress has the power "to make all laws which shall be necessary and proper for carrying into execution the foregoing powers." This is known as the **elastic clause.**

The elastic clause allows Congress to stretch its delegated powers to cover many other subjects. It implies, or hints, that Congress can do other things besides those actually listed in the Constitution. Spending money for school breakfasts is one example. One part of Article I, Section 8 says that Congress can "provide for the . . . general welfare of the United States." That means that Congress can look after the health and well-being of the people. Well-fed schoolchildren would be healthy citizens. Thus, by using its **implied powers** through the elastic clause, Congress can pass a law that allows the spending of money on a breakfast program.

Not everyone likes the idea that Congress can stretch its powers. Some people feel that the federal government interferes too much in daily life. They think that government should do as little as possible. Many arguments about whether federal laws do too much are settled by the Supreme Court. You will learn more about this in Chapter 9.

Other Powers

The powers of Congress go beyond the making of laws. Congress can play other important roles in national life. The following are five other important powers held by Congress:

By using its implied powers through the elastic clause, Congress is able to fund the building of aircraft without having the delegated power to do so.

Impeachment and Trial The Constitution gives Congress the power to play the role of judge. Congress can accuse and try federal officials for serious crimes committed in office. In this process, the House of Representatives and the Senate have two different jobs.

It is up to the House to make the charges. This is known as **impeachment.** First, a list of charges is drawn up by the members of the House. The list is read before the House. Then a vote is taken. If two-thirds of the House members who are voting agree with the charges, then the official is formally accused, or impeached. This does not mean that the official is guilty. The official still has the right to a trial.

The Senate runs the trial. It acts just like a court, calling witnesses and hearing all the evidence. Then, if two-thirds of the

The Watergate hearings showed Congress using its power to accuse, impeach, and convict officials found guilty of suspected wrongdoing.

senators who are present vote "guilty," the official who has been convicted is removed from office.

Impeachment and trial are rare. Only one President has been impeached by the House. He was Andrew Johnson in 1868. The Senate failed to find him guilty, falling short by one vote. In 1974, the House began drawing up impeachment charges against another President—Richard Nixon. The charges never came to a vote, however. President Nixon resigned. Eleven lower-level officials have been impeached. Only four of them—all federal judges—were found guilty and forced to resign.

Electing a President and a Vice President In special cases, Congress has the job of choosing the nation's highest officials. This happens in an election when no candidate gets a majority in the electoral college (see page 151). The House chooses the President from among the three top candidates. The Senate chooses the Vice President. Congress has not been called upon to do this job since 1837, when the Senate chose the Vice President.

Confirming Appointments and Treaties The Senate shares in two of the President's powers. One of those is appointing, or naming, certain federal officials, including Cabinet members and judges. The second is making treaties with other nations.

When the President appoints a person to a job, the person's name is sent to the Senate. There, the name must be voted on. A majority vote is needed to make the appointment official. Likewise, the President must send any treaty to the Senate for a vote. Two-thirds of the senators who are voting must approve the treaty before the President can put it into effect.

Before making a decision on a vote—such as on the Panama Canal Treaty— senators often take government-sponsored trips to review the subject at hand.

Making Investigations Congress has the power to investigate important public matters. It can send people notices requiring them to appear at a hearing, just as a judge can require people to appear in a court case. Usually, an investigation is held to aid Congress in its lawmaking role. For example, an investigation may try to find out if a proposed law is really needed or whether a present law is being carried out correctly.

Changing the Constitution Congress also plays a part in adding amendments to the Constitution. Congress may propose an amendment by getting a favorable vote from two-thirds of the members of both the Senate and the House. The amendment must then be approved by two-thirds of the states. It is also possible to amend the Constitution by means of a national convention. It is then up to the convention to propose amendments. (For further details, see page 309.)

REVIEW
---

1. List four of the delegated powers of Congress.
2. Name an action that Congress has taken under its implied powers.
3. What congressional power is the case of Andrew Johnson an example of?
4. Name two other powers of Congress that do not involve lawmaking.
5. Of all the powers granted to Congress and discussed in this section, which *one* power do you feel is the most important? Why?

Words to Know

bicameral legislature —— a lawmaking body that has two parts—from the Latin for "two chambers"
expel —— throw out; remove
presiding officer —— the person in charge of the meetings of a group

Speaker of the House —— presiding officer of the House of Representatives
president of the Senate —— the Vice President of the United States, who serves as presiding officer of the Senate
president pro-tempore —— officer who presides over the Senate when the Vice President is not there

A Balanced Congress

Congress is a **bicameral legislature.** This means that it is a lawmaking body that is divided into two houses, or parts. One part, known as the "lower house," is the House of Representatives. The other, or "upper house," is the Senate.

There were a number of reasons for giving the legislature two parts. First, England and a number of the colonies had bicameral legislatures. The writers of the Constitution felt comfortable with that form of lawmaking body. Second, the two-house Congress was helpful in settling arguments between large states and small states. The large states had more representatives in the House of Representatives. But all states had the same number of representatives in the Senate, which made the small states equally as powerful as the large states. Third, the writers felt that the two parts of Congress would check and balance each other, so they said that one house of Congress could not pass a law by itself. Both houses had to agree. This would give the legislators more time to think and talk about what was needed and prevent hasty or careless action.

Before looking more closely at the House of Representatives and the Senate, study the accompanying Fact Block. It contains important information about the two parts of Congress.

Fact Block: The Bicameral Congress

Congress	House of Representatives	Senate
Total membership	435	100
Number of members for each state	Depends on population; varies from 1 to 43	2
Elected by	Voters of congressional districts (Sometimes a representative-at-large is elected by voters of the entire state.)	Voters of the entire state
Term of office	2 years	6 years (One-third of the senators are elected every two years.)
Vacancy	Filled by special election or at the next national election	Special election or temporary appointment by governor of the state until the special or regular election
Salary	$60,662.50	$60,662.50
Presiding officer	Speaker of the House	Vice President of the United States
Special powers	To impeach federal officials, to introduce bills regarding money, to choose the President of the United States when the electoral college fails to do so	To vote on the President's appointments of high officials, to vote on treaties, to conduct the trials of impeached officials, to choose the Vice President when the electoral college fails to do so

The House of Representatives

Basis of Representation The House of Representatives was meant to reflect the interests of the people. The number of representatives for each state is based on the number of people who live there. Because of this, the Constitution says that the federal government must take a census, or count, of the population of the country every 10 years. The number of representatives is then changed as the population of each state changes.

The Constitution says that every state must have at least one representative. It also suggests that each member of the House should represent about 30,000 citizens. The first session of the House began with only fifty-nine seats. As new states joined the Union and the population grew,

the House grew too. People began to worry that if the number of representatives continued to rise, the House would be too crowded to do its work. So in 1929, Congress voted to hold the size of the House to 435 members. It is the same size today. Now each member of the House represents about 520,000 people. Each state is split into congressional districts—one for each seat in the House. The voters within a district elect only one representative.

Because the population of the United States has lately been moving toward the South and the West, states in those regions have been gaining representatives. States in the North and the East have lost representatives after recent censuses.

Today, California has the most representatives. Alaska, Delaware, Nevada,

To be totally effective, a member of Congress must adequately represent and reflect the interests of all the people in his or her congressional district.

North Dakota, Vermont, and Wyoming have one representative each. Also, there are nonvoting delegates from Puerto Rico, the Virgin Islands, and Guam (which are territories that are all owned by the United States), and from the District of Columbia.

Members of the House Members are elected to the House of Representatives in November of every even-numbered year. The term of office is 2 years. All seats in the House are up for election at the same time. Thus, it would be possible for the voters to elect a House of Representatives with all new members. Except for the First Congress, however, this has never happened. Usually about 80 percent of the members are re-elected.

The Constitution lists a number of qualifications that House members must meet. Every member must be at least 25 years old. Every member must also have been a citizen of the United States for at least 7 years. Every member must be a resident of the state where he or she is elected. Usually the member also lives in the district he or she will represent, but this is not required.

It is up to the House to decide whether a member-elect meets all qualifications. The House can refuse to seat someone if, for example, that person cheated to win election. In such cases, a majority vote of the House may keep the person from taking a seat. Then a new election must be held to choose another representative.

Even after being seated in the House, members are still subject to discipline. A majority of the House may vote to punish a member for "disorderly behavior." Two-thirds of the House may vote to **expel,** or remove, a member for serious misconduct.

Members can run for re-election as often as they want. If a representative dies or resigns, a special election is held to fill the seat.

Each representative receives a salary of $60,662.50 a year. In addition, representatives get many benefits free or at reduced cost. Each member of Congress gets a fully equipped suite of rooms in one of the five office buildings on Capitol Hill. Each member has a yearly telephone and telegraph allowance. Each has a stationery allowance. All members get allowances for their local district offices, and they all get yearly travel allowances. A representative is permitted thirty-two round trips home per session, a senator from forty to forty-four round trips per year. Both are also free to do considerable foreign traveling.

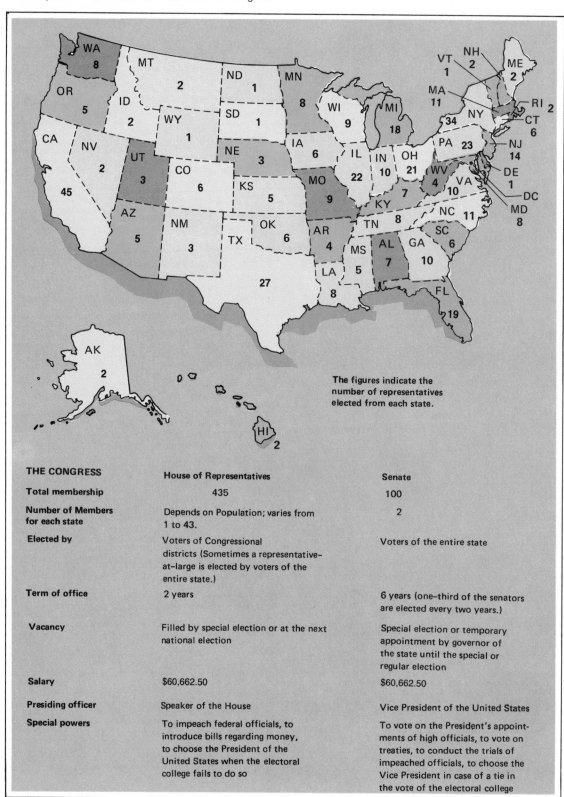

The figures indicate the number of representatives elected from each state.

THE CONGRESS	House of Representatives	Senate
Total membership	435	100
Number of Members for each state	Depends on Population; varies from 1 to 43.	2
Elected by	Voters of Congressional districts (Sometimes a representative-at-large is elected by voters of the entire state.)	Voters of the entire state
Term of office	2 years	6 years (one-third of the senators are elected every two years.)
Vacancy	Filled by special election or at the next national election	Special election or temporary appointment by governor of the state until the special or regular election
Salary	$60,662.50	$60,662.50
Presiding officer	Speaker of the House	Vice President of the United States
Special powers	To impeach federal officials, to introduce bills regarding money, to choose the President of the United States when the electoral college fails to do so	To vote on the President's appointments of high officials, to vote on treaties, to conduct the trials of impeached officials, to choose the Vice President in case of a tie in the vote of the electoral college

Members are entitled to use the two military hospitals in Washington at half the cost of a private hospital. In addition, members can get free medical treatment, checkups, ambulance service, x rays and EKGs from the Capitol physician.

Members have their own dining rooms, where prices are low. And they have their own barber shops and hairdresser's salons, where the rates for a haircut and for a wash-and-set are half of that elsewhere.

Each member also gets a congressional license tag, which permits almost unrestricted parking in the city. Each House member receives five underground parking spaces. There are separate gyms for the House and Senate and congressional recording studios—where a member can go to videotape TV reports. There is also the botanic gardens' nursery, which supplies the members with their house plants.

Officers of the House   At the beginning of each session of Congress, the members of the House elect a number of officers. These people help the House carry out its business smoothly.

The **presiding officer,** or leader, of the whole House of Representatives is the **Speaker of the House.** The Speaker settles questions of rules, decides who can speak, sends bills to the committees, and has some control over all the business carried on in the House. In addition, if the President and Vice President of the United States are both unable to continue in office or if they die, the Speaker of the House becomes President of the United States. Because of these important duties, the Speaker of the House receives a salary of $79,125 a year.

Other officers also help in the work of the House. They include a clerk, a doorkeeper, a postmaster, a sergeant-at-arms, and a chaplain. These people are not members of the House, but are hired by House officials.

The Speaker of the House—shown here at his desk with his aides—is both the Presiding Officer and third in line for the Presidency of the United States.

Special Powers In order for the House of Representatives to check and balance the Senate, the writers of the Constitution gave the House three special powers. First, as we have seen, the House can impeach officials of the federal government. Second, bills to raise money for the federal government *must* be introduced in the House, not the Senate. The Senate can approve, disapprove, or change the bills, but they must start in the House. Third, the House can choose the President of the United States when no candidate receives a majority of the votes in the electoral college. (This will be talked about in Chapter 6.)

The Senate

Basis of Representation The Senate is the branch of Congress that was originally planned to reflect the interests of the states. Each state has two members in the Senate. The size of the state and the number of people who live in it do not matter. Each state must have two senators. Today, there are 100 members of the Senate.

Members of the Senate Once, Senators were elected by the state legislatures. Since 1913, they have been chosen by the people of the state. The voters elect senators at the same time that representatives are elected—in November of every even-numbered year. But senators are elected to a longer term—six years. Only one-third of the Senate is chosen at each election. Two Senate seats from the same state are never up for election in the same year unless a Senator has resigned or died.

Because of this system, the Senate never has an all-new membership. Two-thirds of any Senate are experienced members. The writers of the Constitution felt that this system would make the Senate the more experienced and more stable branch of Congress.

The qualifications for senator that are given in the Constitution are slightly differ-

ent from those for House members. First, a senator must be at least 30 years old. Next, a senator must have been a citizen of the United States for at least 9 years. Finally, the senator must be a resident of the state where she or he is elected. The Senate judges its own members' qualifications. By the same voting practices, it may punish, expel, or refuse to seat a member.

Senators can run for re-election as often as they wish. If a senator dies or resigns, the governor of the senator's state can name someone to fill the seat until the next regular election or a special election can be called to fill the seat.

Senators receive the same salary as House members—$60,662.50 a year. They also get the same free offices, staff allowances, and benefits that members of the House receive.

How the Senate Is Set Up The Senate does not elect a Speaker. Instead, the Constitution says that the Vice President of the United States is to be the presiding officer—the **president of the Senate.** The Vice President is not a member of the Senate and cannot join the debates on bills. The Vice President's job is to see that the proper rules for debate and procedure are followed. As president of the Senate, the Vice President can only vote when there is a tie.

The Vice President is often away from the Senate on other duties. Therefore, there is a stand-in, known as the **president pro tempore** (or *pro tem*)—the temporary president. The president *pro tempore* is a leader of the majority party. Because of the extra duties, the president pro tempore receives a salary of $68,575 a year. Other members of the Senate may also have the honor of presiding from time to time.

The Senate also has other officials, including a clerk, a chaplain, a sergeant-at-arms, a postmaster, and a doorkeeper. These people are not members of the Senate, but are hired by Senate officials.

Among other Senate officials is the sergeant-at-arms, who keeps order during meetings of Congress.

Special Powers To help the system of checks and balances in the government, the Senate was given four special powers (they were already mentioned on page 106): (1) to approve or reject a President's choices to fill important offices in the executive and judicial branches, (2) to approve or reject treaties with foreign countries, (3) to act as a court for impeachment cases sent to it by the House, and (4) to choose the Vice President of the United States when no candidate receives a majority of votes in the electoral college.

Senate has the right to approve Presidential appointees, such as head of the Federal Reserve Board.

REVIEW

---

1. Define the following terms:
   bicameral
   legislature
   presiding officer
   president *pro tempore*

2. How long is the term of office for a member of the House of Representatives? For a member of the Senate?

3. What does the Speaker of the House do?

4. What are three qualifications that must be met by anyone elected to the House of Representatives? By anyone elected to the Senate?

5. What do you feel is the most important special power of the House? The most important special power of the Senate? Explain.

How the United States Works

Printing-press Operator

Suppose you wanted to know what your senator said yesterday. Or you wanted to read a speech that William Jennings Bryan made in the House in 1893. You could find these records very easily. The *Congressional Record* keeps track of everything that goes on in the national legislature. It is something like the minutes of your student-council meetings. It is much longer and more complete, however, and many copies are made of it.

No one could do all this printing and copying by hand. Instead, a printing press is used. The *Congressional Record* could never be made without the work of printing-press operators and the apprentices, assistants, and other workers who help them.

Part of the job of the printing-press operator is preparing the forms that hold the type. Later, the operator uses the forms to make final press plates. From these plates, large numbers of pages are printed. Printing-press operators spend a great deal of time standing near the presses and making any adjustments or repairs that are needed. When all the printing is done, they clean and oil the machines.

Most of the printing-press operator's day is spent standing in the noisy, busy pressroom. Some pressrooms are so noisy that the workers wear protection for their ears. They also need to protect themselves from the running machines. There is some danger at close range. But with all these drawbacks, operating a printing press is a good job. The work is varied and it takes skill and knowledge. The pay is good also—$20,000 to $22,000 a year. Some people add as much as $3,000 or $4,000 to that by working overtime. Night-shift workers earn even more.

To become a printing-press operator, you need a high-school degree and 4 to 5 years of on-the-job training as an apprentice. Few apprentices are hired directly out of high school. Most printing shops give these positions to people who have already been working in the pressroom—as assistants or unskilled workers—for 2 or 3 years.

An apprenticeship opens up when an apprentice becomes an operator, when a printing shop expands and hires more workers, or when a new shop goes into business. Some jobs are being lost because of the use of more advanced machines. New presses need fewer workers to run them. Despite this, the total number of jobs in printing is rising. That is because the industry is growing.

Reading About . . .

What a Member of Congress Must Do for the Folks Back Home

Lawmaking is only a part of the job of a member of Congress. This reading explores some of the tasks of the members of Congress.

As you read, think of the following:

● Are the duties described here more or less important than the lawmaking duties of Congress?
● Should members of Congress spend as much time as they do on these duties?

If they don't know it already, the freshmen members of the House and Senate will soon discover that serving in Congress involves a lot more than debating the great issues of the day.

To be reelected, they will have to devote a large share of their time to two other duties for the folks back home:

● Acting as trouble shooters for constituents with problems in Washington.
● Fighting to insure that their states or districts get their fair shares—if not more than their fair shares—of growing federal expenditures.

These tasks are not new. They go back to the beginning of Congress almost two centuries ago. But the job of serving as a kind of "Mr. Fixit" on the Potomac has become bigger and bigger in recent years as the United States government has ballooned into a bureaucratic giant touching on the lives of everyone.

This job has gotten so enormous that lawmaking itself is sometimes crowded into the background.

"There is an image of members of Congress sitting around in overstuffed chairs, sipping tea, reading great documents, pondering what policy should be," declares Representative Patricia Shroeder, a third-term Democrat from Colorado. "The truth is that if you find three minutes of time like that, you're lucky."

Most members are fortunate if they can spend as much as half their time in committee meetings, and voting or debating on the House or Senate floor. Much of their time is spent meeting with a stream of daily visitors and coping with stacks of mail from back home.

In a year, about 60 million pieces of mail flow into Capitol Hill offices. The volume ranges greatly from office to office. It runs as high as 6,000 to 8,000 letters a week in the offices of senators from the most populous states.

Some of the letters offer constituents opinions on issues or solicit the personal views of a member of Congress. Others may ask for help in making hotel reservations in Washington for a planned visit, for an official congressional calendar, or a flag that has flown over the Capitol, which lawmakers provide at cost.

The biggest share of mail, however, comes from persons who need help in their dealings with the federal government. They turn to their congressional representatives for it—often as a last resort. As one congressional staff member describes their problems:

"Usually, it's a problem of some sort with the bureaucracy. A Social Security check doesn't come. Or a veteran's claim is held up. Maybe it's a slip-up by a computer, or maybe it's a case of a regulation that could be waived. But getting action out of a massive, impersonal bureaucracy is tough for the average person."

chapter
Review

Fact Review

1. Once Congress has adjourned, how can it be called back into session?
2. What is the main job of Congress?
3. Which of the following are among the delegated powers of Congress?
   a. making money
   b. providing school lunches
   c. passing *ex post facto* laws
   d. giving people patents
   e. taxing imports
   f. taxing exports
   g. declaring war
   h. admitting new states to the Union
4. Which of the following are among the powers denied to Congress?
   a. passing bills of attainder
   b. granting copyrights
   c. passing laws that violate the Constitution
   d. passing *ex post facto* laws
   e. providing school lunches
   f. granting titles of nobility
5. Give three reasons why the writers of the Constitution provided for two houses of Congress.
6. Which of the following terms apply to the House and which apply to the Senate?
   a. impeachment
   b. congressional districts
   c. votes on treaties
   d. introduces money bills
   e. conducts trials of impeached officials
   f. upper house
7. How is the presiding officer of the House chosen?
8. Is there any way that the House can discipline unruly members? Explain.
9. Do you think that Congress should be denied any powers that it now has? Explain.
10. Some people believe that the terms of House members should be increased from 2 years to 4 years. Do you think that this would be a good idea? Why or why not?

Developing Your Vocabulary

Choose the correct words from this list to complete the paragraph that follows. Write your answers on a separate sheet of paper.

> elastic clause
> bicameral legislature
> implied powers
> delegated powers

The writers of the Constitution divided Congress into two houses, or parts. This means that Congress is _____ . The writers knew that a lawmaking body had to have certain powers. They gave Congress the power to tax, to borrow money, and to control trade. These powers are known as _____ . The writers also knew that not all powers could be listed by name in the Constitution. The powers of Congress that are not listed are known as _____ . Congress gets its authority to use these powers from the _____ of the Constitution.

Developing Your Reading Skills

Read the following paragraph and then answer the questions that follow:

Congress does not have the power to pass any law that its members may want. It cannot take away the right to a writ of *habeas corpus,* except in time of war or rebellion. It cannot pass bills of attainder or *ex post facto* laws. It cannot put taxes on exports from any state. Also, Congress is forbidden to take any money from the federal treasury except by passing a law. Congress cannot grant any citizen a title of nobility, such as *king.*

1. Which of the following do you think is the main idea, or point, of this paragraph?

a. Congress cannot pass a law about export taxes.
b. Congress cannot pass *ex post facto* laws.
c. Congress cannot grant titles of nobility.
d. Congress has limits to its lawmaking powers.

2. Why did you select either *a, b, c,* or *d* above?

Developing Your Writing Skills— Forming and Supporting an Opinion

In this chapter, you have examined the basic powers of the federal Congress. You have seen what each house of that Congress can do and what it cannot do. Now consider the following questions:

Forming an opinion
1. Do you think that it is a good idea to have different powers granted to the House of Representatives and the Senate? For example, does it seem wise that the House can impeach officials but that the Senate must conduct their trials?

Supporting an opinion
2. After thinking it over, write a paragraph that answers the questions above. Begin with a topic sentence that sums up your opinion. Then continue with evidence or arguments to support your opinion.

Reading Tables

Study the following table showing the profile of the Ninety-seventh Congress and then answer the following questions.

1. How many women served in the Ninety-seventh Congress?

2. Which professional group had the most members in the Ninety-seventh Congress? Which had the least?
3. How many members of the House were in business or banking? How many in the Senate?
4. How many members of the House were in farming or ranching? How many in the Senate?
5. What was the third-largest profession among members of the House? Of the Senate?
6. In what age group are most members of Congress? What was the largest age group for the general population?

Profile of the 97th Congress

House		Senate
435	**Total Membership**	100
	Sexes	
416	Men	98
19	Women	2
	Professions*	
194	Law	59
130	Business, banking	32
28	Farming, ranching	9
21	Communication	6
50	Education	6
7	Medicine	1
1	Workers, craftworkers	0
48	Other	5
	Ages	
% of Members of Congress		**% of Total U.S. Population**
18	Under age 39	38
63	Ages 40–59	35
19	Age 60 or older	27

* In 1981, some members of Congress listed more than one profession or business.
SOURCE: *Congressional Quarterly,* January 10, 1981.

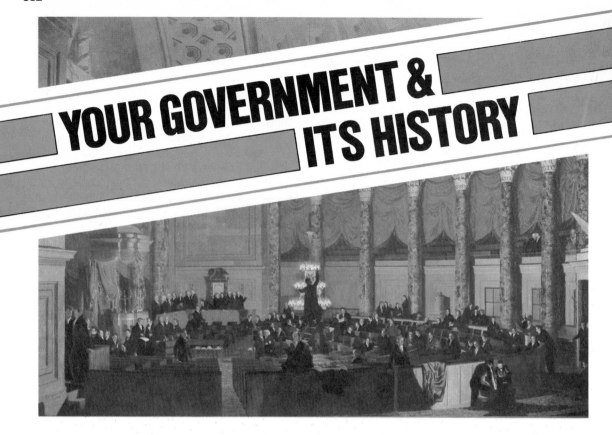

YOUR GOVERNMENT & ITS HISTORY

Our First Congress

Upon New Hampshire's approval of the Constitution in 1788, the job of the Confederation Congress was completed. Now it had only to choose a temporary home for the new government and to pick a date for the first meeting of Congress. New York was chosen as the seat of government. The first Wednesday in March—March 4—was selected for the first meeting of the First Congress of the United States. Noted historian Alvin M. Josephy, Jr., described the first gathering.

When the members of the new House of Representatives assembled in their chamber on the ground floor of Federal Hall on that first morning, warm-ing themselves at the fireplaces and then taking seats at desks arranged in two crescent-shaped rows, they numbered only thirteen of the fifty-nine men elected from the eleven states. Upstairs, in the smaller Senate chamber, it was no better. Scattered in a semicircle of chairs facing the seat to be occupied by the still-unnamed Vice President were only eight senators from five states. In accordance with the constitutional directive that "Each House shall keep a Journal of its Proceedings," the first minutes were recorded that day. "The number," read the first entry in the Senate Legislative Journal, "not being sufficient to constitute a quorum, they adjourned."

So it was the next day, and on each day thereafter during the entire month of March. Travel could be difficult at that season, when winds and ice delayed coastal mail, and rain mired the road. As the days passed, the legislators, housed in private homes and boarding houses and meeting each morning at Federal Hall for idle conversation, grew impatient. . . .

From day to day, the missing legislators at last began to arrive, more of them members of the House than of the Senate. But there were still no quorums. By March 25, the Senate was up to ten members; twelve made up a quorum. The delay in getting started angered Representative Fisher Ames from Dedham, Massachusetts. "This is a mortifying [embarrassing] situation," Ames wrote a Boston friend. ". . . We lose credit, spirit, everything. The public will forget the government before it is born."

On Wednesday, April 1, a thirtieth representative, Thomas Scott from western Pennsylvania, arrived in New York. A quorum was finally declared. The members took their seats and prepared, at last, to deal with the first order of business. This business was the organization of the House. Fisher Ames looked around and observed his fellow legislators. They were "sober, solid, old-charter folks, as we often say," he wrote. Many of them had served in a state legislature or in one of the previous Congresses and were experienced in government. On the whole, they were well educated. There were many college graduates among them (eleven in the first Senate and nineteen in the House) and numerous lawyers.

On the evening of April 5, one of the best-known political leaders in the nation, Richard Henry Lee of Virginia, reached New York. When he took his seat in the Senate the next day, a quorum had finally been made.

Lee's arrival was the signal for both houses, finally, to get down to the business of the nation. The Senate quickly accepted the twelve members who were present. It elected Senator John Langdon, a merchant from Portsmouth, New Hampshire, as temporary president.

Every step Congress took was a first. The members of Congress followed the instructions of the framers of the Constitution. The framers, in one of their compromises, had worked out the difficult problem of who would vote to choose the President and Vice President.

Senator Langdon completed the counting for President. It was no surprise to anyone when Langdon announced to the group that George Washington was everyone's choice for President. He had received a vote from each of the sixty-nine electors who had voted. John Adams, with thirty-four votes, was second and would become Vice President.

1. In what city was the first meeting of Congress held?

2. What delayed the two houses of Congress in getting down to business?

3. What sort of men were part of the first U.S. Congress? Give three examples.

4. What sort of people do you think should be in Congress today? Explain.

SKILLS Developing your basic civic education skills

(fact, opinion, and conflicting viewpoints)

Distinguishing Fact from Opinion

Citizens often need to tell the difference between fact and opinion. The word *fact* means something that is known with certainty. Its accuracy can be tested by checking other sources of information. A statement of fact might be: "Christopher Columbus arrived in the Americas in A.D. 1492" or "Members of the United States House of Representatives serve 2-year terms of office."

The word *opinion* refers to a belief that may or may not be based on facts. It is a conclusion held with confidence, but not necessarily proven. A statement of opinion might be: "Columbus was the greatest of all explorers" or "The current members of the House of Representatives are the best we have ever had in Congress." Both statements are opinion rather than fact. A case could also be made that there were explorers greater than Columbus and members of past sessions of Congress who were better legislators than the current ones.

Separating fact from opinion is something each of us does daily. Consider, as another example, the following paragraph:

Our high school football team is great. This past season, we won eight games. We lost only two games. In the eight games we won, we scored a total of 130 points. Our opponents in those eight games scored a total of only 20 points.

In this example, the topic sentence, or first sentence, in the paragraph is a statement of opinion. This opinion, however, is based on the use of facts: The team won eight of ten games, and in those eight games scored 130 points to the opposition's 20.

1. Define the terms *fact* and *opinion*.

2. Can a sentence contain both a statement of fact and a statement of opinion? If not, tell why not. If so, give an example.

3. Do you see any value in separating fact from opinion? Explain.

Dealing with Conflicting Viewpoints

Thinking critically also involves the ability to deal with conflicting viewpoints. It is the ability to separate fact from opinion when you have statements that do not agree. This problem occurs often in our lives.

Consider the following stories. How would you resolve the conflicts of opinion, or differing viewpoints?

Story 1

Our high school football team is great. This past season, we won six games. We also lost four games. But in the six games we won, we scored a total of 130 points. Our opponents in those six games scored a total of only 20 points.

Story 2

Our high school football team is not too good. This past season, we lost four games and won six. The games lost were the last four of the season. When we won, we scored amazingly well against our opponents. But when we lost, it was because we could not seem to score at all. In those last four games, we only scored a total of 6 points. Our opponents in those last four games scored a total of 110 points.

As you can see by these two stories, there is a difference of opinion as to whether the high school football team was "great" or "not too good." If you were to hear two such different views about anything, one way you might form your own opinion would be to use the following guide.

STEP 1   Determine the points on which the two versions agree.

STEP 2   Determine what points were made in one version but omitted in the other.

STEP 3   Determine the points on which the two versions disagree.

STEP 4   If the two versions disagree on a point, on the basis of available evidence, decide on the probable cause or causes for the disagreement.

STEP 5   Determine what else might need to be considered about the topic.

STEP 6   Determine how you would use both versions to construct a third version.

Suppose you were to apply the six steps to the two stories about the high school football team. Here's how your first four steps would look.

STEP 1   Points of agreement
a. Number of games played = 10.
b. Number of games won = 6.
c. Number of games lost = 4.

STEP 2   Points omitted by one source
a. Story 1 did not mention: Team lost last 4 games, scoring a total of only 6 points and allowing opponents a total of 110 points.
b. Story 2 did not mention: Team scored 130 points in first 6 games, allowing opponents only 20 points.

STEP 3   Points of disagreement
a. Story 1's topic sentence: "Our high school football team is great."
b. Story 2's topic sentence: "Our high school football team is not too good."

STEP 4   Your decision and the reason(s) behind it as to the probable cause(s) for disagreement
The author of Story 1 focused on the winning games. The author of Story 2 focused on the losing games. Story 1 could have been written by the coach. Story 2 might have come from an unhappy fan.

Now you can fill in the last two steps.

4. STEP 5   What else should you consider or what other questions should you ask about the topic?
a.
b.

5. STEP 6   How would you use both versions to write a third version? You might begin by completing the following topic sentence. You might then offer reasons for your choice of endings.

The high school football team featured in the two stories was _____ .

Conflicting Viewpoints in Civics

As you have learned, the 435 voting members of the House of Representatives serve 2-year terms. In November of each even-numbered year, such as 1984 or 1986, any member of the House who wishes to remain there must run for re-election.

In recent years, some representatives have wanted their terms of office extended from 2 to 4 years. Their election cycle would correspond to the election of the President, such as in 1984, 1988, and 1992. The following selection debates this issue.

Should a U.S. Representative's Term Be Extended from 2 to 4 Years?

YES.   Representative Morris K. Udall, Democrat from Arizona:

The House of Representatives is truly the "people's house," and this is as the nation's founders

intended. But Congress has become a full-time job, something the founders never anticipated. Representatives no sooner finish one election campaign than they have to begin to worry about the next one. I believe the nation's founders, if brought back today, would agree that a 4-year term [half up for election every 2 years] would still give voters a chance to make some changes every 2 years while giving members at least 3 years to concentrate on legislation.

NO.   Representative Barry M. Goldwater, Jr., Republican from California:

In contrast to the deliberately slower-paced Senate, the "people's house" often makes dozens of daily decisions that affect the lives of all Americans. The House also controls the nation's purse, since it decides where taxes will be collected and spent. Such enormous power must not be allowed to go unchecked for more than 2 years at a time. The voters must be given the opportunity to give approval, or to "throw the bums out" in regular, closely spaced intervals. Think about it: Would you want your Representative loose for 4 years at a time?

6. Which four of the following statements are fact?
a.   There are 435 voting members in the House of Representatives.
b.   The nation's founders would agree that a 4-year term of office would be a good idea for members of the House of Representatives.
c.   Members of the House of Representatives have too much work to do.

d. Members of the House of Representatives serve 2-year terms of office.

e. Members of the House of Representatives are elected to office during even-numbered years.

f. Members of the House of Representatives should not be given 4-year terms of office.

g. At least some members of the House of Representatives call that legislative body the "people's house."

h. The people should be given the opportunity at least every 2 years to decide whether a member of the House of Representatives should be reelected to office.

7. Briefly, tell why you selected the four statements you did in question 6.

8. In question 6, which four statements are mainly opinion?

9. Briefly, tell why you selected the four statements you did in question 8.

10. On which one of the following points did Udall and Goldwater agree?

a. Working in Congress is a full-time job.

b. The House of Representatives deals with budgets.

c. The House of Representatives is the "people's house."

11. Which two of the following points were made by Udall? Which two were made by Goldwater?

a. The House decides what taxes will be, and this power needs to be held in check by the voters.

b. Serving in the House has become a full-time job.

c. The voters should be allowed to evaluate House members at least every 2 years.

d. Members of the House now have to use valuable work time to campaign for reelection.

12. On which one of the following points did Udall and Goldwater disagree?

a. The House of Representatives is the "people's house."

b. The best length of term for a member of the House of Representatives.

c. Whether or not the House of Representatives should deal with budget matters.

13. What else might you wish to consider about this topic? Can you think of any other arguments that could be made to (a) favor an extension of a representative's term of office to 4 years and (b) oppose an extension of that term of office? List them.

14. Of the arguments noted in your answers to questions 10–13, which two seemed to be most important? Why? Which two seemed to be least important? Why?

15. How would you now complete the following topic sentence? Write a paragraph supporting your selection.

A United States representative's term of office (should/should not) be extended from 2 to 4 years.

Special Note: As you read this book, you will continue to be asked to develop your skills of distinguishing fact from opinion and dealing with conflicting viewpoints. Thus, from time to time, you might wish to review pages 114—117.

5 How Congress Makes a Law

The United States is a big country. Its citizens live in places as different as the cold North Slope of Alaska and the hot, sunny Florida Keys. They live in crowded cities, in cozy suburbs, and on remote ranches. They make their livings in many ways. Some punch cattle, others punch time clocks. Some work with their brains, others with their brawn. Some people pound the pavements day after day looking for work and not finding any. Some citizens are too young to work, while others are too old or too sick to work.

All these citizens have interests and needs. An Illinois farmer's main interest may be getting a good price for a corn crop. A Detroit factory worker may worry that Japanese cars will lure people away from cars made in the United States and cause the automobile plants to close. A person without a job wants to find a way to put food on the table. An investor in oil wells wants to make a quick fortune. Students may want to know if their school will have enough money for after-school sports next year. People who have retired watch the cost of food and rent go up and wonder how they can make their dollars stretch farther.

These different wants and needs are the source of many of our federal laws. People talk about their wants and needs. They make them known to their senators and representatives. Because the senators and representatives wish to serve the people they represent and because they wish to be re-elected, they pay attention. In sessions of Congress, the senators and representatives try to turn the wishes and needs of the people they represent into laws. But can they please both rich and poor,

both old and young? Often, different groups of people want conflicting things. This makes it harder for the members of Congress. They must work out compromises. Naturally, they can not please everyone.

This chapter is about how Congress passes federal laws. You will follow a bill through Congress step by step. In doing so, you will see some of the pressures that affect our senators and representatives as they study new laws.

I. How Congress works
    A. Who has the ideas for bills?
       1. The President
       2. Organized groups
       3. The public
       4. Members of Congress
    B. How a bill is introduced
    C. The committee system
       1. Standing committees
       2. Select committees
       3. Subcommittees
       4. Joint committees
       5. Conference committees
       6. Public hearings
    D. Political parties and committees

II. From idea to law: One bill's journey
    A. Birth of an idea
    B. House of Representatives: first stage
       1. Committee action
       2. Rules Committee: the traffic cop
       3. To the floor of the House
       4. The vote
    C. Senate: second stage
       1. In committee again
       2. To the Senate floor
       3. The vote
    D. Conference committee: third stage
    E. The President: fourth stage
    F. The bill becomes a law.

Words to Know

bill —— a plan or proposal for a law

committee —— a small group of lawmakers (Congress turns over much of its work to many types of committees.)

political party —— an organized group of people who have joined together to win elections and, thus, place their members in government office

majority party —— the political party with more members in Congress

minority party —— the political party with fewer members in Congress

caucus —— a meeting of the Democratic members of the House

conference —— a meeting of the Republican members of Congress

floor leader —— a member of Congress chosen by a political party to help put the party's bills through Congress

whip —— a person who helps the floor leader put bills through Congress

Handicapped students speak to a government representative in a bid to get a bill into Congress.

How Congress Works

All federal laws begin as **bills** in Congress. A bill is a plan or proposal for a law. A bill can begin in either the House or the Senate (remember, though, that money-raising bills can begin only in the House). Each bill must be passed in the same form by a majority in both the House and the Senate. Then Congress sends the bill to the President. If the President signs the bill, it becomes law. If the President returns the bill to Congress without signing it, the bill must be passed again. This time, it needs a two-thirds vote in both houses. Then it becomes a law without going back to the President.

Who Has the Ideas for Bills?

Only a senator or a representative can introduce a bill in Congress. But the ideas for bills can, and often do, come from other people. In fact, you could write a bill yourself. You could put it in your own words and give it to your senator or representative in Congress. If the representative agrees with the bill, he or she may introduce it.

The President The source of many bills is the President of the United States. Each January, the President speaks to Congress in a State of the Union message. This message states the goals that the President would like the nation to work for in the coming months. High officials in the executive branch of the government help give the President ideas for this message. These officials and members of the President's staff draw up bills to help the nation reach these goals. Members of Congress who are friendly with the President then introduce the bills in Congress.

Organized Groups Another important source of bills is organized groups. For example, a labor union such as the United Mine Workers might want stricter laws about mine safety. An environmental group

Listening to speeches about new legislation is an important part of the work done by a member of Congress.

such as the Sierra Club might want a piece of land turned into a national park or wildlife refuge. Very often, such groups will draw up bills for a senator or representative to introduce in the Congress.

The Public Another starting point for bills is public pressure. People who feel strongly about something often write to senators and representatives. For example, large numbers of people might write to Congress to demand better mail service. Representatives who received many such letters might decide that this was a popular issue. Then the chances are good that some member of Congress would soon introduce a bill to improve mail service.

Members of Congress Finally, senators and representatives may draw up bills themselves. They have many ways of learning what laws might be needed. Some of them are specialists in certain subjects. A representative may have worked for years on laws dealing with atomic energy, so he or she may see a need for a new law on safety

in nuclear power plants. A senator may also have taken part in an investigation of corrupt politics. She or he may see a need for a new law to prevent secret campaign contributions, for example. Of course, all members of Congress are specialists in pleasing "the folks back home." A representative from a coastal state knows that fishing is important to the people there. He or she may introduce a bill to keep foreign fishing ships farther out to sea.

How a Bill Is Introduced

Once a bill is written, it is introduced in either the House or the Senate. In the House, a representative drops a bill into a box that hangs on the side of the clerk's desk. This is known as the "hopper." A representative may drop a bill in the hopper at any time.

In the Senate, the procedure is more formal. A senator must request permission to be called on. Only after the President or

After a bill is introduced, it is sent to a committee, where its contents are carefully studied.

President *pro tem* of the Senate has called on a senator can a bill be introduced.

The Committee System

As we have seen, many different people want many different types of bills passed. In a normal 2-year term, 20,000 bills are introduced. It would be impossible for each senator or representative to study each of these 20,000 bills. To handle this large amount of material, both the Senate and the House have a system of committees. **Committees** are the small groups of lawmakers to whom Congress turns over much of its work. Whenever a bill is introduced, it is sent to a committee.

Standing Committees Most of the work of Congress is done by standing committees. These are permanent committees. Each standing committee deals with one range of topics. For example, one standing committee in the House spends all its time on foreign affairs. There is a similar committee in the Senate. Standing committees study bills, hold hearings, and conduct investigations. They are often in the headlines, because their work is very important.

The number of standing committees changes from time to time. At the present time, there are twenty-two standing committees in the House and eighteen in the Senate. The Fact Block on page 123 shows the names of these committees and the number of members that are on each.

Each member of the House may serve on one major committee. The most important committee in the House is the committee on rules. The Rules Committee decides when (or if) a bill is to be considered by the full House. The importance of the Rules Committee comes from the fact that it has a say in what happens to almost every bill in the House. The other important House committees include: Appropriations—which decides how much money each government program or agency will be given; Education and Labor, Foreign Affairs, Judiciary—which handles amendments to the Constitution and impeachments; and Ways and Means—which handles tax bills and other money bills.

Each member of the Senate may serve on two major committees. The most important committees in the Senate are the following: Appropriations, Labor and Public Welfare—which is like the Education and Labor Committee in the House; Foreign Relations, Judiciary, and Finance—which is like the House Ways and Means Committee. The Senate has a Committee on Rules and Administration, but this committee is much less powerful than the House Rules Committee.

STANDING COMMITTEES OF CONGRESS

House of Representatives		Senate	
Agriculture	(43 members)	Agriculture, Nutrition and Forestry	(17 members)
Appropriations	(54 members)	Appropriations	(29 members)
Armed Services	(45 members)	Armed Services	(17 members)
Banking, Finance and Urban Affairs	(44 members)	Banking, Housing, and Urban Affairs	(15 members)
Budget	(32 members)	Budget	(22 members)
District of Columbia	(12 members)	Human Resources	(16 members)
Educational and Labor	(34 members)	Foreign Relations	(17 members)
Energy and Commerce	(44 members)	Government Affairs	(17 members)
Foreign Affairs	(36 members)	Commerce, Science and Transportation	(17 members)
Governments Operations	(41 members)	Judiciary	(18 members)
House Administration	(20 members)	Environment and Public Works	(16 members)
Interior and Insular Affairs	(42 members)	Rules and Administration	(12 members)
Judiciary	(28 members)	Energy and Natural Resources	(20 members)
Merchant Marine and Fisheries	(36 members)	Veterans Affairs	(12 members)
Post Office and Civil Service	(25 members)	Finance	(20 members)
Public Works and Transportation	(46 members)		
Rules	(11 members)		
Science and Technology	(42 members)		
Small Business	(39 members)		
Standards of Official Conduct	(12 members)		
Veterans Affairs	(30 members)		
Ways and Means	(34 members)		

Select Committees Congress sometimes sets up select, or special, committees to handle problems that are not covered by the standing committees. Often, a select committee will investigate a topic of special interest. For example, select committees have investigated organized crime, using televised hearings that have brought the workings of Congress into the home. Other select committees have investigated government scandals, the problems of the aging, and nutrition. After studying a problem, a select committee suggests laws for dealing with it.

Subcommittees Both standing and select committees can have subcommittees. These are smaller groups within a committee. These subcommittees often study some very specific part of a larger problem and report the findings to the whole committee.

If there is a problem approving a single version of a bill, then a committee or subcommittee may hold either public or private hearings on the subject.

Select committees usually have fewer members than standing committees. Subcommittees usually have fewer members than select committees.

Joint Committees Sometimes the two houses of Congress form a single committee with members from both the House and the Senate. There are both standing and select joint committees. A joint committee usually has an equal number of members from each house.

Conference Committees It is the job of another kind of committee to work out a compromise when the House and Senate pass two versions of the same bill. This is a conference committee. Each house must approve the same version of a bill before the bill can be sent to the President. Conference committees include members from both houses. These committees are temporary and work only on one bill.

Public Hearings Committees and subcommittees often hold public hearings to gather information on a problem. The hearings also give private citizens the chance to speak out. If committee members wish to, they can require people to appear before a committee.

Sometimes a committee chooses to hold a closed, or private, meeting. This might happen if the committee is discussing military secrets. At such times, only witnesses called by the committee are allowed into the hearings. No record of such hearings is published.

Political Parties and Committees

To understand how the committee system works, we have to take a brief look at political parties. (The workings of political parties will be taken up in more detail in Chapter 14.) A **political party** is an organized group of people who have joined together to win elections and, thus, place their members in government office.

For most of this country's history, there have been only two major political parties at any one time. The party with more members in Congress is the **majority party.** The party with fewer members in Congress is the **minority party.** Today, the two major parties are known as the Democratic and the Republican parties.

Members of the same political party generally share similar views on public mat-

In addition to party meetings, members may belong to other groups. The women in Congress hold their caucus to decide their position on legislation.

ters—but only in the broadest sense. "Put ten Democrats together and you'll have ten different opinions," one saying goes. The same thing could be said about Republicans. Among members of both the House and the Senate as much bargaining goes on *within* one political party as between the two parties.

The members of each party who are in Congress meet together to decide which bills the party will support and which bills it will fight. Often, there is some disagreement among party members, and the party as a whole takes no stand. The Democrats call their meeting a **caucus.** All the others call their meeting a **conference.**

At the start of each session, the parties in Congress choose their leaders. Each party in each house has a **floor leader.** This person's job is to guide the party's bills through Congress. The most important floor leaders are those of the majority party, because they can usually put together the most votes. They are sometimes called the *majority leaders.* Both the majority and minority floor leaders receive extra pay for their additional duties. Their salary is $68,575 a year.

Assisting each floor leader is a person called the **whip.** The term comes from the British sport of hunting with hounds. The "whipper in" is the person who keeps the hounds from leaving the pack. In Congress, the whip is the party official who rounds up party votes. With the help of various deputy whips, the whip also "counts noses"

The Republican minority leader plays a vital role in guiding party bills through Congress.

and tells party leaders how many members are likely to vote for or against a bill.

The party caucus or conference elects a small group of members to form a policy committee, or steering committee. Its main job is to help guide party members' decisions on whether or not to support bills.

In each house, each party also has a committee on committees. Its job is to name the party members who will serve on the standing committees and on other official committees. For example, the Republican Committee on Committees in the Senate names all of the Republicans who will serve on each Senate committee.

The two parties usually divide up the seats on official committees according to the strength of each party in each house. There might be sixty senators from the majority party and forty from the minority party in the Senate. Then a Senate committee of ten would have six members from the majority party and four members from the minority party.

The majority party has one more job to fill. Because it has the controlling votes in the House, the majority party chooses the Speaker of the House—the presiding officer. The actual election, though, is by a vote of all members of the House. As we saw in Chapter 4, the Speaker has an important job that can help move the bills of the majority party through the House and slow down the movement of the minority bills.

REVIEW
---

1. Define the following terms:
   committee
   political party
   floor leader
   caucus

2. Name three ways in which an idea for a bill can start.

3. Name two types of committees in Congress. What does each type do?

4. What is the job of the party whip?

5. Do you think that all hearings that congressional committees hold should be open to the public? Why or why not?

Words to Know

pigeonhole —— kill a bill by holding it in committee and not returning it to the floor for debate and vote

discharge —— bring a bill out of committee against the committee's will, by majority vote of the whole House

quorum —— a majority of the members of a legislative body who must be present in order to conduct official business

rider —— an addition to a bill that is unrelated to the subject of the bill

filibuster —— a drawn-out Senate speech that is aimed at killing a bill

cloture —— a vote to end debate on a bill and stop a filibuster

pocket veto —— the way a President may kill a bill by "pocketing" it for 10 days and not signing it; only possible if Congress adjourns during the 10 days

presidential veto —— the way a President kills a bill by returning it to Congress unsigned, with a list of reasons for not signing

From Idea to Law: One Bill's Journey

You saw, in the last section, where the ideas for bills come from. You also studied how the committees that work with the bills are put together and learned a little about how they are run. Now it is time to follow one idea on its way to becoming a law. In this *imaginary* example, the bill will start in the House. Remember, though, that except for tax bills any bill can start in the Senate. The steps to its passage would be the same.

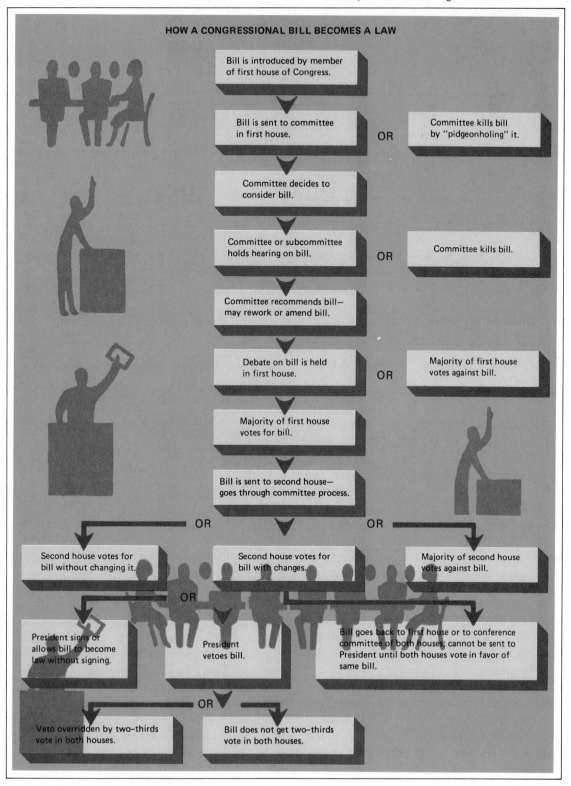

HOW A CONGRESSIONAL BILL BECOMES A LAW

Bill is introduced by member of first house of Congress.

Bill is sent to committee in first house. OR Committee kills bill by "pidgeonholing" it.

Committee decides to consider bill.

Committee or subcommittee holds hearing on bill. OR Committee kills bill.

Committee recommends bill— may rework or amend bill.

Debate on bill is held in first house. OR Majority of first house votes against bill.

Majority of first house votes for bill.

Bill is sent to second house— goes through committee process.

OR   OR

Second house votes for bill without changing it. | Second house votes for bill with changes. | Majority of second house votes against bill.

OR

President signs or allows bill to become law without signing. | President vetoes bill. | Bill goes back to first house or to conference committee of both houses; cannot be sent to President until both houses vote in favor of same bill.

OR

Veto overridden by two-thirds vote in both houses. | Bill does not get two-thirds vote in both houses.

When a special interest group, be it conservation society or school class, wishes to have its idea known to Congress, it first has to have that idea sponsored by a local representative. Pictured here is a congresswoman discussing just such an issue with a group of interested students.

Birth of an Idea

For 10 years Dorothea Muldoon has been taking her biology classes from the Coastal School on field trips to lonely Crawdad Island. It is the best place in the area to see how different kinds of animals live together in nature. One fall, after visiting the island, members of the class decide they should see if a way might be found to keep the island as it is. Other nearby islands are being turned into vacation communities. Developers are cutting down trees, draining swamps, and laying out golf courses. It seems only a matter of time before the same thing will happen to Crawdad Island.

"Let's see if there isn't some way to have the federal government turn the island into a park or something," says one class member. The others agree. So the class writes a letter to its local representative in Congress, Maria Fenton.

Representative Fenton is encouraging. She says she has already heard a similar idea from a local conservation group, the United Wildlife Watchers (UWW). Some of the class members go to a meeting of the UWW. Soon, the two groups are working together to collect signatures on a peti-

tion to Congress. More than 20,000 people sign it.

The students and the UWW leaders write to another conservation group in Washington, D.C. It has experience in dealing with Congress. The group helps write up a bill to preserve the island as a wildlife refuge. The conservation group takes the bill to Representative Fenton's office and discusses it with her and her staff. Representative Fenton suggests a few changes. She agrees to sponsor the bill. "It's just the kind of forward-thinking legislation I want to be identified with," she says.

House of Representatives: First Stage

Representative Fenton drops the bill into the hopper beside the desk of the Clerk of the House. The Clerk gives the bill a short title and a number, "H.R. 770." The *H.R.* stands for House of Representatives. The *770* means that the bill is the 770th bill introduced in the House this term. A notice of the bill is placed in the House *Journal* and in the *Congressional Record*. When all this is done, the bill has received its *first reading*. It will go through two more readings before it leaves the House.

The Speaker of the House receives the bill next. It is up to the Speaker to decide which committee will study the bill. In this case, the Speaker decides to send the bill to the Interior and Insular Affairs Committee for review.

Committee Action　The Interior and Insular Affairs Committee gets the bill and looks it over carefully. The committee re-ceives many bills and must decide which are the most important. Sometimes a number of different bills are proposed on the same subject. The committee can combine those bills into one new bill. Sometimes a bill seems unimportant and the committee sets it aside. The bill has been **pigeon-holed,** or forgotten. It has "died in commit-tee." This is the fate of most bills.

H.R. 770 does not die in committee. It has received lots of publicity. National con-servation organizations have backed it. From all over the country, people have written their representatives in favor of it. But the bill has also drawn opposition. A group of contractors—the people who build vacation communities—is against it. So is a national labor union with many members who are construction workers. The workers think that the bill might cost them jobs. The bill might also encourage people in other parts of the country to block con-struction in undeveloped areas.

Once a bill is received, it is sent to a committee for study and review. Hearings are often held to allow all sides to express their views.

The committee schedules hearings on the bill. Three students from Dorothea Muldoon's class make a special trip to Washington, D.C., to attend the hearings. One of them, Michael Smithers, is given a chance to tell the committee why the students want the bill. He reads a statement. Then Representative Fenton asks friendly questions. The committee chairman, Roscoe Mercer, is a little tougher. "Do you think you students have a right to impose your will upon others just to save a few birds and posies? Don't people have a right to build homes where they want?" the chairman asks. Michael Smithers draws applause when he responds: "Mr. Chairman, all the bills you pass here in Washington impose some people's will upon other people. I think this bill will do more good than harm. I think you should pass it."

Many other people speak before the committee. A man from the labor union tells how many jobs he thinks the bill will cost. A woman from a group called Cut Our Taxes says she thinks the federal government spends too much money on parks and wildlife refuges. "We taxpayers don't want the government wasting our money," she says.

After listening to all the witnesses, the committee members talk the bill over. Several of them want to refuse to report the bill back to the House. That is, they want to pigeonhole it. This would most likely kill the bill. Only if a majority of the House votes to **discharge,** or release, a pigeonholed bill from committee can it be brought up for debate by the full House.

Some committee members want to report the bill back to the House with an unfavorable recommendation. Usually, the House does not pass bills that get an unfavorable recommendation in committee.

Roscoe Mercer, the chairman, does not like the bill, but he owes Representative Fenton a favor for supporting another bill that he introduced. Mutual favors are the grease that keeps the wheels of Congress turning. Mercer says he can support a wildlife refuge that takes up only half of Crawdad Island. Representative Fenton decides half is better than none. She accepts Mercer's proposal, and the committee votes to change the bill. Then a majority of committee members vote to send the bill back to the floor of the House with a favorable recommendation.

Rules Committee: The Traffic Cop The House Rules Committee gets the bill next. People sometimes speak of the House Rules Committee as the "House traffic cop." It plays an important part in the life of any bill at this point. It can give the bill "a red light" by refusing to place it on the House calendar, or schedule. This could kill the bill altogether. The Rules Committee may, instead, give the bill a police escort by scheduling an immediate debate, rather than having the bill wait its turn. This would speed the bill through the House. The Rules Committee may also set a time limit on debate. Remember that there are 435 representatives and thousands of bills. Only a limited amount of time can be allowed for talking about a bill.

H.R. 770 is placed on the regular House calendar. This means that it will have to wait its turn.

To the Floor of the House Finally, H.R. 770 has its day on the floor of the House. Those in favor of the bill and those against it are given equal time to express their points of view. Then the whole bill is read, paragraph by paragraph. This is the *second reading.* As the bill is read, members suggest amendments, or changes, to the bill. Each representative is usually allowed 5 minutes to speak on each amendment. After all who wish to speak have been heard, a vote is taken to accept or reject the amendment. Then the next paragraph of the bill is read and other amendments are offered.

Representative Fenton wants to add an amendment to make the bill once again cover all of Crawdad Island. But the amendment loses, as do two other amendments.

When the whole bill has been read and all amendments voted on, the time for the final vote has arrived. Sometimes a member will first ask for a *quorum call* to see if there is a **quorum,** or a majority, of members present. Without a quorum, neither house of Congress can officially do business. If a quorum is present, the bill can go on to its *third reading*. This is usually just a reading of the bill's title. Then a vote is taken.

The Vote There are three ways of voting in the House. The most common is the *voice vote*. Representatives say "aye" if they are in favor of the vote and "no" if they are opposed. The votes are not actually counted. The Speaker of the House decides which side sounds like it has the most votes.

If some representatives feel that the Speaker has made a mistake, they can ask for a second type of vote. This is a *standing vote,* or a division of the House. First, all in favor of the bill stand. Next, those who are opposed stand. Both sides are counted by the Clerk of the House.

Using a computerized voting system, members of the House of Representatives register their approval or rejection of a bill by simply pushing buttons, thus electronically registering their votes. The votes are then totaled by the same mechanism.

After a bill is read for the last time on the House floor, computers may be used to tally the vote.

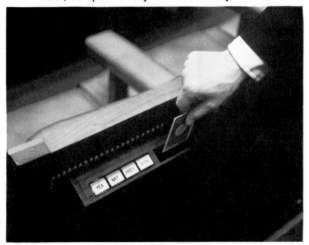

The third type of vote is the *roll-call vote.* This is the only type of vote in which each representative's vote is recorded and printed in the House *Journal* and the *Congressional Record.* Each representative has a computer card. The representative puts the card into one of the computer stations on the House floor and pushes a button to record her or his vote.

H.R. 770 is an important bill and gets a roll-call vote. A majority of those present favor the bill, and it passes by a vote of 203 to 185. The approved bill is next sent on to the Senate.

Senate: Second Stage

In the Senate, the bill becomes S. 1440. The *S* stands for Senate. The number means that it is the 1440th bill introduced in the Senate this term. The bill gets a title and a first reading and is sent to a committee.

In Committee Again The steps that the bill follows in a Senate committee are just like those in the House. The committee can hold hearings. It can change parts of the bill or rewrite it completely. It can pigeonhole the bill. It can recommend it unfavorably, or, as is the case with S. 1440, the committee can make a few changes and recommend the bill favorably to the Senate.

With S. 1440, the changes include an amendment to give dogcatchers a special tax reduction. This has nothing to do with the original subject of the bill. Such an addition is called a **rider.** A member of Congress who introduces a rider feels that a bill on the subject of the rider would not get through Congress on its own, so she or he adds the rider to a bill that has a good chance of becoming a law.

To the Senate Floor S. 1440, along with the rider and a small change in the boundary of the wildlife refuge, finally makes it to the Senate floor. As soon as the bill has its line-by-line second reading, debate starts.

Debate in the Senate is different from debate in the House. The time for debate is not limited in advance. The senators can talk as long as they want for or against a bill. In fact, senators sometimes try to talk bills "to death." Senators who are opposed to a bill have been known to talk around the clock, until their voices are hoarse, trying to stop a vote on the bill. Often, many senators take turns talking. This is known as a **filibuster.** Finally, another senator may call for a special vote to limit the debate and end the filibuster. This is called **cloture.** Cloture needs the approval of three-fifths of the senators present and voting. It is rarely used, however, because senators take pride in their history of unlimited debate.

The Vote In the case of S. 1440, there is a great deal of serious debate but no filibuster. When all the senators have had their say, the bill is in the same form as when it came out of the Senate committee. Now the bill gets its third reading and a vote is taken. As in the House, there can be voice votes, standing votes, and roll-call votes. S. 1440 passes the Senate on a roll-call vote of 50 to 41.

Conference Committee: Third Stage

The bill is not yet through the Congress. Any bill must be passed in exactly the same form by both the House and the Senate. The Senate changed S. 1440, so now it must go back to the House. The House does not like the rider added to S. 1440 and will not approve it.

To avoid coming to a dead end on the bill, members of the House and Senate form a conference committee. This group has an equal number of members from each house. It seeks to work out a compromise that both the House and the Senate can accept. The conference committee soon resolves the differences on the bill. It drops the Senate rider, but keeps the boundary change made by the Senate. The compromise is sent back to both houses. At last, the bill passes in the same form in both houses, by a majority vote.

The President: Fourth Stage

Before becoming law, the bill must be sent to the President. If the President signs it, the bill is law. But a President can do other things. For example, the President might keep the bill and not sign it. In 10 days, if Congress is still in session, the bill will become law without the President's signature. But if Congress adjourns during those 10 days, the bill does not become law. The bill has been killed by a **pocket veto.** One other course the President can follow is to send the bill back to Congress unsigned, with the reasons for not signing it. This is known as a **presidential veto.**

When a bill is killed by pocket veto, Congress can do nothing. It has already adjourned. If Congress really wants the law to pass, it must start the bill again in the next session and go through the whole process once again.

If a bill is killed by presidential veto, Congress has a way of fighting back. If it wants the bill badly enough, Congress can pass it over the President's veto. To do this, two-thirds of the House and two-thirds of the Senate must vote to pass the bill. It is much harder to get a two-thirds vote than a majority vote, especially when the President is strongly against a bill. This is why Congress rarely passes a bill over a veto.

If the bill is approved by both the House and Senate, it is then sent to the President for final approval—in which case it becomes law—or for veto.

The Bill Becomes a Law

The problem of the veto does not come up with S. 1440. The President is in favor of it and signs the bill into law. The signed bill is sent to the National Archives and Records Service. There it is given another number. Shortly after that, the law is published in the *Statutes at Large of the United States.*

So the bill that Dorothea Muldoon's class dreamed of has become a law at last. It is clear that the process has been a long one, and no one is completely happy with the law. The class thinks that the wildlife refuge is too small. The construction unions wish the bill had been defeated.

Still, the length of time it takes to pass a bill and the addition of ideas to a bill were allowed for by the writers of the Constitution. They are part of the system of checks and balances. The writers knew that it would take time for bills to pass both houses of Congress. This meant that one house would have the chance to study seriously a bill that the other house might have passed in the excitement of the moment. By requiring both houses to approve a bill, the writers of the Constitution gave each house a check on the power of the other. By giving the President a chance to veto bills, they added another check on Congress's power. Also, by giving Congress the means to pass a bill over the President's veto, they provided a way to avoid a deadlock over important bills. The final goal of all these checks and balances was to make a lawmaking process that both reflected the people's will and protected the people's rights.

----------------------------------- REVIEW ------------------------------------

1. Define the following terms:
   pigeonhole
   filibuster
   rider
   cloture
2. What are three things that a committee of Congress can do with a bill?
3. What are the types of vote used in the House and the Senate?
4. Can you see any ways to speed up the process in which a bill becomes a law? Do you think that speeding up the process would be a good idea?

How The United States Works

Librarians

Many, many bills come before Congress every year. Legislators have to study each one before deciding how to vote. That calls for a great deal of information and many hours of research. The Library of Congress was set up to help with this task. Its most important job is researching the facts that lawmakers need.

This is the work of professional librarians. With 4 years of college and a 1-year master's degree in library science, they know how to get around in the Library of Congress—that storehouse of books, magazines, newspapers, pamphlets, flyers, posters, and records. They do the research the lawmakers need, and then they prepare a report.

Research is not the only job that librarians do. Most libraries, among them the Library of Congress, supply many services to the public. Librarians direct these services. They also buy books and other materials. They store and catalog the materials so that they are easily found.

Professional librarians do not do all the work needed to run a library, though. Most of the people you see checking books and shelving them are called library technicians, or assistants. Library technicians also help out by repairing books, films, and other materials. They can answer most of the questions that people ask about a library.

The federal government is the most generous employer for professional librarians. It pays $14,000 to $23,000 a year. In neighborhood, school, or college libraries, the salary is usually $10,000 to $15,000 a year. However, these jobs are hard to get, and many people are earning master's degrees in library science.

The job market is much better for library technicians. Many new jobs are opening up in large public and college libraries. Most library technicians are trained in 2-year junior colleges.

Reading About . . .

Debate in Congress ———————————————————

If you visit Washington, D.C., you may have a chance to sit in on a meeting of the House or the Senate. As you listen to the senators or representatives debate, you may notice that their words often seem stuffy and formal. Phrases such as "the honorable representative from Iowa," and "the very able junior senator," and "the distinguished minority leader" are heard again and again. As the following reading indicates, this formality serves a purpose.

As you read, think about the following points:

● What reasons does the reading give for the formal politeness?
● Do you think that Congress would work more or less smoothly if the rules mentioned here were not followed?

One senator once laid down a "tongue-in-cheek" rule for the benefit of new members. He said that a senator who is thought to be stupid should always be referred to as "the able, learned and distinguished Senator"; one who is *known* to be stupid, as "the *very* able, learned and distinguished Senator."

At the bottom of this concern for the senators' feelings is, in part, a real concern about allowing what another senator once described as that "nasty debate one can hear in many parliamentary bodies around the world." That kind of debate, in his judgment, destroys the senators' effectiveness. Probably more basic is the simple fact that an offended senator may some day use his or her influence to make serious trouble for one of the offender's personal bills or for a local project that is vital to the offender.

In addition, there is a rule in both houses forbidding language that insults a member of either house. A violator of the rule who does not quickly withdraw the remarks can be forced to take his or her seat and have the comments taken off the record. But where there is a will to insult, there's a way.

"I wish to know if there is any way under the parliamentary rules of the Senate," once came an inquiry from the floor, "whereby one member may refer to another as a willful, malicious liar." Under the threat of having to take his seat, the senator switched to the proper form: "The charges made by the senator from Michigan, I will say, in parliamentary language, are as much without foundation as it is possible for any charges to be."

Another method was used by a senator who was taken to task for denouncing a member of the House. The senator pleaded: "I did not discuss this person's conduct in the House. I never said one word yesterday, nor will I today, about this person having relatives on the public payroll who are not working. I am not calling attention to it today."

"I will not mention the fact that his wife is on his payroll, nor will I raise any question as to whether she does any work. Neither will I say that he is not fulfilling his duties and is guilty of a great deal of absenteeism."

chapter
Review

Fact Review

1. Which of the following people can introduce a bill in Congress?
   a. the President
   b. any citizen
   c. a representative
   d. a senator
   e. an organized group
   f. the Clerk of the House
2. What is the one reason for using the committee system in Congress?
3. Why are conference committees sometimes needed?
4. What are the checks and balances involved in the process of passing laws in Congress?
5. What are some good points and some bad points of the Senate's tradition of unlimited debate? Do you think it should be made easier or harder to stop a filibuster?

Developing Your Vocabulary

What are the differences between the following pairs of words?
   a. bill and law
   b. caucus and conference
   c. floor leader and whip
   d. standing committee and select committee
   e. filibuster and cloture

Developing Your Reading Skills

Read the following paragraph and then answer the questions that follow:

All of the powers granted to the House of Representatives and the Senate have one very basic goal. That goal is the passing of laws for the good of the United States and its citizens. All laws passed by our Congress start in the form of bills. The ideas for these bills can come from a member of Congress, from the President, or from other people inside and outside the federal government. But only a member of Congress can actually introduce a bill in Congress.

1. Which of the following do you think is the main idea, or point, of this paragraph?
   a. Congress has many legislative powers.
   b. The most important business of Congress is making laws.
   c. All laws passed by Congress first appeared as bills.
   d. Anyone can suggest a bill, but only a member of Congress can introduce a bill in the House or the Senate.
2. Why did you select either *a, b, c,* or *d* above?

Developing Your Writing Skills— Forming and Supporting an Opinion

In this chapter, you have seen what goes on in making a bill into a law. Now consider the following questions:

Forming an opinion

1. What sort of person should be responsible for passing our federal laws in Congress?
2. Can you think of four qualities that a member of the Congress should have?

Supporting an opinion

3. After thinking about these questions, write a paragraph telling what qualities you would look for in a member of Congress. Begin with a topic sentence that sums up your views. Continue with at least one reason for choosing each of the four qualities.

YOUR GOVERNMENT & ITS HISTORY

The Tariff Issue, 1829–1831

Before Andrew Jackson became President, Congress passed the Tariff Act of 1828. A tariff is a tax on goods imported into a country. Many Southerners were against the tariff. They felt it favored the manufacturing interests of the North.

The tariff became the subject of much debate and dispute. In 1830, Jackson supported the tariff, but he recommended changes. Congress then passed a new tariff law in 1832. It was milder than the previous one, but the act still angered many Southerners. The following selection, from Clara Ingram Judson's book about Andrew Jackson, describes the debate.

New Englanders wanted a high tariff. "How can factories make money when Americans buy cheap things made abroad?" they asked. "Slap on a high duty, and make people buy home goods."

Southerners disagreed. They sold cotton abroad and bought things overseas. They had very few factories of their own. "Why should we pay a high duty?" they asked. "We don't need protection."

A bill about another matter brought the dispute into the open. This bill proposed to restrict land sales in the West. Westerners wanted settlers, so they were against the bill. Easterners wanted to stop the movement west, so they were for the bill. Southerners were quick to turn the dispute to help their tariff problem. They said that no section of the nation had a right to force a law on any other section.

Daniel Webster, a New Englander, chanced to enter the Senate chamber one day. Senator Robert Y. Hayne of South Carolina was ending a passionate speech favoring states' rights. On the spur of the moment, Webster took the floor and talked on the side of a strong Union—and against states' rights. He closed with a bold challenge to Hayne to rally. Hayne accepted the chance to explain his views.

"Is the federal government to be the judge of its own power?" Hayne cried. "Is it without limitations? High tariff would ruin the South."

Five days later, the chamber was again crowded when Daniel Webster replied. "The Constitution by the will of the people is the supreme law of the land. It must be obeyed or changed." His audience listened intently through the 4 hours of his speech. He told them that the Constitution had created a Supreme Court. The Constitution, not the states, should decide what laws were right. He ended with ringing words: "Hayne says, 'Liberty first and union afterward.' I speak another sentiment, dear to every American heart—liberty and union, now and forever. . . .

April came. With it came the annual birthday banquet in honor of Thomas Jefferson, who had died 4 years earlier. South Carolinians had charge of the affair. They made sure that the speakers and the toasts would favor states' rights. Of course, the President would speak. . . .

The President sat silent and thoughtful. He was introduced—and for seconds, he did not move. Then he unfolded his long legs and stood tall before them. He lifted a glass, cast his eyes around the hushed room—and spoke fateful words: "Our federal Union, it must be preserved!"

Men gasped. John C. Calhoun of North Carolina leaped to his feet and tried to save the day for the South. "The Union, next to liberty, most dear! May we all remember that it can only be preserved by respecting the rights of states."

After the election of 1831, South Carolina passed a Nullification Act. [The act canceled the tariffs of 1828 and 1832 and prohibited the collection of duties within the state.] Jackson decided to write a speech giving his ideas about this dangerous act. In his message, Jackson stated: "I consider the power to cancel a law of the United States . . . not in keeping with the existence of the Union, not in keeping with every principle on which it was founded, and destructive of the great objective for which it was formed. . . ."

In Jackson's next message to Congress, he reported the excellent state of the nation's finances. Debt was about paid. Soon the treasury would have more money than it needed. A high tariff was not needed for income. Duties on goods were slowly reduced. Peace came with this compromise. Both sides claimed victory. The North said that federal law was upheld. The South said that the tariff had come down; they would obey federal law—on their own terms.

1. Why was the tariff so great an issue during the years from 1828 to 1831?

2. What did each of the following have to say about the tariff and states' rights issues: John C. Calhoun, Daniel Webster, Robert Y. Hayne, and Andrew Jackson?

3. What is meant by *compromise*? What do you think it has to do with the passage of bills in Congress?

SKILLS Developing your basic civic education skills

(types of questions for civics education)

A Look at Committees

In this chapter, you have learned about some of the roles played by committees of Congress. A committee is a group of people elected, appointed, or assigned to consider, investigate, or report on a specific matter.

Committees are a part of our lives. They exist in places other than Congress. They exist in your own school. Think about your student council and other student groups. They probably have committees.

Think about the role committees might play in the operation of your student council. Suppose a member of the student council convinced other members of the need to conduct a used-clothing drive for needy people. Once the idea received approval, plans would have to be formed. How would publicity for the drive be handled? Who would be responsible for collecting the clothing? Where would the used clothing be collected? How would the used clothing be distributed to needy people?

To solve these problems successfully, the student council might form a committee of several students. The committee's task would be to find answers to the questions just asked.

Furthermore, the General Clothing Committee might decide to assign tasks to subcommittees. One subcommittee could be responsible for handling all publicity for the clothing drive. Another might deal with collecting the clothing. Another could be responsible for gathering the clothing in one place. A final group might have the task of distributing the clothing to needy people or taking it to an agency that could do this. Whatever their assignments, all subcommittees would report to the General Clothing Committee. Then it would report to the student council.

1. What is the meaning of the word *committee?*

2. How do committees work within your own school? Cite one example.

3. How does the work of committees in your school compare with the work of committees in Congress?

4. Is having committees a good idea? Explain.

Identifying Types of Questions

Thinking critically requires the ability to ask a variety of questions about a topic. Every day, we all ask many questions. Many questions are asked of us as well. These questions usually fall into several different categories.

Recall questions ask you to remember information previously presented. They often call for the simple repetition of information in its original form. Recall questions usually have only one right answer. Examples of recall questions are: Who is President of the United States? What are the three main branches of the federal government? In what year did Christopher Columbus first arrive in the Americas?

Application questions require the ability to compare and contrast, relate, identify, organize, or classify data or ideas. Many application questions have only one right answer, but sometimes the answers may vary with the individual. Examples of application questions are: What were the similarities and differences between causes for the American Revolution of 1776 and the Texas Revolution of 1836? How does the population of the United States today compare with the population in 1880?

Judgment questions ask you to decide the worth, importance, or effectiveness of an idea, event, or action. Judgment questions can allow you to express your own ideas. They help with responsible decision-making. Judgment questions help you examine the worth of other possible choices and arrive at a conclusion supported by well-thought-out reasons. Examples of judgment questions are: Which one of our Presidents was most effective while in office? Why? Of all the ideas offered for saving our natural resources, which one seems to be the best? Why?

5. Classify questions 1–4 as either a recall, an application, or a judgment question.

6. Using the information you have just read about committees, write one new recall question, one new application question, and one new judgment question.

7. Of the three main types of questions, which one is easiest to ask? Which one seems most difficult to ask? Why?

8. Do the three types of questions seem related in any way? Explain your answer.

9. Do you think there is any value in asking each of these three types of questions about a topic? Why or why not?

Developing Your Questioning Skills

The following accounts and cartoons contain differing views of Congress in recent years. As you examine them, first determine what seems to be the main point of each.

Newspaper Editorial 1

The nation's founders thought Congress should mirror the population. As John Adams put it, "The Congress should be a portrait in miniature of the American people."

To find out how closely this expectation is being met, *American Demographics* magazine [in 1980] made these comparisons of the outgoing Ninety-sixth Congress and the United States population:

—The United States is 49 percent male; Congress is 97 percent male.

—The nation is 86 percent white; Congress is 97 percent white.

—While 38 percent of the United States population is under 39, only 18 percent of Congress falls into that age group. Those between 40 and 59 make up 35 percent of the population but a whopping 63 percent of Congress. And

27 percent of the population is 60 or older while 19 percent of Congress is in that group.
—Only 0.1 percent of the American people are lawyers; 52 percent of the members of Congress hold law degrees.
—The typical American earned $13,333 [in 1979]; the typical member of Congress was paid $60,600. . . .

10. What did John Adams think Congress should represent?

11. How did the Ninety-sixth Congress in 1980 compare with the general population in each of the following areas?

    a. sex
    b. race
    c. percent under age 39
    d. percent age 40–59
    e. percent 60 years and older
    f. number of lawyers
    g. typical salary

12. At this point in your investigation, consider: How close to the general population should Congress be?

Newspaper Editorial 2

Congress is improving its standing with the public.

An Associated Press–NBC News poll [in 1981] found that 29 percent of those interviewed rated Congress's work as excellent or good, up from 14 percent in January 1980.

Only 15 percent rated congressional work poor, compared to 32 percent in 1980. Fifty percent rated Congress fair in both polls. . . .

13. According to the Associated Press–NBC News poll, what percent of those interviewed rated Congress's work as excellent or good in 1981? What percent in 1981 rated Congress's work as poor? What percent in 1981 rated it as fair?

14. How did the 1981 poll results compare with those of 1980?

15. Which one of the following is the main point of the cartoon below?

    a. Some members of Congress have a bad image with the public.
    b. Some members of Congress are well known to the public.
    c. Congress passes many bills each year.

16. Why did you select *a, b,* or *c* in question 15?

SCOOPS   **by Doug Sneyd**

B.C.

re·cess *n.* a rest period enjoyed by kindergarteners and congressmen

WILEY'S DICTIONARY

© Field Enterprises, Inc., 1981

17. Which one of the following is the main point of the cartoon above?

   a. A recess is a rest or play period.
   b. Members of Congress do not work very hard.
   c. Congress has recesses.

18. Why did you select *a, b,* or *c* in question 17?

19. Consider: What could be a fair way to rate the work of Congress?

Report by a Tax Foundation

The Tax Foundation, Inc., of Washington, D.C., reported in 1980 that for the third year in a row the cost of running Congress was over $1 billion a year. The same was true in 1981–1982. The exact sum for 1980 was $1,330,648,000. That is eight times what Congress cost in 1960. It is four times what Congress cost in 1970 and twice what it cost in 1975.

Two Newspaper Editorials on Congressional Costs

In 1981, Henry B. Gonzalez, the San Antonio congressman, tried to get an amendment to an appropriations bill that would require members of the House and Senate to pay the full price for meals served in congressional dining rooms.

Among the many privileges our senators and representatives have voted themselves are meals in the Senate and House restaurants, partly paid for by the government. This is not bad for people making $60,622 a year.

Gonzalez's measure was aimed at requiring equal sacrifice from those who have been cutting federal benefits. It was only fair that members of Congress join in the sacrifice by paying for the full cost of their food instead of allowing the taxpayers to pick up part of the tab.

Unfortunately, Gonzalez's House colleagues managed to kill the amendment on the grounds that it was an attempt to legislate in an appropriations bill, something supposedly not allowed.

Gonzalez's idea is sound, and not only for congressional meals. Congress could set an example in this time of reduction—which we fully support—by eliminating such luxurious perks as congressional barbershops and gyms, along with reducing overblown staffs. Why, Congress could gain a lot of believability by voluntarily taking, say, a 10-percent pay cut. That would encourage a lot of us common folk to believe that budget-cutting is being applied to everyone.

In 1981, U.S. Senator Roger Jepson, a Republican from Iowa, almost became a folk hero. He introduced legislation to eliminate nearly $1 million in salaries for operators to run automatic Capitol Hill elevators.

A few years back, Congress spent $3 million converting the elevators to automatic operation. However, it kept half of the operators, even though the elevators do just fine if a representative or senator pushes the button.

Jepson says taxpayers still shell out more than $10,000 a year for each of the remaining eighty-nine operators. Though this would eliminate some lower-grade patronage, Congress could stiffen its upper lip and do without the operators as it cuts billions in spending elsewhere.

Jepson, we are pleased to note, has been recognized by the Ada Report, a publication that pokes fun at government workers and honors those who save public money. The Ada Report is sending Jepson a 6-foot hero sandwich.

20. What did the Tax Foundation report on the costs of running Congress?
21. Why did Representative Gonzalez introduce an amendment to the Constitution?
22. What bill did Senator Jepson introduce? Why?

23. What did both Gonzalez and Jepson seek to do?
24. Consider: How do you think the costs of operating Congress can be reduced?

A Defense of Congress by Norman J. Ornstein, Professor of Politics at Catholic University:

I have watched Congress and Washington closely for more than a dozen years, most of it from the outside, and I can add with total confidence the following startling beliefs.

—Congress is clean and honest. I would bet a lot of money that the proportion of lawbreakers is no greater in Congress than it is among *any* other group of people with similar, high-pressured jobs, whether they be doctors, lawyers, dentists, journalists, bankers or industrialists. In fact, it is probably less. But a member of Congress breaking the law is news, while a businessperson's affair is not—and even if the latter makes the headlines, it is not generalized in the same way. The plain fact is, however, that the overwhelming majority of people in Congress are of the basic, dull, family-oriented variety.

—Congress works hard. The average member of Congress works 70 to 80 hours a week on public business, ranging from committee hearings to floor debate to meetings with concerned voters. The work week is usually 7 days, 4 or 5 in Washington and the weekend back in the district—a lonely existence that strains family life and physical well-being. Everyone makes fun of congressional recesses, including the President. . . . Newspeople are especially fond of poking fun at the Congress's own term for them, "district work periods." In fact, they *are* district work periods. Most legislators go back to their districts and work long hours— meeting with individuals, visiting senior-citizen homes or community centers. We all try to have it both ways: We accuse members of Congress of "losing touch" if they do not spend a lot of time back home, and of "laziness" if they miss a vote or a meeting in Washington—but then we make fun of them when they try to meet all our demands. . . .

—Congress's working conditions should be improved. Capitol Hill is filled with uncomfortable offices. It may be hard to believe—for those who read about expensive, posh office buildings (and the cost overruns are inexcusable)—but, despite the odd exception, legislators and their staffs do not work in offices with fancy furniture. They sweat and strain in overcrowded offices with too many people and too much noise. Few, if any, businesses would tolerate such a setup. Congress should have better office arrangements.

—Members of Congress are underpaid. Every attempt to increase federal pay results in a chorus of screams of outrage. Of course, it is hard for the average citizen to feel sorry for a poor member of Congress trying to get by on "only" $60,000 a year. But the fact is that in Washington— where a truly modest family home in a decent location goes for $200,000 and up—$60,000 does not go very far. This is especially true for a member of Congress, who must maintain two homes, including one in the district. For most members, serving in Congress means a great financial sacrifice; their government co-workers of equal rank earn anywhere from two to five times a congressional salary. . . . We should keep congressional pay at a level where legislators with eight kids waiting to go through college are not forced out of public life because they cannot afford it. . . .

25. What did Ornstein have to say about each of the following?
    a. the honesty of members of Congress
    b. the working hours of members of Congress
    c. the working conditions of members of Congress
    d. the pay of members of Congress

26. Review the definitions of the three types of questions on page 140–141. Then classify questions 10–25 as either recall, application, or judgment questions.

27. What else might you consider before you form a more definite decision about the following?
    a. the makeup of Congress
    b. a fair way to rate the work of Congress
    c. how much Congress should cost

Special Note: As you read this book, you will continue to develop your questioning skills. Thus, you might wish to review pages 140–145.

UNIT 2 REVIEW

Fact Review

1. How many representatives and senators were in the First Congress? How many are in Congress at the present time?
2. Where did the First Congress meet? Where does Congress meet today?
3. Name six powers that are delegated to Congress and four powers that are denied to Congress.
4. What limits does the Constitution put on Congress's power to raise money?
5. In which house of Congress do the big states have more power? In which house do the small states have more power?
6. How were the members of the Senate chosen up until 1913? How are they chosen now?
7. How do the methods of taking roll-call votes differ in the House and Senate?
8. Give three examples of when a two-thirds majority vote is required in the Senate.
9. Name two kinds of committees that have members from both the Senate and the House.
10. Do you think that there should be a limit on the number of terms a senator or a representative may serve? Why or why not?

Developing Your Vocabulary

1. Match the words in *a* to *d* with the phrases in *(1)* to *(4)*.
   a. impeachment
   b. adjourn
   c. rider
   d. quorum
      (1) amendment unrelated to a bill's subject
      (2) formal House vote leading to a trial
      (3) end a meeting or session
      (4) majority of legislative body's members
2. What is the difference between the words in the following pairs?
   a. term and session
   b. committee and political party

Developing Your Reading Skills

Read the following passage and then answer the questions that follow.

Congress makes laws that touch our lives in many ways. It receives the power to do this from the Constitution. The Constitution lists many powers that are delegated to Congress and many powers that are denied to Congress. Some other powers are implied, although they are not mentioned by name.

Congress does not act alone in making laws. The President also plays a part. Each bill that is passed by Congress is sent to the President. If the President vetoes the bill by refusing to sign it, the bill dies. But if two-thirds of the members of each house vote for it a second time, the bill becomes a law.

1. Which of the following statements are supported by the reading?
   a. Congress is a lawmaking body.
   b. Committees often pigeonhole bills they do not like.
   c. Congress often passes bills over the President's veto.
2. According to the reading, which of the following kinds of powers belong to Congress?
   a. implied
   b. delegated
   c. unlimited
   d. veto

For many people in the United States, the idea of the executive branch of government is clear and simple. The executive branch is the President, who runs the country. In contrast, the legislative branch, with its 100 senators and 435 representatives, is confusing. There are so many committees and subcommittees. There are so many facts to keep straight. Many people in the United States do not know the name of the Speaker of the House or the majority leader of the Senate. In fact, many do not know the names of the senators from their own state or the representative from their own district.

But almost all citizens know who the President is. The President is always in the news. The President's name and picture appear in the papers almost every day. Television stations drop their regular programs to carry a speech by the President. Magazines run long stories studying every action of the President. The public knows what their President eats, what clothes the President wears, and when the President has a cold. The President's family, hobbies, and pets are all in the spotlight. Because they see so much of the President, people think that they know about the executive branch.

But the executive branch is more than one person. It is more than 2.9 million people—not counting members of the armed forces. It is hundreds of departments and bureaus. It is an organization that spends more than $500 billion a year. It is the largest branch of the United States government.

In this unit, you will look closely at the executive branch. You will learn what all those people do and where much of that money goes. To begin to understand the executive branch, we must start with a study of that one person who stands out so clearly—the President.

6 The President

Chapter

In 1789, the people of the United States had never had a President before. They did not even know how to address their new leader. Should they call him simply "President"? It sounded like what people might call the head of a shoe company. Members of the First Congress puzzled over the problem. Some wanted a fancy-sounding title. One suggested: "Your Highness the President of the United States of America and the Protector of the Rights of the Same." Others wanted something royal, like "Your Majesty." But the members of Congress did not feel comfortable with such a title. It reminded them of the king they had revolted against. In the end, no one really decided anything. People just started calling George Washington "Mr. President," and it has been used ever since.

Today, there are also other titles that are used for the President: Chief of State, Chief Executive, and Commander in Chief. In a way, these titles grew out of a question that Washington faced: "What should the President do?" The Constitution had outlined some ideas. For the most part, though, Washington had to answer that question as he went about performing his duties as President.

Washington's answer fulfilled the vision of the Constitution. His actions as President helped to create a real office with real powers. The Presidents after him have added their own ideas of what the President does and can do. All their actions together make a definition of the word *President*. This definition can change with each new President. In this chapter, you will see how the job of President is defined today.

I. A look at the Presidency
  A. Qualifications
    1. Constitutional requirements
    2. Unwritten rules?
  B. How the President is elected
    1. Electoral-college system
    2. Inauguration
  C. How long can a President serve?
  D. Salary and other benefits
  E. What happens if a President dies or resigns?
  F. The Vice President: the President's helper
  G. Impeachment
II. Powers and duties of the President
  A. Executive powers
  B. Legislative powers
    1. Messages to Congress
    2. The veto
    3. Other legislative powers
  C. Military powers
  D. Diplomatic powers
    1. Exchanging diplomats
    2. Making treaties
    3. Making executive agreements
  E. Judicial powers
    1. Reprieves and pardons
    2. Judicial appointments
  F. The Chief of State
  G. Growth of the President's power
    1. Reasons for growth of power
    2. Checks on President's power

Words to Know

electors —— people elected by voters in a presidential election (They, rather than the voters, actually elect the President.)
electoral college —— all the electors
popular vote —— the votes cast by citizens in an election
President-elect —— a person who has been elected President but has not yet taken office
inauguration —— ceremony at which a new President takes office

presidential succession —— the replacement of a President by another person, according to a set order, whenever the office becomes empty

A Look at the Presidency

Qualifications

It is often said that anyone can grow up to be President of the United States. This statement shows our belief in democracy. We like to think what everyone has an equal chance in our country. We work to make this true. But *can* anyone be President?

Constitutional Requirements The writers of the Constitution did not try to keep people out of the job. They only put three conditions into the Constitution. All Presidents—and all Vice Presidents—must meet these three conditions.

First, the President must be a natural-born citizen of the United States. Second, the President must be at least 35 years old. Third, the President must have lived in the United States for at least 14 years. These are the only requirements.

People from many walks of life have met these requirements. Jimmy Carter had been a peanut farmer and a governor. Dwight Eisenhower had been a general in the Army and the president of a university. Herbert Hoover had been an engineer. Warren G. Harding published a newspaper.

Did people from such different backgrounds have anything more in common than the three things listed in the Constitution? Do people have to meet other standards to become President?

Unwritten Rules? It is sometimes said that there are also some unwritten rules about who can become President. So

far, all of our Presidents have been men. All have been white. All have been Christian. Many people say that only someone who meets these unwritten requirements can be elected President.

Maybe they are right. But we must remember that unwritten "rules" can change. Once there was a "rule" that the President must be a Protestant. John F. Kennedy, a Roman Catholic, broke that rule when he was elected President in 1960. After the Civil War, another unwritten rule said that a Southerner could not be elected President. Lyndon Johnson broke that rule in 1964, and Jimmy Carter broke it in 1976.

As time goes by, the other unwritten rules may be broken. Then the only things that count will be the talents of the person running for President—and the requirements written in the Constitution.

How the President Is Elected

Electoral-College System In the United States, a President is elected every 4 years. Citizens cast their votes in November of leap years—for example, 1980, 1984, and 1988. The system of electing a President is a complicated one. The writers of the Constitution worried about the kind of leader that people would choose. They tried to make sure that the President would be the best person for the job by starting a two-step system. The writers thought that voters should first elect able citizens known as **electors.** These citizens would then meet as an **electoral college.** The electors in the electoral college would actually be the people who would elect the President.

Today, the electoral-college system works like this: An election year comes. In midsummer, the major political parties choose their candidates for President and Vice President (you will read more about this in Chapter 6). Candidates tour factories, shake hands on street corners, and speak at county fairs. Every night, the can-

Dorothy Zug won a seat in Pennsylvania's electoral college in 1976 so that she could cast an official ballot for Jimmy Carter. Once this was done, her job as an elected official was over.

didates are seen on television. Sometimes they debate each other on television before millions of people. Newpapers print page after page of news and pictures of the campaign. Finally, on the first Tuesday after the first Monday in November, the voters make their choice. But they are not really electing the President. They are voting for the electors who, in turn, will make the final choice.

The Constitution gives each state a number of electors. The number is equal to the number of senators and representatives that the state has in Congress. If South Carolina has two senators and six representatives, it will have eight electors.

All presidential candidates have electors who promise to support them. When a voter in South Carolina chooses a candidate, that voter is casting a ballot for the eight electors who support that candidate. The candidate who receives the greatest number of votes (the popular vote) in South Carolina wins all eight electoral votes. This is known as the "winner-take-all" system. It is the same in all the states except Maine. (In Maine, it is possible for two presidential candidates to split the electoral vote.)

It might be said that the electoral college has fifty "campuses"—one in each state. The electors meet in mid-December in the state capitals. There, they officially vote for their candidates. Then their job is done. The votes are sealed and sent to the Senate in Washington, D.C.

On January 6, the President of the Senate opens the votes from all the states. Both houses of Congress are present as the votes are counted. The candidate who has a majority of the electoral votes is declared elected. The candidate is now officially called the **President-elect.**

Of course, most people know the winner back in November—even before all the popular votes are counted. Thanks to computers and special sampling methods, television and radio stations can predict the winner on the night of the election. Usually, the candidate with the most popular votes wins the most electoral votes—and so, the Presidency.

But this is not always so. It can happen that no candidate receives a majority of the electoral votes. For example, the electoral votes may be split among three or more candidates. Then, the House of Representatives must elect the President. This has happened twice—once in 1800 and again in 1824. It could happen again.

There is another problem with the electoral-college system. One candidate may win a majority of the popular votes,

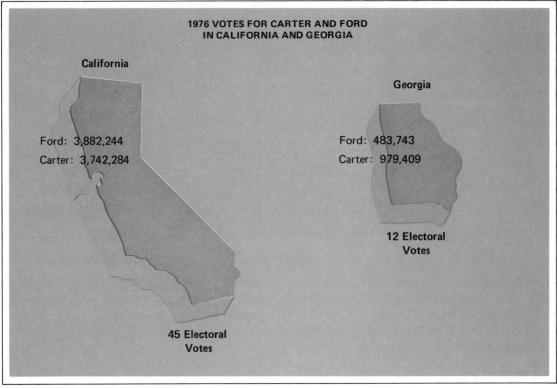

**1976 VOTES FOR CARTER AND FORD
IN CALIFORNIA AND GEORGIA**

California

Ford: 3,882,244

Carter: 3,742,284

45 Electoral
Votes

Georgia

Ford: 483,743

Carter: 979,409

12 Electoral
Votes

The maps above show the voting results in the states of Georgia and California
in the 1976 presidential election.

but not a majority of the electoral votes. How can this happen? Look at the maps on this page. They show the voting results in the states of Georgia and California in 1976. Jimmy Carter has won almost 400,000 more popular votes in those two states than Gerald Ford. But, because of the "winner-take-all" system, Ford is ahead 45 to 12 in the electoral votes. In this case, Carter won the election when the votes from all fifty states were counted. Twice in our history, though—in 1876 and in 1888—candidates who were behind in the popular vote have won the Presidency.

These problems have led people to look for ways to change the electoral system. That system was changed once, in 1804. At that time, the Twelfth Amendment created the system we have today.

Now some people want another system— direct election of the President by popular vote. They think that this system would be more democratic. Others are against changes. They think that changes might weaken the role of the states in the government.

Inauguration Regardless of the method used to elect the President, one step remains before the winning candidate can take office. This is the **inauguration**— the ceremony at which the oath of office is given. The ceremony is held on January 20 of the year following the election. It usually takes place on the steps of the Capitol. There, the Chief Justice of the Supreme Court leads the President-elect in the oath: "I do solemnly swear (or affirm) that I will faithfully execute the office of President of

On a crisp January day, millions of people watched as Chief Justice Warren Burger swore in Ronald Wilson Reagan as the fortieth President of the United States.

the United States, and will, to the best of my ability, preserve, protect, and defend the Constitution of the United States." The President-elect is now the President.

How Long Can a President Serve?

The President and Vice President are elected to 4-year terms. At first, the Constitution said nothing about how many terms a President could serve. George Washington was elected twice. He decided not to run for a third term. This started a custom that lasted for more than 150 years. No President had more than two terms in office.

Franklin D. Roosevelt broke this custom, however. He was first elected in 1932. He was re-elected in 1936, during the Great Depression. When the election of 1940 came, the Depression was still with us. Europe was at war. Roosevelt decided to run again. The voters of the United States did not want to change Presidents at such time,

so they elected Roosevelt to a third term. In 1944, the United States itself was at war. The voters elected Roosevelt to a fourth term.

Many people were upset by the idea of one person's holding office for such a long time. They feared that a President who held office too long might take complete control of the government. Not everyone felt this way, however. Some thought that a President should be able to serve any number of terms—as long as the people continued to re-elect him or her.

In 1951, those who had worked to limit the President's time in office won, and the Twenty-second Amendment was passed. It said that a President could be elected to office only twice.

Salary and Other Benefits

How much should a President be paid for doing one of the most difficult jobs in the world? It is up to Congress to decide.

However, Congress cannot raise or lower the salary during a President's term of office. This rule was made so that Congress cannot use the salary to reward or to punish a President.

Since 1969, the President has received a salary of $200,000 a year. Congress has voted pay raises for the President only four times in the country's history. When George Washington took office, his salary was $25,000 a year.

The salary is not all that the President receives, however. Congress has voted an additional $50,000 a year for expenses. Because a modern President must travel a great deal, there is also a travel allowance of up to $100,000 a year.

Other benefits come with the office. The President and family live in the White House, which is fully furnished and has a large staff. For vacations or weekends, the President can rest at Camp David in the mountains of Maryland. There are offices and aides for the President in the White House and in the Executive Office Building. If the President must travel, fleets of cars, airplanes, helicopters, and boats are ready and waiting.

After leaving office, the President receives a pension of $69,630 a year for life. Also, former Presidents receive money to pay for an office and a staff. Finally, the widow of a former President can receive a pension of $20,000 a year.

What Happens If a President Dies or Resigns?

Since 1900, four of our Presidents have died during their term of office. A fifth President resigned. Who becomes President in such cases? The Constitution and laws passed by Congress provide an answer. They give a **presidential succession**—the replacement of the President by another person, according to a set order, whenever the office becomes empty. This prevents the government's falling into confusion when a President dies or resigns.

The Vice President is first in line of succession. The writers of the Constitution had created the office of Vice President with the problem of succession in mind. The Constitution says what happens if the President dies, resigns, or is unable to carry out the duties of office: the Vice President is to take on the *title* of President. That point caused confusion the first time that a President died in office, in 1841. The President was William Henry Harrison. Vice President John Tyler took over both the duties and the title. He became President Tyler. No one objected strongly, and thus a custom was set. The custom has been followed ever since.

Other questions remained, however. What if both the President and the Vice President should die or become disabled at the same time? When the Vice President becomes President, who becomes Vice President? A number of amendments to the Constitution have answered those questions.

The most recent on this subject is the Twenty-fifth Amendment. It was passed after President John F. Kennedy was killed in 1963. The amendment cleared up any confusion about the language of the Constitution. It says: "In case of the removal of the President from office or of his death or resignation, the Vice President shall become President." This made official the custom that had been practiced all along.

The amendment also deals with the problem of an empty Vice-President's office. If the Vice President dies, resigns, or becomes President, the President of the United States nominates a new Vice President. Both houses of Congress must approve the nomination by a majority vote.

This section of the amendment had its first test in 1973. Vice President Spiro Agnew resigned from his office after a scandal. President Richard Nixon named Gerald

Standing beside a stunned Jacqueline Kennedy, Vice President Lyndon B. Johnson succeeded to the presidency just 99 minutes after John Kennedy's death.

Ford to take Agnew's place. Congress gave its approval.

Within a year, this section of the amendment was used again. President Nixon, threatened with impeachment, resigned in 1974. Gerald Ford then became President. He chose Nelson Rockefeller for Vice President. The House and the Senate approved his choice. For the first time in history, the country had a President and a Vice President who had not been elected by the people.

What if both the President and the Vice President should die or be removed from office at the same time? This has never happened, but one day it might. The Constitution gives Congress the right to determine the order of presidential succession after the Vice President. Congress has set the following order: the Speaker of the House, the president *pro tempore* of the Senate, and then the members of the President's Cabinet—those people who head the top departments in the executive branch. The members of the Cabinet follow in the order in which their departments were created: the Secretary of State, the Secretary of the Treasury, the Secretary of Defense, the Attorney General (Department of Justice), the Secretary of the Interior, the Secretary of Agriculture, the Secretary of Commerce, the Secretary of Labor, the Secretary of Housing and Urban Development, the Secretary of Transportation, the Secretary of Energy, the Secretary of Health and Human Services, and the Secretary of Education.

What if a President is too sick to do the job? The Twenty-fifth Amendment says that the Vice President can become Acting President until the illness has passed. If the Vice President and the members of the Cabinet think that the President is not well, but the President wants to serve again, the Congress must decide. Unless there is a two-thirds vote of both houses in favor of the Vice President, the President will take back the office.

The Vice President: The President's Helper

This is a good time to take a closer look at the office of the Vice President. Not much has been said about the job so far.

As Vice President, George Bush must preside over the Senate as well as act as the President's personal representative at ceremonial functions.

is the highest office in the eyes of the people. The Vice Presidency is the next highest and the lowest. It isn't a crime exactly. You can't be sent to jail for it, but it's a kind of disgrace. . . ."

The fact is, though, that the job is important. Vice Presidents do become Presidents. Nine Vice Presidents have become President so far. There needs to be a good, able person filling the office. In the past 40 years, three Vice Presidents have suddenly become President. So people have begun to pay more attention to the job. Candidates for Presidents are choosing their running mates with more care. Presidents are giving Vice Presidents more tasks and greater responsibilities. All this helps to prepare Vice Presidents for the huge job that might one day be theirs. It also helps to justify their salaries. Vice Presidents receive a salary of $79,125 a year, plus $10,000 for expenses.

Vice Presidents who take over the Presidency are the only persons allowed to serve more than 8 years, or two terms, as President. They can serve up to 10 years. This is only possible if half of the term of office remains when they take over the Presidency. They can then still be elected twice as President.

Impeachment

The Constitution provides only one way to remove a President or a Vice President from office. That is impeachment and trial by Congress. You read how this is done in Chapter 4.

An official can only be removed from office for treason, bribery, or "high crimes and misdemeanors." *Treason* is giving aid to the enemies of the country. *Bribery* is an illegal payment for doing or not doing a certain thing. The third charge, "high crimes and misdemeanors," is a little vague. People agree that the phrase refers to serious matters. They do not always agree on what is a serious matter.

The reason for this is that when the President is healthy, the Vice President—according to the Constitution—does not have that much to do. The only official duty of the Vice President is to preside over the Senate. This is not a full-time job. As President of the Senate, the Vice President rarely gets a chance to affect laws. A Vice President can only vote in case of a tie. Many senators would resent an attempt by the Vice President to take part in Senate business.

Many Vice Presidents grow restless in the office. Often, the job is treated as a kind of joke. One person wrote: "The Presidency

A few hours before he formally became the first President to resign, Richard Nixon explained his decision and bid his supporters an emotional farewell.

No President or Vice President has ever been removed from office by impeachment. President Andrew Johnson was impeached in 1868, but the Senate found him "not guilty." The House Judiciary Committee voted in favor of impeaching President Richard Nixon in 1974. But Nixon resigned before the whole House could vote on the charges against him.

REVIEW
---

1. What are three constitutional requirements for becoming President?
2. The election of a President involves four steps—one in November, one in December, and two in January. What are these four steps?
3. How many terms can a President serve? How long is each term?
4. Who becomes President if both the President and the Vice President should die in office?
5. Would you say that the job of Vice President is important or unimportant? Explain your answer.

Words to Know

program —— the laws and actions that a President recommends to Congress

diplomat —— an official representative of one country in its dealings with another country

ambassador —— the highest rank of diplomat

recognize —— to formally deal with a nation or its government, usually by exchanging diplomats with it

treaty —— a formal written agreement between nations

executive agreement —— a written agreement between nations, usually dealing with routine matters

reprieve —— an official act that stops the carrying out of a criminal sentence

pardon —— an official act that forgives an individual for a crime

amnesty —— a pardon that is given to a group of people

Powers and Duties of the President

A hurricane tears into the Gulf Coast states. The President declares the states a disaster area. The President calls in the National Guard to help these states.

Thousands of young men flee the country to avoid serving in the armed forces. They have committed a federal crime and face prison sentences if they return. The President offers to pardon them and allow them back into the country.

Oil supplies are running short. The country must cut down on the amount of oil it uses. The President raises the tax on all imported oil. This makes the oil more expensive, so that people will use less.

These are just a few examples of the President's powers. These powers come from Article II of the Constitution. Only four paragraphs and a little over 300 words are needed to list the powers. From that short list, the most powerful job in the world has developed.

The President's powers fall into five types. There are executive powers, legislative powers, military powers, diplomatic powers, and judicial powers. The lines between these categories are not always clear. Most often, the powers overlap.

Executive Powers

The Constitution directs the President to carry out the laws of the country. The powers used for this purpose are the execu-

Congress gave the President the power to send aid to any area struck by disaster. This power was used when mud slides caused great damage in California.

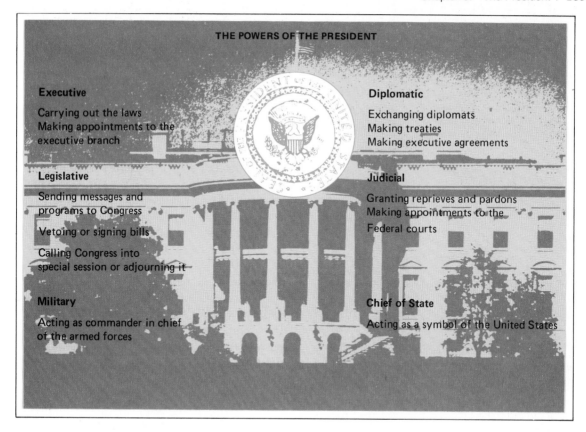

THE POWERS OF THE PRESIDENT

Executive

Carrying out the laws
Making appointments to the
executive branch

Diplomatic

Exchanging diplomats
Making treaties
Making executive agreements

Legislative

Sending messages and
programs to Congress

Vetoing or signing bills

Calling Congress into
special session or adjourning it

Judicial

Granting reprieves and pardons
Making appointments to the
Federal courts

Military

Acting as commander in chief
of the armed forces

Chief of State

Acting as a symbol of the United States

---

tive powers. Executing, or carrying out, the law is the highest duty of the President.

Congress makes the laws. The President must see that they are enforced. Congress can pass a law saying that a dam must be built in Oregon. The law can say where the dam must be placed, how much water it can hold, and how much power it must produce. The law can also say how much the dam can cost.

But Congress cannot build the dam. The site for the dam needs to be surveyed. Plans need to be drawn up. Materials have to be bought. Work crews need to be directed. The President has the responsibility for seeing that these things are done.

Of course, the President alone cannot make sure a dam is built. The President needs helpers. These helpers are the 2.9 million members of the executive branch. We will explore the many parts of this branch in the next chapter.

Legislative Powers

In addition to carrying out the law, the President has a part in writing it. The President shares certain lawmaking powers with Congress. These are known as the President's legislative powers.

Messages to Congress Article II of the Constitution says that the President "shall from time to time give to the Congress information on the state [condition] of the Union." Today, a President does this yearly in a State of the Union address, which is usually given in late January. The President also sends Congress a budget for the federal government and information about the nation's economy. The President

As Commander in Chief, the President has the power to order this ship into action at any time.

gathers up-to-date facts from all the divisions of the executive branch for these messages.

The messages do more than give information about how the President sees the state of the country. They carry out another part of Article II. This part tells the President to recommend to Congress "such measures as he shall judge necessary." In other words, the President must recommend laws.

In the message to Congress, the President suggests a **program.** A program is a group of laws and actions that the President thinks will help the country. After the program is presented to Congress, people in the executive branch write bills that will carry out the program. These bills are sent on to Congress. The members of Congress who favor the bills then introduce them.

Congress does not have to pass the bills. Usually, though, it studies them carefully. Congress can reject the bills, or change them, or write its own bills in place of the President's. It is very unlikely that Congress will follow a President's program exactly.

The Veto The President can block laws that are passed by Congress. This is done through the President's veto power, discussed in Chapter 5. The veto is a strong weapon. When the President kills a bill by veto, that bill is usually "dead." Congress can rarely put together the two-thirds vote needed to pass a bill over a veto. Fewer than 100 bills have ever been passed over a presidential veto.

Members of Congress usually try to avoid a veto. They try to find out what a President thinks about a bill before they pass it. If they learn that the President does not like part of a bill, they will often change or remove that part so that the rest of the bill can become law.

For much the same reason, the President keeps in touch with members of Congress. Their support is needed if the President's program is going to pass. They may have to be coaxed and wheedled, invited to the White House for a meeting over breakfast, patted on the back before television cameras, and promised a favor in return for their votes. Keeping on good terms with Congress helps to smooth the way for the President's program.

A President's Rule for Dealing with Congress

Lyndon Johnson, who served in both houses of Congress before becoming President, knew how to win votes in Congress for his program. He had years of practice in dealing with senators and representatives. One of the main rules for suggesting new bills was: Prepare the way. Do not surprise the members of Congress with a new bill if you want to get their votes.

He once told how he learned this rule. It was during his first term as a representative:

"I was standing in the back of the House behind the rail as Speaker Sam Rayburn listened to the House Clerk read an important new message President Franklin Roosevelt had just sent to Congress. Several dozen Democrats were gathered around him. As he finished, a chorus of complaints rushed forth:

'Why, that message is terrible, Mr. Sam—we can't pass that.'

'That last suggestion is awful.'

'Why in the world did you let the President send one up like that?'

'Why didn't you warn us?'

"Speaker Rayburn listened to all the criticisms and then responded softly: 'We'll just have to look at it more carefully. That's all I can say now, fellows. We'll have to look at it more carefully.'

"The crowd scattered. The Speaker and I were left alone in the back. I could see that something was wrong.

'If only,' he said, 'the President would let me know ahead of time when these controversial messages are coming up. I could pave the way for him. I could create a base of support. I could be better prepared for criticism. I could get much better acceptance in the long run. But I never know when the . . . messages are coming. This last one surprised me as much as it did them.' He shook his head sadly and slowly walked away.

"I could see that his pride was hurt. So was the President's prestige—and his program. I never forgot that lesson."

Adapted from Lyndon Johnson,
The Vantage Point:
Perspectives of the Presidency, 1963–1969,
Holt Rinehart and Winston, New York, 1971, p. 272

Other Legislative Powers The President has other legislative powers that are not used as often. For example, in times of trouble or danger, the President can call Congress into a special session. Another power allows the President to adjourn Congress, but only if the two houses cannot agree to adjourn by themselves. This has never happened in the country's history.

Military Powers

"The President shall be commander-in-chief of the army and navy of the United States, and the militia of the several states. . . ." From these words of Article II of the Constitution come the President's military powers. Today, the President commands more than 3 million members of the armed forces. Nuclear bombs, jet fighters, aircraft carriers, and missile-carrying submarines are just some of the weapons that a President can control.

The President commands these forces both in times of war and in times of peace. During World War II, in 1945, President Truman ordered the dropping of atomic

Friends from earlier days in politics, Johnson and Rayburn stayed friends even as their positions rose in importance.

bombs on Japan. During peacetime, in 1975, President Ford ordered the Marines to retake a United States ship that had been seized by Cambodia. Many Presidents have called out the National Guard to aid in floods, riots, or other emergencies in the United States.

The President receives regular reports from military commanders. Often, their advice is followed. But many military decisions are complicated. Some military acts can start wars or cause wars to spread. For this reason, the final decisions rest with the President alone.

Some members of Congress worry that the President may have too much military power. According to the Constitution, Congress also has some military powers. Only Congress can approve the spending of money for the armed forces. Only Congress has the right to declare war. Yet some military decisions must be made quickly. This means that Congress does not always have time to act. Also, the members of Congress do not always agree on what to do in a military crisis. The President can act more quickly.

Presidents made most of the major decisions about the war in Vietnam in the 1960s and the early 1970s. They ordered the buildup of United States troops in that country. The fighting went on for almost 12 years. More than 50,000 Americans died. In all that time, Congress never declared war. But Congress did take many actions that affected the United States' role in the war. Sometimes it supported the President: it voted money for the fighting or praised his actions. Sometimes it opposed the President: it held back money or required a change in policy.

Both the speed and the secrecy with which a President can act are useful in a time of war or danger. But the open debate and the airing of all sides of an issue in Congress are needed in a democracy. One important question that remains to be an-swered is: How can a proper balance of power between the President and Congress be reached?

Diplomatic Powers

Article II of the Constitution also gives the President certain powers to shape foreign policy. These are the President's diplomatic powers. The powers are used in working out problems between nations.

Exchanging Diplomats The President appoints people to represent the United States government in other countries. These people are called **diplomats.** The top diplomat in any foreign country is usually called an **ambassador.** The United States sends ambassadors to more than 100 countries around the world. These ambassadors pass on messages and requests between the United States government and other governments. Sometimes they help people from the United States, such as tourists or business people, who run into problems in foreign countries.

The President has the power to send or not send diplomats to a country. This power may be used for two purposes. One is to express approval or disapproval of a government. For example, if a friendly government is overthrown by a revolt, the President may call the diplomats to that country home. The President may refuse to **recognize**—exchange diplomats with—the new government. That is what President Dwight Eisenhower did when a Communist government took over Cuba in 1958.

A second purpose of exchanging diplomats is to make smoother dealings possible between nations. The President may recognize a government even while disapproving of that government's actions. For example, the United States and the Soviet Union are not often on friendly terms. Since 1933, however, every President has recognized the Soviet government and had dealings with it. The fact that the United States exchanges diplomats with a country does not necessarily mean that it supports that country's government.

Making Treaties   The President also has the power to make treaties. **Treaties** are formal written agreements between nations. They can cover a wide range of subjects. For example, two or more nations may write a treaty to make rules about trade, or to settle a boundary between countries, or to limit the kinds of weapons each nation may test or build. Treaties are often signed to end wars.

Any treaty that the President signs must be approved by a two-thirds vote of the Senate. Sometimes a President makes a treaty that the Senate refuses to approve. President Woodrow Wilson signed the Treaty of Versailles at the end of World War I. This treaty would have made the United States a member of the League of Nations—an organization similar to the present United Nations. The Senate would not approve the treaty, and the United States never did join the League of Nations.

More recently, President Jimmy Carter had a difficult time getting approval of a treaty to give the Panama Canal back to Panama. The Senate debated long and hard on the treaty. Finally, in 1978, the Senate approved it by one vote more than the necessary two-thirds.

Making Executive Agreements Presidents may make other types of agreements with foreign nations that do not need Senate approval. These are **executive agreements.** Usually they deal with routine matters. For example, the President might want to make it possible for United States citizens to visit nearby countries without a passport. Arrangements might be made for this by executive agreement. Sometimes, however, executive agreements are not routine. President Franklin Roosevelt made an executive agreement in 1940 to send Great Britain some warships in exchange for building United States military

One month after Truman signed the UN charter, the Senate voted its approval of the treaty.

bases in Canada and elsewhere. At the time, Great Britain was fighting in World War II, but the United States was not.

Judicial Powers

The President has certain powers in dealing with judges and the courts. These are the President's judicial powers.

Reprieves and Pardons   The Constitution allows the President to give reprieves and pardons in federal criminal cases. A **reprieve** stops the carrying out of a sentence. A pardon forgives an individual for a crime that he or she may have committed.

A President can also offer a pardon to a group of people. This pardon is sometimes called an **amnesty.** Finally, the President can shorten a convicted person's sentence.

President Gerald Ford used judicial power in 1974 to pardon Richard Nixon for any crimes he might have committed while he was President. Presidents Ford and Carter offered forms of amnesty to those who fled the country to avoid serving in the war in Vietnam.

When President Nixon made this historic visit, the United States did not recognize the government in mainland China. However, Nixon was not exercising his diplomatic powers. He was acting as Chief of State.

Judicial Appointments The President can influence the judicial system by appointing federal justices and judges. Whenever an opening occurs on the Supreme Court or on a lower federal court, the President may fill it. The President makes an appointment. Then the Senate debates it. The appointment must be approved by a majority vote of the Senate.

Presidents usually appoint men and women who share their ideas about the laws. Once an appointment is made, however, the President has no control over the judge or justice. The President cannot fire a federal judge or a Supreme Court Justice. Federal judges and justices serve for life.

The President also appoints other people who work in the judicial system. Many lawyers work for the executive branch. They often follow the President's orders in bringing cases to the courts. These lawyers can be fired if they do not do what a President wants.

The Chief of State

The President has another role in the government. This role is not set down in the Constitution, but it is an important one just the same. It is the role of Chief of State.

As Chief of State, the President is a symbol. The office and the person in it stand for the United States as a whole. For this reason, the words and acts of the President take on a special power.

The President stands for the United States in its dealings with other nations. Look at what happens when the President travels abroad. A visit to a friendly country such as Japan strengthens ties with that country. It shows that the President and other people in the United States value their friendship with Japan. A visit to an unfriendly country has its own meanings. Such a visit could show that the United States wants to be friendlier with the country. President Nixon's visit to China in 1972 is an example of such a visit.

At home, too, the President is a symbol. The President may award medals to war heroes. This act shows that the whole country is grateful to those heroes. The President may invite poets and musicians to dine at the White House. This act shows that the arts have an important place in the life of the country. As a symbol of the nation, the President may encourage others to act in certain ways. For example, the President may be photographed with a handicapped child. This encourages people to give to charities that aid in research.

The President is most important as a symbol of the people of the United States. Who can speak for all the people? The members of Congress? Each member of Congress represents one state or one part of a state—not the whole nation. The nine Supreme Court Justices? The Supreme Court Justices are respected, certainly, but no one elected them. They do not really represent the people. Only the President, along with the Vice President, is elected by all the people.

The President is also highly visible. The President makes television speeches, holds news conferences, tours the country. As the center of attention within the federal government, the President becomes the way that many citizens stay in touch with that government.

The people of the United States have an almost personal relationship with the President. That is why the death of a President is so shocking. When President Kennedy was killed in 1963, the country mourned for a long time.

That relationship is a special one. If a President behaves badly, the people's trust in government can be hurt. Many people felt betrayed by President Nixon's part in the Watergate affair from 1972 to 1974. They thought that their government had failed them. Gerald Ford's actions as President helped to renew the people's faith in the President and in the government.

Growth of the President's Power

The powers of the President have grown since 1789. Most of this growth has not come from amendments to the Constitution. Instead, it is due to events in the country's history and changes in the way the people see the office.

Reasons for Growth of Power First, the country itself has grown since 1789, and the tasks of government have grown with the size of the country. People began to ask more of government. Roads and railroads were built. New lands were added. New types of businesses were started. Congress made laws to meet new conditions, and the Presidents had to carry out these laws. To do so, Presidents needed more money and more workers in the executive branch. Control of this money and these workers strengthened the President's powers.

Second, the country became more complicated as it grew. A federal law that encourages nuclear power plants in New England may have unwanted side effects. Nuclear power plants may cause problems in Colorado, where nuclear wastes are dumped. To pass good laws, Congress needs

These *New York Times'* lawyers have just presented a winning argument against President Nixon's order to keep their paper from printing secret documents about the Vietnam war.

to have information about the effects that the laws will have.

More and more, Congress turns to the executive branch for this information. Members of that branch are experts in many fields. Under the President's direction, they can give Congress the information it needs. More and more, Congress has based its decisions on such information. Congress has also passed laws that leave many decisions up to the President and other members of the executive branch.

Third, the United States has had to face wars and many other times of danger. At such times, decisions have to be made quickly. Congress, with its two houses and many members, is not set up to make quick decisions. The President, on the other hand, is one person. One person can decide and act more swiftly than 535 people trying to work together. For this reason, Presidents have increased their power in times of emergency.

Finally, the President's special relationship with the people of the United States has played a part in the growth of presidential power. This country has had great Presidents, such as Washington, Jackson, Lincoln, and Wilson. They have inspired the people. At times, their acts may have saved the country. The people of the United States have been grateful. They have made some Presidents into heroes. This public gratitude has been passed on to other Presidents. It has allowed them to gain and use greater powers.

Checks on President's Power The power of the President does have limits. The checks and balances of the system hold back any President. The writers of the Constitution feared having a President who would be too strong. They wanted ways of stopping a President who tried to do too much. To keep some control, they wrote the checks and balances into the Constitution. We have mentioned some of these checks and balances in passing. Here is a brief list:

The Supreme Court is free of the control of the President once its members are appointed. The Court can review the actions of a President. The Court has the right to declare a President's actions illegal.

Congress has several checks on the President's power. Congress controls the budget and decides how money will be spent. The Senate must approve the appointments of many members of the executive branch. The Senate must approve any treaties with foreign nations. Congress can pass a bill over the President's veto with a two-thirds vote of both houses. Finally, the Congress can remove a President from office through impeachment.

It is not easy to decide how great a President's powers should be. Those powers have increased a great deal over the years. Congress has accepted and often aided this growth. But the Constitution still allows Congress to say a firm "no" when it feels that the powers of the President are getting out of control.

REVIEW

1. What are two purposes of a President's messages to Congress?
2. Name two ways in which Congress can check the powers of the President.
3. What is a treaty? How is it different from an executive agreement?
4. Do you think that Presidents have about the right amount of power? Too much power? Or not enough power? Explain your answer.

How the United States Works

Interpreter

In order to do a good job at carrying out foreign relations, the President sometimes meets with heads of foreign governments. Often, the President and the foreign leaders do not speak the same language. For this reason, when visitors come to the United States or when the President travels, interpreters are used. These people translate from one language to another.

Two kinds of interpreting are done. In one kind, the speaker and the interpreter take turns speaking. In the other kind, the interpreter listens and translates at the same time. In this method of interpreting, the speaking and the listening are done over microphones and earphones. In that way, no one but the interpreter hears both languages.

Interpreters usually have a college degree. But more important is a good knowledge of at least two languages. All this knowledge must be at the interpreter's fingertips. There is no time to stop and think about which word is the best one to use.

Most full-time interpreters work for the United Nations or for parts of the executive branch. Some work for international groups. All together, though, there are only about 150 full-time interpreter's jobs in the United States. The salary goes from about $9,000 to $20,000. There are more full-time jobs in Europe.

But most interpreters do not work full time. They are free-lancers. That is, they are hired when there is a specific job to do. That usually means traveling around with a foreign visitor. Free-lancers receive about $40 to $80 a day, plus expenses. If they know more than two languages, they have a better chance of getting steady work.

Reading About . . .

Information for the President ─────────────────

In this chapter, you have looked at the separate parts of the President's job—the powers and the duties. To make the different parts of the job work together smoothly and efficiently, the President needs information. How the President gets this information is the subject of this reading.

As you read, think about these points:

● What seems to be the most important task that a President faces each day?

● What personal qualities would help a President deal with conflicting information?

The President may start the day with a summary of the latest news or take time in the early morning to be with the family, for they will not be seeing much of each other during the rest of the day. In any event, work starts with the news, for the President's very first business is to be informed about what is going on.

That does not sound very difficult, but actually it is the most difficult thing that the President has to do. The information must be as exact and as accurate as is humanly possible. If you and I are a little uncertain about who is fighting whom in a country on the other side of the Earth, it does not matter much, because nobody expects us to do anything about it. This is not so with the President. If anything important happens anywhere in the world, the President may have to do something about it. Unless accurate information is available, the President may do the wrong thing, thereby bringing trouble upon the country.

The President must know the truth. If an action is taken on the basis of rumors, gossip, and guesses—which is what happens to most of us most of the time—the results will be serious and may be terrible. Unfortunately, the President cannot know the exact truth at all times. It is hard to get at the truth of any event that is important, because there are always two opinions as to what really happened, frequently there are twenty, and there may be two hundred—and sometimes they are all wrong.

The best that the President can do is to choose the opinion that seems most closely in line with the known facts. Therefore, all the known facts must be available, and even the President can make the wrong decision.

Thus, one of the most valuable qualities that a President can have is good judgment—especially about which person to believe when different people are saying different things. The President must have the ability to tell who is a reliable source of information and who is not.

But the finest judgment will be wrong when it is based on false information, so every effort is made to assist the President by making available all the facts. At a certain time in the morning, usually after reading the news, the President goes down a corridor from the main part of the White House to the private office in the West Wing. In the meantime, many members of the President's stafff have been reading not only the newspapers, but reports from the various departments of the Cabinet, dispatches from ambassadors, teletype reports, and letters from individuals.

The staff mark passages containing information that the President needs.

Fact Review

1. What is the "winner-take-all" system in presidential elections?
2. What would happen if a President became too ill to finish the term of office?
3. What is a President's program? Why is it important?
4. Which power of the Presidency do you think is the most important? Explain your answer.

Developing Your Vocabulary

Use each of the following terms in a sentence about the Presidency. Then tell what each term means.

a. inauguration
b. ambassador
c. amnesty
d. President-elect

Developing Your Reading Skills

Read the following paragraph and then answer the questions that follow:

The real power of the executive branch of the federal government is in the hands of the President. All other parts of the executive branch must answer to the President, who has many types of powers. The President, for example, can either veto or approve a bill from Congress. The President can call special sessions of Congress or send messages to it. The President can order the armed forces to go into action. The President can make treaties and some appointments, with the approval of Congress. The President can have the United States recognize other countries. Above all, the President can see to it that all of the laws of the United States are carried out.

1. Which one of the following do you think is the main point, or main idea, of the paragraph above?
   a. The President cannot pass laws.
   b. The President can make treaties with foreign countries.
   c. The President has many powers.
   d. The President is Commander in Chief of the armed forces.
2. Why did you select either a, b, c, or d in question 1?

Developing Your Writing Skills—Forming and Supporting an Opinion

In this chapter, you have read about the qualifications needed for a person to become President of the United States. You also examined the powers that a President has. Now consider:

Forming an opinion

1. What sort of person should a President be in order to exercise, or use, those powers? Think of four qualities that a President should have—for example, "fairness."
2. What other qualities can you suggest?

Supporting an opinion

3. After thinking it over, write a paragraph that answers the questions above. List at least one reason for choosing each quality.

YOUR GOVERNMENT & ITS HISTORY

The First Occupants of the White House

John Adams was the second President of the United States. But he was the first President to live in the White House in Washington, D.C. The following selection from *In and Out of the White House*, a book by Ona Griffin Jeffries, describes Adam's stay there.

The President's Palace . . . was still being built when President John Adams and his wife, Abigail, moved into it. Three and a half years of his four-year term were already over. Since Congress was due to meet for the first time in Washington on November 17, 1800, it was important that the President begin to live in the Federal City. . . .

When they moved into the Executive Mansion in 1800, Abigail found only six of the rooms in any condition to live in. The walls were newly plastered, the fireplaces were cold, and the rooms were damp. Of these six rooms, two were used as offices by the President and his secretary.

George Washington had picked the site for the new mansion. The plan for the Federal City was designed by the French engineer Pierre L' Enfant. James Hoban, an Irish-born architect, designed the house. Its cornerstone was laid on October 13, 1792.

The plan of the building included reception rooms on the first floor and the President's apartments on the second. On the first floor was the East Room. It was to be used for public receptions. Next to it was the Green Room, which was smaller. In the original plans, the Green Room was the Common Dining Room. The centrally located Oval Room (now the Blue Room) was known as the Drawing Room. It opened onto the Green Room on the east and the Red Room on the west side of the entrance. . . .

The family dining room today was the Public Dining Room in the early days.

It connects with the State Dining Room on the west end of the building.

At the time the Adamses moved in, Abigail needed all her . . . skill to meet the demands of her role as First Lady. She found the President's Palace barn-like and unfriendly. Not a single apartment was finished. Not even the East Room, which she put to use for drying clothes, was completed. The grounds were rough and muddy. The house had no water supply, and so, of course, no bathroom. There was no wood for the fireplaces. Abigail wrote that candles were struck here and there for light—neither the chief staircase nor the outer steps were completed, so the family had to enter the house by temporary wooden stairs and platform.

At that time, the capital . . . had a population of only 3,000. There was a scattering of about 450 houses, the greater number of which were in George-town. Travel was by coach and carriage, mostly over foot- and cowpaths. . . .

On New Year's Day, 1801, the President's Palace was formally opened to the public. Abigail . . . sat in a chair and greeted her guests. The President, dressed in black velvet, silk stockings, silver knee buckles, and a high stock collar, his hair powdered . . . stood at her side. After the guests paid their respects to the President and Mrs. Adams, they were served refreshments. They were entertained by the Marine Band, which made its official debut at that same housewarming. . . .

John Adams—unlike George Washington—had never been a rich man. During his stay abroad, the United States government had been forced to cut expenses. Adams had found his salary reduced from about $6,000 to $5,000 a year. Abigail, hard put to keep expenses down, cut out suppers and attended as few gatherings as possible. She found formal dinners (which averaged one a week) quite expensive.

1. When did Congress first meet in Washington, D.C.?

2. What was the White House like when John and Abigail Adams moved into it? Give three examples.

3. How is life in the White House today different from when the Adamses lived there?

4. What do you think the White House should stand for? Why?

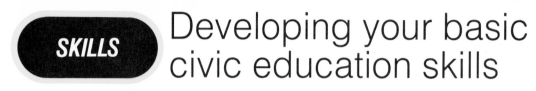

SKILLS Developing your basic civic education skills

(conflicting viewpoints)

A President's Term of Office

As you have learned, a person can serve at least two full terms as President of the United States. This is according to the Twenty-second Amendment to the Constitution. A full term is 4 years. It is still possible, however, for a President to serve up to 10 years. That can happen if the President takes office during a term to which someone else was elected. If a President dies in office, is unable to continue due to ill health, is impeached, or resigns, the Presidency goes to the Vice President. If this happens more than halfway through the term of office, the new President can still seek election twice.

The following readings contain different points of view about changing the length of a President's term of office. The proposed change would limit any President to a single 6-year term. As you consider each reading, keep in mind the kinds of arguments presented about that issue.

Arguments in Support of the Proposal

Representative Dan Quayle, Republican from Indiana:

The time has come to limit the Presidency to one 6-year term. One 6-year term would allow the President to function as a states-person and not as a politician. Special-interest pressures, too, would be reduced. Our leader should be free of political considerations in facing complex and difficult national and international problems. Presidential decisions are often based on what will register at the ballot box. By making the President's term longer, our nation and the world would have a leader free to do what is right instead of what is politically demanded.

Representative John Conyers, Jr., Democrat from Michigan:

A single 6-year term would free the President from electoral and political pressures. . . . It would allow the President to decide the tough issues of governing without the fear of burning a reelection bridge. It would limit the role that money and the media play in the election process. A 6-year term has been encouraged by all recent Presidents, Democrats and Republicans, from Eisenhower to Carter.

Former President Jimmy Carter:

I think that if I had a 6-year term, without any prospect of reelection, it would be an improvement. It would also strengthen my hand with Congress.

No matter what I do as President now . . . a lot of the things I do are colored through the news media and in the minds of the American people by, "Is this a campaign trick, or is it genuinely done by a President in the best interest of our country?"

Jack Valenti, former assistant to President Lyndon Johnson:

The idea is indeed an old one. The framers of the Constitution toyed with a single-term condition in their debates at Philadelphia. Thomas Jefferson was among those who encouraged such a limitation.

No sooner does a President enter the White House than he begins his reelection campaign. Anyone who tells you differently tells you wrong.

The President is deeply involved in all that is being said and decided. Mind you, this is politics in the raw, jungle-smell sense of the word.

1. Match the statements that follow with the people who made them. You may use an answer more than once.

_____**a.** A single 6-year term of office for the President would limit the pressure from special-interest groups.

_____**b.** A single 6-year term of office would allow the President to do what is best for the nation and not just for a political party.

_____**c.** A single 6-year term of office for a President would limit the amount of money spent on elections and limit the role of the media.

_____**d.** Presidents from Dwight D. Eisenhower to Jimmy Carter have favored a single 6-year term of office for the President.

(1) Quayle
(2) Conyers

2. Which two of the following statements were added by Carter or Valenti?

a. Thomas Jefferson favored a single term for the President.

b. The President now has to devote time to reelection.

c. A single 6-year term of office would allow the President greater time before the media.

d. A single 6-year term would help the President work with Congress.

3. At this point in your investigation, consider: Do you think the term of office for a President should be changed to a single 6-year term?

Arguments Opposed to the Proposal

Senator Clifford P. Chase, Republican from New Jersey:

When a system has worked as well as ours for nearly 200 years, there is a strong burden of proof on those who would change it. Where there is no such proof, I lean strongly toward making no change. Relieving the President of the need to run for reelection may make that office less responsive to popular pressures. If pushed to the extreme, this could destroy democracy. A good President is one who feels the people's needs. . . . It would be no service to the country to lift the President above the battle.

Senator Orrin G. Hatch, Republican from Utah:

> A single 6-year presidential term is too long for a poor President and too short for a good President. The present system has worked fairly well for two centuries. I do not agree that only politicians who do not have to face reelection can act as "statespersons." . . . It is equally important that Presidents be held accountable for the electorate. There is no evidence that second-term Presidents . . . have acted in any more "statesmanlike" a manner than first-term Presidents.

A political columnist:

> Two arguments usually are advanced against a single 6-year term: A President is not . . . serving merely as chief executive of the nation. He is also the unofficial leader of his party. He should not remove himself from party politics.
>
> Second, a single-term limit would make a president a lame duck [unable to help his cause or get anyone to pay attention to what he wished to accomplish].

Patrick J. Buchanan, a syndicated columnist:

> The argument most commonly used for the single 6-year term is that it would raise the President above party politics. By removing the possibility of a future campaign, the President could concentrate on the nation's business. His decisions would be taken, and be seen to be taken, only in the national interest.

> Freed of the responsibility of running again, a decent President might become a great President.
>
> If, when someone becomes President, every decision and action involves a concern over the next election, the problem is not in the office, but in the person. You cannot, through constitutional change, turn a person of no great ability into a great President.
>
> A presidential nomination is the highest honor a party can give. The nominating convention is by custom the only time the national party gathers to choose its new leaders and to create the platform on which they will run and it will stand.
>
> A single 6-year term would relieve the incoming President instantly of debt and duty to the people who nominated that person and the platform on which that person ran. Would it be wise, and politically responsible, to have our Presidents free to ignore what the party promised? To appoint high officials without regard to party service, to set policy according only to political beliefs?
>
> The 6-year term could be the final, fatal blow to the nation's political parties. On Inauguration Day, the elected President—to maintain a nonparty image— would immediately transfer the role and duties of party leader to the Vice President. This would cut the ties between the nation's highest political office and its greatest political parties.

4. Match the statements that follow with the people who made them. You may use an answer more than once.

_____**a.** The present system for a President's term of office has worked well for many years.

_____**b.** A President who is not forced to run for reelection could be less willing to respond to popular pressure.

_____**c.** Presidents should not have to remove themselves from what their own political party wants.

_____**d.** Presidents who could not be reelected to office have not acted any differently from those who could be reelected.

_____**e.** A single term of office for a President would make him or her a lame duck.

_____**f.** Presidents should have to answer to the wishes of their political party, and a single term of office could make that impossible.

(1) Chase

(2) Hatch

(3) The political columnist

(4) Buchanan

5. Did the persons on opposite sides agree about anything? If your answer is yes, what did they agree on?

6. Can you add any other arguments to either side?

7. Of all the arguments examined about this issue, which two do you regard as most significant? Which two are least significant? Why?

8. How would you complete the following topic sentence? Write a paragraph supporting your selection.

The present system for a presidential term of office (should/should not) be changed to a single 6-year term.

9. Review the process of inquiry on pages 61–62. Then, match the statements in *a* to *d* with the statements in *(1)* to *(4)*.

_____**a.** Recognize a problem.

_____**b.** Form a hypothesis in answer to the problem.

_____**c.** Test the validity of the hypothesis.

_____**d.** Form and support a generalization in answer to the problem.

(1) When you examined all of the arguments presented in this lesson.

(2) Should the President be limited to a single 6-year term of office?

(3) When you *first* considered an answer to the main question posed in this lesson.

(4) When you arrived at a more definite answer to the main question posed in this lesson.

A Woman President?

Since the early 1970s, the United States has seen many women enter job occupations previously held mainly by men. Women now serve as drill instructors in the armed forces, attend military academies, work in oil fields, cut timber, and labor in steel mills. More and more, women are assuming positions of greater responsibility in federal and state governments as well. In 1975, Carla Anderson Hills was appointed Secretary of Housing and Urban Development. [She followed in the footsteps of Frances Perkins, Secretary of Labor under Franklin Roosevelt, and Oveta Culp Hobby, Secretary of Health, Education, and Welfare under Dwight D. Eisenhower.]

In recent years, Ella Grasso was elected governor of Connecticut. Mary Anne Krupsak was elected lieutenant governor of New York State. In the House of Representatives, women such as Barbara Jordan of Texas and Bella Abzug and Shirley Chisholm of New

York have served. In 1972, Frances "Sissy" Farenthold of Texas came in second on the balloting for the Democrat's vice-presidential nomination. By 1981, the United States had over 1,000 female mayors.

There have recently been women rulers in India, Argentina, Israel, and Sri Lanka [formerly Ceylon]. In Great Britain, Margaret Thatcher became the leader of the Conservative Party in 1975 and was elected Prime Minister in 1979.

In the United States, in 1872, Victoria Woodhull was the first woman ever to run for President. She ran as the candidate of the Equal Rights Party. Since then, other women have sought the presidency, including Shirley Chisholm in 1972 and Ellen McCormack, an anti-abortion candidate, in 1976.

In these readings you will learn about some of the feelings Americans have regarding whether the United States should have a woman President. As you read, consider how you would use the six steps for dealing with conflicting views (page 115) to arrive at a decision on this topic in as nonemotional or objective a way as possible.

The following arguments appeared in an article entitled "It's Time We Had a Woman President." The article appeared in the San Antonio *Express-News, Star*.

Some Arguments for Having a Woman President

1. I believe we have a good number of capable women in this country who would be up to the job. Being female may even prove to be advantageous as far as wars go anyhow. The aggressive little boy never grows out of the man. I believe a woman as head of our country would do some long, hard thinking before allowing us to embark in a war. This is a great time historically to have a woman run for President or Vice President. I think it will happen sooner or later. Sooner than most people think, we will have a woman President.

2. I can see no reason that the President has to be a man. Although there have been many who did great things, and accomplished much while in office, there have been others who have made great mistakes. If a person is intelligent, educated, and dedicated, that person could qualify to hold this high office, regardless of sex.

3. I think a woman is as good as any man is, and who knows, maybe even better.

4. Women are needed not to override or support men but to supplement and bring new qualities to the foreground. The most capable leaders of either sex must be available to the nation.

Some Arguments against Having a Woman President

1. How would you like to wait 10 minutes or longer for a TV speech because the woman President's nails are not dry, or suffer a delay while the President picks out the right color dress in which to announce we are going to war? Women are not qualified to deal in the heavy decisions necessary in running the country.

2. Women are too emotional.

Instead of "power corrupts," it would be "power erupts."

3. A woman President would be a threat to our country. I do not believe she could do the job without blowing her cool.

4. I hope I never live to see a woman President. I know I am a woman, and women are not strong enough. They will even vote for a man if he is good-looking. It will take a good man, very strong, to straighten out the mess in our government.

Public Attitudes about a Woman President— Polls Taken Since 1937

Since 1937, results of various opinion polls of Americans on the subject of a woman President have revealed the opinions shown in Part I of the chart when people are asked: Would you vote for a woman for President if she were qualified for the job? Part II of the chart shows the results of a recent Gallup Poll taken among teenagers.

10. Did the two sides in this issue agree about anything?

11. What points made by those in favor of having a woman President were omitted by those opposed?

12. What points made by those opposed to having a woman President were omitted by those in favor?

13. On which two of the following basic points did the two sides in this issue disagree the most?

    a. The ability of men always to be effective Presidents.

    b. The ability of women to govern the country effectively.

14. What else might you wish to consider about this issue? What other arguments could you add to both sides of this issue?

15. Which two points in questions 11–14 did you consider most important? Why? Which two did you consider least important? Why?

16. How would you complete the following topic sentence? Write a paragraph supporting your answer.

We (should/should not) have a woman President.

WOULD YOU VOTE FOR A WOMAN PRESIDENT? PART I		
	Yes	**No**
1937	34%	66%
1945	33%	55%
1955	52%	44%
1958	52%	43%
1967	57%	39%
1971	66%	29%
1976	76%	20%

WOULD YOU VOTE FOR A WOMAN PRESIDENT? PART II			
	Yes	No	Don't know
Nationwide	86%	11%	3%
Boys	83%	13%	4%
Girls	89%	9%	2%
Both sexes:			
13–15 years	88%	9%	3%
16–18 years	85%	12%	3%
Whites	86%	11%	3%
Nonwhites	89%	8%	3%
Family income:			
Under $10,000	88%	8%	4%
$10,000–14,999	87%	10%	3%
$15,000 & over	88%	10%	2%
East	88%	8%	4%
Midwest	85%	11%	4%
South	85%	12%	3%
West	88%	10%	2%

SOURCE: George Gallup Poll

Chapter 7 The Executive Department and the Cabinet

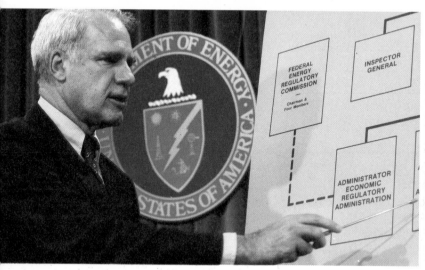

A President working alone would be like a quarterback without a football team. The President needs helpers. The President's helpers are the people who work in the executive branch of the federal government. When President John Adams moved to Washington, D.C., in 1800, he had about a thousand such helpers in all. Many of those were postal workers or diplomats who worked in faraway places. Only 120 worked in the nation's new capital. Without much trouble, the President could have known every person by name.

It was a different story when Ronald Reagan moved into the White House in 1981. The staff of the White House alone numbered more than 500. There were 400,000 federal employees working in the capital and 2,500,000 more scattered around the world. Almost all of them—98 percent—worked for the executive branch. Needless to say, President Reagan knew very few by name.

With so many helpers, there needs to be a way to organize them efficiently—and there is. Federal employees are arranged in a huge number of departments, agencies, commissions, boards, services, bureaus, divisions, and offices. Many of these are known by their initials: FBI, CIA, CAB, FCC, HHS, HUD. As someone once observed: "We don't have a government; we have alphabet soup."

In this chapter, you will take a look at the executive branch. You will study the different parts of the executive branch and see how they work together. You will also learn about the jobs in the executive branch,

the people who hold them, and how they got their jobs. Finally, you will see how the size of the executive branch affects the way the government works.

Words to Know

Cabinet —— advisers to the President who serve as the heads of executive departments

executive department —— a department of the federal government that is headed by a Cabinet member (There are thirteen all together.)

Attorney General —— head of the Department of Justice

embassy —— the most important government office of one country in a foreign country

civilian —— a person who is *not* serving in the armed forces

trademark —— a special word or symbol that stands for a product

passport —— an official travel document

The Executive Departments and the Cabinet

Origins of the Cabinet

The Constitution says little about what the executive branch should include. At one point, Article II says that the President "may require the opinion, in writing, of the principal officer in each of the executive departments . . . ." The Constitution does not say what those departments should be, and it does not list their duties.

The First Congress set up three executive departments and gave each certain duties. It also gave titles to the department heads: Secretary of State, Secretary of the Treasury, and Secretary of War. These department heads met often with President George Washington. They became known as the **Cabinet.** The word *Cabinet* is not in the Constitution, but the Cabinet is now a part of the federal government. All Presidents after Washington have held Cabinet meetings.

Departments headed by Cabinet members are known as Cabinet-level departments, or **executive departments.** The number of these departments has changed over the years. Sometimes new departments are added. The newest is the Department of Education, which was formed in 1980 when the Department of Health, Education, and Welfare was split up. The other department formed from this split is the Department of Health and Human Services. Sometimes departments are dropped. The Department of the Post Office was removed from the list of departments in 1971. It became an independent agency. Sometimes departments are rearranged. The Department of War and the Department of the Navy joined as the Department of Defense in 1947. Today, there are thirteen executive departments.

The Executive Departments

Specialized Jobs The executive departments carry out tasks in specific areas. Limiting a department to one kind of work helps get the work done more quickly. The members of each department become specialists. They learn all about their field. If a problem arises in foreign affairs, the President knows that the Department of State will have useful information. If Congress passes a change in tax laws, the President knows that a part of the Department of the Treasury will enforce that law.

Each department is divided into many parts. These parts have a number of different names. The most common names are *bureau, service,* and *administration.* Dividing a department in this way helps it to run more smoothly. To see how, look at the Department of the Treasury. One of its jobs is to collect money that is owed to the government. Two parts of this Department are the Bureau of Customs and the Internal Revenue Service. The Bureau of Customs collects duties, or taxes, on goods brought into the country. The Internal Revenue Service

The Department of State runs border-inspection stations at every possible point of entry to the United States.

collects income taxes from people and businesses.

The President Appoints Top Officials The President names the heads of the executive departments. The choices must be approved by a majority vote of the Senate. Usually, the President acting alone can name the other high officials in each department. Lower-level jobs are filled by a merit system of hiring (this system will be discussed later in the chapter).

The people in the lower-level jobs in a department report to higher officers. Their reports and information are passed on to still higher officers. Chiefs of the major bureaus and services report to the department head. The department head reports to the President. This process works in reverse when the President gives an order or makes a request.

The Thirteen Cabinet-level Departments

Now let's look at the thirteen departments. We will discover the fields they work in. The most important parts of each department will also be given. Remember that the head of a department is known as the *Secretary*. For example, the Secretary of Energy heads the Department of Energy. This is true for all the Departments except

the Department of Justice. The head of the Department of Justice is called the **Attorney General.**

Department of State The Department of State helps to carry out the diplomatic powers of the President. It was the first department to be set up by Congress in 1789. The Secretary of State is the highest-ranking Cabinet member. Thomas Jefferson, James Madison, James Monroe, and John Quincy Adams all served as Secretary of State before becoming President.

The Department of State directs programs that deal with other countries. Its most important division is the Foreign Service. The Foreign Service has offices in some 270 foreign cities. The most important of these offices are the **embassies.** Other offices are called *legations* and *consulates*. The embassies are the homes of the ambassadors. Ambassadors are the highest-ranking foreign diplomats. Other diplomats are called *ministers* and *consuls*.

Diplomats have many duties, some of which were mentioned in Chapter 6. One duty is to collect facts about foreign countries. Another is to try to increase trade with other countries.

The Department of State also helps people of other countries to become familiar with the United States. One way it does this is by sending singers or artists from the

The person who carries out the President's diplomatic powers in Kenya is the Ambassador. Part of that duty includes being friendly and available to the people.

United States to perform in other countries. For example, the Department might send a jazz group to tour the Soviet Union. In exchange, the Soviet Union might send a ballet company on a tour of the United States. These are known as cultural exchanges.

The Department of State helps send food and needed equipment to poorer nations. That is, it carries out United States foreign aid programs. The Agency for International Development (AID) handles most of this work. At one time, the State Department also ran the Peace Corps. The Corps is made up of United States citizens who volunteer to live and work in other countries. Since 1971, the Peace Corps has been part of another agency of the executive branch, called ACTION.

You would probably deal with the State Department if you wanted to take a trip to another country. The State Department issues **passports,** which are official travel documents. When you enter a foreign nation, you must show your passport and have it stamped by an official. Most nations require foreign visitors to do this, so that they have a record of who has come into their country. But United States citizens can visit some nations, such as Canada and Mexico, without a passport.

The Secretary of State is in charge of the Great Seal of the United States. This stamp must be put on official papers.

Department of the Treasury The Department of the Treasury was also set up by the First Congress. The Secretary of the Treasury manages the money of the United States. Most of the money that the government receives or pays out goes through some part of the Treasury Department. The Department also looks after the records of receipts and payments.

The money that you carry in your pocketbook or wallet is turned out by this Department. The Bureau of the Mint produces coins. The Bureau of Printing and Engraving prints paper money. The Bureau of Printing and Engraving also prints savings bonds, postage stamps, food stamps, and other items.

The Bureau of Customs collects duties on goods, or products, that are brought into the country. For more than 100 years, these duties were the government's main source of income. This is no longer the case. Still, the Customs Service collects well over 5 billion dollars a year. The Customs Service also watches for smugglers—people who try to bring goods into the country without paying the proper duty.

The main source of the government's income today is taxes. The Internal Revenue Service collects these taxes. Most of the money comes from income taxes on people and businesses. Income taxes give the government more than 200 billion dollars a year. The Internal Revenue Service also collects taxes on liquor, tobacco, gasoline, airplane tickets, and other goods.

The Fiscal Service keeps the government's accounts. Sections of this service make sure that all income is properly recorded and spent. The Treasurer of the United States is responsible for the payments of money.

One other branch of the Department of the Treasury is the United States Secret Service. The Secret Service tracks down counterfeiters—people who print fake money. There is another important job of the Secret Service. That is to protect the President and the Vice President and their families. In recent years, the Secret Service has also guarded candidates for high office as well.

Department of Defense   The First Congress set up a Department of War in 1789. In 1798, Congress added a separate Department of the Navy. These departments were made into one department in 1947. All military matters are now handled by the Department of Defense.

The Secretary of Defense, like other members of the Cabinet, is always a **civilian**—someone who is not a member of the armed forces. In addition, the Secretary cannot have served in any branch of the armed forces for 10 years before taking office. Thus, the nation's two highest military leaders—the President and the Secretary of Defense—are both civilians. Decisions about military matters, which often are questions of war or peace, are always in civilian hands.

The Secretary of Defense heads the largest department in the executive branch. More than 1 million civilians work in the Department of Defense. There are nearly 2 million more people working for the Department as members of the armed forces.

The Secretary of Defense keeps the President informed on all military matters. Where should troops be stationed? What kinds of weapons should the armed forces use? Is the United States prepared to meet a surprise attack? These are a few of the questions that the Secretary of Defense must be ready to answer.

Department of Justice   The Attorney General heads the Department of Justice. The First Congress created the office of Attorney General in 1789. However, the Department of Justice was not formed until 1870. The Attorney General is responsible for enforcing federal laws. The Attorney General also gives legal advice to the President and to the other executive departments.

The Department of Justice is divided into several parts. We can take a quick tour of the Department by following an imaginary crime: A bank is robbed. This breaks a federal law. It is a federal crime and, therefore, a matter for the Department of Justice. The Federal Bureau of Investigation, or FBI, handles such cases. The FBI's trained agents can use many tools to track down the robber. The FBI has more than 100 million fingerprint cards in its files. Its labs use the most modern equipment to analyze clues.

FBI agents arrest a suspect. Because a federal crime was committed, the case is tried in a federal court. An attorney in the Department's Criminal Division serves as the government's lawyer by prosecuting the

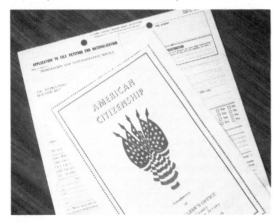

Citizenship papers give naturalized citizens the benefits and duties of natural-born United States' citizens.

Before receiving citizenship papers, applicants pledge their allegiance to their new country.

case: the attorney trys to convince a jury that the suspect is guilty. The Criminal Division assembles evidence and witnesses in the case.

The suspect is found guilty and sentenced to prison. The prison she goes to is run by the Bureau of Prisons, which is also part of the Department of Justice. Her behavior in prison is good. She has a chance for an early release from prison—a *parole*. Whether or not she gets the parole will be decided by another part of the Department, the Board of Parole.

The Department of Justice also handles noncriminal matters. It has a Civil Division that provides lawyers to represent the government in civil disputes. Also, it operates the Immigration and Naturalization Service, which runs the programs that admit foreigners to the United States.

Department of the Interior The Department of the Interior was set up by the Congress in 1849. The United States has great wealth in its land, forests, rivers, minerals, fuels, and wildlife. The Department of the Interior looks after these natural resources. The Secretary of the Interior advises the President on conservation issues.

The Department of the Interior deals with people too. The Bureau of Indian Affairs tries to help Native Americans in their daily lives. The Bureau works with them in planning the use of their lands. The Bureau also runs schools and health programs for Native Americans.

The Office of Territorial Affairs looks after United States land overseas. These lands include the Virgin Islands, Guam, and the islands of the Pacific Trust Territory. The Office gives the governments of these lands advice and aid. The Office also helps the growth of business in these lands.

The National Park Service is a well-known part of the Department of the Interior. Geysers, cactus plants, sequoia trees, and sand dunes are some of the natural wonders that the Park Service cares for. The National Park System—which is run by the Park Service—is made up of more than 300 parks, monuments, historic sites, memorials, battlefields, seashores, and parkways.

The Fish and Wildlife Service also maintains lands, many of which are open to visitors. About 300 wildlife refuges help the Fish and Wildlife Service preserve the country's fish, birds, and animals.

The Department of the Interior promotes other outdoor activities as well. The

National Scenic Rivers and the National Trails systems allow hiking and boating in some of the country's most beautiful areas. The Bureau of Outdoor Recreation studies the use of federal lands. It then sets up recreational programs, with the aid of the states.

Other sections of the Department help to increase the value of land. The Bureau of Reclamation watches over irrigation projects in the West. Its dams produce water for farming and electricity for industry. The Bureau of Land Management supervises mining, grazing, and logging on some federal lands.

Department of Agriculture The Department of Agriculture was set up in 1862. Today, United States farmers are among the most productive in the world. One-quarter of all the world's beef is raised on this country's ranches. One-fifth of all grain and eggs come from its farms. Agriculture is a key to this country's wealth. The Department of Agriculture works with farmers to keep their crops and livestock healthy and their level of production high.

The Agricultural Research Service looks for ways to improve crops and livestock. It also fights plant pests and diseases. The Farmer Cooperative Service and the Federal Extension Service spread knowledge of new farming methods. The Soil Conservation Service fights to protect farmland from destruction by soil erosion.

The Department of Agriculture aids people in farming areas in several ways. The Farmer's Home Administration gives loans for buying or operating farms. The Rural Electrification Administration brings telephone and electric lines to farming areas.

The Department of Agriculture has other duties that are not directly connected to farming. The Forest Service looks after more than fifty national forests. The Food and Nutrition Service runs the food stamp program and the school lunch program. The

The Forest Service received the help of 1,000 young volunteers after a fire destroyed a national forest in Virginia.

Department also checks and rates the quality of food products. This lets buyers know they are getting safe, high-quality food.

Department of Commerce In 1903, Congress created a Department of Commerce and Labor. In 1913, Commerce and Labor became separate departments. The Department of Commerce oversees the nation's trade and business. The sections mentioned here will give you some idea of the broad range of the Department's duties.

The Patent Office protects ideas and inventions. People can file plans of inventions or designs with the Office. They receive patents. A patent gives a person the sole right to use an invention or a design. People or companies can also ask the Patent Office to help protect their trademarks. A **trademark** is a word or a symbol that identifies a product. A person who files a trademark with the Office gets the sole right to use that trademark. For example, the Coca-Cola Company is the only company allowed to use the trademark "Coke" for its products.

Imagine that you are building a shed. You need some 3-inch bolts to finish the job. You go to a hardware store and buy some. When you get home, you find that the bolts are not the right size. The boltmaker's idea of 3 inches was not yours at all.

People need a common system of measurement. If the nation's businesses and factories are to run smoothly, they must be able to depend on standard weights, volumes, and sizes of the products they buy and make. The National Bureau of Standards keeps the standards of measurement for the country. It also does scientific research that aids businesses.

The Maritime Administration watches over the country's merchant ships, which are involved in international trade. It also runs the United States Merchant Marine Academy at King's Point, New York. This school trains officers for the merchant ships.

The Census Bureau counts the population of the country every 10 years. It also gathers much information about incomes, education, and styles of life in the United States.

The National Oceanic and Atmospheric Administration does the nation's weather forecasting. The Administration also makes maps and charts of the nation's lands and waters.

Department of Labor The Secretary of Labor is in charge of the Department of Labor. In 1933, Frances Perkins became the first woman to hold a Cabinet post when she became Secretary of Labor. The Secretary's job is to report to the President on problems facing workers in the United States. The Secretary also directs members of the Department to carry out federal laws that protect workers.

The Bureau of Labor Statistics collects facts about work and the economy. It publishes unemployment figures. The Bureau figures out the "cost of living"—how much an average person must spend for food, shelter, and clothing.

The Wage and Hour Division enforces federal laws on minimum wages. The Division studies and maintains standards about the length of the workday and workweek.

The Unemployment Insurance Service runs programs for workers who have lost their jobs or are unable to find work. These workers receive payments for several months to help them while they search for jobs.

The Office of Comprehensive Economic Development is in charge of several programs. Many of these programs train unskilled workers or help people keep their jobs.

Department of Health and Human Services In 1980, the Department of Health, Education, and Welfare (HEW) was split in two. The Department of Health and Human Services kept under its control all programs formerly under HEW with the exception of those involving education.

Most of the money in this department goes to the Social Security Administration. The Administration provides economic assistance for the old and the sick. Workers have money taken out of their paychecks to help pay for this assistance. Employers also contribute. Medicare is a program that helps people over 65 with their medical bills. Medicare is paid for with tax dollars.

The Social and Rehabilitation Service looks after this country's needy citizens. Its Medicaid plan helps those who are below a certain income with their medical bills. The Service also gives cash to people whose incomes are below a certain figure.

Other programs in this department research the causes, prevention, and treatment of diseases; enforce pure food and drug laws; and aid the handicapped.

Department of Education The other Cabinet-level department created by

Samuel R. Pierce (second from right), Secretary of Housing and Urban Development (HUD), has frequent meetings with his aides to discuss department policies and actions.

the splitting up of HEW is the Department of Education. This new agency directs the flow of federal money into school programs across the country. These funds help pay for books, school buildings, student loans, and much more. In addition, the Department of Education oversees adult education and job training programs. It also sets up special education and rehabilitation programs for gifted, problem, or handicapped students.

Department of Housing and Urban Development The rapid growth of cities in this century led Congress to form the Department of Housing and Urban Development (HUD) in 1965. HUD works to improve the living conditions of United States citizens. It also tries to solve the problems that have arisen as more and more people have moved to urban areas.

The Federal Housing Administration (FHA) insures loans for people who wish to buy homes. With this insurance, banks are more willing to lend money for homes. The insurance lowers the payments that borrowers make on their loans. The Department also runs a program that makes it easier for people to get loans to buy homes.

Other Department activities put money into building new, low-rent housing or repairing run-down neighborhoods. Still other sections of HUD are responsible for showing cities and their surrounding areas

how to work together to solve common problems.

Department of Transportation The people of the United States are always on the move. Passenger jets crisscross the skies. Trucks carry food to the cities. Trains pull carloads of coal to factories. The whole country depends on systems of transporting people and goods.

Recognizing this fact, Congress set up the Department of Transportation in 1966. Divisions of the Department help pay for interstate highways. The safety, fares, and schedules of the airlines are watched over by this Department. The Department inspects railroads and pays for public transportation systems. The Coast Guard is a branch of this Department in peacetime. The Coast Guard inspects ships, opens icebound harbors, and rescues ships in trouble at sea.

Department of Energy The United States is truly a nation "on the go." Energy is needed to keep it going. Gasoline runs its cars and trucks. Electricity drives its trains and subways. Oil and gas drive turbines. Coal produces the power for industry.

People in the United States have often acted as if these fuels would last forever. In 1973, however, many nations stopped shipping oil to the United States for a time. Suddenly, people saw what could happen if the nation's supplies ran low. Harsh winters in following years caused other fuel shortages. The nation's economy suffered from these shortages. It was clear that better planning for energy supplies was needed.

In 1977, Congress created the Department of Energy. The Department plans and carries out the energy policy of the government. The Department has the power to set fuel prices. It can enforce laws for the saving of energy. In times of fuel shortage, it will decide how fuel is to be distributed around the country.

―――――――――― REVIEW ――――――――――

1. What is the Cabinet?
2. How are Cabinet members appointed?
3. What is the title of the head of the Department of State? The head of the Department of Justice?
4. What is the newest executive department? What is the oldest?
5. Of the thirteen departments of the Cabinet, which *three* do you think are the most important? Why?

Words to Know

intelligence —— information that affects a nation's safety

domestic —— relating to one's own home or country; opposite of *foreign*

budget —— a plan showing expected income and expenses

independent agencies —— parts of the executive branch that handle jobs that are not in either the executive departments or the Executive Office

regulatory agencies —— independent agencies that help to control the nation's economy

stocks —— shares in the ownership of a business

bonds —— promises to repay given by businesses in exchange for loans

securities —— stocks and bonds

Other Executive Agencies

Independent Agencies

Congress has set up other parts of the executive branch called **independent agencies.** Many of these agencies handle jobs that do not fall clearly under the Executive Office or any of the executive departments.

Some of the independent agencies are called **regulatory agencies.** These help to regulate the nation's economic activities. The regulatory agencies are independent in two ways. First, like other independent agencies, they are not part of any executive department. Second, they are not under the day-to-day control of the President. They are given this special independence because of their special powers.

Regulatory agencies have certain lawmaking powers. For example, they write rules that people and businesses must obey. Regulatory agencies also have judicial powers. For example, they may hold a hearing—much like a trial—to decide if someone is breaking a rule. The decisions of regulatory agencies may be appealed to the federal courts.

Congress has set up a system of checks and balances to guard the independence of the regulatory agencies. It created a board or commission to run each agency. Each board or commission has from five to eleven members. The President appoints the members. Then, the Senate must approve them by majority vote. The appointments can be for as long as 14 years.

This means that one President will rarely appoint more than one or two members to each board or commission. In addition, the President cannot remove members except for specific reasons. Congress lists the reasons whenever it sets up a new agency.

The regulatory agencies often cause arguments. Some people say that the agencies often serve those people that they are supposed to control, rather than serving the public. Others argue that the agencies make rules and regulations that interfere too much with our daily lives. All the agencies and departments of the federal government together make enough rules in 1 year to fill a 10-foot-high bookshelf. One President called these rules "a nightmare of red tape."

But some people defend the rules and the agencies that make them. They say that some rules are needed to protect the health and safety of the public. They say that other rules are needed to keep large businesses from cheating the average person.

Interstate Commerce Commission When you ride a bus between two states, the fare that you pay is set by a regulatory agency—the Interstate Commerce Commission (ICC). The ICC is the oldest regulatory agency. Congress set it up in 1887 to watch over the railroads. Since then, the ICC has come to regulate interstate buses and trucks, plus shipping on rivers and lakes. The rates that these *carriers* charge are set by the commission. The services and schedules of shippers are also watched over by the ICC.

Civil Aeronautics Board The Civil Aeronautics Board (CAB) has tasks that are similar to those of the ICC. The difference is that the CAB supervises airlines. The Board hears evidence from the airlines and passengers before it makes its decisions.

Federal Communications Commission Millions of people watch television or listen to the radio every day. Most of the stations that broadcast programs are privately owned. The air through which the programs are sent, however, belongs to the public.

The Federal Communications Commission (FCC) is the regulatory agency that protects this public airspace. Radio and television stations must get licenses from the FCC before they can broadcast. After licensing, a station must follow FCC rules about the times of broadcasting and the strength of the station's signal. Other rules apply to the content of programs. Stations must give all political candidates equal time.

The FCC licenses short-wave, or "ham," radios. The millions of citizen's band radios in cars and homes are also under the control of the FCC.

Federal Trade Commission Free and fair trade is a key to the economy of the United States. Businesses should not make deals that unfairly hurt other businesses. A company should not have an unfair edge on its competition. A business should advertise its products honestly. Rules on these subjects have been written for businesses to follow. The Federal Trade Commission (FTC) enforces many of these rules.

Securities and Exchange Commission Businesses need money in order to operate. Some companies raise this money by selling shares in the ownership of their business. These shares are known as **stocks.** Companies can also borrow money. The promises they make to repay the money are known as **bonds.** Stocks and bonds are known as **securities.** Millions of dollars in securities are traded every day at stock exchanges. The most famous stock exchanges in the country are in New York City and Chicago.

Securities are important to business. Business is important to the country's well-being. For this reason, the federal government has set up an agency to watch over the sale of stocks and bonds. This is the Securities and Exchange Commission (SEC). The SEC's rules protect buyers of stocks and bonds from careless and dishonest business practices.

Federal Reserve System The Federal Reserve System works to keep the

The New York Stock Exchange is regulated by the Securities and Exchange Commission.

country's banks strong. A seven-member Federal Reserve Board runs a system of banks for banks. The country's economy is closely tied to the decisions of the Board. The Federal Reserve System controls the amount of money in circulation. It sets the interest rates paid on bank deposits at member banks. It decides how much money banks must have on hand. We will explore how these things affect the economy in Chapter 19.

Many Other Agencies All together, there are more than 100 independent agencies. The National Aeronautics and Space Administration (NASA) plans the United States' space program. It has landed people on the moon and sent ships to Mars and Jupiter. The National Labor Relations Board (NLRB) handles problems that arise between workers and employers. The Environmental Protection Agency fights pollution and polluters. The Veterans Administration runs programs for those who have served in the country's armed forces.

=========== REVIEW ===========

1. Why are regulatory agencies also known as independent agencies?
2. What agency regulates interstate buses?
3. What agency would you deal with if you wanted an amateur radio license?
4. What agency controls the amount of money in circulation?
5. Do you think it is a good idea for the government to have agencies that help control the economy? Why or why not?

Words to Know

civil servant —— someone who works for the government in a nonmilitary job

patronage —— giving out government jobs as political rewards

civil service system —— a merit system for government jobs

bureaucracy —— a system of jobs organized into specialized departments or bureaus, and ranked in a chain of command, with each rank taking orders from the next-higher rank

bureaucrat —— a white-collar worker in a bureaucracy

Federal Employees

The Merit System

So far in this chapter, we have been looking at the various parts of the executive branch. But what about the people who work there? Remember that 2.9 million civilians are employed in the executive branch. They are this country's **civil servants.** Civil servants perform a variety of jobs. Lawyers go to court for the Department of Justice. Artists design stamps for the Bureau of Printing and Engraving. Accountants study tax figures for the Internal Revenue Service. Physicists probe the mysteries of the Sun for the National Aeronautics and Space Administration. Chemists try out new medicines for the Food and Drug Administration. Typists turn out federal reports. Janitors scrub federal buildings. In all, there are more than 2,000 types of jobs within the federal government.

Early in the country's history, the President could make all the appointments to jobs in the executive branch. Washington named fewer than 800 government employees in 1792. Then the number of federal workers began to rise. The jobs came to be treated as political rewards, or **patronage.** A job would not go to the best worker, but to the person with the best "connections." Often, such people were unqualified, and the work of the government suffered.

People began to demand reform. In 1883, Congress passed the Civil Service Act. This act set up a merit system for many federal jobs—the **civil service system.** The skills of those who wanted federal jobs would be measured by tests. The role of politics in the appointment process would be reduced. Changes have been made in the Civil Service Act since 1883, but much of it remains in effect. Today, most but not all government workers get their jobs through this sytem.

In 1978, the Civil Service Commission was replaced by two separate agencies. The Office of Personnel Management took over the hiring role of the existing commission. The other, the Merit System Protection Board, was established as an independent regulatory agency. It helps to protect federal workers' rights on the job.

Tests are written to measure the skills needed for each type of job. Some tests are multiple-choice, matching, or true-and-false questions. Others might involve typing or taking dictation. Applicants for some jobs go through a personal interview.

All those who score above 70 on a test are put on a list for a specific job classification. Extra test points are given to certain people, such as armed forces veterans, widows of soldiers, and mothers of disabled veterans.

Let's say the Department of State needs a typist. The Office of Personnel Management sends a list of those people who did best on the tests for typists. The Department of State can choose from that list. Once all the people on the list have jobs, new tests are given and another list is drawn up.

Those who are hired by the federal government get a salary that compares well with that for similar jobs in private business. They also receive such benefits as life and health insurance, paid vacations, and sick leave.

Those who hold jobs through the civil service cannot run for political office or work in political campaigns. These rules were written to avoid the problems that caused the system to be set up in the first place.

Once in the civil service system, a person can be promoted to a better job or higher pay. Some raises are based on length of service. Other raises are based on the quality of a person's work. Civil service employees cannot be fired for political reasons. But they *can* be fired if they fail to do their jobs.

The civil service system has spread. The federal government now requires that jobs in state or local government using federal money be filled by merit. Today, about 18 percent of all jobs in the country are in some part of state or local government. Many of these jobs are filled through the use of some form of the civil service system.

The Bureaucracy

All the departments, bureaus, and agencies that carry out the work of the federal government are known as the federal bureaucracy. A **bureaucracy** is any system of jobs organized into specialized departments or bureaus, and ranked in order, with each rank taking orders from the next-highest rank.

With a large and complex system such as the federal government, rules and guidelines are needed for carrying out different tasks. A federal employee who orders concrete for a dam must follow the guidelines. All workers who order concrete follow the same guidelines. That way, other employees who have to use the concrete can be sure that it will do the job.

Workers in a bureaucracy—called **bureaucrats**—are given specific tasks. In an organization as big as the federal government, it is hard to get an overall picture of what is happening. Without carefully assigned tasks, workers in different areas might be doing the same task, or some important job might go undone.

Each level of worker in the bureaucracy reports to a worker on a higher level. The President is at the highest level. This is the *chain of command*. The chain of command helps assign the responsibility for jobs. It is also a way to check on progress. If something goes wrong with a highway in Alaska, each link in the chain can be examined until the error is found.

Unfortunately, all the reasons for having a bureaucracy can become reasons for not having one. When the way to do a job is set by firm rules, it is hard to introduce a new and better way of doing that job. The narrow tasks that are given to workers can keep them from being original or creative. The chain of command can grow so long and complicated that it covers up responsibility instead of locating it.

—————————— REVIEW ——————————

1. How many people work for the executive branch of the government?
2. Why was the civil service system started?
3. Do you think that it is a good idea for a bureaucracy to have firm rules about how things should be done? Why or why not?

How the United States Works

Forest Ranger

The words *forest ranger* may bring to mind pictures of people battling raging forest fires and searching for lost children. The pictures are true, but they are only part of the job of the forest ranger. Let's see what else is involved.

Forest rangers work for the executive branch—the largest employer in the United States. They are hired by one of its agencies, the Forest Service. Rangers run complex communications systems that include lookout towers with radios and telephones. Roads, airstrips, and storage areas are also part of the system. Together, they make it possible for forests to be watched carefully and reached quickly. To make sure that everything is in order, forest rangers spend many hours traveling through their districts—often on foot, skis, or horseback.

Another part of the ranger's job has nothing to do with emergencies. Forest rangers make sure that the environment is protected. They see that the forest is put to good use. They must know how to save forests from insects and disease, as well as from fires. They must also know how to harvest trees. Rangers decide which parts of the national forest will be cut and where plants should be thinned. They also direct replanting. They must know which soil and weather conditions the different kinds of trees need. All this takes a good deal of training. The minimum schooling needed to become a forest ranger is 4 years of college, with a degree in forestry.

There are only about a thousand forest rangers working for federal or state agencies. However, other foresters can find jobs working for timber companies—which locate and cut down trees for wood—or teaching in colleges or vocational schools.

Reading About . . .

Executive Departments at Work

The executive departments handle a wide variety of jobs, and the range of jobs is always growing. In this reading, you will look at one way in which the executive departments are trying to solve the energy crisis.

As you read, ask yourself these questions:

● Which executive departments are working on this project?
● Should departments of the government handle a project like this, or should the project be left to private companies?

On a windswept plain at the edge of Clayton, New Mexico, a brand-new orange, white, and blue windmill is more than a local curiosity. Whenever the speed of the wind is more than 12 kilometers (8 miles) per hour, the machine's two 63-foot blades start to turn—and feed enough electricity into the power supply for 60 of the town's 1,300 homes. "We have wind practically always," says a town spokesperson. "We figure that the windmill will be producing 90 percent of the time."

A joint project of the Department of Energy and the National Aeronautics and Space Administration, the Clayton windmill is just the first in a promising line of wind machines to be built in United States. Windmills like Clayton's will soon start working on Block Island, Rhode Island, and Culebra Island in Puerto Rico. By the year 2000, some optimistic experts believe, windmills could supply as much as 10 percent of the United States' electrical energy needs.

The windmills are hardly free from problems. For one thing, the high towers interfere with television reception. More importantly, electricity from even the largest windmills now in action costs more than three times as much as electricity from oil generators. But, according to the Department of Energy, "early studies show that costs should come down as the size of the wind machines goes up."

Wind, of course, can be undependable. So energy companies that invest in windmills will have to have some way of producing spare power when the wind dies. But one Deputy Secretary of Energy says, "If you can find a place where the wind blows at 27 kilometers (17 miles) per hour for 80 percent of the time, you've got a deal." Some projects are also being planned to link up with existing power supplies. For example, the Department of the Interior's Bureau of Reclamation is studying plans for a grouping of windmills near Medicine Bow, Wyoming, to add to the power produced by six dams on the Colorado River.

Clearly, the federal government sees great possibilities for harnessing the wind. Not only is wind power free from pollution, but it promises great savings as oil prices rise. If the wind provides just 1 percent of the nation's energy, it could reduce the costs of importing oil and natural gas by millions of dollars.

chapter
Review

Fact Review

1. How many executive departments does the federal government now have?
2. Match the jobs in *a* to *d* with the departments in (*1*) to (*4*).
   a. running Medicare
   b. issuing passports
   c. protecting wildlife
   d. running the Army
      (1) Department of State
      (2) Department of the Interior
      (3) Department of Defense
      (4) Department of Health and Human Services
3. What department of the government is especially concerned with the problems of cities?

4. Why are federal civil service employees not allowed to run for political office?
5. Do you think that the executive branch is too big? Why or why not?

Developing Your Vocabulary

1. Choose the word that best completes the following sentences:
   a. Stocks and bonds are examples of (trademarks / securities).
   b. In the civil service system, job appointments are based on (merit / influence).
2. Match the terms in *a* to *e* with the phrases in (*1*) to (*5*).
   a. budget
   b. civil servant
   c. embassy
   d. Cabinet
   e. passport
      (1) a group of official advisers to the President
      (2) a diplomatic office in another country
      (3) an official travel document
      (4) a plan showing expected income and expenses
      (5) a government employee

Developing Your Reading Skills

Read the following paragraph and then answer the questions that follow:

Your life is affected in many ways by what the regulatory agencies do. Each agency has its own job. The Federal Communications Commission licenses radio and television stations. The Federal Reserve System controls the amount of money that is available. The Interstate Commerce Commission sets rules about railroad, bus, and train fares. The Civil Aeronautics Board sets rules about air fares. Each agency operates under powers given to it by Congress.

1. Which one of the following do you think is the main point, or main idea, of the paragraph above?
   a. Regulatory agencies do many things.
   b. Congress has a say about what regulatory agencies do.
   c. The jobs of regulatory agencies are specialized.
   d. Air fares and bus fares are handled by two different agencies.
2. Why did you select either *a, b, c,* or *d* in question 1?

Developing Your Writing Skills— Forming and Supporting an Opinion

In this chapter, you have read about how the people who work in the executive branch are part of a bureaucracy. The chain of command starts with the President at the top. Each person in the bureaucracy must follow rules of procedure. Now consider:

Forming an opinion

1. What are the good and bad features of a bureaucracy?
2. How might the federal bureaucracy be improved?

Supporting an opinion

3. After thinking it over, write a paragraph that answers the questions above.

YOUR GOVERNMENT & ITS HISTORY

A Split in the First Cabinet

Every President sets up a Cabinet for advice and assistance. Members of the President's Cabinet work together for the good of the President and the country. Sometimes, Cabinet members do not agree. Disagreements date back to the first Cabinet of George Washington. The two men in dispute were Alexander Hamilton, who was the Secretary of the Treasury, and Thomas Jefferson, who was the Secretary of State.

Hamilton supported a strong and active federal government. Jefferson feared a strong federal government. He usually opposed most of Hamilton's proposals.

Hamilton wanted to set up a national bank. It would serve as a safe place for both individuals and government to deposit money. He felt that a national bank would also provide the country with a sound system of money. The bank would lend money to businesspeople. In this way, it would encourage the growth of industry.

Hamilton's policies tended to increase the power of the federal government. The establishment of the national bank helped enlarge the powers of Congress. The Constitution did not delegate to Congress the power to establish a national bank. Hamilton argued that this power was implied in the powers granted to Congress. He favored a "loose construction," or broad interpretation, of the Constitution.

Jefferson believed in giving as much power as possible to state governments. He also believed in developing agriculture more than industry. He felt that giving the government more financial power would increase federal power at the expense of the states. He felt, too, that Hamilton's program helped business interests but ignored agricultural interests.

Jefferson opposed Hamilton's plan for a national bank on constitutional grounds. Wishing to limit federal power, Jefferson supported a "strict construction," or narrow interpretation, of the Constitution. He insisted that setting up a national bank was unconstitutional.

There was a series of arguments between the two men. Hamilton showed how he felt about Jefferson in the following letter, written to a friend. In the letter, Hamilton referred to James Madison, a close friend and political ally of Jefferson.

Philadelphia, May 26, 1792

I became . . . convinced of the following truth. . . . Mr. Madison, cooperating with Mr. Jefferson, is at the head of a party decidedly hostile to me . . . and moved by views, in my judgment, against the principles of good government and dangerous to the Union, peace, and happiness of the country. . . . In various conversations with others, Jefferson has shown disapproval of my principles of government. . . . 'Tis obvious beyond a question, from every moment, that Mr. Jefferson aims, with strong desire, at the presidential chair.

Jefferson also had his opinions about Hamilton. Those opinions are shown in the following letter to George Washington.

Philadelphia, May 23, 1792

The final object of Hamilton's program is to prepare the way for a change. It would be a change from the present republican form of government to that of a monarchy, of which the English constitution is the model. It would also produce, in the future, a king, lords, and commons, or whatever else those who direct it may choose.

President Washington then wrote to Jefferson.

I regret, deeply regret, the difference in opinions that have . . . divided you and Hamilton; and wish, sincerely, there could be a settlement of them by compromise. . . . A measure of this sort would produce harmony and . . . goodwill in our public councils. The opposite will, in the end, introduce confusion and serious mischiefs, and for what? Because mankind cannot think alike, but would adopt different means to achieve the same end. For I will frankly . . . declare that I believe the views of both of you are pure, and well meant, and that experience alone will decide who is right.

Washington also wrote to Hamilton.

Differences in political opinion are as hard to avoid as, to a certain point, they may, perhaps, be necessary. But it is very much to be regretted that subjects cannot be discussed with temper on the one hand, or decision, submitted to without having the motives distorted by the other party. Here we find that men of abilities, eager patriots, having the same general objects in view and the same upright intentions to carry them out will not exercise more charity in deciding on the options and actions of one another. . . . Having stated these things, I would gladly hope that liberal allowance will be made for the political opinions of each other; and instead of those wounding suspicions, and irritating charges . . . there might be mutual restraints . . . on all sides.

1. What position did Alexander Hamilton hold in the first Cabinet? What position did Thomas Jefferson hold?
2. How did Hamilton and Jefferson differ in their views of what the new federal government should be doing?
3. What advice did Washington offer both men?
4. How do you think a President should deal with members of the Cabinet?

 **SKILLS**

Developing your basic civic education skills

A Closer Look at Bureaucracies

(distinguishing fact from opinion)

If you completed the writing exercise on page 195, then you are familiar with the good and bad features of a bureaucracy. Now you will consider more information about bureaucracies.

As you have learned, each government has many bureaus and agencies to help carry out its programs. (This is also true of businesses and educational systems.) Those bureaus and agencies make up the bureaucracy. A government bureaucracy is the part of any government that is run by nonelected officials. People who work in bureaus and agencies are called bureaucrats. For example, the staffs of the members of Congress are made up of bureaucrats. Unlike the legislators, the staff members are not elected to office. Instead, they are appointed by the legislator.

Bureaucrats perform many duties. They help elected officials in planning new laws and enforcing laws and programs. They sometimes assist judges in interpreting laws. Other tasks include serving the poor, the aged, the sick, the handicapped, and people unable to get work.

In recent years, the bureaucracy has increased in number and size. Many bureaus and agencies that were created for only a short period of time have remained in operation. Few bureaus or agencies are done away with. Yet they cost money to operate. And in recent years, tax money to operate the government has become more and more difficult to obtain.

To do away with bureaus and agencies that are not needed, Colorado became the first state to approve a sunset law. A sunset law gives an agency or bureau a life of 6 years. Within that time, the legislature must be shown that the agency or bureau does a necessary job.

If the legislators are satisfied, the agency or bureau will continue for another 6 years. The process is then repeated. If witnesses cannot prove the value of either the jobs or the program, the bureau or agency will be given a year to complete its business, with no reduction in its authority. At the end of that year, the bureau or agency ceases to exist. In other words, if a bureau or an agency cannot justify its existence, the "sun will set on it."

1. What is a government bureaucracy?

2. Why do government bureaucracies exist?

3. What is a sunset law? Why have some local governments adopted them?

4. Which three of the following statements are fact?

a. A government bureaucracy is the part of a government that is run by nonelected officials.

b. The bureaucracy of the United States government has grown too large.

c. Businesses and educational systems have bureaucracies.

d. Colorado became the first state to pass a sunset law.

e. All bureaucracies need to be evaluated every year.

f. Any bureau or agency that cannot prove its value should be done away with.

5. Briefly, tell why you selected the three statements you did in question 4.

6. Tell which three of the statements in question 4 are opinion.

7. Briefly, tell why you selected the three statements you did in question 6.

The Humorous Side of Governmental Bureaucracy: The Use of Satire

(thinking critically)

Comedians such as Will Rogers and Bob Hope, writers such as Mark Twain and Art Buchwald, and political cartoonists such as Gary Trudeau and Bill Maulden have had great fun showing the humorous or ridiculous side of the workings of government.

Much of the humor relating to government has been in the form of *satire* (SAT ire). This is a tongue-in-cheek, or exaggerated, use of wit, humor, or ridicule to expose what the satirist regards as foolishness or wickedness.

Comic Strips as Satire

Many comic strips are satiric; that is, they have satire as their content. Three such comic strips are shown here. They deal with how some political cartoonists view the federal bureaucracy.

8. What is satire?

9. Match the main points that follow with the main points in comic strips *1* to *3*:

_____ **a.** The government bureaucracy sometimes creates more problems than are necessary.

_____ **b.** Many persons think the government requires too much paperwork of them.

Comic Strip 1

Comic Strip 2

CROCK   by Rechin and Parker

_____ **c.** The government has a habit of issuing too many rules to suit most people.

(1) comic strip 1

(2) comic strip 2

(3) comic strip 3

10. How did the authors of these comic strips use satire to make a point?

Newspaper Editorials as Satire

Editorial 1

Recently, a Washington newspaper held a contest to find the bureaucrat with the longest title.

The winner was an employee of the National Oceanic and Atmospheric Administration. That employee had the title of "administrative assistant to the administrative assistant to the assistant administrator for administration." Honest.

Since the bureaucracy does not appreciate having fun poked at it, the folks at NOAA promptly gave the office an even longer title. The employee has become the "administrative assistant to the administrative assistant to the assistant administrator for management and budgets." Honest.

Editorial 2

Even bureaucrats cannot win against the bureaucracy.

Raul de Armas is a special Internal Revenue Service agent who goes after drug traffickers. In a case that led to the conviction of a major trafficker for not paying $2.6 million in taxes, de Armas made a rush trip to Spain to collect vital evidence.

He took a direct Iberia Airlines flight from Miami, where he is stationed, at a cost of $791, round trip. That is where de Armas got into trouble.

Comic Strip 3

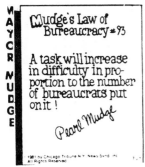

If he had followed government regulations, he would have taken a United States carrier. He would have flown to New York and then to Spain at a cost of about $1,800 to the government.

The General Accounting Office, tut-tutting about the rule violation, made de Armas pay for the Iberia ticket himself. In saving time and about $1,000 for the taxpayers, de Armas lost $791. Fellow agents made up his loss.

11. Which of the following is the main point of Editorial 1?

    a. The federal bureaucracy can sometimes be self-defeating.

    b. The federal bureaucracy has workers with absurd job titles.

    c. The federal bureaucracy has too many employees.

12. Which one of the following statements is the main point of Editorial 2?

    a. The federal bureaucracy can sometimes be self-defeating.

    b. The federal bureaucracy has workers with absurd job titles.

    c. The federal bureaucracy has too few employees.

13. In what way are Editorials 1 and 2 forms of satire?

A Tongue-in-Cheek Request

In recent years, the problems of unemployment have come up in rulings from the federal bureaucracy. The attitudes of many of the unemployed toward work are seen in the following reading.

Although many people believe that some jobs are so unpleasant that only illegal aliens will take them, a *Los Angeles Times* poll has found that this is not true.

Seventy-five percent of people interviewed who were unemployed said they would apply for jobs paying them between $3.35 an hour, the legal minimum, and $4.50 an hour.

More than 48 percent of the unemployed polled said they would seek restaurant jobs. Forty percent said they would apply for clothing-industry jobs. Both industries hire large numbers of illegal aliens.

The *Los Angeles Times* poll interviewed 1,681 American adults—employed and unemployed—in an 8-day period. The poll was conducted by telephone. Special measures were taken to interview many Hispanics, blacks, and poor whites to make sure that the sample was balanced.

The poll also shows that the public's view of the number of Americans willing to take poor jobs is far different from reality. Nearly half (48 percent) of all those polled said that illegal aliens take only those jobs that Americans will not accept. Forty percent believe that Americans can be found to do the jobs. Twelve percent were not sure.

Yet the poll also showed that a large majority of the unemployed would take such jobs— nearly 5 million people, particularly blacks, poor whites, and women. (About 7.8 million Americans are now unemployed.)

In 1977, Woody Glasscock (the mayor of Hondo, Texas) attracted national attention with a letter he sent to President Carter. Vickie Davidson, a reporter for the San Antonio *Express-News,* reported on Glasscock's request.

Notice: You regularly unemployed who will not work even if work is available—Hondo wants you. Hondo Mayor Woodrow Glasscock, Jr., figures he needs 180 unemployment roll regulars to push his community's 3 percent unemployment rate up to 6 percent. Maybe the higher unemployment rate would help the small city west of San Antonio get federal funds, he says.

Hondo's requests for federal funds to build a civic center have been turned down repeatedly. This is due to the low unemployment rates in the community of some 6,000 people.

Now, Glasscock calls this a policy that gives no consideration to those who work for a living and pay their bills.

But if unemployment is what it takes to get federal assistance, then he wants it. Mayor Glasscock is asking for President Jimmy Carter's help.

"I want a list of people who will not work under any circumstances," reads a letter the newly elected mayor wrote to the President.

"I intend to write them letters to move here. We want enough people to allow us to qualify for some of your programs.

"We are a proud people here, with a proud heritage born of hard work and enterprise. Trying to get enough locals to quit work so we can qualify is out of the question. We will have to import the unemployed," reads the letter.

The way the 37-year-old Glasscock, who served on the City Council before being elected mayor, sees it, Hondo cannot afford to pass a bond issue and build a $1 million center themselves. "Most people are on a low wage scale, and the tax burden would be too heavy."

Glasscock says the community has no public building for meetings, displays, or conventions.

"It just kind of angered me that we had people employed, so they were going to turn us down," explained Glasscock.

His letter to Carter says as much.

"Since our town was established in 1881, the only federal

assistance grant we have ever received was $200,000 for a flood-control project. I feel, and so do the members of our community, that this was precious little interest on your part for our needs."

Glasscock does not have all the details worked out yet.

He's not sure how they would handle the unemployed if they did come. "We've got an old air base out there. We could make barracks out of it," he suggests.

And he admits he's "mostly" trying to get his point across with the letter to Carter. "But," he says, "I'm going to be interested to see what my response is from Washington."

Glasscock's main argument was this: Aren't people who are working and paying taxes as deserving of federal funds as the unemployed? "My main crusade with this is the nonwork ethic that it is promoting," he stated. "If you are a working-class citizen, you are going to be turned down for federal funds."

His request for federal funding was rejected. Glasscock's attempt to attract 180 unemployed people to Hondo was also a failure. Two unemployed individuals did come to Hondo, but both ruined Glasscock's plan. They found work in Hondo within a day of their arrival.

14. What did the poll results show about the attitudes of the unemployed toward work? Give three examples.

15. Who is Woodrow Glasscock, Jr.? What did he request of President Jimmy Carter and the federal bureaucracy?

16. What was the main point Glasscock was trying to make through the use of satire?

17. When do you think a community should be eligible to receive government funding? Under what conditions? Explain.

18. Obviously, there are arguments against the points made in this lesson. Consider what might be the result if no bureaucracies existed in our society. How could needed programs be created? What if there were no bureaucratic rules to serve as guides? What would be the result for the sick, the aged, the poor, the handicapped, or for businesspeople, farmers, people in educational institutions, or others who sometimes must rely on governmental aid? We must also continue to consider the problems of people who want to work but cannot find a job no matter how much they search for one. What can be done to help them, especially if they do not have enough money to move to parts of the country where jobs are available? In considering these questions, review and use the parts of the critical-thinking process on page 62. Then, tell which one of the following is the most important issue discussed in this lesson on bureaucracy.

    a. the number of American citizens who were unemployed in 1981
    b. topics that newspapers should include in their coverage of the activities of the federal bureaucracy
    c. how to justify the existence of a government bureaucracy

19. Why did you select *a, b,* or *c* in question 18?

20. Write your answer to question 18 either in the form of a hypothesis or in the form of a generalization. Which did you use? Explain.

UNIT 3 REVIEW

Fact Review

1. What is the main job of the President?
2. Name five types of powers that the President has.
3. Name three ways in which the President's powers are subject to checks and balances.
4. Give the order of presidential succession by putting a number next to each official below who is part of that succession. Begin with the number 1 for the official who is first in line.
   a. Secretary of State
   b. Speaker of the House
   c. Vice President
   d. president *pro tempore* of the Senate

Developing Your Vocabulary

1. Give a definition for each of the following words. Then use the words in a paragraph about the executive branch of the federal government.
   a. popular vote
   b. electoral college
   c. President-elect
   d. inauguration
2. Four terms in the paragraph below are misused. First find the terms. Then choose the correct terms from the following list to replace them.

ambassadors	foreign
military	recognized
treaties	civilians

The President uses the diplomatic powers of the Presidency to shape the nation's domestic policy. For example, the President may appoint embassies to other countries. These officials are only sent to countries that the United States has officially pardoned. Sometimes these officials help to write executive agreements, which must then be submitted to the Senate for approval.

Developing Your Reading Skills

Read the following passage and then answer the questions that follow:

The executive branch contains one President, thirteen executive departments, and 2.9 million employees. To make it easier to control all those people, the government organizes the people into a bureaucracy. The bureaucracy is made up of hundreds of agencies and bureaus, all linked in a chain of command. Each worker and each official is responsible to someone who is higher up. The President is at the top of this chain of command. At one time, there was a sign on a President's desk: "The buck stops here." The President cannot pass the buck. The President has final responsibility for what happens in the executive branch.

The main parts of the executive branch are the executive departments, the Executive Office of the President, and the independent agencies. Each part has a special job to do. This is true of all bureaucracies. People in a bureaucracy work in specialized jobs. They are supposed to follow set rules of procedure. Sometimes this makes it very difficult to deal with a bureaucracy. There always seem to be so many rules.

1. Which of the following questions cannot be answered from the reading?
   a. What are the main parts of the executive branch?
   b. How many people work for the executive branch?
   c. What are the names of the executive departments?
   d. How are the jobs in a bureaucracy organized?
   e. What are people who work in a bureaucracy called?
   f. Who is in charge of the federal bureaucracy?
2. Which questions can be answered from the reading? Identify the sentence or sentences which continue the answer to each.

You have seen how the Constitution gives Congress the power to make laws. You have also seen how the President and members of the executive branch put the laws into effect.

Now you will see how the law is applied to people and their disputes. What happens when a person breaks a law; when two people cannot settle a dispute by themselves; when a person believes his or her rights under the law have been violated; or when someone feels that a law is wrong?

The writers of the Constitution understood that questions such as these would arise. They knew the importance of settling disputes fairly. They knew that people might disagree about whether the law itself was fair. They had their own argument with the laws of England. They knew that a good system of government must have some way of making sure the laws were carried out fairly. They provided for this in the Constitution. They did so by setting up a third branch of the federal government—the judicial branch, which is made up of the federal courts.

unit 4

The Judicial Branch

The Federal Courts

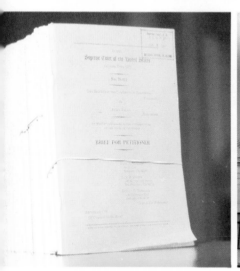

In Chapter 2, we discussed some of the reasons why societies have laws. One reason is to help settle disputes. Disputes can arise between people, between people and the government, and between governments. A **court** is a part of government that works to settle disputes by applying laws and precedents to specific cases.

In this chapter, you will examine the courts that make up the federal court system. You will also see how state courts fit into the federal system. To begin, let's look at the way a typical court case might work.

Words to Know

court —— a part of government that works to settle disputes by applying laws or precedents to specific cases

lawsuit —— court case

complaint —— written statement presented to a court to start a lawsuit

plaintiff —— person who takes a case to court

defendant —— person against whom a court case is brought

trial —— formal court proceeding at which evidence is heard and a case is decided

judge —— the official who presides over a trial

jury —— a group of citizens chosen to hear evidence in a court case and decide on questions of fact

evidence —— facts and testimony given by one side or the other in a court case

verdict —— a jury's decision

statutory law —— laws, or statutes, passed by lawmaking bodies and regulations made by executive departments and agencies

jurors —— members of a jury

petit jury —— a trial jury; gives a verdict in a trial

grand jury —— an investigating jury; decides whether there is enough evidence to hold a criminal trial

The Courts—An Overview

How a Court Works

You will probably take part in many disputes in your life. Most of these will be settled privately. For example, you have an argument with a neighbor. You throw a ball that breaks the neighbor's window. It is an accident. You agree to pay for a new window. You and the neighbor shake hands. That dispute has been settled privately.

Some disputes are not so easily settled. One afternoon, Maria Byrne is driving in her car on the expressway. Suddenly, a large sofa falls off a truck just ahead of her. Her car hits the sofa and goes into a spin. Maria is thrown against the windshield. Her skull is fractured.

The medical bills are more than Maria can pay. Maria believes the accident was not her fault. Maria gets in touch with the truck driver. The driver says it was not his fault either. He did not load the truck. He will not pay. If Maria is going to get any money, it looks as if she will have to file a **lawsuit**—that is, a court case.

To start the court case, Maria hires a lawyer, Deborah Smith. Ms. Smith gives the court a written statement of Maria's side of the dispute. The statement is called a **complaint.** Since Maria is making the complaint, she is the **plaintiff.** The truck driver is the **defendant.**

Court officials will now set a date for a **trial.** A trial is a formal method of deciding a lawsuit. On the day of the trial, Maria and her lawyer go to the court building. Many trials are going on there at once. They finally find the room where Maria's case is to be heard. The truck driver and his lawyer are already there.

The official who presides over the trial is a **judge.** In many cases, a **jury** will take part in the trial. A jury is a group of citizens chosen by the court to listen to both sides in a case and decide which side is right. Before the trial begins, the judge and the jury promise that they will give both sides a fair hearing.

The start of a trial is usually taken up by the choosing of people for the jury. Then Maria and the truck driver—or their lawyers—present **evidence,** or facts about the case. For example, Maria may have had other people in the car with her. These people will tell what happened. Ms. Smith may show the court Maria's medical bills. The truck driver will also present evidence. For

In a trial, the judge presides over court proceedings and must, in each case, interpret the law.

example, he may tell what happened just before the accident. He may tell the court that he thinks Maria's car was following his truck too closely.

When all the evidence has been given, the judge explains to the jury what the law says about cases like this. Then the jury goes to another room to talk the case over. It is up to the jury to decide the facts of the case.

When all the members of the jury have agreed, they return to the courtroom and give their decision, or **verdict.** The verdict tells who wins the case. If Maria wins, the jury will also decide how much money the truck driver should pay her. If she loses, she will have to pay all the hospital bills herself. In addition, she will have the lawyer's bills and court costs to pay.

Judges

The judge's job is an important one. The judge must run the trial, deciding who can speak and when. The judge must rule on which evidence can be used. The judge must keep order in the court. Most importantly, the judge must decide the law in each case. That is why judges must be highly trained, with a broad knowledge of the law.

As we saw in Chapter 2, judges in the United States depend on two sources of law. One is *precedent*—the decisions of judges in past cases. We have seen that precedent is part of common law. In our example, the judge may know of an earlier case that was like Maria's. A crate bounced off a truck causing an accident. In that case, the injured person filed a lawsuit. Perhaps in this earlier case, the plaintiff lost because the jury decided that the driver of the car had been following too closely. The jury felt that the driver of the car was as wrong as the driver of the truck. The judge might explain this earlier case to the jury. Then the judge would tell the jury to apply this common-law rule to Maria's case. You should note, however, that two cases are never exactly alike. Precedents must be used under different conditions in every case.

Another source of law that judges must know is **statutory law.** This is made up of all the laws, or *statutes,* passed by lawmaking bodies. It includes the Constitution, the laws passed by Congress and state legislatures and by city or other local governments, and the rules made by the executive departments and agencies. In Maria's case, there might be a statute making it unlawful to drop anything onto a public highway. The judge would explain to the jury what law specifically means in terms of this case.

In some trials, there is no jury. The judge takes on the jury's part. For example, the plaintiff and the defendant in a trial may sometimes agree to let the judge decide without a jury. Also, as we shall see shortly, juries are never asked to rule on cases that have come to a higher court from a lower court. That job is left solely to judges.

Juries

Juries are made up of people from the community. The people who make up a jury are called **jurors.** Court officials keep a list of people in the community. Often, the list is made up of the names of voters. The officials draw names from the list and send notices ordering the people to come to the court for "jury duty." Serving on juries is one of the responsibilities of United States citizenship. It helps to protect an important right: the right to a trial by jury that is guaranteed in the Constitution.

There are two kinds of juries. The kind in the case we have been following is a **petit jury.** This is the jury that is used in trials. Another kind of jury is the **grand jury.** The grand jury holds investigations. It decides whether there is enough evidence in a criminal case to hold a trial. It may also look into possible wrongdoings by public officials.

At a trial, the judge and the jury each have a job to do. The judge rules on points of *law*. The jury rules on points of *fact*. Was the car following too closely behind the truck? Was the truck driver careless? Was Maria hurt as badly as she claims? These are among the questions that the jury would have to decide in Maria's case.

In a civil case like Maria's, the jury would not have to be totally sure of the facts. It would weigh all the evidence that had been presented. Then it would decide if most of the evidence was on Maria's side or on the truck driver's side.

To experience the legal system in action, some schools set up a mock court, which includes an acting judge, jury, defense, and prosecution.

In a criminal case, it would be different. A criminal case, as we have seen, involves a person who is accused of breaking a law. The jury must decide if the person really broke the law and should be punished. In such a case, "most of the evidence" is not enough. The jury must be quite sure of its facts. It must be certain "beyond a reasonable doubt" that the person is guilty.

In the past, petit juries in this country have been made up of twelve persons. This is no longer the case. In some places, juries now have nine, eight, six, or even five persons. In criminal cases, however, a jury must have at least six persons.

========= REVIEW =========

1. Who is the plaintiff in a lawsuit?
2. What are three jobs of a judge in a court trial?
3. What kind of jury would investigate wrongdoing by an official?
4. In what kind of case do you think a jury has to be more sure of the facts—in a civil case or in a criminal case? Why?
5. Is serving on a jury an important job or not? Explain your answer.

Words to Know

jurisdiction —— the authority of a court to consider a case

original jurisdiction —— the authority of a court to start a case

appellate jurisdiction —— the authority of a court to review a decision made by a lower court

concurrent jurisdiction —— the authority over a case shared by both federal and state courts

circuit —— region (The United States is divided into eleven circuits, each of which has a United States Court of Appeals.)

affirm —— uphold a lower court's decision
court-martial —— a trial conducted by military officers under military law

The Federal Court System

A Two-Level Court System

Under the federal system, there are two levels of government—the federal government and the state governments. There are also two court systems. One system is the federal court system. The other is the state court system, which also includes city and county courts.

Maria's lawsuit against the truck driver would have been filed in a state court. State and local courts handle cases that result from violations of state and local laws. More than 90 percent of all court cases are at this level.

Federal courts deal with cases that result from violations of federal laws and the Constitution. They also handle cases that go beyond the limits of one state, as well as disputes between states.

Federal and state courts are like two railroad tracks that run alongside each other. A court case is the train. If a train starts out on the federal track, it stays on that track. If it starts out on the state track, it usually stays on that track. But sometimes a case from the state track can be switched over to the federal track.

Cases can be switched from state to federal courts only when a federal question is involved. For example, let's say a movie theater shows a movie that contains nudity. The theater owner is charged with violating a city law against "public display of obscene materials." The case starts in a state court, because the law is a local one. The court convicts the theater owner, saying that he

Most federal cases begin here in a district court. They are the only federal courts that use juries.

broke the law. The owner *appeals,* or takes his case, to higher state courts, but loses. Finally, the theater owner asks the Supreme Court to review the case. The owner claims that the local law violates the federal Constitution's freedom-of-the-press and freedom-of-speech clauses. It would be up to the Supreme Court to decide whether there is, indeed, a federal question involved.

The federal Constitution is the law of the United States. So are the laws of Congress made under that Constitution. A state law may not conflict with a federal law or with the Constitution. The nudity case raises the question of whether or not a local law does conflict with the Constitution. It is up to federal courts—not the state courts—

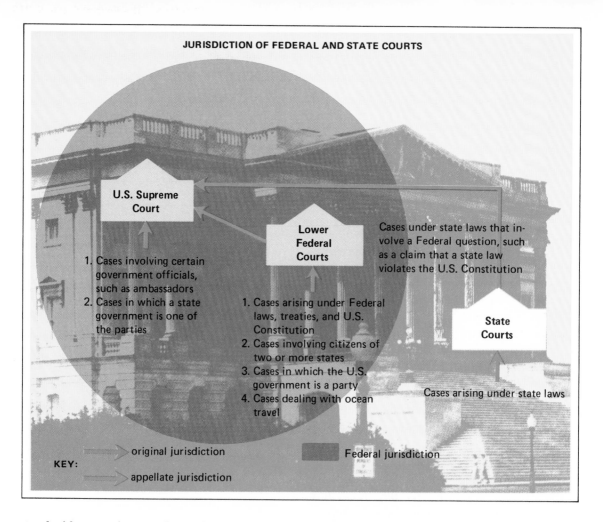

JURISDICTION OF FEDERAL AND STATE COURTS

U.S. Supreme Court

1. Cases involving certain government officials, such as ambassadors
2. Cases in which a state government is one of the parties

Lower Federal Courts

1. Cases arising under Federal laws, treaties, and U.S. Constitution
2. Cases involving citizens of two or more states
3. Cases in which the U.S. government is a party
4. Cases dealing with ocean travel

Cases under state laws that involve a Federal question, such as a claim that a state law violates the U.S. Constitution

State Courts

Cases arising under state laws

KEY:
→ original jurisdiction
→ appellate jurisdiction
Federal jurisdiction

to decide questions such as this. The decision of a federal court would be followed over the decision of a state court.

Jurisdiction

Look again at Maria's case against the truck driver. She filed the suit in a state court. That court had **original jurisdiction** over her case. That means that Maria could start her case in that court. She could not have started the case in the United States Supreme Court because it does not have original jurisdiction over such cases.

The suit over nudity involves another kind of jurisdiction. The theater owner was not pleased with the verdict of the first court. So the owner appealed the case to a higher court. A court that can take cases on appeal has *appellate jurisdiction*.

Federal courts have jurisdiction only in certain kinds of cases. These are described in Article III, Section 2 of the Constitution. They are: (1) cases arising under the Constitution, federal laws, and federal treaties, (2) cases involving certain government officials, such as ambassadors, (3) cases involving two or more states, or the citizens of two or more states, (4) case in which the United States government is involved, (5) cases dealing with ocean travel.

The fact that a federal court has jurisdiction does not mean that a case will be tried in federal court. In some matters, both federal and state courts share authority over a case—**concurrent jurisdiction.** In such cases, the parties, or sides, to a suit may choose either a federal court or a state court. For example, a suit between citizens of two different states may be tried in a state court if both parties agree.

Parts of the Federal Court System

The federal court system has several levels. At the top is the Supreme Court, which is mentioned by name in the Constitution—Article III, Section I. Below the Supreme Court are many lesser courts. These have been set up by Congress. Some have special jobs, such as deciding only tax cases. Others can hear many kinds of cases. Some courts, at the bottom levels, have only original jurisdiction, some have only appellate jurisdiction, and some—like the Supreme Court—have original jurisdiction over some cases and appellate jurisdiction over other cases.

We will begin at the bottom level and take a quick tour of the federal courts. The flow chart below will give you an idea of how cases may be appealed from one level of federal court to another level.

District Courts Most federal cases begin in the district courts. These courts have only original jurisdiction. They cannot take appeals from other courts. They are

the only federal courts that use juries. The first district courts were set up by the First Congress in 1789.

There is at least one district court in each state and one in the District of Columbia. Some states have as many as four. Altogether there are almost one hundred district courts. A district court may have only one judge, or it may have as many as twenty-seven judges.

About one-third of the cases handled by district courts are criminal cases. They involve trials of persons who are accused of breaking a federal law, such as the law against kidnaping. The other two-thirds are civil cases. For example, a business might start a lawsuit in district court to get back money owed by someone who is living in another state.

Most federal cases begin and end in district court. The loser in the case usually does not file an appeal. One reason is the expense. It can cost a good deal of money to carry an appeal to one or more higher courts. In one case out of twenty, however, an appeal is filed.

United States Courts of Appeals Most appeals from district courts go to the United States Courts of Appeals. Appeals from decisions of federal regulatory agencies go there too. Congress set up this level

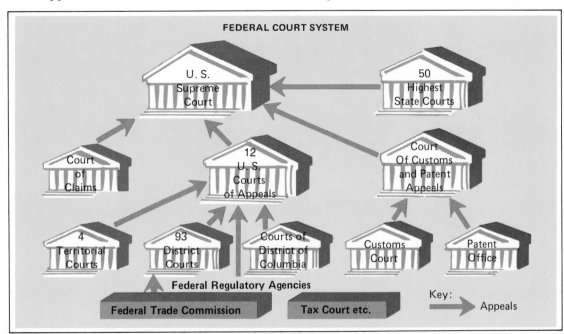

of court in 1891 to take some of the workload from the Supreme Court. Up to that time, appeals from district courts went directly to the Supreme Court.

The nation is divided into eleven regions, or **circuits.** Each region has its own Court of Appeals. There is also a Twelfth Court of Appeals, which handles only cases from the District of Columbia. Arizona is part of the Ninth Circuit. A case appealed from a district court in Phoenix would be heard by the Ninth Court of Appeals.

Courts of Appeals have only appellate jurisdiction. They do not hear new evidence. They do not hold trials. They do not use juries. Most cases are decided by a panel of three judges. The job of these judges is to review the record of the case and hear arguments by the lawyers. The judges ask themselves: Did the district court or regulatory agency act properly? Did it apply the law correctly?

If the Court of Appeals finds that the district court made a mistake, it will send the case back to the lower court for a new trial. Often, however, the Court of Appeals finds no mistakes. In that event, it **affirms,** or upholds, the original decision. That usually ends the case. But a losing party has one more chance. It may ask the Supreme Court to review the decision. But before examining the Supreme Court of the United States, let's look at some of the special federal courts.

Court of Claims If you were a federal employee who believed that you had some back pay coming to you, you might file a case in the Court of Claims. This court hears suits by people who claim that the federal government owes them money. Sometimes a company takes the federal government to court over a contract. Perhaps a company claims that the government did not pay for materials it ordered. The Court of Claims would hear that suit too. The Court has a chief judge and six other judges. After the court approves a

claim, Congress must then vote to approve the payment.

Customs Court Let's say that you visit a foreign country and buy a camera and some equipment for a darkroom. You must pay a duty to bring it into the United States. A customs official will tell you what the duty is, based on the value of the goods. If you think that the duty is too high, you may file a suit in Customs Court. The Court is based in New York City, but it may also meet in other port cities. It has a chief judge and eight other judges.

Court of Customs and Patent Appeals If you appeal a decision of the Customs Court, it will go to the Court of Customs and Patent Appeals. Another kind of case might also go there. Let's say that you invent a fuel-saving engine. The Patent Office, however, will not give you a patent. You could appeal that decision in the Court too. The Court of Customs and Patent Appeals is in Washington, D.C. It has a chief judge and five other judges.

Territorial Courts Congress has set up territorial courts in Guam, the Virgin Islands, the Panama Canal Zone, and Puerto Rico. These are like district courts—they handle cases that would usually go to state courts. The decisions of territorial courts may be appealed to the United States Courts of Appeals.

Courts of the District of Columbia Because the District of Columbia is not a part of any state, it has federal courts to handle local criminal cases and lawsuits. A superior court holds trials. A Court of Appeals hears appeals. There is also a district court for the District of Columbia.

Tax Court A taxpayer may receive a notice from the Internal Revenue Service saying that more income tax is due. If the person thinks the IRS made a mistake, an appeal can be made to the Tax Court. This is an independent agency that is part of the executive branch, but it works just like a court. It has nineteen judges and can hear

The armed services police themselves. A member of any branch accused of breaking military law can be tried at a court-martial. In this picture, a military officer (middle) is led into the courtroom to face trial.

cases anywhere in the country. If the Tax Court decides against the taxpayer, an appeal can be made to a Court of Appeals.

Court of Military Appeals People in the armed services are under military law. If they are accused of breaking military law, they may be tried at a **court-martial.** This is a trial that is run by military officers. In serious cases, the decision at a court-martial may be appealed to the Court of Military Appeals. The Court is made up of three civilian judges and is located in Washington, D.C. Its decisions are final. They may not be appealed.

Officials of Federal Courts

The federal courts employ some five hundred and twenty-five full-time judges and more that one hundred part-time judges. While judges in state courts are often elected by the voters, *no* federal judge is elected. All federal judges are named by the President. They must be approved by a majority vote of the Senate. Most federal judges do not serve a set term. Once appointed, they stay in office for life, or until they resign or retire. They can be removed by impeachment only if they commit a serious offense.

The salary of federal judges is about equal to that of members of Congress. Judges on the United States Courts of Appeals receive about $65,000 a year. Judges on the district courts receive $61,500. Congress may not lower the salary during a judge's time in office.

Judges are aided in their duties by many helpers. For example, a court may have clerks, court reporters, and stenographers. Also, each district court has a marshal, who is named by the President with the Senate's consent. The marshal's job is to make arrests, deliver court papers, and see that court decisions are carried out.

Until recently, each district court also had a United States Commissioner to hear evidence in a federal criminal case and decide whether the case should go to a grand jury. New officials, called United States Magistrates, are taking the place of the Commissioners. They have the same duties, plus an additional one: they may try minor criminal cases themselves.

Some members of the executive branch work closely with the federal courts. For example, the President names a United States Attorney to each district court. The Attorney works for the Justice Department and serves as the government's lawyer. In a

The statue of Justice outside the Supreme Court Building in Washington,
D.C., symbolizes the law as enforced by the nation's highest court.

criminal case, the United States Attorney—
or an assistant—presents evidence in court.
The Attorney tries to prove that an accused
person is guilty. Unlike a judge, who is supposed to take no side, a United States Attorney takes an active part on one side of a
case.

REVIEW

1. If a federal law conflicts with a state law,
which law must be followed?
2. Which of the following cases would be
held in state courts and which would be
held in federal courts?
   a. a trial for the crime of kidnaping
   b. a trial about a ticket for speeding
   c. a lawsuit between two state governments
   d. an appeal of a conviction for speeding
3. Which level of federal court is the only
one to use juries?

4. Name two levels of federal courts that
have appellate jurisdiction.
5. Do you think it is a good idea that federal judges are appointed, rather than
elected? Why or why not?

Words to Know

Justice —— member of the United States
Supreme Court
opinion —— a statement issued by a court
to explain the reasoning behind a decision
majority opinion —— opinion issued by
the majority in a Court case; has legal force
dissenting opinion —— opinion issued by
one or more Justices to explain why they
disagree with the majority opinion

The Supreme Court

The United States Supreme Court is the highest court in the country. Everything about it suggests the majesty of the law—from the marble temple where it meets to the ceremony that calls it to order. The black-robed Justices treat each case with a seriousness that is appropriate for the Court's importance. The Supreme Court is the court of last appeal. Its decisions cannot be appealed.

The Supreme Court is at the top of the federal court system. It hears appeals from other federal courts. It may also hear appeals from state courts when a federal question is involved. In addition, a few cases may start in the Supreme Court. We will read about them shortly.

When the Court Meets

The Supreme Court begins its session each year on the first Monday in October. It meets throughout the fall, winter, and spring. It adjourns toward the end of June.

The Justices divide their time among three activities. First, they hold public sessions. This is when they hear lawyers present their cases. Second, they "do homework." They read the papers that the lawyers have submitted. They do research. They handle other business. And third, the Justices hold private meetings at which they discuss and vote on cases. These meetings are held on Fridays. Court decisions usually are announced on Mondays and Tuesdays.

The public sessions gleam with pomp and ceremony. They are held in a high-ceilinged room on the main floor of the Supreme Court building in Washington, D.C. At 10 A.M., a court crier calls out: "Oyez! Oyez! Oyez!" This ancient English term means "Hear ye!" The Justices take their seats. Lawyers, many of them in striped pants and formal coats, then present their cases. The Justices may break in from time to time to ask questions. But the Justices reach their decisions behind closed doors. The public is not allowed to hear their discussion.

The Justices

Members of the Supreme Court are called **justices,** not judges. There are nine of them—eight Associate Justices and a Chief Justice of the United States, who presides.

Congress can change the number of Justices, but it has not done so since 1869. In the 1930s, President Franklin D. Roosevelt wanted to increase the number of Justices. He was angry because the Court had ruled some laws unconstitutional. Congress refused to go along with the President. Crit-

Franklin D. Roosevelt angered Congress by trying to increase the number of Supreme Court Justices.

ics said that Roosevelt was trying to "pack" the Court with Justices who would support him.

Supreme Court Justices, like other federal judges, are appointed by the President. The appointments must be approved by a majority vote of the Senate. The Justices serve for life. The only way they can be removed from office is through the process of impeachment.

There is no minimum-age requirement for Justices, and a Justice need not have served as a judge. In fact, a Justice does not even have to be a lawyer (so far, though, all the Justices have been lawyers). The salary of the Chief Justice is $84,675 a year. The Associate Justices receive a salary of $81,288 a year.

Duties of the Court

The Supreme Court hears the most important cases in the nation. Like most other federal courts, the Supreme Court has no power to start a case itself. It must wait until someone files a lawsuit or brings a case before it for review.

The Constitution lists two kinds of cases in which the Supreme Court has original jurisdiction. They are: (1) cases that involve ambassadors and other high officials of the foreign service and (2) cases in which a state government is one of the parties. All other cases reach the Supreme Court from some lower state or federal court.

The Supreme Court must, by law, hear certain cases on appeal—for example, when a lower court has struck down a federal or state law as unconstitutional. But the Court can pick and choose among other cases. The Court accepts only those cases that raise a federal or constitutional question of major public interest.

Each year, about five thousand cases are placed on the Supreme Court's schedule. Only about two hundred of those cases receive the Court's full attention.

How the Justices Reach Decisions

The Supreme Court makes its decisions by majority vote. All the Justices do not have to agree. To reach a decision, the Court must have at least six Justices present. In the event of a tie vote, the decision of the lower court remains in effect. Ties are rare, however. In most cases, there is a majority vote.

Why the Court reaches a decision is just as important as *what* the Court decides. For this reason, the Justices write an explanation of the reasoning that led to the decision. This explanation is called the Court's **opinion.** Lower-court judges read Supreme Court opinions carefully. These opinions are used to help reach decisions in other cases.

The Court often issues more than one opinion. Let's say, for example, that the Court is split 5 to 4 on an important case. One of the Justices will write the **majority opinion.** This gives the reasoning of the majority. This opinion may be used by lower courts as a precedent. In addition, one or more of the Justices who voted with the minority may write a **dissenting opinion.** It will tell why they disagree with the majority's decision. A dissenting opinion has no binding force. It is the reasoning of the losing side in the case. The reasoning in such an opinion may still have an influence, however. The Supreme Court has been known to change its mind. It may one day accept the reasoning that it rejects today.

━━━━━━━━━ REVIEW ━━━━━━━━━

1. What are three main activities of Supreme Court Justices?

2. List the kinds of cases in which the Supreme Court has original jurisdiction.

3. In what kind of case does the Supreme Court have appellate jurisdiction? What courts would such cases start in?

4. Do all the Justices of the Supreme Court have to agree on a decision? Or can a decision be made by majority vote?

5. Do you think that a Justice who disagrees with the majority should write a dissenting opinion? Why or why not?

How the United States Works

Court Reporter

Judges and lawyers are not the only people who work in the courtroom. A record must be kept of everything that goes on in court—whether it is a simple trial or a complicated lawsuit. This is the job of the court reporter.

Court reporters sit somewhere near the witness stand. Most of them use a Stenotype machine. A Stenotype machine looks something like a typewriter, but the keys make no noise. Clanging keys would disturb the court and make it harder for the reporter to hear. As you can imagine, court reporters cannot jump up and say: "Hold it a minute! I didn't catch that." Nothing must get in the way of their hearing.

The Stenotype machine differs from a typewriter in another important way: the keys print word sounds instead of single letters. This makes it possible for a trained person to work very fast. Speed is very important for court reporters. Many jobs call for taking notes at the rate of 225 words a minute. The Stenotype notes cannot be read by many people though. So when the court hearings are over, the reporter has to go over the notes and type them on a standard typewriter. This copy then becomes the official court record.

Most courts of law will only hire certified shorthand reporters. These people take a 2-year course in shorthand reporting after finishing high school. Then, to be certified, they pass a test of their speed and accuracy. The test is given by the National Shorthand Reporters Association. Once a person has passed this test, there are plenty of good jobs available. Court reporters start at over $12,000 a year.

Reading About . . .

The Life of a Supreme Court Justice ————————————————

In this chapter, you have learned some of the powers and duties of a Supreme Court Justice. What is a Justice's life like, though? Part of the answer can be found in the reading that follows.

As you read, ask yourself the following questions:

● Does Justice Powell seem to enjoy being a member of the Court?
● What was one thing that Justice Powell did not feel he could do after being appointed to the Supreme Court? Why did he feel that way?

Lewis F. Powell, Associate Justice of the Supreme Court, would like to be able to have lunch or dinner with some of his old friends. He would like to talk politics. He would even like to have time to read a "trashy" book or at least, as he says, "I still would like to be able to just read a book, whether it is trash or not."

There are trade-offs for being a Supreme Court Justice, however. Lewis Powell says that he has "come to feel very deeply about the Court." He says: "It does something to you after you've been there for a while. All of the negatives are outweighed by the opportunity to be at the Court."

He likes his fellow Justices and the rest of the Court personnel—and their spirit. He likes the Court's traditions and his own role in the Court. But the job has changed his life—keeping him apart from friends he has known for years and making demands on his time and his family that he had not had or expected to have before he took his seat on the high Court.

In Washington, Justice Powell almost never eats lunch or dines with any of his old friends from the legal profession. This is an enormous loss to his personal life, for he is 68 years old now and was in private practice for almost 40 years. As with a lot of his fellow lawyers, his friends tend to be other lawyers.

He was invited by a former client to see the horse Secretariat race. He wanted to go, because he knew the horse's owner. But the former client was going to fly him to the race in his company plane, so Justice turned the invitation down. "I thought about it," he said, "and decided someone would probably write a column saying that Justice Powell was 'Riding Around in a Company Plane.'"

Joining the Court has also affected Justice Powell's family. Justice Powell and his wife had been only "moderately social" over the years, but his social life is far more limited now than it ever was.

Justice Powell said that he spends six days a week at Court when the Court is in session. On Saturday, he goes in to work an hour or so later than usual, often carrying a sandwich. On Sundays, he does some work at home.

Once a week or so, he goes out to lunch with a clerk, or a former clerk, or a fellow Justice. His other lunches during the week are mostly at Court.

Justices have work to do even when they are in recess, because they continue to receive petitions asking for review of cases at a rate of 100 a week. "Reading briefs and Supreme Court opinions is not unpleasant to me," he said, adding that he would remain on the Court as long as he felt "fit."

Fact Review

1. What two sources of law can a judge in the United States refer to?
2. Which of the following courts would use a jury?
   a. district court
   b. Court of Appeals
   c. Tax Court
   d. United States Supreme Court
3. Which courts in (1) to (5) would handle cases in *a* to *e*?
   a. appeal of a district-court decision
   b. dispute over a tax refund
   c. appeal of a Customs Court decision
   d. appeal of a Court of Appeals decision
   e. appeal of a soldier's conviction in a court-martial
      (1) Court of Customs and Patent Appeals
      (2) Court of Military Appeals
      (3) United States Court of Appeals
      (4) Tax Court
      (5) United States Supreme Court

Developing Your Vocabulary

1. What is the difference between the words in the following pairs?
   a. plaintiff and defendant
   b. verdict and opinion
   c. common law and statutory law
   d. petit jury and grand jury
   e. original jurisdiction and appellate jurisdiction

Developing Your Reading Skills

Read the following paragraph and then answer the questions that follow:

The federal Constitution set up a system of checks and balances. The legislative branch makes federal laws. The executive branch carries out the laws. The judicial branch explains the meaning of laws. The judicial branch does this in order to make sure that federal laws do not conflict with any parts of the Constitution.

1. Which one of the following do you think is the main idea of the paragraph above?
   a. The federal Constitution gives Congress the power to make laws.
   b. The executive branch enforces laws.
   c. The federal Constitution places some restrictions on each branch of the government that it set up.
   d. The judicial branch explains the meaning of laws.
2. Tell why you selected either *a, b, c,* or *d* in question 1.

Developing Your Writing Skills— Forming and Supporting an Opinion

In this chapter, you have examined the powers of the judicial branch. You also learned that the judicial branch, along with the legislative and executive branches, is part of a system of checks and balances. Now consider:

Forming an opinion
1. Do you think that any one of the three branches of the federal government should not have any checks and balances placed upon it?

Supporting an opinion
2. After thinking it over, write a paragraph that answers the question above. Give arguments to support your position.

YOUR GOVERNMENT & ITS HISTORY

The Daniel Shays Rebellion

In this chapter, you have learned about the federal court system. You have even learned some of its history. Now you will get another view of the court system. It is a view of a time when courts were not peaceful, orderly, and quiet. The time was the late 1700s. A rebellion took place against court actions. This rebellion occurred while the United States was still governed by the Articles of Confederation. It was led by a man named Daniel Shays. An account of this rebellion follows:

After the American Revolution, the established farmers in the older sections of the country did well. As long as British, French, and American forces needed supplies, the farmers made money. By 1785, however, the American army had been broken up and the foreign troops had left. The farmers' market shrank. Wartime moneylenders began to press farmers for the interest on their loans. To make matters worse, the state legislatures began to raise taxes. They also demanded that they be paid in cash. This was so that the states could pay back the interest on their Revolutionary War debts.

The farmers and small business owners were surprised by the actions of the legislatures. They cried out for relief. As they had done in colonial times, they demanded that the states issue paper money. This money would serve for the payment of all debts, public and private. They also demanded that the states pass laws that would save their farms from being taken over by the moneylenders. This would happen if the farmers could not pay their debts.

Captain Daniel Shays was an American officer during the Revolution. Shays became a spokesperson for the angry farmers, especially those in the western counties in Massachusetts. In some counties, the people were too poor to afford to send delegates to the state legislature in far-off Boston. The farmers, most of them veterans of the Revolution, were unable to have any voice in the state government. And the people of great wealth (usually merchants or shippers in Boston and other port towns) backed laws forcing farmers to pay what they felt was more than their share of taxes.

To make their protests heard, the farmers organized county conventions. People from neighboring towns gathered at the county seats. They expressed their political feelings in petitions, which they sent to the legislature. In July 1786, the legislature adjourned, ignoring the petitions of the farmers. Soon, more and more county conventions were called—this time, in all parts of the state.

Members of the conventions were warned by ex-officers like Shays. They were told not to form mobs and unlawful assemblies. A lawful way to protest must be agreed upon. But anger soon won out over these cautions. Hotheads took advantage of the situation to organize protestors.

The rioting mobs focused on courts, where many cases about the farms were scheduled. Mobs had already succeeded in forcing the closing of many of these courts. Other courts were also attacked in an effort to prevent the trials of rioters.

Finally, the protestors could delay action no longer. Leaders had to put themselves at the head of the mobs to keep them from greater violence. Thus, Shays became the leader of the movement. Soon, the militia were called out to put down "Shays' Rebellion," as it was called.

Fighting between Shays' forces and the militia continued from mid-January until the end of February 1788. At this time, the rebellion was finally crushed. Shays fled to Vermont. Later in 1788, Shays was offered clemency, or official forgiveness for his crimes, by the state. Most of the other rebels were also pardoned.

1. What was the cause of Shays' Rebellion?
2. Who was Daniel Shays? What part did he play in the rebellion?
3. What did the courts have to do with Shays' Rebellion?
4. What was the outcome of the rebellion?
5. Do you think there could ever be a good reason for a group to use force to close a court or stop its sessions? Explain. What do you think could result if just any group chose to close a court?

SKILLS Developing your basic civic education skills

Making Judgments

(determining sequence and cause-and-effect)

Making a fair judgment is usually a difficult task. Some examples of judgment making, from stories researched by Margaret Stimmann Branson, follow.

Story 1

There is a folktale that has been told for hundreds of years throughout central Europe. It is about a young girl so wise she is able to solve problems that her elders could not—and achieve justice in the bargain. In the German and Russian versions of the story, the girl has no name. She is known simply as Daughter. In this retelling of the story, she is known as Tatianna.

Once there was a man whom everyone thought was very poor. He had neither horse nor wagon. His clothes were ragged. His meals were small. He lived in an old, cold cabin on the edge of the forest. But the man did not consider himself poor. He thought of himself as rich, because he had a daughter, Tatianna.

Although Tatianna was just 9 years old, she was very wise. . . . In time, a judge heard of her. He sent word to the father: "Bring your daughter with you to my court tomorrow."

The next day Tatianna and her father went to the village court. The judge motioned for them to be seated. They listened while two brothers spoke of a quarrel. Their father had died. In his will, he had said that his farm should be divided between his sons. The soil on one part of the farm was deep and black. Rich crops grew on it. The soil on the other part was thin and rocky. Nothing would grow on it. The brothers could not agree on how to share the farm. Even when the judge tried to divide the land between them, they were dissatisfied. So, at last, the judge called Tatianna before him.

"I hear you are a wise girl," he said. "Tell me, what would you do, if you were judge?"

Tatianna hesitated for a moment. Then she said, "Let one brother divide the farm. Let the other brother take first choice."

It was done. The brothers went away in peace.

Story 2

It is interesting that a similar case actually happened in the early nineteenth century. The person making the judgment gave a decision similar to Tatianna's. For it, he was praised by the peoples of southern Africa. That person was the feared and fearless warrior-statesman Shaka Zulu.

Shaka Zulu is not as well known to the general public in the Western world as he deserves to be. By 1810, Shaka had built up one of the most highly skilled and well-trained armies the world has known. With it, he conquered a great empire—and he did it all in the space of 12 years.

One of the ways in which Shaka Zulu [*Zulu* means heaven] kept the peace among the different kinds of people in his empire was by taking part in the settlement of disputes. He held court at the new Bulawayo, his capital, in what is now Zimbabwe.

At the new Bulawayo, Shaka's court met under a huge, spreading fig tree in the 5-acre yard in front of his Great Council hut. Every morning, shortly after sunrise and before breakfast, Shaka served as judge. He was colorfully dressed in his chief's clothes, his *assegai* in hand. [An *assegai* is a shield combined with a heavy, wide blade.]

One day, two chief herdsmen came before him to discuss their disagreements.

Each herdsman accused the other of moving in on his grazing lands. Because of this, fights had occurred among their herdsmen. Shaka told each of them to show the boundaries of his land. He found that there was indeed a considerable overlap in the rival herdsmen's claims. He asked the first one to swear on oath that justice would be done if his boundary were granted. The herdman did so. Then, turning to the other chief herdsman, Shaka obtained a similar oath.

"Good!" said Shaka. "You will now, each of you, with all your herdsmen and cattle, exchange lands. On your own showing, that will leave you both with considerable space, and if any member of either party moves in on this, he will eat earth. I have spoken."

"Ruler! Your decision will be done" said the two men. Thus, the herdsmen, by exchanging lands, exchanged each other's lies.

1. Rearrange the following sequence of events in the story about Tatianna in the correct chronological order.

a. The brothers went away in peace.

b. The judge sends for Tatianna.

c. Tatianna listens to the two brothers quarrel.

d. Tatianna decides to let one brother divide the farm and to let the other brother take first choice.

e. The judge asks Tatianna to make a decision in the case.

2. Which one of the following from the story about Tatianna's decision could be called a cause?

a. why Tatianna's father had little money

b. the decision made by Tatianna about the quarrel between the two brothers

c. why Tatianna had to be brought to the court

3. Which one of the following from the story about Tatianna's decision could be called an effect?

a. the age of the folktale about Tatianna

b. the decision made by Tatianna about the quarrel between the two brothers

c. why Tatianna had to be brought to the court

4. Rearrange the following sequence of events in the story about Shaka Zulu in the correct chronological order.

    a. The herdsmen vow to uphold Shaka Zulu's decision.

    b. Shaka Zulu has each herdsman swear on an oath that justice will be done.

    c. Two chief herdsmen appear before Shaka Zulu.

    d. Shaka Zulu has each herdsman exchange sections of land.

    e. The two chief herdsmen accuse each other.

5. Which one of the following from the story about Shaka Zulu's decision could be called a cause?

    a. why Shaka Zulu had to make a decision about the disagreement between the two herdsmen

    b. the decision made by Shaka Zulu in regard to the disagreement between the two herdsmen

    c. the meaning of the word *zulu*

6. Which one of the following from the story about Shaka Zulu's decision could be called an effect?

    a. why Shaka Zulu had to make a decision about the disagreement between the two herdsmen

    b. the decision made by Shaka Zulu in regard to the dispute between the two herdsmen

    c. the name of one of Shaka Zulu's biographers

7. What do you think makes a judgment fair?

Problems Faced by Female Judges
(distinguishing fact from opinion)

In 1977, there were only 5 female federal judges in the United States. Two years later, 28 of the nation's 605 federal judges were women. By August of 1981, there were 44 female federal judges out of a total of 667 federal judges.

Some of the problems faced by female judges were discussed in a newspaper article. The article concerned the creation of the National Association of Women Judges in 1979. At the first meeting, many of the judges pointed out the low number of women in the judiciary. This low number was especially telling since there were more than 46,000 women lawyers in the United States. The account of that meeting noted the following.

    The reason for the low number, according to Susan Ness, a lawyer with the National Women's Political Caucus, is that women are underrepresented on judicial screening panels. . . .

    "The association is needed since women judges are experiencing special problems because there are so few of them, and they are meeting opposition from the male judges," said Joan Dempsey Klein, a California Courts of Appeal judge who was elected president.

    Several female judges at the conference objected to what they considered the control by men of the fourteen-member American Bar Association Committee on the Federal Judiciary. This committee advises the White House on nominees and selection standards.

    The stress, they said, is on experience as a trial lawyer.

    "In 5 years, I do not think trial experience will be the problem it is today because an increasing number of women are gaining such experience," Leonard S. Janofsky, president of the American Bar Association told the group.

Margaret McKenna, deputy counsel to President Jimmy Carter, urged the members to become politically active.

"One reason that senators do not come up with women's names," she said, "is that many of them do not consider women politically workable on the local level."

Women are at a disadvantage in going after judicial posts because of heavy responsibilities at home, said Beverly B. Cook, professor of political science at the University of Wisconsin–Milwaukee.

Cook had surveyed both male and female trial judges on the state courts in 1979. She found that 38 percent of all female trial judges do all or most of their own housework. She also found that female judges feel all alone.

Of the 500 surveyed, 22 percent had never met another female judge outside their states, she said. Except for the metropolitan areas, the majority of female judges worked in courthouses where there were no other female judges.

Only a third of the women reported that they were accepted by their male co-workers, she said. And many of those surveyed felt that male judges objected to women on the bench or regarded being female as a disadvantage.

Rose Elizabeth Bird, chief justice of the California Supreme Court, told the group to expect criticism.

"Those who are breaking ground in any given area—as women and minorities so often do as they enter the judiciary—are open to particularly close inspection. They are allowed little or no room for error," said Bird.

"This inspection is not unwelcome," she said. "But it does make the complex role of a judge even more difficult and the responsibility to fulfill the oath of office all the more solemn."

Bird urged the organization to support the continuing appointment of women and minorities as judges so that "the makeup may truly show the differences of our society."

8. Which one of the following is a statement of fact?

a. There are not enough women judges in the United States.

b. In 1979, there were twenty-eight female judges in the United States.

c. Women in the United States need to be more active in politics.

9. Tell why you selected the statement you did in question 8.

10. Which of the statements in question 8 are statements of opinion?

11. Tell why you selected the statements you did in question 10.

12. Use information in the reading to write two other statements of fact about female judges.

13. Use information in the reading to write two other statements of opinion about female judges.

14. What would you recommend on the subject of appointing more women to be federal judges? Explain.

9 The Federal Courts in Action

The last chapter gave an outline of how the court system works. In this chapter, you will explore that system in greater detail. You will follow one case up to the Supreme Court to see the kinds of issues the Justices must deal with.

It is important to remember that the federal court system was not described in detail in the Constitution. The federal court system has grown through the years as cases were argued and new issues came up.

This chapter will start with a brief review of the growth in power of the Supreme Court. Then we will consider one particular case and some general problems of the courts.

I. The power of the Supreme Court
    A. Judicial review
    B. Arguments over the Court
    C. The Court can change its mind.
    D. History of the Supreme Court
    E. Checks and balances
II. A case for the courts
    A. Setting the scene
    B. Issues in the case
       1. Freedom of speech
       2. Discipline

C. The case in the courts
   1. U.S. District Court
   2. U.S. Court of Appeals
   3. U.S. Supreme Court
   4. The dissent
III. Some problems of the courts
    A. Too many cases
    B. The ability of juries
    C. The ability of judges

Words to Know

judicial review —— the right of a court to review the actions and set aside the decisions of other branches of government

unconstitutional —— in conflict with the Constitution, and therefore illegal

reverse —— overturn an earlier decision

segregated —— separated by race

interpret —— explain the meaning of a law; apply the law to a specific case

The Power of the Supreme Court

It is hard now to imagine it, but there once was a time when little attention was paid to the Supreme Court. During its first 10 years, the Supreme Court had three Chief Justices. None of them stayed long, because the job did not seem challenging.

But the fourth Chief Justice, John Marshall, made the Court stronger. He wrote some decisions that made the Court the number one referee in arguments involving federal laws and the Constitution. He made the Court a strong and important part of the federal system.

Judicial Review

Chief Justice Marshall established the Supreme Court's power of **judicial review.** This means that the Court can review the actions of other branches of the government. The Court makes sure that the other branches obey the Constitution. If a law passed by Congress violates the Constitution, the Court can set the law aside. If the President is acting illegally, the Court can order the President to stop. The Court has the final word on what the Constitution means and on what laws mean.

John Marshall, our fourth Chief Justice, established the Supreme Court's power of judicial review.

Under Chief Justice Roger B. Taney, the U.S. Supreme Court made a surprising defense of slavery.

Marshall's idea of judicial review started with the case of *Marbury v. Madison* in 1803. The case was about an act of Congress that was passed in 1789. That act had a short section stating that some court cases against federal officials might be filed directly with the Supreme Court. Marshall said that the law conflicted with the Constitution. The Chief Justice noted that the Constitution gave the Court original jurisdiction in only two kinds of cases. The Court thus declared the federal law to be **unconstitutional.** Therefore, the law could not be followed. This decision made the Supreme Court more powerful.

Marshall helped to make other important decisions during his 34 years as Chief Justice. In 1809, the Court ruled that no state legislature could set aside a federal court decision. In 1819, the Court ruled that Congress has "implied powers," as well as those listed in the Constitution. In 1821, it took upon itself the power to review decisions made by state courts. This meant that the Supreme Court was truly the highest court in the country.

Arguments over the Court

Because of its great powers, the Supreme Court has often caused arguments. Chief Justice Marshall's decisions started many arguments. The decisions pleased those who believed in a strong federal government. They displeased those who—like Thomas Jefferson—believed in states' rights and a limited federal government.

Roger B. Taney followed Marshall as Chief Justice. He served from 1836 until 1864. Taney also caused arguments. Under Taney, the Court dealt directly with the question of slavery. In the Dred Scott Case of 1857, the Court made a surprising decision in defense of slavery. First, it ruled that a black person could not be a citizen of the United States. Second, it ruled that Congress could not forbid slavery in the United States. People who opposed slavery were shocked and angry.

The Court's decision did not settle the slavery question. Only the Civil War did that. After the war, two amendments were added to the Constitution. The amendments **reversed,** or overturned, the Court's decision. In 1865, the Thirteenth Amendment put an end to slavery. In 1868, the Fourteenth Amendment said that "all persons born or naturalized in the United States . . . are citizens."

This example shows some important facts about the Supreme Court. The Court plays a major role in the federal system of checks and balances. It can strike down laws that are passed by Congress and stop practices of the executive branch. But while the Court's decisions are final, they are not permanent. They can be changed. Congress can pass a new law. An amendment can be added to the Constitution. The Court itself can change its mind.

The Court Can Change Its Mind

In 1954, the Supreme Court made another surprising decision. It ruled that states could no longer have two separate systems of schools—one for blacks and one for whites. Why was this surprising? It was surprising because the decision said the exact opposite of an earlier decision of the Supreme Court.

In the 1890s, a Louisiana law said that railroad cars must be **segregated.** This meant that there had to be cars just for whites and other cars just for blacks. This law was not unusual at the time. Many states in the South had passed such laws. The laws destroyed any hope that freed slaves might become truly equal.

In 1896, the case of *Plessy v. Ferguson* came before the Supreme Court. It came from a challenge to the Louisiana law. Homer Plessy was seven-eighths white and one-eighth black. He had been thrown out of a "white" railroad car. He argued that the Louisiana law broke the Fourteenth Amendment, which says that no state can deny any person the equal protection of the laws. The Supreme Court disagreed with Plessy. It upheld the Louisiana law. The Court declared that public places such as trains and schools could be segregated. All a state had to do was provide "separate but equal" places for whites and blacks.

For 58 years, this opinion of the Supreme Court was the law of the country. The Justices did not all agree on the decision, however. A dissenting opinion was written by Associate Justice John Marshall Harlan. Harlan made some points that would be backed up by later Courts. He said that the 1896 decision would be as harmful as the Dred Scott case. Harlan felt that the Court's decision set up a ruling class—and that the Constitution should not allow that. He said, "Our Constitution is colorblind . . . ."

In many states for the next 58 years, blacks rode in separate railroad cars. They went to separate schools. They ate in separate restaurants. Few people would have said that these places were "equal." Indeed, some states did not try to make them equal. Some states did not even have 4-year high schools for blacks. Still, courts upheld the "separate-but-equal" rule.

By the 1950s, however, conditions were changing. Many states had acted to end segregated places. The federal government had changed some of its practices. For example, the United States Army had stopped putting black soldiers into separate fighting units. The world, too, was changing. Nations in Africa and Asia were gaining independence. Allowing segregated places to exist in this country was becoming

The people pictured here await the decision of the *Brown v. Board of Education of Topeka* case in 1954. In a decision that altered the course of United States history, the court ruled that separate places for different races did not display equality. This ruling started the movement toward desegregation.

an embarrassment. It endangered the role of the United States as a world leader.

The Supreme Court was aware of these changes. In 1954, it reversed itself. In the case *Brown v. Board of Education of Topeka,* the Court ruled that separate places could never be equal. This time, it based its decision on the Fourteenth Amendment. Segregated schools, said the Court, do not permit equal protection of the laws. Such schools must be desegregated.

The nation's history has been changed a great deal by the Court's decision in 1954. An important change had been made. But the painful process of gaining true equality for blacks is still going on.

History of the Supreme Court

The power of the Supreme Court can change over time. Sometimes the Court has more power. Sometimes it has less. The amount of power the Court has often depends on the Chief Justice. For this reason, people often refer to the Supreme Court by the name of its Chief Justice. For example, there was the "Marshall Court" from 1801 to 1835. It was followed by the "Taney Court" from 1836 to 1864.

The Supreme Court can **interpret,** or read, the Constitution very strictly. In such cases, the Court will not allow any branch of government to act unless that action is described clearly in the Constitution. The Taney Court often gave strict interpretations of the Constitution.

The Supreme Court can also permit freer readings of the Constitution. At such times, the Court will grant powers or permit actions that it feels are implied, or hinted at, in the Constitution. The Court under Chief Justice John Marshall often gave these freer readings.

When a Court gives strict readings, the Court's power is decreased. When a Court gives freer readings, its power is increased. In the country's history, the Supreme Court has shifted back and forth from strict to freer readings.

For a long time after the Taney Court, strict readings were common. This was especially true between 1888 and 1937. The Court repeatedly upheld the rights of property owners. It ruled income taxes unconstitutional. It ruled laws against child labor unconstitutional. It struck down many other federal and state laws that tried to control businesses.

With the coming of the court of Chief Justice Earl Warren, the Constitution was given a more liberal reading. As a result, the court defended the rights of people accused of crimes. Police officers—such as the one in this picture—are now obliged to read to suspects a person's rights before booking them.

After the 1930s, a change started. The Court began to give freer readings. Now it upheld laws to control businesses. From 1953 to 1969, the Chief Justice was Earl Warren. The Warren Court became known for its free, or liberal, readings of the Constitution. The Warren Court made the 1954 decision against segregated schools. It defended the rights of people accused of crimes. It forced states to make congressional districts equal in population. Such decisions pleased many people.

But the decisions angered many others. They felt that the Warren Court was too liberal in its readings. They said that the Court did more than just interpret the law. They said the Warren Court was taking on the job of Congress and writing its own laws.

In 1969, Earl Warren resigned. President Richard Nixon named Warren E. Burger as Chief Justice. Burger seemed to favor stricter readings of the law than Warren did. Under Burger, the Court began to move away from some of the decisions made during the Warren years. The Court seemed less eager to defend the rights of

people accused of crimes. It seemed more likely to uphold the actions of law officers. Again, its decisions angered many people.

Checks and Balances

The Supreme Court causes arguments because it is powerful. All three branches of the federal government—the President, Congress, and the Supreme Court—sometimes do things that make some people mad. This is natural. "You can't please all of the people all of the time," as President Lincoln once said.

Remember, however, that anything the Supreme Court does can be changed if enough people want it changed. People can urge Congress to write a new law. People can work for the adoption of a constitutional amendment. People can work to elect a President who will appoint Supreme Court Justices with different views.

The Supreme Court does not work in isolation. Its members pay attention to public opinion. And in our democracy, no branch of government has the final word. The people do.

1. What is the power of judicial review?
2. Under what Chief Justice did the Supreme Court first become a powerful part of the federal government?
3. Name a Supreme Court decision that has been reversed by a constitutional amendment.
4. Name a Supreme Court decision that has been reversed by the Court itself.
5. Do you think it is possible for Supreme Court Justices to keep their feelings from affecting their decisions? Why or why not?

Words to Know

symbolic speech —— an action that uses a sign or symbol, rather than actual words, to make a point

damages —— payment of money ordered by a court to make up for a wrong

The time has come to look more closely at the Supreme Court doing its job. We will follow one case on its way through the federal court system. To understand the case and why it was important, some background facts are needed.

A Case for the Courts

Setting the Scene

It was the holiday season—Hanukkah, Christmas. The year was 1965. Carols were being played on radios, and cards said "Peace on Earth." But it was not a peaceful time. During 1965, a quiet, lingering war in Vietnam had burst into widespread violence. In February, President Lyndon Johnson had sent United States bombers into action. He also sent United States ground troops to that far-off country. By the Christmas season, there were nearly 185,000 United States troops in Vietnam.

Where is Vietnam? That is what many people in the United States were wondering early in 1965. By the Christmas season, they knew. Vietnam was a divided nation in Southeast Asia. One-half of the country, North Vietnam, had a Communist government. The other half, South Vietnam, had a government that was pro-United States. Rebels in South Vietnam were fighting against their own government. They had support—troops and weapons—from North Vietnam.

People in the United States were sharply divided over the United States' part in the war. A majority in Congress supported President Johnson. He said that the war would keep Communists from taking over a small, weak country. In Johnson's view, North Vietnam had started the fighting by sending troops into South Vietnam. Others strongly disagreed. They saw the war as a civil war in South Vietnam. In their opinion, the United States had no business there. It had stepped into a "family dispute."

Arguments over the war were bitter by late in 1965. Later, they would become even more bitter, as half a million United States troops were sent to fight in South Vietnam. The United States finally withdrew its troops. In 1975, the government of South Vietnam collapsed. The two Vietnams were reunited, under a Communist government.

In Des Moines, Iowa, people knew a lot more about the Vietnam war by December 1965 than they had known the year before. Some young men from Des Moines had been drafted into the armed forces to help fight the war. Others had volunteered.

The people against the war hoped that Christmas time could be a time of peace. A United States senator had called for a stop in the fighting. The idea was to get peace

Dissent in the United States over its involvement in Vietnam led to massive antiwar demonstrations, such as the one in this picture.

talks going. Maybe the war could be settled that way, some people in Des Moines who were against the war thought. To show their concern, they planned to wear black armbands—2-inch strips of black cloth wrapped around their arms. The armbands would show that they were mourning those who were dying in the war. They wanted to show support for the peace talks. The people agreed to wear the armbands until New Year's Day.

Some of those who wanted to wear armbands were students in the Des Moines Public Schools. They wanted to wear the armbands to school. The school board met on December 14—two days before the arm-

bands were to be put on. The board announced that no one could come to school wearing an armband. The black armbands might disturb classes. They might distract students from their studies.

A handful of students disobeyed the school board and wore armbands. Five of the city's 18,000 students in the public schools were suspended for wearing armbands. Three of them—John F. Tinker, 15, his sister Mary Beth Tinker, 13, and Christopher Eckhardt, 16—filed a suit in the U.S. District Court. They asked the Court to keep school officials from disciplining them. Before the case was settled, it would go all the way to the U.S. Supreme Court.

Issues in the Case

What were the issues in the case? To the students, it was a question of freedom of speech. To the school authorities, it was a question of discipline, order, and safety.

Freedom of Speech The students argued that the First Amendment to the Constitution protected them. That amendment says: "Congress shall make no law . . . abridging (diminishing) the freedom of speech." State and local governments have to obey the same rule. The school board is part of government. Therefore, the school must respect students' rights to free speech.

In the words of one student: "We did not believe . . . that rights are provided only for adults, just as the colonists did not believe that . . . wealthy landowners were the only Americans with rights. We thought that everyone in America, including students, had certain rights, and that no one . . . could take them away."

Is wearing an armband the same thing as "speech"? The students thought so. They said that the armbands let people know how they felt about the Vietnam War. It was **symbolic speech**—making a point by using a sign or symbol.

The students pointed out that school authorities did not stop students from wearing political buttons during election campaigns. Some students had even worn the swastika—a symbol of the Nazi movement. Such buttons clearly showed political opinions. If they were permitted, why not black armbands?

School officials rejected the students' argument. In the first place, they said, wearing armbands is not "speech." In the second place, students are still children. They do not have all the rights that adults have. They must wait until they are adults before they have all the rights in the Constitution.

Discipline To the school board, the issue was not freedom of speech, but freedom to learn. They had to keep order in class so that students could get an education. To keep order, there must be rules. There must be discipline. School officials had made many rules about classroom behavior. That was their job. It was not up to the students to make their own rules. And

Freedom of speech was the issue when Mary Beth and John Tinker were suspended from school in 1965 for wearing black armbands signifying the desire for peace in Vietnam. Suit was filed in the U.S. District Court asking the court to stop school officials from disciplining them for exercising their rights.

During the time of the Vietnam war, school classes—such as the one in this picture—discussed the pros and cons of United States' involvement in Southeast Asia. Today, social studies or civics classes discuss other issues equally as important with just as much vigor.

it was not up to the courts to interfere in the school's business.

To the school officials, wearing armbands was a political demonstration. Such a demonstration could disturb classrooms. After all, the Vietnam War was causing many arguments. Some students firmly supported the United States' part in the war. What if they started to wear armbands of a different color? What if the school became split into two hostile sides?

School officials pointed out that one former high school student from Des Moines had been killed in the war. Some of his friends were still in school. Would the armbands make them angry? Would there be fights?

Questions such as these had to be studied carefully. Students go to school to learn. Only by keeping order can the schools be sure that all students will be able to learn.

Part of education is learning to form political ideas. School officials said that there was a proper time and place for this. Public issues were discussed in social studies or civics classes. If a student wanted to speak on public issues, such classes were the proper place.

The students argued that citizenship is a central part of education. It is good citizenship to take a stand on important matters. The schools should encourage political actions. Finally, the wearing of armbands had not disturbed classes. No fights had broken out. Classes had gone on without interruption. The rule against armbands had no useful purpose.

The Case in the Courts

U.S. District Court The first court to hear the case of *Tinker v. The Des Moines Independent Community School District* was the U.S. District Court in Des Moines. The Court agreed with the students on one point: wearing an armband to make one's views known *is* an exercise of free speech. But the court agreed with the school officials on a second point: the schools had a right to make reasonable rules to prevent disturbances. Thus, the Court ruled against the students.

Since at least the year 1800, it has been traditional for Justices to wear black robes while in court. John Jay, the first Chief Justice of the Supreme Court, lent a colorful air to early sessions of the Court by wearing robes that were trimmed in scarlet and gold.

Unlike British judges, the Justices of the Supreme Court do not wear wigs. When the first session of the Court met in 1790, Justice William Cushing arrived wearing the white wig that he had worn as a Massachusetts judge. It is said that the laughter of small boys as they followed him through the streets convinced judges to accept the views of Thomas Jefferson: "For heaven's sake," he urged, "discard the monstrous wig which makes English judges look like rats peeping through bunches of oakum [a fiber used to stuff the seams of ships]."

U.S. Court of Appeals Next, the students appealed to the Eighth Circuit Court of Appeals. All eight judges of the court listened to the arguments. They could not reach a decision. Four of the judges agreed with the students and four agreed with the school officials. This meant that the District Court ruling remained in effect. The students had lost again.

U.S. Supreme Court Finally, the students asked the Supreme Court to hear the case. The Justices agreed to do so. They felt that the questions raised by the case were important. By 1968, protests against the Vietnam War had spread to all parts of the country. In some schools and colleges, students had used violence in making protests. They had seized buildings. They had destroyed property. Police had sometimes used more violence in return. The question of how and when people might make public protests was an important one.

Lawyers for both sides appeared before the Court. In brief statements, they made many of the points already mentioned. The Justices listened to the lawyers and asked some questions. After that hearing, the Justices studied the case. They looked at the records of the lower courts and at records of similar cases.

The Supreme Court announced its decision early in 1969. This time, the students won by a vote of 7 to 2. Both the majority and the minority on the Court wrote opinions. A look at those opinions will help us to see just how the Court reaches its decisions.

The majority opinion was based on many sources. The First Amendment was the heart of the case. Justice Fortas agreed with the District Court that wearing an armband was like "pure speech." It was protected by the First Amendment.

In the Tinker case, Justice Abe Fortas said that the youth of the United States have the same basic rights as adults.

Next, Justice Fortas referred to a number of earlier Supreme Court cases. He used these cases to answer questions that were raised by the students' case.

Do First Amendment rights apply in the schools? Yes, said Justice Fortas. In an earlier case, the Court had decided that under the First Amendment, a student could not be made to salute the flag. At that time, the Court said that the Constitution protects the citizen against the State and all of its parts, including boards of education.

Justice Fortas said, "It can hardly be argued that either students or teachers shed their constitutional rights to freedom of speech or expression at the schoolhouse gate."

Can free speech sometimes lead to arguments or disturb classes? "Yes," said Justice Fortas, "but our Constitution says we must take this risk." He said that this, too, had been covered in an earlier case.

But don't school officials have a right to make rules to keep a school in order? Yes, again, said Justice Fortas, but only so long as they respect the rights of students and teachers. Justice Fortas said that the Court has agreed that school officials have wide powers. He suggested that school officials probably have the power to stop some expressions of opinion. But *only* in very limited cases.

In another case, the Court decided that a right could be limited only if using that right would greatly get in the way of the need for proper discipline in the school.

That brought Justice Fortas to the facts of the Des Moines case. He found that the armbands were not a threat to school discipline. There was no disruption. "School authorities," he said, "simply felt that the schools are no place for demonstrations."

Justice Fortas made it clear that freedom of speech in the schools has limits. Students cannot disturb class work. They cannot cause great disorder. They cannot deny the rights of others. Freedom of speech does not, by any means, give students unlimited freedom to do as they please. He said that in the Des Moines case, however, students were within their rights.

In closing, Justice Fortas said that the District Court's decision was reversed: the earlier losers became the winners. The Tinker case was sent back to lower courts for a final decision.

The students had asked for **damages**—a payment of money. They had also asked for a court order to stop school officials from punishing the students involved. It would be up to the lower court to settle the details.

The Dissent Two Supreme Court Justices disagreed with this decision. Justice Hugo Black wrote a dissenting opinion. Like Justice Fortas, Black referred to earlier Court cases. He also gave his own reading of the facts in this case.

Black said that the armbands did keep students' minds off their lessons. He said that an argument between Beth Tinker and a teacher almost "wrecked" a mathematics class. Other students made fun of the students with armbands. Justice Black felt that students could not concentrate on lessons when black armbands were reminding them of the wounded and dead of the war. The purpose of wearing armbands, he added, was "to distract the attention of other students."

Justice Black stressed the limits on First Amendment rights. In an earlier case, he said: "the Court clearly stated that the rights of free speech . . . do not mean that anyone . . . may address a group at any public place and at any time."

Black also questioned the wisdom of telling school officials what to do. It was their job to keep discipline, and the courts should not step in.

Justice Black argued: "School discipline . . . is . . . part of training our children to be good citizens." If students were allowed to break school rules, schools would be unable to control them.

As you can see, two people can look at the same set of facts and see different things. That is one reason why there are courts and judges in the first place.

The case of *Tinker v. The Des Moines Independent Community School District* is now part of the nation's laws. Judges may refer to it in cases to come. It is possible that the Supreme Court might one day change its mind on the matter. At that time, Justice Black's dissenting opinion might become support for a new decision. Until that happens, Justice Fortas's opinion stands. It is the law of the country.

1. What did the Vietnam War have to do with the Tinker case?
2. What did the students claim was their right?
3. What did school officials do? Why?
4. Name, in order, the courts in which the Tinker case was heard.
5. Do you think the Supreme Court majority made a wise decision in the Tinker case? Why or why not?

Words to Know

oath —— sworn statement
recall —— a procedure by which a judge may be removed from office by the voters
censure —— to reprimand, or give a verbal spanking to, someone

Some Problems of the Courts

Not everyone is happy with the way the courts in the United States work. Many people think there is room for improvement. Some high officials agree. Chief Justice Warren E. Burger, for one, has suggested a number of ways to improve our system of justice. Let's take a look at three problems that trouble the courts today.

Too Many Cases

What happens if you are charged with a crime? A judge will probably set *bail.* This is an amount of money that an accused person pays the court. It is a promise that the person will return for trial. The more seri-

ous the crime, the higher the bail. If you can afford the bail, you will be released until the trial. If you cannot, you must stay in jail. If you believe that you are innocent, you will probably want the trial to begin as soon as possible. The Constitution says that you have the right to a speedy trial.

In many courts, however, there is a backlog of cases. Trials often are delayed because judges are busy with other cases. Sometimes people who cannot afford bail wait a year or more in jail before their case is heard. Under the system of law used in the United States, accused people are innocent until proven guilty. Is it fair to keep them in jail for long periods?

Court decisions have said "No." Appeals courts have put time limits on criminal cases of many kinds. If a case is not brought to trial within a certain time—for example, 6 months—then it must be dropped.

That idea works for criminal cases. It may not be perfect. It may even make the crime rate go up, as some people charge. But it frees the courts' schedules.

Civil cases are another matter. They cannot just be dropped. They must be dealt with. Long waits for trials may cost a lot in lawyers' fees and other expenses.

Between the 1950s and the 1970s, the number of criminal and civil cases in United States courts doubled. The number of appeals increased even more. In 1957, the United States Courts of Appeals handled 3,700 cases. That number went up to 19,000 in 1977. The Supreme Court is also busier now. It hears twice as many cases as it did 20 years ago.

Why are there so many court cases? One professor of law says that we seem bent on "waging total law." People use any excuse to go to court. Did your neighbor back over your rosebush? Sue him. Did a factory pollute your air? Sue the factory. Did a police officer give you a traffic ticket? Sue for violation of your constitutional rights.

Chief Justice Burger feels that part of the problem is United States society. It is becoming more complicated. Congress has passed laws protecting the environment. It has set up rules to safeguard the health and safety of people at work. It has tried to protect people's civil rights. Each time a new law or rule is passed, there is one more subject for court action.

The Chief Justice said that Congress should think about how a new law would affect the courts before passing the law. Congress might do a study of each new bill. The study would try to tell how many more court cases a law might cause.

There have been other ideas for dealing with busy courts. One is to increase the number of judges. That costs more money, of course. Also, Chief Justice Burger has proposed setting up a National Court of Appeals to take some of the workload from the Supreme Court. It would sort out cases from the United States Courts of Appeals and the state courts. Only the most important cases would go to the Supreme Court.

Another idea is to take some subjects for cases out of the courts. Is it really necessary to go to court to adopt a baby? To get a divorce? To get back expenses brought on by an automobile accident? Some people feel that such matters might be removed from the courts in cases that are not out of the ordinary.

One more idea is to remove criminal punishment from some acts that are treated as crimes. Do we need to put people on trial for becoming drunk in public or for gambling in private? Perhaps such matters might be treated like breaking a traffic law. People might pay their "ticket" without having to go to trial. Other people argue that punishment in such cases should be removed altogether.

The Ability of Juries

How well do juries do their job? Can we expect twelve—or eight, or six—ordinary people to understand the confusing issues in a modern court case? Some people

The question of the competence of juries has always been subject to debate. Does this drawing give you any indication as to the illustrator's opinion?

say that juries are the weak spot in the court system. Others see juries as the strongest protection of people's rights and liberties. Which view is more correct?

The critics of juries say that jurors are not able to do their job well. We take twelve average people and ask them to make difficult legal decisions. One case may involve payments of millions of dollars. Another case might be a matter of life or death for the accused person. One case might depend on evidence about medical subjects. Even trained doctors might not agree on what the evidence means. Should we let twelve average people make a decision in such a case?

Other critics argue that jurors may not take their duties seriously. They say that some juries decide cases by the flip of a coin and other juries make up their minds before hearing the evidence.

The defenders of juries answer that juries do not have to be experts. Their main job is to decide who is telling the truth. They do not have to be experts to be able to tell who is lying. Besides, say the defenders, juries are needed in a democracy. They help to protect the people from leaders who might make unjust decisions. They help to keep the experts honest.

The defenders of juries question the stories about coin-flipping in the jury room. Most jurors, they say, take their job seriously. They take an **oath**—a sworn statement—to uphold the law. They promise to hear each case fairly. In most cases, say the defenders, jurors do at least as well as judges at being fair.

The Ability of Judges

How well do judges do their jobs? Some people with good backgrounds in the law think the answer is "not well" too often. One writer publishes a yearly list of New York City's "ten worst judges." He says that he has no trouble filling out the list. One college law professor says that truly able judges are hard to find. On the other hand, many people have high praise for judges. Chief Justice Burger, for example, says that only a handful of some seven hundred federal judges are "problem judges."

The critics of judges point out many examples to prove their opinion. There was the judge who did not like the coffee sold in the court building. He sent three officials to bring the person who sold the coffee to court in handcuffs. The judge then scolded him severely. That judge was later removed from office.

Another judge misbehaved in court. Once, he did not believe what a defendant was saying. The judge "gave him the raspberry"—blew air through his lips to show contempt. That judge was also removed from office.

Judges have also fallen asleep in court. One 82-year-old judge on the California Supreme Court fell asleep often. Lawyers said that the judge did not pay attention during trials. They said that the judge was too old to do his job well. Finally, a special panel of judges was asked to hear these charges. The panel forced the judge to retire.

These examples raise the question of how such judges can be removed from office. The only way to remove federal judges from office seems to be impeachment. But only four federal judges have ever been both impeached and convicted. Impeachment is too serious and difficult to be used in most situations. Judges in state courts can be disciplined more easily. In some states, judges can be removed by a vote of the people. Such a procedure is called a **recall.** California adopted another way to "judge the judges." In 1960, it set up a commission to look into charges against state judges. If the commission recommends punishment, then the California Supreme Court takes up the case. Some judges have been removed from office. Others have been

In defending persons or beliefs that are controversial, judges often find themselves just as unpopular. Chief Justice Earl Warren's stand on desegregation in the 1950s and 1960s made him just such a target for those demanding his impeachment.

censured—given a verbal spanking. Almost all states now have panels like California's. A bill has been introduced in Congress to set up a federal commission as well.

Some people say that a problem might result from making it easier to remove judges. They ask: Would this threaten the independence of judges? Judges often play a difficult role. They must defend the rights of people who are unpopular. If it were too easy to remove judges, they might not be able to protect the rights of the people.

The courts do have problems, as we have seen. Still, they manage to deal with an amazing assortment of cases day after day. The Courts play a major role in settling disputes, and they help to maintain the checks and balances upon which the federal system of government depends.

REVIEW

1. Why do you think jams in the courts are a problem for the United States' legal system?

2. Why are there more court cases today than ever before?

3. What proposals have been made for dealing with the overload of cases in the courts?

4. Why do some people think that juries are not able to do their job?

5. Which do you think might be the greater problem—the inability of juries to do their job or the inability of judges to do their job? Explain.

How the United States Works

Police Officer

Many cases that go through the courts start with an arrest by a police officer. Police work is not as exciting as it seems to be on television. The danger is real enough at times, however. The injury rate is higher than in most jobs. But a good deal of police work is dull routine.

Let's follow the day of a city patrol officer to see what the job is like. That is the job that most new officers have when they finish police cadet school. Our officer's day starts at midnight. The police usually work a 40-hour week. But since their services are needed around the clock, officers have to work shifts. After being told about the conditions in the area where they will work, the officer joins his partner, a woman patrol officer. Today, more and more women and members of minority groups are being hired. Towns and cities want their police forces to represent fairly the people who live there.

Our officers spend most of their time driving around looking for trouble—that is, anything unusual or unsafe. They also watch out for other things, such as speeders and drunk drivers. After 2 A.M., the streets are nearly empty. A store alarm goes off. The alarm may have gone off by itself, or it may mean that a burglar is in the store, or it may mean that the burglar has fled.

This time, the store was broken into. A witness gives a description of the burglar. The officers ask more questions and send the description of the burglar over the radio so that other patrol officers can watch for him. If a suspect is taken in, the officers fill out detailed reports.

At 4 A.M., a call comes in to ask the police to settle a family fight. These calls are often received in big cities. Many times, they mean danger. When people are angry, someone can get hurt. The officers try to calm the people and settle the argument. Police officers are well trained for dealing with such problems.

At 8 A.M., the officers return to fill out reports about their shift. If any arrests have been made, one or the other of them may have to appear in court.

All police officers must be United States citizens. They usually have to be 21 years old. They also have to pass certain tests—both physical and mental. Beginning officers make between $9,000 and $18,000 a year, depending on where they work. They generally receive regular raises. The services of police officers are always in demand. But it is the city government that runs the police force, and the number of new jobs that are available often depends on the size of the city budget.

Reading About . . .

How Judges Learn

One of the problems with the United States' system of justice is judges who do not do their job well. One way to deal with this problem is to make sure that judges learn the job well in the first place. How does a person learn such a difficult and complex job? This reading gives one answer.

As you read, think about the following:

● Should all judges have to take a course like the one described?
● Can you think of another, better way for judges to learn?

The professor begins by offering a made-up case. Most of the students quietly concentrate on the facts. A few of them scribble on yellow legal pads. The professor's questions become pointed: "Now you're a fair man," the professor says to one student, "How would you decide?" After a long silence comes a hesitant answer, but that sets off a lively debate among the students. Finally, the professor—a Dallas judge—tells the students that he has tricked them. The case is not made-up. It was decided by the Supreme Court in 1974. Perhaps the students should have known better—for they are all judges—but they have come to the National Judicial College to learn.

The National Judicial College in Reno, Nevada, teaches judges how to be judges. "The responsibilities are so complex," says the dean of the college. "The judge is dealing with crowded courtrooms and constant changes in the law. He or she can learn by trial and error, but at whose expense?" No judge is required to attend the college, but enrollment has grown rapidly since it opened.

The college offers both basic programs for new judges and courses for veteran judges who want to keep up with rapidly changing laws. The courses, some held in mock-trial form, range from matters such as organizing a staff to complex issues such as sentencing.

Classes begin at 8 A.M.—not 8:01—and last until 5 P.M. Bells signal the beginning and end of classes, and the faculty uses seating charts to check attendance. Two-hour group discussions follow dinner each evening. "This is not a vacation," the dean says, "and those who come here thinking that don't last long." The dean has been known to scold judges who are late to class and has even expelled students.

Thanks largely to the National Judicial College, which has awarded more than eight thousand graduation "certificates," the idea of education for judges appears to have taken hold. Forty-five states now offer some type of training for new judges.

chapter
Review

Fact Review

1. Tell which of the following statements are true and which are false.
   a. The federal courts are described in detail in the Constitution.
   b. The Supreme Court can order a President to stop an action that the Court considers to be unconstitutional.
   c. A state legislature can set aside a federal court decision.
   d. The Supreme Court cannot review any decisions made by state courts.
   e. John Marshall's decisions pleased those who believed in a strong federal government.
   f. A decision made by the Supreme Court can never be changed.
   g. The Warren Court favored loose interpretation of the Constitution.
   h. The Supreme Court ruled in the Tinker case that "symbolic speech" is not protected by the First Amendment.
2. What was the importance of each of the following Supreme Court cases?
   a. *Marbury v. Madison*
   b. *Plessy v. Ferguson*
   c. *Brown v. Board of Education of Topeka*
   d. *Tinker v. The Des Moines Independent Community School District*
3. What is the biggest problem facing the United States legal system?
4. What are the two points of view regarding juries? Which point of view do you agree with? Explain your answer.
5. Now that you have read about *Tinker v. The Des Moines Independent Community School District,* put the following courts in the order in which they were appealed to in the case. After each court you list, tell what decision was reached there.
   a. U.S. Court of Appeals
   b. U.S. Supreme Court
   c. U.S. District Court

6. Tell whether you agree or disagree with the following statements. Give reasons to support your point of view.
   a. Supreme Court Justices base too many decisions on their personal beliefs rather than on the law and the Constitution.
   b. A good way to solve the problem of the overload of cases in the courts would be to remove punishment from many actions that are now treated as crimes.

Developing Your Vocabulary

1. Match the terms in *a* to *e* with the definitions in (*1*) to (*5*).
   a. segregated
   b. reverse
   c. remand
   d. damages
   e. oath
      (1) overturn an earlier decision
      (2) a payment of money to make up for a wrong
      (3) separated by race
      (4) sworn statement
      (5) send a case back to a lower court
2. Which of the following are examples of symbolic speech?
   a. carrying a flag to show patriotism
   b. wearing an armband to express an opinion on a public issue
   c. shouting in a crowd
   d. making a public speech
   e. wearing a campaign button to show support for a candidate

Developing Your Reading Skills

Read the following paragraph and then answer the questions that follow:

The case of *Tinker v. The Des Moines Independent Community School District* marked a victory for the rights of students. It showed that students do not leave their constitutional rights behind them when they go to school. But the case showed that students' rights are not unlimited. Students cannot disrupt classes while exercising their rights. They cannot cause great disorder. They cannot disturb the rights of others.

1. Which one of the following do you think is the main point, or main idea, of the paragraph above?
   a. The Tinker case spelled out definite rights for students in school, but pointed out that those rights are not unlimited.
   b. The Tinker case gave students the same constitutional rights as adults.
   c. The Tinker case indicated that a student who disturbs a class has no constitutional rights.
   d. The Tinker case showed that school officials have no right to keep students from speaking out.
2. Tell why you selected either *a, b, c,* or *d* in question 1.

Developing Your Writing Skills— Forming and Supporting an Opinion

In this chapter, you have read about a number of controversial cases decided by the Supreme Court. In some cases, the Court's decision has later been changed, either by a constitutional amendment or by the Court itself. Now consider these questions:

Forming an opinion
1. Do you think it is too easy for people to change a Supreme Court decision that they do not like?
2. Do you think it is too hard?
3. Are there ever any times when an unpopular decision is better left unchanged?

Supporting an opinion
4. After thinking about those questions, write a paragraph telling whether or not you think there might be a better way to bring about changes in unpopular Supreme Court decisions. Explain your reasons for thinking the way you do.

YOUR GOVERNMENT & ITS HISTORY

The Power of Judicial Review

In this chapter, you have learned about the United States Supreme Court. Now you will read about one of the Supreme Court's more important powers—the power of judicial review. Judicial review is the right of the Supreme Court to decide whether laws passed by Congress follow the principles of the Constitution.

The Supreme Court did not always have the right of judicial review. That right was first established in the court case of *Marbury v. Madison* in 1803. The case was important for political, as well as judicial, reasons. At the time, there were two strong political parties—the Federalists and the Republicans. These parties had opposing views about how the Constitution could be explained. The Federalists believed that there was only one correct explanation of the Constitution. The Republicans believed that there were many possible explanations. The direction that the law of the land would take depended upon Chief Justice John Marshall's historic decision.

The conflict that led to judicial review began in 1801. As President John Adams prepared to leave office, he appointed forty-two justices of the peace for the District of Columbia. These appointments were accepted by the Senate. The commissions (legal documents giving official permission for an act to be carried out) were not sent out before Adams's term of office ended.

When Thomas Jefferson became President, he told his Secretary of State, James Madison, to give out only twenty-five of the commissions. The other seventeen were held up because the individuals chosen were considered enemies of the new administration.

Four of the people whose appointments were held up sued. They wanted the

Supreme Court to force Madison to give out the remaining commissions. William Marbury, one of the four, became the main defendant in the case. Chief Justice John Marshall ordered Madison to show some reason why the appointment should not be made. Thus began the case of *Marbury v. Madison* in 1803.

According to the Judiciary Act of 1789, the Supreme Court had the power to decide matters such as this. Marshall found himself in a difficult position. On one hand, Madison had openly ignored the order of the Court by blocking Marbury's appointment. If the Court ruled in favor of Marbury, the Jefferson administration would ignore that ruling, too. The Court would then be put in the position of issuing an order it had no way to carry out. On the other hand, a decision in favor of Madison would look as if the Court were backing the Jefferson Administration's position, which it was not.

Chief Justice Marshall had to find a way to show that Marbury had reason to sue Madison without allowing Marbury to become a justice of the peace. He also had to criticize the Jefferson Administration for trying to deny Marbury his appointment. Above all, Marshall had to secure the Supreme Court's right to judicial review. He did all this by asking and answering three questions.

"First," he asked himself, "has the applicant a right to the commission he demands?

"Second, if he has a right, and that right has been violated, do the laws of his country afford him a remedy?

"Third, if they do afford him a remedy, is the remedy a *mandamus* (a document issued by a higher court directing someone to perform an act) issuing from this court?"

Marshall answered "yes" to the first two questions, and "no" to the third. He then ruled that Section 13 of the Judiciary Act of 1789 went against the Constitution and was not legal. Section 13 gave the Court the power to issue a writ (a legal document) forcing the Jefferson Administration to grant Marbury his appointment. This was the first time the Supreme Court ruled that a law of Congress was unconstitutional.

In ruling as he did, Chief Justice Marshall was able to decide the *Marbury v. Madison* case while also ruling that the Supreme Court had no legal authority to judge the case. But at the same time, Marshall established that the Supreme Court has the right to declare a law unconstitutional. It was a historic decision whose impact has been felt in the court system ever since.

1. What action led to the case of *Marbury v. Madison?*

2. Why was the Judiciary Act of 1789 important in this case?

3. Why was Chief Justice Marshall's decision so difficult? How did Marshall make his decision?

4. Why is the case of *Marbury v. Madison* important?

5. Why do you think the power of judicial review is important?

SKILLS Developing your basic civic education skills

Do We Need a National Court of Appeals?

(distinguishing fact from opinion)

In this chapter, you read that Chief Justice Warren E. Burger proposed setting up a National Court of Appeals. He wanted to take some of the workload off the United States Supreme Court. A National Court of Appeals would sort out cases from the United States Courts of Appeals and the state courts. Only the most important cases then would go to the United States Supreme Court. Arguments for and against such a proposal follow.

For the Proposal

Charles Alan Wright, McCormick Professor of Law, University of Texas Law School:

With four times as many cases as it had 40 years ago, the Supreme Court is badly overworked. Most cases it dismisses without a hearing. Important issues are left unsettled. The Court cannot increase the number of cases to which it gives a full hearing. Lower courts are crowded, too, but there, additional judges have been added to lighten caseloads. There is an urgent need to give the Supreme Court relief. This could be done by creating a new court that can speak to the country and for the country in cases the Supreme Court simply cannot hear.

Against the Proposal

Eugene Gressman, Professor of Law, University of North Carolina Law School:

Certainly not. A second Supreme Court is unconstitutional, unwise, and unnecessary. The Constitution says there shall be one Supreme Court, no second or auxiliary one. Nor can the Court delegate any of its . . . duties. The Court now has enough . . . ways to handle fast-moving caseloads and remain consistently current in its work. Another Court would do nothing to help the work of the nine Justices. It would make court cases more expensive and longer. It would take away from the constitutional role and dignity of our one Supreme Court.

1. Which two of the following statements are fact?
   a. Members of the Supreme Court are badly overworked.
   b. Chief Justice Warren E. Burger proposed the creation of a National Court of Appeals.
   c. The Supreme Court has four times as many cases as it had 40 years ago.
   d. A National Court of Appeals would be unconstitutional and very expensive.
2. Briefly, tell why you selected the statements you did in question 1.

3. Match the main points noted in *a* to *d* with the individuals who made them.

    a. Creation of a National Court of Appeals would be unconstitutional since it would allow for two Supreme Courts.

    b. The already-overworked United States Supreme Court cannot add many more new cases to which it can grant full consideration.

    c. There is an urgent need to create a new court to make decisions the United States Supreme Court cannot handle.

    d. A National Court of Appeals would only make court cases longer and more expensive for courts to handle.

        (1) Wright

        (2) Gressman

4. Which two of the following were included in the arguments by Wright but left out by Gressman?

    a. The United States Supreme Court now has four times as many cases as it had 40 years ago.

    b. Creation of a National Court of Appeals would only cost the government more money.

    c. The United States Supreme Court must dismiss many cases without even giving them a hearing.

5. Which two of the following were included in the arguments by Gressman but left out by Wright?

    a. The United States Supreme Court now has ways to handle effectively all cases to come before it.

    b. There can be only one United States Supreme Court.

    c. The number of Justices on the United States Supreme Court has not been increased, but its caseload has increased four times over what it was 40 years ago.

6. Would you favor or oppose the creation of a National Court of Appeals?

Tenure of Federal Judges
(conflicting viewpoints)

In Chapter 8, you learned that federal judges receive lifetime appointments. In this chapter, you read about some of the problems associated with the lifetime appointments for federal judges. During the past few years, some citizens have questioned whether we should continue to let the President appoint federal judges for such long terms. Others have defended the practice. Arguments for each side follow.

Should Federal Judges Continue to Receive Lifetime Appointments?

YES. Senator Birch Bayh, Democrat from Indiana:

> When the framers of the Constitution declared that federal judges were to hold office without time limit . . . they did so knowing that lifetime tenure [appointment] was necessary to keep the delicate balance of power. Congress was to reflect the will of the people. The judiciary was to protect individual justice through standards of law tested over time, without regard to popular will. It was to act as a check on congressional or executive actions. The President and Congress were given checks on the judiciary through appointment, confirmation, and impeachment. Only by keeping judges from the same political pressures as elected legisla-

tors could the framers hope to maintain this system of checks and balances.

YES. Representative Robert W. Kastenmeier, Democrat from Wisconsin:

The nation's founders, in the United States Constitution, provided for the lifetime tenure of federal judges. I strongly agree with the wisdom of that decision, which is of more importance today than it was 200 years ago. Basically, the promise of lifetime tenure attracts very qualified individuals to the judiciary. Also, once on the bench, judges are kept from powerful political and economic pressures. It gives them the necessary independence to decide difficult and emotional cases in an ever-changing society. Lastly, judicial tenure provides the weaker third branch with a check on the extremes of the more political legislative and executive branches.

NO. Representative Henry J. Hyde, Republican from Illinois:

Federal judges, being only human, are sometimes not effective or not qualified. We need a workable way to remove those who do not measure up, other than the impeachment process. A 12-year term, for example, would be long enough to keep judges from political interference. At the same time, it would assure the public that uncontrollable and unqualified judicial behavior will not be accepted without time limit. In 1951, the Twenty-second Amendment limited a President to two terms, setting a new pat-

tern. A constitutional amendment limiting the tenure of federal judges would be a clear signal that they must be held responsible for their behavior.

NO. Senator James B. Allen, Democrat from Alabama:

Rather than having a government of three equal branches, we face the danger of the federal judiciary being the most powerful branch of government. There must be meaningful and lasting reform to restore balance in our government. This must be done without compromising the basic independence necessary for judges to interpret the Constitution and to apply the law fairly. I have proposed . . . the reapproval of federal judges at certain times. There would be no limit to the number of terms that might be served. I simply do not believe it is in the best interest of the American people to have any public official appointed for life and to be accountable to no one.

7. Match the main points that follow with the individuals who made them. You may use one name more than once.

a. A better way to get bad judges out of the court system is needed.

b. Lifetime tenure of judges is needed to preserve the balance of power within the federal government.

c. Federal judges should be evaluated regularly, and those judges who do not pass the evaluation should be removed.

d. Lifetime tenure of judges attracts good people to the judiciary.

   (1) Bayh
   (2) Kastenmeier

(3) Hyde

(4) Allen

8. What did Bayh and Kastenmeier agree about? Disagree about?

9. What did Hyde and Allen agree about? Disagree about?

10. Did Bayh and Kastenmeier agree with anything Allen said? Explain.

11. Which one of the following was the most important point of disagreement between the two sides on this issue?

    a. whether federal judges should continue with the present system of lifetime appointments

    b. whether federal judges should be evaluated regularly

    c. whether federal judges should have the power now granted to them in the Constitution

What Might Be Done about Bad Judges?

(determining types of questions)

What to do about a federal judge who no longer has the confidence of the public is a very difficult issue.

Article III of the Constitution states that all federal judges shall hold their offices during good behavior. Article III allows a judge's removal by impeachment for, and conviction of, treason, bribery, high crimes, and lesser crimes.

The House of Representatives is granted sole power to impeach, or accuse, a judge. Impeachment requires a majority vote in the House.

Then it is up to the Senate to try the judge. A conviction requires a two-thirds vote.

As early as 1819, President Thomas Jefferson called the impeachment process "a bungling way of removing judges . . . an impracticable thing." And in the 1960s, Chief Justice Warren E. Burger declared: "I would not presume to say how many United States judges now in active service are not physically able to perform their work well. But every observer knows that there are more than a few."

In 1979, Congress considered a proposed law that would allow the judicial branch to police its own ranks. The proposed Judicial Tenure Act—often called the Nunn bill for its sponsor, Senator Sam Nunn—offered a way to make a judge's removal possible without impeachment.

The bill would have set up a council of federal judges to consider firing judges. Grounds for firing would have included a continued failure to perform the duties of the office. They would also have included continued bad behavior in office. The Nunn bill had a host of critics. Some say the bill would have crushed individuality on the bench and stripped judges of the independence a lifetime job is supposed to foster.

12. What did Senator Sam Nunn propose in regard to the possible removal of federal judges? Why?

13. What was the main point of disagreement between those who supported Nunn's bill and those who opposed it?

14. Classify each of questions 12 and 13 as either a recall question or an application question.

UNIT 4 REVIEW

Fact Review

1. Arrange the following steps in the order in which they would occur in a typical court case:
   a. An appeal is filed.
   b. The trial begins.
   c. A complaint is filed.
   d. The verdict is given.
   e. A jury is chosen.
2. Can a federal court decision be appealed to a state supreme court? Explain.
3. In what cases does the Supreme Court have original jurisdiction?
4. Explain why the Supreme Court's decisions in the following cases are no longer in effect:
   a. Dred Scott case
   b. *Plessy v. Ferguson*
5. Name three ways in which judges who are not able to do their job may be removed from office or reprimanded.
6. Do you think that the Supreme Court should have the power of judicial review, as it does now? Or do you think that each branch of the federal government should have the last word on its own actions and powers? Explain.

Developing Your Vocabulary

1. Four terms in the paragraph below are misused. First find the terms. Then choose the correct terms from the following list to replace them.

twelve	petit jury
plaintiff	activist
a complaint	defendant

   A person who wishes to take a case to court must first file an appeal. For example, let's say you sue your landlord. You are known as the defendant. Your landlord is the prosecutor. The person who presides over the trial is called the judge. Questions of fact will be decided by a grand jury. There may be anywhere from five to sixteen persons on the jury.

2. Give a definition for each of the following terms. Then use each in a sentence about the judicial branch of the government.
   a. court
   b. court-martial
   c. judicial review
   d. dissenting opinion

Developing Your Reading Skills

Read the following passage and then answer the questions that follow:

The judicial branch of the federal government has many courts. The Supreme Court is at the top. It has the final word in cases involving the United States Constitution, federal laws, and federal treaties. It may review cases that have been decided by lower federal courts. It may also review cases that have been decided by state courts, provided that a federal question is involved.

There are several kinds of lower federal courts. Some handle a variety of cases. District courts, for example, have wide jurisdiction. Other lower federal courts handle special cases. The Tax Court, for example, handles only tax cases.

The exact role of the federal courts was not detailed in the Constitution. It has developed over the years. At first, there was confusion as to what powers the Supreme Court had. Chief Justice John Marshall helped to define those powers. He used the Court's power to review the actions of Congress and the executive branch. This is the power of judicial review. It has given the Supreme Court a major role in the federal system of checks and balances.

1. Which of the questions below can be answered from the reading?
   a. How many federal judges are there?
   b. What court has the final word in cases involving the Constitution?
   c. How can Congress check the power of the Supreme Court?
2. Now give the answers that can be found in the reading.

Up to now, we have been looking mainly at one level of the federal government. The President, the Congress, and the Supreme Court are all parts of the national government. The national government affects your life in many ways. Yet the national government is only one of several governments in your life. You also live under a state government and one or more local governments. These local governments might include a county government, a town or city government, and several special districts, such as a school district.

The actions of these governments rarely touch the lives of all 226 million people in the United States. But they do touch your own life, even as you are reading this textbook. Perhaps your state's department of education says that you must take a course in civics. The department of education might have decided that this is one of the textbooks your teacher could use for the course. Your town or city government probably raises money to support local schools by taxing the property that people own. Then, your local school board decides how much of that money is to be spent for books, new buildings, buses, or teachers' salaries. You could make a long list of ways in which your state and local governments affect your daily activities.

Since state and local governments play such an active role in your life, you should understand how they work. In the first chapter of this unit, you will study state governments. In the second chapter, you will learn about the many types of local government.

unit

5

State and Local Government

10 State Government

The fifty states that make up the United States of America are a diverse group. Texas, for example, is 220 times larger than Rhode Island. Some states, such as New Jersey, are very densely populated. Others, such as Nevada, have large areas of land where no people live. The state of Michigan is known for its industries. Yet its neighbor, Wisconsin, is most famous for its dairy products. When the temperature is $-37°C$ ($-35°F$) in Iowa, it may be $21°C$ ($70°F$) in Florida.

The fifty state governments also differ from each other in many ways. However, their basic structures are alike. Every state has a constitution that divides the government into three branches—legislative, executive, and judicial. This gives each state a system of checks and balances like that of the national government. States also offer many of the same services to their citizens.

In this chapter, you will read about how state governments work and how they can affect your life.

I. The states in the federal system
A. The powers of the states
B. How states join the Union
C. State constitutions
D. What state governments do

II. How state governments work
A. State legislatures
B. The state executive
C. State courts

Words to Know

policing power —— a state's right to pass laws to protect the health, safety, and welfare of its people

Northwest Ordinance —— a law, passed in 1787, that told how parts of the Northwest Territory—the land between the Ohio River and the Great Lakes—could become states

The States in the Federal System

When the delegates from the original thirteen states met in Philadelphia in 1787, most of them knew that the Articles of Confederation were not working very well. The thirteen states had not been able to work together. They quarreled with each other and refused to cooperate with Congress.

During the long weeks in Philadelphia, the delegates struggled to write a constitution that would solve the problems faced by the new nation. The Constitution that they finally created gave many powers to a strong central government. This national government does not replace state governments, however. Instead, the Constitution sets up another level of power. As you have learned, this combination of state and national governments is known as the federal system.

The Powers of the States

Many citizens of the first thirteen states wanted to protect the rights and powers of their state governments. They wrote the Tenth Amendment of the Constitution to do just that. It keeps for the states all powers that the Constitution does not give to the national government or stop the states from holding.

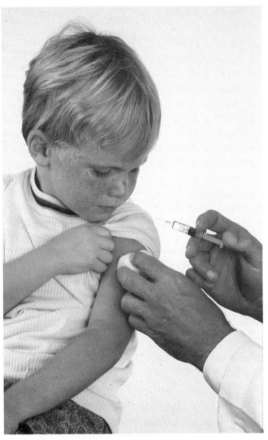

This child benefits from his state having the Constitutional right to look after his well being.

Because taxation is a concurrent power, state residents have the right to petition for tax relief.

Thus, each of the states has the power it needs to govern its own citizens. These *reserved powers* include such powers as the power to hold elections and to set up a school system. States also have **policing power.** This means that a state has the right to provide for the health, safety, and well-being of its people. For example, states may set speed limits, keep stores from opening on Sundays, or require that children attend school.

States share some powers with the federal government. These are called *concurrent powers.* For example, both levels of government can tax citizens and both have their own systems of courts and jails or prisons.

These are only a few of the powers of state governments. It would not be possible to list all the powers, because they are not all known. A state's powers grow and change as the needs of its citizens grow and change. Remember that a state may take any action that is not given to the national government or withheld from the states by the United States Constitution or by the state's own constitution.

How States Join the Union

The nation grew rapidly after 1789, as more states joined the first thirteen. Article IV, Section 3 of the Constitution allows the addition of new states. However, a way of joining the Union had been set up even before the Constitution was written. In 1787, Congress—under the Articles of Confederation—passed the **Northwest Ordinance.** This law told how the lands between the Ohio River and the Great Lakes could someday become states.

The ordinance stated that once the population of a territory was large enough, the people could apply to Congress for statehood. The first step was to write a state constitution. The constitution had to follow certain guidelines. It could not violate the federal constitution in any way. A majority of voters in the territory and in the Congress had to approve the constitution. Once these steps were completed, Congress could vote to admit the territory as a new state.

A method like this was followed for admitting thirty-seven states—from Vermont, in 1791, to Hawaii, in 1959. New states can

With congressional approval, the Hawaiian people voted on and approved United States statehood in 1959.

still join the Union today. Any United States territory, such as Samoa, Guam, the Virgin Islands, or Puerto Rico, could apply for statehood. In 1967, for example, 39 percent of the people in Puerto Rico voted in favor of applying for statehood. A majority, however, wanted to keep their present status. A large group of Puerto Ricans want independence for the island, but most of them did not vote in 1967.

State Constitutions

A territory must have an approved constitution before it can become a state. Most of these state constitutions are modeled after the United States Constitution. They come in many different lengths. Vermont's constitution is the shortest. It has just 8,000 words, which makes it a little longer than this chapter. Georgia's constitution is the longest, with over half a million words—more than three times the size of this textbook.

Your state's constitution tells how the state government will work. It probably explains the organization of the government. It lists some of the government's duties and powers. A state constitution might also outline how local governments will be formed. In addition, most state constitutions have a bill of rights.

An important part of all state constitutions tells how the constitution can be changed. Such changes may be large or small. If large changes are needed, voters in the state elect delegates to a special convention. The delegates then decide how to change, or rewrite, the constitution.

If only small changes are needed, amendments may be added to the constitution. In all the states, the state legislature can suggest amendments. In about one-third of the states, citizens can also suggest amendments. If the required number of voters sign a petition, the suggested amendment is voted on during the next election.

Every state—except Delaware—requires that all amendments be approved by the voters.

In most states, there is at least one amendment to vote on during each election. Some of these changes are needed because state constitutions were written so long ago. Almost half of them are over 100 years old. The oldest constitution, in Massachusetts, was written in 1780—almost 10 years before the United States Constitution.

Since the time when they were first written, many state constitutions have collected a large number of amendments. Often, these amendments deal with problems that no longer exist. It takes a long time to change or remove these outdated sections by adding other amendments. As a result, several states have adopted new constitutions since 1964. They include Michigan, Connecticut, Florida, Hawaii, North Carolina, Virginia, Illinois, Montana, and Louisiana.

Among its duties, state government is responsible for many aspects of public and private transportation.

What State Governments Do

Your state government is involved in many areas of your life. One way that it affects you directly is through education. State governments work with local school districts to run your school system. In some areas, local property taxes provide most of the money to run the schools. When the money from local taxes is not enough, however, state governments usually give money from state funds to the schools.

Your state government may also affect what you study. It may say that you must take certain courses before you can graduate, or it may say that you must be able to pass a test of basic skills. In some states, the state department of education decides which textbooks teachers can use and the courses they will teach at each grade level. If you continue your education beyond high school, you might go to a technical school, college, or university that the state runs.

Other important areas in which state government can affect your life include health, transportation, work, and public aid. State government protects your health in many ways. The state government probably required you to have shots against polio, measles, and other diseases before you started school. State governments can stop the sale of any food or drug that is harmful to its citizens. They can close businesses that do not meet health standards.

In most states, some hospitals are run by the state government. Also, health professionals, such as doctors and nurses, must have licenses from the state.

State government is involved in transportation in many ways. All cars, buses, trucks, and motorcycles must be registered with the state. The states issue licenses to all drivers. States build and keep up highways. They also work with the national government to plan and build federal roads and highways. In some places, the state pays for buses and trains that are used as public transportation.

State governments regulate the work of many of their citizens. For example, the state might set a minimum wage—the lowest salary that a person can be paid. A state government sets safety standards for factories, mines, and other places of work. It also controls the way that companies can do business within the state.

Public aid, or assistance, is an important job of the state. State governments usually give help to citizens who cannot support themselves. This help might go to people who cannot work or for children who have no families. It can also go to people who are out of work for a short time.

In all of their tasks, state governments rarely act alone. They work with local governments and with the national government. You have already seen how both the local government and the state department of education work together to run schools. The federal government can also help. It might pay for a career education program, for example. Funds from the federal government are also a large source of support for many school lunch programs.

The state plays a major role in the smooth working of the levels of government. It is often a connection between the federal and local levels. A state agency, for example, may receive federal money that it uses to help a local program. In case of a flood or an earthquake, state officials often work to coordinate the actions of local and federal groups.

======= REVIEW =======

1. Define the following terms:
   concurrent powers
   policing power
2. Why was the Tenth Amendment added to the Constitution?
3. How can a territory become a state?
4. Describe three ways in which state constitutions can be changed.
5. Which of the activities of state government do you think are the most important? In what way does your state government affect you the most?

Words to Know

unicameral legislature —— a legislature made up of one house

initiative —— the right of voters to propose bills by collecting signatures on petitions

referendum —— the right of voters to approve or reject bills that are passed by the legislature

item veto —— a governor's power to reject a part of a bill and approve the rest of it

executive ordinance —— a governor's orders that tell how a law will be carried out

How State Governments Work

Three branches of government share power in the states, just as they do in the federal government. The legislative branch makes the laws. The executive branch executes—or carries out—the laws, and the courts interpret them. This separation of powers prevents any person or group from becoming too powerful.

State Legislatures

General Assembly, State Legislature, Legislative Assembly, and *General Court* are all names used to describe the lawmaking branch of state government. The term *State Legislature* is used in twenty-seven states. *General Assembly* is used in nineteen states. In this section, we will use the term *state legislature*.

IMPORTANT STATE OFFICIALS

Governor:	the head of the executive department of state government
Lieutenant Governor:	serves as acting governor when governor is out of the state, becomes governor if present governor dies or is removed from office, is president of the state senate
Secretary of State:	keeps the official records of the state, supervises elections, publishes state laws
Attorney General:	serves as chief law officer of the state, advises state officials about the meaning of the law, represents the state in court
Treasurer:	is in charge of state funds, pays state bills
Auditor:	examines state financial records, approves all payments from state funds
Superintendent of Public Instruction:	is in charge of the state school system

With one exception, all states have a two-house, or *bicameral,* legislature. The lower house is usually called the house of representatives and the upper house is called the senate. Election districts for both houses are based mainly on population. A state senator represents more people than a member of the lower house.

Nebraska has the only **unicameral legislature**—or one-house legislature. Supporters of this system say that the bicameral system makes passing state laws too difficult. They say that a one-house legislature can save time and money. Attempts to start unicameral lawmaking bodies in other states have failed, however. For example, in 1972, voters in Montana and North Dakota rejected the idea.

A "typical" state legislature is as difficult to describe as a typical student or a typical citizen of the United States. You saw earlier that states do not even use the same name for their lawmaking body.

State legislatures come in many sizes. The lower houses in Alaska and Nevada have only forty members each. The New Hampshire house of representatives has 400 members. Most lower houses have between 90 and 150 members. The number of senators ranges from twenty in Alaska and Nevada to sixty-seven in Minnesota. Senates are most likely to have between thirty and fifty members.

Nearly all members of the lower houses serve terms of 2 years. State senators most often have 4-year terms. The salaries that lawmakers receive differ greatly. Some states pay their legislators a flat yearly salary. Other states pay their legislators by the number of days they work. Still other states pay a combination of a yearly salary and a daily fee. Legislators also receive a travel and expense allowance to cover costs relating to their position.

People can serve at a younger age in state legislatures than in Congress. Usually, a person must be 21 years old to serve in the lower house and 25 years old to serve in the senate.

In addition to being a given age, state lawmakers must be citizens of the United

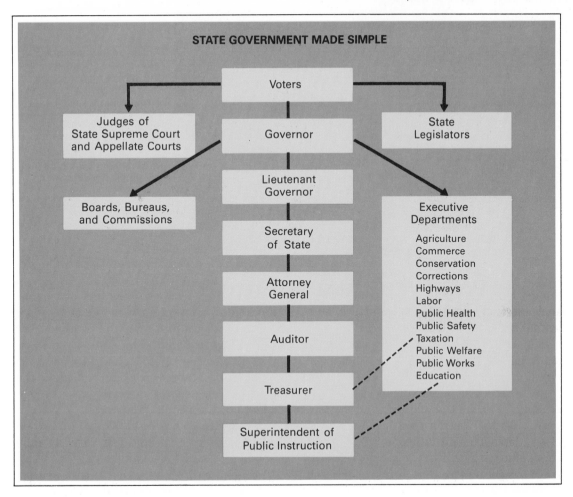

STATE GOVERNMENT MADE SIMPLE

States and must live in the state. Many states also require that the members of the legislature live in the district that they represent.

In more than half of the states, the legislature has a session, or meeting, every year. Sessions may be limited to as few as 20 days, or they may last several months or more.

When state lawmakers meet in the state capitol at the beginning of a new term, their first task is to organize. They must choose leaders and set up committees. In most states, the lieutenant governor serves as the president of the senate. (The job of lieutenant governor is like that of Vice President.) If a state has no lieutenant governor, the senators elect one of their members to be president of the senate.

The lower house in bicameral legislatures elects a member as speaker of the house. Speakers may have many of the same powers as the Speaker in the United States House of Representatives. They control the day-to-day business of the house. They keep the house running smoothly. State speakers, however, can also choose the heads and members of all committees. Thus, the speaker of the house is a very important person in state government.

Acting as the lawmaking branch of state government, the state legislature bears the responsibility of sifting through the many bills up for approval, studying them through committees, and then voting on them. Here in the House, representatives debate the merits of a bill up for consideration.

Committees are just as important in state legislatures as they are in Congress. Hundreds of bills may be introduced in a single session. Standing committees help lawmakers sort through this large number of bills. Committee members study bills in depth and report on them to the other legislators.

The method of passing laws in state legislatures is like the method used in Congress. (Review the material in Chapter 4.) After a lawmaker introduces a bill, the presiding officer sends it to the proper committee. If the committee reports on the bill, the members talk about it on the floor.

In most state legislatures, the bill must be read three times in each house. It is read once when it is first introduced, and it is read two more times during the floor debate. These readings take a lot of time.

Once one house has passed a bill, it sends the bill to the other house. Here, the same process is followed. After both houses have approved the same bill, they send it to the governor for action.

Members of state legislatures represent the state's citizens when they vote to pass or defeat a bill. In some states, however, citizens can take a direct part in making laws. Twenty states allow citizens to start laws through the **initiative.** When a group of people think that a certain law is

needed, they can draw up a petition describing the law. Then they ask voters to sign it. After a required number of persons have signed, action must be taken.

In a *direct initiative,* the proposed law appears on a ballot. The state's voters either accept it or reject it. In an *indirect initiative,* the state legislature considers the bill. If the legislature does not pass the bill, it goes to the people for a vote.

Initiatives are most likely to succeed when a group of people feel very strongly about an issue. For example, the voters of Utah used a direct initiative to ban, or stop, the use of the chemical fluoride in the state's drinking water. In many parts of the country, fluoride has been added to drinking water to help prevent tooth decay. A majority of the voters in Utah, however, did not want fluoride in the water. They voted for the ban.

In twenty-four states, voters can also take a direct role in state lawmaking by using the **referendum.** In a referendum, bills that are passed by the legislature go to the voters before they become law. A state constitution may say that some measures have to be sent to the voters—constitutional amendments, for example.

A *popular referendum* is one in which voters demand that a bill passed by the legislature be approved by them. They make

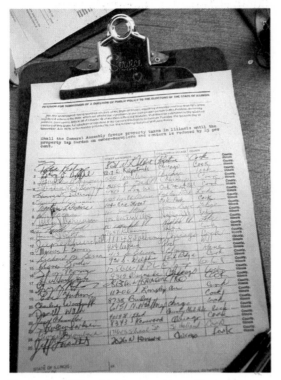

Through petition drives, voters are able to give voice to demands for change in state government.

Do you know which state was an independent country before its citizens voted to join the United States? Do you know which state is the only one that can divide itself into five separate states?

The answer to both questions is "Texas." Texas was a part of Mexico until 1836. In that year, settlers revolted against the Mexican government. They declared their independence. Sam Houston led the Texans to victory and became President of the Republic of Texas.

Shortly after this, a majority of Texans voted to join the Union, but their application was rejected by the United States. Some politicians in the United States feared a war with Mexico if the United States allowed Texas to become a state. Also, politicians in the North did not want a large, powerful Southern state to join the Union.

Finally, in 1845—almost 10 years later—the Congresses of both Texas and the United States agreed on the question. The following year, in 1846, the Republic of Texas became the state of Texas. Its first governor was Sam Houston.

Unlike other new states, Texas did not completely give up its independence when it became a state. For one thing, Texas kept control of its public lands. Public land in all the other states became the property of the United States when the state joined the Union.

Also, if it wishes, Texas can divide itself into as many as five separate states. Texans are unlikely to do this, however. The size of the state, its vast natural resources, its farm land, and its large cities make Texas an important and powerful state.

their demand known by signing petitions. For example, many voters in Oregon opposed a bill to raise the tax on gasoline by 1 cent a gallon. They drew up petitions and collected signatures. When the bill appeared on the ballot, a majority of the state's voters voted against it and it was defeated.

The State Executive

You have probably seen your state's governor many times on television or in newspaper pictures. What was she or he doing? What do most governors do? Who can be governor?

The governor is the chief executive of a state. This can be a powerful position, yet the requirements for being governor are not difficult to meet. A governor must be a United States citizen and must live in the state for a certain number of years. Most states also say that a governor must be at least 30 years old. In some states, however, persons who are 25 years old may run for governor.

As chief executive of a state, the governor has to function as both a personable public figure and a strong executor of the laws of the state. Other duties include promoting the state's interests, proposing a state budget, and coordinating the actions of state officials and agencies.

The governors of Arkansas, New Hampshire, Rhode Island, and Vermont serve 2-year terms. In all the other states, a governor's term lasts for 4 years. Constitutions in half of the states limit the number of terms that a governor can serve. This is done to keep one person from becoming too powerful. In nineteen states, governors can serve only two terms in a row.

A governor plays many different roles. He or she might cut the ribbon when a new state highway opens. A governor might have to order the closing of state offices when there is a shortage of fuel for heating and lights. A governor often serves as the state's public leader. The governor meets with important visitors and represents the state in Washington, D.C. The governor travels to other parts of the country and the world to promote the state's interests.

Most governors have a powerful part in the state government. They play an important role in lawmaking. A governor can recommend bills to the legislature. A governor can call the legislature into special session if the lawmakers have not passed an important bill, such as the state's budget. In every state except North Carolina, governors can also veto bills that have been passed by the legislature.

You learned about the President's veto power in Chapter 6. The President has to accept or reject the whole bill. On the other hand, a governor can veto only one part, or item, in a bill and approve the other parts. This is known as an **item veto.** State legislatures can pass a bill over the governor's veto, however. Two-thirds of each house must vote favorably in order to pass a bill over the veto.

A governor's main job is to carry out, or execute, the laws of the state. When the legislature passes a law, the governor gives orders telling how the law will be carried out. These orders are called **executive ordinances.**

Governors work to make sure that the state government runs smoothly. They try to coordinate the many actions of state officials and agencies. Many governors also play a major role in state spending. First, a governor proposes a state budget to the legislature. Then, once the legislature approves the budget, the governor must usually see that the money is spent properly.

Governors have the power to shorten the sentences of or give pardons to persons convicted of crimes. This power is usually used if a governor is sure that the behavior of the person has improved.

Like the President, a governor is the commander in chief of the state's "armed forces." These forces include the state police and the militia, or National Guard. The governor can call up the National Guard, for example, during a large demonstration or during a natural disaster, such as a blizzard or a tornado. In the event of a flood, the governor could call up the National Guard to rescue people who were trapped by the water. Guards would also protect the property that people would have to leave behind.

As the chief executive, a governor appoints certain state officials. The number of persons he or she can name differs from state to state. In general, a governor has limited control over the state's executive branch. This is because many important officials are elected directly by the voters. In most states, these officials include the lieutenant governor, the secretary of state, the attorney general, the treasurer, the auditor, and the superintendent of public instruction.

The executive branch of your state government also includes many boards and commissions. They deal with areas such as agriculture, highways, insurance, welfare, and health. Usually, they help the governor carry out the laws and rules of the state.

State Courts

Most court cases in the United States are heard in the state courts. The courts in

Always at the availability of the governor, the National Guard may be called upon in many instances for a variety of reasons, including rescue work.

your state hear many types of cases every day. These include both criminal and civil cases.

Each of the fifty states has its own system of courts for interpreting and applying the law. Although the courts differ from state to state, they can be described in general terms.

There are several types of local state courts. They usually hear minor cases. In rural areas, a justice of the peace might handle traffic violations or civil cases that involve small amounts of money. In towns and cities, police or magistrate's courts handle these kinds of cases.

A third type of local court is the city-wide municipal court. Municipal courts are often divided into smaller courts that hear only certain kinds of cases. These might include traffic, small claims, domestic relations, or juvenile courts.

Above the local state courts are the general trial courts. In some states, people call these circuit courts. In other states, they are known as district courts, county courts, or superior courts. Trial courts hear major criminal cases and civil cases that involve large amounts of money.

In the local courts, a single judge usually hears the cases that are brought before the court. In a general trial court, a judge and a jury of local citizens hear most cases.

Two types of juries exist in the state court system. A *grand jury* is a group of citizens who decide whether there is enough evidence to bring a person to trial. The *trial jury* listens to the evidence in court and decides what the facts are.

Most United States citizens between the ages of 18 and 70 can serve on a jury. Every year, local or county officials make a list of people who can serve on juries. They write the names on slips of paper and put them in a locked box. When a jury is needed, an officer of the court draws names from the box. Then each person whose name is drawn is called for jury duty.

The trial jury's verdict in a general trial court is usually final, as far as the facts of a case are concerned. Sometimes, however, a person may think that the court made a mistake in the way that the trial

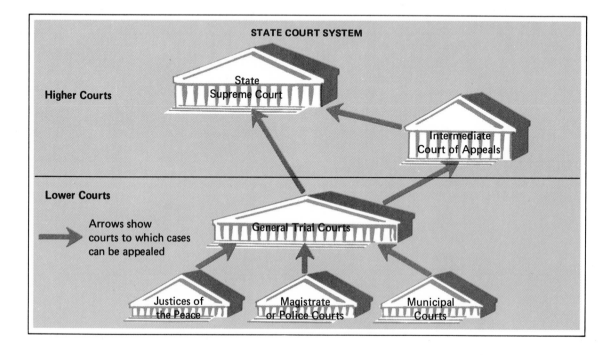

STATE COURT SYSTEM

Higher Courts

State Supreme Court

Intermediate Court of Appeals

Lower Courts

Arrows show courts to which cases can be appealed

General Trial Courts

Justices of the Peace

Magistrate or Police Courts

Municipal Courts

was held. Perhaps she or he feels that the judge did not apply the law correctly.

When this happens, the person can appeal the decision to higher state courts. In most states, this means a state supreme court. A judge or panel of judges then reviews the lower court's decision.

Some states have found, however, that the workload of the supreme courts has grown to be much too large. These states have set up courts of appeals to share the work. In these states, the first appeal would be made to the court of appeals, and many cases end there. However, if a person is still not satisfied, he or she can appeal to the state supreme court. In cases that involve a question about the United States Constitution, the case may be further appealed to the United States Supreme Court.

The diagram on page 268 shows the organization of many state courts. As you look at it, remember that there are many differences among the state systems.

Voters elect most state court judges. Some are also appointed by the governor or the legislature. Elected judges, unlike judges in the federal courts, serve limited terms which differ in length from state to state. Many judges, however, are easily reelected and serve for a long time. Most states require that judges be lawyers, but this requirement usually does not apply to justices of the peace.

REVIEW

1. Define the following terms:
   initiative
   item veto
   referendum

2. List four ways in which state legislatures may differ from each other.

3. What is the most important job of a governor?

4. In which type of state court do a judge and a jury usually hear the cases?

5. In your opinion, which branch of your state government has the most power? Explain your answer.

How the United States Works

Civil Engineer

State governments spend more money on education than on any other single thing. But they have other big tasks. One of the biggest is building and taking care of roads. To do this work, many kinds of workers are needed. Among these are civil engineers.

A great deal of planning goes into the building of a road. This planning is the job of civil engineers. They have to think about such things as the amount of damage that trucks and weather will do to the road. This helps them choose the right materials to use. Civil engineers also decide whether the road will go over or under rivers, around or through mountains. They design the bridges and tunnels that are needed. When the road curves, a civil engineer has to figure out how much of a slant to give it so that cars going the proper speed will be able to go safely around the curve. These are only some of the things that are studied in the planning stage. Once the work gets under way, more questions and problems always come up. This means that civil engineers are also needed to direct the building of the road itself.

Civil engineers have to know physics, chemistry, and mathematics. They

learn most of this in college. All civil engineers are required to have a bachelor's degree in engineering. Many of them go on to get advanced degrees.

Until recently, there were more civil engineers getting degrees than there were jobs available. This kept many people from studying civil engineering. Now there are a number of jobs open to each graduate.

Most beginning civil engineers make about $13,000 a year. Those with graduate degrees may start out making as much as $20,000. The knowledge that a civil engineer has is very valuable to industry. Some civil engineers are offered high-level jobs in industry. These pay anywhere from $30,000 to $300,000 per year.

Reading About . . .

How State and Federal Problems Sometimes Overlap —————

Each of the fifty states has its own problems. Sometimes those problems also involve the federal government. The following reading concerns one of those problems—the interstate highway system.

As you read ask yourself:

- Why does the interstate problem overlap?
- Is the problem getting better or worse?

"The whole Interstate 80 isn't worth the powder and lead you'd need to blow it apart," declared a trucker as he waited to cash a check just off the highway.

Though he was exaggerating, he was echoing the feelings that many haulers, business people and recreation motorists voice about interstate highways these days. They, along with state transportation officials, have found parts of I-80, which stretches from the George Washington Bridge to the San Francisco-Oakland Bay Bridge, to be as rutted, soft-shouldered, and pot-holed as the most battered side streets in Brooklyn.

The problems with I-80 point out those of the entire interstate network of nearly 39,000 miles, begun in 1956 and designed to connect every major city in a web of smooth, wide, safe roads. The web is almost complete.

The older parts, however, have begun to wear out. Many were built before the interstate system was created and have reached or passed the 20-year life expectancy of a well-traveled road.

So many parts of the network are reaching serious stages of decay that in 1976, Congress appropriated $175 million a year specifically for the "3 Rs"—rehabilitation, restoration and reconstruction.

The "3 R" program, in which the Federal Government pays 90 percent of the costs and the states 10 percent, was the first sign that the government felt the interstates needed major maintenance work, more than the individual states could afford.

Nevertheless, states like Pennsylvania, which are most in need of rehabilitation funds, may not be able to take advantage of them because they cannot always come up with their 10 percent share of the costs.

Meanwhile the cost of such maintenance rises steadily. Not only have labor costs risen greatly in recent years, but so has the price of oil, a major part of asphalt.

The construction costs of the system—90 percent of it financed by the Federal Government—have passed the original estimates by tens of billions of dollars.

Now, in many cases, rehabilitation work costs more than the original construction.

"It's just a drop in the bucket," Dale Janik, an Illinois Transportation Department unit chief, said of the "3 R" program. "In the early 1980s, all interstates in our state will be coming of age for resurfacing."

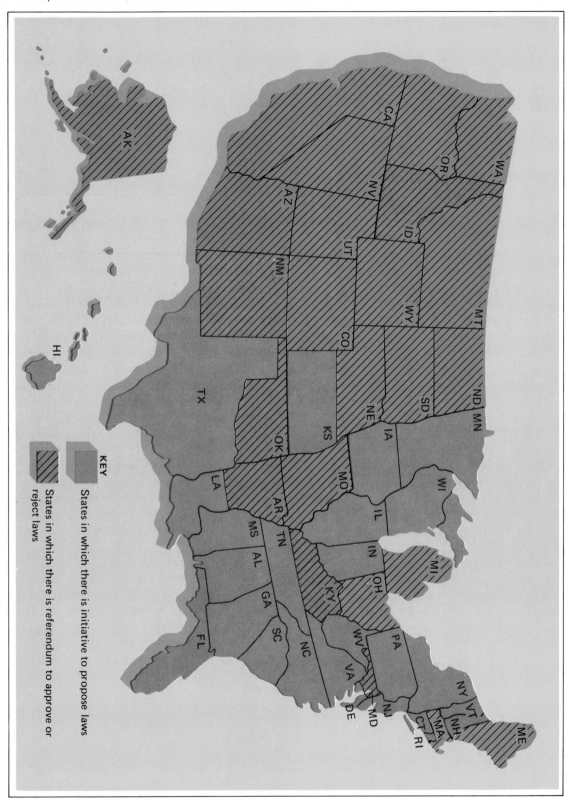

KEY

States in which there is initiative to propose laws

States in which there is referendum to approve or reject laws

Fact Review

1. Why do all the states have written constitutions?
2. Describe two ways in which voters can take a direct part in state lawmaking.
3. Give at least one example of how a governor plays each of the following roles:
   a. public leader
   b. lawmaker
   c. enforcer of laws
   d. commander-in-chief of the armed forces
4. List two differences between local courts and general trial courts.
5. How are state legislatures different from the United States Congress? How are they similar? Consider the following points:
   a. requirements for membership
   b. length of members' terms
   c. salaries of members
   d. power of speaker of the house
   e. the way in which a bill becomes a law

Developing Your Vocabulary

Explain the difference between the words in each pair below.

   a. initiative and referendum
   b. unicameral and bicameral
   c. reserved powers and concurrent powers

Read the following paragraph and then answer the questions that follow:

Each of the state governments is basically like the federal government. Each state government has a legislative branch for making laws. Every state government has an executive branch to carry out the laws. Each state has a judicial branch to interpret state laws.

1. Which one of the following do you think is the main point, or main idea, of the paragraph above?
   a. Like the federal government, state governments are divided into three branches.
   b. Like the federal government, state governments have a legislative branch.
   c. State governments have judges to interpret state laws.
   d. Each state government has a governor.
2. Tell why you selected either *a, b, c,* or *d* in question 1.

Reading a Map

Study the map on the facing page and then answer the questions below.

1. Name five states that allow the use of the initiative.
2. Which is allowed in more states, the initiative or the referendum?
3. Name four states that allow the referendum but not the initiative.
4. In which part of the country do voters have the greatest chance of playing a direct part in the lawmaking of their states?
5. In your opinion, why do states that allow the initiative also allow the referendum?

YOUR GOVERNMENT & ITS HISTORY

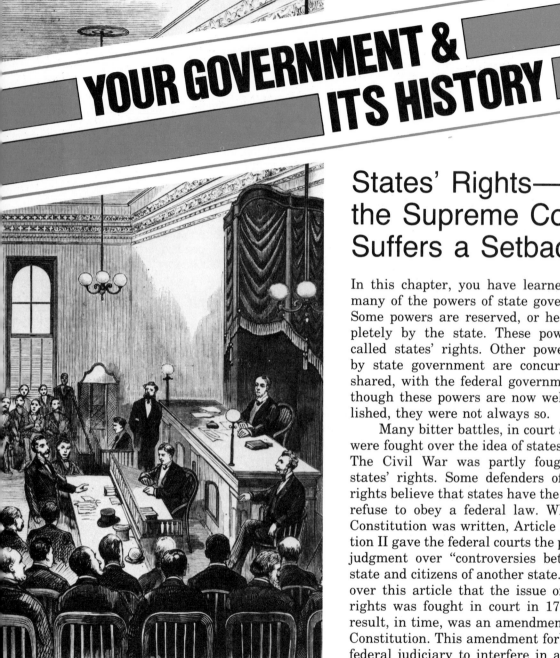

States' Rights— the Supreme Court Suffers a Setback

In this chapter, you have learned about many of the powers of state government. Some powers are reserved, or held, completely by the state. These powers are called states' rights. Other powers held by state government are concurrent, or shared, with the federal government. Although these powers are now well established, they were not always so.

Many bitter battles, in court and out, were fought over the idea of states' rights. The Civil War was partly fought over states' rights. Some defenders of states' rights believe that states have the right to refuse to obey a federal law. When the Constitution was written, Article III, Section II gave the federal courts the power of judgment over "controversies between a state and citizens of another state." It was over this article that the issue of states' rights was fought in court in 1793. The result, in time, was an amendment to the Constitution. This amendment forbids the federal judiciary to interfere in any lawsuit brought against a state by a citizen of another state.

Soon after the Revolutionary War, states began to fight the federal government for more control. The Supreme Court became involved in several disputes over states' rights. The most important of these cases was *Chisholm v. Georgia* in 1793.

Chisholm v. Georgia was a lawsuit brought against the state of Georgia by two South Carolina citizens representing a British creditor. The purpose was to recover property taken during the Revolutionary War, or be paid a sum equal to the value of that property.

When the suit went to the Supreme Court, the Georgians refused to enter a plea. In a written document, the state of Georgia denied the authority of the Supreme Court to judge such a case.

Chief Justice John Jay approached the case of *Chisholm v. Georgia* by contrasting life in Europe and America. In Europe, he pointed out, sovereignty, or absolute power, was held by rulers over their subjects. In America, sovereignty was in the hands of the people. To Jay's way of thinking, any individual could sue another individual or group of individuals. He wrote:

> In the State of Delaware, there are fifty-odd thousand free citizens, and what reason can be assigned why a free citizen who has demands against him should not prosecute them? Can the difference between forty-odd thousand and fifty-odd thousand make any distinction as to the right? . . . In this land of equal liberty, shall forty-odd thousand in one place be forced to do justice, and yet fifty-odd thousand in another place be allowed to do justice only as they think proper? Such objections would not correspond with the equal rights, with the equality we profess to admire and maintain, and with that popular sovereignty which every citizen shares in.

Georgia was not convinced by Jay's speech. The state refused to obey the Court's order to pay the claim. The Georgia House of Representatives introduced a bill warning that anyone who tried to carry out the order of the Court would be judged "guilty of felony and shall suffer death, without benefit of clergy, by being hanged." The Supreme Court's order was never carried out.

The Supreme Court's decision had gone against Georgia. But in the end, it was a setback for the Court rather than the state. The Court was powerless to enforce its decision. Later, partly as a result of this decision, an amendment to the Constitution was passed. The amendment forbids the federal judiciary from hearing any suit that involves a state being sued by a citizen of another state or nation. This was the Eleventh Amendment to the Constitution.

1. Briefly describe the case of *Chisholm v. Georgia*.

2. What was the main issue in *Chisholm v. Georgia*?

3. How did Chief Justice John Jay view the case? What was his judgment?

4. In what two ways did the Supreme Court suffer a setback after the decision?

5. How has the issue of states' rights made an impact on the history of the United States?

Developing your basic civic education skills

A State Trooper's Workday
(determining sequence and cause-and-effect)

In this chapter, you have read about some of the services provided by state governments. Now you can learn about one function of state government in more detail. It concerns a service you can see any time you travel on a highway. The story is about a typical workday of a state trooper.

Just before 11 o'clock on a Friday night, Trooper Roland Wildey swings into the darkened drive of a closed service station for a routine check. Wildey, 29, is a 7-year veteran of the New York State Police. If everything is secure, he will turn his black-and-white police car back toward his trooper barracks. A night-shift trooper is already waiting to relieve him. It has been 9 hours since Trooper Wildey began his tour of duty. He is eager to go home to his wife, Emily.

Wildey hits the windows and doors with the car's spotlight. All the glass is in place. He is heading back toward County Route 9H when he sees a yellow convertible pull out from a brightly lighted tavern across the road. Except to Wildey's trained eye, there is nothing apparently unusual about the car. It moves strangely, just as the driver finds his lane.

Wildey is due for relief in 10 minutes. But he starts cruising behind the yellow car. The convertible moves smoothly on, well within the speed limit. Wildey's attention is completely focused. Another car appears from the opposite direction—and suddenly the convertible drives sharply left, directly into its path. Wildey throws on his flashing red light in a desperate attempt to prevent what is about to happen. He tenses as, tires screaming, the approaching car cuts right at the last possible second onto the dusty shoulder of the road. It escapes with inches to spare. As Wildey passes, he can see several small children in the back of the car on the shoulder.

The driver of the yellow car rolls on and slowly returns to his lane. Wildey must wait another minute before the driver becomes aware of his flashing red light and the convertible eases to a stop. Looking into the car, Wildey sees a dulled and expressionless face. The smell of alcohol pours out. The trooper asks for license and registration.

Within 10 minutes, Wildey has placed the car's driver under arrest for driving while drunk. He has explained the driver's rights, taken him to the troop car, locked up the yellow convertible, and headed back to the barracks. He must forget about going home. He now faces hours of tests, reports, and further investigation.

Removing his trooper's wide-brimmed gray hat, Wildey settles his 6-foot, 2-inch body into a chair. Lines of tiredness lightly form on his face. The stress of the day has begun to show. He explains to the arrested driver that under New York law he has 2 hours to decide whether to take a breath test. The test determines the amount of alcohol in his blood. If he refuses, he will lose his license for 6 months. If he agrees, the test results can be used either for or against him. The man says he will do nothing until his lawyer arrives.

Wildey nods and goes across the hall to a machine that is linked to a central computer in Albany, the state capital. He punches in the arrested man's name and date of birth. Result: a long list of serious traffic violations. The latest, not quite a year old, is a conviction for drunk driving. A look of satisfaction crosses Wildey's face. He has pulled a problem drinker off the road.

It is past midnight when the arrested man's attorney arrives. There are only 15 minutes left in the 2-hour time limit. The lawyer announces that his client will take the test. Wildey has already made the necessary preparations. The man breathes into a tube. His breath mixes with a chemical in the machine, and a thin, black needle rises on the scale. The lawyer's client has a 0.25 on a scale where 0.11 is considered drunk, and 0.40 is often an alcohol level that can kill.

Wildey has made a solid arrest. The man's second charge of driving while drunk in a 10-year period is, under New York law, a serious crime.

It is 1:45 A.M. Saturday, 12 hours and 15 minutes since Wildey came on duty. He can now begin thinking about much-needed rest.

1. List in chronological order what you feel is the sequence of events in this story. Begin when Trooper Wildey made a routine check of the service station.

2. Which one of the following from the story about the state trooper could be called a cause?
   a. the arrest of the man driving the yellow car
   b. how the driver of the yellow car drove down the highway
   c. the time Trooper Wildey went off duty

3. Which one of the following from the story about the state trooper could be called an effect?
   a. the arrest of the man driving the yellow car
   b. how the driver of the yellow car drove down the highway
   c. how long Trooper Wildey was on duty

4. What were two of the duties of this state trooper? What role did he play as part of a state government?

Welfare Programs
(distinguishing fact from opinion —asking questions)

In recent years, the subject of welfare has been a controversial issue. Welfare is the assistance people get from a government. People depend on this help.

The term *welfare* covers a great variety of government programs that give help to individuals and groups.

Sometimes people differ over what public funding to call welfare. Are federal subsidies [grants of money] to businesses and farmers a form of welfare? What about tax laws that aid mainly middle- and upper-income citizens? What about Social Security benefits to which people have contributed from their earnings? Some people would include these under welfare, and some would not. On the other hand, nearly everybody would agree that welfare does include the food-stamp program and aid to mothers with dependent children.

The subject of welfare at the state level in 1980 is discussed in the following account. As you read it, keep in mind the definitions of the terms *fact, opinion, hypothesis,* and *generalization.*

Welfare is a controversial and often emotional subject. Some people argue against any type of welfare. Others argue that it is the responsibility of the state to care for its less-fortunate individuals. Critics point to publicized abuses of the system. Defenders call for changes to assure the fair distribution of welfare funds. In the midst of the pros and cons, generalizations emerge that often become accepted as facts.

To clear up such generalizations, the Texas Department of Human Resources has published a pamphlet entitled "Facts about Texas Welfare." The pamphlet gives statistical information guaranteed by state welfare officials to be based in fact, documented, and 100 percent accurate. The information allows readers to draw their own conclusions.

"Illegal aliens on welfare . . ." —Illegal aliens are entitled to no welfare benefits. Any illegal alien found to be on the Texas welfare rolls is reported to the local district attorney for prosecution on theft charges.

"More and more welfare babies . . ."—The size of the Texas welfare family has dropped from an average of 4.12 persons in 1971 to 3.39 persons in 1976.

"Getting rich off welfare . . ." —Texas pays its average welfare family $104 per month. Forty-seven states have a higher average monthly payment.

"Able-bodied men on welfare . . ."—Ninety-five percent of all Texas welfare checks go to female head-of-household families. A Texas family with both father and mother living in the house does not qualify for any cash assistance. Thirty states do allow both parents to live in a welfare household.

Widespread fraud and errors . . ."—Less than 1 percent of all food-stamp cases in Texas have been found to be unqualified for food stamps. The total of all errors equals 8.5 percent. The national average is 13.4.

"The growing welfare bureaucracy . . ."—In 1970–71, Texas welfare accounted for 19.7 percent of the entire state budget. In 1980–81, it accounted for 17 percent. Nationwide, there are 17 state and local welfare employees per 10,000 population. In Texas, there are 11 per 10,000.

"A lifetime on welfare . . ."

—In Texas, the average length of stay on the welfare rolls is 4 ½ years. Two-thirds of all welfare families are on the rolls only once.

"Everyone is on welfare . . ." —In 1976, the average number of Texas people on welfare was 27.3 per 1,000 population. The national average was 52 per 1,000. The District of Columbia had 139.8 people on welfare per 1,000 population.

"With all the benefits, they are rich . . ."—Combined welfare and food-stamp benefits for the average Texas welfare family amounts to $238 per month. This is less than half the poverty level. Of all welfare families, 16.6 percent receive housing partly paid for by the government. Even with the cost of paid medical coverage for welfare families included, they receive less than two-thirds the poverty-level wage.

"Welfare payments are going to break the state . . ."—Of a total Texas welfare budget of $1.37 billion in 1979, only $35 million in state funds went for welfare payments. The state budget for welfare payments equals 2 percent of the entire welfare budget.

"Welfare administration is much too high . . ."—In the 1981 Texas welfare budget, 7.8 percent of the monies went for agency administration. If the 1983 budget is approved, as is, by the Texas Legislature, that 7.8 percent will drop to 4.3 percent.

"The food stamp Cadillac . . ." —Anyone under the age of 60 receiving food stamps whose automobile is worth $6,250 is not qualified for any assistance. This is true even if they have not a single penny in cash, resources, or income.

5. Why is welfare often a controversial and emotional subject?

6. Which five of the following statements could best be classified as fact?
   a. Illegal aliens cannot get welfare.
   b. There are too many illegal aliens on welfare.
   c. Many people get rich living on welfare.
   d. The average Texas welfare family gets $104 per month.
   e. Of people on welfare in Texas, 8.5 percent cheat the welfare system.
   f. Many people cheat to get on welfare rolls.
   g. Most families stay on welfare for a lifetime.
   h. In Texas, the average length of stay on the welfare rolls is 4 ½ years.
   i. In the 1981 Texas welfare budget, 7.8 percent of the monies went for agency administration.
   j. Too many people are employed to run welfare programs.

7. Which five statements in question 6 could best be classified as opinion? Why?

8. What could make those five opinion statements in question 6 into statements of fact?

9. Suppose you wanted to evaluate the information presented in this account about state welfare. What are two recall questions, two application questions, and one judgment question you might pose?

11 Local Government

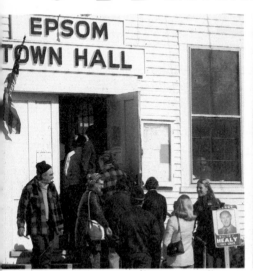

When the United States was first settled, people needed a government that was within their reach. They valued their right to take an active part in governing their lives. State governments were important to them—as you saw in the last chapter—, but even state governments were too far away from most people in the days before airplanes, cars, and superhighways.

To fill their need, colonists set up many local governments. These ranged from small village governments to larger county governments. They included governments for cities, boroughs, towns, and townships.

Local governments have a different place in the federal system than the states have. States form a partnership with the federal government. Each state has its own powers and responsibilities, but they also share some powers. Local governments, on the other hand, have only the power and authority that the state gives them in their constitution or charter.

In this chapter, you will explore the different types of local governments, how they affect your life, and how you can have an effect on them.

I. Local communities and you
   A. A variety of local communities
   B. Local services
   C. The citizen's role in local government

II. Organization of local governments
   A. Three forms of local government
      1. Mayor-council form
      2. Commission form
      3. Council-manager form

B. County government
C. Town government
D. Special district government

Local Communities and You

What type of local community do you live in? Are you one of the 170 million people in the United States who live in a city or in its suburbs? Do you live in a town, a township, a borough, or a village? Perhaps you live in a rural area. No matter what type of community you live in, you have at least one local government. In every part of the United States, local governments are closest to the people. Citizens also have the greatest opportunity to influence their local governments.

Words to Know

county —— the largest unit of local government

town —— a unit of local government within a county

township —— a division of a county found in some mid-Atlantic and Midwestern states

municipality —— a city, town, village, or borough that a state sets up as a unit of local government

special district —— a unit of local government that performs a specific public service

block association —— a group of citizens who work together to improve their neighborhood

A Variety of Local Communities

Local communities in the United States have grown over nearly 400 years. It should not be surprising that they differ from each other.

The largest unit of local government is usually a **county.** County boundaries were set up so that everyone living in the county could reach the county seat—the place where the government does business—in a day by carriage or on horseback. Today, every state except Alaska, Connecticut, Louisiana, and Rhode Island is divided into counties. These come in every possible shape and size. Texas has the largest number of counties—254—but one of them, Loving County, has less than 150 people. Los Angeles County in California, on the other hand, has about 7 million people.

Counties are both urban and rural. A few counties—such as Cook County, Illinois—contain one large urban area. The city of Chicago is located in Cook County. In fact, one-fifth of the people of the United States live in just sixteen of over 3,000 counties. Most counties have a population of less than 50,000 people.

In some states, counties are divided into smaller units called towns and townships. One type of town is found only in New England. Early settlers there built homes near one another for protection. They farmed the surrounding land. The village area and the farm land together were known as the **town.** These towns, begun during the colonial period, are still the basis of government in much of New England.

Townships are found in the mid-Atlantic states and in several Midwestern states. In New York, New Jersey, Pennsylvania, and Delaware, townships grew during colonial times, much in the same way that New England towns did.

In the Midwest, however, townships were mostly set up by Congress in the Northwest Ordinance of 1787. The ordinance divided the Northwest Territory into townships that were 6 miles long and 6 miles wide. This dividing up of the land was done to control land sales in the territory. In many areas, these townships became the unit of local government.

You probably live in a county, and perhaps in a township. Like more than 70 percent of the people in the United States, you may also live in a municipality. A **municipality** is a city, town, village, or borough that is set up by the state as a unit of local self-government. Cities are usually large municipalities. In Georgia, however, a community of only 200 people can be a city. *Town, village,* and *borough* are names for small municipalities in different parts of the country.

Like most people, you are probably not aware of another local government, even though it is the most common. This government is called a **special district.** A special district is a unit of government that is set up to perform a single public service. The service might be management of the schools, fire protection, soil conservation, treatment and disposal of sewage, or one of many others. The boundaries of special districts do not have to match those of the municipality or the county. One fire-protection district, for example, might cover only part of a city. A soil-conservation district might cover an area larger than one city or county.

Local Governments

Local Government	Number in U.S.
Counties	3,042
Municipalities	18,862
Townships and New England towns	16,882
Special districts	41,136

SOURCE: The Municipal Yearbook, 1981.

Local Services

Each of the above can have a major impact on your life. One of the jobs of any government is to give services to its citizens. You use these services every day, even though you may not think about them.

Local government provides a number of services to its citizens. One such service is sanitation, which includes everything from supplying clean water to homes to removing water wastes and keeping main streets clear of rain and snow.

Often, it is local government that gives the services that touch your daily life. In fact, local governments often carry out state and federal programs.

To become more aware of some of these services, think about a normal day. Your contact with local services might begin as soon as you wake up. The water you drink or use to wash could come from the local government. Local water departments pump water from lakes, rivers, or reservoirs. The water is cleaned and pumped through miles of underground pipes to homes. Sanitation departments often supply a system of pipes to take waste water away from the homes. This water is usually cleaned, or treated, before it is pumped back into the lake or river. Bringing clean water to homes and removing water wastes is a huge task.

The electricity for your lights, television sets, and refrigerators may come from a special power district or from a private utility company. Usually, however, the state or local government closely controls the companies, the way they are run, and the prices that they charge.

Local governments also repair streets and keep them clean. Often, this means collecting garbage. Street lights, traffic lights, and road signs are other examples of services that a local government might give to its citizens.

Your school itself is a service of local government. The local school district—a special district—keeps up the school and runs it. A local board of education hires teachers and sets policies for the schools within the district.

The school building, like other local buildings, must meet building codes, or laws. These might cover the materials used to build the school, its size, the number of doors it has, and many other items. Buildings also have to pass fire inspection.

Fire protection is an important local service. Members of the fire department inspect homes and public buildings to find fire dangers. In this way, they try to keep fires from happening. They must also fight those fires that do break out.

After school, you might visit the public library, play baseball or soccer at a nearby park, or perhaps go swimming. In many communities, local governments provide these types of services. They might also support a golf course, youth centers and senior citizen centers, and museums or art galleries.

These students benefit from another service of local government—the setting up, structuring, and maintenance of a district school system.

The local police department must protect the public. Police officers keep the peace by enforcing the laws. They arrest those persons who break the laws. You will recall from Chapter 10 that local courts are part of the state judicial system.

These are just some of the services that local governments can give us. All communities, of course, do not provide the services in the same way. For example, a large city probably has its own sanitation department for garbage collection. In a suburb, citizens might pay a small fee for a private collector. A small town might hire a private company to do this. In a rural area, the county government may run a dump, where citizens take their own garbage.

Another example is fire protection. Many communities have full-time, salaried fire fighters. Other communities use volunteers. Some communities use both.

Schools also differ among communities. In some areas, the eighth grade is part of a junior high school. In others, it is in a middle school. In still other places, the eighth grade may be the last grade in elementary school. Sometimes these differences appear in the same community.

The Citizen's Role in Local Government

In colonial times, people valued their local governments. They felt they could have more of a say in the local government than in the state or federal government. Citizens today can often have an even greater effect on a local government. One reason for this is that most people live closer to the county seat or to the city hall than to Washington, D.C. It is easy for them to visit the city hall if they want to ask a question or make a complaint. Citizens can also attend many meetings of city councils or school boards. Also, a person's vote often has a greater effect in a local election, since there are fewer voters.

Many people, however, do not take part in their local government. Often, as few as one-fourth of those who are qualified vote in a municipal election. One reason for this lack of interest is that people often are not aware of the important role that local governments play in their lives. Citizens may also feel that their actions will not mean anything, even at the local level.

This last feeling is strong in large cities. Urban problems tend to be very complex, and urban populations are very large. Individual citizens sometimes feel helpless.

You may have heard the saying, "You can't fight city hall." This means that people feel that they cannot have any effect on the way the city is run.

Even in large cities, however, many citizens do take part in their local government. They often act together with other citizens in community groups. One such group, in Baltimore, Maryland, is the Southeast Community Organization. Citizens formed it in 1970 to fight the building of a new highway through part of the city.

In New York City, citizens have formed many **block associations** to improve their neighborhoods. They clean up parks and streets. Some block associations fix up older buildings so that people will want to stay in the city.

Community involvement functions on many different levels. Here a Greenwich Village block party brings neighbors together and fosters community pride.

Local neighborhood groups such as these are active all over the country. They can be found in large and small cities, as well as in small towns. By working in groups, citizens increase their influence on the government. A busy city council is more likely to listen to a group with a plan than to one person's ideas.

In at least one city, community groups have become a part of the city government. In Dayton, Ohio, each of the city's six neighborhoods has a *priority board*. Local citizens elect between twenty-five and thirty-five people to serve on their board. The board meets at least once a month and talks about problems and goals of the neighborhood. The board then tells the city government how the government can help the neighborhood solve its problems and reach its goals.

─────── REVIEW ───────

1. Define the following words:

   county
   municipality
   township
   special district

2. Describe four different kinds of local governments.

3. What are three services that local governments can give?

4. How can citizens take part in local government?

5. Do you think it is important for citizens to take part in local government? Give at least three good reasons for your answer.

Words to Know

mayor-council form ── a system of local government in which voters elect a mayor and a city council

ordinances ── laws passed by a local government

commission ── a group of officials—usually elected—who have duties and jobs that are described by law

council-manager form ── a system of local government in which voters elect a city council, which hires a city manager

commission form ── a system of local government in which voters elect a small number of commissioners

Organization of Local Governments

Local governments differ as much as the communities they serve. Even two cities with the same population and the same kinds of problems can have very different governments. In spite of these differences, however, we can list the general types of governments used in municipalities, counties, townships, New England towns, and special districts.

Three Forms of Local Government

Mayor-Council Form Over half of the cities in the United States have a **mayor-council form** of government. Voters elect a mayor and a city council. The city council may have as few as five members, or it can have as many as fifty, like the Chicago City Council.

Distribution of the Three Forms of Municipal Government

Form of Government	Number of Cities
Mayor-council	3,640
Council-manager	2,410
Commission	194

SOURCE: The Municipal Yearbook, 1981.

A city council is the legislative branch of the mayor-council form of government. It passes laws called **ordinances.** The mayor makes sure that these laws are carried out. She or he is the city's chief executive. The mayors in some cities, however, have much more power than mayors in other cities. A "strong" mayor can veto ordinances passed by the council. He or she can also appoint and remove most city officials. These officials usually include the police and fire chiefs, the heads of departments—such as housing, sanitation, parks, and traffic. "Weak" mayors often have veto power, but they are not able to appoint or remove as many city officials as "strong" mayors.

During the 1800s almost every city in the United States had a mayor-council form of government. Today, almost half of these cities have a different type of city government. Some cities found that the mayor and the city council were not able to work well together. In other cities, sometimes voters thought that the mayor was too pow-

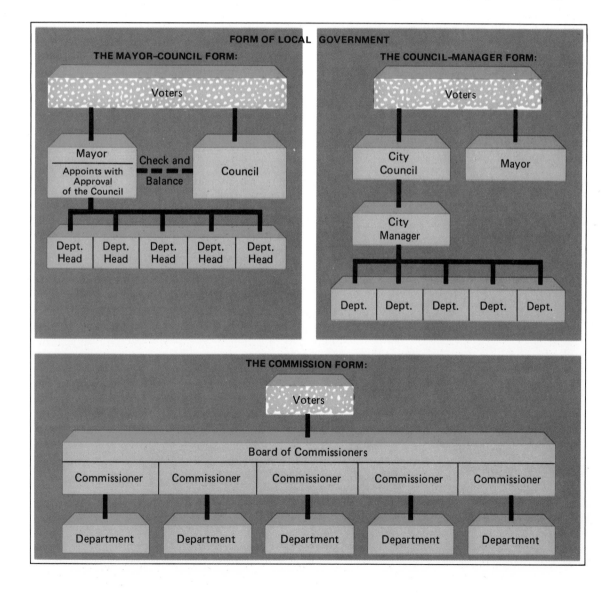

erful. They found that political parties had too much influence over the mayor. Sometimes mayors were not able to run the city well because problems had grown too complex. For one or all of these reasons, many cities turned to one of two other forms of government—either a commission form of government or a council-manager form of government.

Commission Form The **commission form** of government has no chief executive. Voters elect between three and seven persons to a city **commission.** Like a city council, the city commission passes ordinances. Each commissioner also serves as the head of a city department.

There is no separation of powers in this type of government. The same group passes the laws and makes sure that they are carried out. Because there is no chief executive, commissioners sometimes com-pete with each other for city money and for power. This can make it difficult to get good government.

The commission form was popular early in this century. Today, only a few cities still use it. Some of the largest cities include Portland, Oregon; Tulsa, Oklahoma; and St. Paul, Minnesota.

Council-Manager Form A growing number of cities use the **council-manager form** of city government. Under this plan, voters elect a small city council. The council then hires a manager who is an expert in city administration. The city manager appoints most other city officials and runs the city government. If a city manager does not do a good job, she or he can be fired by the city council.

Medium-sized cities are most likely to prefer a council-manager form of government. Some large cities also use it, how-

This scene of a city-council meeting in progress is typical of the mayor-council system found in the majority of local governments.

ever—Cincinnati, Ohio, and Dallas, Texas, for example.

A major problem with this type of city government is finding a good city manager. Some cities, mostly small ones, have found that they cannot afford to use this plan. In other cities, voters feel that they have more control over the government if they elect the important officials.

Governments in villages, towns, and boroughs are like city governments. Most use a mayor-council form of government with a "weak" mayor. Often, the mayor and the council members serve part time, without pay. As small communities grow, however, governing them becomes more difficult. Local officials are finding that they need to spend more time on their jobs.

County Government

Many county governments seem to be a confusing mixture of boards and elected officials. One reason is that county governments have not changed much since colonial times. If a new service was needed, a department or official was often "tacked on" to the government. Few county governments have been reorganized to meet new problems.

The governing body of a county is most often an elected board. It might be called such names as the *county board, board of supervisors, or county commissioners.* The county board is the lawmaking body for the county. It may also carry out the laws that it passes.

Most counties do not have a chief executive, such as a mayor. Voters do elect many officials, however. These often include a sheriff—who keeps the peace and serves as an officer of the county court—, a clerk—who keeps the public records—, and a coroner—who looks for the cause of death in suspicious cases.

In many areas, people look to the county government to give more services

The Women of Walthourville

Walthourville is a town so tiny folks in that part of Georgia would call it a wide place in the road. A couple of new stores with gas pumps are the visible heart of the community of 433, which got its start back in 1795 under the leadership of men. For 179 years nothing much happened. Then, in 1974, the women took over and Walthourville became a little more than a couple of friendly lights for the night driver.

Mrs. Lyndol Anderson, who is 51 and a grandmother, got together with other women and decided Walthourville should become a real city, with real services like streets and sewers. They planned and talked it up until just about everyone in town was with them. They enlisted the services of a former judge who helped them organize and petition for incorporation as a separate town. He pushed the petition through and Walthourville became a certified town governed by women.

The first notes of discord came when Thomas Edward (Ed) Rogers decided to run for mayor in the first election. "I don't think," Rogers said, "women should be in politics." Male opponents went on the ballot against all but one councilwoman. The election shaped up as a man-woman conflict.

The result was a landslide for the women candidates. What began as a male-female fight developed into an election by people. "More men were pulling for us than against," said Mayor Anderson. "More came and encouraged us."

So if Walthourville is only a wide place in the road motorists might miss if they blinked, they will be able to find it now even in the dark.

than in the past. This is most true where the population is growing rapidly. Local officials are finding that old types of county government do not work well today. A major problem is the lack of strong leadership.

To solve this problem, some counties have reorganized their governments. Two new types of county governments have appeared. In one type, voters elect a county board and a county mayor, or president. The county mayor is the chief executive. He or she appoints most other county officials. Several urban counties, such as Westchester County in New York, St. Louis County in Missouri, and Cook County in Illinois, use this type of county government.

In the second type, some counties have hired a manager who is like the city manager. The manager runs county programs. Twenty states have at least one county with a council-manager type of government. North Carolina has the largest number of counties using this form. California and Virginia have the next largest number.

Town Government

If you live in a New England town, you might have the chance to take part in one of the few direct democracies in the world. Remember that in a direct democracy, citizens suggest and vote on laws and policies themselves. They do not elect other people to represent them in the government.

The heart of the New England town government is the town meeting. Voters attend a town meeting, usually once a year. They discuss and vote on important policies. They also elect town officials. These can include a clerk, a tax collector, the school board, a treasurer, and a board of selectmen. The board of selectmen runs the government between town meetings.

Direct democracy works best in a small community with common interests

and problems. However, many New England towns are growing rapidly. Their populations are becoming more varied. A large meeting is often not the best way to handle the new problems created by this growth.

A second problem facing New England towns is that fewer citizens attend the meetings now. A study in Rhode Island, for example, showed that only about 9 percent of the voters regularly come to town meetings.

As a result of these problems, the board of selectmen in many towns plays more of a role in town government. In some towns, voters elect representatives who then attend a smaller town meeting. A few towns have also hired managers to deal with problems and supply services.

Governments in townships are like those in New England towns in many ways. Town meetings are held in about half the states with townships. In most townships, voters elect a board of trustees or supervisors to govern the township.

The power of township government, however, has been decreasing. Often, county governments have taken over many of their jobs. Townships in urban states, such as New Jersey, are difficult to pick out from nearby city or borough governments.

Special District Government

You probably live in several special districts. In a rural area, one of the most important special districts, is the soil-conservation district. Cemetery districts and housing authorities are the most common special districts in suburban areas. The chart on page 292 shows many of the services that special districts give.

Like local governments, special districts are set up by the state. They are governed by a small board. Voters elect some of the boards, such as the school board. But in many cases, state or local officials appoint

Small-town governments are more responsive to the needs of their constituents. The reverse is also true. These two photos show both sides of the picture—private citizens operating as a volunteer fire brigade and a mobile counseling unit staffed by a career counselor.

Services of Special Districts

Type of District	Number of Districts
School district	15,781
Fire protection	3,872
Soil conservation	2,564
Urban water supply	2,473
Drainage	2,192
Housing	2,270
Cemeteries	1,496
Sewage treatment	1,406
School buildings	1,085
Water conservation	966
Parks and recreation	749
Highways	698
Flood control	677
Hospitals	655
Libraries	498
Others	2,280

SOURCE: Bureau of the Census, Census of Governments.

board members. This means that citizens often have little control over the actions of special districts.

Yet special districts serve an important purpose. They often handle problems that go beyond the reach of local governments. Also, special districts are useful in dealing with short-term problems. They have more freedom of action, since special districts are independent of other local governments.

──────────── REVIEW ────────────

1. Define the following words:
   commission
   ordinances
   direct democracy
   town meetings

2. What are the three basic forms of municipal government found in the United States today?

3. How are some county governments changing to meet the challenge of a growing urban population?

4. List five services that are given by special districts.

5. The different types of local government can be very confusing. Should all communities be made to use the same type of government? Why or why not?

How the United States Works

Fire fighter

A fire is always exciting and dangerous. People crowd around to watch the smoke, the flames, and the fire fighters, who risk their lives to save others' lives. Fire fighters are in danger of cave-ins, burns, and smoke injuries. Nevertheless, they save thousands of lives and millions of dollars of property every year.

Fighting fires is not just risky. It is also very demanding. Fire fighters do their jobs rain or shine, whether its 100°F or 20° below zero. At a fire, they carry heavy gear up and down stairs or ladders. They search for trapped people. They hack holes in the roof to release smoke and gas. They hold hoses on the fire. The hoses are heavy, and the water in them shoots out under great pressure. In fact, it usually takes two fire fighters to hold one hose.

Fire fighters also have many other duties. Sometimes they have to give first aid, and their equipment must be kept in order. They must visit factories and public buildings to check for fire dangers.

Most fire fighters are on duty about 50 hours a week. Not all that time is spent at fires, however. Much of it is spent in the firehouse. There, fire fighters can eat, sleep, or read. They must clean and take care of their equipment. Whatever they do, they must be ready to rush to a fire at any moment.

Fire fighters are hired by local governments. Some small cities and towns use volunteer fire fighters. Fighting fires is an important job. That means there will always be jobs for fire fighters. However, the number of jobs available and the rate of pay depend upon the budget. Beginning fire fighters make between $11,000 and $14,500, and they generally receive regular raises.

A person has to pass certain tests in order to be hired as a fire fighter. Among these are tests of intelligence and strength. The tests are given to men and women who meet the height and weight standards and have high school degrees. Applicants must also

be at least 18 years old. After they are hired, new fire fighters spend a few weeks in a training school. Then they are assigned to a fire company.

Reading About . . .

A Member of a Town Council

The author of the following reading is a member of a town council in an Eastern state. The reading will give you an idea of the both simple and complex problems that come up every day in local government.

As you read, think about the following:

● What kinds of problems does the author think are the toughest?
● Does the author seem to like the job?

"What sort of things do I dislike? Mrs. Garfield's drainage. It represents all the simple problems that are impossible to settle simply. In the beginning I assumed I could help people who had problems—water running off a town road and wrecking

Mrs. Garfield's lawn, say. Now I know the odds are against me.

"First I have to get the Highway Superintendent and Town Engineer to figure out what's wrong. They have to take time off from a million-dollar water study to do that. Then, if it is the Town's fault, we must find out how much it will cost to fix and whether the harm being done to Mrs. Garfield justifies spending that much of the other taxpayers' money.

"Everybody in politics sours a bit on the populace sooner or later. Some politicians conclude that the voters are loony, and when a complaint comes in they assume it's exaggerated or groundless. I still assume that the problem is real and important to that person at least. But I know there's a discouraging chance that we can't or shouldn't do anything about it.

"Yet, if we drove around town, I could point out places every few hundred feet where I've had some sort of impact: here's where I helped the Supervisor set up a con-

nection for emergency water supply, here are four tennis courts we built, here's where we kept New York City from building a large garage, here's where we got the state to fix a dangerous curve. But some of those things would have happened regardless of who was in office.

"So I ask myself a really tough question: Is it worth being a grassroots politician in America today?

"Here's how I see it. If more work is better than less, and more reason better than less, and more honest public discussion better than less, then it has been worth it and I've accomplished something.

"As to how I feel about what I've accomplished, that's easy: I feel disappointed and proud. That's politics."

chapter
Review

Fact Review

1. Describe each of the forms of local government listed below. Include one advantage and one disadvantage in your description.
   a. council-manager form
   b. town meeting
   c. special district
2. List the ways in which local government touches your daily life. Which way do you think is most important?
3. Why are a growing number of cities using the council-manager form of government rather than the mayor-council or commission form?
4. How have New England town governments changed in recent years?
5. What are block associations? What do block associations do? Do you have a block association in your neighborhood?
6. What is a priority board? Is a priority board similar to a block association? If so, in what ways are they similar? If not, in what ways do they differ?

7. Which of the following are examples of special districts?
   a. cemeteries
   b. shopping centers
   c. school buildings
   d. housing projects
   e. movie theaters
   f. parks

Developing Your Vocabulary

1. For each word or phrase listed below, write a complete sentence that shows how the word is related to local government.

mayor	borough
county board	block association
town meeting	school district
ordinance	city council
city manager	community

2. Match the terms in *a* to *c* with the definitions in (*1*) to (*3*).
   a. county
   b. township
   c. municipality
   (1) a division of a county found in some Mid-Atlantic and Midwestern states
   (2) a city, town, village, or borough that a state sets up as a unit of local government
   (3) the largest unit of local government

Developing Your Reading Skills

Read the following paragraph and then answer the questions that follow:

In some areas of the United States, counties are becoming more urban. Some counties, in fact, are made up of one large city. Many county governments have had to change to meet the needs of their urban populations. Some have introduced an elected county mayor. In other counties, the county board hires a county manager whose powers are like those of city managers.

1. Which one of the following do you think is the main point, or main idea, of the paragraph above?
   a. Urban populations need more services than rural populations.
   b. Some counties have a manager form of government.
   c. County governments have had to change because they are becoming increasingly urban.
   d. Some counties are made up of one large city.
2. Tell why you selected either *a, b, c,* or *d* in question 1.

Reading Tables

1. About what percentage of the population of the United States was urban in 1880?
2. About what percentage was urban in 1950?
3. When was the first time that more than half of the population of the United States lived in urban areas?
4. Between which two dates did the percentage of urban population grow the most?
5. In what ways is it easier to use this graph than to use a table of numbers?

URBAN POPULATION GROWTH 1880–1980			
Census	Total Population	Urban Population	Percent Urban
1880	50,155,783	14,129,735	28.2
1890	62,947,714	22,106,265	35.1
1900	75,994,575	30,159,921	39.7
1910	91,972,266	41,998,932	45.7
1920	105,710,620	54,157,973	51.2
1930	122,775,046	68,954,823	56.2
1940	131,669,275	74,423,702	56.5
1950	151,325,789	96,847,686	64.0
1960	179,323,175	125,268,750	69.9
1970	203,211,926	149,280,769	73.5
1980	226,504,825	166,965,380	73.7

YOUR GOVERNMENT & ITS HISTORY

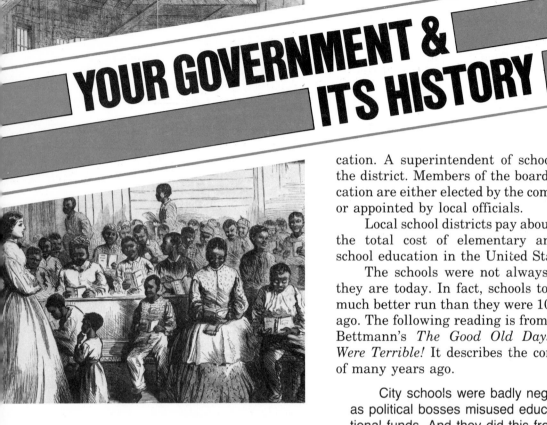

Early Education in America

In this chapter, you have learned that special districts are a part of local government. Special districts are set up to perform a specific public service. One service performed by a special district is the creation and control of public schools. Under rules set up by the state, school districts are responsible for running the schools in their areas. Their responsibilities include maintaining the school buildings, setting policies and procedures for the schools, and hiring teachers. In the United States, there are nearly 16,000 school districts.

In all states except Hawaii, each local school district sets up its own board of edu-cation. A superintendent of schools runs the district. Members of the board of education are either elected by the community or appointed by local officials.

Local school districts pay about half of the total cost of elementary and high school education in the United States.

The schools were not always run as they are today. In fact, schools today are much better run than they were 100 years ago. The following reading is from Otto L. Bettmann's *The Good Old Days—They Were Terrible!* It describes the conditions of many years ago.

City schools were badly neglected as political bosses misused educational funds. And they did this freely, since the board of education was appointed by aldermen [city council members] who were appointed by the mayor, who was controlled by the bosses. . . .

As a result, city schools were too crowded and did not provide enough fresh air. . . . Many teachers confessed that the best they could do was to "maintain order." . . .

One hundred years ago, most states did not allow black students and white students to attend the school. As a result, separate schools were set up for each race.

Many early schools did not have good buildings. Those that did exist were poorly built and poorly kept up. They were filthy, and usually too crowded. The crowding was the most dangerous problem. Schools built for 1,000 pupils had twice that number in their classrooms. A survey of one school in 1893 listed 18 classes with 90 to 100 students. One class had 158 students. There were not enough desks. Those that they had were badly made. Often, three children shared a desk built for two.

A visitor to another school in the same year found one schoolroom where "the furniture was so closely packed that the children were forced to squeeze their little bodies in between the desks. There was barely room enough . . . to breathe, much less to move their limbs about freely."

To one observer, the city school was a factory of hunchbacks. The children's "chests were sunken, their shoulders rounded," the observer said.

And one slum school, located over a live chicken market, lacked chairs and benches. The students studied on their knees.

Many city schools were also hurt by their location. These locations did not allow for decent lighting or air flow. They were often crammed into narrow streets in the shadows of taller buildings or elevated railroads. The schoolrooms were often lighted by only a single gas jet.

Air quality proved as poor as the lighting. A Massachusetts law required 1,800 cubic feet of fresh air per hour per child. But in many city schools in other eastern states, students got closer to 70 cubic feet. "The air . . . became so filthy, foul, and unhealthy that teachers were forced to suspend the studies."

A risk of spreadable disease was present in the classrooms in the absence of cleanliness. "The teachers . . . found themselves giving hundreds of baths each week." One small student answered his teacher's criticism of his appearance with, "Don't never wash—ketch cold."

In 1890, only 20 percent of all black children received any education at all. Their lifetime schooling averaged 100 days.

W. E. B. DuBois, the educator, has left an account of the black school. He described one as a log hut where Colonel Wheeler used to shelter his corn . . . chinks between the logs served as windows. . . . My chair, borrowed from the landlady, had to be returned every night." There were no desks, and crude backless boards served as seats. These "had the one virtue of making napping dangerous," DuBois wrote.

State constitutions, amended to give blacks separate but "equal" education, were ignored. Promised funds were simply never paid. School facilities remained totally unequal.

1. What public service do special districts serve in regard to education?

2. In the examples cited, what was school like for many white students 100 years ago? Give three examples.

3. In the examples cited, what was school like for many black students at that time? Give three examples.

4. Under what conditions do you think learning best occurs? Explain your answer.

Developing your basic civic education skills

A City Council Member

(asking questions)

As you have learned, citizens serve on councils and commissions in city and town governments. The following story concerns Henry Cisneros. In 1975, Cisneros was a member of the city council in San Antonio, Texas. That city has a mayor-council type of local government. Since the publication of the following story, Cisneros was elected mayor of San Antonio.

City Councilman Henry Cisneros worked as a garbage man. Cisneros collected garbage for about 4 hours one day. He accompanied a city crew as it made its rounds in southeast San Antonio. He and a partner regularly picked up about 11,000 pounds of garbage from some 900 homes. In the past Cisneros also had ridden with patrolling police and emergency medical service workers. He said he worked at these jobs to get an understanding of the departments and their services.

"You can sit on the City Council. . . . But if you are serious about it, you have to understand the job from the point of view of the people who do it," he said.

Cisneros came out of the garbage-collecting experience with sore muscles and a bruise on his face from a low-hanging tree branch. He also picked up a new respect for garbage collectors.

"I learned a lot," Cisneros said. "Those guys really work hard. I thought I was in pretty good physical shape, but they test you."

He said he saw at least three ways citizens can help out garbage collectors and, at the same time, help save on the city's labor bill:

Get a strong but lightweight garbage can, and keep it in good shape. "It makes a lot of difference to pick up a solid can with a handle as opposed to an old can with no handles and a rusted-out bottom."

Keep lids on garbage cans. Cisneros said open cans only invite dogs. They also catch rain, which "about triples their weight."

Use plastic bags as garbage-can liners when possible, Cisneros suggested.

Cisneros said by working as a garbage collector, he hoped not only to learn about the needs of the department but also enough so he could answer citizens' questions about trash collection.

With a new budget now being considered by the city council, Cisneros plans to study the pay scales of garbage workers. Indicating that they might deserve a raise, Cisneros said of the garbage collectors: "They really work hard. . . . It is a tough job; it really is."

Cisneros praised what he called "dignity and team spirit" among the garbage collectors. He urged citizens to be considerate in the way they leave their trash for pickup. He urged them not to look on garbage collectors as mere "machines."

"Something nasty and foul-smelling is nasty and foul-smelling to them," he said.

Cisneros said he encountered his share of nasty things as a garbage man—"dead animals and stinking water from a couple of days of rain." The worst thing, he said, was the weight lifting.

"Basically, garbage is heavy. People put two cans out there, with a little bit of water in them—you must be lifting 50 pounds a shot."

1. What kind of work did Henry Cisneros do for about 4 hours one day?

2. What were two reasons he gave for doing that work?

3. How did the work of the garbage collectors compare with that of a state trooper? (See pages 276–277.)

4. Do you think more city council or commission members should do the kind of thing Cisneros did? Support your answer.

5. Classify the questions you just answered according to whether they are recall, application, or judgment questions. Give reasons for your choices.

Women Police Officers
(distinguishing fact from opinion)

Police departments around the country began to experience some dramatic changes in the late 1960s and early 1970s. Crime rates soared from coast to coast. Police work was becoming more dangerous than it had ever been. More police officers were being injured or killed in the line of duty than ever before. And, for the first time, women began to take on law enforcement responsibilities in police departments around the country that they had never been allowed in the past.

The first city in the United States to allow women to assume the same responsibilities as their male counterparts in police work was Indianapolis, Indiana. There, in 1968, police officers Betty Blankenship and Elizabeth Coffal were assigned to patrol duty for the first time. This assignment came as a result of years of requests for such work.

Previously, female police officers were used primarily as office workers, guards in women's prisons, and as juvenile officers. Women were viewed as being too emotional and physically unfit to handle the same assignments as men. Many male officers refused to patrol with women. These officers argued that they would not feel as confident and secure if they were to need assistance as they would with a male partner.

When officers Blankenship and Coffal were finally assigned to patrol duty by their superior officer, Police Chief Winston Churchill, it came with one day's notice. Because no women had ever been given this sort of assignment before, the two officers were forced to take on their new role with no training whatsoever.

Although training for patrol officers varies from area to area, there are certain requirements that must be met. In New York City, for example, patrol officers must pass a minimum of 6 months of instruction. This instruction includes 4 hours a day in the classroom and 3 hours a day of physical training. Among the subjects covered in the physical training segment are first aid, the use of firearms, and hand-to-hand combat.

For two officers with no prior patrol experience or training, Blankenship and Coffal did extremely well. In responding to calls of all descriptions, from domestic quarrels to robberies to murder, the two new officers proved to be more than able to handle a role that was formerly assumed to be beyond their capabilities. As a matter of fact, their work as patrol officers proved to be so successful that it came to be used as a model for other cities—such as Washington, Detroit, and Los Angeles—to follow.

By the early 1970s, opposition to female patrol officers within police departments had weakened considerably. Male hostility toward patroling with women lessened as women proved to be equal to their tasks. In some situations, such as family fights, female officers actually showed themselves to be superior to males in calming potentially explosive situations.

In a published interview on the subject of female patrol officers, Catherine Milton, assistant director of the Police Foundation, is quoted as saying that, in domestic situations, women are less threatening to violent males than are male officers.

"Take a policeman who answers a domestic call and finds a violent male. The male may feel the need to prove his manhood by not backing down from the officer. The officer, in turn, may feel a need to prove his manhood by coming at the offender head-on. Often, with a female officer in that situation, the male offender is caught off balance. He would lose face by attacking a woman."

In 1974, the Police Foundation, a Washington D.C.-based research organization, conducted a survey comparing 86 female officers with 86 male officers. The results of the survey showed that, in the span of a year's observation, there was very little difference noted between the abilities of men and the abilities of women to deal with violent, or potentially violent, confrontations. Similarly, women were found to be equal to men in the number of injuries suffered on the job, in the percentage of arrests made that resulted in convictions, and in the number of involvements in situations that required requests for back-up assistance.

A later study by the Urban Institute in Washington, D.C., stated that policewomen were able to deal with violent situations with considerably less violence than males. This was due, according to the Institute, to a willingness to talk a situation out before resorting to violence. On the whole, women police officers have proven to be less aggressive and less violence-provoking than their male counterparts.

Officers Blankenship and Coffal have not been the only policewomen to achieve recognition for their work. In 1974, Washington, D.C., policewoman Gail A. Cobb became the first female police officer to die in uniform. Officer Cobb was shot while chasing a criminal through an underground parking garage. Critically wounded, Officer Cobb died 45 minutes later at George Washington Hospital.

In August, 1979, two patroling policewomen in downtown Detroit encountered an unclothed man standing in the middle of the street. The man, standing with his Doberman pinscher, was burning dollar bills. Officers Katherine Perkins and Glenda Rudolph radioed for assistance. Then they tried to talk the man into coming along with them quietly. Before they were able to do so, Sergeant Paul Janness arrived and became involved in a bloody fight with the man, who was finally overcome and arrested. However, Sergeant Janness, who had been badly beaten in the struggle, claimed that the two policewomen had not come to his aid when he needed them. Witnesses agreed and Perkins and Rudolph were charged with cowardice in the face of duty by the department.

Although witnesses came forward to back each side's story, a police trial board found both women guilty. It was recommended that the two officers be dismissed from the police force.

Whether Officers Perkins and Rudolph were guilty or innocent of cowardice, the case left the impression that women were not up to the same responsibilities as men. After concluding a study of her own on female police officers, Sociologist Patricia Weiser Remmington said, "Either the view of females as weaker or the view and self-image of American police as symbols of physical power will have to change."

6. Which three of the following are statements of fact?

a. In 1974, Gail A. Cobb became the first policewoman to die in the line of duty.

b. The use of policewomen on patrol was pioneered in Indianapolis in 1968.

c. Women police officers should not be assigned dangerous duty.

d. A study by the Urban Institute found that women police officers usually did not provoke citizens deliberately as much as male police officers did.

e. Women police officers must be as exposed to hazardous work as men police officers are.

f. Female police officers should command as much respect from the public as male officers.

7. Tell why you selected the three statements you did in question 6.

8. In question 6, which three statements are opinion?

9. Tell why you selected the three statements you did in question 8.

10. In the past, what duties were policewomen assigned?

11. How have the roles of policewomen changed since 1970? Cite two examples.

12. Why have many cities begun to place policewomen on active duty?

Brady and the EPA
(conflicting viewpoints)

As you learned in Chapter 7, the federal Environmental Protection Agency (EPA) has the job of fighting pollution and polluters. Readings about one action of the EPA and the town of Brady, Texas, follow. As you read, think about the issue and the arguments that might be used by each side in the issue.

A Newspaper Account:

People in this town of 6,000 located east of San Angelo are proud of their plentiful underground water. It is a rare find in dry West Texas.

But the Environmental Protection Agency says Brady's water contains dangerous amounts of radiation. And it has ordered the small city to build a $3 million treatment plant to remove it.

City officials argue that such an expense would double the

water rates in a town where the annual city budget is barely $5 million.

The radiation occurs naturally in the Hickory Sand machinery from which six city wells draw water. The radiation has been there since the wells were first drilled 60 years ago, state health officials say. The level of radiation is just barely beyond the limits the EPA allows. At that level, one study estimated, a town the size of Brady can expect one radiation-caused death every 7,000 years.

"It is ridiculous," Mayor Sherrod Kilmer said Monday.

Kilmer reported that EPA officials believed the health risk was about the same as eating 100 grilled charcoal steaks.

"We are all exposed to so many things. We expect to take a certain level of risk," Kilmer said. "It is a matter of what you can afford for insurance."

Brady must find a way to afford a plant that can reduce the radiation to acceptable levels. . . . A treatment plant must be in operation by January 1, 1984. If not, the city faces penalties as high as $10,400 a day. . . .

"A study to determine the extent of the problem and options available will cost $15,000," said City Superintendent Dennis Jones. "We were concerned that the people would get excited about radioactivity in their water. They did not. I do not believe there is anybody in this town who thinks there is anything wrong with our water. They just think it is more federal regulations."

Tongue-in-Cheek Responses through Satire

Excerpt from an editorial:

Brady should ignore the EPA and its guidelines and deadlines. When January 1, 1984, comes around, let the federal agency start figuring the penalties, which Brady should not pay.

When the penalties match the figured property values in Brady, officials should announce that the EPA owns Brady. They should force EPA to either foreclose and build its own plant or forget it.

Roddy Stinson, a newspaper columnist:

Washington's brilliant bureaucrats . . . have come up with a unique idea.

Only the federal government's strongest defenders could have suspected that the faceless bureaucracy was capable of such a warm, feeling act.

I am referring to the Environmental Protection Agency's order forcing the small—population 6,000—Texas town of Brady to build a $3-million water treatment plant.

Why?

Because Brady's current water supply . . . contains a "dangerous level of radioactivity."

So what will happen if the radiation level is not reduced?

That is the kicker.

If the $3-million water treatment plant is not built, Brady can expect one radiation-caused death every 7,000 years.

You can see the problem.

Unfortunately, not everyone is as aware as you.

"It is ridiculous," says Brady's mayor.

"Just more federal regulations," echoes the town's superintendent.

And the jesters at the newspaper had a field day the morning the story came out in the paper.

"Boy, wouldn't it be tragic if the day before the chosen person died of radiation, a train ran over him on his way to work? Then there would only be one death every 14,000 years."

"Yeah, or imagine what life will be like in the spring of 8981 if nobody has died of radiation in the last 7,000 years. Everyone will figure it is time for somebody to go. . . .

Newspaper people have no feelings.

That is why they rarely go into government work. It takes a warm-hearted person to look beyond the $3 million, the doubled water bills, and the cries of Brady's 6,000 consumers to the 80-year-old guy in the ninetieth century who will drop dead of too much radioactivity.

You would not worry about him.

I would not worry about him.

Only a federal bureaucrat could come up with something so uniquely humane.

OK, I know what you are thinking. The same thought went through my mind. Why should the citizens of Brady pay for the next 70 centuries to prevent one death?

Well, it is easy to question the EPA's judgment if you are not involved. But if you were the 80-year-old guy who is going to drop dead in 8981, then you would figure the plant was worth every penny.

Of course, there is one other way to handle the problem. According to Brady officials, the EPA has said that the health risk of drinking Brady's water is about the same as eating 100 charcoal-grilled steaks.

Which presents a possible compromise. The EPA could issue an order requiring all Brady citizens to eat 100 charcoal-grilled steaks on or before their seventy-ninth birthdays. That way, the weakest individuals would get knocked off before the water could do them any serious damage.

13. What did the EPA order Brady to do?

14. How did the editorial use humor or satire to illustrate the problem? How did Roddy Stinson use humor or satire to illustrate the same point?

15. Suppose you were the person who had to make the final decision. What would you consider before arriving at your decision? Complete the following by pretending you are a supporter for each side of the issue, whether or not you agree with any of those arguments.
Arguments for the EPA Ruling
  a.
  b.
  c.

Arguments against the EPA Ruling
  a.
  b.
  c.

16. What would you decide? Why?

UNIT 5 REVIEW

Fact Review

1. Draw diagrams of (a) the organization of a state government and (b) the organization of one form of local government. Explain how the governments are alike and how they are different.
2. Many governors and "weak" mayors do not have the power to appoint and remove officials. How does this decrease their authority?
3. Describe how part of the state judicial branch operates on the local level.
4. States give local governments all of their powers. How does this differ from the relationship between a state and the national government?
5. One of the foundations of United States government is the separation of powers. Several different governments are listed below. For each one, decide whether a separation of power exists. Explain your answers.
   a. a state government
   b. a county government with a board of supervisors
   c. a mayor-council government
   d. a New England town meeting

Developing Your Vocabulary

Match the words in *a* to *e* with the phrases in (*1*) to (*5*).
a. initiative
b. referendum
c. township
d. municipality
e. special district
   (1) the right of voters to approve or reject bills passed by the legislature
   (2) a unit of local government that performs a specific public service
   (3) a city, town, village, or borough a state sets up as a unit of local government
   (4) the right of voters to propose bills by collecting signatures on petitions
   (5) a division of a county found in some mid-Atlantic and Midwestern states

Developing Your Reading Skills

Read the following paragraphs and then answer the questions that follow:

When the public thinks about the "government," it is usually the federal government. It is the federal government that handles all the dramatic affairs that often result in national headlines, while the state and local governments concern themselves more with doling out goods and services and with making up the rules and regulations to be observed by government agencies and officials as well as those governed by them.

Sometimes, however, the responsibilities of both the federal and state-local governments overlap, as is the case in the areas of housing, public welfare, and urban renewal. The governments are separate and distinct; yet they all work together for the common good.

1. Which of the following statements are not supported by the reading?
   a. The federal functions of government are more important than state and local functions.
   b. The federal government tends to be involved in issues of more national interest.
   c. The responsibilities of the federal and state-local governments never overlap.

"We hold these Truths to be self-evident, that all Men are created equal, that they are endowed by their Creator with certain unalienable Rights. . . ."

Those stirring words are from the Declaration of Independence. Their meaning is simple. People have certain rights that can neither be given up nor taken away from them. Governments must respect those rights, and so must other people.

The founders of the United States government put great faith in the idea of rights and freedoms. We still do today. We sing songs praising the "land of the free" and urging people to "let freedom ring." We pledge allegiance to a country "with liberty and justice for all." We work hard to make sure that the United States lives up to those ideals.

But the founders of the nation did not see just the *rights* that came with citizenship. They also emphasized the *duties* that go with those rights. They pictured a nation of independent people, sharing in the tasks of governing themselves. They saw the people keeping informed, voting, obeying the laws—and above all, thinking for themselves.

This unit is about the rights and duties of citizenship. Chapter 12 will focus on rights. Chapter 13 will focus on duties.

unit

6

Rights and Duties

12 Our Constitutional Rights

Several years ago, a group of people felt very strongly about a social issue. When they tired of waiting for help from their local government, these people got together and marched around the block where the mayor lived. They chanted slogans and blamed him for not taking any action on their issue. The area's residents came out of their houses and some threatened the demonstrators. Some even threw rocks and eggs at them.

After a while, the demonstrators were outnumbered by the area residents. Even the police officers who were present were outnumbered by angry spectators. The police told the demonstrators to stop the march. They kept marching. The police then arrested the demonstrators, charging them with disorderly conduct.

The leader of the demonstration protested. She argued that the demonstrators had not been disorderly. It was the spectators who were disorderly.

The leader was right. A few years later, the Supreme Court ruled that the arrests had been illegal. The Court said that the First Amendment gives all United States citizens the right that this group was using—the right to speak out and express opinions. They can use this right even when they make other people angry. Sometimes they can even use this right when the police tell them to stop.

The Constitution and the laws of the United States give us many *rights*. Some of those rights protect us against the government—against

the police, for instance. Some of the rights protect us against other individuals or groups—for example, against angry mobs. Protesters have a right to speak out peacefully and say things that other people might disagree with. Just as people who oppose them have a right to voice *their* opinions peacefully.

Rights are a precious part of our democratic heritage. In a democracy, rights belong to everyone—not just to a privileged few. This chapter will explore how the United States feels about rights, how rights were built into our system of government, and what those rights are today.

I. The sources of our rights
A. The Bill of Rights
B. The living Constitution
   1. Amending process
   2. Flexibility
II. Our Rights
A. First Amendment
   1. Freedom of religion
   2. Freedom of speech
   3. Freedom of the press
   4. Freedom of assembly and petition

B. Legal rights
   1. Freedom from unreasonable searches
   2. Right to grand jury indictment
   3. Right to due process
   4. Right to a speedy trial
   5. Right to confront witnesses
   6. Right to a lawyer
   7. Right to jury trials in civil suits
   8. No excessive bail
   9. No excessive fines

C. Voting rights
  1. Freed slaves are given the vote
  2. Women's suffrage
  3. Rights for voters in Washington, D.C.
  4. Poll tax outlawed
  5. Voting age lowered to 18
D. Rights dealing with weapons and soldiers
  1. Right to bear arms
  2. Quartering of soldiers
E. Civil and other rights
  1. Civil rights
  2. Abolition of slavery
  3. Citizenship for blacks
  4. Due process and equal protection of the laws
  5. Other rights

Words to Know

amendment —— a formal change in a document such as the Constitution
Bill of Rights —— first ten amendments to the U.S. Constitution
ratify —— approve, put into effect

The Sources of Our Rights

The founders of the United States government had fought a war to escape a government that denied their rights. Their goal was to create a land of liberty. In the Declaration of Independence (1776), they had committed themselves to the idea that people have "Unalienable rights"—rights that could not be taken away. What were those rights? How could they be protected?

The Bill of Rights

Some people wanted to list the people's rights in the Constitution. They pointed to Virginia's state constitution, adopted in 1776. It had a "bill of rights." Why not put such a list into the federal Constitution?

The writers of the Constitution did not include a bill of rights. Some of them thought it was not necessary. After all, the new national government was going to have only limited powers, so how could it threaten people's rights? Others argued that, listing the rights might be dangerous. If *all* rights were guaranteed, it might mean that the government could take away any right that was not on the list. It might be better not to list the rights at all.

When the Constitution went to the states for adoption, there was no bill of rights. The Constitution made only passing mention of certain rights—such as the right to a trial by jury (Article III, Section 2). The Constitution dealt mostly with how the new national government was going to work.

Many people were disappointed with the new Constitution. They said that it should not be adopted without a bill of rights. Finally, when it looked as if some states might refuse to adopt the Constitution, a compromise was reached. The supporters of the Constitution agreed to work for a bill of rights. First, however, the states would have to approve the Constitution.

The compromise worked. The states approved the Constitution as written. Then, the First Congress started to work on a bill of rights to add to it.

The Living Constitution

The writers of the Constitution had built into the Constitution a way to change it. They allowed for **amendments**—or formal changes—in the Constitution. They knew that changes would be needed to suit the peoples' needs. The Bill of Rights was added in 1791, only two years after the Constitution took effect. The **Bill of Rights** is the term we use for the first ten amendments to the Constitution. But before we discuss those amendments, let's take a look at how amendments are made.

The Amending Process Article V of the Constitution tells how amendments are made. The process is rather complicated. Both Congress and the states must take part. Changing the Constitution is much more difficult than passing a law. This helps to make certain that the rights that become a part of the Constitution cannot be changed too easily.

There are two different ways in which an amendment can be proposed, or suggested. There are also two different ways in which an amendment can be **ratified,** or approved, by the states.

One way of changing the Constitution begins with Congress. Either the House of Representatives or the Senate proposes an amendment by a two-thirds vote. Then the other house of Congress must pass the amendment, also by a two-thirds vote. Next, the amendment goes to the states for approval.

Another way of changing the Constitution begins with the states. The legislatures in at least two-thirds of the states—that is, thirty-four out of fifty—must request a national convention. The states' requests go to Congress. When it receives requests from thirty-four states, Congress has no choice. It must call a convention. Then, each state sends delegates to the convention to draw up a constitutional amendment.

This second method has never been used. Recently, many states have sent requests to Congress for such a convention.

In an effort to amend the Constitution, these people are marching to drum up state support for the Equal Rights Amendment.

As many as thirty-two states have acted. So far, the required two-thirds has not done so.

No matter how an amendment is proposed—whether by Congress or by a national convention— it must still be approved by three-fourths of the states: thirty-eight out of fifty. There are two ways of ratifying an amendment. Congress chooses which one will be used.

Congress may send a proposed amendment to the fifty state legislatures for approval. Of the twenty-six amendments that have been adopted, all but one were approved in this way.

Congress may, instead, call upon each state to hold a convention to act upon the proposed amendment. This method has been used only for the Twenty-first Amendment, which repealed the federal ban on alcoholic beverages.

If the required number of states approves an amendment, it automatically becomes part of the Constitution. The amendment does not go to the President for signing. The President has no formal role in the amending process, and no veto.

Congress often sets a time limit when it sends a proposed amendment to the states. It usually sets a limit of 7 years. If the amendment is not ratified within that time limit, it dies, unless Congress votes to lengthen the time limit.

Flexibility The amendment process gives flexibility to the Constitution. It makes it possible to meet new situations and new needs. Some of the twenty-six amendments that have been added to the Constitution made changes in the way the government worked. Others described the basic rights of citizens or gave those rights to people who had been denied them.

=== REVIEW ===

1. Why did some people think that the United States Constitution needed a bill of rights? Why did others disagree?

2. Explain the compromise that led to the adoption of the Bill of Rights.

3. What is an amendment?

4. Describe briefly two ways in which the Constitution can be changed.

5. Do you think that it is too easy to amend the Constitution? Too hard? Explain your answer.

Words to Know

abridge —— limit

seditious libel —— stirring up opposition to a government by criticizing or making fun of it

warrant —— a search order granted by a judge

indictment —— a grand jury's written statement charging someone with a crime

due process of law —— government action taken fairly and in line with procedures set down in the law

bail —— amount of money that an accused person puts up to guarantee that he or she will be present at a trial

suffrage —— the right to vote

servitude —— condition of being a servant to another, like a slave

poll tax —— a tax on people who want to vote

militia —— an army of citizens

Our Rights

The Bill of Rights marked the first use of the amending process to add to the basic rights of United States citizens. It was not the last such use. Court decisions and actions by Congress have also added to those rights. These decisions and actions have made clear the sometimes vague words in which the Constitution and its amendments are written. They help us to under-

These elementary-school students show their eagerness to learn the latest developments in the controversy over prayer in public schools.

stand exactly what our rights mean in everyday life. Let's take a look at the rights that are described in the Constitution, in its amendments, and in court decisions about those amendments.

The First Amendment

The First Amendment holds an honored place among our basic rights. It guarantees *freedom of conscience* and *freedom of expression*. Without those freedoms, other freedoms would lose much of their meaning. Note, however, that the courts have said that First Amendment rights have some limits. They are accompanied by certain responsibilities. They cannot be used to invade other people's rights.

Here is what the First Amendment says: "Congress shall make no law respecting an establishment of religion, or prohibiting the free exercise thereof; or **abridging** [limiting] the freedom of speech, or of the press; or the right of the people peaceably

to assemble, and to petition the Government for a redress [removal] of grievances."

The First Amendment begins: "Congress shall make no law. . . ." The Bill of Rights at first applied only to Congress—that is, to the federal government. It did not apply to state or local governments. A later amendment, the Fourteenth, changed this. The First Amendment and some—but not all—of the other parts of the Bill of Rights now apply to *all* levels of government.

Freedom of Religion Many of the early settlers in what is now the United States were seeking freedom to practice the religion of their choice. Often, however, they wanted that freedom only for those who shared their own beliefs. The Puritans who controlled the Massachusetts Bay Colony banished Quakers and others who were not Puritans. Other colonies acted in the same way. Some colonies allowed religious freedom only to the members of an official church. Others allowed all Protestants—but no one else—to worship freely. In 1700, Pennsylvania extended freedom of worship to all who believed in God. Slowly, the idea grew that all people should be allowed to worship in their own way.

Today, the First Amendment guarantees this right. People may practice Buddhism, a Native American religion, Judaism, Christianity, Islam, or any other religion. If they wish to have no religion, that is also their right.

What happens if a religious practice breaks a law? For example, in the 1800s, men of the Mormon faith often had more than one wife. Church leaders encouraged this practice, and it was common in Utah territory, where many Mormons had settled. Then, the United States Congress passed a law against having more than one spouse at a time.

Mormons claimed that the law violated their religious freedom. George Reynolds, for instance, refused to give up his second wife. He was tried, found guilty, fined $500, and sentenced to 2 years in prison. He appealed. The Supreme Court ruled against him. The Court agreed that laws cannot interfere with religious beliefs and opinions, but said that laws can interfere with religious *practices*. Not long after that, the Mormon church gave up this practice.

The First Amendment also says that government may not favor one religion over another. What does this mean in real life? For example, can a public school require that an official prayer be said in a classroom? Would the wording of such a prayer favor one religion over another?

In 1962, such a case came before the Supreme Court. A school board in New Hyde Park, New York, had directed the public schools to use a prayer written by a state board of education. Here is how it went: "Almighty God, we acknowledge our dependence upon Thee, and we beg Thy blessings upon us, our parents, our teachers, and our Country." The board said that no

child should be made to join in the prayer unwillingly. But the parents of five children filed suit to bar the prayer from the schools. They claimed that it violated the First Amendment.

The Court said that although the prayer did not favor one religion over another, its use in the schools amounted to official support of certain religious beliefs. Thus, it was unconstitutional.

Freedom of Speech If our government is to work, people must be able to say what thoughts are on their minds. Most people would agree with that statement. But when and where can people speak out? Can a person speak out when the police say to stop? These questions are not always

In a democracy, freedom of speech means being able to voice your opinions without fear.

easy to answer. The Supreme Court has ruled that the government can, indeed, put certain limitations on the time, place, and manner of speech.

The Supreme Court has said that there are differences between speech that expresses *ideas* and speech that moves people to *action*. In general, the Court has said, people may express any idea they want to. But if that speech causes actions, some limits may be put on it. Here is how one Supreme Court Justice put it: "The protection of free speech would not protect a man in falsely shouting fire in a theater and causing panic."

What rights do people who are speaking in public have? One case involved a university student, named Irving Feiner, who made a speech of a street corner in Syracuse, New York. He urged people to go to a political meeting that night. During his speech, he called the President a "bum" and the city's mayor "a champagne-sipping bum." He urged black people to "rise up in arms and fight" for their rights.

A crowd of about seventy people gathered. It included both blacks and whites, and two police officers. The police said that the crowd was blocking the sidewalk and had spilled into the street. One onlooker shouted a threat at Feiner. The police officers, who said they had feared trouble, asked Feiner to stop speaking. He refused. The police then arrested him and charged him with disorderly conduct.

Feiner's case reached the Supreme Court. The Court ruled that Feiner was not arrested for what he had said in his speech. It also declared that "the ordinary murmurings and objections of a hostile audience cannot be allowed to silence a speaker." But it concluded that Feiner had gone too far, that his speech was causing a riot. To keep order, the police had the right to make him stop.

A minority of the Court strongly disagreed. Three Justices argued that the police had violated Feiner's rights. They said it was the job of the police to protect Feiner from the threats of the crowd.

The Tinker case, which you read about earlier, deals with still another side of free speech (see page 236).

Freedom of the Press The writers of the Constitution believed that democracy could only work if the people were well informed. In the eyes of these early citizens, that knowledge would have to be spread by a free and independent press. At the time, the *press* meant newspapers, pamphlets, and books. Today, it also includes radio, television, magazines, and movies. As Thomas Jefferson said: "Were it left to me to decide whether we should have a government without newspapers or newspapers without a government, I should not hesitate a moment to prefer the latter."

One question that came up in those days—and is still an issue today—was how far the press could go in criticizing the government. At first the answer was "Not very far." English law did not allow the press to criticize or make fun of government or public officials. This was a crime known as

The Constitution upholds the right of the media to express views that are critical of the government.

Freedom of the Press?

The Secret Service spied him in the middle of the night, moving through the darkness outside the Secretary of State's home in Georgetown, Virginia. He was carrying away—of all things—five bulging bags of the Secretary's garbage. It took 2½ hours for the reporter to persuade the puzzled agents that what he was doing involved the new science of garbology—the art of studying about a person by carefully inspecting what he or she throws away—and that taking rubbish was perfectly legal in any case. The agents finally let him go, after which the reporter spent another 8 hours digging into the Secretary's garbage.

seditious libel. *Sedition* was stirring up opposition to the government's authority. *Libel* was publishing a statement—even a true one—that would harm someone's reputation.

In 1734, a famous court case in the American colonies gained new freedom for the press. John Peter Zenger, a New York editor, had sharply criticized the royal governor. According to past cases, he was guilty of seditious libel. But a jury found him not guilty. The jury agreed with Zenger's lawyer, who argued that Zenger had only written the truth.

Today, we look upon the Zenger case as a landmark in the history of a free press. One case did not change the law, however. People were still punished for seditious libel. The truth of their statements was rarely considered to be a defense.

Opinions changed slowly. In time, the idea was accepted that a true statement could not be libel. The idea of seditious libel faded away.

Today, the press has great freedom to criticize public officials. Even an untrue statement about a public official is not necessarily libel. An official has to prove either that the press knew the statement was false or that it published the statement without caring whether it was false or not. Only then can libel be proved.

The law of libel allows the press to be punished for something that it has already printed or broadcast. But can the press be kept from publishing a story?

That question arose in 1971, during the Vietnam War. A federal employee took a set of secret papers from the Pentagon—the building that houses the Department of Defense. The papers filled forty-seven volumes and told the story of how the United States became involved in Vietnam. Someone passed the documents on to various newspapers.

The New York Times printed parts of the secret papers. It printed more of them the next day. Then the federal government obtained a court order to stop *The Times* from publishing more of the papers. The government argued that publishing the papers harmed the nation's safety.

The secret papers became known as "The Pentagon Papers." Did the government have a right to stop the newspaper? The newspaper argued that the government's act was unconstitutional. They said that the government could only go to court *after* publication. Anything else would be censorship.

Soon, the question was before the United States Supreme Court. The Court held emergency sessions. It acted much more quickly than usual. Finally, the Court ruled in favor of the newspaper—by a 6-to-3 majority. Said Justice Hugo Black: "The First Amendment says that the press must be left free to publish the news—without censorship."

Freedom of Assembly and Petition
People have a right to gather and to express their views—freedom of assembly. They also have a right to let public officials know those views—freedom of petition. The important question is: When and how can people do this?

No matter what the cause or conviction, every individual or group in the United States has the right to gather and express its views. This is freedom of assembly.

The protest demonstration has a long history in the United States. In colonial days, it was used to protest some British acts. More recently, it has been used by many groups—civil rights groups, antiwar groups, pro-administration groups, Nazis, left-wingers, welfare parents, farmers, log-truck drivers, veterans' groups, and many others.

A major problem with protest demonstrations is that they sometimes interfere with other people. A line of marchers crossing a street can hold up traffic. A group of shouting people can disturb people who want silence. Can rules be made to prevent such inconveniences? Would such rules violate people's freedom of assembly?

The Supreme Court has ruled that *reasonable* rules may apply to demonstrations. For example, a city may require either advance notice or a permit. But the rules must have a proper purpose. Advance notice, for example, must help prevent traffic jams.

The rules cannot be used to block all demonstrations, and they cannot be used at random. For example, a city cannot refuse parade permits to one group while giving them to another.

The Court has also said that the police must protect people who assemble to express their views. In 1961, an angry crowd gathered around a group of students demonstrating at the South Carolina State House. The students were protesting discrimination against blacks. The police told the students to go home. The police said they had feared that there would be trouble. The students kept up their demonstration, and 200 of them were arrested. The Supreme Court ruled that the arrest was unconstitutional.

Legal Rights

Now that we have taken a close look at the First Amendment, let's turn to other rights that the Bill of Rights lists. Some of these can be called "legal rights." They have to do with our rights in dealing with the police and with the courts.

Freedom from Unreasonable Searches The Fourth Amendment guarantees "the right of the people to be secure in their persons, houses, papers, and effects, against unreasonable searches and seizures." Before 1776, the royal governors sometimes sent troops to search colonial Americans' homes. Sometimes they were searching for hidden weapons or smuggled goods. Sometimes they were looking for letters or papers criticizing the King of England. The soldiers did not need permits. Many people believed that these searches were a danger to liberty. The Fourth Amendment was adopted to make sure that this did not happen in the United States.

The Fourth Amendment does not prohibit all searches—just "unreasonable" ones. How do the courts decide what is a reasonable search?

First, a reasonable search has a stated purpose. The authorities cannot just guess that they will find something. They must be able to say exactly what they are looking for. They must also be able to say why they think they will find it in a certain place.

Second, the search must be approved in advance by a judge. The judge must sign a search order, called a **warrant.** The warrant must describe the place to be searched. It must also state just what (or whom) can be seized.

Warrants are not needed for *all* searches. For example, a police officer who is chasing a suspect can follow the suspect into his or her home. Warrants are not always needed to make an arrest. Most arrests, in fact, are made without a warrant. An arresting officer must have a "reasonable belief" that a person has committed a crime or is about to commit one.

What happens if the police do make an illegal search? Can the thing, or things, that they find be used in court? The answer is "No." The Supreme Courts says that this rule is needed to give the Fourth Amendment rights practical meaning. If evidence from an illegal search *is* used to convict someone of a crime, the courts can overturn the conviction. Then, the case has to be tried again without the illegal evidence.

Right to Grand Jury Indictment The Fifth Amendment contains a number of rights that have to do with trials. One right protects a person who has been arrested on weak evidence and charged with a serious crime. Before the person can be put on trial, the evidence must be shown to a group of citizens known as a *grand jury.* A grand jury is made up of sixteen to twenty-three persons. It hears the evidence. If the evidence is very weak, the grand jury may decide that a trial is not called for. The accused person may then go free.

If the evidence is strong, the grand jury issues an **indictment.** This is a written statement that charges a person with a crime. A person who has been indicted must then stand trial. The grand jury does not hold the actual trial. It only decides whether there should be a trial. As you saw earlier, the jury that serves during the trial is called a petit jury. The right to a grand jury indictment does not apply to members of the military services in war or in time of public danger.

The Fifth Amendment also guarantees other rights. It says that nobody can be tried twice for the same crime. It says that nobody can be forced to give evidence against himself or herself. It says that no private property can be taken for public use without a fair price being paid for it.

Right to Due Process The Fifth Amendment also says that no person shall "be deprived of life, liberty, or property without **due process of law.**" If the government is to take someone's life, liberty, or property, it must first go through the rules —and these rules must be fair.

Right to a Speedy Trial The Sixth Amendment gives anyone accused of a crime the right to a speedy trial. This trial must be before a jury, unless the accused person asks that a judge try the case without a jury. The trial must be held in the state and district where the crime was committed. The accused person has the right to be told plainly what crime he or she is accused of.

Right to Confront Witnesses A person who is accused of a crime has a right to hear and question all witnesses. The person may also order witnesses who can tell his or her side of the story to appear. This, too, is part of the Sixth Amendment.

Right to a Lawyer The Sixth Amendment also says that anyone who is accused of a crime has the right "to have the assistance of counsel." Having counsel—a lawyer—can be a big help to someone accused of a crime. A lawyer can find mistakes in the way a trial is being held. A lawyer usually knows the best questions to ask at a trial. But what about someone who has no money to pay a lawyer? Is such a person protected by the Sixth Amendment?

Up until 1932, the answer was "No." If you could not afford a lawyer, you did not get one. In recent years, the Supreme Court has read the Sixth Amendment more freely. Today, if you are accused of any serious crime—that is, one for which you might be sent to jail—, you have a right to a lawyer at your trial. If you are too poor to pay the lawyer, he or she will be provided free. It does not matter whether you are being tried in a federal court or in a state court.

Right to Jury Trials in Civil Suits The Seventh Amendment guarantees the right to have a civil lawsuit tried by a jury. This applies to any dispute involving more than $20.

No Excessive Bail The Eighth Amendment states that "excessive bail shall not be required. . . ." **Bail** is money that an accused person puts up to guarantee that he or she will be present at a trial. The person is freed after the bail is made. A judge may set the bail low or high, depending on the seriousness of the crime. The bail must not be "excessive," or too high. Its purpose is to make sure that the person will be at the trial, not to punish the person.

Under the "due process of law," anyone accused of a crime—such as the boy in this picture—has a number of legal rights. Among those rights is the right of legal counsel. If the accused cannot afford legal counsel, a lawyer may be provided by the court.

No Excessive Fines or Unduly Harsh Punishment The Eighth Amendment also protects us against "excessive fines" and "cruel and unusual punishments." At first, the ban on cruel punishments was aimed at torture and burning at the stake. In recent years, some people have argued that the death penalty is cruel and unconstitutional. The Supreme Court has rejected that argument. But in 1972, the Court ruled that the death penalty could not be applied unfairly. Since then, most states and the federal government have passed new laws to make sure that the death penalty is applied fairly.

Voting Rights

In order to take full part in the United States' system of government, a person must be able to vote. Voting is one of the most important ways in which a citizen can affect what the government does. By voting, the citizen helps choose the people who will run the government. In some cases, the voters may even decide on laws or government actions.

The Constitution originally made no attempt to say who could or could not vote. It left that up to the states, and most states followed practices from colonial days. As a rule, the only people who were allowed to vote were white males over the age of 21 who owned a certain amount of property. Some states only allowed those who held certain religious beliefs to vote. In the first election held under the Constitution, only one out of every thirty people in the United States cast a ballot.

The struggle for voting rights centered first on the religious and property requirements. By 1850, those requirements for voting had, for the most part, been removed by the states. Most white males over the age of 21 could vote.

Freed Slaves Are Given the Vote The federal government became involved in the issue of voting rights, or **suffrage,** in 1870. In that year, the Fifteenth Amendment was added to the Constitution. It said: "The right of citizens of the United States to vote shall not be denied . . . or abridged [limited] by the United States or by any State on account of race, color, or previous condition of **servitude.**" The amendment applied to former slaves. They were guaranteed the right to vote. But many states, especially in the South, found ways to keep blacks from voting.

Women's Suffrage Women were the next to win a federal guarantee of the right to vote. Many women had been seeking this right since colonial days. Only in New Jersey had they been successful. Women with property had the vote there from the Revolution until 1807, when voting was again limited to men. The number of supporters of women's suffrage slowly grew. In 1869, the territory of Wyoming decided to allow women to vote. Then, other states began to adopt women's suffrage.

In 1920, the Nineteenth Amendment was added to the Constitution. It said that neither the United States government nor any state could deny women the right to vote.

Rights for Voters in Washington, D.C. Up until 1961, those who lived in the nation's capital—Washington, D.C.—could not vote in national elections. The Twenty-third Amendment changed that. It allowed people in the District of Columbia to vote for President and Vice President. In 1970, Congress passed a law allowing the capital's residents to elect one nonvoting member to Congress. In 1978, Congress passed an amendment allowing Washington, D.C., to have two senators and at least one representative in Congress. This amendment has not yet been approved by the states.

Poll Tax Outlawed Some states limited voting by making people pay a tax in order to vote. This was called a **poll tax.**

Due to the tireless efforts of women's suffrage groups, women were granted the right to vote in 1920.

The tax was usually small—only a few dollars. That was a lot of money to many poor people. It kept many of them from voting. In 1964, the Twenty-fourth Amendment outlawed poll taxes in federal elections. Two years later, the Supreme Court held that poll taxes were also illegal in other elections.

Voting Age Lowered to 18 For many years, the usual age at which United States citizens could vote was 21. Only a few states set a lower voting age. The Constitution left the matter to the states.

During the 1960s, the Vietnam War focused new attention on the issue. Many of those fighting in the war were young men aged 18, 19, or 20 who had been *drafted*—required to perform military service. Supporters of a lower voting age said that it was unfair to order young men to risk their lives for a nation that did not allow them to vote. In 1971, the Twenty-sixth Amendment settled the question. It lowered the voting age to 18 in all elections.

Thus, the right to vote has been expanded in many ways. State laws still put

As a direct result of the United States' involvement in Vietnam and the consequent drafting of 18-, 19-, and 20-year-olds to perform military service, the Twenty-sixth Amendment was passed in 1971, lowering the voting age to 18 and thus giving a whole new generation a say in the governmental system.

some limits on the right to vote, however. Those who cannot always vote include insane persons, people convicted of serious crimes, and people dishonorably discharged from the armed forces.

Rights Dealing with Weapons and Soldiers

Right to Bear Arms The Second Amendment has been the subject of much argument. Here is what it says: "A well-regulated militia, being necessary to the security of a free State, the right of the people to keep and bear arms, shall not be infringed."

A **militia** is an army of citizens. In time of peace, its members are civilians. But they have weapons ready in case they are called upon to defend their government. Each of the thirteen colonies had its own militia. The militias served an important role in the American Revolution. Today, the nearest thing to state militias are the units of the National Guard.

Can the federal or state governments control or limit the ownership of guns? Some people argue that the Second Amendment gives all people an unlimited right to keep arms such as rifles and pistols. They object to state and federal laws that take away that right. For example, some states say that certain guns must be registered, or listed, with the state. A 1968 federal law bars mail-order sales of guns and ammunition. It also outlaws the sale of handguns to persons under the age of 21 and the sale of rifles and shotguns to persons under 18.

Other people argue that the Second Amendment was not meant to keep the government from making such regulations. They say that the amendment was meant to protect the right of state governments to keep a militia. They say that the amendment has little meaning today.

Quartering of Soldiers The Third Amendment says that no one can be forced

The National Rifle Association believes strongly in the right of individuals to bear arms.

to quarter, or give housing to, a soldier in his or her home in peacetime. In time of war, however, the right is limited. A homeowner may then be required to house soldiers, but only under the terms named in laws.

Civil and Other Rights

Civil Rights Civil rights are those rights that promise all citizens equal treatment under the law. That is the usual meaning of "civil rights," but not the only one. Sometimes the term is used to refer to *all* a citizen's rights.

The United States is often referred to as a "melting pot." Its citizens have many backgrounds and national origins. Its people differ in many ways. Certain parts of the Constitution and of the laws are meant to make sure that all of these people have an equal chance in our society.

Amendments That Guarantee the Rights of Citizens

Freedom of Conscience and Expression
First Amendment—guarantees freedom of religion, freedom of speech, freedom of the press, freedom of peaceable assembly, and freedom of petition.
Legal Rights
Fourth Amendment—protects people from unreasonable searches and seizures.   *Fifth Amendment*—protects people from being held for trial without a grand jury indictment and from being tried twice for the same crime; says that no one can be forced to give evidence against himself or herself; protects property rights; requires the federal government to follow "due process of law" in taking anyone's life, liberty, or property.   *Sixth Amendment*—guarantees the right to a speedy trial by jury, the right to confront witnesses, and the right to have a lawyer.   *Seventh Amendment*—guarantees the right to jury trials in civil suits.   *Eighth Amendment*—bars excessive bail, excessive fines, and cruel and unusual punishments.
Voting Rights
Fifteenth Amendment—gives suffrage to freed slaves.   *Nineteenth Amendment*—gives suffrage to women.   *Twenty-third Amendment*—gives people who live in Washington, D.C., the right to vote for President and Vice President.   *Twenty-fourth Amendment*—outlaws poll taxes in federal elections.   *Twenty-sixth Amendment*—gives suffrage to persons who are the age of 18 or over.
Rights Dealing with Weapons and Soldiers
Second Amendment—guarantees the right to bear arms.   *Third Amendment*—says that no one can be forced to quarter soldiers in peacetime.
Civil and Other Rights
Thirteenth Amendment—outlaws slavery.   *Fourteenth Amendment*—gives citizenship to blacks and to all others who are born or naturalized in the United States; requires state governments to observe due process of law and to give all persons equal protection of the laws.   *Proposed Twenty-seventh Amendment*—would keep any government from denying or limiting rights on account of sex.   *Ninth Amendment*—limits the powers of federal government by reserving powers for the states and for the people.

Abolition of Slavery In 1865, the Thirteenth Amendment abolished, or put an end to, slavery. It declared that no one was to be forced into being a servant to another person. The only exception was a person being punished for a crime. President Lincoln had declared an end to slavery in many of the Confederate States during the Civil War. The Thirteenth Amendment ended slavery in *all* states.

Citizenship for Blacks The Fourteenth Amendment followed the Thir-

teenth Amendment by giving citizenship to black people. In 1857, the Supreme Court had ruled in the Dred Scott case that a black person could not be a citizen of the United States. In 1868, this decision was overruled by the Fourteenth Amendment, which provided that "all persons born or naturalized in the United States" could be citizens.

Due Process and Equal Protection of the Laws The Fourteenth Amendment also says: "No State shall . . . deny to any person within its jurisdiction the equal protection of the laws." This clause has been used to stop discrimination against blacks, other minorities, and women.

Many people believed that this amendment did not go far enough in protecting the rights of women, however. In 1971, Congress proposed a Twenty-seventh Amendment. It said: "Equality of rights under the law shall not be denied or abridged by the United States or by any State on account of sex." A debate over adopting the Equal Rights Amendment has gone on for years.

Other Rights   Two amendments to the Constitution make clear that we have even more rights. The Ninth Amendment says that other rights not listed in the Constitution are "retained by the people." The Tenth Amendment limits the powers of the federal government. It says that any powers that are not given to the United States government by the Constitution or taken away from the states "are reserved to the States respectively, or to the people."

—————— REVIEW ——————

1. To what government, or governments, does the Bill of Rights apply? Explain.

2. Give an example of a use of freedom of speech that is protected by the Constitution. Give an example of a use of freedom of speech that is *not* protected.

3. Consider this statement: "A family's home is its castle." How does the Fourth Amendment support that statement?

4. Do you think that government should be able to control the ownership or use of guns in any way? Explain.

How the United States Works

Radio News Director

When the Constitution was written, no one would have imagined that we would someday get most of our news from television and radio reports. This is why the writers did not include freedom of broadcast in the rights they listed. Nevertheless, the First Amendment has been applied to these new forms of communicating the news.

At the larger radio stations, people have specialized jobs. Many reporters, writers, and newscasters work under the news director. At small stations—for example, some educational stations on the FM band—, the news director may do many jobs.

One job is gathering the news. Some stories come in from a news service. The director chooses the stories to be used. If the service has provided enough information, the director writes the story. If not, the director sends a reporter out to cover the story. Other news items are called in from reporters who are located in different places around the world.

While the stories are coming in, the director edits them and writes an introduction to each one. As broadcast time comes closer, the pressure grows. When the news is finally on the air, the news director also acts as the announcer. All the reports are on tape, but the introductions and news-service stories are read live.

There are always plenty of people trying to get jobs like these, even though the pay may be low. A news director at a small FM radio station may make only $7,000 a year. At larger stations, the pay is much better. Some radio news directors make as much as $50,000.

Many people get started in radio by taking low-paying clerical or assistant jobs. Once they have some experience, they may be able to take advantage of better jobs that become available.

By law, you have to have an FCC Radiotelephone Third-Class Operator License to work a radio transmitter. You can get the training needed to pass the licensing test in most colleges, in broadcasting schools, or by working as a technical aid at a radio station. A good speaking voice and a dramatic or pleasant personality are also useful.

Reading About . . .

A Right to Privacy? _____

So far in this chapter, you have looked at the rights that are listed in the Constitution. But do people have other rights that are not listed? This reading explores an area that has troubled many people recently—privacy. *Privacy,* in this case, means controlling the number of people who can have very confidential information about a person's life.

As you read, ask yourself the following questions:

● Do people have a right to privacy?
● Should such a right be protected by laws or by a constitutional amendment?

To show how precious little privacy Americans have, Hanna Weston, an economics instructor in Cedar Rapids, Iowa, set out to learn everything she could about the personal affairs of her friend—a state senator. The Johnson County auditor's files showed that the senator's house was valued at $47,110 and that her property taxes were $1,252.94 a year. An official at an Iowa City bank did not hesitate to tell Ms. Weston that a 500-dollar check on the senator's account would clear, meaning that she had a balance of at least that much money. Just as readily, an employee at Blue Cross-Blue Shield looked up the senator's file—with the help of her Social Security number, which Weston obtained from the county voting roles—and reported that she had not filed a claim in the past 18 months. From a marriage certificate, Weston discovered that the senator had been married only once. From her birth certificate she was a housewife when her children were born, in 1948 and 1951. Motor vehicle records showed that she had used a $2,000 loan from the Hawkeye State Bank to buy her 1976 Plymouth Valiant and also revealed that she is 54, blond, blue-eyed, 5 feet 6 inches tall, and 140 pounds. Weston's search, which took only 3 hours, illustrates the variety of information about a typical American that is readily available to any snoop. "And I am only an amateur," says Weston. If she had been a professional investigator, she could have tapped the files of banks, credit bureaus, insurance companies, and Government agencies even more heavily—and sometimes illegally. Details could have been learned about the senator's investments, debts, shopping patterns, charities, hobbies, social life, medical history, drinking habits, and morals.

A government commission that studied the invasion of privacy for nearly 2 years has issued a report showing that the problem is far worse than most people think. The report touches on the threat to privacy from government gumshoes but concentrates chiefly on the danger posed by private firms, most of which operate with no controls on the information they collect and the way in which they use it. The head of the commission says: "We are an information-spoiled society. It's been so easy to collect that we just keep on collecting. Tens of millions of names are being pushed around from one organization to another for whatever purposes they want them, and we don't know anything about it."

chapter
Review

Fact Review

1. Why was the Zenger case important for a free press?
2. Does a newspaper have to be able to prove the truth of any statement it makes that criticizes a public official? Explain.
3. Does a group of people have the right to stage a protest demonstration whenever and wherever they wish? Explain.
4. In what kinds of cases must a lawyer be provided free of charge to a defendant who cannot afford one? Why?
5. Describe four groups of people to whom voting rights have been extended by amendments to the Constitution.

Developing Your Vocabulary

Match the words in *a* to *e* with the definitions in (*1*) to (*5*).

a. right
b. indictment
c. warrant
d. bail
e. suffrage

(1) a grand jury's written statement accusing someone of a crime
(2) the right to vote
(3) an amount of money put up by an accused person to guarantee that he or she will be present at a trial
(4) a search order granted by a judge
(5) a privilege; something that is due to a person

Developing Your Reading Skills

Read the following paragraph and then answer the questions that follow:

The federal Bill of Rights is the first ten amendments to the Constitution. It went into effect in 1791. The Bill of Rights guarantees citizens of the United States many basic freedoms. Perhaps the most important are freedom of conscience and freedom of expression. Other basic freedoms involve the right to bear arms and the right of people who are accused of crimes to due process of law. In addition, the Bill of Rights protects people from cruel and unusual punishments. Finally, it reserves certain rights and powers for the people and for the states.

1. Which one of the following do you think is the main point, or main idea, of the paragraph above?
   a. The federal Bill of Rights guarantees us freedom of conscience and freedom of expression.
   b. The Bill of Rights took effect in 1791.
   c. The Bill of Rights allows United States citizens to enjoy many freedoms.
2. Tell why you selected *a, b,* or *c* in question 1.

Developing Your Writing Skills— Forming and Supporting an Opinion

In this chapter, you have examined the basic freedoms that are guaranteed us by the Constitution. Now consider:

Forming an opinion
1. Suppose the First Amendment were removed from the Constitution. Could that affect our freedoms under the Constitution and its other amendments?

Supporting an opinion
2. After thinking it over, write a paragraph that answers the question above. Tell why you decided on that answer.

YOUR GOVERNMENT & ITS HISTORY

The Nineteenth Amendment—a Brief History

As American citizens in the twentieth century, we often take for granted the right to vote. Yet, all Americans did not always have this right. The Constitution left voting rights to each state until the Fifteenth Amendment was passed in 1870. Even then, the right of women to vote was not assured. Their right to vote was not guaranteed until the passage of the Nineteenth Amendment in 1920.

Voting rights in colonial times were reserved strictly for adult, white, male property owners. Exceptions were rarely made. In some colonies, widows were granted voting rights if they became property owners upon their husbands' deaths. Property owners were seen as having the most interest in government and thus, being the best qualified to make decisions.

After the Constitution gave the states the right to decide who could vote, property requirements were slowly removed. By 1830, all white males could vote.

As women received more education and got involved in various reform movements, they began to question why they had no right to vote.

In 1848, Elizabeth Cady Stanton and Lucretia Mott called a Women's Rights Convention in Seneca Falls, New York. Elizabeth Cady Stanton used the Declaration of Independence as a model to write a Declaration of Sentiments. It called for equal rights for women in education, voting, property, and other matters. It read, in part:

> When, in the course of human events, it becomes necessary for one portion of the family of man to assume among the people of the Earth a position different from that they have hitherto occupied . . .
>
> We hold these truths to be self-evident: that all men and women are created equal; that they are endowed

by their Creator with certain unalienable rights: That among these are life,
liberty, and the pursuit of happiness.

The history of mankind is a history of repeated injuries and usurpations [taking possession of by force or
use] on the part of man toward
woman, having in direct object the
establishment of an absolute tyranny
over her.

Leaders of the suffrage movement
felt that the right to vote was the key to
gaining other important rights.

In 1869, the National Woman Suffrage Association and the American
Woman Suffrage Association were formed.
The National Woman Suffrage Association
was led by Elizabeth Cady Stanton and
Susan B. Anthony. Their aim was an
amendment to the Constitution that would
give women the vote. In 1872, Susan B.
Anthony and a group of suffragists voted
in the presidential primary in Rochester,
New York. They were arrested and fined
for voting illegally.

The American Woman Suffrage Association was led by Lucy Stone and her husband, Henry Blackwell. Their aim was to
convince individual states to give women
the vote. In 1890, the two suffrage associations merged and became the National
American Woman Suffrage Association.

In 1915, Carrie Lane Chapman Catt
became president of the National American Woman Suffrage Association. In 5
years, she organized a force of 2 million
women. They worked in local political districts and developed a national campaign.

Also, the many contributions made by
women to the war effort during World War
I increased support for a suffrage amendment to the Constitution.

A women's suffrage amendment had
first been introduced, and turned down, in
1878. For the next 40 years, the amendment was brought up again in Congress
every 2 years. In 1918, the House of Representatives finally passed a suffrage
amendment. The House was packed for the
vote. One representative left his wife's
deathbed, at her request, to vote for the
amendment. Another representative was
carried in on a stretcher. However, the
Senate defeated the amendment. In 1919,
the Senate changed its vote and approved
the amendment. It was then passed on to
the individual states for approval.

In 1920, thirty-six states ratified
what came to be the Nineteenth Amendment to the Constitution.

About the struggle for suffrage,
Carrie Lane Chapman Catt said that it
had been "a continuous, seemingly endless, chain of activity. Young suffragists
. . . were not born when it began. Old suffragists . . . were dead when it ended."

1. Who had the right to vote in colonial
times? What were the requirements to
vote then?

2. What event opened the drive for wom-
en's suffrage? Who were its leaders?

3. What two organizations pushed for voting rights in the late 1800s? What was the
difference in their goals?

4. When did women finally win the right
to vote? What amendment gave the right?

5. Why do you think it is important that
we not take for granted the right to vote?

SKILLS Developing your basic civic education skills

Amending an Idea
(thinking critically)

In this chapter, you have learned how the federal Constitution can be amended. An amendment is something that is added or changed. But why might amendments to a constitution be needed? Why should a people provide for amendments to their form of government?

To begin to answer such questions, think about the following situation. Consider what happens when you meet a new person at school. You probably ask yourself: Could this person become a good friend of mine? After getting to know the person a little, you form a hypothesis or temporary opinion: This person could become a friend of mine. Your temporary opinion is an idea that has not been proven true. Yet, for the time being, you assume it to be true. It is a temporary explanation.

During the school year, you get to know that person better. In doing so, you test the correctness of your first impression or your hypothesis. Finally, at the end of the school year, you form a more definite opinion or conclusion about that person: He or she is (or is not) a good friend of mine. You then can make some needed changes or additions to your first opinions about that new person at school.

The framers of the Constitution were much like you when you meet new people at school. The framers were not absolutely certain about some things. One concern was whether the Constitu-tion should remain exactly as it was when first approved. The men who wrote that document thought that the passage of time would bring many new events and problems. These could mean that changes or additions might be needed in the Constitution. They were right. New events and problems have resulted in twenty-six amendments to the Constitution.

1. How are the following similar?
   a. meeting a new person at school/feelings about change on the part of the authors of the Constitution
   b. getting to know that new person at school/the provision for an amending process in the Constitution
   c. forming a more definite opinion about that new person at school/the passage of twenty-six amendments to the Constitution

2. Do you think you need to plan to make amendments in your own views and ideas sometimes? Explain your answer.

Conflicts over Basic Freedoms
(conflicting viewpoints)

Example 1

When you talk about dealing with conflicting viewpoints, two words often come to mind: *value* and *dilemma*.

As you learned in chapters 1 and 3, we value something when we place great importance on it. As citizens of the United States, we value the ideas stated in the Constitution, the Bill of Rights, and the Declaration of Independence. Objects as well as ideas can also be valued. One person might place great value on owning a coin or stamp collection, a private letter from a friend, a particular kind of car, or perhaps an outstanding report card.

A dilemma is a situation that requires one to choose between two equally balanced, or almost equally balanced, choices. Often, a dilemma is a problem that seemingly has no satisfactory solution. You might be in a dilemma if you had to choose between these two things: Whether to go to a very special event with your best friend on a Saturday night or whether to accept a part-time job on that Saturday night. The job will provide you with just enough money to buy something special.

Keep the definitions of value and dilemma in mind as you read the following selection.

On the morning of May 25, 1979, the state of Florida executed convicted murderer John Spenkelink. At the moment the switch was thrown on the electric chair, twelve people sat down on the steps of the Supreme Court building in Washington, D.C. They sat in a silent protest against the death penalty, and they were promptly arrested.

That demonstration was the opening round in a legal battle. The battle was over the constitutional right of free speech centering on a single square block of land on Capitol Hill.

The battle is the kind that takes place when First Amend-ment guarantees clash with the government's right to operate free of interference. The protest would have been perfectly legal had it occurred just across the street from the Supreme Court building. At issue was Title 40, Section 13K, of the U.S. Code, which bans any form of political demonstration on Court property.

In November 1980, a federal appeals court heard the case. The government argued that the Supreme Court is not the proper setting for expression of political views. Protesting on the steps of the Supreme Court interferes with the government. The protesters' attorneys argued that their clients' right to free speech was interfered with by this law.

The protesters' attorneys insisted . . . that the protesters' actions . . . were not the kind of conduct that can be controlled by statute. Lawyer Brad Stetler told a district court that the demonstration did not, and was not intended to, interfere with justice. Thus, it could not be prohibited under the Constitution.

But Benjamin Sendor, arguing the government's case, replied, "The Supreme Court is a unique institution. It has a tradition of strict political neutrality that must be strictly, jealously guarded."

Stetler observed that vending machines sell newspapers on court property every day. Do newspapers represent political speech?

No, said the government. The newspapers are merely a commercial convenience, insisted attorney

Sendor. "It is clear under the Constitution that Congress can control the time, place, and manner of expressive conduct."

Stetler, however, insisted that the government could only prohibit loud or disorderly behavior or demonstrations deliberately planned to interfere with the administration of justice.

3. Define the terms *value* and *dilemma*.

4. Which one of the following is the main issue in the story?

    a. whether or not a federal court should rule on First Amendment freedoms

    b. First Amendment freedoms versus the federal government's right to operate free of interference

    c. First Amendment freedoms versus the sale of newspapers

5. What had the protesters been arrested for?

6. What arguments were made in support of the protesters?

7. Which one of the following shows what the protesters valued?

    a. the right of the government to function free of any interference

    b. the right to peacefully protest an action of the government anywhere

    c. the right of Congress to ban any form of political demonstration on Court property

8. Tell why you selected the answer you did in question 7.

9. What arguments in question 7 were made in support of the position taken by the federal government? Could these arguments also have included the events of the Daniel Shays Rebellion? (See pages 222–223.)

10. Which one of the following shows what the federal authorities valued?

    a. the right of the government to operate free of any interference

    b. the right to protest peacefully an action of the government anywhere

    c. the right of Congress to ban any form of political protest on government property

11. Tell why you selected the answer you did in question 10.

12. How might a judge asked to rule in this case have been faced with a dilemma?

Example 2

Susan is a junior at Wetmore High School. She transferred to Wetmore at the start of her sophomore year. Susan is a popular student with the teachers and her peers. Encouraged by her friends, Susan has decided to run for a student council office.

Harry, the editor of the school newspaper, is looking for information about the candidates for a special article on the election. A friend of Harry's attends the same school Susan attended when she was a freshman. Because Harry's friend works in the school office, he often knows a lot about some students. For example, he says he knows that Susan was a discipline problem at that school. She had been caught smoking on school grounds and had been disciplined for talking back to teachers.

Harry has doubts about the way he received this information. He also has some doubts about the truth of this information. As a result, Harry has to decide whether or not to print the information in the school paper.

13. Who is Susan? Harry? What did Harry find?

14. Even if the unproven charges against Susan are true, do you think the problems that Susan had in the past will have any effect on her ability to perform in the student council? Explain.

15. In this situation, does Harry face a dilemma? Explain.

16. Should information like this be printed in spite of the way it was obtained?

17. When do you think the press should make information available to the public? What sort of information should be made available to the public by the press? What responsibilities does the press have in deciding what should be made public? Who should decide what those responsibilities will be? Why? How would your answers to these questions show what you value?

Example 3

Should America's Student Press Be Subject to Censorship?

Rodney F. Page, School Board Chair, Fairfax County, Virginia:

A tide of court decisions in the last decade has extended the constitutional guarantees of the Bill of Rights and due process of students. Freedom of the student press remains a . . . disputed area, however. Where students have established and published their own newspapers and are financially responsible, the full protection of the First Amendment

seems right. But many student newspapers, especially in high schools, are, in fact, published by the school system. The students are working and learning journalists. In these cases, should the decisions of the student reporters and editors override contrary policies of the school system? Clearly not.

Alan N. Sussman, lawyer and author of *The Rights of Young People:*

The First Amendment guarantees all Americans—including students—freedom of the press. If there were any doubt, the Supreme Court recently declared that students do not "shed their constitutional rights to freedom of speech or expression at the schoolhouse gate." Freedom of the press insures that information will flow freely among those who seek knowledge. Therefore, when school officials interfere with the free exchange of ideas, they deny students the right to read as well as the right to publish. Censorship of student newspapers not only violates the Constitution but also seriously interfers with the process of education itself.

18. What issue did Page and Sussman consider?

19. Did the two agree about anything? What was it?

20. On what did the two disagree? Could that show what each valued most? Explain.

21. Do you think anyone attempting to make a decision on this issue could face a dilemma? Explain. Does a dilemma ever involve a conflict of values?

Chapter **13** Our Responsibilities and Duties

In the last chapter, you learned about the rights that are guaranteed all citizens. The citizens of the United States also have responsibilities and duties. Some of these are set down in laws.

Among our duties and responsibilities are the following: obeying the laws, paying taxes, serving in the armed forces when asked to do so, attending school, serving on juries or appearing in court as a witness, and voting. You will explore these duties and responsibilities in this chapter.

The duties and responsibilities are not so simple and straightforward as this list may make them seem. They are filtered through and changed by another responsibility. This responsibility is perhaps the most important one for us to take on, if the Constitution is to continue to protect our rights. This is our duty as citizens to think for ourselves.

I. Laws and taxes
  A. Obeying the law
    1. Reasons for obeying the law
    2. Thinking about obeying the law
  B. Paying taxes
    1. Reasons for paying taxes
    2. Thinking about paying taxes

II. Other responsibilities
  A. Serving in the armed forces
    1. Reasons for military service
    2. Thinking about military service
  B. Attending school
    1. Reasons for attending school
    2. Thinking about attending school

C. Court duty
1. Reasons for court duty
2. Thinking about court duty
D. Voting
1. Reasons for voting
2. Thinking about voting

Words to Know

civil disobedience —— concept according to which a person may—or *should*—break a law that he or she considers unjust, accepting arrest and even imprisonment without trying to escape punishment

initiative —— a vote in which the public can make laws directly, without action by the legislature

Laws and Taxes

Obeying the Law

Laws are the binding rules that a society lives by. They are set up and enforced by the government. We have already discussed the reasons why laws are needed. You may wish to review these reasons (see Chapter 2).

Reasons for Obeying the Law Our responsibility to obey the law is the foundation of our social system. Without laws, there would be anarchy. But there can be anarchy even with laws, if the laws are not obeyed. By obeying laws, we help our society to work in an orderly manner.

Imagine what would happen if just one person in ten disobeyed the law that says drivers must stop for a red light. It would be almost as bad as *everyone* disobeying.

RESPONSIBILITIES OF
UNITED STATES CITIZENS

To Obey the Law

To Vote

To Serve in the
Armed Forces

To Pay Taxes

To Attend School

To Serve as a Juror
or Witness in Court

To Think About One's Duties as a Citizen

Laws help us to avoid disorder. We obey the law because it makes sense to do so. Obeying the law helps our society to run smoothly.

As members of a democratic society, we have another reason for obeying the laws. They are *our* laws. We make them through our elected representatives. The laws are supposed to represent the will of a majority of the people. If a majority wishes to change the laws, it may do so. But we have a responsibility to obey the laws that are in force at any particular time.

Thinking about Obeying the Law

Is obedience to the law always a mark of good citizenship? Should you obey *all* laws unquestioningly?

From 1933 to 1945, Germany was ruled by Hitler's Nazis. The Nazis passed a number of laws to eliminate the Jewish people from Germany. The laws set up concentration camps, or prisons, where millions of Jews were confined and murdered. After World War II, some Germans were put on trial for their actions in these camps. Most of them defended their actions. They said that they had only obeyed orders. The orders had been given under laws made by their government. It was not their responsibility to question whether the laws or the orders were right or wrong, they said.

The questions that were raised at these trials are worth thinking about. When would *you* follow an order? When would you question it? No one would deny that we have a responsibility to obey the law. But should we obey *all* laws in *all* cases?

Some Americans have argued that it is as important to *disobey* an unjust law as it is to *obey* a just law. During the 1760s and 1770s many people in the American colonies disobeyed laws they thought unjust. For example, they refused to pay the taxes set by the Stamp Act. In the 1840s, some people in the United States refused to pay taxes to support a war against Mexico. One of the people who refused was Henry David Thoreau, a writer and philosopher living in Massachusetts. Thoreau went to jail rather than pay a tax. In a famous essay called "Civil Disobedience," Thoreau explained his actions. He set forth arguments that were often used by other people in the United States in later years.

Civil disobedience is the idea that a person may—or *should*—break a law that he or she considers unjust. The person in this case is not trying to "get away with something." Such a person is not like a thief who steals money and tries to escape. In-

Is there an obligation to obey laws and orders without regard to morality or conscience? This was the central focus of the Nuremburg Trials after World War II.

stead, the person accepts arrest and perhaps jail. The person may be trying to test the law in court or trying to set an example, hoping that other people will be encouraged to resist the law and finally change it.

Martin Luther King Jr., the black civil rights leader, practiced civil disobedience. King fought laws and practices that discriminated against blacks. King first came to the attention of the public in 1955. In that year, he led a movement by blacks who refused to ride on buses in Montgomery, Alabama. A black woman, Rosa Parks, had been arrested there for not obeying a bus driver's order that she stand up and give her seat to a white person. The law required her to do that.

King himself went to jail many times. His movement and ideas spread to other parts of the nation. He helped to persuade national leaders to change many of the state and local laws that discriminated against blacks.

Civil disobedience on the part of Rosa Parks in the 1950s did much to further racial integration.

The use of civil disobedience always causes arguments. Some people say that it can lead to anarchy. They ask: What if everyone in the United States took it upon themselves to decide which laws they would obey and which they would disobey? Even those who support civil disobedience usually urge people to use all possible legal methods to change a law before turning to civil disobedience. They look upon civil disobedience as a last resort.

Paying Taxes

Reasons for Paying Taxes As citizens, we have a responsibility to pay for the services that the government provides. For example, the government builds streets and highways, and we are taxed to pay for them. The government has armed forces and police to protect us. It pays for aid to needy families and to older people who cannot meet their medical bills. Taxes pay for all of these things.

It is fairly easy to see the role of the government in building highways. Each time we use a highway, we see our taxes at work. But we cannot *always* see the direct results of government actions. The results may take the form of freedom to take a walk through a park without being robbed or freedom from worry about the well-being of an aging parent. These results, while not as clear, are no less real.

The Constitution and the laws have set up the tax system. Some taxes hit directly—and hard. For example, the federal income tax may take one-half, or more, of a

Always an effective campaign technique, stickers such as this were seen across California in 1978.

For every issue, there are two sides. These young people represented the opposing view to the taxpayer's revolt in California.

wealthy person's income. State and local taxes on income and property may take another large amount of money. Other taxes take a little bit of money at a time. For example, a sales tax may be just a few cents on each item. But all the taxes add up.

Thinking about Paying Taxes Are we paying too high a price for what the governments give us? Some people think so. And they are willing to do more than just argue. They are willing to work to change things.

Howard Jarvis is a retired manufacturer in California. For years, he urged the state legislature to hold down taxes. He was not satisfied with the results, so he and another businessman organized a group of volunteers to collect signatures on a petition. The petition called for a statewide **initiative.** This is a vote in which the public can make laws directly, without action by the legislature.

The volunteers had no trouble gathering the 498,000 signatures needed to put the initiative on the ballot. In fact, they got 1,263,699 signatures. Many Californians were upset and angry about their property taxes. These taxes are set by local governments and are based on the value of a home or a piece of land. During the 1970s the value of homes shot up. So did taxes. Some families received tax bills that were two or three times what they had been the previous year.

Many homeowners supported Jarvis' idea. It called for rolling back the property taxes on homes and businesses. It also limited the amount by which local governments could raise taxes.

Some people disagreed with Jarvis. They said that decreased taxes would lead to cutbacks in government services. The poor and the elderly, who needed government services the most, would suffer most. They said that other taxes—such as the state income tax—would have to be increased to make up for a property-tax cut.

In June 1978, California voted in favor of the initiative. Jarvis and his supporters had won. One California politician said, in effect, that the voters had hit state officials over the head with a two-by-four in order to get their attention. They got it. Property taxes went down, and people in other states started calling for lower taxes.

The California example shows that people do not always have to accept the taxes that government places on them. People can work together to make changes. This is an important responsibility in our system of government.

———————— REVIEW ————————

1. What are two reasons why you should obey the law?

2. Who was the author of a famous nineteenth-century essay on civil disobedience?

3. What did Howard Jarvis do about taxes in California?

4. Do you think that a person would ever be right in refusing to pay his or her taxes? Explain.

Words to Know

military draft —— a system for requiring people to enter the military service

pacifist —— someone who believes that taking part in war is wrong on religious or moral grounds

conscientious objector —— a pacifist who refuses to be drafted as a military fighter

compulsory schooling —— the policy of requiring children to attend school until they reach a certain age

jury duty —— the responsibility of serving on juries when asked to do so

subpoena —— a court order instructing someone to appear in court or to produce a document

This recruitment poster asks for volunteers, yet military service is a duty of all eligible citizens.

Other Responsibilities

Serving in the Armed Forces

Reasons for Military Service If you live in a country and enjoy its freedoms, you have a duty to help that country in time of danger. This may mean serving in the armed forces.

The United States has sometimes used the **military draft.** This system requires people to enter military service. In the United States, the draft has applied only to men. A few countries draft both men and women.

The first United States draft laws were passed in colonial times. The governments of the colonies sometimes drafted men to serve in the state militia. Some men served in militia units that fought in the American Revolution. After the Revolution, Congress turned down a plan for a peacetime draft. The draft reappeared at the time of the Civil War. It was used again in World War I.

In 1940, Congress adopted a draft system that was in effect until 1975. The law said that all men had to register for the draft within 5 days of their eighteenth birthday. Each man then received a rating. A "1-A" rating meant that the man could be drafted at any time. A "4-F" meant that he was mentally or physically unfit. Full-time high school and college students received special ratings that let them finish their studies before being drafted.

Since 1975, the United States has used only volunteers in its armed forces. No one has to sign up for the draft. But this could change. A new draft would probably be started if a war or some other crisis required larger armed forces.

Thinking about Military Service Does a person have to answer any time the nation calls him or her to military service? Might that duty be limited in any way?

Some people believe that taking part in war is wrong on religious or moral grounds. These people are known as **pacifists.** A pacifist who refuses to be drafted as a fighter is called a **conscientious objector.**

United States draft laws let conscientious objectors choose another way of serving the country. For example, many conscientious objectors have served in the armed forces. But they went on the battlefield as medics. They cared for the wounded, but did not carry weapons. Others, who objected to being in the armed forces altogether, were given work in hospitals or with charities.

So far, we have been talking about people who object to serving in *all wars*. They believe that war is always wrong. Some people object to a *particular war*. For example, some men refused to serve in the Vietnam War. They disapproved of that one war. But the law did not allow for such dissenters. If they were drafted and refused to go, they were put in prison. Some fled the country in order to avoid the draft.

In 1974, President Gerald Ford offered draft evaders an *amnesty*. Ford said that if they turned themselves in, they would be assigned to 1 or 2 years of "alternative service." By that he meant a nonmilitary job that would help the country. In 1977, President Jimmy Carter went further. He pardoned almost all draft evaders. Both Presidents claimed that these actions would help to unite the nation.

Attending School

Reasons for Attending School We go to school to learn. We also go to school to obey the law. Parents must, by law, send their children to school through a certain age. In most states, that age is 16. This is known as **compulsory schooling.**

Compulsory schooling came about because people believed that only educated people would make good citizens. Someone who cannot read has a hard time keeping up on public issues. Such a person is at a disadvantage in modern life.

Compulsory schooling goes back as far as 1647 in Massachusetts, but it did not become widespread until the nineteenth century. At that time, free public schools appeared in many states. By the 1850s, all states had at least some public elementary schools. Public high schools came later. Only after World War I did most states begin to require education beyond grade school.

We have a duty to attend school, at least until the age that the law requires. School can help make us better citizens and more intelligent voters.

Thinking about Attending School Should *everyone* be required to obey compulsory schooling laws? Or should exceptions be made in certain cases?

In 1968, three Wisconsin couples refused to follow a state law requiring parents to make sure that children from the ages of 7 to 16 attend school regularly. The couples were believers in the Amish religion, a form of Protestantism. Like the other 60,000 Amish in this country, they believe in a simple life. Most Amish refuse to use automobiles, telephones, or even electricity. They live in Amish farming communities. When they go into the outside world, they

Should education be compulsory for all children until age 16? The Amish, who believe in the greater value of plain hard work, fought the system all the way up to the U.S. Supreme Court for the right to determine how much formal education their children must have. In the end, they won.

still use horse-drawn wagons and wear simple clothing.

The Amish couples had sent their children to public school through the eighth grade, but they objected to sending the children to high school. They felt that 8 years of school was enough to teach the children reading, writing, and arithmetic. That was all they would need for life in the Amish community. To send them to high school would expose them to "worldly" knowledge that would be against Amish beliefs. For example, they might be taught that working in an office is "more desirable" than working in a field. The Amish place great value on manual labor—plain hard work. The parents feared that the children would be torn between the Amish community and the outside world.

Wisconsin officials went to court to force the parents to send their children to school. The parents lost at first and were fined $5. But they won their case at the highest level, in the Supreme Court.

Chief Justice Warren Burger said that it would violate the Amish couples' freedom of religion to force them to send their children to high school. It might undermine the Amish community and its religious beliefs.

The Wisconsin officials had argued that the state must protect children from "ignorance." The Justices agreed, but said that the argument did not apply in this case. The Amish way of life involved "learning by doing." It did a good job of preparing children for life in the Amish community. The Court said that was what counted.

The Court seemed to be saying that religious beliefs can be more important than educating a citizen for a role in an industrial society.

Court Duty

Reasons for Court Duty Some day you may receive a notice in the mail asking you to appear in court on a certain day. The notice will instruct you to appear for **jury duty.** Serving on juries is our responsibility, just as having a trial by jury is our right. We would not have this right if citizens did not take on the responsibility of serving as jurors.

Citizens may be asked to serve either on grand juries or on trial juries. Jury duty may, at times, involve great personal sacrifice. It may take time that you would rather be spending in other ways. Still, jurors are needed if our system of trial-by-jury is to work. And jurors do receive payment for each day they serve.

Another type of court duty involves serving as a witness when called. For example, if you see an accident, you may be called as a witness. You would receive a **subpoena**—a court order instructing you to appear in court. You are legally required to obey the subpoena. What you saw may help the court to decide the case. You have a responsibility to serve as a witness when called, just as you have a right to call witnesses if you yourself were on trial.

Thinking about Court Duty Being a juror or a witness is not always easy. Look at some possible cases.

First, what if you are a juror at a criminal trial? The defendant is accused of breaking a law. But you do not agree with the law. You think that what the defendant is accused of doing should not be called a crime at all. Do you ignore your personal beliefs and make your decision based on the law as it is written? Or do you follow your personal beliefs and ignore the law?

The answer is: You must follow the law as it is described by the judge. Many people find this difficult to do at times. If they are opposed to a given law, they might refuse to convict someone of breaking that law. This has happened a number of times in our nation's past. Can you think of any laws that you disagree with? Could you convict someone of violating such a law? What else could you do?

In a representative democracy, only through voting can people make their opinions known and choices in matters of government felt. Recruitment drives—such as the one in this photo—help those who don't speak English well or understand the voting system to take part in the democratic process.

Second, what would happen if you see one person murder another person? You are close to the scene. You think you can identify the killer. But you know that the killer has connections with organized crime. What happens if the killer is arrested and you are called to be a witness at the trial? Would you name the suspect? Would you worry that the killer's partners might try to harm you? Would you protect yourself by "forgetting" what you had seen?

There are no simple answers to these questions. Each of us must think them through carefully. We must also remember that unless people accept their responsibilities as citizens our society will suffer.

Voting

Reasons for Voting Voting is one of our most precious rights—and, at the same time, a heavy responsibility. The decisions that we make in the voting booth shape what the government does, how it does it, and who does it. Voting makes our system of representative democracy work.

Voting means more than just stepping into a booth and throwing some levers or making some *x*'s. It is a full-time job. We cannot vote responsibly unless we keep up with public issues. Who is running for office? What do the candidates believe? What are the arguments for or against the public issues on the ballot? Watching the news on television the night before the election is not enough to make you an informed voter. There is a responsibility to *stay* informed.

Voting goes beyond election day. We have a responsibility to let our elected representatives know what we think about issues. That may mean writing a letter to a member of Congress or to a local official. It may mean going to hearings on a public issue in the community. Those are ways of making your views known where they can do some good. Another way is to take an active part in the work of a political party. That is what is known as "grassroots involvement." If the roots are healthy, the whole plant will be healthy. Without roots, the plant will weaken and die. And so it is with the democratic system.

Thinking about Voting Imagine that it is election day. You have followed the race closely. The latest public opinion polls say that the candidate you favor—Candidate A—is far behind the other candidates. You like one of the other candidates—Candidate B—, but think that the rest are poor choices. What should you do?

342 / Chapter 13: Our Responsibilities and Duties

Should you stay with Candidate A to the bitter end? Would that be "wasting" your vote? Should you, instead, vote for your second choice and try to "make your vote count"? What if the polls are wrong? What if *everyone* voted for his or her second choice?

Decisions about voting are not always easy. Sometimes they are harder than other times. What if you do not like *any* of the candidates? Should you write in a name—add it to the ballot? Should you avoid voting at all? Not voting does not really do much. It simply allows a candidate to be elected with fewer votes.

Nevada offered its voters a special choice in the 1976 elections. It gave them more than a list of candidates. For each office, there was a line marked "None of the above." Some voters used the extra line. "None of the above" received 47 percent of the vote in one race. The winner received 29 percent of the vote and the runner-up, 24 percent.

"I guess that gave the politicians a message," some people said. Do you agree? What was the message? What might it do?

=========== REVIEW ===========

1. At what different times in its history has the United States had a military draft?
2. What was the difference between President Ford's amnesty for draft evaders and President Carter's pardon?
3. What constitutional right was at issue in the Amish school case?
4. How did Nevada give voters an extra choice in one recent election?
5. Do you think that a person would ever be right in refusing to obey a subpoena to be a witness at a trial? Explain.

How the United States Works

The Armed Forces

In this age of missiles and jets, trouble between nations can happen suddenly. The government must keep its armed forces ready at all times, even when there is no clear threat. Therefore, serving in the armed forces is a citizen's responsibility in peacetime as well as in time of war. It is a voluntary responsibility, however, so the armed forces have to be able to attract great numbers of people. They have to offer some benefits.

The main benefit is the training. The armed forces need people to do all kinds of work in addition to the military jobs. The Navy, for example, does not hire a local electrician to fix a ship's generator. Nor does the Air Force hire civilians as air-traffic controllers. Instead, the armed forces enlist people, train them, and have the use of their services for 3 to 6 years. The length of time depends on the amount of training. Most tours of duty are for 3 or 4 years.

To get into the armed forces, you must be at least 17 years old. A high school degree is not required. In fact, you can receive that, too, after you have joined. Some people even receive college degrees while in the armed forces.

If you are interested in joining the military service for the educational benefits, make sure that you will receive training that can be used after you leave the service. The type of training you can take part in depends on job openings and on your abilities.

Reading About . . .

Making Your Views Known

This chapter has said that you have a responsibility to make your views on important matters known to your elected representatives. In this reading, Morris K. Udall, a representative from Arizona, tells how to do it.

As you read, ask yourself the following questions:

● Do you know the name of your representative in Congress?
● On what issue do you feel strongly enough to write to a representative?

Not long ago a letter reached my office written by an 8-year-old girl in Tucson who had been directed to "write your representative in Congress" when she complained about an 8 o'clock bedtime to her mother. She wrote. While I don't think my response was entirely satisfactory, at least she did write—something that 90 percent of all Americans do not do.

Why this reluctance? Perhaps it comes from a feeling that members of Congress are too busy to read their mail, that one letter won't make a difference. Speaking for myself, I can say flatly those ideas are wrong.

Letters *are* important. Mail is the hot line between the Washington office and home. Perhaps setting down some basics of writing your member of Congress will get more people to exercise this 'right to write.'

"*Address the letter properly:* When writing, send the letter to 'Hon. _____, House Office Building, Washington, D.C. 20515' or to 'Senator _____, Senate Office Building, Washington, D.C. 20515.'

Identify the issue: With some 20,000 bills introduced in each Congress, and a dazzling number of issues, it's vital to identify the bill by number or popular title—'minimum wage' or 'strip-mine bill,' etc.—in your letter.

Concentrate on your delegation: Don't waste time writing 535 members of Congress. Your representatives and your senators cast *your* vote. Stick with them.

Be brief: Letters have a much better chance of being answered fully and promptly if they are short and readable. You don't have to type, but write clearly.

Some do's and don't's: Do write your own opinions. A personal letter is far better than a form letter.

Do explain why you are taking a stand. A letter that simply says you are for or against a bill is not very helpful.

Do be constructive. If you see that a problem exists, but think that a certain bill is the wrong answer, help the representative by suggesting another answer.

Do say "well done" when it's deserved. The men and women who serve in the Congress are people, too. They appreciate compliments once in a while.

Don't threaten. Most representatives want to do what is right for the country. This may not always be popular at home. It sometimes brings letters threatening political action or withdrawal of past support. You have a right to do this, but it is my experience that reason works better than threats.

Don't be a "pen pal." The person who sends a long letter every few days on a vast number of issues becomes what is known as a "pen pal" in congressional offices. "Pen pals" get answered last.

chapter
Review

Fact Review

1. Choose a law that you consider to be important. Tell what might happen if people stopped obeying that law.
2. Give three reasons why people should obey the law.
3. Why did Martin Luther King, Jr., use civil disobedience? How did he use it? Do you think that his use of civil disobedience accomplished its purpose? Why?
4. Give two other historical examples of the use of civil disobedience.
5. Governments use tax money in order to give treatment to people who are mentally ill. In what way might this benefit a person who is not mentally ill?
6. Why did many California voters feel that their property taxes were too high? What did they do to voice their protest? Who led the fight to roll back California property taxes?
7. Which of the following are responsibilities of an American citizen?
   a. military service
   b. attending school
   c. attending a place of worship
   d. court duty
   e. respect for points of view different from your own
   f. voting
8. What were two reasons for which a man might be excused from military service under the draft law that was in effect between 1940 and 1975?
9. For about how long has at least some elementary schooling been offered in the United States?
10. What are three reasons for making school attendance compulsory?
11. What constitutional right does jury duty help protect?
12. You are a juror in a criminal trial. The defendant is accused of breaking a law. If you do not agree with the law the defendant is accused of breaking, do you:

   a. follow your personal beliefs and ignore the law?
   b. ignore your personal beliefs and base your decision upon the law as it is written?
13. Which of the following statements about voting are true and which are false?
   a. A responsible voter keeps informed about public issues.
   b. A responsible voter must get actively involved in political campaigns by handing out leaflets or helping out at polling places.
   c. "Grassroots involvement" means running for public office.
   d. A responsible voter considers his or her choices before entering the voting booth.
14. At various times, government officials have been accused of breaking the law while carrying out their official duties. Do you think that an official who breaks the law while following orders from a superior should be punished? Why or why not?
15. Do you think that compulsory schooling is necessary to produce educated voters? Why or why not?

Developing Your Vocabulary

1. Tell which of the following are examples of civil disobedience, which are examples of conscientious objection, and which are neither.
   a. A person who is hungry steals food.
   b. A pacifist refuses to serve in the armed forces.
   c. A soldier runs away for fear of being killed in battle.
   d. A citizen goes to jail rather than pay taxes that might help pay for war.
   e. A black civil rights demonstrator requests service at a "white" lunch counter, is refused service, stays seated, and is quietly arrested for trespassing.

f. War protesters go to jail rather than be drafted to fight a war they do not believe in.

2. Match the words in *a* to *e* with the phrases in *(1)* to *(5)*

a. civil disobedience
b. subpoena
c. jury duty
d. compulsory schooling
e. military draft

(1) a system for requiring people to enter the military service
(2) the policy of requiring children to attend school until they reach a certain age
(3) a court order instructing someone to appear in court or produce a document
(4) concept according to which a person may—or should—break a law that she or he considers unjust
(5) a responsibility to serve on juries when ordered to do so

---

Developing Your Reading Skills

Read the following paragraph and then answer the questions that follow:

As citizens, we have not only rights but also responsibilities. One such responsibility is that of obeying the law. In a democracy, we have a part in helping to make the laws under which we are guided. But once these laws are made, we have a responsibility to obey them. If we disobey them, we must be willing to accept the punishment. Those who take part in civil disobedience are often trying to change laws that they do not like. Both obedience to the law and civil disobedience are features of living in a democracy.

1. Which one of the following do you think is the main point, or main idea, of the paragraph above?
   a. Our freedoms come with certain duties.
   b. It is never right to disobey a law.
   c. Civil disobedience is useful in a democracy.
   d. We have a duty to help make our laws.
   e. Citizens who do not obey the laws of our country should not be allowed to be citizens.

2. Tell why you selected either *a, b, c, d,* or *e* in question 1.

Developing Your Writing Skills— Forming and Supporting an Opinion

In this chapter, you have studied several responsibilities that accompany our constitutional rights. Now consider:

Forming an opinion

Supporting an opinion

1. What one responsibility is the most important for the citizen of a democracy such as ours?

2. After thinking it over, write a brief paragraph that answers the question above. Tell the reasons why you chose that responsibility.

YOUR GOVERNMENT & ITS HISTORY

A Nation of Immigrants

In this chapter, you have read about the rights and responsibilities of all American citizens. As you have learned, almost all Americans have their roots in other countries. With that in mind, let us learn about the migrations that brought most of our families to America. Then, let us look at the steps required for an immigrant to become a United States citizen.

The United States is often called a nation of immigrants. This is because it has accepted more people from other lands than any other nation.

Until 1882, the United States had no laws governing immigration. At first, about 10,000 settlers arrived per year.

But in the 1830s and 1840s, millions came from Great Britain, Germany, and Ireland. They came to escape persecution, poverty, and famine. They were attracted by America's abundance of rich farmland, need for workers, and political and religious freedom.

From 1860 to 1890, more than 10 million immigrants poured onto American soil. This second wave of immigrants mostly came from Denmark, Norway, Sweden, Poland, Russia, Austria, Hungary, Czechoslovakia, Italy, and China.

Some of these new immigrants took advantage of the Homestead Act of 1862. This act offered complete ownership of 160 acres of land. Any settler willing to live on it for 5 years was given the land for free. Any settler willing to work the land for 6 months could buy it for $1.50 an acre.

The majority of immigrants settled in the cities and new industrial centers in the Northeast. They lived in small communities based on ethnic and national background. Italians migrated to the Little Italies of New York and Boston. Finns went to the copper and iron mines of the Midwest. Bulgarians headed for the steel towns of Illinois. Poles were drawn to the meat-packing industry of Chicago and, later, to the automobile industry of Detroit.

These newcomers to the United States contributed to its great economic growth. They also brought with them many diverse cultural and religious traditions. Many of these traditions are still with us today.

In the 1880s, the rising rate of immigration led to resentment among many Americans. New immigrants were blamed for the evils of urban growth and industrial expansion. In 1882, immigration to America was restricted for the first time.

From 1890 to 1930, nearly 22 million immigrants entered the country. Many of this group came from Greece, Hungary, Italy, Poland, Portugal, Russia, and Spain.

In 1924, a law was passed restricting the number of immigrants to 150,000 each year. Each nationality was allowed a certain number of immigrants. This number depended on how many from each group were in the United States when the law was passed. This was known as the national-origin system.

Today, the United States limits the number of immigrants to 170,000 from the eastern hemisphere and to 120,000 from the western hemisphere. It also limits the maximum number of immigrants from any one country to 20,000 per year.

Becoming an American Citizen

The legal process of becoming an American citizen is called naturalization. To qualify for citizenship, one must be at least 18 years old and a permanent resident of the United States. He or she must have lived in this country continuously for 5 years and at least 6 months in the same state. Anyone under 18 years of age be-comes a citizen automatically when his or her parents become citizens. Husbands and wives of citizens qualify for citizenship after 3 years in the United States.

The first step toward becoming a citizen is to fill out an application provided by the Immigration and Naturalization Service. It is returned, along with a fingerprint card, a biographic information form, and three unsigned photographs.

Next, the applicant appears before a naturalization examiner who asks questions about American history and government. Applicants must read, write, and speak simple English. Two witnesses must testify about their character, loyalty, and length of time in the United States. A petition for naturalization is filed, and a $25 fee is paid.

When an application for citizenship has been approved, the applicant must return to the Immigration and Naturalization Service. This time, he or she takes an oath of allegiance to the United States and receives a certificate of naturalization. This person is now a naturalized American who has all the rights and duties of a citizen by birth, with one exception: Naturalized citizens cannot become President or Vice President of the United States.

1. Why is America often called a nation of immigrants?

2. When were the three great waves of immigration to America? Who came in each of these waves?

3. Where did most immigrants settle?

4. What steps must you take to become a citizen? What are the qualifications?

Developing your basic civic education skills

Another Look at Taxes

(thinking critically—
asking questions)

In this chapter, you have learned about taxes and the reasons we pay them. Political cartoonists and comic strip artists have long made fun of paying taxes. They have also made fun of how those taxes are spent by the government. Three comic strips about paying taxes are on the next page.

1. Match each point that follows with one of the three comic strips.

   a. Getting tax money is often more important than anything else in government.

   b. Someone can always find a way to increase taxes.

   c. The government does not always spend tax money wisely.

     1. Comic strip 1
     2. Comic strip 2
     3. Comic strip 3

2. Why do you think some comic strip artists draw these kinds of strips? What sorts of questions can be asked about such comic strips? Ask two such questions.

Now imagine the following situation:

The Middleton High School Student Council voted 21–12 to create a fund for an annual senior class trip. The council was made up only of juniors and seniors. This fund was to be paid for by charging all the students at Middleton High a fee at the beginning of each year. The council voted to charge freshmen $0.50, sophomores $1.00, juniors $1.50, and seniors $2.00.

After the council voted in favor of the proposal, many students expressed concern over the new tax. Unhappy students argued that any money charged them should be spent on other things the school needed. These things included picnic tables for students to use while eating lunch, providing more money for the school newspaper, or buying plants for the school grounds. The unhappy students also argued that the taxing method was unfair. Freshmen and sophomores were not allowed to vote for or against the tax proposal. Yet, they were to be taxed, even though they would not benefit from it.

Some students went even further. They questioned whether it would be fair for anyone except seniors to pay the tax. What if a student moved to a new school district before becoming a senior? In such a situation, the student would not benefit at all from the taxes that had been paid.

The uproar over the tax finally proved so great that the student council agreed that they should reconsider the tax proposal at the next meeting.

3. What fund did the Middleton High

GOOSEMYER

Comic Strip 1

Comic Strip 2

Comic Strip 3

School Student Council establish? What were students to pay each year?

4. What did some of the students think of the new tax? Would you have agreed with them? Explain.

5. As shown by the three comic strips, many people have complaints about paying taxes or about how taxes are spent. Yet what would happen if local, state, and federal governments never collected any taxes? List four results. Could the same thing happen if the citizens refused to pay taxes?

6. What do you think makes a system of taxation fair? Do you suppose that all the citizens would agree? Why or why not? Would that present any problems? Explain.

Jury Duty
(conflicting viewpoints)

In this chapter, you have read about serving on a jury. The following readings offer some additional observations about jury duty.

Reading 1

You have been summoned to jury duty. What goes through your mind?

Probably, "Why me?" You probably greet the summons with as much enthusiasm as a tax bill or a statement that your bank account is overdrawn.

Your second thought might well be, "How am I going to get out of this?" You do not jump for joy about the prospects of "fulfilling your civic duty."

Your mind moves to the obvi-

ous solution: The boss will just have to explain to some clerk at the courthouse how necessary you are on the job.

But it nags at your memory that work is no excuse. And (horrors!) what if boss decides the shop would not close down if you had to be absent a few days?

I know those feelings. I was called. I was seated. I served—but not without a struggle.

Certainly, I thought, a talk with my old buddy, the district clerk, would be enough to get my name removed from the call.

He replied, "I'm sorry, Bill, but there isn't a thing I can do. But I'll see you in the jury meeting room; you see, I have been called, too." There went my inside pull and political influence.

I answered the call, as did about 600 other citizens, that Monday morning. We had only one thing in common: we were all registered voters. This irritates me no end. The law ought to be changed. If you use your right to vote, you open yourself to the time-consuming, expensive bother of jury duty. Do not register to vote, and you are home free.

That requirement keeps loads of people from voting. It seriously penalizes civic involvement. It blocks the democratic processes.

There are plenty of other sources for names to be fed into the jury-wheel or computers that fill the list of possible jurors. Other states use voters' lists but also . . . obtain names from school records, lists of utility customers, employment records, telephone listings, tax records, drivers' licenses, and car titles. This guarantees a much more representative cross-section of the entire community. It also aids the concept of being judged by one's equals.

As it is, nonvoters are excused. So are several other groupings of people, such as persons more than 65 years old. Certainly, senior citizens are a growing percentage of our society. Except for juries, it would be impossible to bring together twelve typical citizens without two or three oldsters being present.

But surely a professor (like me), busy with daily classes, would be excused, I thought. After all, students attending high school or college, otherwise qualified, are freed from their civic duty. Since the learning process is so highly regarded, pure logic demands that this way out must also be granted to their teachers.

Ha! My students were free to attend class, but I was not allowed to be there to teach them. That just does not make sense. Are you listening, state legislators?

The excused left, and I stayed, my plea having fallen upon deaf ears. The district judge addressed us all, stressing how important juries were to our system of justice.

The announcement that we would receive $5 a day did little to increase our sense of importance. Try parking all day within walking distance of the courthouse and having lunch downtown. Then count your change from your $5, and you will appreciate the burden of being important.

We waited—for hours. Finally, I heard my name called and joined a party of thirty-three others. . . . We were marched to an upstairs hallway. We were informed that we would form a group from which twelve would be seated in a murder case.

We waited. We never entered the courtroom. Finally, we were marched back to the assembly room, where we were told that our experience had just proved how well the jury system worked.

This . . . made some sense when it was explained. The defendant's attorney, having learned we were standing outside the courtroom, had suddenly decided to accept the District Attorney's offer that his client plead guilty to a lesser charge.

Look at the expense and time saved by our merely being outside. But was justice served? I felt as if I were being used in a legal game of blackmail and bluff. And I didn't like it.

But at least I had been called. I had marched forward, ready to answer questions openly and freely as to my ability to serve without bias as an all-important juror. Now I was through. I could collect my $5 and return to my classroom. No. We had to stay for yet more calls. And the second day, the call came.

7. Which three of the following were observations made in the reading?

a. Jury duty is something most people try to avoid.

b. Jury duty is very enjoyable for most people.

c. Jury duty does not pay well.

d. The system of choosing jurors is fair.

e. Jury duty pays well.

f. Jury duty often requires an individual to spend much time waiting to serve on a case.

8. Do you think the expense and time spent on jury duty should be considered as a contribution of civic duty?

Reading 2

It took 28 years, but the county finally tagged me for jury duty. To my surprise, it was really an enjoyable experience. It was a surprise because everything I had heard about jury duty was negative.

My friends did not tell me about the continuing coffee breaks, the 2-hour lunch periods and the chance to meet new people. They also did not tell me about the absence of ringing phones and the delightful opportunity to read a novel or play cards.

Sounds like a vacation? It is, unless you are assigned to a difficult case. Then, you have another unique life experience.

But, back to us "rejects," the gang in the central jury room who were sent out but not selected to serve.

The central jury bailiff sends groups of fifteen, twenty-eight, or thirty-six jurors, picked by computer, to one of the six county or fifteen district courts. The prosecuting and defense attorneys choose a jury from the panel. The remaining jurors return to the central courtroom to await another call.

Once at the courthouse, most people want to serve on a jury. While the "rejects" joke about it, they are just a little let down.

The old sayings "Many are called, but few are chosen" and "Those who stand and wait also serve" often ran through my mind. Except for 1½ hours when I was called into a courtroom, I spent 2 days in the central jury room.

The hardest part of jury duty is finding a parking place. After the first day, I discovered that many jurors ride the bus.

A jury summons arrives by mail with a warning that gets your attention. The fine for being late or failing to respond is from $10 to $100. If you are qualified to vote, can read and write, and have not been convicted of a felony or theft, you are qualified to serve on a jury.

If you are lucky, your employer will pay your salary while you serve. But if not, or even if you run a one-person business, do not expect to be excused.

But why me? Why a jury summons? Once a year, in August, a computer picks possible jurors from the current voter registration list.

You cannot be chosen twice in 12 months unless you are registered more than once or had jury duty rescheduled.

The county sheriff issues about 1,000 jury summons a week. Jury calls begin on Mondays and Wednesdays. This means citizens report on Monday or Wednesday and normally are released at the end of the second day.

Under the old system, jurors reported on Monday and were not released until Thursday afternoon. Persons chosen for juries continue to serve until their work is complete.

My first day in the central jury room began with a 1-hour talk by the supervising judge. He covered the beginning of the jury system, the lack of voter interest, the need for a new spirit of patriotism, and what we jurors could expect.

"You will be unhappy here," he said. There is not much happening here, but something is happening elsewhere. Cases are being heard and judged peacefully. Your being here is important to the handling of cases whether or not you get to court."

Continuing with good humor, the judge said, "A lot of people enjoy being here. They speak with old friends and make new ones. Every once in a while, a romance springs up. If this happens, and you get to the marrying stage, I'll marry you free of charge."

The judge explained that the jury system started with Henry II in the twelfth century and that originally the jury were witnesses as well as judges.

I was sent to court. The attorneys selected a jury of six for a reckless-conduct case. I was not chosen. Another "reject" was a police officer.

"No defense attorney in his or her right mind would choose a police officer," he said. "But I have to come here and sit two days anyway."

The officer was the only one of us who had ever heard of a reckless conduct charge. The assistant district attorney explained that reckless conduct is putting another's life in danger.

My two days on jury duty were like a brief vacation. I enjoyed reading my book and sipping coffee. I made a couple of new friends. At noon, I went shopping and sightseeing and visited the library. The salary of $5 a day paid for lunch and parking.

On the afternoon of the second day, jurors were released in groups. It was amusing to watch the farewells as the little groups broke up. . . . Eventually, we all went home and back to the daily routine.

9. What three observations were made about jury duty in the reading?

10. Did the two writers agree about anything concerning jury duty? Explain your answer.

11. Did the two writers disagree about anything about jury duty? Explain.

12. More potential jurors are called than are needed for a case. This is so lawyers for each side in a case can select the best jury possible for their cases. Do you think having more possible jurors than will actually serve is a good idea? Would you feel that way if you were going to be on trial before a jury?

13. How representative do you think a jury should be?

14. How important do you think jury duty is? What could happen if everyone suddenly refused to serve on juries?

UNIT 6 REVIEW

Fact Review

1. Tell which amendment, or amendments, to the Constitution protect our right to do each of the following things:
   a. have a jury trial in a civil lawsuit
   b. practice the religion of our choice
   c. keep and bear arms
   d. vote without paying a poll tax
2. Name five groups of people to whom rights have been extended by amendments to the U.S. Constitution. Explain how these people have benefited.
3. Name one *right* that comes from the First Amendment. Name one *responsibility* involved in the First Amendment.
4. What requirement must a government meet before it can take a person's property? Where in the Constitution is this requirement mentioned?

Developing Your Vocabulary

Four terms in the paragraph below are misused. First, find the terms. Then, choose the correct terms from the following list.

probation	witnesses
punishment	convicted
indicted	bail

The Constitution guarantees certain rights to someone arrested for a crime. The person has a right to be acquitted by a grand jury. Between arrest and trial, the person may be released on libel. The trial must be speedy. At the trial, the defendant may call jurors to testify. If convicted, the person may not be sentenced to cruel or unusual servitude.

Developing Your Reading Skills

Read the following passage and then answer the questions that follow:

The Constitution and its amendments guarantee us many rights. These are privileges to which we are entitled. As citizens, we also have duties and responsibilities.

Many of our rights are set forth in the Bill of Rights. This is made up of the first ten amendments to the Constitution. The Bill of Rights was adopted in 1791, after many people complained that the Constitution did not do enough to guarantee people's rights.

Some of our most important rights are included in the First Amendment. This guarantees freedom of conscience and freedom of expression. Religious freedom is part of this amendment, as are freedom of speech, freedom of the press, and freedom of assembly.

We have rights if we are accused of a crime—the right to have a lawyer, for example, and to have a speedy trial. We have rights that protect us if we should be found guilty of a crime. One such right is not to be given cruel and unusual punishments.

Amendments to the Constitution have greatly increased the number of people who have the right to vote. At one time, blacks, women, people who lived in the District of Columbia, people between the ages of 18 and 21, and poor people were kept from voting. Now, their right to vote is protected.

Balancing these rights are a number of responsibilities and duties. We have a duty to obey the law. We have a duty to pay taxes. If required, we have a duty to serve in the armed forces.

As free citizens, we must think about our responsibilities. We do not need to carry them out unquestioningly. In fact, true citizenship requires that we always think before acting.

1. Tell which of the questions below can be answered from the reading:
   a. How many amendments are part of the Bill of Rights?
   b. Which amendment guarantees freedom of expression?
   c. Which amendment guarantees the right to a speedy trial?
2. Now answer the questions above that can be found in the reading.

The word *politics* brings to mind many images. To some people, politics is a struggle for power. They see it as being dirty. "I don't even try to keep up with what goes on down at city hall. It's all politics anyway," someone might say. You might also hear comments such as: "They never fix the potholes out this way. That's politics for you."

To other people, politics is something exciting—almost a game. It is brass bands, and straw hats, and bumper stickers.

To still others, politics is a very serious business—the business of governing the United States. "If you want to improve your lot in life or improve society, get into politics" is a piece of advice that is passed on by many worldly-wise people. In this view, politics is the process by which roads are built, laws are passed, and rights are won. It is the process by which conflicts are settled.

In truth, politics is all of these. It has its dark side and its bright side.

We are all involved in politics, whether we want to be or not. Our lives are closely affected by the decisions made in the voting booths and in the halls of government. That is why we have a responsibility to participate in politics for our own good, as well as for the good of society.

In this unit, you will examine some of the ways in which people participate in our political system—by voting, by joining political parties, by campaigning, by forming and expressing opinions, and by working with others for a common goal.

unit
7

The Process of Politics

Chapter

14 Voters and Politics

Every 4 years, "presidential fever" strikes. The hopefuls shake hands, kiss babies, pat backs, and make promises. For months, the people hear presidential politics discussed nightly on the television news. State by state, the people go to vote. First come the primary elections, then the November presidential election. All this is part of the way in which the people of the United States choose their President.

Most of our interest in voting and elections focuses on presidential elections. The stakes are biggest there, and the excitement reaches its highest peak. But there are many other types of elections. State elections decide who will build our highways and run our state governments. Local elections decide who will build our sewers, control our schools, and run our city halls. There are votes to put people in office and votes to remove people from office. There are votes to raise or lower taxes. There are also votes to decide other issues.

In this chapter, you will take a close look at what goes on in an election. You will see how people vote and how people run for office. In short, you will see how the voters rule in a democracy.

I. Voters and voting
   A. Expressing our wishes
   B. Who can vote?
   C. The ballot

II. Political parties and elections
   A. The two-party system
     1. History
     2. Advantages of a two-party system

Words to Know

voting —— the formal process by which people express their choice about the way government should be run

candidate —— a person who seeks to be elected to public office

recall —— an election in which voters can put an elected official out of office before the official's term ends

register —— to have one's name put on a list of qualified voters

electorate —— all the people who are qualified to vote

polls —— voting places

Voters and Voting

Expressing Our Wishes

The word *vote* comes from a Latin word meaning "wish." When someone casts a vote, that person is expressing a wish or a choice. **Voting** is the formal process by which people express their choice about the way government should be run. Those people who do not vote do not have their wishes taken into account.

Voters may express their wishes in a number of ways. The most obvious way is to elect government officials at national, state, and local levels. The people who are running for office are called **candidates.** The voters can vote *for* candidates who share their own views about how government should be run. Or they can vote *against* candidates whose views they op-

pose or who have failed to live up to their promises in the past.

In some states, voters can remove an elected official from office before the official's term ends. They can vote yes or no on a question such as: "Should Jane Doe be removed from the office of treasurer?" This process is known as **recall.** If an official is recalled, another election is held to choose a replacement.

There are also two ways in which voters can take a direct part in lawmaking. First, they may be asked to approve or reject a law that has been passed by the state legislature. This kind of election is known as a *referendum.* It is often used with suggested constitutional amendments as well. Second, the voters may themselves propose, or initiate, a law and adopt it. This is known as an *initiative.*

Who Can Vote?

Each state makes its own rules about who is qualified to vote. But all states must follow certain basic guidelines. These are set down by the United States Constitution, by federal laws, and by decisions of the Supreme Court. As a result, voting qualifications in the fifty states are much alike.

Some states and communities require that you live in one place for a certain amount of time before you can vote. This is usually not more than 30 days.

In almost all states, you must **register** before you can vote. That is, you must have your name put on a list of qualified voters in your voting district. In most states, a person must be registered for 10 to 30 days before being able to vote.

All together, the people who are qualified to vote make up the **electorate.**

In general, the only people who cannot vote are: (1) persons under 18 years of age, (2) convicted criminals, and (3) people who are not citizens.

Enrolling to vote at a registration table is the first step to becoming a qualified voter.

The Constitution states that the right to vote of a citizen 18 years of age or older cannot be taken away because of race, color, sex, previous condition of servitude, or failure to pay a poll tax. If your eighteenth birthday is the day of an election, you are qualified to vote in that election.

In the past, election officials sometimes tried to keep certain people from voting. Blacks, recent immigrants, and poor people were kept off many voting lists as recently as the 1960s. Federal laws and court rulings have tried to change this. For example, literacy tests have been outlawed in the United States. These tests used to be given to make sure that all voters knew how to read and write in English. Often, the tests were unnecessarily hard to keep certain citizens from voting. Now Congress requires ballots in certain areas to be printed in two languages. This is done to help citizens whose first language is not English.

The Ballot

What happens when you go to the **polls**—the voting places? In the early nineteenth century, you might have been questioned out loud by a voting official. Everyone present would have known how you voted. Today, voting is done in secret. This is required by federal law.

The names of the people who are running for the offices are listed on a *ballot,* an official list. The ballot may also contain issues—such as constitutional amendments—to be decided by the voters.

The ballot that we use today is called the Australian ballot. It is a uniform ballot that is printed by the government and used by all voters. It is called that because it was first used in Australia. Voters used to write their own ballots. They listed only the names they wanted to vote for. Sometimes a political party would print up a ballot listing only its candidates. Occasionally, a

By reading an advance sample ballot, this woman will already have had her choices in mind before actually voting.

group might print fake ballots. The ballot would appear to list, for example, all of the Whig Party's candidates. But it would leave off some important names. Unsuspecting voters would use the ballot, thinking that they had supported all of the Whigs, when they had really not voted at all for some important offices. The Australian ballot got rid of such abuses.

In some places, the ballot is a piece of paper. The voter takes the ballot into a booth and closes a curtain. Then the voter places a mark—such as an x—beside the desired candidates' names. If the voter does not like any of the candidates, he or she can write in a name. Then, the voter folds the ballot, leaves the booth, and deposits the ballot in a closed container.

Today, however, many places use voting machines. The voting procedure is different with machines. The voter enters a booth and closes a curtain. The names of the candidates are located beside a series of levers on a machine inside the booth. To vote for someone, the voter pulls the lever beside the candidate's name. There is also a slot where a voter can write in another name. When finished, the voter pulls a handle that opens the curtain and records the vote. This action also clears the machine so that the next voter can use it.

No matter what method of voting is used, voting officials always check each voter's name off a list of the qualified voters. This is done to make sure that no one votes twice.

─────── REVIEW ───────

1. In what ways does the federal government limit the freedom of states to decide who may and who may not vote?
2. What persons are generally denied the right to vote?
3. What kind of thing, other than candidates' names, might be on an election ballot?
4. Do you approve of a minimum age of 18 for voting, or do you think that age should be set higher or lower? Why?

Words to Know

political party —— a group of people who have joined together to take part in elections with the goal of winning control of the government
GOP —— "Grand Old Party," the Republican Party
coalition —— an alliance of two or more parties
third party —— a minor party, not one of the two major parties
primary election —— a preliminary election to choose a party's candidates
general election —— the final election

closed primary —— a primary election that is open only to members of a political party and closed to all others
open primary —— a primary election that is open to all voters, regardless of what party they belong to
run-off primary —— a second election between the top candidates in a primary in which no candidate won a majority of the votes
nominating convention —— a meeting of the members of a political party to choose their candidates for an election
keynote speech —— a kickoff speech at a political-party convention
party platform —— a statement of principles and promises that is drawn up by a political party
plank —— a principle or a promise in a party platform
favorite son or daughter —— an important person who is nominated for President by his or her state's delegation to a national convention. (Such a nomination is made primarily as a bargaining tactic.)

Political Parties and Elections

Most of the candidates on an election ballot are backed by political parties. We will see shortly how their names come to be placed on the ballot. But first, let's take a look at political parties.

The Two-Party System

A **political party** is a group of people who have joined together to take part in elections with the goal of winning control of the government. Members of a political party do not always agree with each other. In fact, they often argue among themselves. The thing that holds parties together is the common goal of winning elections.

History The Constitution does not mention political parties. In fact, some of the founders of the United States thought that we did not need political parties. But from the first, people did group together in order to follow common political interests.

The fight over whether or not to adopt the Constitution divided people into two groups. People who liked the Constitution were known as Federalists. People who opposed it were called Antifederalists. This division into two parts sets a long-lasting pattern. Today, we still have a two-way division. The two major political parties are the Democratic Party and the Republican Party.

The political-party system began to take shape between 1789 and 1800. People who wanted a strong federal government formed the Federalist Party. Its leaders were Alexander Hamilton and John Adams. People who wanted a limited federal government and strong state governments formed the Democratic Republican Party. Its leaders were Thomas Jefferson and James Madison.

Out of arguments and agreements made in this small frame schoolhouse, the Republican party emerged.

In 1827, the Democratic Republican Party changed its name to the Democratic Party. Their leader, Andrew Jackson, was President from 1829 to 1837. He wanted to see the Democrats identified with the "common people." The party had great strength in the South and the West.

By that time, the Federalist Party had died out. To take its place, opponents of Jackson formed the Whig Party. It included some former Federalists and some Democrats who had broken with Jackson. Among its leaders were Henry Clay and Daniel Webster. The Whigs won only two presidential elections, in 1840 and 1848.

The Republican Party was formed in 1854. It quickly replaced the Whigs as the second major political party. The Republicans opposed the spread of slavery. In 1860, their candidate—Abraham Lincoln—was elected President. Ever since, the Democrats and the Republicans have been the two major political parties in the United States.

The Republicans became known as the "Grand Old Party," or **GOP,** because they had a grand time for many years. The Democrats had become divided over the issue of slavery at the time of the Civil War and did not build up their strength again until the 1930s. Between 1860 and 1932, all except two Presidents were Republicans.

But after that, things changed. Since 1932, the Democrats and the Republicans have taken turns electing Presidents. But the Democrats have controlled Congress most of that time. The Republicans have not had a majority in Congress since the 1953-to-1954 session.

Advantages of a Two-Party System A two-party system gives voters a choice between the "ins" and the "outs." If the voters do not like what the party in power—the "ins"—is doing, they have a clear choice. They can elect the "outs."

In a two-party system, however, both parties tend to have moderate programs.

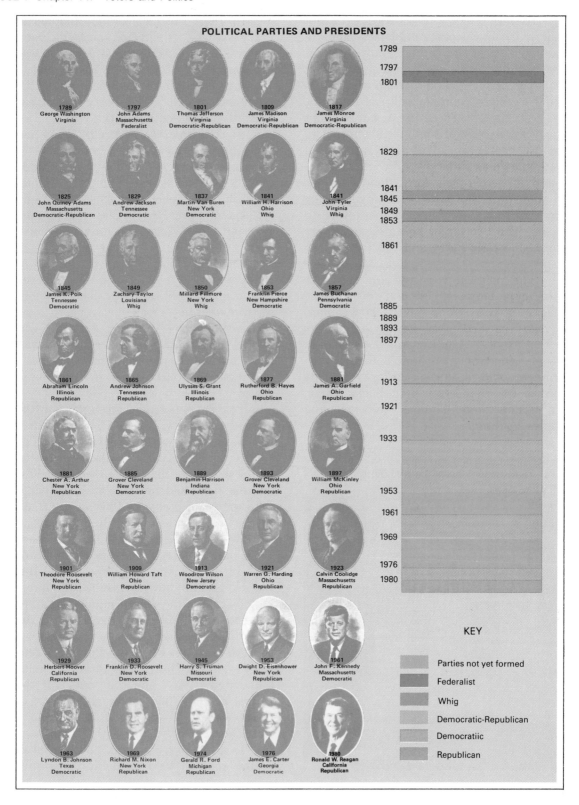

POLITICAL PARTIES AND PRESIDENTS

1789 George Washington, Virginia

1797 John Adams, Massachusetts, Federalist

1801 Thomas Jefferson, Virginia, Democratic-Republican

1809 James Madison, Virginia, Democratic-Republican

1817 James Monroe, Virginia, Democratic-Republican

1825 John Quincy Adams, Massachusetts, Democratic-Republican

1829 Andrew Jackson, Tennessee, Democratic

1837 Martin Van Buren, New York, Democratic

1841 William H. Harrison, Ohio, Whig

1841 John Tyler, Virginia, Whig

1845 James K. Polk, Tennessee, Democratic

1849 Zachary Taylor, Louisiana, Whig

1850 Millard Fillmore, New York, Whig

1853 Franklin Pierce, New Hampshire, Democratic

1857 James Buchanan, Pennsylvania, Democratic

1861 Abraham Lincoln, Illinois, Republican

1865 Andrew Johnson, Tennessee, Republican

1869 Ulysses S. Grant, Illinois, Republican

1877 Rutherford B. Hayes, Ohio, Republican

1881 James A. Garfield, Ohio, Republican

1881 Chester A. Arthur, New York, Republican

1885 Grover Cleveland, New York, Democratic

1889 Benjamin Harrison, Indiana, Republican

1893 Grover Cleveland, New York, Democratic

1897 William McKinley, Ohio, Republican

1901 Theodore Roosevelt, New York, Republican

1909 William Howard Taft, Ohio, Republican

1913 Woodrow Wilson, New Jersey, Democratic

1921 Warren G. Harding, Ohio, Republican

1923 Calvin Coolidge, Massachusetts, Republican

1929 Herbert Hoover, California, Republican

1933 Franklin D. Roosevelt, New York, Democratic

1945 Harry S. Truman, Missouri, Democratic

1953 Dwight D. Eisenhower, New York, Republican

1961 John F. Kennedy, Massachusetts, Democratic

1963 Lyndon B. Johnson, Texas, Democratic

1969 Richard M. Nixon, New York, Republican

1974 Gerald R. Ford, Michigan, Republican

1976 James E. Carter, Georgia, Democratic

1980 Ronald W. Reagan, California, Republican

1789
1797
1801
1829
1841
1845
1849
1853
1861
1885
1889
1893
1897
1913
1921
1933
1953
1961
1969
1976
1980

KEY

Parties not yet formed

Federalist

Whig

Democratic-Republican

Democratiic

Republican

They must appeal to business owners as well as workers, to city dwellers as well as farmers.

In countries with only one political party, the voters have no choice. But in countries with more than two major parties, there may be too many choices. Dissatisfied voters may not be able to agree on which of the "outs" to elect. The result may be a government that is made up of two or more parties. Such a government is called a **coalition.** Often, coalition governments do not last long. Even while they last, they may not be able to get together on a plan of action.

Criticisms of a Two-Party System
Some people argue that our two-party system does not offer a significant choice. They say that Democrats and Republicans are often as alike as two peas in a pod.

Critics also tend to see the moderate views of the two major parties as a sign of weakness. They claim that the parties are afraid to speak out strongly on the issues. As a result, the critics say, the two parties give the voters only vague promises.

The Party System and Compromise
In any sort of political system, some form of compromise is necessary. In a system of many parties, compromise usually takes place after a coalition is formed. In our two-party system, political bargaining and compromise often take place *within* a political party.

For example, let's say that the Democrats control Congress. A bill to cut defense spending is suggested. A liberal Democrat might favor the bill on the grounds that it would make more money available for social programs. A Democrat from the West might argue that the bill would cause unemployment in the big defense industries located there. Another Democrat might argue that the bill would dangerously weaken the nation's defenses.

In order to build the widest possible support for the bill, Democratic leaders might work out a compromise. They might reduce the size of the defense cut to please one section of the party. They might add a provision to decrease the threat of unemployment. They would try to do all this in such a way as to avoid losing the support of the different members of the party.

In a sense, then, each of our two major parties is itself a coalition. Each party includes people with a wide range of ideas. But members of each party agree on one thing: that is, that their own party is the best and should be helped to win elections.

Third Parties

When we say we have a two-party system, it means that only two parties have a good chance of winning elections. However, there are often many parties competing. A voter in Pennsylvania in 1976, for example, had a choice of seven candidates for President. Two were the Democratic and the Republican candidates. In addition, there were candidates from the Socialist Workers Party, the Communist Party, the Constitution Party, and the U.S. Labor Party—as well as an *independent,* Eugene McCarthy. An independent is a person who runs for office without the aid of a political party. In other states, various other parties entered candidates for President.

Minor parties have played a major role in history. Sometimes they win elections. Often, these parties take enough votes away from another party to influence the outcome of an election. Minor parties are often referred to as **third parties.**

Third parties serve as a safety valve. They give voters a chance to express dissatisfaction with the two major parties. If enough voters switch their votes to third parties, the major parties take notice. They try to win back the third-party voters—often by adopting the minor parties' views. As a result, most third parties eventually die out.

Third parties have never won a presidential election, yet their ideas and the votes they've taken from the other parties have influenced United States politics.

Many laws that we take for granted today started as campaign issues that were raised by "far-out" third parties. A graduated income tax was called for by the Greenback Party. The direct election of United States senators was demanded by the Populist Party. Women's suffrage was fought for by the suffragists. Social security and unemployment insurance was suggested by the Socialist Party.

No third-party candidate has ever won the Presidency in this century. Theodore Roosevelt came the closest. He ran as a Progressive in 1912. He won eighty-eight electoral votes, beating Republican William Howard Taft—who had eight electoral votes—but losing to Democrat Woodrow Wilson—who had 435 votes. The most recent third-party candidate to win any electoral votes in a presidential election was George Wallace, the 1968 candidate of the American Independent Party. He came in third with forty-six electoral votes and 13 percent of the popular vote.

Before confinement to a wheelchair, George Wallace was the most popular modern third-party candidate.

What Do Political Parties Do?

Political parties have a number of important jobs to do in our system of government.

Nominating Candidates Political parties are the main means by which people's names are placed on election ballots.

Each party *nominates,* or formally suggests, the people who will be the party's candidates on the ballot. Thus, parties help to supply leadership for the government.

Focusing Issues and Suggesting Action The different levels of government deal with many issues. Some are dull issues—such as picking up garbage. Others are exciting issues—such as sending people to the moon. Political parties help to make sense of the many issues. They also choose certain issues as a focus of debate, for example: "Infrequent garbage pickups are a threat to our health" and "The moon race is too costly."

But political parties do more than just raise issues. They also offer voters a course of action, for example: "Increase the number of garbage pickups" and "Cut spending on space exploration."

Informing the Public By debating public issues, political parties help to inform the public, for example: "Our garbage collection occurs only half as often as River City's" and "It would raise taxes by $10 a year per family to double the frequency of garbage collection." Such statements give voters the facts on which to base their voting decisions. Such statements also help to keep voters interested in public issues. When there is high interest, more people take an active part in government.

Governing Once its candidates have been elected, a political party shares the responsibility for the way in which the government is run. If a Democratic President makes a political mistake, the whole Democratic Party will suffer. After all, the party wants its people to be reelected.

Whistle-Blowing If a Democratic President *does* make a mistake, you can be quite sure that the country will hear about it. Republicans will be the first to talk. The party that is out of power often "blows the whistle" on the party in power. This is an important job. It helps to keep any party from putting itself above the law.

The Donkey and the Elephant

Cartoonists often use a donkey to stand for the Democratic Party and an elephant to stand for the Republican Party. Why are these particular animals used? Why not something more noble?

A man named Thomas Nast started it all. He was the most famous political cartoonist of the nineteenth century. He first used a donkey to represent the Democratic Party in the *Harper's Weekly* of January 15, 1870. He showed it kicking a dead lion—Edwin M. Stanton, a controversial Republican who had recently died.

Nast also used the elephant as a symbol of the Republican Party. It first appeared in 1874. Nast intended the symbol to be a criticism of the Republican Party. He thought the party had grown unwieldy and timid.

Today, both the Democrats and the Republicans use these symbols with pride. Observes former United States Representative Wright Patman: "Democrats consider the donkey a symbol of homely, down-to-earth appeal. Republicans look upon the elephant as standing for intelligence and impressive strength."

Adapted from Wright Patman,
Our American Government, Barnes and Noble
Books, New York, 1974, p. 46.

The Organization of Political Parties

Like the federal government, our major political parties have national, state, and local levels. Usually, no one on the national level can give an order to someone on a local level. Each level of a party is basically concerned with the elections at its own level of government.

National Committees Each party elects a national committee every 4 years. This committee includes at least one man and one woman from each state, each territory, and the District of Columbia. The main job of the national committee is to help in the presidential campaign. The committee chooses a city for the party's presidential nominating convention. It also decides rules for the convention and helps to run it. We will talk more about the national conventions shortly.

The presidential candidate picks the head of the national committee. This is the national chairperson. The chairperson directs the party's presidential campaign and raises money for the national party. She or he names an executive committee to

run party affairs in between presidential elections.

State and Local Committees Each state party has its own organization, which is about the same from state to state. At the top of the organization is a state committee, headed by the state chairperson. Below it are committees at each level of government—county, city, and ward. At the bottom is the *precinct*—or polling district—committee, which is often elected directly by voters who are party members.

Members of the precinct committee are sometimes called precinct captains, or district leaders. One of their jobs is to see that the party's voters come out to vote on election day. Another is to help party members to cut through government "red tape." For example, a precinct captain might urge city officials to investigate a fire danger in an apartment building.

In theory, power in each political party is organized from the bottom up. Each level elects the next higher level. Representatives from the precincts elect the ward committees, which elect the party's city committee, and so forth.

In practice, however, things are more complicated. A powerful individual—called

Behind each presidential candidate stands a large organization. At the head of this organization, known as *the national committee,* is the national chairperson. His or her role takes in everything from party figurehead and campaign fundraiser to manager of party affairs between elections.

A political campaign cannot run on promises alone. It takes a lot of money—money that comes from a wide crosssection of individuals and special-interest groups. In this photo, California Congresswoman Yvonne Braithwaite Burke speaks to her supporters at a fund-raising rally for her reelection in 1978.

a party boss—may control a party's city or county organization—or "machine." This boss may be able to "pack" precinct or ward elections with loyal supporters and so keep firm control over the local party organization.

Money and Politics

Where Does the Money Come From? It takes a great deal of money to run a political campaign—money for advertisements, money for travel and office expenses, money for campaign buttons, money for computer letters to voters asking for money or for votes. In 1976, the candidates for President spent $114 million on their campaign. The candidates for Congress that year spent $99 million.

That is where someone such as Muhammad Ali comes in. Ali was a boxer. But he had political opinions, and he was a good "drawing card" for political candidates who were in need of campaign money.

That is why Ali arrived one evening, along with the Speaker of the House of Representatives and other important people in Washington, at a fund-raising party for Yvonne Braithwaite Burke. She was a member of Congress from California. In 1978, she needed money for her reelection campaign, so she held a party. For a 50-dollar contribution, guests dined on roast beef and steak tartare. They also had the chance to shake hands with Muhammad Ali and various well-known politicians. Three hundred people came to the party, and the Burke campaign was off and running.

Until recently, all money for election campaigns came from private contributions. Most campaign money still does. The biggest givers are special-interest groups—businesses, labor unions, farmers, public employees, and so forth. But many individuals also contribute. Wealthy people write 1,000-dollar checks. Other people send in 10-dollar or 20-dollar contributions.

Controlling Corruption Whenever large amounts of money change hands, people worry about corruption. Do contributors "buy" politicians by giving them money? Is democracy well served by a system that depends so heavily on money from special-interest groups?

To decrease the chances of corruption, the federal and state governments have passed laws regulating contributions and campaign spending. For example, the Federal Elections Campaign Acts of 1972 and 1974 apply to *federal* elections. These laws affect both contributors and candidates.

Suppose you want to give money to Candidate A, who is running for Congress. You may give $1,000 to be used in a primary election. You may give another $1,000 to be used in a general election. That is all you may give to Candidate A. However, you may give like amounts to Candidates B, C, and so forth.

You may also contribute to political-action committees. But you may give no more than $25,000 to all candidates running for federal office in any one year.

Political-action committees are set up by business and labor groups, because these groups cannot make direct contributions to a federal candidate. Such committees may give up to $5,000 to any one candidate.

Candidates and political-action committees must keep a record of all contributions, no matter how small. The names, addresses, and occupations of all persons or groups contributing more than $100 are made public. No gift of cash may exceed $100.

Public Financing In 1974, the federal government introduced a new idea in campaign financing: let the public pay part of the bill. The idea is to use tax money to pay for the campaigns of people who are running for President. This system was first tried out in the 1976 presidential election. A number of states—fourteen, as of early 1978—have introduced plans such as this to help candidates who are running for certain state offices. But in 1978, Congress refused to discuss a suggestion for public financing of congressional campaigns.

Here is how the presidential-election plan works. Each federal income-tax form has a special box. By checking that box, a taxpayer can request that 1 dollar of her or his tax money go to pay for presidential campaigns. This neither raises nor lowers the person's total tax due.

The money goes to the Federal Election Commission (FEC), which by law is made up of three Democrats and three Republicans. The FEC gives the money to the different candidates.

In order to receive federal money for a political campaign, a presidential candidate must first raise $100,000 from private contributors. The candidate then becomes qualified for up to $5 million in matching funds. The more money the candidate's own fund raisers can get, the more money the FEC contributes. But in the 1976 election, the most that a candidate who accepted federal money could spend on a primary campaign was $10 million.

Once the major parties have nominated their candidates, all private fund raising must stop. The presidential nominees must sign a pledge to accept *only* what the FEC gives them from that time on. They must also observe a spending limit—about $28 million for each party in 1980.

Federal campaign funds for the general election are paid only to political parties, not to individuals. This means that an independent candidate for President is not qualified for a contribution from federal campaign funds. A third party must receive at least 5 percent of the vote nationally in order to qualify for a partial contribution. It must receive 25 percent of the vote in order to get a full contribution.

Elections

In most parts of the country, elections for all levels of government take place in two steps. The **primary election** and the **general election.** Primary elections are usually held in the spring and general elections in the fall. Sometimes there is an additional step—a nominating convention.

In an age of electronic journalism, national party conventions have risen from the scene of presidential nomination to the status of television spectaculars.

The Primary Election Until the late nineteenth century, most nominations of candidates were made at meetings held by each party's leaders. But reformers claimed that this was not democratic. They said that party bosses were controlling the process.

Primary elections give the voters a direct say in who a party's candidates will be. There are two kinds of primary election. The **closed primary** is limited to registered party members. So if, for example, you are a Democrat, you can only vote in the Democratic primary. This is the most common type of primary. It is sometimes used to choose party leaders as well as nominees for public office.

The **open primary** is open to all voters. Whether or not a person has registered with a party, he or she can decide on the morning of the primary to vote in either the Republican or the Democratic primary. In

two states, Alaska and Washington, a person can even vote in *both* primaries—but only once for each office. For example, if you voted on the Republican ballot for governor, you could not vote on the Democratic ballot for governor. But you *could* vote for a member of Congress on the Democratic ballot.

Sometimes there are five or six—even as many as fifty or sixty—candidates for an office in a primary election. In most states, the winner is the candidate with the most votes. The winner does not have to have a majority—more than 50 percent of the votes. But in some states, a majority is required. If no one gets a majority, then a **run-off primary** is held between the top two candidates.

Nominating Conventions Sometimes a political party chooses its candidates at a **nominating convention.** This is a meeting of delegates chosen by party members. For example, voters in a polling precinct might elect delegates in a closed primary election. These delegates would hold a precinct convention to elect delegates to a county convention. At the county convention, delegates would choose the party's nominees for county offices and for the legislature or Congress. They would also elect delegates to a state party convention. The state convention would choose the party's candidates for high state offices. It might also elect delegates to the party's national convention.

The General Election The nominees of the major political parties automatically go on the general election ballot. But third-party candidates and independents may have trouble getting on the ballot. That is because the major parties have supported election laws that discourage small parties and independents.

To get on the ballot, a minor-party candidate might have to first get voters to sign nominating petitions. The state may require that a minimum of 5 percent of the voters in the last election sign the petition. Second, the party may have to pay a filing fee.

Electing a President

Primaries and conventions both play a part in electing a President. The general election for President is held in November of every fourth year. The primaries begin in February or March. But the actual campaign starts long before that. It begins when the first candidate stands before the television cameras and announces: "I am running for President."

Running in the Primaries Often, several candidates try to get a party's nomination for President. They go from state to state, seeking votes in primary elections or in state conventions. Each state controls its own primaries, and the rules differ from state to state.

In 1980, thirty-six states had presidential primaries. That was a record number. The first primary was in New Hampshire in February. The last was in California in June. In general, these primaries had two purposes. One was to elect party delegates to the national conventions, where the actual nominations of candidates would be made. The other was to give the voters a chance to show which candidates they wanted. In some states, the delegates to the national convention have to vote for the presidential candidate who wins the most votes in the state's primary. In other states, the delegates are free to vote as they please. In states that do not hold primaries, delegates to the national convention are chosen by state party conventions or by state party committees.

Many voters are confused by the present system. Even the candidates can become confused. They must handle a heavy schedule and travel back and forth across the country, campaigning the same week in such widely separated states as California and Ohio. Some people have suggested ways to change this system. One idea is to have a single presidential primary for the whole nation. The winner would automatically become the party's nominee. Another idea is to hold a series of regional primaries—one in New England, then one in the Midwest, and so forth. During the 1970s, these ideas gained a good deal of attention in Congress and among the voters.

In any event, the long primary campaign ends as summer begins. Soon, it is time for the national nominating conventions.

The National Conventions The presidential nominating convention is a United States phenomenon. No other nation has anything quite like it. In the middle of the summer, thousands of politicians—either Republicans or Democrats—take over a major city such as Miami Beach or Kansas City. They talk and listen, make

The *keynote*, or opening, address at a national convention must be presented by a rousing speaker.

deals and compromises. By the end of the week, they nominate candidates for President and Vice President, and then they go home exhausted. A few weeks later, the same scene is repeated in a second city by the other major political party.

Since 1952, all Democratic and Republican conventions have been televised. The conventions are staged as television spectaculars. One of the first events is a **keynote speech.** This is a stirring address by an important member of the national party. Throughout the convention, television reporters go around the convention floor asking delegates how they will vote and trying to obtain information on behind-the-scenes action. Partly because of the demands of television, convention rules ask that speeches be brief and to the point. The presidential candidate's acceptance speech is scheduled for prime-time viewing. Banner-waving demonstrations no longer go on for hours, as they did in earlier times. They usually end after a few minutes.

Nominating conventions do not always go smoothly. There may be bitter battles. These battles usually center on three questions: Who can vote at the convention? What will the party promise the voters? Who will the party nominate?

It is not uncommon for two rival groups of delegates from a single state to show up at a convention. This is what happened to the Democrats in 1964 and 1968. Some of the groups of delegates from the Southern states were all white. Some were of mixed races. The convention had to decide which groups would vote. This sort of decision is usually made by a credentials committee.

The next item of controversy will be the party's promises to voters, which are contained in a **party platform.** The platform is a statement that sets forth the party's principles as well as its promises. Each principle or promise is called a **plank.** A committee of the national convention fits the planks together. It writes and rewrites them to appeal to as many voters as possible. This process begins months before the convention meets. It ends with a vote of all the convention delegates to accept or reject each plank of the platform. Often, a fight over a platform plank amounts to a test of the strength of the rivals who are seeking the presidential nomination.

The choosing of the nominees for President and Vice President is the climax of the convention. The process begins with a roll call. As each state is called, its delegation can propose a candidate for the nomination. Usually, there are flowery speeches. Then, the candidate's supporters parade around the convention floor, waving signs and tooting horns.

Sometimes a state will nominate a **favorite daughter or a favorite son.** This person is an important state party member. Often, such a nomination is not a serious attempt to win. It is a bargaining tactic. The state's delegates vote for their favorite on the first round to see how the vote is going. Then they can change their vote to a more promising candidate, hoping to win special favors.

After the nominations are completed, the voting begins. Once again, there is a roll call. One delegate from each state stands up and announces how many votes the state is casting and for whom. To win, a candidate must get a majority of the votes. Often, no candidate gets a majority on the first round, or first *ballot*. Then the voting begins again. It is repeated as many times as necessary. In 1924, the Democrats took 103 ballots before there was a majority to nominate John W. Davis for President. Since then, rule changes have made it easier to obtain a majority. Most nominations are now made on the first or second ballot.

The nominee for President appears before the cheering delegates to make an acceptance speech. The nominee decides who the candidate for Vice President will be. Then the roll is called, and convention delegates vote to confirm this choice.

The Presidential Campaign The traditional date for the start of the presidential campaign is Labor Day, in early September. The following 2 months are a busy time for many people. The candidates travel back and forth across the country in search of votes. Reporters run after the candidates for news items or travel the country in search of typical voters to interview. Television commentators try to explain the new shades of meaning in a candidate's latest speech.

Other citizens also become involved in the excitement. Grade-school students pass around campaign buttons. Older students go from door to door urging people to vote for one candidate or another. People organize parades, rallies, parties—anything to communicate their message: "Vote for Candidate X."

Candidates always welcome volunteer help. Many a presidential hopeful has gone through the primaries depending almost entirely on students for the hard work of door-to-door vists. In 1976, more than one thousand students helped out in the New Hampshire primary. One candidate, Birch Bayh, flew college students in for weekend

The stirring end to every national convention is the nomination of a presidential candidate. After the candidate's acceptance speech, the traditional round of cheers and waving kicks off the campaign.

work that went far into the night. "When they leave, they're basket cases," said one of Bayh's staff members. "This just chews people up." Yet the volunteers were glad to help out.

As the election date approaches, the candidates turn more and more to television to give their message to the voters. They run mood commercials—much the way oil companies do—to build an attractive image. They buy television time for call-in shows, during which they answer questions from callers. They make televi-

Unpaid campaign workers are usually young, energetic people with a firm commitment to the ideas and goals of a particular political candidate.

sion speeches. Perhaps, as in 1960, 1976, and 1980, the two major-party candidates meet on television in a debate.

Finally, it is election day. The nation goes to the polls. Many people are just beginning to vote in the West when the polls close in the East. Within minutes, the television networks begin to report the results. Computers make projections—guesses about how the vote will go—based on sample results from a few carefully-chosen precincts. The reporters focus on state-by-state returns, since it is the electoral vote in each state that counts. (The electoral-college voting system is explained in Chapter 6.)

Late on election night, the result is usually known. The voters have chosen a President.

REVIEW

1. What are three measures now in effect that were first made popular by third parties?

2. From whom do candidates for Congress receive most of the money that they need for election campaigns?

3. Describe the system of public financing of presidential campaigns.

4. What are two suggestions for changing the present system of nominating presidential candidates?

5. Do you think that the United States would be better served by a three- or four-major-party system than it is by the present two-party system? Why or why not?

How the United States Works

Political Scientists

You have certainly heard or read about public-opinion polls. Politicians can use these polls, or surveys, to find out how popular they are. Other polls tell how the country feels about different issues. The people who write the questions for and explain the results of these polls are political scientists.

Political scientists are interested in the causes and effects of political actions. A great many of them study the relations between governments. Others are interested in the workings of the United States' political system. Still others are interested in the political values and beliefs of the general public. These political scientists use polls and voting results as the raw materials for their studies. Their research tells us a great deal about our society.

Most political scientists only do research or consultation work on a part-time basis. Four-fifths of all political scientists have full-time jobs as teachers in colleges. To get such a job, a person needs to have a Ph.D. However, there are many graduates competing for every teaching position, so the value of a degree in political science is really based on its usefulness in other fields. Lawyers, journalists, diplomats, and—of course—politicians are able to make good use of it.

The salaries of political scientists vary widely. Beginning college teachers may make between $12,000 and $20,000 a year. The federal government hires some political scientists to do research on a full-time basis. The average salary paid by the government is $25,800. However, the starting salary for someone with only a bachelor's degree may be as low as $10,700.

Reading About . . .

Political Speechmaking

Political speechmaking has been a traditional campaign custom for generations now. The reading below explores how one speechmaker, Paul Douglas, sees the difference between speeches of the past and those of today.

   As you read, think of the following:

● What are the major differences between speechmaking of the past and today?

● What special qualities did the great speakers of the past have?

The first and most obvious difference between the political speeches of today and those of a century ago is that today's are much shorter. Television and radio have no doubt limited the tolerance of the listeners. When Lincoln and Douglas crossed words, each was allotted an hour and a half and, if the contemporary accounts can be believed, the crowds listened with close attention throughout the three hours' struggle. It was not unusual then for orators to speak for two or three hours. In my youth I can remember how "Old Bob" LaFollette would frequently exceed even this limit and once, the legend goes, he started as the moon rose and only stopped as the sun appeared over the Wisconsin prairies.

Today no one dares to speak an hour. If you go over thirty-five minutes you are unpopular, while twenty minutes is considered right. This is especially hard for those of us who are Senators and accustomed to develop our arguments in some detail. My wife, who served in Congress before me, sometimes remarks, a little wryly, that a Senator can condense into an hour what an ordinary man can say in five minutes. Certainly a political speech today, if it is to bear fruit, needs a lot of pruning.

A second great difference between the speeches of today and those heard by our grandfathers is that the crowds are now much smaller. In the days of Lincoln and Douglas, there were few, if any, competing attractions. Politics and religion were the chief intellectual interests of the people, and orators and politicians attracted almost as much attention as do the movie stars and television personalities of today. A Lincoln-Douglas debate in 1958 would not draw the 12,000 who a century ago came to Charleston, or the still greater numbers who listened through a chilling October day in Galesburg. Outside the big cities a gathering of 200 is respectable today and an attendance of 500 is really heartwarming.

Another notable change is in the places of public meetings. County rallies were formerly held in the courthouses, while the rural precinct meetings were held in the schools. But since the seats were hard, the rooms poorly lighted and either too hot or too cold and always at the top of long flights of stairs, attendance at these meetings declined rapidly during the Forties. Today a more common gathering is the potluck supper put on by women. In warmer weather, the men often take over with their fish fries. At these meetings, good food and sociability give a great lift to political morale.

Still a third difference between the speeches of today and those of a century or more ago lies in their style. The great pre-Civil War orators in this country, such as Webster, Clay, Calhoun, Benton and Douglas, were schooled in the literary traditions of the eighteenth century. Their oratory was involved and magniloquent. In the mouth of a Winston Churchill or a Bryan this manner of speaking has, even in modern times, thrilled millions. But it is today almost obsolete. The late Senator Neely of West Virginia was probably the last great exemplar.

Today the emphasis is upon exposition rather than oratory. And here again radio and television have had their effect. Clarity, directness and logic are the qualities which the public wants in a speaker. Short words of Anglo-Saxon origin are preferred to Latinisms, and to be effective the sentences and paragraphs should be brief and to the point.

Finally, the tone of modern speaking is far more moderate than it was. We have had some vituperative speakers in Congress during the last two decades but even at their height these men could not match the stinging bitterness and personal abuse that marked the speeches of John Randolph and Charles Sumner. Even the victims of McCarthyism were not heaped with the poisonous epithets that were showered upon William Jennings Bryan when he first ran for the Presidency in 1896.

There is today an increasing desire for fair play and a recognition that no one party or cause is either wholly good or evil. The result is that the bitter demagogue, who seeks to stir up hatred, generally and in the long run destroys himself. Joyce Cary's political character who stated that his aim was not to inform, but to arouse, still has his followers, but I believe they are far fewer than before.

But perhaps the simplicity of style and the greater moderation in tone have reduced the excitement in politics. The rise of competing interests for men's time and attention has certainly shifted the attention of the public away from questions of foreign and domestic policy.

chapter /Review

Fact Review

1. How has Congress tried to protect the voting rights of United States citizens who speak a language other than English?
2. How long have the Democratic and Republican Parties been the two major political parties? Explain how this happened.
3. Describe five jobs that political parties do in our system of government.
4. How are the major political parties organized? Explain.
5. In what ways do the laws limit contributions and spending in federal election campaigns?

6. How might a third-party candidate for President qualify to receive federal money for his or her campaign?
7. What are two ways in which delegates to a national party convention can be chosen?
8. How does a political party prepare its party platform?
9. Do you think that a national primary to choose presidential nominees would be a good idea? Why or why not?
10. Do you approve or disapprove of public financing of election campaigns? Why?
11. What are the two ways that voters can take a direct part in lawmaking?
12. Voters in some states can remove an elected official from office before that official's term ends. By what name is this process known?
13. What is one advantage of our two-party system? What do some people feel is one disadvantage of the two-party system?
14. Name the four major differences between political speechmaking of the past and of today.

Developing Your Vocabulary
1. Explain the difference between the terms in the following pairs:
   a. referendum and initiative
   b. major party and third party
   c. primary election and general election
   d. closed primary and open primary
   e. plurality and majority
2. Match the words in a to e with the phrases in (1) to (5).
   a. candidate
   b. electorate
   c. keynote speech
   d. plank
   e. polls
      (1) all the people who are qualified to vote
      (2) part of a party platform
      (3) kickoff speech at a political convention
      (4) voting places
      (5) someone who is running for a public office

Developing Your Reading Skills

Read the following paragraph and then answer the questions that follow:

The whole group of voters is called the electorate. When much of the electorate fails to vote, government "by the people" suffers. It is only through voting that informed citizens can keep their final political power. If large numbers of people fail to vote, it is difficult for our elected representatives to know the people's wishes.

1. Which one of the following do you think is the main point, or main idea, of the paragraph above?
   a. Elected representatives need to know what people think.
   b. Informed citizens who vote help continue the people's control of the government.
   c. Not all qualified voters cast their ballots on election days.
   d. Voters need to be informed about political issues.
2. Tell why you selected either a, b, c, or d in question 1 above.

Developing Your Writing Skills— Forming and Supporting an Opinion

In this chapter, you have examined the roles of voters and of political parties in our democracy. Now consider the following:

Forming an opinion
1. What might happen if we had only one political party in the United States?
2. Should we always have a system of competing political parties?

Supporting an opinion
3. After thinking about these questions, write your answers in a brief paragraph. Give at least two reasons to support your opinion.

YOUR GOVERNMENT & ITS HISTORY

Davy Crockett— Political Speechmaker

In this chapter, you have learned about the political party process in the United States. One part of that process involves political speeches made by candidates for public office. The following reading is taken from the autobiography of David "Davy" Crockett. It was published in 1834, two years before he died defending the Alamo during the Texas Revolution. In this reading, Crockett tells what he remembers about a campaign speech given before the voters of Tennessee. He was running for the Tennessee House of Representatives. The year was 1821.

As you read Davy Crockett's story, keep in mind that in frontier times, many political speeches were more for entertainment than for providing information on issues. Many people voted for political candidates on the basis of their personalities or past accomplishments rather than on their goals for government.

I went first into Heckman County to see what I could do among the people as a candidate. . . . About this time, there was a great squirrel hunt on Duck River. . . . People were to hunt for two days, then to meet and have a big barbecue, and what might be called a tip-top country frolic. I got a gun ready for the hunt. I killed a great many squirrels, and my party was victorious.

The party had everything to eat and drink that could be furnished in so new a country, and much fun and good humor prevailed. But before the regular frolic commenced, I mean, the dancing, I was called on to make a speech as a candidate. . . .

How to begin I could not tell. I made many apologies and tried to get off, for I knowed I had a man to run against who could speak very well and I knowed, too, that I was not able to keep up with him. He was there, and knowing my ignorance as well as I did myself, he also urged me to make a speech. The truth is, he thought my being a candidate was a mere matter of sport. He did not think for a moment that he was in any danger from an ignorant backwoods bear hunter. But I found I could not get off, and so I determined just to go ahead, and leave it to chance what I should say.

I got up and told the people I reckoned they knowed what I come for, but if not, I could tell them. I had come for their votes, and if they did not watch mighty close, I would get them too. But the worst of all was, that I could not tell them anything about government. I tried to speak about something, and I cared very little what, until I choked up as bad as if my mouth had been jammed and crammed chock-full of dry mush. There the people stood, listening all the while, with their eyes, mouths, and ears open to catch every word I could speak.

At last, I told them I was like a fellow I had heard of not long before. He was beating on the head of an empty barrel near the roadside when a traveler who was passing along asked him what he was doing that for. The fellow replied that there was some cider in that barrel a few days before and he was trying to see if there was any then. But if there was, he could not get at it. I told them that there had been a little bit of speech in me awhile ago, but I believed I could not get it out. They all roared out in a mighty laugh and I told some other anecdotes, equally amusing to them; and believing I had them in a first-rate way, I quit and got down, thanking the people for their attention. But I

took care to remark that I was as dry as a powder horn, and that I thought it was time for us to wet our whistles a little. So I put off to the refreshment stand and was followed by the greater part of the crowd.

I felt certain this was necessary, for I knowed my competitor could open government matters to them as easy as he pleased. He had, however, mighty few left to hear him. I continued with the crowd . . . telling good-humored stories till he was done speaking. I found I was good for the votes at the hunt. When we broke up, I went on to the town of Vernon.

The thought of having to make a speech made my knees feel mighty weak and set my heart to fluttering. . . . But as good luck would have it, these big candidates spoke nearly all day, and when they quit, the people were worn out with fatigue, which afforded me a good apology for not discussing the government. . . . When they were all done, I got up and told some laughable story and quit. . . . But to cut this matter short, I was elected, doubling my competitor and nine votes over.

1. According to Davy Crockett, how did he manage his speechmaking before the people of Heckman County? Before the people of Vernon?

2. Do you really think that Crockett was as ignorant of government as he made himself out to be? Explain your answer.

3. What would you recommend that anyone consider when listening to a political speech? Why?

Developing your basic civic education skills

The Feast

(determining sequence and cause-effect)

In chapters 13 and 14, you learned about voting in elections. As you read the following story, think about what it has to do with whether one votes or not. This is a tale told by a tribe in Cameroon, a country in west-central Africa.

This is the story of a chief who ruled over many villages. He decided to give a great feast for all his people. The chief sent messengers to the villages announcing the event. They asked everyone to bring a bottle of palm wine.

The great day of the festival came. Hundreds of people with their families came to the house of the chief. As each person entered the chief's house, his or her bottle of wine was poured into a large pot.

There was one man who wanted very much to attend the feast, but he had no palm wine to take. His wife said, "Why don't you buy some palm wine from someone who has plenty?"

The man replied, "What? Spend money so that I can attend a feast that is free? No, there must be another way." And after a while, he said to his wife, "Hundreds and hundreds of people will pour their wine into the chief's pot. Could one bottle of water spoil so much wine? Who would know the difference?"

He filled his bottle with water and went with the others to the chief's village. When he arrived, he saw everyone pouring their wine into the big pot. He went forward, poured in his water, and greeted the chief. He sat down, to await the serving of the palm wine.

When all the guests had arrived, the chief ordered the servers to fill everyone's cup. The cups were filled, and each awaited the signal to begin drinking.

Finally, the signal came from the chief, and the guests tipped their cups to their lips. They tasted. They tasted again. Again they tasted. And what they tasted was not palm wine, but water. Each of them had thought, "One bottle of water cannot spoil a great pot of good palm wine." And each of them had filled a bottle at the spring. Thus, the large pot contained nothing but water.

1. List in chronological order the sequence of events in this story. Begin when the chief first decided to give a feast.

2. Which one of the following from the story was a cause?

    a. The guests had only water to drink.

    b. The guests brought only water to the feast.

    c. The chief called for a great feast.

3. Which one of the following was an effect?

a. The guests had only water to drink.

b. The guests brought only water to drink.

c. The chief had many people attend the feast.

4. Which one of the following is the main point of the story?

a. If many people attend a feast, they all must be fed.

b. If none of the people do their share of a task, nothing will be accomplished.

c. Most people like to be a part of a large social event.

5. Do you think there is a relationship between the main point of the story and whether or not people vote? Explain.

Voter Turnout in the United States

Voter interest and participation have not usually been very high in the United States. James J. Kilpatrick, a newspaper columnist, commented in 1977 that "every American schoolchild once was taught the meaning of the right to vote. Voting was the most important of our political rights. It was what distinguished free societies from societies where government had complete control over people's lives. It was the very character of a republican form of government."

Kilpatrick added that in the 1976 presidential election between Gerald Ford and Jimmy Carter "only 54.4 percent of the qualified adults bothered to vote. Put another way, 68.5 million persons who might have voted were no-shows at the polls."

After the 1980 presidential election, in which Ronald Reagan defeated Jimmy Carter, one newspaper article noted:

Americans showed their unhappiness by staying away from the polls in great numbers last November. The election day saw the lowest turnout in more than 30 years, according to a new study of voting patterns.

The Committee for the Study of the American Electorate reported that 86,495,678 people went to the polls in November, 53.9 percent. That is the smallest percentage turnout since 51.1 percent voted in 1948.

By contrast, a record 62.8 percent of qualified Americans cast ballots in 1960.

The 1980 contest also marked the first time since 1948 that a majority of qualified voters did not vote for either major-party presidential candidate.

In 1976, poll-taker Peter D. Hart interviewed 1,486 nonvoters. Although qualified, these persons had neither registered to vote nor planned to. The results of Hart's poll are on page 382. On page 383, are the results of a 1977 Gallup poll of 1,035 teenagers' interest in politics.

Two cartoonists also give their views of the low voter turnout on pages 382–383.

6. What percentage of the qualified voters voted in each of the following presidential elections?

a. 1948 **b.** 1960 **c.** 1976 **d.** 1980

7. In the poll taken by Peter Hart, what were the five most important reasons given for not voting?

8. Why do you think McFeatters drew Cartoon 1? Why do you think Hulme drew Cartoon 2?

WHY PEOPLE DON'T VOTE

Nearly 1500 nonvoters were given a list of possible reasons for choosing not to vote. They were asked to determine their own reasons. Here is a sample of responses.

	Important	Not Important	Not Sure
Candidates say one thing and then do another.	68%	27%	5%
It doesn't make any difference who is elected because things never seem to work right.	55%	38%	7%
All candidates seem very much the same.	50%	43%	7%
It is hard to find reliable and unbiased information on the candidates.	49%	42%	9%
One person's vote really won't make any difference.	46%	49%	5%
I don't feel qualified to vote.	31%	64%	5%
I couldn't get to the polls during voting hours.	18%	76%	6%

SOURCE: *Newsweek,* September 13, 1976

9. In the poll taken by the Gallup organization:

a. What percentage of those polled in your age group were very interested in politics?

b. What percentage in your age group were not at all interested in politics?

c. What percentage in your age group knew the name of their congressperson?

10. Look at Cartoon 1 again. What do you think would be the effect if 95 percent of all qualified voters did what the woman in the cartoon is doing? What problem could that cause?

Cartoon 1

STRICTLY BUSINESS   McFeatters

"I'm not voting this year. I want to see how they make out without me."

POLLING TEENAGE INTEREST IN POLITICS

HOW INTERESTED ARE YOU IN POLITICS?						DO YOU KNOW THE NAME OF YOUR VICE PRESIDENT? YOUR CONGRESSPERSON? YOUR GOVERNOR?			
	Very	Fairly	Not Very	Not at All	Don't Know/ No Answer		Vice President	Congress-person	Governor
Total	7%	32%	32%	29%	★	Total who Knew	52%	27%	63%
Boys	9%	34%	31%	36%	★	Boys	55%	31%	69%
Girls	5%	29%	34%	31%	1%	Girls	50%	23%	57%
Both Sexes						Both Sexes			
13–15 years	4%	30%	30%	36%	★	13-15 years	48%	20%	57%
16–18 years	10%	33%	34%	23%	★	16-18 years	56%	32%	67%

SOURCE: George Gallup Poll   ★ Less than 1 percent.

Cartoon 2

Reprinted by permission of NEA, Inc.

Public Opinion, Pressure Groups, and Propaganda

Chapter **15**

In the last chapter, we discussed voting. When we vote, we make a choice. We express our opinion on a candidate or an issue.

In this chapter, we will look more closely at what opinions are. How are our opinions formed? How can they be measured? We will also take a look at groups that try to shape opinions and study some of the methods they use.

I. Public opinion
   A. What is an opinion?
   B. The importance of public opinion
   C. Measuring public opinion
      1. Choosing a sample
      2. Possible shortcomings of polls
   D. Forming public opinion
      1. Agents of socialization
      2. The mass media
      3. Pressure groups
   E. Expressing opinions
      1. Working for a political party or candidate
      2. Contacting officials
      3. Writing to newspapers
      4. Forming or joining a pressure group

II. Pressure groups
   A. What they are
   B. Types of pressure groups
      1. Business groups
      2. Labor groups
      3. Farm groups
      4. Professional groups
      5. Groups with a cause
   C. How pressure groups work
      1. Grassroots lobbying
      2. Stirring up public opinion
      3. Wooing the regulators
      4. Wining and dining
      5. Campaign help
   D. Laws about lobbying
   E. Are pressure groups a blessing or a curse?

III. Propaganda
    A. What is propaganda?
    B. Techniques of propaganda
       1. Name-calling
       2. Glittering generalities
       3. Transfer
       4. Testimonial
       5. "Plain folks" appeal
       6. Card-stacking
       7. Bandwagon appeal
       8. Stereotype

Words to Know

opinion —— a judgment or a belief; something that someone thinks is true

public opinion —— judgments about any public matter that are shared by a large number of people

pollster —— someone who takes polls

mass media —— public channels of communication—such as newspapers, magazines, television, radio, books, and films

Public Opinion

The word *opinion* comes up in our conversations in many ways. You might hear someone say: "In my opinion, Mayor Benchfinckle is a disaster" or "Public opinion won't stand for higher taxes." What do the terms *opinion* and *public opinion* actually mean?

What Is an Opinion?

An **opinion** is a judgment or a belief. The statement about Mayor Benchfinckle was one person's opinion. Another person might disagree: "On the contrary, Mayor Benchfinckle is the best mayor we have ever had." That, too, is an opinion. It cannot be proved true or false, as a factual statement could: "Mayor Benchfinckle has curly green hair."

There are many different opinions on many different subjects. What is the most exciting movie that you have ever seen? Where can you get the tastiest hamburgers? Who is the most talented singer?

Your opinions about movies and hamburgers and singers are opinions about private matters. They are of interest mainly to you. (Of course, if you play music at ear-shattering volume, your opinions about recording stars may be of great interest to your neighbors.) But your opinions about some other matters are different. Are taxes too high? Do some people face discrimination? These are opinions about *public* matters—matters of concern to all the people of your community or nation. As a citizen, you have a responsibility to think seriously about such public matters and to form your own opinions.

Though public-opinion polls are often accused of shaping opinion as well as tallying it, they are still the preferred form of measuring general consensus.

The Importance of Public Opinion

When we add together the opinions of a large number of individuals about a public matter, we come up with **public opinion.** As you might expect, public opinion is never unanimous—in complete agreement. But we sometimes talk as if it were. We may say: "Public opinion won't stand for higher taxes this year." What we mean is that *many* members of the public share this opinion about taxes. These people may make up a majority or only a plurality. There will always be some people who disagree. Thus, the term "public opinion" often refers to what a majority or a plurality of the public believes about public matters.

Public opinion is the driving force in a democracy. We have invented complex ways of finding out just what the public wants. Elections are one of those ways. We have elections to see what the largest number of people want. We settle our differences by the principle of majority rule.

But elections are not the only way to measure public opinion, which is lucky for politicians. Their election to public office may depend on how well they shape their platforms to fit public opinion.

Measuring Public Opinion

One way of measuring people's opinions is to go around and ask them their opinions. You might do this among your classmates. For example, ask all the students in your class whether or not the school needs a new gymnasium.

If the general public were as small as your class, this might be a good way to measure public opinion. But the public is too large, so a selected few—a sample of the public—are asked their opinions. An effort to measure public opinion by asking a sample of the public for its opinions is called a *public-opinion poll.*

Choosing a Sample Taking an opinion poll is more complex than holding an election. If you hold an election, the people come to the election. If someone comes to vote, that is fine. That person's vote will be counted. If the person does not come, that is just too bad.

In order to take an opinion poll, however, you must seek out the people to ask them questions. It also makes a great deal of difference *whom* you seek out. Suppose that you want to know whether people prefer buses to airplanes. If you were to do the poll in an airport, it would not be surprising if you found a large majority who preferred airplanes. But if you asked the same question in a bus terminal, the results might be just the opposite.

Of course, no one would be careless enough to choose such a poor sample. But errors in sampling are a real problem.

A famous case of sampling error occurred in 1936. A magazine called *Literary Digest* conducted a poll in the midst of our worst economic depression to predict the outcome of that year's presidential election. The magazine sent ballots to several million people. Their names had been taken from telephone books and from automobile registration lists. Two million people replied. A large majority favored the Republican candidate for President, Alfred Landon. But who won the election? The Democratic candidate, Franklin D. Roosevelt, won by a large majority.

What went wrong with the poll? Think about who was most likely to own a car or a telephone in 1936. A worker on a low salary? This was not likely. A business executive or a professional person? This was much more likely. Now consider another piece of information. Traditionally, workers on a low salary are more likely to vote for the Democrats. Business executives and professional people are more likely to vote for the Republicans. The poll had a built-in bias. The people who made up the poll had chosen a poor sample. As a result, the poll was a failure.

Today's public-opinion polls are carefully designed to try to avoid such errors. **Pollsters**—people who take polls—try to choose a sample that is representative of the public they want to measure. If 11 percent of the people in the United States are black, then 11 percent of the sample is black. If 23 percent of the people are Roman Catholic, then 23 percent of those people are polled too.

Such a sample would be representative of the public as a whole. But it might not be representative of the *voting* public. Blacks are somewhat less likely to vote than whites. Roman Catholics are somewhat more likely to vote than Protestants. If a pollster wanted to predict how an election would come out, he or she would change the sample to represent just the voting public.

In taking a poll, questioners try to obtain as random and representative a sample as possible.

But how large a sample is necessary? Pollsters claim that they can get an accurate reading of public opinion with a national sample of 1,500 persons. They say that their results will be correct to within 3 percentage points. Suppose they find that 52 percent of their sample holds a certain opinion. This means that somewhere between 49 and 55 percent of the whole public holds such an opinion. Pollsters base their claims on mathematical probability—the same reasoning that tells you that if you flip a coin 1,500 times, you will come up with heads and tails in almost equal proportions.

Possible Shortcomings of Polls Sampling errors are not the only potential problems with polls. Think about the questions in the following paragraphs:

Are the questions in a poll phrased in a neutral manner? Sometimes the answer one receives to a question depends on the way in which the question is put. For example, "Should taxes be cut?" might receive one answer. "Should taxes be cut if it means a cutback in government services?" might receive another answer.

Do some people give the answers that they think the pollsters want, rather than their own opinions? Imagine that a pollster is asking questions about people's reading habits. The pollster is a young woman. Do you think this would affect the answers she receives to a question such as: "Do you favor equal rights for women?"

Do polls merely *measure* public opinion, or do they also *shape* it? Imagine a hard-fought election race between two candidates, Argus and Barkley. A week before the election, a public-opinion poll is published. It shows that 49 percent of those questioned will vote for Barkley and 43 percent for Argus. The other people are undecided. Will undecided voters decide to support Barkley so as to go with a winner?

Might politicians become slaves to public-opinion polls? Imagine a public official who has devoted a great deal of study to questions about national defense. This official believes that the nation's safety requires an increase in military spending. But a poll shows that the public wants tax cuts—even if military spending must be decreased. Does the official have an obligation to go along with public opinion? Should politicians be leaders or followers?

Forming Public Opinion

What are some elements that shape public opinion? Two of these seem especially important. One is information. For example, you were not born with an opinion about tariffs. In school, you learned that a tariff is a tax on goods that are imported from another country. That gives you some information. But you still may not form an opinion about tariffs if tariffs do not affect your life.

A personal interest in a public matter is the other major element that goes into shaping public opinion. Now suppose you get a job in a shoe factory. One day the management announces that the factory can no longer make shoes cheaply enough to compete with shoes from other countries. Unless Congress raises the tariff on shoes, the company says, the factory will close in 6 months. Suddenly, you have a great interest in tariffs. You are likely to have a very strong opinion—and to let other people know about it.

Now let's take a look at some of the influences that provide us with information and help mold our attitudes about our interests and the public issues that affect them. In other words, let's see what helps shape public opinion.

Agents of Socialization In Chapter 1, you learned about the agents of socialization that help prepare us for our roles in society. Our family, friends, school, and work groups are powerful influences in shaping the way we see public issues.

The agents of socialization give us information about how the world works. School is an obvious example. By studying this book, you gain information about how the United States resolves public issues. Family, friends, and work groups also give us information. Where did you first learn about racial discrimination? About religion? About what it takes to be a leader?

The agents of socialization are even more powerful in shaping our attitudes than in giving us information. Schools try to give students democratic values. Parents pass on their own attitudes about political parties, race relations, economic values, and many other matters. This does not mean that we pattern *all* of our attitudes after those of our teachers, parents, and friends. We do think for ourselves. But opinion polls show that *your* attitudes about public matters are very likely to be similar to the attitudes of your parents and your closest friends.

The Mass Media   Suppose that Congress is considering an important bill of great interest to you. There is to be a vote this afternoon. How will you find out the result? Will you go to Washington, D.C., to be present for the vote? Will you phone a member of Congress? If you are like most people in the United States, you will not. You will learn about it from the mass media.

We need information to help us form intelligent opinions. Most of our information comes from the mass media. A *medium* is a channel of communication—something that passes along information. In the plural, the *media* are all the channels of communication—newspapers, television, radio, books, films, and so forth. They are called the **mass media** because they communicate information to millions of people.

It is from television and radio that most people learn the news. These media bring major events right into our living

Of all forms of media, television communicates ideas and opinions to the largest possible audience.

room. With a television, we can study the expression on the face of a politician making a speech, see the anguish of people uprooted by war, hear the cries of people trapped in burning buildings. Television has made us more aware of what is happening in the world.

But television news has shortcomings. Of necessity, news reports are usually brief. They concentrate on the drama of a story. They rarely can provide a detailed background to the story. Moreover, television may put less emphasis on important but dull stories. Today's balance of payments report may affect whether or not many people in the United States have jobs next year. A tornado in the Midwest may affect only a small area of the country. But which is more likely to make the evening newscast, a report on the balance of payments or an action film of a tornado? Which would *you* rather watch?

Newspapers and magazines supply most of the in-depth news that we read. There are some 1,800 daily newspapers in the country. They range from *The New York Daily News,* which sells some 2 million copies each day, to small home-town papers that sell only a few thousand. Magazines come in many forms. There are general news magazines, such as *Time, Newsweek,* and *U.S. News and World Report.* There are journals of opinion, such as *The Nation* and *The National Observer.* There are also specialized magazines, such as *Farm Journal* and *Motor Trends.* These sources provide a great variety of both news and opinion.

Newspapers today are very different from what they were in the early days of our nation. Then, they were generally small—from two to four pages—, poorly printed, and full of second-hand news taken from other newspapers. As a rule, a newspaper in those days voiced the opinion of one individual. The paper often made no attempt to separate fact from opinion.

Here is an excerpt from a news story that appeared in 1858 in *The New York Tribune.* It is a Northern correspondent's comment on a Southern senator's speech in Congress: "It is . . . sad . . . that a man like Mr. Toombs should feel himself compelled to rise as he did today, in the face of the American Senate and the American people, and lower himself by using his powers of speech and argument to the vain task of proving that to be true which he knows to be false, and that to be sound which he knows to be rotten . . . ."

Today, such outright editorializing is unlikely to appear in the news columns of a newspaper. Opinion is generally kept to the editorial page and to identifiable columns of opinion. But readers must still read newspapers with a cautious eye.

Here are some points to think about:

Do all candidates for a political office receive equal coverage? In 1970, one medium-sized daily newspaper supported a local member of Congress so openly that it failed to mention the name of his opponent in its news columns. The only way that the opposing candidate could get his name in the paper was by buying an advertisement.

Do the news articles that appear in the newspaper reflect the interest of all parts of the community? Some newspapers ignore news that is of interest to minority groups.

Are advertisers given favored treatment? Newspapers depend on advertising for two-thirds of their income. (Television and radio receive virtually *all* of their income from advertising.) Some advertisers do not hesitate to threaten to withdraw their advertisements if a newspaper—or a television program—carries a controversial story. Some newspaper owners give in to this kind of pressure, and some carry the story anyway.

Newspapers and magazines have no legal obligation to be fair. The First Amendment protects a publisher's right to publish

Newspapers, both home-delivered and sold from machines and stands, supply the most in-depth news coverage.

or refuse to publish any story. But television and radio stations operate under different rules. They use public airwaves and, therefore, must be licensed by the Federal Communications Commission (FCC). Under the FCC's fairness doctrine, a radio or television station must give equal time to all candidates for public office and to all sides of controversial issues. If it fails to do so, a station can lose its license.

Controversy over the fairness of the mass media comes up again and again. President Thomas Jefferson, known as a supporter of freedom of the press, observed in 1807: "Nothing can now be believed which is seen in a newspaper." More recently, President Richard Nixon said of coverage of the Watergate Affair: "I have never heard or seen such outrageous, vicious, distorted reporting in 27 years of public life."

Almost every recent President has had a disagreement with the news media. Some people see this as normal. They say that the press and government officials are natural enemies. It is the job of the press to report *all* the news, both good and bad, so that

citizens can reach informed opinions. Government officials, on the other hand, would be happier if the press concentrated on their successes and overlooked their mistakes.

Others say that the press distorts events for its own purposes—to sell newspapers or to make a more exciting television program. They argue that the press has gone too far in being an enemy.

Pressure Groups   A third major influence on public opinion is pressure groups. Their biggest impact on the public is through the mass media. We will devote a later section of this chapter to pressure groups.

Expressing Opinions

As a responsible citizen, you have a duty not only to *have* opinions on public matters, but also to *express* them. Voting is one way of expressing your opinions. What are some other ways?

Working for a Political Party or Candidate   You have to be 18 years old to vote, but not to do campaign work. Visit the office of a political party or its campaign headquarters. Ask what you can do. It may be handing out pamphlets. It may be getting signatures on a petition. Such jobs are not always exciting. But they can lead to contacts with interesting people and give you a better understanding of what politics is all about.

Contacting Officials   When was the last time you wrote to a member of Congress or a mayor? Letters from the public give government officials an idea of what people want. When you write, be brief. Use your own words. Be polite and reasonable, not threatening. Include your full name and address on the letter itself, not just the envelope. Then follow up your letter. If you urge a legislator to vote a certain way, send a letter of thanks later if the legislator follows your wishes.

Public officials are responsive to the needs and desires of their constituents. Letter writing is a good way to make your opinions known to officials.

Contacts do not have to be by letter. You might also telephone a representative. If the representative is out, tell your message to an assistant. Do not forget to give your name and address. Some members of Congress have regular call-in times when people can call without paying the telephone charge. Watch your newspaper to see if this applies to your area. In addition, some state legislatures have toll-free numbers so that you can call to check on a bill's progress. Western Union offers several kinds of messages. These vary from a regular telegram, which is delivered immediately by telephone, to a mailgram, which comes in the next day's mail.

Personal visits to representatives are also a good way to express your opinions. Also, members of Congress often visit their home districts just to get people's opinions. Call the local office of your representative or senator to make an appointment.

Writing to Newspapers Most newspapers publish letters to the editor. You can write and give your opinion. Keep it brief, limit the letter to one topic, and sign your name and address. Give your telephone number as well. Many papers check out letters to make sure that they are actually from the person whose name is signed.

Forming or Joining a Pressure Group One of the most effective ways of expressing your opinions is to form or join a pressure group. Then you will work with other people who share your opinions about an issue. The next section of this chapter discusses pressure groups in detail.

––––––– REVIEW –––––––

1. Why is public opinion important in a democracy?
2. What are two ways of measuring public opinion?
3. Why was the *Literary Digest* poll in 1936 a failure?
4. Some people have opinions about tariffs and others do not. Give two reasons why this is so.
5. Which sources of information do you think people should depend on for the latest news? Why?

Words to Know

pressure group–––– an organized group of people who share common goals and try to influence the policies of government

special-interest group–––– a pressure group

lobbyist–––– a person who acts as an agent for a pressure group in trying to influence the policies of government

Pressure Groups

What They Are

Pressure groups are organized groups of people who share common goals and try to influence the policies of government. They are sometimes called **special-interest groups.**

Pressure groups are different from political parties. Their main interest is not winning elections. What is important to pressure groups is not *who* is in office but *what policies* a government adopts. This does not mean that pressure groups do not care who wins elections. On the contrary, they often work very hard to help elect the people who, they hope, will support their policies.

The right of people to join pressure groups is protected by the First Amendment. A pressure group is a form of peaceable assembly. By joining a pressure group, people can make their right of free speech more effective.

Pressure groups have been around since this nation was formed. Manufacturers formed pressure groups to demand a protective tariff. Abolitionists formed pressure groups to fight for an end to slavery. Farmers formed pressure groups to demand regulation of the railroads. Labor unions formed pressure groups to work for the right to bargain collectively.

Types of Pressure Groups

A pressure group can be found on one side or another of almost every major political issue. Perhaps the greatest number of pressure groups represent economic interests—business, labor, and so forth. But a wide range of organizations act as pressure groups at one time or another. Religious groups sometimes try to influence public policy on issues such as civil rights and foreign policy. A group of hunters may lobby for conservation measures or against stronger gun-control legislation. A garden club may urge a city council to create more

Arguments Favoring Use of Pressure Groups and Lobbyists	Arguments Opposing Use of Pressure Groups and Lobbyists
1. The First Amendment gives all citizens the right to organize into groups and petition the government.	1. Not everyone is represented by a pressure group or by lobbyists. This is unfair to those who are not represented.
2. Lobbyists and pressure groups can offer much-needed information that can affect legislation, executive orders, and regulations. This is especially true if lobbyists from the opposing side of the issue are at work.	2. At times, there are so many lobbyists in state legislatures that they slow down the process of making laws.
3. Our laws safeguard against abuses by lobbyists. A dishonest lobbyist can be tried, convicted, and jailed or fined.	3. Lobbyists usually give one-sided information that only supports their cause.
4. Any group of citizens can form its own pressure group and use lobbyists.	4. Dishonest lobbyists can sometimes bribe lawmakers or other officials to make decisions in their favor.

Of all pressure groups, the greatest number represents business interests. These interests—like the Chamber of Commerce in this photo—attempt to influence congressional opinion in favor of their particular concern through the employment of professional lobbyists.

parks. These organizations may or may not see themselves as pressure groups. But when they try to influence government policies, that is what they are.

Business Groups Businesses may compete against each other in the market-place. But when it comes to government policies, they often find that they have common interests. That is why businesses form pressure groups.

For example, oil companies have formed a group called the American Petroleum Institute (API). It seeks to influence federal policies that affect oil companies. Will the gasoline tax go up? Will solar energy have government support and so compete with oil as a fuel? These are some of the questions that interest the API.

The API represents one industry. Many other industries have similar groups.

Some business groups represent a wide range of business interests. For example, there is the Chamber of Commerce of the United States. It has a great interest in labor laws and work-safety regulations that may affect thousands of small businesses.

Business groups do not always agree with one another. What is good for the rail-

Professionals also hire lobbyists. Here a member of the police and fire fighter's lobby talks to a senator.

roads may not be good for the bus lines. What is good for big manufacturers may not be good for small retail stores. Thus, business groups do not always speak with one voice.

Labor Groups Labor unions are another form of pressure group. The American Federation of Labor (AFL) was founded in 1886 by skilled workers such as carpenters and machinists. The Congress of Industrial Organizations (CIO) was founded in 1938 by industrial workers, such as steel workers. In 1955, the two unions merged to form the AFL-CIO. Today, the AFL-CIO includes some 16 million workers in 120 different unions.

Another 4 or 5 million workers belong to independent unions. These include the International Brotherhood of Teamsters, the United Auto Workers, and the United Mine Workers.

Labor unions seek to promote legislation that makes it easier for them to organize workers, that raises minimum wages, that promotes safety in the work place, and so forth. But unions, like businesses, sometimes disagree.

Farm Groups Farmers discovered long ago that they could best protect their interests by organizing into pressure groups. Three major farm groups today are the American Farm Bureau Federation, the National Farmers Union, and the National Grange. In addition, there are groups that represent particular types of farmers.

Professional Groups Professionals in many fields have organized into pressure groups. One of the best known is the American Medical Association (AMA). The AMA has opposed plans for national health insurance for a long time. Other professional groups include the American Bar Association (lawyers), the National Education Association (teachers), and the American Association of University Professors.

Groups with a Cause All of the groups discussed so far are based on eco-

Lobbies don't always concern business. Here Lillian Carter (left) speaks out on behalf of the elderly.

nomic interests. Farmers can gain or lose money, depending on the policies that the government adopts. This is also true of members of labor unions, oil companies, doctors, and other pressure groups. But some pressure groups are made up of people whose main interest in government policies is ideologic rather than economic.

There are literally hundreds of causes, each with its own pressure group. The National Association for the Advancement of Colored People promotes policies that are aimed at ending racial discrimination. The American Civil Liberties Union seeks guarantees for constitutional rights. The Women's Christian Temperance Union wants to limit the use of alcoholic beverages. Common Cause wants to limit the strength of economic interests in influencing legislation. The list of groups with a cause goes on and on.

How Pressure Groups Work

Pressure groups seek to influence government both directly and indirectly. Direct approaches are aimed at government officials. Indirect approaches are aimed at

Lobbying by single-issue groups, or political action committees, can often influence congressional decisions. Pictured above is John T. Dolan, head of the National Political Action Committee (NPAC).

public opinion, which in turn helps influence government officials.

To get their point of view accepted, pressure groups often use **lobbyists.** These are persons who act as agents for pressure groups. Lobbyists can be found at all levels of government. The greatest concentration of lobbyists is in Washington, D.C. One estimate is that there are 10,000 lobbyists in Washington. Some lobby Congress and some lobby the executive branch.

Lobbyists have many jobs. They may help fight or support bills. They testify before congressional committees. They may even write a bill and ask a member of Congress to introduce it. They also try to make social contacts with influential people.

Here are some examples of how lobbyists work:

Grassroots Lobbying Many pressure groups ask members or sympathizers to write their members of Congress when an important vote is coming up. A few years ago, Congress was considering whether or not to build a new kind of bomber, the B-1. Rockwell International, a large company, would be building many parts of the plane, so Rockwell handed out hundreds of postcards to its employees. It urged them to send Congress a message: "Please build the B-1." One member of Congress, whose district in the Midwest includes a town with a factory that is run by a Rockwell subsidiary, reported receiving 400 postcards in a single day.

Stirring Up Public Opinion Sometimes grassroots lobbying is aimed at the public. In 1974, the residents of Dade County in Miami, Florida, voted in a referendum on a bottle bill—one that would require soft drinks and beer to be sold in returnable containers. Many environmentalists supported the bill, claiming that it would help to stop littering. But the beverage industry overwhelmingly opposed it and spent at least $150,000 on advertisements. The beverage industry argued that the bottle bill would raise prices by requiring people to pay a deposit. Supermarkets put stickers on six-packs, claiming that the bill would add 30 cents to the price. The industry's television commercials told viewers that the bill would not help to save the environment. When the vote took place, a majority agreed with the lobby and rejected the bill.

Arguments aimed at stirring up public opinion are often called "propaganda." We will turn shortly to an examination of the different kinds of propaganda.

Wooing the Regulators The way in which a law is put into practice is often just as important as what the law says. During the energy crisis of the 1970s, the federal government put price controls on gasoline. When the government decided to end price controls, the Department of Energy worked out a method of monitoring, or watching, price changes. Lobbyists for the oil industry kept a close watch on this development. One lobbyist, employed by the American Petroleum Institute, said in a memo to his company that he had "worked closely" with Department officials and "got them to agree to a number of important changes." The memo became public and caused an investigation in Congress. An official study found that one of the changes that the lobbyist claimed to have brought about would add ½ cent to the price of each gallon of gasoline—or an estimated $500 million a year.

Wining and Dining Lobbyists may invite legislators out for a meal. This gives them a chance for informal discussion and informs the legislators of the lobbyists'

Wining and dining legislators in order to influence their votes and interests is an accepted part of lobbying. This is especially true of foreign concerns, which aren't allowed to make monetary contributions to government officials. The introduction of carefully catalogued facts and figures during a meal can often be very persuasive.

wishes. Sometimes these activities become public when lobbyists file the reports that are required by law. In 1977, for example, the Pennsylvania Farmers Association said that it spent $1,000 on a dinner for 100 state legislators. The Pennsylvania Association of Realtors reported spending more than $3,000 on an "informal get-together" for 128 legislators at an elegant hotel.

Campaign Help Elected officials always welcome contributions at campaign time, and lobbyists are willing to give contributions. Business corporations have established some 600 political-action committees, each of which can legally contribute $5,000 to each candidate in a federal election. Labor unions have some 250 such committees. Said Ben Vandergrift, a former special counsel to the Federal Election Commission, "I can't help but think that if you put $5,000 into a congressman's campaign, when you come in and talk to him, his door will be open." Pressure groups that do not have much money but have a large membership can volunteer their members for campaign jobs.

Laws about Lobbying

Federal and state governments have had laws for a long time that require lobbyists to register and file reports on their activities. The purpose of these laws is not to stop lobbying. That would violate the First Amendment. The purpose is to bring lobbying activities into the open.

The main federal law about lobbying is the Regulation of Lobbying Act of 1946. It requires lobbyists to register with Congress. But is has a big loophole, or weakness: it applies only to organizations whose "principal purpose" is to influence legislation. Thus, it does not apply to many pressure groups that have purposes besides lobbying, such as running a business. Congress has recently introduced new legislation that would strengthen the laws on lobbying.

Are Pressure Groups a Blessing or a Curse?

Pressure groups are usually controversial. If you agree with them, you like them. If you disagree with them, you may see them as a threat.

Many people believe that pressure groups and lobbyists are basic in a democratic government. This view says that government officials must balance the interests of all parts of society. How can they balance those interests unless someone tells them what the interests are?

But other people point out that pressure groups represent only *organized* interests. What about everyone else? People who live near a factory that is polluting the air or the water are rarely organized into a pressure group. Will *their* interests be taken into account when legislation to control pollution is considered? People who do not have jobs are usually not members of labor unions. Will *their* interests be considered when Congress is discussing labor laws?

A new type of pressure group has appeared in recent years. It claims to represent the public as a whole. For example, Ralph Nader's group claims to represent consumers. Another group, Common Cause, calls itself a "public-interest lobby." It finances its activities by asking for small contributions from thousands of individuals. Like other pressure groups, these organizations take sides on public issues. Thus, they are also controversial. Some people do not agree with their idea of what the public interest is.

=== REVIEW ===

1. How does the First Amendment apply to the activities of pressure groups?
2. Should a pressure group be allowed to give money to political campaigns?
3. Give an example of a pressure group that represents the business interests of one industry or trade.

4. Give an example of a pressure group that represents workers in many different jobs.

5. Do you think that a pressure group should be allowed to contribute money to political campaigns? Why or why not?

Words to Know

propaganda —— the art of shaping other people's opinions for one's own purposes

stereotype —— an oversimplified picture of a group of people or of an idea

Propaganda

What Is Propaganda?

Have you ever heard someone say "I'd know propaganda if I saw it"? Perhaps you feel the same way. Read the following statements. Which statements look like propaganda to you?

"We are morally superior to any other race."

"People in Great Britain are capitalist, warmongering pigs."

"Senator Brigg is a veteran of World War II."

"Volkswagon Diesel gets 52 miles to the gallon on the highway."

"The United States is the world's leading democracy."

"Johnny's folks let him stay out till midnight."

The fact is that *all* of the statements above could be propaganda. It depends on the purpose for which they are used. **Propaganda** is the art of shaping other people's opinions for one's own purposes. If a statement is made for this reason, then it is propaganda. Propaganda may be true or false, reasonable or unreasonable, obvious or hidden.

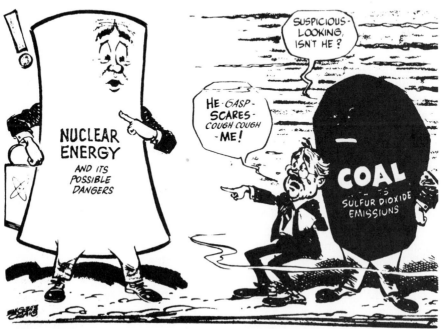

EUGENE CRAIG
Courtesy Columbus (O.) Dispatch

Propaganda is used almost everywhere. The United States government uses it as often as any other government. Our politicians use it, our advertisers use it, and *you* use it. For example, when you try to get your parents to let you stay out late, you are using propaganda.

Propaganda can be used for good purposes or bad purposes. It can be used through proper techniques or shockingly improper techniques. It all depends.

Techniques of Propaganda

Certain techniques are commonly used by propagandists. It helps to know these techniques so that you can recognize propaganda for what it is.

Name-Calling   If you call a group or an idea a bad name, people may reject it. Examples of such names are: corrupt business interests, power-hungry liberals, and evil oil companies.

Glittering Generalities   If you associate a person or an idea with something good, people may accept it without examining the evidence. Some examples of glittering generalities would be:

"I believe in the sanctity of the family."

"We must abolish exploitation."

"Like millions of red-blooded Americans, Representative Krutch answered his country's call in the war."

"We must fight a war to end wars."

Transfer   Transfer is a method that associates a product, a person, or an idea with something that has high prestige. Some of this prestige is shifted, or transferred. For example, a brand of golf clubs might be displayed in a plush, country-club setting. A candidate for Congress might arrange to be photographed with the President or with a group of religious leaders. A pressure group might quote Thomas Jefferson to lend prestige to its policy.

Testimonial   You are using the testimonial method when a well-known person

TYPES OF PROPAGANDA

Name-calling

Glittering Generalities

TRANSFER

Testimonial

Plain-folks Appeal

Card-stacking

Bandwagon Appeal

agrees with you on an issue, and you say so. Examples are: "Jane Fonda will vote for . . . ", or "Ronald Reagan believes, as I do, that . . . ", or "Our astronauts always drink Gloopo."

"Plain Folks" Appeal   This kind of appeal lets people know that you are just like them—just plain folks. Examples of "plain folks" appeal are: "I had to go to work in a factory when I was only 16" and "I wouldn't know one fancy food from another." Being photographed fishing or hunting and buying a puppy and tickling its ears for the television cameras are other examples.

Card-Stacking   Card-stacking uses only those arguments that support one side of an issue or tear down the other side of the issue. For example, if you wanted a cut in school taxes, you would point out how much money the average family would save, but you would not mention that the schools might deteriorate. If you were fighting a pressure group, you would point out that many of its supporters are "fat cats," but you would not mention that it also has thousands of supporters who are ordinary working people.

Bandwagon Appeal The bandwagon appeal tries to convince people that *everybody* is on the same side of the issue—or, in political jargon, has climbed on the bandwagon. Examples are: "This year, the most popular car is the new . . .," or "We've got the labor movement, big business, and the feminists behind us on this one, Senator," or "The troops were met by cheering crowds of peasants."

Stereotype A **stereotype** is an over-simplified picture of a group of people or an idea. A stereotype may or may not be an accurate description, for example:

"Kids today have no respect."

"Those people are all racists."

"Socialism leads to communism."

"The people of the United States are a generous people."

All of the above methods can be used honorably or dishonorably. They can be used with truths or falsehoods. They have only one thing in common: all of them are methods of persuasion. Therefore, they are all propaganda.

When you encounter propaganda, ask yourself: Who is selling what? Why? What technique are they using? What should I know that they are not telling me? If you are cautious, you can find your way through the various propaganda claims. But you must keep your eyes and ears—and your mind—open.

═══════════ REVIEW ═══════════

1. Give an example of propaganda that might be used by a government.
2. Give an example of propaganda that might be used by a politician.
3. Give an example of propaganda that might be used by an advertiser.
4. Give an example of propaganda that might be used by a pressure group.
5. What do you think would be an improper use of propaganda?

How the United States Works

Public Relations

You may have heard about a candidate for President who changed his style of dress in order to get more votes. There have also been a number of local politicians who have spent millions of dollars advertising one accomplishment. These politicians hired public-relations people to help shape the public's ideas about them. Of course, politicians are not the only people who worry about what the public thinks. Private companies and government agencies also care about public opinion. A bad image can be very damaging, so they hire public-relations people to make the public aware of what the company has done or is doing.

Public-relations people do everything from planning and researching advertising campaigns to writing speeches and managing fund-raising events. They also use news reports to shape the client's image. Then they contact newspapers, magazines, and radio stations that might be interested in using the material.

Almost all public-relations people have a college degree. However, the experience of working on a school newspaper is probably more valuable than any one course. That is because work experience is the only thing that interests employers. People get into the field of public relations by taking advantage of an opportunity that opens up. However, a good deal of experience is needed in order to do that, because there is so much competition for every job.

How does a person get experience? There are many ways. One way is by working for a public-relations company in a low-level job. Another way is by working in a related field such as advertising. A third way is by working on political campaigns.

Depending on a person's experience and ability, the pay in public-relations jobs is fairly good. Beginners can make between $9,000 and $15,000 a year. Experienced people at large companies may make between $30,000 and $50,000. Those with their own successful consulting firms can make $100,000 or more.

Reading About . . .

How a Lobbyist Works

This chapter has explored the different types of pressure groups and their methods. Now it's time to see how lobbyists do their job.

As you read, ask yourself the following questions:

- Do you think that any of the actions described in this reading show unfair pressure?
- What qualities are needed to make a good lobbyist?

"A good part of my work," said a lobbyist for one of the United States' largest corporations, "consists of constantly broadening my contacts—getting to know more people and establishing friendly relations with them. It's like throwing a stone into a pond. One contact leads to another. Suppose I need some information about a particular matter. I think of a guy I know on the Hill who may have it, so I call him. He doesn't have it, but he refers me to another man, whom I don't know. I call the second fellow, introduce myself, and ask him the question. But I don't drop it there. I invite him to lunch and get to know him. Making new contacts is an endless process."

This lobbyist specializes in three areas of government for his corporation. He estimates that he spends 60 to 75 percent of his time dealing with the members and staffs of the congressional committees that handle legislation in these three areas. When other chores come along, he is adaptable.

"I catch whatever comes along," he said. "There's a good deal of variety. The other day, for instance, my boss called from New York and said he was sending two men down to Washington to look into the automatic vending business. The company was thinking of going into automatic vending machines.

"So I spent a day at the Commerce Department putting together information on automatic vending machines and over at the Agriculture Department getting a lot of stuff on institutional feeding. You know, feeding large numbers of people with a batch of these machines, some for sandwiches, some for coffee, and so on.

"Another part of my job is to iron out disputes between company plant managers who come to Washington with congressional problems. Two of them will come in. They're both planning a particular section of a bill, but they have different ideas of how to go about it, what approach to take. I sit down with them and try to persuade them to agree on one tack. I tell them I don't care what they decide, as long as they go up there with one approach. I don't want it to appear that the company can't make up its mind.

"Then you have this kind of thing. An assistant to a congressman called me the other day and said the congressman wanted to poll his constituents on how they felt about various issues. He said they were short of money for the poll and needed another $250. My firm has plants or facilities in more than 100 communities, and one of them is in this congressman's district. I called the manager of that plant and told him about it. About a week later, I ran into

the assistant, and he said: 'I don't know who you called, but it certainly did the trick. We got the $250 in a few days.' "

Most examples of this type involve direct-contact lobbying—personal contact between the lobbyist and the legislator or his aides. This is the lobbyist as persuader.

A Lesson in Winning the Public's Support

How does a pressure group go about winning the public over to its side? To find out, let's look at the campaign to cut California property taxes. Here are some of the steps that were taken by supporters of the campaign for Proposition 13.

1. *Organize:* Taxpayers who wanted to cut high taxes first formed pressure groups. One was headed by Howard Jarvis. Another was headed by Paul Gann. These groups helped to organize volunteers to gather signatures on an initiative petition.

2. *Raise Money:* Television commercials and other types of publicity cost money. Jarvis hired a company that specializes in raising money for causes. It collected $1.2 million to pay for the campaign.

3. *Get Well-Known Supporters:* One of the leading economists in the country is Milton Friedman, a winner of the Nobel Prize. He shares the conservative philosophy of those who organized the California initiative. As someone who lives in California, Friedman was anxious to give his support to the plan. He appeared on television commercials to urge a yes vote. Other big-name backers included Ronald Reagan.

4. *Get Out the Message:* Supporters of the initiative were not shy about speaking out. Some people put signs on their front lawns saying exactly how much their property taxes had increased.

The supporters of the initiative must have done *something* right. Sixty-five percent of the voters went along with them in the 1978 vote.

chapter
Review

Fact Review

1. In choosing a sample for a public-opinion poll, is it more important that the sample be large or that it be representative? Explain.
2. What are four possible problems with public-opinion polls?
3. How do the agents of socialization help to mold public opinion?
4. Your school is considering adding a course in woodworking as an elective. Which of the following do you think are effective ways of measuring the opinions of your classmates on the subject?
   a. asking every member of the student body how she or he feels about adding the woodworking class
   b. putting an advertisement in the school paper requesting that students send in their opinion on having a woodworking class added as an elective
   c. asking only the male members of the student body whether they would like a woodworking class since they would be more likely to sign up for it than the females in school would
   d. asking an equal number of male and female members of the student body whether they would like to see a woodworking class offered as an elective
5. Give two examples of pressure groups that are based on economic interests and two examples of pressure groups that are based on ideological interests.
6. What are five ways in which lobbyists do their work?
7. How have state and federal governments tried to control lobbying?
8. In the following examples of propaganda, tell which technique is being used:
   a. "Mayor Blatt is a defender of liberty."
   b. "The enemy's bloodthirsty soldiers overtook the villagers."
   c. "All the other kids have a class ring."
   d. "Five prominent doctors endorse our product."
9. Do you think that the press and government officials should be enemies or partners? Explain your answer.
10. Do you think that it is possible for a pressure group to represent the public interest, or do you think that pressure groups usually represent special interests? Explain.

Developing Your Vocabulary

1. What is the difference between a pressure group and a political party?
2. Which of the following statements are statements of opinion and which are statements of fact?
   a. Senator Garflower has let down the voters.
   b. Senator Garflower voted for the tax-cut bill.
   c. Senator Garflower has been in office for 8 years.
   d. Senator Garflower has been in office too long.
3. Which of the following are examples of stereotypes?
   a. Nureyev is a good dancer.
   b. Blacks are good athletes.
   c. Girls are sissies.
   d. The girls in fourth-period gym class are terrible basketball players.
   e. Boys are brave.
4. Match the words in *a* to *e* with the phrases in (*1*) to (*5*).
   a. opinion
   b. public opinion
   c. pollster

   (1) a pressure group
   (2) a person who takes polls
   (3) a judgment or a belief; something that someone thinks is true

d. special-interest groups

(4) judgments about any public matter that are shared by a large number of people

e. lobbyist

(5) a person who acts as an agent for a pressure group in trying to influence the policies of government

a. Television and radio broadcasts are not reliable sources of news.
b. Books and films are part of the mass media.
c. Newspapers and magazines give less detailed coverage of the news than television and radio.
d. We receive much of our information from the mass media.

2. Tell why you selected either *a, b, c,* or *d* in question 1 above.

Developing Your Reading Skills

Read the following paragraph and then answer the questions that follow:

Most of us get the news from television and radio broadcasts, but many other sources help to inform us. Nothing is better than newspapers and magazines for in-depth coverage of news events. They can provide more background information and help fill in the details of events that we learn about first from television or radio. Books and films also provide us with information and help to shape our opinions about public matters. In short, the mass media are vital sources of information for today's citizen.

1. Which one of the following do you think is the main point, or main idea, of the paragraph above?

Developing Your Writing Skills— Forming and Supporting an Opinion

In this chapter, you have studied public opinion and some ways in which people and groups try to influence it. Now consider the following sets of questions.

Forming an opinion

1. Why might it be important for unorganized interests—that is, people who are not represented by existing pressure groups—to organize and try to influence government policies?

Supporting an opinion

2. After thinking it over, write a brief paragraph that answers the question above. Give reasons to support your opinion.

YOUR GOVERNMENT & ITS HISTORY

Predicting Elections by Polls

In this chapter, you have learned about the value of public-opinion polls. You have read how public opinion can be shaped and how it can be measured. Now, you will read about the history of the public-opinion poll.

In 1824, the *Harrisburg Pennsylvanian* asked voters in Wilmington, Delaware, whom they thought the next Presi-

dent would be. The survey was the first recorded public-opinion poll. It was not a good beginning. Using its poll as an indicator of public support, the newspaper announced that Andrew Jackson would win the presidential election. Jackson did receive more popular votes than any of his three opponents. He did not win a majority of the votes, though. The election was decided by the House of Representatives, which elected John Quincy Adams as America's sixth President.

It was not until 1935 that public-opinion polls acquired a scientific base. In that year, an American named George H. Gallup opened the American Institute of Public Opinion in Princeton, New Jersey. A year later, pollster Archibald M. Crossley began using scientific polling methods. By 1940, the first center for the development of polling methods was opened by Hadley Cantril at Princeton University.

At the time, two methods of conducting public-opinion polls were used. In the first method, called probability sampling, pollsters would divide the area to be sampled into small sections. They would then select areas and neighborhoods at random and conduct interviews equally at random within the chosen neighborhoods. In the second method, quota sampling, individuals were selected as representatives of a specific segment of society. They might be rich, poor, white, black, male, or female, and so on.

The results of two presidential polls during the mid-1900s proved the quota-sampling method to be embarrassingly wrong. In 1936, the magazine *Literary Digest* predicted that Governor Alfred M. Landon of Kansas would defeat President Franklin Delano Roosevelt. This prediction was based on the results of a questionnaire mailed out to 10 million individuals. (Two million of the questionnaires were returned.) Using probability sampling, pollsters Gallup, Crossley, and Elmo Roper correctly predicted Roosevelt's return to office. Roosevelt was reelected by a landslide vote. The *Literary Digest* prediction was wrong because the questionnaires were mailed out to people picked from telephone books and from lists of automobile owners. By this method, too many rich Americans were sent questionnaires. The poll takers did not get a balanced view.

In 1948, polls based on quota sampling once again gave poor results. This time, the polls predicted that Governor Thomas E. Dewey of New York would defeat President Harry S. Truman. Truman, the Democratic candidate, had failed to win the strong support of his own party. Some Democrats split off to form a new Progressive party. They nominated Henry A. Wallace for President. Many Southern Democrats left the party when its platform included a firm pro-civil-rights stand. They formed the Dixiecrat Party. The Republicans nominated Senator Robert A. Taft of Ohio to oppose Truman. Against these odds, Truman won reelection and succeeded in one of the greatest upsets in political history.

Few polls predicted Truman's victory. The *Chicago Daily Tribune* was so sure that the polls and the early election returns were correct that it went to press the morning after the election with the headline "Dewey Defeats Truman." A correction was printed later that day.

As for the polls, they failed for two reasons. First, the last polls were taken too far in advance of the election. By the election, many voters had changed their minds. Second, the quota samples did not truly represent the majority of the voting public. After the 1948 election, probability sampling became the accepted method of polling in presidential elections.

1. Who conducted the first recorded public-opinion poll? How accurate were the results?

2. Who is George H. Gallup?

3. What are the two methods of conducting public-opinion polls? Which method is more accurate? Why?

4. What roles did the *Literary Digest* and the *Chicago Daily Tribune* play in the elections of 1936 and 1948, respectively?

5. Do you think public-opinion polls have a place in American politics? Explain your answer.

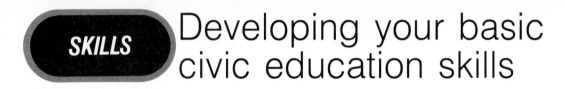

SKILLS Developing your basic civic education skills

A Closer Look at Political-Poll Results
(conflicting viewpoints)

In this chapter, you began to consider the value of poll results. The subject has been one of continuing debate, as shown in the following arguments.

Do the Results of Political Polls Influence the Average Citizen?

Senator Robert J. Dole, Republican from Kansas:

Polls clearly affect the average citizen's judgment. In campaigns, they influence views about who is ahead and who is gaining. They do not determine who will be elected, only who should be taken seriously. But polls influence the person on the street in another way. They give people a sense of being involved even before a single vote is cast. They suggest where or whether people should make a campaign contribution. They suggest whether their votes are necessary.

Thomas E. Mann, codirector, Congress Project, American Enterprise Institute:

Certainly not, if we mean that the average citizen will jump on the leading candidate's bandwagon or get behind the underdog. Many studies show the lack of a need to vote for the favorite or support a likely loser. Some elec-

tions get closer after the release of polls. For others, the difference in candidate support increases. Polls influence citizens by encouraging or discouraging volunteers, by leading to media attention or lack of attention, and by changing campaign strategies.

1. On the subject of the influence of political poll results, what arguments were made by Robert Dole? Can you add any other arguments in support of Dole's position?

2. What arguments were made by Thomas Mann? Can you add any other arguments in support of Mann's position?

3. Suppose you have an opinion about an issue or a political candidate. Some poll results show that your opinion is in the minority. Would that cause you to change your opinion? Should it cause you to change your opinion?

Your Future Role in Politics
(thinking critically)

In chapters 14 and 15, you learned about the parts of the election process. Have you considered what role you will play in that process? Think about that as you read the following two accounts. The first account, by Lamar Smith, deals with how he thinks people should view politics. The second account, by Marcy Meffert, includes advice offered by a county Women's political caucus to possible candidates.

Lamar Smith:

Public opinion polls regularly announce that "the least desirable career" is politics. John Kennedy observed: "Mothers may still want their favorite sons to grow up to be President, but . . . they do not want them to become politicians in the process."

Politics, it seems, is the unpleasant job of a few based on power, control of others, and self-interest.

Yet politics enters our lives, and so involves us all. The groceries we buy, the house we sell, and the taxes we pay are all under the control of government regulations and laws. Government also involves us because it provides services. If citizens want better schools or a repaved street, they must talk to their school board or city council.

For politicians, it is often a question of what should be done next. Public officials have to decide how to divide the resources at hand. Usually *resources* means "taxpayers' dollars." Individuals underestimate the effect they can have on politicians and their judgments.

One concerned mother, walking into a city council meeting, can have an effect on whether she and her neighbors get a new traffic light.

Local politicians rarely get much feedback from their voting public. And when they do, they usually listen—and respond. If

they do not put up that new street light, they are going to continue to hear about it.

People also can have an impact on state and national politics. Sometimes, though, it requires a lot of organization and large numbers of people.

What is important is that, from the local decision to pave a street to the national decision to make war, people can have an influence if they get involved in the political system.

Speaking to the founders of democracy in the ancient city-state of Athens [now a city in Greece], Pericles said: "We do not say that a man who takes no interest in politics minds his own business. We say he has no business here at all."

If citizens will not shape politics and point its direction, who will? To leave politics to certain politicians is to give up our right to expect better government. Active and interested citizens will prevent government from becoming a shelter for those people who use others for their own gain. It is well for Americans to expect more from their public officials. But in a democracy, they must also give more of themselves.

President Theodore Roosevelt described the reactions of family and friends to his attending political meetings. He said: "They laughed at me, and told me that politics was 'low.' . . . They assured me that the men I met would be rough and brutal and unpleasant to deal with." Roosevelt responded, "If they proved too hard-bit for me, I supposed I would have to quit, but I certainly would not quit until I had made the effort."

Politics is worth the effort. Political activity—voting, giving time or money, going to public hearings, making your views known—is important. How else is a politician to find out what people want?

The best politics spring from leaders who have worthy goals and the ability to achieve them. Guided by the goal of justice and the rights of the individual, politicians can transform politics from mere power-holding to the most inspiring type of public service.

Politicians speak of confidence in themselves when their need to achieve a goal is greater than the fear of making mistakes.

"My own judgment," Theodore Roosevelt confessed, "is that it is dangerous to begin to do anything, but it is fatal not to begin it."

Real leaders must take action. They must know where they are headed and how they will get there.

When the goals and the ability of a politician to achieve them blend, and are driven by right reasons, we get leaders who involve us in a group effort to achieve our ideals.

When we insist on these kinds of leaders, and are willing to help them, we have politics with honor.

4. In the account by Lamar Smith, which six of the following points did he stress?

a. For many people, politics is not a good career.
b. Many people help to elect a President of the United States.
c. Politics has a great influence on how people live.
d. Politicians must decide which jobs they must attend to first.
e. Pericles lived in Athens, Greece.
f. Politicians do not often hear from many of their voting public.
g. All citizens should take an active interest in politics.
h. By being involved in the political process, citizens can help build the confidence and goals of their leaders.

5. Review the six points you selected in answering question 5. Do you disagree with any of those points? Explain.

6. What do you think might happen if more than 95 percent of citizens failed to have anything to do with politics?

Marcy Meffert:

Are you one of those folks who has often said, "Now if *I* were on that city council or that school board . . ."

Are you one of those voters who would like to step into the booth on election day and find your name on the ballot?

To be a good candidate, you must have a goal and a desire to win. You must also have strength to see you through the criticism and tension. You need to have confidence in your ability to be a good officeholder.

Successful campaigners can adjust to changing situations. Good candidates realize that opponents today can be friends tomorrow.

To be a good candidate, you must be willing to listen to others. You must not be so rigid in your ideas and opinions that you are unable to take advice.

If you are married, you need the enthusiastic support of your family. According to one booklet about running for office, many candidates have guilt feelings about time spent away from home. "A guilty candidate is a loser," the booklet says.

What about your background? Consider your education, experience, financial resources, acceptability to the voters, organizational memberships and previous political experience. Be realistic, the booklet advises, about any drawbacks you have or any enemies you may have made.

"A good cross-section of personal friends is one of the most positive features of a good candidate," the booklet advises. A candidate needs "real friends" to make an honest judgment of whether or not to run. Friends who fear the candidate's disapproval and are not honest in judging the candidate's qualities are no help. A person who has worked with many economic, social, and racial groups is likely to have a wide base of support.

Close involvement with professional groups . . . may be a financial advantage. They also offer support. Involvement with service groups may help a candidate get volunteer help in the campaign.

A candidate must carefully judge his or her opponents. The candidate must judge whether the expected support will be split by an opponent who shares his or her philosophy.

Candidates need to make a campaign plan, get organized, and raise funds. If you will be a candidate, are you ready to meet the voters at coffees and receptions? Are you willing to walk door-to-door to meet people? Do you know how to get publicity, paid and free? Can you gather the support of your family, trusted friends, and advisors with experience to help you carry out your plan?

Do you really want to run for office?

7. Which six of the following points were stressed in the account by Marcy Meffert?

    a. A good candidate needs a goal.

    b. Good candidates must want to win at all costs.

    c. Good candidates must want to win yet be able to change.

    d. Good candidates must realize that today's opponents may be tomorrow's friends.

    e. Married candidates need the support of their families.

    f. Good candidates should not be bothered with having a good cross-section of friends.

    g. Good candidates should consider any drawbacks they may have.

    h. Good candidates need involvement with professional groups.

8. Review the six points you selected in question 7. Do you disagree with any of those points? Explain.

9. Imagine the following: In an upcoming election, so few people run for political office that all of those who do become candidates run without opposition in their races. What might result from such an event?

UNIT 7 REVIEW

Fact Review

1. In what way can voters sometimes remove an elected official from office before the official's term ends?
2. Why do voting rules differ from state to state? What voting rules do not differ?
3. What are four ways—other than voting—of expressing your opinions on public issues?
4. For each of the following issues, name two pressure groups that might lobby on the issue:
   a. a bill to make it easier to organize labor unions
   b. a bill to limit contributions to political campaigns by pressure groups
   c. a regulation that would set strict safety standards for coal mines
   d. a bill that would make teachers' strikes illegal
5. What could be one worthwhile result of the use of propaganda? What could be one harmful result?

Developing Your Vocabulary

Use complete sentences to tell how each of the following terms relates to the ways in which voters influence public affairs:

a. democracy   c. pressure groups
b. voting   d. initiative

Developing Your Reading Skills

Read the following passage and then answer the questions that follow:

Voting is the process by which people in our society can formally make decisions on public issues. But it is really only one of the many ways in which people help govern themselves.

There are two major political parties competing for public office in the United States. They are the Democratic and Republican parties. In addition, minor parties often enter into the competition, bringing up issues that the major parties have ignored. We call these minor parties third parties.

The major political parties are organized on a decentralized basis—that is, the national party organizations have little direct control over state and local party organizations. The national party chooses the party's nominees for President and Vice President. This is done at a convention attended by delegates from all over the country. Many of these delegates are elected directly by voters in primary elections. Others are chosen by state party conventions.

Political candidates and public officials pay close attention to public opinion. We have developed complex ways of measuring public opinion. Elections are one way. Public-opinion polls are another.

Expressing opinions on public issues is an important responsibility of each citizen. One way to express your opinions is to join a pressure group. A pressure group is an organized body of people who seek to influence the policies of government. Some pressure groups are organized around common economic interests. Others are organized around a common idea or cause.

Pressure groups often use propaganda—that is, they seek to shape public opinion for their own purposes. In itself, propaganda is neither good nor bad. It can be used for good purposes or bad purposes. You yourself have used propaganda whenever you have tried to persuade someone to do something.

1. Tell which of the questions below can be answered from the reading:
   a. What are the two major political parties in the United States?
   b. What are two ways of measuring public opinion?
   c. What was wrong with the *Literary Digest* poll in 1936?
   d. What are two main types of pressure groups?
2. Now give the answers to the questions above that can be found in the reading.

Any time you read a newspaper, you find stories about people and the law: "Suspect Arrested in Smuggling Ring," "Trial Opens in City Hall Bribery," "Woman Wins $1 Million in Accident Case," "Juveniles Rounded Up in Drug Crackdown," "Divorce Rate Soars."

When we think of the law, many of us think immediately of crime. Indeed, crime is a major reason for having laws. Also, in recent years, crime has been increasing.

But the law deals with many matters other than crime. In particular, it helps to find answers to arguments involving the rights and responsibilities of individuals.

The next two chapters will introduce some of the issues of the two main types of law—criminal and civil.

unit
8

You and the Law

Chapter 16 Criminal Law

The sound of shattering glass pierces the night air, followed by a scream. You stumble sleepily to the window and see two shadows racing toward a dark corner. By the time you reach the door, they have vanished. "Was I dreaming?" you wonder. You hope so. But now you hear the sound of sirens, and you know it was no dream. There has been a crime. But what crime? What will happen next?

You have seen plenty of crimes on television. But this is real. Do you know what to expect? Just what *is* a crime? How is crime dealt with? What happens to those who commit crimes? What would happen to *you* if you were the victim of a crime—or if you were accused of a crime?

Words to Know

rob —— to take something from a person by force, against the person's will

crime —— any action that violates a law and for which the law provides punishment

criminal-justice system —— the part of society that deals with crimes and their effects; includes law-enforcement agencies, criminal courts, and corrections agencies

corrections agency —— an agency, such as a prison, that deals with persons who have been convicted of crimes

felony —— a serious crime, such as murder or robbery

misdemeanor —— a minor crime, for which the penalty is 1 year or less in prison

infraction —— a minor law violation, punishable by a fine; sometimes not even considered to be a crime

victimless crime —— a crime, such as drunkenness or gambling, that affects mainly the lawbreaker

white-collar crime —— a crime committed by someone of high social status, without the use of force—for example, price-fixing

arson —— the crime of deliberately setting a fire with the intent to damage property

The Basics of Crime

What Is a Crime?

One night, Joe bought a gun and held up a liquor store. It just was not Joe's night. A police car came by just as he ran out of the store carrying the gun and a fistful of money. The police officers yelled to Joe to stop. They drew their guns. Joe was no fool. He stopped.

Joe had committed a crime. He had **robbed** a clerk at the liquor store—that is, he had taken something from the clerk by force, against the clerk's will. The law says that anyone who commits robbery can be sentenced to prison. This makes robbery a crime. A **crime** is any action that violates a

This suspect is being fingerprinted by police, who may use those prints to determine his guilt.

law and for which the law provides punishment.

We all know that robbery is a crime. But some crimes are not so obvious. Do you know whether it is a crime to make a U-turn? To fail to pay federal income tax? To fail to pay the rent?

Making a U-turn is usually against the law, and it can be punished by a fine. Thus, it is a crime.

Failing to pay federal income tax is also a crime. If you owe a tax, you must pay it. If you do not pay, you can be sent to jail. Therefore, something that you *do not* do can also be a crime.

Failing to pay the rent is not a crime. It is a violation of a contract between you and the landlord. It is a *civil* dispute. Thus, the landlord could not have you arrested. He or she would have to follow the procedures of civil law, not criminal law. Civil law and its procedures will be discussed in Chapter 17.

Criminal law, as we saw in Chapter 2, is law that deals with crimes. The **criminal-justice system** is the part of our society that deals with crimes and their effects. The system includes law-enforcement agencies, criminal courts, and **corrections agencies**—prisons, probation officers, and so forth.

Categories of Crime Crimes are classified into three major categories. The most serious crimes are **felonies.** Joe's liquor-store holdup was a felony. Murder and kidnaping are also felonies. Under federal law, a felony is a crime for which the penalty is 1 year or more in prison.

People who are accused of felonies have the right to a jury trial and a lawyer. If they cannot afford a lawyer, one will be provided free. These are constitutional protections. They are provided because of the seriousness of the charge. Someone who is convicted of a felony may lose more than freedom. A felony conviction may also mean the loss of the right to vote, the right to hold public office, and the right to hold certain jobs.

Less serious crimes are called **misdemeanors.** Vandalism—the deliberate destruction of property—is an example of a misdemeanor. Other examples might be stealing hubcaps or being drunk in public.

People accused of misdemeanors do not have as many constitutional protections as people accused of felonies. They do not have a right to a free lawyer, for example. Also, in some very minor cases, they may not have a right to a trial by jury. People convicted of misdemeanors serve 1 year or less in prison.

The least serious crimes are called **infractions.** They call for fines rather than jail sentences. Making a U-turn and parking illegally are examples of infractions. In some states, infractions are not legally crimes at all.

Victimless Crime Some crimes have no victims in the sense that murders and robberies do. Gambling is such a crime. The only people who are directly affected by **victimless crimes** are the lawbreakers themselves. But these acts are considered harmful to society, and so the lawbreakers are punished.

White-Collar Crime Another special type of crime is **white-collar crime.** This is crime committed by people of high social status who do not use violence in their crimes. A bank clerk who takes money from the bank is a white-collar criminal. A corporation executive who steals money from consumers by breaking the law is also a white-collar criminal.

One of the most common forms of white-collar crime is *fraud.* Fraud means causing damage or injury to another person through the use of a false statement. Each year millions of dollars are lost as a result of an individual or a business misrepresenting the facts about a good or service being offered for sale. One classic example of this type of white-collar crime is the garage owner who charges her or his customers for repairs that were not needed. People who file false claims for unemployment payments or false insurance claims are also guilty of fraud.

The Costs of Crime

At the age of 72, Mary Fellini lives in fear. She does not go out at night anymore. In fact, she rarely leaves her apartment even in the daytime. She is afraid of being *mugged.* She was already mugged once. One of her friends was struck on the head in a mugging and is permanently scarred.

Roger Booth, age 47, has no money. He used his life savings to buy a new home in the suburbs. The week after he moved in, the house was burglarized twice. Booth had to borrow several hundred dollars to have bars put on the windows and a burglar alarm installed. Now nighttime noises cause him to wake up in a sweat.

Harry's Department Store has an employee who walks around the floor all day watching for shoplifters. The store loses $200,000 a year in goods to shoplifters. The owner has to charge higher prices to make up for the losses. Thus, the store's customers pay for the crimes of a few people.

These fictional examples cover a few of the costs of crime to society. Fear is one big cost. But the actual losses in lives and money are enormous. Take one crime as an example—**arson.** In a typical year, 1,000 people die in fires that someone has set deliberately. Another 10,000 people are injured. Property losses caused by arson in one recent year added up to an estimated $1.4 billion.

Each year, some 10 million serious crimes are reported. But the figures do not tell the whole story. Many victims never report crimes to the police. People who are robbed may not do anything about it. They may not wish to testify in court. They may just not want to get involved.

Nowhere is the cost of arson—both in dollars and lives—more evident than in New York's South Bronx.

Many people believe that crime is a bigger problem today than ever before. They *may* be wrong. Crime has always been a problem, especially in crowded cities. But people worry and talk about crime much more these days. Fear haunts many people. It lowers the quality of their lives. Fear also leads to anxious demands for the authorities to "do something" about crime. But the authorities are not sure what to do, partly because they are not sure why people commit crimes.

The Causes of Crime

Experts have many theories about what causes crime. But no one has been able to prove or disprove any of them. One reason for this is that we do not know who most criminals are. It is thought that most crimes go unreported. In only one out of ten reported cases is anyone arrested. Of those arrested, six out of ten are eventually convicted. Thus, it can be said that for every 100 crimes reported, only six are solved. How can we learn the causes of crime if we cannot even learn who commits crimes?

There is another aspect to the problem. One study, involving 1,700 people, showed that 91 percent of them had committed a criminal act at some time in their lives. If they had been caught, they could have been arrested. But most of them were not caught. What causes supposedly law-abiding people to commit crimes?

Keep those questions in mind as you consider the following suggested causes of crime:

Poverty Most of the people who are arrested for crimes are poor. Most of the victims of violent crime are also poor people. Thus, many people have argued that poverty causes crime. They have supported government programs to help the poor, and thus remove poverty as a cause of crime.

Social Problems Many social problems besides poverty are sometimes listed as causes of crime. Do people turn to crime because they are somehow disadvantaged? Because their parents are alcoholics or are divorced? Because they cannot get jobs or are kept in dead-end jobs?

Permissiveness Are crimes caused by permissive child-rearing techniques and by permissive courts? Some people feel that parents let their children do anything they want to do. These people say, "No wonder children think that stealing is all right." Others say, "Even if the police catch the criminals, the judges let them off with a slap on the wrist."

Instead of jail, this traffic offender has been given the job of washing police cars as his sentence.

A variation on the permissiveness theory applies to white-collar crime. In this view, the law does not treat such crimes as seriously as it should. Therefore, some businesspeople try to ignore the law. They know it is unlikely that they will go to jail—or even be fined as much as they profit from the crime—if they are caught.

Maladjustment Another theory is that criminals are poorly adjusted to life. They commit crimes because they have personality problems. Perhaps criminals lack self-respect, feel inadequate, or feel unloved. Perhaps they want attention.

Changes in the Population The people most likely to get into trouble with the law are 15- to 24-year-olds. Because of the "baby boom" after World War II, the number of people in that age group in the United States almost doubled between 1950 and 1975. In one view, recent rises in crime can be explained largely by the increase in that age group. But the birth rate has been decreasing. During the 1980s fewer people will be between the ages of 15 and 24. Some people think that this will bring a decrease in crime.

Prisons Some people argue that our prison system itself helps cause crime. They call prisons "schools for crime." A person may go to prison for a minor crime, learn from hardened criminals, and start out on a life of crime.

═══════ REVIEW ═══════

1. Who have more legal rights, people accused of felonies or people accused of misdemeanors?

2. In what way is the crime of gambling different from the crime of murder?

3. Which of the following are white-collar crimes?
   a. Executives from three dairies talk it over and agree to jointly raise the price of milk.
   b. A corporation president murders her husband.
   c. A bank official takes money from the bank.
   d. An automobile company makes and sells cars that do not meet federal safety standards.

4. Describe six theories about the causes of crime.

5. Rank the following crimes according to how serious you think they are. Name the most serious crimes first. Then tell why you rank them as you do.
   a. murder
   b. getting drunk in public
   c. price-fixing
   d. burglary
   e. gambling
   f. armed robbery

Words to Know

night watch —— a volunteer force that watched the town or city streets at night before police forces came into being

book —— to write the charges against a person into the police records

bail-bonding agent —— a person who supplies bail so that accused persons may be freed before trial

waive —— to give up voluntarily

plea —— an answer to a criminal charge

arraignment —— the court process during which an accused person enters a plea to the charges against him or her

prosecution —— the government's side in a criminal case

defense —— the accused person's side in a criminal case

plea bargaining —— a deal between the prosecution and the defense in which the defense agrees to plead guilty to a reduced charge

Crime, Arrest, and Trial

To describe the criminal-justice system, we are going to follow one fictional case. We will look first at the role of the police, then at the position of the accused, and finally at what happens in a trial.

The Role of the Police

Case Study Anne Johnson is a police officer. She is in her first year on the force. Her partner, Ralph Flannigan, is a 10-year police veteran. Together, the two were cruising the streets of Middle City on the night of October 4.

It was a normal night—not too dull, but not exciting either. The police radio crackled with reports of lost children and family quarrels. At about 10 o'clock the pair calmed down three belligerent drunks who were taking pokes at each other.

Next came a call about a traffic accident. It was minor—no injuries, little damage. Flannigan and Johnson directed traffic until a tow truck came. There were also calls about prowlers, a group of kids standing on a street corner, and an unattended baby outside a bar.

At 2:08 A.M., Flannigan and Johnson were sent to an alley in a run-down neighborhood. Someone had reported a fight between two men.

When the officers drove up, they saw a man leaning over a person who was lying on

Directing traffic is one way in which the police enforce society's rules. In this way, both law and order are kept.

the pavement. A scattered pack of cards and a broken bottle lay nearby. The man straightened up, but stayed in the same spot. He was swaying a bit. When Flannigan came closer, he could smell whiskey on the man's breath. The man's speech was slurred as he asked, "Whatcha want?"

Anne Johnson stooped over the person who was lying face up on the pavement. It was an unconscious man. A knife lay beside him. "We'd better get an ambulance," she said quietly.

While Johnson used the police radio, Flannigan snapped handcuffs on the bleary-eyed man. He patted the man's clothes, searching for a weapon. "We're going to arrest you for assault," he said. "You have a right to remain silent. If you talk, anything you say can be used against you in court. You have a right to a lawyer. The lawyer can be with you when we question you. If you can't afford a lawyer, the court will appoint one, free of charge. Do you understand your rights as I've explained them?"

The man mumbled "Yes." He did not say another word. After the ambulance had taken the wounded man away, the officers led the handcuffed man to the police car and drove him to the police station.

Police Have Two Jobs Flannigan and Johnson had started the night dealing with one of the police officer's main jobs—keeping order. They had tried to settle disputes between individuals. They had kept traffic moving at an accident scene.

But eventually they had to deal with their second main job—enforcing the law. From what they saw, Flannigan and Johnson concluded that the bleary-eyed man had stabbed the second man. They followed the rule book. Before asking the suspect any questions, they told him his rights.

Flannigan and Johnson were lucky. They did not have to bring a violent suspect under control, as sometimes happens. They did not have to deal with hostile members of the suspect's family.

Many Police Agencies Flannigan and Johnson work for one of some 40,000 police agencies in the United States. Our federal system spreads law-enforcement responsibilities over many levels of government. Almost all law-enforcement agencies are local—run by a city or a county. Many states have state police forces. In addition, there are about fifty different federal law-enforcement agencies. The most famous of these is the FBI, or Federal Bureau of Investigation. But many other federal agencies have law-enforcement officers. A few examples are Border Patrol agents, Secret Service agents, and alcohol-tax agents.

Our law-enforcement agencies have expanded gradually over the years. The first city police department was not created until 1857, in New York. Before that time, towns and cities had only small forces of volunteers to watch the streets at night. These forces were called the **night watch.** Today, police officers are professionals who often have advanced education and special training. Their job is neither simple nor safe. In an average year, some 100 police officers are killed in the line of duty—ten of them while making an arrest for a traffic violation.

The Accused

Being Booked At the police station, Flannigan and Johnson **booked** their suspect on a charge of assault and battery. He said his name was Henry Fleet. The police took his fingerprints and photographed him.

A Lawyer Fleet spent the night in jail. He was unemployed and could not afford a lawyer. The next afternoon, a lawyer who was provided by the court talked with him. The lawyer was present while the police questioned Fleet.

Fleet said that he and the other man—he called him Sam—had been drinking and playing cards. According to Fleet, Sam had accused him of cheating. Sam had come at him with a broken bottle, and Fleet had

pulled out a knife to defend himself. He was not sure how Sam had been stabbed.

The hospital reported that Sam was now out of danger. He had a skull fracture and a nasty gash in his stomach, but the knife had not struck any vital organs.

Bail Fleet's lawyer arranged for him to be released on $2,500 bail. Fleet did not have that much money himself. But his wife came down to the jail with $300, and a **bail-bonding agent** posted the rest. Such agents have offices near most jails. They charge a fee, or premium, of 10 to 15 percent. If Fleet is present at the trial, the bonding agent will get back the $2,500. If Fleet does not come to the trial, the bonding agent will lose the $2,500. Needless to say, the agent wants to make sure that Fleet is present at the trial.

At this point, Fleet is presumed to be innocent. He is a *defendant* in a criminal case. By arranging *bail,* he is able to be free until his court case comes up. If he had owned his own home, Fleet might have been able to pledge his property against his bail. But, like most criminal defendants, Fleet is poor. Many are even too poor to pay a bail-bonding agent's premium. For these people, the constitutional right to bail has little meaning. Unless the court can be persuaded to release them without bail, they must remain in jail until their trials take place.

Under the Constitution, the accused in a serious criminal case has a right to have the evidence considered by a grand jury before the case is brought to trial. This protects innocent people against the expense of going to trial unnecessarily. In this case, Fleet **waived,** or gave up, the right to a grand jury on his lawyer's advice.

Preliminary Hearing Instead, Fleet had a preliminary hearing. The police officers had turned in their reports. Officer Johnson had visited Sam in the hospital and heard his side of the story. The judge studied the reports and decided that there

Booking a criminal suspect is the first step the police take in bringing the guilty party to trial. After the suspect is checked for weapons, he or she is fingerprinted, photographed, and jailed.

was enough evidence to send the case to trial. If there had been too little evidence, the judge could have dismissed, or dropped, the charges.

Arraignment Fleet now had to enter a **plea,** or answer, to the charge. If he pleaded *guilty,* he would be admitting that he had committed assault and battery. Then there would be no need for a trial. But Fleet pleaded *not guilty*. His lawyer told the court that Fleet had acted in self-defense. The formal making of a plea by the accused is the first step in the trial process. It is called the **arraignment.**

The Rights of the Accused Our case study has touched on a number of rights that are enjoyed by every person who is accused of a crime. One right is freedom from unreasonable search. If the police officers had not had reason to believe that Fleet had committed a crime, they would have had no right to frisk him—that is, search him for weapons. But they were arresting him. That called for a search.

Officer Flannigan informed Fleet of his right to be silent and his right to a lawyer. The right to be informed of one's rights is

an important one. The police are required by law to tell a suspect her or his rights. They must also be sure that the suspect understands those rights. If the police fail to follow the required procedures, a judge can throw the case out of court. This protects suspects from abuses such as the old practice of beating a suspect until he or she confessed to a crime.

The Trial

The People v. Fleet Fleet went on trial on December 10, slightly more than 2 months after the alleged crime. The trial was held before a judge and a jury of twelve people. Mrs. Fleet and thirteen other people were also in the courtroom. One of those present was a court reporter, who wrote down everything that was said at the trial. By that time, Sam was out of the hospital. He was called to be a witness for the **prosecution**—the government's side of the case. "We were playing poker," Sam told the court. "That little lizzard pulled a card out of his sleeve. I slugged him, but only with my fist. That's the last thing I remember. I

In any criminal court case, the police officers involved will testify for the prosecution. Their testimony is often the strongest evidence the government has against the defendant.

don't know where the knife came from. It wasn't mine."

Fleet's lawyer questioned Sam. "How much do you weigh?" the lawyer asked. "Two-fifty," Sam replied. Later, the lawyer pointed out to the jury that Fleet himself was a small man. The lawyer suggested that Fleet had feared Sam would harm him and had lawfully defended himself. The prosecution argued that using a knife in such a situation was uncalled-for.

Fleet himself did not testify at the trial. This is his constitutional right. Fleet's lawyer told him that it would be better for him not to testify.

Both police officers testified at the trial. In addition, the prosecution introduced two items as evidence. One was the broken bottle. The other was the knife. A laboratory test had failed to find any identifiable fingerprints on the knife.

When the testimony was over, the prosecution summed up the arguments against Fleet. Fleet's lawyer summed up the case for the **defense**—that is, for the accused. Then the judge explained the law to the jury. The judge said that the law allows a person to use a reasonable amount of force if the person fears that his or her life is in immediate danger. This is self-defense. It was up to the jury to decide, beyond a reasonable doubt, whether Fleet had used reasonable force. It was also up to the jury to decide if Fleet had, in fact, stabbed Sam with the knife.

The jury found Fleet guilty of assault and battery.

The Rights of the Accused Fleet had the rights that are due to all accused persons. His trial was speedy and public. He was represented by a lawyer. The lawyer was allowed to question the witnesses against the accused. No one forced Fleet to testify against himself.

Plea Bargaining Before the trial, Fleet was confident that the jury would find him innocent. He had ignored his lawyer's suggestion that he bargain with the prosecution. In many cases, the accused person agrees to plead guilty if the prosecution makes the charge less serious. For example, rather than charge Fleet with assault and battery—a felony—the prosecution might have charged him with disorderly conduct—a misdemeanor. This is known as **plea bargaining.**

Plea bargaining is an important means of settling criminal cases. As many as 85 percent of all cases end in guilty pleas, often after a plea bargain. Many prosecutors say that the practice is necessary in order to keep the courts from becoming hopelessly overloaded with trials. But some people argue that because of plea bargaining, criminals manage to avoid proper punishment. Others say that plea bargains pressure innocent people into giving up their constitutional right to a trial by jury. The state of Alaska banned plea bargaining in 1975.

REVIEW
---

1. What are the two main jobs of a police officer? Give one example of each job.
2. List the rights that an arresting officer must explain to a suspect.
3. Describe how the system of bail works.
4. What are four rights belonging to a person who is being tried on a criminal charge?
5. Do you think that plea bargaining should be allowed? Why or why not?

Words to Know

sentence —— the punishment given to a person convicted of a crime
retribution —— paying back someone for a wrong
rehabilitation —— preparing a convicted person for a life of useful activity
probation officer —— an official whose job is to study a convicted person's record and recommend whether or not the person should be placed on probation; also, an official who supervises persons on probation
probation —— a type of sentence that lets a convicted person go free, but requires the person to follow certain rules under supervision
prison —— a place operated by a state or federal government where people convicted of serious crimes are held
jail —— a small prison run by a city or a county
parole —— release from prison under official supervision and before completion of a sentence
indeterminate sentence —— a prison sentence for an indefinite period of time, such as 2 to 8 years
fixed sentence —— a prison sentence for a definite length of time

Paying the Penalty

The Purpose of the Sentence

How should someone who breaks the law be punished? That question has bothered people through the centuries. Most people believe that the answer is to make the punishment fit the crime. If the crime is serious, the punishment, or **sentence,** should be severe. If the crime is minor, the punishment should be lighter. That has generally been the approach in the United States.

The sentence is usually decided by a judge. In some cases—especially crimes that may involve the death penalty—the sentence is fixed by law. In most cases, however, the judge has some freedom to decide the punishment.

In the case that we have been following, Judge Roscoe Lamb was responsible for setting a sentence for Henry Fleet. The judge's decision could have been influenced by how he viewed the *purpose* of the sen-

Only the most dangerous criminals are sent to maximum-security prisons such as the Statesville Penitentiary near Chicago, Illinois (shown above).

At the Framingham model prison in Massachusetts, this inmate lives under minimum-security conditions.

tence. Let's look at four common attitudes about the purpose of sentences in criminal cases.

Retribution In one view, the purpose of a sentence is **retribution**—paying back the criminal for the harm done to others. Fleet broke the law by assaulting Sam. Justice demands that he pay for the crime.

Deterrence A related view is that punishment should be aimed at deterrence—prevention—of further crimes. In earlier days, executions were done in public. The message was: "Look closely. This might happen to you if you do not obey the law." According to this view, by punishing Fleet, the justice system warns others of the consequences of letting fights get out of control.

Rehabilitation Another view is that the sentence should give **rehabilitation**—prepare a convicted person for a useful life in society. For example, before Henry Fleet returns to normal society, he should be given guidance and training so that he can avoid his past mistakes and lead a law-abiding life. Corrections agencies generally take this approach today. They may offer job training, psychological counseling, and other services.

Protection for Society A fourth view of the purpose of the sentence is that it protects society. A murderer who is sentenced to life in prison, for example, is taken off the streets. As long as the criminal is in prison, the public is protected against that person.

Probation

Before Judge Lamb sentenced Fleet, he received a report from a court official called a **probation officer.** Her name was Margaret Fleming. Fleming checked into Fleet's police record. She found that he had been convicted once before on a misdemeanor charge of public drunkenness. But he had no felony convictions. Fleming also talked to Fleet's wife. She learned that Fleet had worked steadily until the previous summer, when his boss fired him for being drunk on the job.

After studying Fleming's probation report, Judge Lamb announced his sentence. Fleet would not be sent to prison. Instead, he would be placed on **probation** for 1 year. This meant that Fleet was free to go home, but for the next year he would have to follow certain rules set by the judge. One of those rules was to report once a month to a probation officer. Another was to get a job. A third rule was to enroll in an alcoholism-treatment program.

As long as Fleet follows the rules, he will remain free. At the end of the year, the sentence is over and the rules no longer apply. But if Fleet breaks the rules, he can be sent to prison.

The idea of probation developed about one hundred years ago. The goal of probation is rehabilitation. Probation is much less expensive than imprisonment and thus saves the taxpayers money. Probation often succeeds. But, as critics claim, the probation system may free dangerous criminals—especially if it is used with criminals who repeat the same crime.

Prison

In gangster movies, it is called "the slammer." In the language of bureaucrats, it is called a "correctional institution." Most of us know it as **prison.**

Imprisonment has been used as a punishment for thousands of years. In medieval times, criminals were put into dungeons. Their legs might be chained. They were often treated brutally. Early United States prisons offered little improvement. Even today public attention is drawn, from time to time, to cruel conditions in one prison or another.

But most modern prisons in the United States have come a long way from medieval dungeons. Today, prisons may offer psychiatric treatment, job training, and even sports programs. One federal prison, at Allenwood, Pennsylvania, is noted for its "country-club atmosphere," complete with tennis courts. It was the prison used for some high government officials who were convicted of crimes connected with the Watergate Affair in the early 1970s.

Maximum-Security Prisons The most dangerous prisoners are sent to maximum-security prisons. More than half of all state prisons are maximum-security prisons. They generally have high walls and heavy bars. They are not at all like country clubs.

In a typical maximum-security prison, prisoners are kept in individual, barred cells. They have a bed, a few other items of furniture, and a sink. There is no hot water, only cold water. For 8 hours each day, the prisoners work at a job—perhaps making license plates or wooden furniture. Then, they go back to their cells. It is a lonely life. Mail is screened. Reading matter is censored. Before seeing a visitor, prisoners are stripped and thoroughly searched.

Life is not always safe in prison. Often, prisoners form gangs and prey on other prisoners. Violence is frequent. Even murder is known to happen.

Prison riots are a repeated problem in maximum-security prisons. In 1971, some 1,200 prisoners at the state prison in Attica, New York, seized thirty-eight guards as hostages. A stand-off lasted several days. When 1,000 state troopers stormed the prison, nine guards and twenty-eight prisoners lost their lives.

Medium-Security Prisons Less dangerous prisoners are often sent to medium-security prisons. There, the emphasis is usually on rehabilitation. Prisoners may attend classes to further their education. They may also receive job training.

Minimum-Security Prisons Prisoners who are not considered dangerous may be sent to minimum-security prisons. There are no high walls there—sometimes no walls at all. Housing is in dormitorylike buildings. Prisoners may even be allowed to leave the prison during the day in order to go to work. But they must report back each evening.

Jails As a rule, **jails** are smaller than prisons and have no rehabilitation programs—only cells. Accused persons who are imprisoned while awaiting trial are kept in jails. Persons who have been convicted of minor crimes and are serving less than a year are also kept in jails. Jails are run by cities and counties.

Prisoners' Rights People who are sent to prison lose many—but not all—of their rights. Since the 1960s, court decisions have stated some of the rights that prison-

Although this jail in Johnson City, Texas, is not representative of detention facilities throughout the United States, it does have two main characteristics—cells for short-term stays and no rehabilitation programs.

ers keep. One is the right to keep in contact with a lawyer. Certain other rights—such as the right of freedom of religion—are also kept by prisoners. But these rights may be limited by prison officials when necessary to maintain security and order.

Parole

Joe—the unlucky man who robbed the liquor store—was found guilty of armed robbery. A judge sentenced him to a period of 2 to 10 years in the state prison. At the end of 2 years, Joe came up for **parole**— that is, release from prison, under official supervision. Parole is much like probation, except that it comes after—not instead of— a prison sentence and before completion of that sentence.

A parole board considered Joe's case. It studied a report on Joe's behavior in prison. He had not been in trouble. He had done well in the prison's training program for computer operators. A psychiatrist who examined him said that Joe had a "constructive" attitude. Thus, the board decided to release Joe on parole.

The parole board set down certain rules for Joe to follow while on parole. He had to report to a parole officer, stay out of bars, stay away from anyone else who has been in prison, and not keep any guns. If Joe violated the rules, he could be sent back to prison.

Joe was pleased to find that his parole officer was "a regular guy." The parole officer helped Joe look for work. Joe was discouraged at first. Several employers refused to hire him because of his conviction for robbery. But the parole officer sent Joe to a volunteer group that helps ex-convicts find jobs. Soon, he was accepted for a trial period as a computer operator for the city school system. Joe had a hard time adjusting to his new-found freedom. He was not used to deciding how to spend his time. But he worked things out. At the end of 6 years,

his sentence—and thus, his period of parole—ended. Joe was then fully free once more.

Joe's sentence of 2 to 8 years was an **indeterminate sentence**—a sentence for an indefinite period of time. Most sentences today are of this sort. But in some situations, the punishment for a crime is set at a specific number of years. For example, someone who is convicted of robbery might be sentenced to 10 years. This is a **fixed sentence.** People who receive fixed sentences usually come up before a parole board after serving about one-third of their sentence.

By holding out the hope of parole to a prisoner, criminal-justice officials hope to give the prisoner a reason to improve.

Failures of the System

Does the United States' criminal-justice system succeed in reforming criminals? Sometimes it does. But all too many times, it does not.

A study done by the FBI a few years ago showed that 63 percent of all released prisoners were arrested again within 4 years. The youngest prisoners—those under 20—were the most likely to get into trouble again. Three out of every four were arrested again.

Statistics such as these increase the public's fears about crime. Some people feel that the figures point to the failure of our prison system. They say that we should deal with criminals in other ways. Some people believe that many criminals could be placed in special programs outside of prisons. This, they say, would be more effective than sending them to prisons—"schools for crime." But others argue that prison sentences are too short. They say that criminals do not fear being sent to prison because they know that they will not have to stay long. In this view, the solution is to give criminals longer sentences.

REVIEW

1. What kind of prisoners would be sent to a maximum-security prison? To a minimum-security prison?
2. Do prisoners have the same rights as other United States citizens? Explain.
3. If a person convicted of a crime receives a fixed sentence of 20 years, approximately when will she or he come up for parole?
4. Of the four purposes of sentences in criminal cases, which *one* do you think is most important? Explain.

Words to Know

juvenile —— someone who is not legally an adult; generally, someone under 18 years of age

status offense —— an offense that can be committed only by juveniles, not by adults—for example, running away from home

delinquent —— a juvenile who is found by a court to have broken a law or committed a status offense

Criminal Justice for Juveniles

Why We Have Juvenile Courts

If you are under the age of 18, you are considered a **juvenile** in most states. (Some states set the age at 16, others as high as 21.) A juvenile is someone who is not legally an adult. Our criminal-justice system provides special courts and special procedures for juveniles who get into trouble with the law.

This was not always so. As recently as 100 years ago, our criminal-justice system treated juveniles and adults alike. A 12-year-old who was accused of shoplifting was tried in a regular court. If sentenced to jail, the juvenile went to the same place as an adult.

But reformers wanted change. They argued that children were not fully responsible for their acts. Therefore, it was not so important to punish a child as to correct the child's behavior. Thus, they suggested that court proceedings for juveniles be kept secret. In this way, a youthful mistake would not give the child a criminal record. Moreover, the reformers wanted the judges in juvenile cases to be more like parents and less like judges. They pictured a kindly judge who would patiently question a child. The judge would try to understand what had gone wrong and seek to correct it.

Between 1899 and 1930, almost all states passed laws requiring special treatment for juveniles. Sometimes, especially in large cities, separate juvenile courts were created. In other places, the same judge who presided over adult trials might also hold court for juveniles.

Juveniles come under two sets of laws. One set applies to adults as well as to juveniles. This set is made up of the ordinary criminal laws. Another set of laws applies only to juveniles. For example, running away from home and skipping school are against the law. These are called **status offenses**—offenses that can be committed only by juveniles. Both criminal violations and status offenses are handled by juvenile-court judges.

How Juvenile Courts Work

Henry Fleet, whom we met earlier, was an adult. We have seen how the criminal-justice system handled his case. The charge, as you will recall, was that he assaulted someone during a fight over a poker game. What would happen if Henry were a 16-year-old?

One characteristic of juvenile courts—like the one above in Orange County, California—is the lack of a jury, which is a right denied to minors by law.

After booking Henry on the assault charge, the police would telephone his parents. The police might even send Henry home with his parents. But if Henry's parents claim that they cannot handle him, he might have to stay in a detention center. It is sometimes harder for juveniles to win release—with or without bail—than it is for adults.

Like an adult, Henry would be informed of his rights—to have a lawyer, to remain silent. A probation officer would talk to him, probably with his parents present. The officer would decide whether Henry should go through further legal proceedings.

Since assault is a serious charge, Henry would probably have to go to a hearing. For juveniles, a hearing takes the place of a trial. A hearing is more informal than a trial. The public is barred, and there is no jury. The only people present would be the judge—sometimes called a "special referee"—, Henry, Henry's parents, the proba-

tion officer, and others directly involved in the case.

As in a trial, any witnesses against Henry would testify under oath. Henry's lawyer—if he has one—may question the witnesses or call others to testify in Henry's favor.

After hearing the evidence, the judge would decide whether or not to declare Henry a **delinquent.** A finding of delinquency would mean that Henry had broken the law.

Let's assume that the judge does find Henry a delinquent. The judge now has several choices. One is to place Henry in a reform school—a prison for juveniles. Another is to send Henry to an adult court for trial. Still another choice is to put Henry on probation.

The Rights of Juveniles

Until just recently, juveniles were considered special in two ways. First, they were not considered fully responsible for their actions. Thus, the law was supposed to treat them with more understanding. Second, their rights were strictly limited. It was believed that court officials and parents would do what was best for the child. There was no need to pay close attention to formal rights, which would only complicate matters. But in 1967, the United States Supreme Court made a ruling that was to bring major changes in our juvenile-justice system.

The Gault Case Gerald Gault was 15 years old. One day, the police picked him up on suspicion of making an obscene phone call to a neighbor, Mrs. Cook. They put Gerald in a juvenile detention center. No one notified his parents. But his mother found out where he was and went to see him. A hearing was held the next day, and a second hearing the following week.

At the hearing, no witnesses were called. Mrs. Gault asked the judge to have Mrs. Cook come and testify. But she did not come. Gerald admitted dialing the phone, but said that he handed the phone to another boy—who was also arrested—who made the obscene remarks.

Two points came up in these hearings. One was that, 2 years earlier, Gerald had been accused of taking a baseball glove from a younger boy. He was found not guilty. The second point was that Gerald was already on probation. He had been "in the company" of a boy who stole a wallet from a woman's purse.

A judge found Gerald to be a delinquent. He sent the boy to reform school for 6 years—until he became 21.

The Supreme Court ruled that Gerald had been denied due process of law. If he had been an adult, the Court noted, he would have been given a lighter sentence. The maximum punishment for an adult who made an obscene call would be a 50-dollar fine and 2 months in jail.

The Court ruled that juveniles must be given the following rights: (1) the right to be told exactly what the charges are, (2) the right to be represented by a lawyer, (3) the right to confront and question witnesses, (4) and the right to refuse to testify. Observed Justice Abe Fortas: "Under our Constitution, the condition of being a boy [or a girl] does not justify a kangaroo court."

Restrictions on Juvenile Rights The Court has made clear, however, that juveniles do not have *all* the rights of adults. For example, juveniles have no right to a jury trial. Some states do allow juries for juveniles, however.

In dealing with juveniles, the courts must determine what is best for a child and, at the same time, protect society. They must respect the accused child's basic rights, while seeing that justice is done.

=== REVIEW ===

1. At what age does a person legally stop being a juvenile?
2. Give two examples of status offenses. Explain the term.
3. What is the reasoning behind our system of separate courts for juveniles?
4. Do you think that it is fair to try juveniles in special courts under the present practices? Why or why not?

Social Service Aide

With more and more young people getting into trouble with the law, social workers are very busy. They try to keep teenagers out of jail and in school. One way to do this is to keep teenagers busy with a satisfying activity. In some places, social workers set up programs to direct creative energy from the drawing of graffiti to the commercial arts. In other places, basketball or baseball teams are set up. Sometimes the young people are organized into patrol groups. Then, they are given the job of protecting older citizens that they might otherwise have robbed and attacked. Social workers set up these youth programs to meet the needs of a particular area.

Social workers are highly trained in solving community problems. They know how to set up programs and get things started. However, the day-to-day workings of the programs are often handled by social service aides. The aides encourage the young artists, train the sports teams, and oversee the patrol groups. They do other kinds of work as well. The tasks depend on the area's needs. Some aides are hired to work in the welfare office. They help out with a variety of tasks, such as paperwork and record-keeping.

As the population of the United States grows and social services are expanded, the need for social service aides will also increase. Social workers usually choose the people to fill these jobs. There are no educational requirements for the job, however. Many social service aides do not have a high-school degree. Some are the same teenagers that social workers are trying to keep out of trouble.

All aides are trained for a few months before starting to work. At first, the pay is low. Most beginning aides make between $6,500 and $8,000 a year. However, with education and on-the-job training, there can be advancement. The social service agency often pays part of any schooling costs. It may even provide classes to help aides pass a high-school equivalency test.

Reading About . . .

An Experiment in Preventing Crime ——————————

Today, close to 45 percent of all serious crimes in this country are committed by children who are 17 or younger. How can crime by youthful offenders be stopped? In Rahway, New Jersey, a prison inmate had an idea for a program that seems to work. Children who have been in trouble with the law go to prison, just for a visit—but a special kind of visit. Only 6 percent of those who have made the visit have been in trouble with the law again. A more usual figure would be 70 percent.

As you read the selection, think about the following questions:

- What are the convicts trying to do with their stories?
- Why do you think a program like this might be successful?

The 12 teenage boys, wearing jeans and flannel shirts or sweatshirts, have long hair and hardened faces. Some have tattooed arms, and one wears three tiny gold earrings in his pierced left ear.

They have come to Rahway State Prison because of misdeeds ranging from running away and truancy to car theft and burglary. They are seated on narrow wooden benches facing 16 similarly dressed and equally tough-looking men, ranging in age from about 25 to 40. The men are murderers and robbers. They are serving prison terms of 25 years or longer. The boys are visiting and will leave after three hours.

Inmate Fred Wilkes stands up to speak. At age 28, he is in prison for the third time, this time doing 15 to 27 years for armed robbery, illegal weapons possession and conspiracy. "Everything you have from doing all that stuff, they're gonna take," he tells the boys. "And when they take all that, then they're gonna take your freedom. That's the last thing you have to lose except your life, and in here, you stand to lose that, too."

Such advice is standard in what is known here as the lifers program, an attempt to steer kids away from crime. The program was begun in September 1976 by a small group of inmates serving life terms. As in-

mate Frank Bindhammer recalls it now, it started after a few inmates watched a college class tour the prison. One of the inmates said he was concerned about his son, who had been picked up by the police for a minor offense. Bindhammer says the inmates watching the tour concluded that any would-be criminal who saw what prison life was really like would do his best to go straight. The inmates suggested to authorities that lawbreaking youngsters be allowed to visit the prison.

About 50 inmates now are involved, giving tours of the prison, talking about their own lives and the high price they are paying for past crimes. More than 5,000 youngsters have been to Rahway since the program began. Typically, youngsters who have been in trouble repeatedly are referred to the program, by police departments and social-service agencies. Sometimes, courts order juvenile offenders to attend the sessions.

The impact is almost universal. "I told my mom when I came back that I wouldn't do nothing bad no more, and I'm not," says a 16-year-old Newark youth who visited Rahway.

Few of the youths who have visited the prison have gotten into trouble again—so far, at least.

At Rahway, inmates see two groups of youngsters a day, five days a week. Working out of a small, paneled office on the fourth floor of the prison, inmates schedule visits of groups from all over the state and from New York and let prison authorities know who is coming when.

The Lifers, with the help of private contributions, pay for their two telephones, office supplies, postage, and other costs. The state pays the $17,000-a-year salary of a corrections officer assigned to the group full time. By comparison, it usually costs more than $15,000 to keep one child locked up for a year.

The shock treatment of the Rahway program begins even before the youngsters enter the prison. A uniformed officer tells them they must turn in their cigarettes, keys, belt buckles, and other metal objects. He reminds them that they can't take weapons or drugs into the prison. Anyone caught with drugs will be charged with attempt to introduce drugs into a state prison, a much harsher charge than just possession, he says.

Once inside the door, the first thing the boys see is the room where the officers' riot gear is stored. Floor-to-ceiling shelves hold helmets, clear plastic shields and billy clubs, which were used just two weeks before, an officer tells the group, after one inmate had stabbed another with a homemade weapon in the mess hall.

The youngsters also see "the hole," the long row of dark, dingy cells, behind a locked screen, where inmates are sent for breaking prison rules. They see living conditions in the oldest wing of the 82-year-old prison—rows of cells that are just four feet by eight feet, crowded with a cot, a table, a sink and a toilet.

The boys, who minutes earlier were laughing and joking while they waited outside, are silent and stony faced when they enter the prison auditorium for their encounter with the inmates.

The talk is about conditions inside the prison—the murders and the suicides—and about how these men got there. Some of the advice is almost parental, although the language is the tough language of the street.

"You want to be cool, you want to smoke reefers, you want to shoot dope," says inmate Edward Bermel, a large, sandy-haired man of 40 who is serving two consecutive life terms for murder. "When I was your age, I wanted to be cool, too. Then you wake up one day and you don't got no trade, you don't got no education. You're forcing yourselves to steal, you're forcing yourselves into a life of crime."

Pacing back and forth, Bermel continues in a softer voice. "We're all a bunch of fools, that's why we're here." The large room is silent.

"It's the first time in my life that I'm doing something worthwhile," explains Frank Bindhammer, who has been in and out of institutions since he was eight. James Irby, 35, who is serving 30 years for murder, kidnapping, robbery and conspiracy, adds, "We want to show society that we aren't animals." The inmates also say they enjoy the contact with the outside world.

Youngsters who have been through the program are encouraged to keep in touch with the inmates by telephone, to call if they have any problems. Some do call, to discuss plans to run away or even to commit another crime, which the inmates then try to discourage.

Among 2,500 of the youngsters who have visited the prison, according to an informal state study, fewer than 200 have later gotten into trouble. The New Jersey Department of Correction says that is about half the usual rate.

"It's naive to think that a kid who's going back to the Central Ward in Newark, with its poverty, its unemployment and its despair, is going to change his life because of a few hours inside a prison," says David Rothenberg, executive director of the Fortune Society, a similar organization in Texas. He suggests that the biggest impact is on middle-class youths.

Still, "If they save one kid, whatever effort we expend has got to be worth it," says prison superintendent Robert Hatrak.

Inmate James Irby adds, "If somebody would have given me that opportunity when I was their age, maybe I wouldn't be here."

chapter
Review

Fact Review

1. Explain this statement: "Some crimes are committed by doing, some by not doing."
2. What are three of the costs of crime to society?
3. If an accused person in a criminal case cannot afford a lawyer, does this mean that the person must do without one? Explain.
4. In what way does the law limit a person's right to act in self-defense?
5. What factors, or purposes, might a judge consider in deciding on a sentence?
6. Many released prisoners quickly get into trouble again. What are two different beliefs about what should be done about this problem?
7. What can be done to a juvenile who has been found to be delinquent?
8. What do you think is the most important reason for high crime rates? Explain.
9. State whether you agree or disagree with the following statement: "Prisons are schools for crime. We would all be better off if fewer people were sent to prison." Explain your answer.

Developing Your Vocabulary

1. What is the difference between the terms in the following pairs?
   a. felony and misdemeanor
   b. prosecution and defense
   c. probation and parole
   d. prison and jail

2. Match the terms in *a* to *e* with the phrases in (*1*) to (*5*).

   a. plea   (1) to give up voluntarily

   b. waive   (2) a minor law violation

   c. fixed sentence   (3) an answer to a criminal charge

   d. indeterminate sentence   (4) 1 to 5 years

   e. infraction   (5) 99 years

Developing Your Reading Skills

Read the following paragraph and then answer the questions that follow:

Crime is often said to be caused by poverty. Put an end to poverty, people say, and you will cut the crime rate. But many other causes for crime have been suggested. Some say that the cause is maladjustment—that troubled minds lead to crime. Some say that the cause is permissiveness. Some say that it is divorce, or unemployment, or alcoholism. Still other people say that crime can be traced to our prison system or to the large percentage of young people in today's population. It would be helpful if we could determine the cause or causes of crime. Then we could attack crime by trying to get rid of its causes.

1. Which one of the following do you think is the main point, or main idea, of the paragraph?
   a. Some say that alcoholism causes crime.
   b. Poverty causes crime.
   c. Some people want to get rid of the causes of crime.
   d. People have not been able to agree on exactly what causes crime.
2. Tell why you selected *a, b, c,* or *d* in question 1 above.

Developing Your Writing Skills— Forming and Supporting an Opinion

In this chapter, you have examined the problem of crime in our society. You have considered the possible causes of crime, the way in which police agencies and the courts deal with crime, and what happens to people who are convicted of crimes. Now consider the following:

Forming an opinion
1. What one step would you suggest as the most effective way to decrease the amount of crime?

Supporting an opinion
2. After thinking it over, write a paragraph that answers the question above. Give arguments to support your position.

Reading Tables

The following table shows the *rate* at which crimes were committed over a 10-year period. For example, in 1970 there were 7.9 murders committed for each 100,000 people living in the United States that year. In 1970 there were about 203 million people living in the United States. If we divide 203 million by 100,000, we get an answer of 2,030. When 2,030 is multiplied by the murder rate for that year (7.9), we find that the total number of murders committed in 1970 was about 16,000.

The reason why rates are used rather than the total number of crimes is that the number of people living in the United States changes from year to year. By using rates it is easier to compare one year with another. Study the table below and then answer the following questions.

1. During the period 1969 to 1978, which type of crime had the highest rate?
2. Are there more crimes committed against people or property?
3. In general, did the crime rate increase or decrease between 1969 and 1978?
4. What was the total number of motor vehicles stolen in 1970?
5. Look at the figures for 1975 and 1978. In what categories did the crime rate go down?

Types of Crime

Rate per 100,000 inhabitants	Violent crime			Property crime		
	Murder	Robbery	Aggravated Assault	Burglary	Larceny (Theft)	Motor Vehicle Theft
1969	7.3	148	155	984	1,931	436
1970	7.9	172	165	1,085	2,079	457
1971	8.6	188	179	1,164	2,146	460
1972	9.0	181	189	1,141	1,994	426
1973	9.4	183	201	1,223	2,072	443
1974	9.8	209	216	1,438	2,490	462
1975	9.6	218	227	1,526	2,805	469
1976	8.8	196	229	1,439	2,921	446
1977	8.8	187	242	1,411	2,730	448
1978	9.0	191	256	1,423	2,743	454

YOUR GOVERNMENT & ITS HISTORY

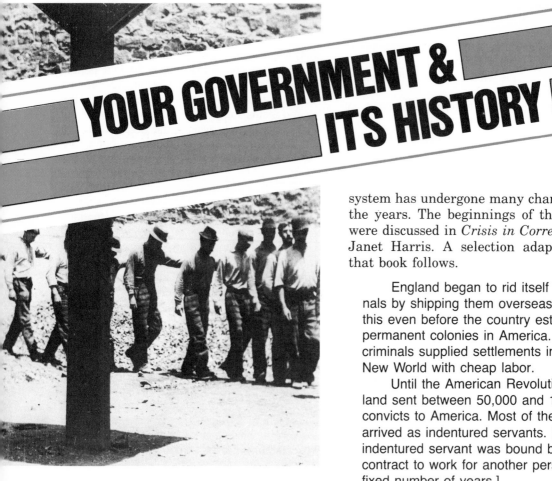

Corrections—a Brief History

There are three main divisions of the criminal-justice system. The police are responsible for enforcing the law and protecting the public. The courts decide whether an individual on trial has committed a crime, and, if so, what the penalty will be. The third division of the criminal-justice system, is the corrections system, has four purposes: punishment, prevention, rehabilitation, and protection for society.

People rarely agree on what is the most effective way to deal with criminals. For this reason, the American corrections system has undergone many changes over the years. The beginnings of the system were discussed in *Crisis in Corrections* by Janet Harris. A selection adapted from that book follows.

England began to rid itself of criminals by shipping them overseas. It did this even before the country established permanent colonies in America. The criminals supplied settlements in the New World with cheap labor.

Until the American Revolution, England sent between 50,000 and 100,000 convicts to America. Most of the convicts arrived as indentured servants. [An indentured servant was bound by legal contract to work for another person for a fixed number of years.]

When indentured servants finished their contract, it was the custom to give each one seeds and plants, clothing, tools, enough food to survive at least one winter, and often a grant of 50 acres of land. Many men and women sent in chains to America were able to make new lives for themselves.

American colonists did not like being forced to adopt British laws. These laws were based on severe physical punishment and the death penalty for some crimes.

In Philadelphia in 1787, a group of Quakers formed The Philadelphia Society for Alleviating [relieving] the Miseries of Public Prisons. The group set to work to plan a satisfactory prison system. Their work was in agreement with the first Pennsylvania State Constitution.

The legislature of Philadelphia, in 1790, ordered the building of a cell house in the yard of the Walnut Street jail. The legislature decided it had complete authority to create a brand new system.

As a first step, prisoners were to be divided into two categories. The "more hardened . . . offenders" were to be housed in small cells in solitary confinement. Suspects, witnesses, and people who had committed misdemeanors were to be kept in large rooms with other prisoners.

But the building plans for the prison had been figured wrong. Prisoners were soon so jammed together that industrial activity (shoemaking, weaving, and so on) became impossible.

The serious flaw in the first American prison was explained by French historians De Tocqueville and De Beaumont: "It corrupted by contamination those who worked together." Anxious to eliminate the problem of "contamination," the Philadelphia legislature turned entirely toward what became known as the "separate system." This system was designed to house prisoners in solitary confinement.

The solitary-confinement system collapsed, and a legislative committee of investigation was appointed. Their report, in 1824, "respectfully recommend[ed] . . . the repeal of the laws for solitary confinement." Meanwhile, local prison officials began working out a new system. This new system had prisoners working together by day and separated by night.

Silence was enforced at all times (the "silent system").

One new idea that remained until 1924 was the lease system of convict labor. Prisoners were "rented," usually for outdoor labor, on contract to private companies. These companies had complete control over the prisoners, including food, housing, and discipline. Although the kinds of work and the length of employment were fixed by lease, under law, there were seldom safeguards to insure that prisoners were properly treated. Often, conditions were horribly brutal.

The American Prison Association was formed in 1870. Its first step was to adopt a declaration of principles. This declaration stated that: "Reform, not revenge, should be the purpose of prison treatment."

Throughout the end of the nineteenth and all of the twentieth century, the methods of correction have swung back and forth between the opposing ends of thought. Long-term trends have been toward rehabilitation rather than revenge. But the earlier methods and purposes survive in one way or another in present correctional practice.

1. What was the role of the American colonies in Britain's correction system?

2. Name three systems of corrections tried in America. How was each set up?

3. What role did the American Prison Association play in the corrections system?

4. What are the two opposing schools of thought on correction? Which do you think is more effective in curbing crime? Explain why you feel this way.

SKILLS Developing your basic civic education skills

Another View of *Scared Straight*

(conflicting viewpoints—asking questions)

In this chapter, you read about the experiences juveniles had at Rahway State Prison. Another view of a similar experience follows. The account is by Dr. Walt Menninger, an authority in the field of mental health.

Several years ago, a television documentary dramatically showed a "new" approach to reducing juvenile delinquency. This approach was to scare the kids straight.

In an hour-long program, seventeen juvenile offenders were followed as they visited Rahway State Prison in New Jersey. There they came face-to-face with the truth about prison life.

After hearing honest and passionate descriptions of prison violence, . . . these youngsters said that they had a different feeling about crime and violence.

It has been reported that 80 percent of the juveniles experiencing the Rahway program committed no more offenses. This figure was to have proved that indeed they had been "scared straight."

Recently, there was new approval of the Scared Straight method for reforming juvenile offenders. This was on a follow-up television program.

Wait a minute! For ages, efforts to reform youths by introducing . . . fear . . . or some terrible fate if they do not stay on the straight and narrow have met with limited success. Why is *this* method so successful?

Apparently, the success has been overstated. That is the conclusion of Dr. James O. Finchenauer and his co-workers at the Rutgers University School of Criminal Justice.

The Rutgers investigators followed eighty-one youngsters chosen to attend a session with the prisoners. They divided the group so that roughly half visited the prison. This was the experimental group. The other group did not visit the prison.

At first, the researchers were struck by a discovery. When the youths were judged according to a delinquency prediction scale, more than 70 percent of them were in the category of "low chance for delinquency."

Thus, the great majority of youths who were being introduced to the Scared Straight program already had a low chance for delinquency. Only 18 percent of the youths scored in the "high chance for delinquency" category.

The Rutgers researchers tested for attitude changes, before and after the Rahway experience, in both groups. Toward law, justice, police, punishment, and self-awareness, there were no important changes in differences between the two groups.

After its Rahway visit, the experimental group did shift slightly toward a more-favorable attitude toward obeying the law. But, strangely enough, the other group, without visiting the prison, improved its attitude toward obeying the law even more than the experimental group did.

A 6-month follow-up found that many more youths who did not attend the prison were offense-free than those who did.

The conclusion: the considerable positive public opinion surrounding the Scared Straight program is for the most part groundless. It is a product of too much hope, not of a well-thought-out strategy.

1. Who is Dr. James O. Finchenauer? What conclusion did he and his co-workers reach about *Scared Straight?*

2. Why did the Finchenauer group reach that conclusion?

3. What conclusion can be formed from the account on page 434? How does this differ from Finchenauer's view?

4. How would you go about conducting a critical examination of the material in both the accounts of the Scared Straight program? For example, what questions would you ask to get started?

5. Do you think this kind of program is worthwhile? Tell why or why not.

What Is Fair and Effective Punishment?
(determining cause-effect)

In the history section of this chapter, you read about some features of crime and punishment in nineteenth-century America. You have also learned that the Eighth Amendment to the Constitution forbids cruel or unusual punishments. But what makes punishment fair? When is it effective? Think about these questions as you read about six examples of punishment in the United States.

Example 1

Because prisons tend to turn young people and first offenders into hardened criminals, some law officers are trying to find ways to combine effective punishment with rehabilitation and service.

In Salem, Massachusetts, District Judge Samuel E. Zoll has set up a schedule of penalties for juvenile offenders. For turning in a false fire alarm, offenders get 80 hours of polishing fire engines. For slashing trees, they get 40 hours of planting seedlings in town parks. For vandalizing school property, offenders must wash school walls and write an essay on citizenship.

Example 2

In Multnomah County, Oregon, a middle-aged first offender caught stealing a $4.95 blouse was sentenced to work 30 hours at an adoption center.

Example 3

When a Phoenix, Arizona, doctor was convicted of illegally selling $40,000 worth of drugs to a state undercover agent, he faced from 5 years to life in prison. Instead, he was sentenced to 7 years of practicing medicine in Tombstone, Arizona. The town had not had a doctor of its own for 4 years.

Example 4

In Miami, a postal worker convicted of manslaughter after running a red light, hitting another car, and killing the driver was not sent to prison. Instead, the judge sentenced him to probation for 5 years and a fine of $1,500 for each year. The money is to go into a special trust fund for the young child of the dead man. The convicted man also has two small children and, on his salary, the $125-a-month payments will be a strain. But if he had been sent to prison, his family would have had to manage without any of his salary. The dead man's family would not have benefited, either.

Example 5

An 18-year-old high school senior from Phoenix, Arizona, was found guilty in an $85 liquor-store robbery. He was sentenced to 5 years probation. Of that time, 2 years were to be spent in college.

The judge included the college sentence as part of the probation at the request of the youth's sister. She was an athletic coach at Phoenix Union High School.

The judge said, "He has his family's support and outside support to see that he makes it. I think all he needs is a little kick."

Example 6

One judge in the state of Washington believes punishment should fit the crime. He also believes that the judicial system should teach offenders something about life.

That is why he sentenced a dentist in a traffic death case to spend a day each week for a year fixing the teeth of the aged and the poor without charge. And he made a carpenter in a drug case agree to provide free maintenance and repair work for the elderly.

The carpenter, who pleaded guilty to possession of cocaine, was being taught a lesson. "I was trying to teach him that drugs tear down society because it reduces the work force," said the judge.

6. What were the offenses committed and the punishments handed out in the following:
   a. Example 1
   b. Example 2
   c. Example 3
   d. Example 4
   e. Example 5
   f. Example 6

7. Do you think those punishments were fair? Tell why or why not.

8. For examples 1–6, how can the term *cause* be applied to what the judge had to consider in each case before deciding on a sentence?

9. For examples 1–6, how could the sentences for those crimes be an *effect*?

American Opinion about Punishment: A Poll

In 1980, the Associated Press and NBC News polled 1,599 adults across the nation. The poll dealt with American attitudes toward the harshness of prison life. The results of that poll are shown in the following graphs.

10. What were the poll results in response to the question: How harsh are our prison systems?

11. What were the poll results in response to the question: What should the main purpose of prisons be?

12. What do you think makes *any* punishment effective?

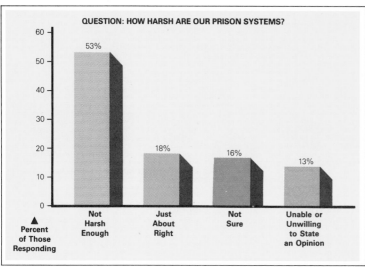

SOURCE: Associated Press

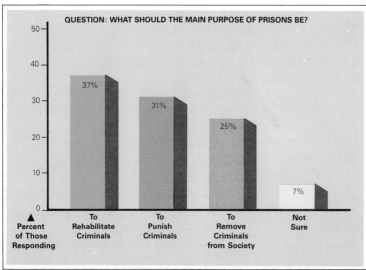

SOURCE: Associated Press

17 Civil Law

It was a fine spring morning. Harold Flores was eager to get to the park for softball practice. He took the steps two at a time—down four flights of stairs and out the door. But he went no farther. A flowerpot fell on Harold's head, hospitalizing him for 2 weeks.

The flowerpot had fallen from Ralph Harrison's fifth-floor window ledge. Ralph had accidentally bumped against the pot, which caused it to fall on Harold.

This fictional case is like many cases that end up in court. Someone was hurt. Someone else caused the hurt. But no crime was involved. There was no law against keeping flowerpots on window ledges. Thus, the state did not take Ralph to court, as it would have done in a criminal case. It was up to Harold and his parents to start a court case—and that is exactly what happened. The Flores family wanted money for paying Harold's medical bills.

The case of *Flores v. Harrison* was filed in civil court, because a dispute between two individuals or groups of individuals falls under civil law. What civil law is and how it works will be covered in this chapter.

I. The basics of civil law
  A. What is civil law?
  B. Contracts
    1. The offer
    2. The acceptance

3. The consideration
4. Oral and written contracts
5. Will a court uphold the contract?
C. Torts
  1. Unintentional torts

Words to Know

civil law —— the type of law that deals with private disputes

contract —— a form of agreement that binds people to do things (A contract must involve an offer, an acceptance, and a consideration.)

offer —— a promise to give something to or do something for someone else in exchange for something else.

offeror —— someone who makes an offer

consideration —— something of value that is exchanged as the result of a contract

oral contract —— a contract made by agreement, with nothing in writing

void —— unenforceable; not legally binding

tort —— a wrongful action that causes someone harm; sometimes called a *civil wrong*

negligent —— failing to take the care that a reasonable person would take

liable —— legally responsible (For example, if you are liable for damages, you are legally responsible for paying for those damages.)

strict liability —— a legal responsibility that exists whether one is negligent or not

battery —— hitting or touching another person in an offensive way

assault —— threatening someone in such a way as to make that person fear that you are about to commit battery

defamation —— spreading false information that harms a person's reputation

slander —— defamation by word of mouth

community property —— property that belongs equally to wife and husband

grounds for divorce —— the reasons that must be present before the state will permit a divorce

annulment —— a court ruling that a marriage never legally existed at all

divorce —— a legal proceeding that ends a marriage

alimony —— support payments given by one spouse—husband or wife—to the other after a legal separation or divorce

legal separation —— a formal, court-arranged separation of a married couple, generally granted when there are grounds for divorce

child abuse —— the physical or mental mistreatment of a child

The Basics of Civil Law

What Is Civil Law?

There are two major divisions of our system of laws in the United States—civil law and criminal law. Criminal law, as we have seen, is the type of law that deals with crimes. **Civil law** helps to determine the rights and duties of each of the individuals in a private dispute. Did Ralph have a duty to be careful with his flowerpots? Did Harold's family have a right to be paid for their medical expenses? These are the kinds of questions that civil courts answer.

You should note two major differences between civil and criminal cases:

1. In a criminal case, it is always the government that starts court action. But civil cases can be filed by an individual, a group of individuals, a business, or a government.

2. A criminal case has one main goal: to punish a wrongdoer. A civil case may

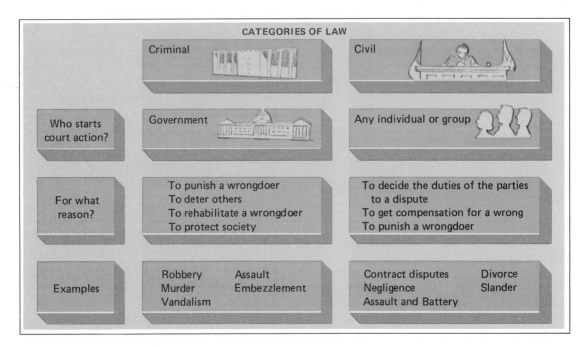

CATEGORIES OF LAW		
	Criminal	Civil
Who starts court action?	Government	Any individual or group
For what reason?	To punish a wrongdoer To deter others To rehabilitate a wrongdoer To protect society	To decide the duties of the parties to a dispute To get compensation for a wrong To punish a wrongdoer
Examples	Robbery　　Assault Murder　　Embezzlement Vandalism	Contract disputes　　Divorce Negligence　　Slander Assault and Battery

When one of these two women offered to sell the other her movie projector, she took the first step in any contract agreement. Because this agreement was made between friends, their contract was oral.

have a number of goals. One is to decide the duties or rights of the individuals in a dispute. Another is to compensate, or pay back, the injured party for a wrong. A third is to punish someone for a wrong.

Civil law covers a wide variety of cases. In this chapter, we will deal with three particular varieties: cases involving contracts, cases involving wrong—as in the case of the falling flowerpot—, and cases involving family duties.

Contracts

Martha had the best collection of eight-track tapes of anyone in her school. She decided to sell twenty rock-music tapes to get money for a bicycle. She told Celeste, "If you'd like my twenty rock tapes, I'll sell them to you for $50." Celeste jumped at the chance. She paid Martha $5 and promised to bring the rest of the money the next day. Martha agreed. But overnight, she had a change of heart. She told Celeste the next day that she had decided not to sell the tapes.

Martha and Celeste might end up in court over the matter. Many civil law cases arise out of disagreements between people over acts that should have been done but were not done, and over things that were promised but not delivered. Martha and Celeste had made a contract. It was legally binding, even though they had not signed any papers or consulted a lawyer.

A **contract** is a form of agreement that binds people to do things. To be legally binding, a contract must result from a clear understanding between two or more people. It must include three things: an offer, an acceptance, and a consideration. Let's examine the case of Martha and Celeste to see what these terms mean.

The Offer Martha made an offer by saying that she would sell the tapes to Celeste in exchange for $50. An **offer** is a promise to give something to someone in exchange for something else. Martha is known as the **offeror**—the person who makes the offer.

An offeror may place conditions on an offer. For example, Martha might have said: "I'll sell you my tapes for $50. But Jim wants them if you don't. You'll have to let me know by 8 o'clock tonight." In that situation, the offer would have a condition: a time limit. If Celeste did not contact Martha by 8 o'clock, the offer would no longer be in effect.

By making an offer, Martha is committing herself to carrying out the deal if Celeste accepts. This can lead to problems. Suppose that Celeste is undecided and says, "I'll call you tonight and let you know." On the way home from school, Martha meets Rose and offers *her* the tapes. Rose eagerly accepts and gives Martha $50. Now suppose that when Martha arrives home from school, her mother gives her a message from Celeste: "I'll take the tapes. You'll get the money tomorrow." Celeste has accepted Martha's offer in good faith. Legally, a contract exists between the two girls. Now Martha is in trouble. She has made *two* contracts and she will be able to only keep one of them.

If Martha had put an advertisment in the school newspaper offering to sell the tapes for $50, the situation would be different. Technically, Martha would be asking *other* people to make an offer. Martha has only one set of tapes for sale, after all. She cannot sell that set more than once. Thus, she informs readers of the school newspaper that she plans to sell the tapes. In effect, she is inviting them to make an offer.

Suppose that Martha had said to Celeste: "I'm thinking about selling my tapes for $50. Would you be interested?" She would not be making an offer in the legal sense of the word. No contract could be made until there was a definite offer.

The Acceptance Celeste accepted Martha's offer by agreeing to pay $50 for the tapes. As soon as she accepted the offer, a contract existed. Celeste owed Martha $50. Martha owed Celeste the tapes.

But suppose that Celeste had said: "I'd like your tapes, but I think $50 is too much. I'll give you $40 for them." That is not an acceptance, since Celeste did not agree to the terms set by Martha. In legal terms, it is a *counteroffer*. Now it is up to Martha to accept or reject the counteroffer.

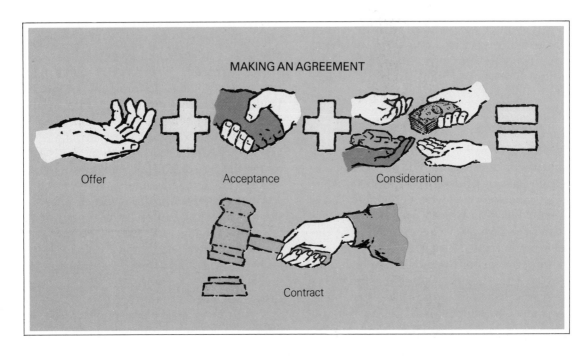

MAKING AN AGREEMENT

Offer   Acceptance   Consideration

Contract

We saw earlier that the person making an offer can place conditions on the offer. Martha might have said: "I'll sell you my tapes for $50 if you pay me right away." Since Celeste only had $5 at the time, she could not have accepted the offer.

An acceptance must be made while an offer is in effect. Let's suppose again that Martha met Rose after school and found out that Rose wanted to buy the tapes. Martha could call Celeste at once and say: "Hey, forget it. I'm taking back my offer. I'm selling the tapes to someone else." Martha has a right to withdraw her offer—as long as Celeste has not yet accepted it. Celeste cannot later claim that Martha backed out of a contract, since no contract ever existed.

The Consideration The third part of a contract is an exchange of something of value. This "something" is called the **consideration.** If there is no consideration, there is no contract.

Suppose that your uncle promises to give you a car when you become 16 years old. He does not ask anything in return.

Since there is no consideration, what he is offering you is a *gift*, not a contract. A promise of a gift is not legally enforceable. If you turn 16 and your uncle fails to give you the car, you cannot take the case to court. You have no legal right to the car.

But suppose that your uncle has a big farm in the country. He tells you that if you work for him every summer until you are 16, then he will buy you a car. You accept his offer and do the work. You and your uncle have entered into a contract. You are both giving up something of value: you are giving him your work, and he is giving you a car. These are considerations. When you become 16, you have a right to the car that he offered you. If he does not give it to you, you can take the case to court.

In the case of Martha and Celeste, Martha's consideration was a set of tapes. Celeste's was $50.

A consideration must be something that is given up now or in the future. It cannot be something that has already been given up. For example, suppose that you have helped a neighbor pull weeds for sev-

With the shaking of hands, the offer of selling the movie projector reaches its second stage—acceptance. Once acceptance has taken place, the offer may not be withdrawn.

eral years. Last fall, she told you that she appreciated your help and would give you her power tiller for your years of help. You had visions of earning money this year by tilling other people's gardens. But last week, you had a quarrel with the neighbor. Now she refuses to give you the tiller. Did a contract exist, giving you a right to the tiller? The answer is "No." The offer of the tiller was a gift, because you were not asked to give a present or future consideration. Your neighbor has no legal duty to give you the tiller.

For you to make a legal contract, you must give a consideration that is rightfully yours to give. For example, suppose that your parents offer to pay you $500 if you do not use alcohol before you are 21. You avoid drinking, and when you reach 21, you ask for the money. They refuse to give it to you. Can you sue them? You cannot sue if your state's laws say that it is illegal for someone under 21 to use alcohol. You had no right to drink alcohol and, therefore, were not giving a consideration.

Oral and Written Contracts Obviously, a contract does not have to be written down. It may either be oral or written. **Oral contracts**—contracts with nothing in writing—are sufficient for many of our daily activities. Suppose that you order a hamburger at a lunch counter. Neither you nor the person taking the order signs a written agreement, but you have entered into a contract.

Oral contracts are not always adequate, however. To have a contract enforced by a court, you must be able to prove that it exists. It may be your word against someone else's.

In some matters, the law *requires* that a contract be in writing. This is true of contracts for the sale of land and for the sale of stocks and bonds. Also, most states require that a contract be in writing if it involves more than $500 or if it is to last for more than 1 year.

But a written contract, too, has certain weaknesses. You should be aware that if a contract is in writing, *only* what is written down is part of the contract. In most instances, oral promises made by either party are not enforceable.

Let's say that you sign a contract to have your home treated against termites. The contract states that the termite-proofing is guaranteed only so long as the soil within 12 inches of the house is left undisturbed. You say, "Oh, but can't I have my flower beds there?" The salesperson waves a hand reassuringly and says: "Oh, sure. Don't worry about the legal language."

You go ahead and plant your flower beds. Does the guarantee protect your house? Do not be too sure. The salesperson's oral statement to you would not be taken into account by a court. The court would assume that the contract was complete as written.

Will a Court Uphold the Contract? Sometimes a court will refuse to uphold a contract. Here are two reasons why a court might declare an agreement to be **void**, or unenforceable:

1. It is not legally a contract at all. One or more of the three essential parts—an offer, an acceptance, and a consideration—is missing.

2. The contract is illegal. For example, two business firms might agree to divide up a territory. Under antitrust laws, such an agreement is illegal. A court would not enforce the contract.

Such contracts are void from the start. Other contracts are defective and may be voided at one party's request. These are known as *voidable* contracts. Here are some examples:

1. A contract is made by a person who is not legally sane or who is under the influence of alcohol.

2. A contract was made unwillingly—for example, under threat of violence.

3. A contract was brought about by fraud. Let's say that John Applegate sells his 3-year-old snowmobile to Peter Friendly. John says that the vehicle has a recently-rebuilt engine. Peter later discovers that it has the original engine, which works poorly. He can sue to cancel the contract because John used fraud.

4. In certain situations, a contract that is made by a minor—someone who is not legally an adult—is voidable. The legal position of minors will be discussed later on in this chapter.

You should note that a voidable contract can only be voided by one party—the insane person, the victim of force or fraud, or the minor. The other party has no reason for voiding the contract.

Torts

The case of the falling flowerpot that opened this chapter is an example of a *civil wrong.* Ralph Harrison was responsible for a flowerpot's falling on Harold Flores's head. This caused Harold and his family pain, suffering, and expense. This led them to sue Ralph for *damages*—that is, for money to pay them back for their troubles.

The legal term for a civil wrong is a **tort.** The word comes from the same Latin root that the word *torture* comes from. The Latin root means "twisted." A tort is a wrongful action that causes someone harm.

Torts come in three main forms:

Unintentional Torts The Flores' lawsuit accused Ralph of an unintentional tort. Ralph did not intend to make the flowerpot fall on Harold's head. It was an accident. But it would not have happened if Ralph had not placed flowerpots on the window ledge and bumped against one of them. Ralph was careless. In legal terms, he was *negligent.* The court ordered Ralph to pay damages to Harold. An unintentional tort occurs when a defendant's negligence causes harm to a plaintiff.

How does a court go about deciding whether a defendant is negligent? The court has to consider whether the defendant took the care that a *reasonable person* would take in similar circumstances. A reasonable person is someone of normal intelligence who uses common sense and keeps control of her or his temper.

Let's say that you are riding your bicycle down a sidewalk and run into a woman. She falls down and breaks her leg. When she is released from the hospital, she files a civil lawsuit. The suit asks a court to order you to pay her damages. The court will probably ask for a certain amount of money for medical expenses, plus money to replace the woman's loss of earnings during the time she was away from work, plus an additional amount for the pain and suffering that you caused her.

At the trial, it will be the woman's responsibility to prove two things. First, she must show that your action—or failure to act—caused her harm. Second, she must

Under our laws, the owner of this dog will be liable if the pet bites the passerby shown in this photo.

show that you were negligent. This means that she must convince the judge or jury that you did not exercise the care that a resonable person would normally exercise while riding a bicycle. Since you are a minor, *reasonable person* means someone your age—not necessarily a "reasonable adult."

What if you claimed that you hit the woman for the following reason: you ran over a broken bottle on the sidewalk and a tire blew out on your bicycle, causing you to lose control? A number of things would have to be considered. Would a reasonable teenager ride on the sidewalk in the first place? The answer is probably not. Is it illegal to ride a bicycle on the sidewalk in your community? If so, you would be considered negligent. Would a reasonable teenager be going slowly enough to stop when he or she saw glass? The answer is probably. Would a reasonable teenager slow down when approaching a person on a narrow sidewalk? Yes, she or he would. In other words, it would seem that the women has a strong case in accusing you of negligence.

If you are *not* negligent, you are not **liable**, or legally responsible. Let's say that you left your bike at a public parking stand along a sidewalk. A woman walked into your bike, fell, and broke a leg. You would not be liable because a reasonable person would expect to be able to park at a bicycle stand. However, the woman might be able to recover damages from whoever it was who placed a parking stand on the sidewalk to begin with.

Strict Liability In certain tort cases, you might be held liable even if you were not negligent. This is because of a legal rule known as **strict liability.**

Many states make owners of pets strictly liable for damage done by their pets. Let's say that you keep your dog in a fenced-in yard. A child carelessly leaves your gate open, and the dog gets out. The dog bites another child. Even though you yourself were not negligent, you would still be liable for the harm done by your dog.

If you carry on dangerous activities, you may also be held strictly liable for an accident in which you were not negligent. Let's say that you operate a construction company. You use dynamite to blast through rock. The blast shatters glass in a nearby house. Even though you took reasonable precautions to avoid accidents, you would be liable for damages to the house.

Another example of strict liability involves the safety of products made by a manufacturer. In recent years, laws and court interpretations have used the concept of strict liability to help protect consumers. For example, suppose that you buy a ladder. A rung gives way, causing you to fall and suffer injuries. You may be able to recover damages, even without proving the maker of the ladder to be negligent.

Intentional Torts Sometimes a person's deliberate actions can cause another person harm. These are intentional torts. It

Should someone fall over this bicycle left in the walk way, its owner will be liable due to negligence.

does not matter whether or not a defendant intended to harm another person. What does matter is that the defendant could reasonably be expected to know that a certain action *might* harm someone else.

Let's say that Oscar is a practical joker. He thinks that it would be cute to scare Harriet, a fellow worker. He places a large spider in her handbag. Harriet opens the bag to pay for her lunch. When she sees the spider, she jumps back and knocks over a pot of hot coffee, receiving severe burns. Oscar would be liable for damages. He should have been aware of the potential dangers of his act, even though he could not have known just when Harriet would open her handbag.

Some intentional torts may be both a civil wrong and a crime. Assault and battery are two examples. Note that word *two*. There is a clear distinction between assault and battery, although the two offenses often occur together.

Battery occurs when one person hits or touches another person in such a way as to be offensive. If you strike someone on the nose, you are committing battery. If you pinch someone's arm, that is battery. If you kiss someone against his or her will, that is also battery. A battery may also occur even though you do not actually touch a person's body. For example, if you rip an item of clothing off a person or knock something from the person's hand, you are committing battery.

Battery does not occur if the "victim" consents to the battery. If a boy puckers up his lips and closes his eyes, he cannot later claim that the girl who kissed him committed battery. If you join in a boxing match, you cannot accuse your opponent of battery.

Assault occurs when one person threatens another in such a way as to cause fear that a battery is about to occur. Even if you take a punch at someone and miss, you are committing assault. The person right-

Is an assault taking place here? If there is reason to believe battery will follow, the answer is yes.

fully feared that you were going to hit her or him. If you swerve your bicycle toward a man, making him fear that you are trying to hit him, then you are committing assault. If you then actually hit him intentionally, you are committing both assault and battery.

For assault to take place, a person must reasonably fear that you intend to harm him or her. Suppose that you stand in your back yard and wave your fist at the man next door. That is not an assault, because you could not hit him from where you stand. But let's say that you angrily point a gun at the neighbor, and he thinks that the gun is loaded. In that situation, you have committed assault.

In a case of assault or battery, criminal charges may be filed by the authorities. But the victim may also file suit in civil court to recover damages. A person may recover damages even if the person did not suffer actual physical harm.

What about someone who tries to protect himself or herself against an attack? What if a bully takes a poke at you and you hit the bully back? Have you committed battery? No, you have only fought back in self-defense. But self-defense can only occur when you are trying to avoid actual physical harm to yourself or to your family. Also, you must not use unreasonable force. You could not, for example, shoot someone who punched you in the mouth. If you did, you would be committing battery. As a general rule, you cannot use any greater force for self-defense than your attacker is using against you.

Another kind of intentional tort is called **defamation.** That means spreading false information that harms another person's reputation.

For example, Jane's former boyfriend, Nat, sees Jane drinking a soda with Phillip. Nat spreads a false rumor about Phillip. Many people who hear the rumor believe it and begin to avoid Phillip. Jane also stops seeing him. In this situation, Nat has defamed Phillip. Because Nat spread the rumor by word of mouth, his action is called **slander.** If he had published the rumor in a newspaper or announced it on television, his action would have been called **libel.**

In order to collect damages for defamation, you must be able to show that the information is false. You must also show that it caused you actual harm—for example, the loss of a job or the loss of friends. In addition, you must show that the information was spread to at least one other person. You would not be defamed if you were the only one who heard a person make a false statement about you.

Family Law

Civil law affects not only our actions outside the home, but also those actions that involve our families. Among the aspects of family life that are controlled by civil laws are marriage, divorce, and the duties of parents and children toward each other.

Most laws about family life are state laws, and the laws often differ from state to

state. Thus, the examples given in this section may or may not apply to the state in which you live.

Marriage Technically, marriage is a contract between two people. But it is unlike other contracts. Each state has regulations to control who may legally marry and how they must go about marrying. All states require that the couple have a marriage license.

Portia and Gene were both 17 when they suddenly decided to get married. They were afraid that their parents would be opposed, so they drove to a nearby town to be married. Then, their troubles began.

Portia and Gene went to a courthouse to apply for a marriage license. First, they discovered that they could not get the license without a blood test. This is to make sure that neither person has a disease that can be passed on to the other person. They also learned that there was a 3-day waiting

By getting married, this couple is entering into a legal and binding contract with each other.

period for a license. (Some states have no waiting period, while others have a waiting period of 4 or 5 days.)

But even after a waiting period, Portia and Gene could not be married. At 17, they were old enough to marry—but only with their parents' consent. If they wanted to marry without that consent, they would have to wait for a year. Only Mississippi allows a 17-year-old couple to marry without parental consent. In some states, a couple—or at least the man—must be 21.

Marriage laws have changed greatly over the years. At one time, the husband was superior in the marriage. He owned all the property. He decided where the family was to live. If he thought it necessary, he could "discipline" the wife by not letting her out of the house.

But those days are over. In many ways, the partners in a marriage are now equal before the law. Many states have **community-property** laws, which say that both husband and wife are equal owners of all family property acquired during the marriage—gifts and inheritances not included, however. Wives can now borrow money and make contracts—two rights that were once denied them. But husbands and wives are not completely equal. In many states, the husband is still considered to be the head of the family. He is responsible for seeing that the family is properly fed, clothed, and housed.

Ending a Marriage When a marriage breaks down, a couple cannot just decide to end it. The state must first grant its permission, and it will do so only on certain conditions. Each state decides for itself what **grounds,** or reasons, **for divorce** are required for ending a marriage. It is up to a civil court to determine whether those conditions have been met.

Marriages can be ended in two ways. One way to end a marriage is by **annulment.** An annulment is a court ruling that a marriage never legally existed in the first

place. Having a marriage annulled is similar to having a contract declared void.

A more common procedure for ending a marriage is **divorce.** A divorce is a legal proceeding that usually includes a decision about how to divide up the property of the couple. It also determines which parent will keep the children, how the costs of rearing the children should be shared, and whether either parent is entitled to **alimony.** Alimony is support payments that are given by one spouse to another to help her or him meet living expenses. In the past, alimony was usually paid by husbands to former wives who did not have jobs. Now many women have jobs, and men sometimes receive alimony.

Sometimes a couple decides to stop living together but does not want to put a formal end to the marriage. In that case, the husband and wife may seek a **legal separation.** This is a court order recognizing that the couple is no longer living together. It can generally be granted only when there are grounds for divorce.

The Duties of Parents Parents have certain legal duties toward their children until those children become adults. One duty is to supply the children's needs—food, shelter, and clothing. Another is to supervise the children so that they do not cause harm to themselves or to others. Still another duty of parents is to see that the children obey school-attendance laws. If parents do not meet their responsibilities, the state can do something about it.

Take the case of Gloria and Walter, for example. They had two children, aged 2 and 6. Neither Gloria nor Walter had a job. What little money they did manage to obtain went mostly for alcohol. Neighbors noticed that the two children were always dirty, had open sores on their bodies, and often seemed hungry. One Saturday night, Gloria took the 2-year-old, who was unconscious, to the hospital. A doctor noticed bruises all over the child's body. An investi-

A parent-teacher conference is one way parents fulfill their legal duties toward their children.

order a child removed from the parents' control and placed in a foster home. Criminal charges may also be filed against the parents.

=============== REVIEW ===============

1. What are two differences between a criminal case and a civil case?
2. Give an example of a contract that *must* be in writing.
3. What two things must a plaintiff prove in order to collect damages in a negligence suit?
4. What are three duties that parents have toward their children?
5. Do you think that it is fair to hold the owners of pets strictly liable for damages caused by their pets? Why or why not?

gation found that Walter had become drunk and had thrown the child against the wall.

Unfortunately, such cases of **child abuse**—the physical or mental mistreatment of a child—are far from rare. All states now require doctors and others to report cases of child abuse. A court may then

Words to Know

small-claims court —— a court that handles civil cases involving small amounts of money, usually without a need for lawyers

arbitration —— a method of settling disputes by submitting them to a person who

These parents have many legal obligations to their children. In addition to feeding, clothing, and sheltering them, they must see that their offspring know wrong from right and do not harm either themselves or others.

is agreed upon by both parties to the dispute

arbitrator —— a person who hears and decides arbitration cases

binding arbitration —— an arbitration in which both sides accept the arbitrator's decision as final and binding

nonbinding arbitration —— an arbitration in which either side is free to reject the arbitrator's decision and take the case to court

Settling Disputes in Civil Cases

Civil disputes can be settled in a number of ways. Some are quite formal, involving lawyers, judges, juries, and so forth. Others are more informal.

Suppose that a person named Ronnie Robineau has had a number of disputes involving civil law. The ways in which they might have been handled follow.

Civil Court

Ronnie and his 18-year-old son were waiting on a street corner for a light to change. A car and a bread van collided in front of them. The van exploded. A piece of metal struck the boy and killed him. An investigation showed that the explosion was caused by a can of gasoline that was being carried beside the van's driver. Ronnie filed suit in his state's District Court. He sought $1 million in damages from the driver of the van and the bread company that employed the driver. The suit alleged that the defendants had been negligent by carrying gasoline in a can inside the van.

Ronnie's case was heard in the civil division of the court. This case differed from a criminal case in several ways. There was no prosecuting attorney representing the state. The object was not to prove guilt, but to prove negligence and the amount of loss. The jury did not have to be certain "beyond a reasonable doubt." It only had to decide whether or not most of the evidence was on Ronnie's side.

Ronnie hired a lawyer, and so did the van driver and the bread company. Expert witnesses were called by both sides. One was a doctor who discribed the victim's injuries. Another was a specialist who told how much money the boy might have earned in his job as a mechanic if he had lived to retirement age. Another witness was an explosives expert. This expert described the danger of carrying gasoline in cans.

Ronnie won a 500,000-dollar judgment. His lawyer's fee took 30 percent of that amount. It is common for plaintiffs' lawyers in tort cases to receive a percentage of the damages. If they lose the case, on the other hand, the lawyers often receive nothing at all.

The expense of a suit in civil court is a big drawback. A plaintiff who is not absolutely sure of winning a case may hesitate before filing such a suit. Appeals by one side or the other may add to the expense. Thus, other solutions to legal disputes are sometimes sought.

Small-Claims Court

Many states have established special courts to try civil cases involving small amounts of money. These are called **small-claims courts**. Typically, they handle cases in which a plaintiff seeks $300 or less. Neither the plaintiff nor the defendant needs a lawyer in small-claims court. There may also be no charge for court costs, which can run into thousands of dollars in a civil court case.

Ronnie filed a suit against his landlord in small-claims court. Ronnie lived in an apartment building. A pipe on the floor above him had burst, sending water flooding down through Ronnie's ceiling and damaging a sofa. The landlord had refused to pay the $250 for repairing the sofa. A judge decided that the repairs were only worth $200, but held the landlord responsible. Ronnie received his $200.

Besides being less expensive, small-claims court has several advantages over civil court. It is often more convenient, holding evening sessions that make it easier for people who work in the daytime. Also, it does not use the formalities of regular courts.

Family Court

Most states provide a family court, or domestic court, to deal with problems involving marriage and divorce. One day, Ronnie Robineau received a summons to

Couples like the one below often have their marital disputes settled in state domestic courts.

appear in family court the following Tuesday.

Ronnie had been divorced several years earlier. As part of the divorce, Ronnie had taken custody of his son. His former wife, Sue, had taken custody of their two daughters. The settlement called for Ronnie to pay $100 a month to help support each of the girls until the age of 18. When Ronnie fell behind in his payments, Sue brought suit in family court. A judge ordered Ronnie to pay $40 extra each month until he had made up the difference.

What happens if Ronnie will not—or cannot—pay? The court could order Ronnie's employer to pay part of Ronnie's wages directly to Sue. This would not happen in Ronnie's case, however, since Ronnie has no employer. He owns his own business. A court might take certain types of property away from Ronnie. As a last resort, the court might order him to go to jail for disobeying a court order.

Arbitration

As a machine-shop owner, Ronnie has signed many contracts. He signed contracts when he ordered supplies, when he made sales, and when he hired workers. In many of these contracts, he put a clause stating that any contract dispute, or argument, would be submitted to **arbitration.** Arbitration is a method of settling disputes by giving them to a person—an **arbitrator**— who is agreed upon by both parties to the dispute. Arbitration is often quicker than going to court and much less expensive. Millions of contracts—including insurance policies and labor-management disputes— have clauses requiring that any dispute be submitted to **binding arbitration.** This means that the decision of the arbitrator is binding on both parties. The losing side cannot appeal the ruling to a regular court.

There was a binding-arbitration clause in the contract between Ronnie and the union that represented the workers in his shop. Ronnie fired one worker for coming in late 3 days in a row. The union claimed that the firing violated its contract. Thus, the two sides submitted the dispute to arbitration. They found an arbitrator through the American Arbitration Association—a private arbitration organization. The arbitrator decided that Ronnie had acted too quickly in firing the worker. The absences had been caused by family difficulties, and the worker promised to be on time in the future. Because Ronnie had accepted binding arbitration, the worker was rehired.

Arbitration is the idea behind a new system of neighborhood justice centers that is being tried out in cities such as Kansas City, Atlanta, and Los Angeles. These centers seek to arbitrate disputes between neighbors that might otherwise be taken to court. Court officials refer people with problems to the neighborhood centers. If both sides to the dispute agree to it, then the center assigns an arbitrator to hear the case. Often, the arbitrator's ruling is accepted by both sides. But in these cases, the ruling does not have to be accepted. If one party still wants to take the case to court, she or he may do so. This type of arbitration is commonly known as **nonbinding arbitration.**

─────── REVIEW ───────

1. What is one disadvantage of taking a case to civil court?

2. What is one advantage of taking a case to small-claims court?

3. Give an example of a case that could *not* be taken to small-claims court.

4. Give an example of a case that might be handled by a family court.

5. Do you think that it is fair to put a person in jail for falling behind in making support payments after a divorce? Why or why not?

Words to Know

minor ──── a juvenile; someone who has not reached the legal age of adulthood

emancipated minor ──── a minor who no longer has a legal duty to his or her parents and whose parents are also freed of legal duties toward the minor

Juveniles and Civil Law

In most respects, civil law applies to juveniles in the same way that it applies to adults. But juveniles do get special treatment in some situations. In civil law, juveniles are usually referred to as **minors.** A minor is anyone who has not reached the legal age of adulthood—18 years of age in most states.

Contracts

Marianne had been eyeing a stereo in the window of a store for several weeks. A sign beside the set promised: "Easy Terms, $25 Down." Marianne went into the store one afternoon with savings from her weekend job and put down $25. "I'd like to buy that stereo," she said.

Marianne signed a contract that required her to pay $15 a week for 30 weeks. The stereo was delivered the next day. It was a big surprise to Marianne's parents. They sat down with her for a long talk. They pointed out that a large part of what Marianne was paying would be interest—a fee for the money that the store was loaning her. They urged her to take back the stereo and save her money in a bank instead. In a couple of months, she could pay cash for a stereo.

After thinking it over, Marianne decided to follow her parents' advice. The stereo would cost less this way. Besides, she thought, the quality of the sound was not

Should this shopper wish to break the contract she signs to buy this stereo receiver, her ability to do so rests on whether she is or is not under the legal age of adulthood in her state.

what she had expected. She realized that it would have been better to shop around before buying.

If Marianne had been an adult, the store might have refused to take back the stereo. But as a minor, Marianne had the right to back out of the contract. An adult does not have the same right. If a minor makes a contract with an adult—as Marianne did—, the minor may cancel the contract. But the adult may not. Under the law, minors are not considered to have enough experience to make mature judgments. Marianne had not realized how much of her money would go for interest. An adult would have been expected to know more about what she or he was becoming involved in.

What if Marianne had lied about her age? Would it make any difference if the salesperson thought that Marianne was already 18? No, it would not. Marianne could still cancel the contract.

There are one or two exceptions to this rule. If a minor enters into a contract to buy necessities, the minor may be required to fulfill the contract. Necessities include food, shelter, and clothing. In addition, a marriage contract is binding on a minor.

Torts

Aaron was a lively 4-year-old who spent most of his waking moments on a tricycle. One evening, he left his tricycle on the sidewalk when his mother called him to dinner. A neighbor, Mr. Billings, tripped over the tricycle in the dim light of dusk and broke a leg. Could Mr. Billings sue Aaron for negligence?

He could sue Aaron, but he would not win the case. Mr. Billings would have to prove that Aaron had not taken the care expected of a reasonable person. But since Aaron is only 4, he can only be expected to be a reasonable 4-year-old. Traditionally, children under the age of 7 are not liable for negligence.

In other words, the law expects a minor to be only as reasonable as a normal person of the same age. A minor is not usually expected to be as reasonable as an adult. (Note that Mr. Billings's might sue Aaron's *parents* for being negligent by not supervising their son's activities.)

In some situations, however, minors *are* expected to meet adult standards. This is so when minors are engaged in adult activities. Driving a car is such an activity.

Flying an airplane and operating a boat are also adult activities.

Even with the special protection of the law, minors are sometimes sued for negligence—and sometimes they lose. What happens if a minor must pay damages of $2,000, but has no bank account and no earnings? Do the minor's parents have to pay? They do not have to pay, unless the parents themselves are also found negligent. But any money that the minor earns or is given during the next 10 years after the decision may have to go toward satisfying the damages.

Family Law

Just as parents have legal duties toward their children, children also have duties toward their parents. In most families, these duties are worked out informally between parents and children and the law has no occasion to intrude. But that is not always so. To understand this better, let's examine two families.

The Millers are an "ideal" family. Sharon, 12, and Ted, 14, get along well with their parents. Since both Mr. and Mrs. Miller have jobs, Sharon and Ted do much of the household work. They did not object because they knew their help was needed.

Sharon was unhappy when her parents asked her to stop seeing a boyfriend, Pete, but she obeyed. She realized that her parents were only doing what they thought best. Besides, Pete scared her sometimes with his rough ways.

Like all children, Sharon and Ted have a duty to obey their parents. They have a duty to perform services that their parents request. This is only fair, since their parents have a legal duty to give them food and shelter.

But the Holton family is not so happy together. Sometimes Carl, 17, and Margaret, 11, refuse even to speak to their parents for days. One weekend, Margaret ran away from home. Mrs. Holton called the police. After that, the Holtons "grounded" Margaret every weekend for 2 months.

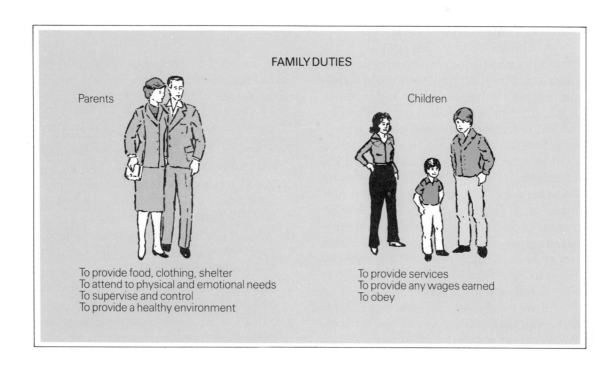

FAMILY DUTIES

Parents

To provide food, clothing, shelter
To attend to physical and emotional needs
To supervise and control
To provide a healthy environment

Children

To provide services
To provide any wages earned
To obey

Preparing a meal is just one of many duties these children may perform as part of their obligation to their mother and father.

Carl earned good money working evenings at a filling station. One day, Mr. Holton ordered Carl to turn over his earnings to him. Carl became really angry. When he had calmed down, Carl had a talk with a social service worker. He was shocked to learn that he had a legal duty to do as his father asked. "The old man doesn't give me his money, and I'm not about to give him mine," he shouted. Carl decided to ask his parents to let him be declared an **emancipated minor.** This meant that he would no longer have a legal duty to his parents. They, in turn, would be released from their duty to house and support Carl.

Some people become emancipated minors when they enlist in the armed services. The status of emancipated minor only effects the legal duties between the child and her or his parents. It does not change the minor's other legal duties or rights.

--- REVIEW ---

1. Why are minors' rights in making contracts different from adults' rights?

2. Could a person recover damages from a 6-year-old who caused an accident by being negligent? Explain.

3. What might happen to a minor who was sued for negligence, lost the suit, and had no money to pay?

4. What are two duties that children have toward their parents?

5. At what age do you think a person should legally be considered an adult?

How the United States Works

Claims Adjuster

Suppose you were walking along the street and a window-washer's bucket fell on your head. Could you sue the window-washing company or the building owner for the cost of your hospital bills? As you have seen, this kind of suit is often settled in civil court. After hearing the case, the judge decides who is at fault. That is the one who pays the bills. Most often, the company that is insuring the person or company at fault will pay the bill. Your family probably has hospital insurance. Most companies and property owners are protected by insurance against accidents.

When an accident takes place, a claim is made on the insurance company. The company then sends out a claims adjuster to investigate. The claims adjuster finds out just how great the loss was, who was at fault, and whether or not the accident is covered by the insurance. To do this, adjusters check bills, read reports, look at evidence, and question witnesses. The adjuster for the window washer, for example, would want to know if the bucket fell because you shook the ladder. Perhaps you walked inside a roped-off area. If so, the insurance company might not have to pay. A case only goes to court when two or more insurance companies cannot agree on who is at fault or how much money should be paid. With many of the claims that an adjuster investigates, the question of fault does not come up. People may want to recover money for flood damage or theft, or they may put in a claim for hospital bills when a new baby comes. In such instances, claims adjusters do not have to reconstruct the event. But they still have to check the insurance policy to go over any bills.

In most states, claims adjusters have to be licensed before they can be hired. To become licensed, they may have to be 20 or 21 years old. They usually have to pass a written test. A course in insurance adjusting may also be needed. These are the only educational requirements. However, insurance companies will usually hire a college graduate over a high-school graduate. Most adjusters make between $11,000 and $17,000 a year.

Reading About . . .

Parents, Children, and the Law ————————————————

What responsibility do parents have for controlling the actions of their children? What happens when the children's acts break some law? These questions have posed problems for people for hundreds of years.

As you read the following, think about the following questions:

● Do you think that a parent can realistically be expected to be responsible for all his or her children's acts?

● Is it fair to hold a parent responsible, especially if the child was doing something that she or he had been told not to do by the parent?

In most communities, children who break the law have only to stand before a judge and receive a stern talking-to. Their parents are legally obligated to pay for any damages. In some communities, however, the local law regarding minors is more strict. Parents there can be arrested as criminals for not properly supervising their children. That was exactly the situation the parents of Peter and Hillary Gable found themselves in when their 13-year-old son and 12-year-old daughter went on a shooting spree with their air rifles. One Saturday afternoon, the two decided they would rather shoot at targets that break and make noise than at the tin cans in their backyard. Before the afternoon was over, they had damaged more than one dozen car windows in their neighborhood. The repair cost was more than $1,000. At the trial, Harold Gable—the children's father and an accountant—and Anita Gable—their mother and a book editor—were convicted of misdemeanors and fined $100 each in addition to paying the damages. Their town is one of many that have passed "parental responsibility" laws over the past few years.

By community standards, the Gables are attentive, supportive parents. Harold spends one night a week working with Peter's boy scout troop as scoutmaster. In the summertime, Mr. Gable takes time out from his busy work schedule to supervise the troop on overnight outings. Anita Gable spends weekends with Hillary going to art museums, theater matinees, and films. She says she wants her daughter to be as well-rounded as she would have liked to have been when she was Hillary's age.

Neither of the Gables has any idea why their children shot holes in car windows. When Peter was 11, his father gave him a BB gun and taught him how to shoot it. When the boy turned 13 earlier this year, Mr. Gable gave him a more powerful gun but made him promise to use it only to shoot at cans in their backyard. When Hillary became jealous, Mr. Gable bought her an air gun as well and taught her just as he had taught his son. In the judge's opinion, the two children, who were out of school for the summer, simply grew bored playing in the backyard. In her own words, "Mischief got the best of them."

In finding the Gables guilty of negligence, local District Judge Martha Evers ruled that they had failed to meet the community's standards of parental responsibility. Six months later, Harold Gable admits he was wrong in allowing his children to own a weapon while they were still so young. "I guess you can't expect children their age to stick to their promises. And if that's the case, then you shouldn't be putting guns in their hands."

Fact Review

1. What is one important difference between a gift and a contract?
2. Give an example of an oral contract.
3. A contract may be declared void if it does not contain three specific parts. What are they?
4. Which of the following might be cases of assault and which might be cases of battery?
   a. Roger punches Tom in the nose.
   b. Harriet swings at Mary with an umbrella, but misses.
   c. Cecile aims a pistol at Dan.
   d. Phil grabs Mia's schoolbooks from her.
   e. Phyllis tries unsuccessfully to run over Todd with her dirt bike.
5. Let's say that Glenn walks up to Roger on the beach and accuses Roger of stealing a radio. What three conditions would be required for Roger to win damages for slander?

Developing Your Vocabulary

1. What is the difference between the terms in the following pairs?
   a. civil law and criminal law
   b. intentional tort and unintentional tort
   c. assault and battery
   d. slander and libel
2. Match the words in *a* to *d* with the phrases in *(1)* to *(4)*.
   a. consideration (1) something of value
   b. void (2) a wrongful action that harms someone else
   c. tort (3) not legally binding
   d. liable (4) legally responsible

Developing Your Reading Skills

Read the following paragraph and then answer the questions that follow:

Minors are given some special consideration in civil law. For example, a minor cannot usually be required to carry out a contract. Also, a minor who is sued for negligence does not have to meet as high a standard as an adult. On the other hand, minors face some special restrictions. For example, a minor may need to have parental permission to marry. Obviously, being a minor has its privileges and its drawbacks.

1. Which one of the following do you think is the main point, or main idea, of the paragraph above?
   a. Civil law treats minors differently from adults.
   b. A minor can be sued for negligence.
   c. Minors cannot usually be required to carry out contracts.
   d. Minors must get their parents' permission for many things.
2. Tell why you selected *a, b, c,* or *d* in question 1 above.

Developing Your Writing Skills— Forming and Supporting an Opinion

In this chapter, you have considered some ways in which civil law helps to handle disputes in our society. You have taken a look at contracts, torts, family law, and the special rules that apply to minors. Now consider the following:

Forming an opinion
1. What do you think life would be like if we did *not* have a system of civil law? In other words, is some kind of civil law necessary for any society?

Supporting an opinion
2. After thinking about those questions, write your opinion in a brief paragraph. Give reasons that support your opinion.

YOUR GOVERNMENT & ITS HISTORY

The Cherokee Nation Sues the State of Georgia

In this chapter, you have learned about civil law. Now you will read about two civil cases concerning the Supreme Court and rights claimed by the Cherokee Indians.

By 1827, the Cherokee Indians were the last large tribe remaining in the South. They had established farms and factories. They published a newspaper. They built schools for their children. Many Cherokees married whites and adopted English names. When they decided to set up their own state, they modeled it on the American states. In 1827, they wrote their own constitution. Treaties with the U.S. government dating back to 1791 had recognized the Cherokees as a nation.

Increasingly, more white settlers had moved into Georgia, as well as into other Southern states. The whites sought more land to set up cotton plantations. These settlers especially wanted lands belonging to the Cherokees and some smaller Indian tribes of the Southeast. They demanded that the federal and state governments move the Indians farther west.

The government of Georgia agreed with the whites. It outlawed tribal government. Georgia said it had the right to regulate the Cherokee state. The Cherokees believed that they had the right to establish their own government on the land that the federal government had given them. They appealed to the federal government for help. The federal government refused.

In 1829, gold was discovered in Cherokee lands. Miners and settlers rushed to claim these lands. They ignored the fact that the lands belonged to the Cherokees. A Georgia law was then passed that forbade the Cherokee council from meeting, except to give land to the whites.

On May 28, 1830, at the urging of President Andrew Jackson, Congress passed the Removal Bill. This law gave the President the power to exchange land west of the Mississippi River for territory still held in the Southeast by Indian tribes.

The Cherokees sought help in the federal courts, without success. The Supreme Court, ruled in 1831 that the Cherokees did not have the legal status of a foreign nation. This case is known as the *Cherokee Nation v. Georgia.*

In 1832, the Cherokees then filed another lawsuit that went to the Supreme Court, *Worcester v. Georgia.* Worcester, a Cherokee, had been sentenced to hard labor for living on what had been Cherokee territory without a permit. In the Court's decision, John Marshall ruled that Georgia had no right to interfere with the Cherokees:

> From the beginning of our government, Congress has passed acts to regulate trade and relations with the Indians. These acts treat them as nations, respect their rights, and show a firm purpose to give the protection that treaties offer. All these acts . . . clearly consider the several Indian nations as distinct political communities. These communities have territorial boundaries, within which their authority is complete. The Indians have a right to all lands within those boundaries. This is not only acknowledged, but guaranteed by the United States.
>
> The Cherokee Nation. . .occupies its own territory, with boundaries accurately described. Within these boundaries, the laws of Georgia can have no force, and the citizens of Georgia have no right to enter but with the permission of the Cherokees themselves in agreement with treaties and with the acts of Congress.

> The acts of Georgia are in direct violation of treaties . . . that mark out the boundary that separates the Cherokee country from Georgia. These acts guarantee to them all the land within their boundary, solemnly pledge the faith of the United States to stop their citizens from trespassing on it, and recognize the preexisting power of the Cherokee Nation to govern itself.

The Cherokees thought they had won. They were soon disappointed. Georgia protested the decision, and President Jackson refused to enforce it.

In 1835, a small group of Cherokee leaders were bribed into signing a treaty. This treaty gave up all remaining Cherokee land in the South. As a result, in 1838, the Cherokees started on their westward trek, now called the "Trail of Tears." On the trip to Oklahoma under U.S. Army guard, nearly a fourth of the Cherokees died of disease, starvation, and hardship. A small band of several hundred Cherokees did not go. They hid in the North Carolina mountains. Their descendants are known today as the Eastern Cherokees.

1. What was the main issue in the case of *Cherokee Nation v. Georgia?* What did the Supreme Court decide?
2. What was the main issue in the case of *Worcester v. Georgia?* What did the Supreme Court decide in this case?
3. Do you think a President should ever refuse to enforce a decision of the Supreme Court? Explain your answer.

SKILLS Developing your basic civic education skills

Cameras in Courtrooms
(conflicting viewpoints)

As you learned in Chapter 12, the Bill of Rights provides many guarantees to citizens. The First Amendment allows freedom of the press. The *press* includes newspapers, magazines, and television and radio stations. The Fifth Amendment guarantees a person accused of a crime a fair trial through due process of law. The Sixth Amendment gives anyone accused of a crime the right to a speedy trial before a jury. The Seventh Amendment guarantees the right to have any civil lawsuit involving more than $20 tried by a jury. Over the years, the states have included these rights in their own constitutions.

Sometimes the rights of one person can come into conflict with those of another. Such a conflict occurred in a Supreme Court case decided in 1981. The case was *Chandler v. Florida*. It involved the 1977 burglary conviction of two men from Miami Beach, Florida. They were convicted just after Florida had begun a year-long experiment in televising court cases. The rules for televising court cases allowed only one fixed television camera in the courtroom. No artificial lighting was allowed, nor could the jury ever be photographed. Members of the jury had to agree that the use of television would not influence their decision. The judge could have the camera shut off whenever he chose.

The local television stations showed only 2 minutes and 55 seconds of the entire trial. Nevertheless, the two con-victed burglars claimed that the use of television denied them the right to a fair trial. They appealed their case all the way to the Supreme Court.

The Supreme Court, in an 8–0 decision, ruled that the presence of cameras in a state courtroom does not automatically hurt a defendant's right to a fair trial. Instead, in future cases, the defendants will have to prove that they have been hurt by television coverage. The two defendants in the Florida case had not proved such damage to the Supreme Court. The Court also ruled that the states could continue to experiment with television coverage. It did *not* rule that camera crews had a First Amendment guarantee to televise state court proceedings. Also, the decision did not allow cameras in any federal courtrooms. This included the Supreme Court.

The Chandler decision meant that state courts could continue to experiment with television coverage of judicial proceedings. By the early 1980s, over thirty states were doing just that. The practice has its supporters and its critics. You will see this in the following accounts.

Some Arguments Opposed to the Use of Television Coverage of Trials

Frank White, columnist:

A reason generally used for forbidding media coverage in the

All arguments were adapted with permission from the San Antonio *Express* and the *Express-News*.

courtroom is that media reports will likely cause the public to be prejudiced about a trial. This would hurt a defendant's chances for a fair trial.

Lawmakers also say that media equipment and practices interfere with the proceedings.

Editorial, San Antonio *Express:*

Allowing TV or newspaper photographers into courtrooms does not serve justice.

Cameras, lights, and crews do not belong in courtrooms. They would be confusing. They could threaten witnesses. And the result would be a little piece on the 10 P.M. news or just another picture in a newspaper.

Courtrooms should be places not only of dignity but of justice. The noise and lights of news cameras would take away from both.

James Reston, columnist:

The argument against cameras is that although physical problems may be overcome, the psychological effects of their being there cannot be.

It is said that:

—They would be a confusing influence. They would make it more difficult to get the truth out of witnesses, whose powers of observing, remembering, and communicating are already limited under the emotional pressures of a courtroom.

—They would encourage jurors to think about themselves on camera rather than concentrate on the evidence. They would also tempt lawyers to play to the cameras rather than to the jury.

—They would open up the process of justice to a much wider audience. They would also, in many cases, if not most, give that audience a distorted picture of court activities.

For even in the most sensational cases, court activities are unbearably long and even dull. It is hard to imagine producers, who measure television time in seconds, accepting these tiresome arguments that usually decide guilt or innocence. They would rather concentrate on the few dramatic moments that seldom settle anything.

The general public would not get a true picture of the due process of law. They would just get a glimpse of the fireworks.

It is hard to argue that the cameras would increase the rights of the defendant by increasing the size of the audience.

And one assumption in the past was that the courts should decide cases on their merits, without being overly concerned as to how their decision would be received by the public.

Some Arguments Favoring the Use of Television Coverage of Trials

James Reston, columnist:

The argument for letting cameras into the courts is that they would enlarge the public's knowledge of the due process of law. It is pointed out that smaller television cameras can now operate without blinding light. Modern courtrooms can also contain television studios that are barely visible from the court chamber.

Frank White, columnist:

A Texas State judge said America's courtrooms will have to open their doors to the media. They must do this to erase the negative attitude the public has about judges and peace officers.

"It is not criticism any more," he said. "People are suspicious. The public does not understand us. People do not know the role each one of us plays in the system of justice. Yet, they are not to blame," he continued. "We must open up our courtrooms to the media—radio, television and press."

The judge said reporters and cameras should be permitted in courtrooms on all levels. He also said that a system should be found to keep them from confusing the proceedings.

"Opening up the courtrooms will not automatically eliminate this attitude," he said. "But it will put us under close watch of the media.

"Let us be dedicated . . . to give a dollar's worth of service for every tax dollar that is paid. Let us be dedicated to the principles upon which this great land was founded."

Letter to the editor, San Antonio *Express:*

Cameras in the courtroom . . . would unquestionably benefit the administration of justice.

Can there be any doubt that everyone involved in the courtroom process would be concerned about achieving perfection if the world were watching?

Certainly the trial lawyer is bound to prepare a case more completely than ever before. A more complete investigation of the facts and the law would be involved. The lawyer would stretch his or her talents to the fullest for a splendid opening statement to the jury. The same would be done at the end of the evidence. This would achieve not only a logical and brilliantly worded closing speech to the jury, but a moving one as well. All this would obviously benefit the client.

Also, the judge would be more completely prepared for the law of the case and for the necessary rulings during trial. The judge would know full well that the viewing audience would include other knowledgeable judges and lawyers who would be well able to recognize any errors.

The judge's speech on the law to the jury would be more carefully prepared. Dignity with proper respect for the court would certainly be seen to.

Careless witnesses would be more careful not to stray in their testimony for fear of exposure by some public viewer or listener. Also, experience teaches us that insincere witnesses, when off guard, are more likely to let the truth slip out. So, if distracted by the cameras, they are more likely to give the truthful answer.

Jurors would also be on their best behavior. And regardless of the effect of other pressures in this process, in the long run they would certainly be concerned to give the proper verdict.

Texas State District Judge Tom Cave:

> With advances in technology, such as the minicamera, television coverage may no longer be as interruptive. More advanced technical breakthroughs, such as unmanned camera systems, may provide an even better possibility for televised coverage.

1. What did the U.S. Supreme Court rule in *Chandler v. Florida?*

2. What are four arguments against the use of television coverage of trials?

3. What are four arguments for the use of television coverage of trials?

4. What do you think is the main point of the cartoon below?

5. What press freedom is guaranteed by the First Amendment?

6. Describe the trial rights guaranteed by the following amendments:

a. the Fifth Amendment
b. the Sixth Amendment
c. the Seventh Amendment

7. Suppose all cases in the future, both criminal and civil, in state and perhaps federal courts, could be televised. Could that present any problems for anyone involved in the cases? Might rights guaranteed in the First, Fifth, Sixth, and Seventh Amendments come into conflict with one another?

8. Review the meaning of the term *dilemma* on page 329. How might a dilemma arise for anyone having to make a decision about whether or not the press rights in the First Amendment should come before trial rights guaranteed in the Fifth, Sixth, and Seventh Amendments?

9. Do you think that court proceedings should be televised? Explain your answer.

'How was I?'

UNIT 8 REVIEW

Fact Review

1. Which of the following situations would be covered by criminal law, which by civil law, and which by *both* criminal and civil law?
   a. You fail to pay your rent on time.
   b. You steal some money.
   c. You injure someone accidentally.
   d. You use an illegal drug.
2. What problem do people who have been in prison often face when looking for a job after being released?
3. Which of the following would be contracts?
   a. You tell a friend that you will give him your tape player because he helped you with a big project.
   b. Your aunt says that she will pay for your college education if you work in her antique shop every summer.
   c. You order a phonograph record from a mail-order company.
4. What consideration does a court or jury use to decide whether a defendant in a tort case was negligent?
5. Do you think it is fair to make people pay for the harm their negligence causes to others? Why or why not?

Developing Your Vocabulary

Explain the difference between the terms in the following pairs:

a. criminal law and civil law
b. fixed sentence and indeterminate sentence
c. divorce and annulment
d. void contract and voidable contract

Developing Your Reading Skills

Read the following passage and then answer the questions that follow:

Our system of laws in the United States is divided into two main types: criminal law and civil law.

Criminal law deals with the prevention and punishment of acts that are considered harmful to society. The most serious crimes are felonies. Less serious crimes are called misdemeanors.

Criminal law tries to protect society. Civil law, on the other hand, deals with the rights and duties of individuals in their dealings with one another and with the government.

One area of civil law deals with contracts. Everyday acts, such as ordering a restaurant meal, involve contracts. Many other activities, from being married to borrowing money, also involve contracts.

Another area of civil law deals with torts. These are actions—or inactions—by one party that result in harm to another party. One example of a tort might be an automobile accident caused by a careless driver. If the driver's negligence caused injury or expense to another party, then a tort occurred. The law states how the injured party can be paid back.

Still another area of civil law deals with family matters. It includes regulations about who may marry and how. It includes rules about how a marriage may be ended.

1. Tell which of the questions below can be answered from the reading:
   a. What are three types of crimes?
   b. What constitutional guarantees protect the rights of people who are accused of crimes?
   c. What are three areas of civil law?
   d. How does a court decide when a tort has occurred?
2. Now give the answers to the questions above that can be found in the reading.

To many people, *economics* is a subject more discussed than understood, more ignored than studied. These people seem to feel that economics is something that goes on around them, yet does not or should not concern them because it is complex and mysterious and far beyond their grasp.

In truth, economics does concern them. It concerns all of us. It affects our lives deeply both as individuals and as Americans.

To put it simply, economics makes the world go 'round. On a global level, it is the basis of the goals of some 150 nations, each having their own methods of achieving those goals.

On a more personal level, economics defines the way we live. It sets us apart from other countries, it distinguishes our attitudes and values, and it determines our future.

In this unit, you will learn about our economic system and have the opportunity to compare it to others. Then you will examine our government's role in the United States economy and see how it functions as both consumer and competitor with private industry.

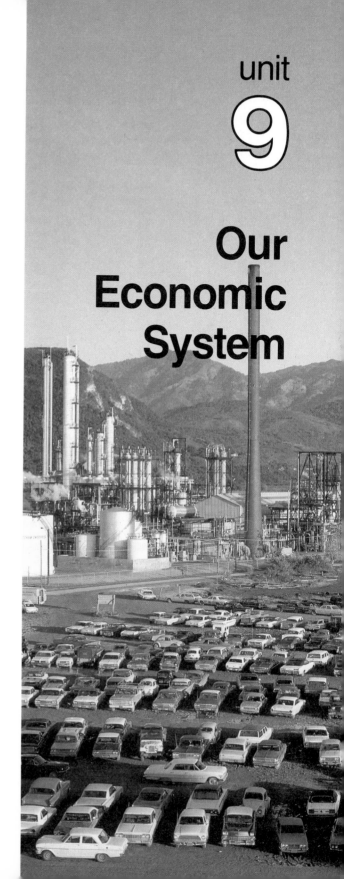

unit

9

Our Economic System

18 The United States Economic System and Your Place in It

What will I do for a living? How much money will I earn? What will I be able to spend it on? These questions probably sound familiar to you. They are questions that most young people wonder about.

To answer these questions, you must know something about how your country's economic system works. Then you will understand how jobs are created, how salaries are set, and how people choose their work.

In this chapter, you will learn about the two major economic systems in the world today—capitalism and socialism. Then you will take a closer look at the United States economic system and its three most important parts: business, agriculture, and labor. The section on labor includes a discussion of where your job opportunities will be.

Words to Know

economic system —— the way in which goods and services are produced, distributed, and consumed

economics —— the study of how economic systems work

economic resources —— the materials and the work that go into producing all things of value

human resources —— the labor of people

labor —— the work that people do in organizing and shaping material resources into goods and services

money —— coins or paper that people accept as having a standard value

material resources —— all the material things that are used to create goods and services

land —— resources including soil, the mineral deposits under the soil, and timber

capital —— the materials and equipment that are used to make and distribute goods and services; the money used to buy equipment, materials, and land

productivity —— the measure of the output of goods or services that a worker produces

technology —— the scientific methods and machinery used to produce goods and perform services

capital formation —— the gathering and combining of economic resources in order to build up a nation's industrial capacity, which then increases productivity and produces wealth

entrepreneurs —— the people who risk their money and time to start and run new businesses

Economic Resources

Suppose you wanted to have a cookout and you planned to serve hamburgers. How would you go about getting the food? You would buy it in a grocery store, no doubt. You would trade money for meat, and buns, and ketchup.

This simple exchange would not have been possible a few thousand years ago. In those days, there was no **economic system** for distributing food. People generally lived on the food that they produced themselves.

Today, there are complex economic systems in use. **Economics** is the study of how these systems work. It examines and describes how resources are used to produce, distribute, and consume goods and services.

What Is an Economic Resource?

If every person could have enough food, clothing, and shelter without working, there would be no need for any economic systems. But food, clothing, and shelter have to be made. The materials and the work that go into making life's necessities—as well as its luxuries—are called **economic resources.** Since economic resources are the basis of all wealth, they are extremely valuable.

Human Resources The most important economic resources are **human resources**—people like you. There can be no goods or services without the work of people who organize and shape the other economic resources.

Human resources are also the basis of all economic systems. People everywhere exchange their **labor**—their time and abilities—for the things they want and need. The exchange is not a direct one, however. You would probably not spend a day sweeping a grocery store in exchange for your hamburgers. Instead, labor is traded for a certain amount of **money**—coins or paper that people accept as having a standard value.

In our society, money is a convenience. It has no real value in itself. But without money, there would be no easy way to distribute the goods and services that are created. How could you trade your labor for shoes, shoes for doctor's services, and doctor's services for a car? Without money, no industrial economy could exist.

Material Resources All the material things that are used by people to create goods and services are called **material resources.** There are two major kinds of material resources: land and capital.

New technology has meant increased output, or productivity, by human resources in our economy.

Land includes soil and timber plus the scarce mineral deposits under the soil, such as oil and iron. **Capital** is all the other materials and equipment that people use to produce other goods and services. Some examples of capital are a harvester, an oil rig, a machine in a factory, and a truck. The word *capital* has another meaning that may be more familiar to you. It also refers to the money that is used to buy equipment, materials, and land.

Resources and Wealth

The fact that a country has large human and material resources does not guarantee the country's wealth. Argentina and Brazil, for example, have far greater resources than the Netherlands or Japan. But Japan and the Netherlands have more productive economies.

Productivity Productivity is the measure of the output of goods or services per worker per hour. Suppose a company named Typeaway employs ten typists. They work 8 hours a day and together produce 240 pages. Typeaway is more productive than Type, Inc. Type, Inc. has ten typists working 8 hours a day, but producing only 160 pages. Typeaway's productivity is three pages per hour. Type, Inc.'s is only two pages per hour.

Why is there a difference in productivity between the two companies? Someone with special knowledge about the capital and organization of typing services would certainly know. That specialist, or *technocrat*, might be a scientist, or an engineer, or an office manager who knows about the technology of typing services. The **technology** of any business includes all the machinery it uses, as well as the methods it uses, to get the work done. Perhaps Type, Inc. would increase its productivity by using a new labor-saving machine, such as an electric typewriter. Perhaps the company's work methods need to be changed. A technocrat would know whether productivity would be improved by dividing the workers into typing and proofreading specialists, for example.

Capital Formation If Type, Inc. can hire technocrats to increase its productivity, can countries like Brazil and Argentina do the same thing? Yes, they can. But it may not do much good. Someone has to have

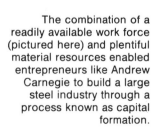

The combination of a readily available work force (pictured here) and plentiful material resources enabled entrepreneurs like Andrew Carnegie to build a large steel industry through a process known as capital formation.

The founding of important industries such as oil by adventurous entrepreneurs like John D. Rockefeller has played a vital role in making the United States the major economic power it is today.

saved enough money to buy the new labor-saving machines. Even more importantly, someone has to have saved enough money to build the factories, roads, and trucks needed to make and distribute those labor-saving machines.

In other words, resources have to be accumulated and combined. This process allows a country to build up its industrial capacity. Expanded industrial capacity increases productivity and produces wealth. This process of gathering and combining economic resources is called **capital formation.** Capital formation has taken place in Japan and the Netherlands, but it has not happened to any great extent in Argentina or Brazil.

Capital formation took place in the United States between 1865 and 1935. During those years, the economy of the United States was built up by entrepreneurs—people such as John D. Rockefeller, who founded the oil industry, and Andrew Carnegie, who founded the steel industry. **Entrepreneurs** are men and women who risk their money and time to start and run new businesses.

Some of the early entrepreneurs in this country made great fortunes. This happened partly because they had good ideas, partly because there were no income taxes then, and partly because their employees worked long hours at low wages. Labor was not only cheap, but plentiful, as well. Many laborers came from the American country-side, eager to make their fortune in the city. Many others were immigrants, who would work long hours for little pay. Since labor was so cheap, entrepreneurs had huge profits that they were able to reinvest in machinery. This, in turn, increased productivity. Between 1865 and 1900, capital formation created a nation of large industries based on steel and railroads.

Capital formation is a great deal like saving. It can only be done if people are willing to make sacrifices in the present for benefits in the future. Most underdeveloped and poor countries today are finding that the process of capital formation is difficult to begin.

—————— REVIEW ——————

1. What are the two kinds of economic resources?
2. Is a coal mine capital? Is the equipment that the miners use capital?
3. What are two ways to increase productivity?
4. Why is capital formation necessary for increased productivity?
5. How would you have felt abut entrepreneurs and the importance of capital formation if you had been a steelworker in 1890?

Words to Know

profit —— the difference between the cost of producing a product and the price at which it is sold

expense —— the cost of producing a good or a service

capitalism —— the economic system in which the means of producing goods and services are privately owned

consumer —— a person who buys goods and services

free enterprise —— the form of capitalism that exists in the United States

socialism —— the economic system in which the means of producing goods and services are owned or controlled by the government

communist economy —— the form of socialism in which the government determines what will be produced and where people will work

Economic Systems

Each of the 150 or so nations of the world has its own economic goals and its own methods for reaching those goals. Basically, however, there are two major economic systems: capitalism and socialism.

Capitalism

The United States is the world's most powerful and successful capitalist country. Two other major capitalist countries are Japan and Germany.

How It Works Suppose you were running a toy factory and you noticed that wind-up toys were selling very well. In response to that demand, you started making a wind-up toy that was bigger and better than anything else being sold. Soon, however, all the children who had been longing for a wind-up toy had bought one. Then, you found yourself left with a supply of toys that you could not sell. In other words, the supply of your 10-dollar specials was now greater than the demand. What would you do? You would lower your price. If you lowered it enough, some of the children who had been only somewhat interested in wind-up toys at $10 might now become interested because of the bargain. At $7, for example, you might find that the demand was great enough to get rid of your supply of wind-up toys.

These workers at a pineapple canning plant fulfill two roles in society—producers and consumers.

Your toy factory is obeying *the law of supply and demand.* Based on demand, you were finding the price at which profits were greatest. **Profits** are the amount of money left over from selling a product after subtracting the **expenses,** or the costs of making the product. The capitalist system is based on the following theory: If people are left free to make the most profit possible, they will, in the long run, produce goods and services at prices that people can afford and are willing to pay.

Under **capitalism,** all the material resources—land and capital—are privately owned and run. Businesses decide what and how much to produce based on the demands of the *market*—the people who buy the products.

The capitalist theory was promoted in the late 1700s by a Scottish philosopher named Adam Smith. In his book, *Wealth of Nations,* he referred to "the invisible hand of the marketplace" as the best way to determine what people should produce.

As you can see, the central person in the capitalist plan is the **consumer**—that is, you and other people who buy goods and services. The consumer creates the demand for a product. But for the system to work, the consumer must have the money to purchase the goods and services that are produced. In other words, consumers must have a share of the wealth. Most people get it by selling the only economic resource they have—their labor.

In the capitalist system, if you wanted to earn money, you would probably go to a privately owned company and try to get a job. However, if you saw a market demand that was not being met, you would have the right to start a business of your own to meet that demand. Then, if you were successful, you would earn money through profit rather than through labor.

The main advantage of capitalism is that it gives people the incentive, or reason, to work hard. They can keep all the money they earn. On the other hand, if they do nothing, they get nothing. In a pure capitalist society, a person's income is directly related to the work he or she does.

Another advantage of capitalism is that it allows people a great deal of freedom. In the United States, for example, no one can tell you what you must produce or what salary you must accept. However, for most workers, this freedom is only partly real. Their labor, like everything else in the capitalist system, has to obey the law of supply and demand. If a worker has a skill that is in great demand, she or he can earn a good salary. However, if a worker has no skill or a skill that is in great supply and low demand, he or she will have to compete with many others in the job market. Such a worker can only compete by working for less.

littering
is
filthy
&
selfish
so
don't
do it!

Because goods are so plentiful and so easily available in a consumer society, waste often becomes a problem.

One final advantage—and this is not to be taken lightly—is that capitalism works. Capitalist nations such as the United States were the first to give large numbers of people not only life's necessities, but also many of its luxuries.

The Modified United States Plan Pure capitalism is strictly a "government— hands off!" system. In practice, there are no pure capitalist economies in the world today. The United States is, however, the nation most committed to capitalism. The United States *free-enterprise* system is a form of modified capitalism. In this system, entrepreneurs, workers, and consumers freely choose what to produce, where to work, and what to buy. However, the government has stepped in to make sure that competition between companies continues and to protect consumers from unsafe products.

The government has also acted to protect people's economic interests. Now workers have the right to unemployment insurance, paid vacations, minimum wages, and maximum hours of work.

Socialism

A toy factory in a socialist country would be run very differently from one in a capitalist country.

How It Works Under **socialism,** the government owns or controls the means of producing wealth. The decisions about what to make, how much to pay workers, and how much to charge for the product are not always based on consumer demand. The government decides these things. It may base its decisions on long-range goals rather than on immediate wants and needs.

Personal profit is not the driving force in socialism. In theory, the government acts as a manager on behalf of the people. The profits of industry are supposed to be spent on such things as food, housing, health care, and schools. However, industrial profits depend on capital formation, and many nations have not yet become industrialized.

The biggest problem with socialism is simple. People's incomes are not related to their productivity. Thus, there is no incentive to work hard. Hard work and high-quality work are not rewarded. This is true for managers and professionals as well as for skilled and unskilled workers. As a result, socialist countries often suffer from poor distribution of resources, poor services, low production, and low-quality products.

Another disadvantage of socialism is that it often goes along with a loss of personal freedom. The poorer nations in the world, for example, are impatient to develop their economies so that they can build up their industrial power. In order to do so, they may set up a form of socialism known as a communist economy.

In a communist economy, people have very little choice about what they can buy and where they can work. The government tells the factories what to produce. It decides how much stores charge for goods. It also strongly encourages—if not commands—people to work in a particular

Under a communist economy, these Chinese women must abide by their government's decision to have them work in the fields on government-owned farms.

place. In China, Cambodia, and Vietnam, for example, everyone is forced to spend a certain amount of time in the country working on government-owned farms. Nevertheless, few communist economies have ever grown enough food to feed their own people year after year. To produce food in abundance, farmers need the incentive of private ownership and the rewards of private profits.

Because people are forced to make such great economic sacrifices, governments that use a communist economy often fear social unrest. This results in another disadvantage of this type of system. It is not unusual for the people to suffer a loss of political freedom along with their loss of personal freedom and economic choice.

Therefore, although the necessities of life are met, the quality of life may not be high because of loss of freedom, poor quality of goods, and frequent shortages.

Socialism on the Modified Plan At present, many nations consider themselves to be socialist. However, there is great variety among socialist countries. Great Britain, for example, permits a great deal of private ownership of industry and as much personal freedom as there is in the United States. But its government has far greater power over the lives of the people than our government does. It can take over a company, close down a company, or start up a government-owned company.

The economy of Great Britain was first built up by capitalist methods. But now the economy's primary objective seems to be focused on social welfare, not profit. Profits and salaries are heavily taxed—far more so than in the United States. The taxes are used to pay for an expensive system of housing, medical care, schools, homes for the aged, and other similar social-welfare programs.

In countries like Sweden, a modified socialist plan calls for heavy taxation in order to provide social-welfare services such as care for the elderly.

━━━━━━━━━ REVIEW ━━━━━━━━━

1. What is the basic way in which capitalism and socialism differ?
2. In which economic system is the role of the consumer more important? How?

Words to Know

sole proprietorship —— a business that is owned by one person

partnership —— a business that is owned by two or more persons as co-owners

corporation —— an artificial being created by law and given the right to carry on a business

charter —— a written document, granted by the government, that defines the rights of a corporation

stock —— a share of ownership in a corporation

shareholder —— an owner of stock in a corporation

limited liability —— a business owner's responsibility for losses that is only as great as her or his investment in the business

agribusiness —— a company that processes and distributes food

farmers' cooperative —— an association of independent farmers that shares equipment and means of distribution

labor union —— an association of employees that works for good wages and working conditions

collective bargaining —— the give-and-take discussions about wages and working conditions between an employer and union leaders, who speak on behalf of all the workers

strike —— an organized work stoppage; labor union's strongest way of trying to get a company to agree to favorable working terms

In its American form, capitalism may be seen as a steady stream of mass-produced commodities, such as these cars at the Ford Rouge Plant in Michigan.

Business, Agriculture, and Labor

You now have an idea of how the two basic economic systems differ. Now it is time to see how capitalism works in the United States. Let's take a closer look at the three primary engines of the United States economic system: business, agriculture, and labor.

Business

"The business of America," President Calvin Coolidge told the nation is 1925, "is business." When he said that, business stood alone at the center of society in the United States. Business leaders were envied and respected.

Conditions have changed in the last 50 years, however. Labor and government have become as powerful as business. And business leaders, as well as government and union leaders, are freely criticized. But business is still at the center of life in the United States. It employs three out of every four workers (the other workers are employed by government and by nonprofit institutions). It generates most of the nation's wealth. It builds our cars, homes, television sets, and airplanes. It runs our movie houses, motels, and restaurants.

Business is all of the work involved in providing people with goods and services at a profit. There are more than 12 million business firms in the United States, ranging in size from a corner grocery store to General Motors. General Motors' sales alone are greater than the total output of all but the seventeen largest nations in the world.

Forms of Business

Remember that toy factory you ran under a capitalist system? That factory may have been a sole proprietorship, a partnership, or a corporation. Those are the three basic forms of business.

Sole Proprietorships Your toy factory is most likely a **sole proprietorship,** a business owned by one person. Nearly four out of every five businesses in the United

SIZE AND WEALTH OF THREE DIFFERENT
KINDS OF BUSINESS

Sole Proprietorship

Number: 10,874,000
Receipts (in billions of dollars): 328.3

Partnership

Number: 1,062,000
Receipts (in billions of dollars): 137.2

Corporation

Number: 1,966,000
Receipts (in billions of dollars) 2,854.8

States—about 11 million in all—are sole proprietorships. This includes most small farms. Many retail stores, such as newsstands, grocery stores, and clothing shops, are also sole proprietorships. Most neighborhood service stores, such as restaurants, laundries, and repair shops, are also sole proprietorships.

A sole proprietorship is the easiest form of business to begin. That is one reason why it is such a popular form of business. Another reason is that many of us want to own our own businesses. We want to make our own decisions and have all the rewards of our efforts.

A single person can work only a limited number of hours, however. Due to this, most sole proprietorships are small. They bring in less than $600 a week in sales. Successful entrepreneurs who want their companies to grow usually change them into one of the other two forms of business.

Partnerships There are only about 1 million partnerships in the United States, but this form of business is very important to the country's economic system. That is because the largest law and accounting firms are partnerships. They perform vital services for the business community.

A **partnership** is a business that is owned by two or more persons as co-owners, or partners. Like sole proprietorships,

As sole proprietor of her candy store, this businesswoman is among the majority of business owners. In contrast to the high finance of big business, she keeps her operation small in order to retain total control over it.

partnerships are easy to form. But partnerships can become much larger. For example, a major accounting firm can have 100 partners, as well as a number of junior accountants and other employees, and bring in $500 million a year.

Partnerships have another advantage over businesses owned by one person. They give two people with different talents in the same field a chance to join forces. For example, a dress-manufacturing company may be owned by one partner who runs the factory and another who travels around the world selling the dresses. In economic terms, the two partners have combined their economic resources—their operating and selling skills—to create more wealth than either could have made by working alone. This combining of economic resources—especially of time and skill—makes partnerships very attractive for doctors, lawyers, and other professionals.

However, none of the largest and most powerful business firms in the United States are partnerships. That is because partnerships have two major disadvantages that limit their growth. One disadvantage is that, as a business form, partnerships have limited life spans. They depend upon the lives and talents of the partners. If one of the partners dies or if there are disagreements between partners, the business is often closed down. The second disadvantage is that a partnership does not have the flexibility that a business needs in order to grow and change. There are too many leaders in a large partnership. For a big business to succeed, it needs firm leadership that has the power to make quick decisions.

Corporations A **corporation** is an artificial being created by law and given the right to carry on a business. This right is granted by a **charter,** a written document that state governments issue to create a corporation.

There are only about 2 million corporations in the United States. However, these corporations control the largest percentage of the nation's business assets and nearly half of all the wealth. A large corporation such as AT&T, Exxon, or General Motors has tens of billions of dollars in sales every year, earns billions of dollars in profits, and employs hundreds of thousands of people.

Corporations are usually formed from sole proprietorships or partnerships that need money to expand. To get this money, the owners divide the ownership of the business into shares and offer some of these shares for sale. Each share of ownership is called a **stock.** If a corporation has issued 1 million shares of stock, each share is one-millionth ownership in the company.

Stock in a corporation is owned by **shareholders.** These partial owners do not run the business as partners or proprietors would. In fact, shareholders rarely have much of a say at all in how the business is run, since they usually own such a small part of the business. AT&T, for example, has 2.9 million shareholders.

Shareholders do, collectively, elect a board of directors. The directors, in turn, select the officers who run the company. The most important of these are usually the chairperson of the board and the president. The chairperson makes policy decisions for the corporation. The president is in charge of the day-to-day business decisions.

A corporation has several major advantages over the other forms of business. First, most corporate charters give corporations great flexibility. They can reorganize whenever they need to. They also have the right to go into new product lines or service lines. This means that corporations can be highly adaptable to changing needs.

Second, corporations have **limited liability.** A corporate shareholder risks only his or her investment—the price of the shares of stock bought. But partners and proprietors can be sued for everything they

Historically, stock shares issued and sold to raise money for business expansion have been bought and saved in hopes of great capital gain.

own if their companies do not make enough profits to pay their bills.

Third, corporations have an unlimited life span. When a shareholder dies, the shares are transferred to someone else. When directors or officers retire, they are replaced.

Thus, corporations have an unequaled ability to combine economic resources, to stay in business for a long time and to keep growing.

Mass Production and the Economy of Scale

Before the industrial revolution, there were no large corporations. The technology of producing in large amounts had not yet been developed. Even if the technology had been available, there would have been no way for factory owners to sell their products other than locally. Communication and transportation systems were slow and unreliable. Therefore, small partnerships and sole proprietorships were able to handle all the work of running the major businesses.

But the times were changing. Around 1800, Eli Whitney—the inventor of the cotton gin—built his first factory in Connecticut for the mass production of rifles. Whitney invented the *machine tool,* a machine that makes parts that workers can fit together, or assemble, into the product—in this case, a rifle. Until then, rifles had been made by hand. But Whitney was able to produce rifles 40 times faster, and much cheaper, than any competitor.

Whitney's workers walked around to the rifle parts, picked them up, and then assembled them. Shortly after 1900, Henry Ford improved upon Whitney's factory system by creating the modern factory system as we know it today. Ford kept his workers in one spot and brought the parts to them. His invention, the moving *assembly line,* made factories even more productive.

At the same time, the birth of nationwide telephone and railroad systems made it possible to sell and distribute products to a nationwide market. Thus, a crate of canned tomatoes from an H.J. Heinz plant in Pittsburgh, Pennsylvania, could be sold

The telephone greatly improved the communication network that was so vital to a growing technology.

by phone and delivered by train or truck to a grocery store in Houston, Texas.

These advances in manufacturing and distributing made economies of scale possible. *Economy of scale* is one of the most important rules of economics. According to this rule, it is cheaper to mass produce 50,000 books than to produce 1 book at a time. But only large corporations with great investments in machinery, thousands of workers, and extensive distribution and management systems could really take advantage of economies of scale. Thus, a new form of business, the corporation, came into being. The ability of corporations to grow and make use of the economy of scale is the key to our nation's success in business. It has allowed us to create the greatest economic system the world has ever known.

Agriculture

In the early days of this country, farming held an important place in our social system, and free land attracted many immigrants. Since the 1920s, families have been selling their farms and moving to the city. They have been attracted by higher income and easier work, with less risk. For those who have remained on the land, farming is still a special way of life. Farmers work hard and take great risks. But they also produce large amounts of food. In fact, food is our nation's most important export.

Capitalism at Work   In an economic sense, farming is one of the most successful industries in American business. It proves the capitalist theory that people are more productive when they are allowed freedom of choice and ownership of their own businesses.

Today, less than 3 million farm families produce more food than 10 million families produced 20 years ago. Some 200,000 produce one-third of the nation's food. Another 2.5 million produce the rest. This comparatively small number of farm families is able to feed our nation and much of the world because farming has become a highly specialized branch of business in the United States.

These farmers, working for themselves and using the most modern equipment, practice economies of scale as successfully as do large industrial corporations. In fact, many family farms are corporations. As with other corporations, these farms offer stock for sale, although ownership is spread among several members of the family. Other farms are owned by **agribusinesses**. These are companies that process and distribute food—for example, the Campbell Soup Company and General Mills.

The large family farms and agribusinesses can afford to buy expensive modern equipment. They are also large enough to have a strong negotiating position with large food distributors. Therefore, they are sure of receiving a fair price for their products.

Smaller family farms achieve economies of scale and bargaining advantages by grouping together to form **coopera-**

tives. These are associations of independent farmers. Some cooperatives buy equipment for their members to use. All cooperatives market the products of their cooperator members. The most famous farm cooperative is Sunkist, an association of California orange and lemon growers. Sunkist markets oranges nationwide and is able to get good prices for its members.

The Government's Role Food production is an important part of the American economy. Because it is, the government controls the amount of goods produced. The government does this because farmers often overproduce. However, farmers cannot hold on to their product until supplies decrease and demand increases. They have to sell soon after they harvest. If the market is oversupplied, prices go down so low that farmers are driven out of business.

To protect the farmers from the problems of overproduction, the government limits the number of acres on which farmers can plant a certain crop in any given year. The farmers accept this regulation because the government, in return, supports farm prices at a minimum level. In this way, the government relieves farmers of some of the risks of the market.

The United States government also helps farmers by distributing information about the latest agricultural methods, such

Improvements in technology since the days of the horse and plow have made it possible for American farmers to produce ever increasing amounts of food. Due to these improvements, farming has become a highly specialized branch of business.

as new fertilizers or a new way of planting. As a result, United States agricultural production continues to be more and more productive per acre, and farming remains a highly valued and rewarding way of life.

Labor

After creating the assembly line, Henry Ford asked himself just who would buy all those cars that he was making. His answer was: the workers. In 1914, he raised his workers' wages to $5 a day, which was more than twice the average day's wage at the time. He began the process of turning workers into the United States economy's best customers.

Labor Unions These days, most workers are paid wages that support a decent standard of living. But before the twentieth century most entrepreneurs were either not willing or did not have enough foresight to give up any of their profits. Workers were not willing to wait for their employers' possible generosity. They grouped together to force the employers to improve their situation.

You can just imagine what an entrepreneur said when a worker came up and complained about pay or working conditions. That worker did not have a job for very long. But when workers later organized into labor unions, or associations of workers, they were protected by their power as a group. Union leaders were able to engage in **collective bargaining** for better wages and working conditions—and they were able to do this as equals with the employers. That is because they had the threat of a strike supporting them. A **strike** is an organized work stoppage. It is one of organized labor's most useful weapons. By striking, the workers try to close down a company so that it will be forced, through economic losses, to negotiate with its workers.

The growth of unions was made easier by the fact that the process of capital formation was well under way by 1900. There were enough profits left over after reinvestment in new machinery to pay better wages. Also, the entrepreneurs who had founded the great United States industries had retired and had been replaced by professional managers. These were men and women who gave orders to workers but were fellow employees, not entrepreneurs. Professional managers were more likely than entrepreneurs to listen to labor's demands. Henry Ford, for example, may have been more generous than other entrepreneurs, but he was just as strongly opposed to unions. He insisted on his right to direct his own business as he pleased.

Between 1865 and 1935, there were many violent struggles in which workers called strikes for higher wages and better working conditions. Many strikes led to violence and death on both sides. Finally, in 1935, the United States enacted the Wagner Act. This law gave workers the right to organize unions that would bargain collectively for them. It also required management to bargain with the unions.

During World War II, the nation began a period of enormous productivity, and labor became a full-fledged partner in the economy. Today, labor unions are one of the three most powerful institutions in the economy, along with business and government. Now, the managers of some industries—such as the automobile and steel industries—are likely to work with the leaders of their unions—the United Auto Workers and the United Steelworkers—to agree on wages. They even work together to plan a united labor-management campaign on certain issues, such as opposition to the import of foreign steel or automobiles.

At their peak—around 1945—, labor unions accounted for one out of every three workers in the United States. Unions were especially strong in manufacturing and in

The women shoe workers' strike in Lynn, Massachusetts, in the 1830s was one of many strikes aimed at securing higher wages and better working conditions.

large-scale service and craft industries, such as steel, trucking, and construction. Unions were never strong among office workers or other service industries.

Recently, there has been a change in emphasis in the United States economy from products to services. Therefore, the percentage of workers who belong to unions has decreased. Now, only about one out of five workers is a union member. Unions are beginning to organize service employees such as teachers and civil servants, but it is not yet known how much progress they will make within service industries.

Where the Jobs Are As recently as 30 years ago, a majority of the people in the United States had not graduated from high school. Today, nearly everyone in the United States graduates from high school, and the majority of people continue their education in trade schools or colleges. Others go from high school to business firms, where they get special on-the-job training. What has caused this change? The more education people have, the more career choices are open to them.

When you finish with your schooling, you will almost certainly spend the greater part of your adult life in the United States labor force. That prediction can be made because the United States is a country that believes in the *work ethic*. That is, we believe that work is good for people, that we should learn to work well, and that hard work should be rewarded. But you are probably wondering what kinds of jobs will be available to you.

The U.S. Census of population and jobs revealed an interesting fact in 1960. For the first time, workers who manufactured products and goods on farms and in factories were outnumbered by workers who provided services in retail stores, offices, repair shops, and classrooms.

In 1900, our major industries were steel and railroads. As farms and industrial plants improved their productivity, they required fewer workers to produce the same amount of goods. Therefore, while the nation will always need factory workers and farm workers, most new job opportunities will be in the service industries. The major employers are the computer industry, the travel industry—hotels, restaurants, airlines, and gas stations—banks, and retail stores. However, there are exceptions. Companies that make *petrochemicals*—plastics and other products made from chemicals—are an expanding manufacturing industry. These companies will employ more workers in the future.

The largest increase in number of jobs available will be in sales. Job opportunities for teachers and civil servants may stop growing as the number of students decreases and as taxpayers question the need for more public services. But the banking and computer industries will be employing more people.

In all these areas, there will be a wide range of salaries. In sales, for example, salaries may range from the $150-a-week salary of a young clerk in a shoe store to the $100,000-a-year salary of an insurance or computer salesperson. Salaries will depend upon level of employment, personal ambition, and education.

Educated people have a better chance of becoming *skilled workers*. Truckers and computer operators are skilled. Messengers and cleaning personnel are unskilled. Skilled workers are capable of doing more productive work. Therefore, they earn higher pay.

Education is important, but it is only one of the things that determine whether you will have a successful career. Others are ambition, luck, good judgment, the ability to work well with people, and the ability to make wise career choices based on your talents and desires.

If you have these qualities, you will find that the United States economic system gives you every opportunity to succeed. There are laws to protect you from being denied a job or a promotion on the basis of your race or sex. Indeed, many large business firms make special efforts to recruit and promote employees from groups of people who have suffered from the lack of job opportunities in the past. In the United States today, modified capitalism gives all of us freedom of choice and a good chance for success.

REVIEW

1. What are two advantages that partnerships have over sole proprietorships?
2. How are the highest officers of a corporation chosen?
3. Explain the following statement: "Large corporations arose in order to take advantage of economies of scale."
4. What is the difference between an agribusiness and a farm cooperative?
5. Do you think that police officers should have the right to join unions and strike for better working conditions? Why or why not?

How the United States Works

Computer Operators

There are almost 100 million working people in the United States. You can imagine all the weekly tax and social security payments the government has to handle. Working people also file tax returns that must be checked. If all this work were done by hand, many workers would have to be hired to do the job. Luckily, much of this work can be processed very quickly by computer. Thousands of people do not have to be hired, for example, to go over the arithmetic on all those tax returns. Computers can be run by considerably fewer people.

The two major computer-operating jobs are those of the keypuncher and the console operator. Console operators usually earn between $8,000 and $13,000 a year. They keep the computers in good running order. They feed the data, or information, into the computer. While the computer is running, the console operator solves any mechanical difficulties that come up. Since more and more computers are being used all the time, the need for console operators is rising.

The data that the operator feeds into the computer is not exactly the material that came into the office. For example, your parents' tax return is not fed into the computer as sheets of paper covered with writing. A computer

cannot read information in that form. It is the job of the keypuncher to change the data into a form that the computer can understand. Keypunchers usually earn between $7,000 and $10,000. However, many of these jobs will become outdated as computers are made that are able to read data in different forms.

Beginning computer operators are usually trained on the job. Most employers, including the federal government, will only train high school graduates. The working conditions of computer operators are always good. The operators work in clean, temperature-controlled areas. This temperature control is necessary because computers break down if they are exposed to dirt or if they become too hot.

Some operators are needed to work odd shifts—for example, throughout the night. That is because computers are run on a 24-hour basis.

Reading About . . .

Specialization —————————————————————————————

This chapter has discussed the American economic system, its labor market, and where you stand in it. Now let's explore one feature of the labor market—specialization.

As you read, ask yourself the following questions:

- What are the advantages of specialization?
- Do you think that there might be some disadvantages to specialization as well?

Solitary hermits living in the wilderness can satisfy their economic wants in only one way: by their own unaided efforts. They must be able to do many kinds of work: growing or finding their own food, building shelter, mending their clothes. This kind of life has certain advantages. People in this situation need to consult only their own preferences to decide whether to take the afternoon off or to clear some land to make a berry patch. They run no danger of "losing a job" or being swindled by wily salespeople. But this sort of life has an enormous disadvantage: a person living completely alone cannot enjoy more than the simplest way of life. Even a primitive village society can achieve a higher level of living than a hermit can. Why? This is because of the division of labor into specialized occupations.

Specialization occurs in its simplest, most primitive form when each person spends his or her full time making a single kind of product. One person weaves cloth, another makes shoes, a third bakes bread, and so on. Goods are better and more quickly made that way, since people can concentrate on doing the things for which they have the greatest aptitude. Also, practice makes perfect. A person who is equally capable of becoming a good carpenter or a good dentist gains greater skill and experience by spending all her or his time in one occupation, rather than working part time in several.

But specialization usually goes farther than this. Today, a worker almost never makes a complete product. Production is split up into many separate operations. The typical factory worker spends the day spray-painting a part that is on its way to the assembly line, grinding the rough edges off a casting, or checking the controls on a complicated automatic machine. By the time the finished product reaches the retail store, nobody can say "I made that."

Another advantageous form of specialization is based on geography: regional specialization. Cranberries will not grow on the Midwestern plains, nor will grapefruit thrive in Maine. Coal obviously cannot be mined in states that have no coal deposits. Steel can be produced anywhere, but it is foolishly expensive to produce it too far away from the souce of iron ore and coke.

Fact Review

1. What resources are necessary for the process of capital formation?
2. Which of the following are capitalist countries and which are socialist countries?
   a. the United States
   b. China
   c. Cambodia
   d. Japan
   e. Germany
3. Name and define the three primary engines of the United States economic system.
4. Who invented the moving assembly line and what impact did it have on production? Explain.
5. For what reasons were labor unions organized? What was their main weapon and why was it so successful?

Developing Your Vocabulary

What are the differences between the following sets of words?
   a. human resources and material resources
   b. capitalism and socialism
   c. sole proprietorship, partnership, and corporation

Developing Your Reading Skills

Read the following paragraph and then answer the questions that follow:

Capitalism in its pure form does not exist anywhere in the world today. Instead, countries such as the United States have adopted a modified capitalism known as the free-enterprise system. This system allows entrepreneurs to produce what they wish, workers to work where they please, and consumers to buy what they want when they want. The government steps in only when it is necessary to protect consumers from unsafe goods or to guard against threats to competition.

1. Which of the following do you think is the main idea, or point, of this paragraph?
   a. Capitalism does not really exist.
   b. Capitalism exists in the United States in an altered form that allows for freedom of choice.
   c. Capitalism is better than socialism.
   d. Government cannot interfere with private industry under the free-enterprise system.
   e. Government may interfere with business whenever the consumer must be protected.
2. Why did you choose *a, b, c, d,* or *e* above?

Developing Your Writing Skills— Forming and Supporting an Opinion

In this chapter, you have examined the three forms of business—sole proprietorships, partnerships, and corporations. You have seen the advantages of each. Now consider the following questions:

Forming an opinion

1. Of the three forms of business, which form do you think is best suited to a person who wants to open his or her own bookstore?

Supporting an opinion

2. After thinking it over, write a paragraph that answers the question above. Begin with a topic sentence that sums up your opinion. Continue with evidence or arguments to support your opinion.

YOUR GOVERNMENT & ITS HISTORY

Samuel Gompers and the Founding of the AFL

The American Federation of Labor, or the AFL, has been one of the largest organizations in the American labor union movement for almost 100 years. It has also been one of the most influential. One of its founders, Samuel Gompers, served as its first president from 1886 to 1925.

Samuel Gompers was an immigrant from England. He came to America with his family in 1863, when he was 13 years old. Gompers went to work when he was only a boy. He eventually became a cigar-maker. The Cigarmakers Union was founded soon after Gompers arrived in this country. He joined the union and worked his way up to become one of its early leaders. The constitution of the Cigarmakers Union outlined its attitudes and goals:

The worker has no protection. All wealth and power is in the hands of the few, and many workers are their victims. The worker . . . deserves more of the leisure that rightfully belongs to workers.

The past teaches us that labor has not been treated justly. This is due to the workers' lack of unity. "In union there is strength." United action is the only way the worker can gain. Good and strong labor unions defend and preserve the interests of working people.

The Cigarmakers Union of America will help its members by the following means:

—By aiding the worker or worker's family in case of sickness or death.
—By getting the government to forbid child labor under 14 years of age.
—By making a normal day's work not more than 8 hours a day.

Gompers believed that there was a need for an organization that would bring together unions from all over the country. Such an organization is called a federation. In 1881, the first attempts were made to set up a federation. More than 100 representatives of various unions met in Pittsburgh. At this meeting, a committee was appointed to organize a new federation. Samuel Gompers was picked to head the committee. The organization Gompers helped to form was the Federation of Organized Trades and Labor Unions.

The Federation tried unsuccessfully to unite a variety of unions having different goals. There was no agreement about tactics. Some rival unions competed with one another. By 1886, it appeared almost impossible to hold the organization together.

In 1886, some of the major American trade unions decided to form a federation of their own. (Trade unions were made up of men and women who performed the same kind of work. The Cigarmakers Union was a trade union.) A meeting was held in Columbus, Ohio. At this meeting, twenty-five unions formed a new organization, the American Federation of Labor. Only trade unions would belong. The new organization would work for the common good of the combined membership of all the unions belonging to the AFL. The Cigarmakers Union was one of these members, and Samuel Gompers played a key role in founding the AFL.

For 37 of the next 38 years, Gompers headed the AFL. Someone once asked him, "What do the working people want, Mr. Gompers?" Gompers replied with one word: "More!" Gompers explained the basic reasons for labor unions this way:

The efforts of the American labor movement to secure a larger share of the nation's income are directed against all who illegally stand between the workers and . . . a better life. Employers and others oppose the efforts of the workers in the AFL. . . . But an additional reason that leads to conflict between workers and employers is that there are employers who live in the twentieth century, but who have the mental outlook of the sixteenth century in their attitudes toward the working people. They still think that they are masters of all they survey. These employers think that any attempt upon the part of the working people to secure improvements in their conditions is a spirit of rebellion that must be frowned down.

The AFL grew slowly until the early 1900s, when its membership increased dramatically. It passed the 1 million mark in 1902 and reached 4 million in 1920. Under Samuel Gompers, the AFL came to be a powerful representative of American trade unions. It contributed to accomplishing many of the goals of the American labor union movement.

1. What were the goals of the Cigarmakers Union?

2. Why was the AFL founded?

3. Who was the AFL's first president?

4. According to Gompers, what was the purpose of the labor movement? What did he feel was the attitude of employers toward attempts to improve working conditions?

5. What do you think should be the purpose of labor unions today? If employees are not happy with working conditions, what do you think they should do about it?

SKILLS Developing your basic civic education skills

(developing your critical thinking skills)

Comparing Economic Systems

In this chapter, you learned that there are two major economic systems—capitalism and socialism. The United States and Japan today are two of the leading capitalist nations. Among the nations having socialist economic systems are Britain and Sweden. Their economic systems are a modified form of socialism. Communism is another form of socialism. The Soviet Union (USSR) and the People's Republic of China are communist economic systems.

How do economic systems differ? To help you form an answer to this question, look at the table below. This table provides economic information about capitalist and socialist countries. Examine the table; then answer the questions on page 500.

HOW ECONOMIC SYSTEMS DIFFER						
	Capitalist		Socialist			
			Modified Socialist		Communist	
	U.S.A.	Japan	Britain	Sweden	China	U.S.S.R.
Population (in millions)	222	115	55	8	1,012	262
Farm land per person (in acres)	2.1	0.09	0.3	0.9	0.3	2.1
Meat production (in millions of metric tons)	17.6	1.5	2.0	0.4	17.0	13.0
Steel production (in millions of metric tons)	123.3	111.8	21.6	4.7	34.4	149.0
Electricity (in billions of kilowatt hours)	2,211	495	287	90	256	1,200
Automobiles in use (in millions)	109	19.8	14.5	2.8	0.03	4.7
Television sets (in millions)	121	26	17.7	2.9	1.0	55.2
Telephones (in millions)	162	50	23	5	—	19
Average annual income per person	$8,612	$7,153	$4,955	$9,274	$232	$2,600
People able to read and write	99%	99%	99%	99%	70%	99%
Number of medical doctors per 100,000 people	176	119	153	178	33	346

SOURCE: *The World Almanac and Book of Facts,*
1981 Edition, © Newspaper Enterprise Association

One difference between capitalist and communist economies is in the availability of consumer goods. In many communist countries, citizens wait in long lines to buy scarce canned goods and fresh fruits, vegetables, and meats. In most capitalist countries, such goods are abundant. In the top picture, a shopper in California chooses among cuts of meat. In the picture below, Polish citizens wait to buy at one of the largest supermarkets in Gdansk.

1. Using the information in the table, select the country in which you think the quality of life is probably most comfortable. Explain your answer.

2. To prove that your answer to question 1 is correct, what additional information about the countries in the table would be helpful?

3. Based on the table, select the leading manufacturer of goods among the six nations listed. Explain your answer.

4. What additional information would be helpful to prove your answer to question 3?

5. Using information in the table, create a hypothesis that could be used to answer each of these questions:

   a. Is the standard of living higher in capitalist or socialist countries?

   b. Is production greater under capitalism or socialism?

   c. Is the average annual income higher in socialist or capitalist economic systems?

6. Briefly, explain the answers you gave in question 5.

7. What additional information would be necessary to make generalizations about a to c in question 5?

Government Regulation of Economic Activities

In this chapter, you learned that our free enterprise system is a modified form of capitalism. Under our system, individuals enjoy great freedom in deciding what to buy, what to produce, and where to work. In recent years, however, these freedoms have been affected by an increase in government rules and regulations. As the federal government has grown in size, the number of federal agencies has grown, too. Along with this has come more federal control of our economic system.

One complaint about increased regulation involves the amount of paperwork the government requires. Each year, federal agencies print ten billion sheets of paper to be filled out by American businesses. This is enough paper to fill a space of 4 million cubic feet. This amounts to ten copies of some government forms for every man, woman, and child in the United States.

Cartoonists have poked fun at the enormous amount of paperwork that private businesses must fill out each year. On the opposite page are two such cartoons. Note that they both make use of satire.

8. Match each statement that follows to the messages in the cartoons. Some statements will apply to both.

   a. Filling out federal forms takes up too much of businesspeople's time.

   b. Government paperwork is a great expense for American business.

   c. Completing government paperwork is not a pleasant job.

   d. There is too much paperwork required by the government.

   e. Many people are involved in filling out federal forms.

   (1) Applies to cartoon 1

   (2) Applies to cartoon 2

   (3) Applies to both cartoon 1 and cartoon 2

9. Briefly explain why you answered a to e in question 8 as you did.

10. Why do you think artists draw cartoons such as these? How else might artists try to accomplish their purposes?

Cartoon 1

Cartoon 2

"HE SPENT MOST OF HIS TIME AT THE OFFICE, FILLING OUT GOVERNMENT FORMS.
THEN, ONE DAY, HE JUST JUMPED ON HIS HONDA, AND DISAPPEARED."

More Thinking about Federal Regulation

The city of Terrell Hills has fewer than 5,000 people. Since the town was founded, the streetlights have been gas operated. Natural gas has been plentiful. In 1980, however, a federal agency in Washington sent notice to the city that natural gas no longer could be used for streetlights. The city of Terrell Hills would have to replace its streetlights with electric ones.

After looking into what it could do, the city sent letters to its residents. It gave them four options (choices):

Option 1 Terrell Hills may have the electric company in a nearby large city put in telephone poles with electric streetlights on them. There is no charge to put in the lights, but the operating cost each year will be $10,000.

Option 2 Terrell Hills itself will put in attractive streetlights similar to the gas lights now in use. The cost to put them in will range from $80,000 to $115,000. The city's monthly fuel cost after that will be from $150 to $350.

Option 3 Terrell Hills will put in lights similar to those in Option 2 on the property of selected homeowners rather than on street corners where the present gas lights are. The cost for placing these new lights in taxpayers' front yards will range from $18,000 to $50,000. The monthly fuel cost after that will be paid by the selected property owners, not by the city. The estimated cost to these property owners will probably be no more than $3 per month.

Option 4 Terrell Hills can turn off its gas streetlights and do without streetlights after that.

11. Match each statement in *a* to *d* with the option (*1* to *4*) to which it corresponds:

    a. It is unfair for some citizens to pay the monthly fuel bill for streetlights that benefit all the residents.

    b. This option can destroy the beauty of the neighborhoods.

    c. The cost to put in the lights is high, but the city's monthly fuel cost is low.

    d. In order to save money, the city would be creating unsafe conditions in the neighborhoods.

12. Briefly explain why you answered question 11 as you did.

13. How much more in taxes will Terrell Hills residents be forced to pay for new streetlights during the first year if they select Option 1? Option 2? Option 3? Option 4?

14. If there are 5,000 persons in Terrell Hills, what would be the cost per person of each of the city's four options?

15. If you were a resident of this town, which option would you select? Why?

16. What are some other ways the money required for new streetlights might be spent? Do you think that the rules and regulations of the federal government's can affect our economic activities? Explain. Is your answer more of a hypothesis or a generalization?

Supply and Demand

You have learned that the law, or principle, of supply and demand helps determine prices in our economic system. The law of supply and demand can be stated this way:

FATHER'S DAY™   **by Nancy & Mario Risso**

© 1981 United Feature Syndicate, Inc.

If the supply of a product increases, while the demand for the product decreases, prices will be lowered. If the supply of a product decreases, while the demand for the product increases, prices will be raised.

To better understand the meaning of this principle, look at the comic strip above. This comic strip is supposed to be amusing. But it is also based on the law of supply and demand. Answer the questions that follow.

17. In this comic strip, what product is *supply* related to?

18. Which character(s) is *demand* related to?

19. Why do you think the seller offers to reduce the price to $6,000?

20. Which statement below do you think is the main point of this comic strip?

   a. Prices of new autos today are high because the demand for them is increasing.

   b. The prices of new cars should be lowered in order to create greater demand for the present supply.

   c. The large supply of new cars and their high prices has brought about an increase in demand.

21. Explain why you answered question 20 as you did.

19 Government and the Economy

The various levels of government in our country play an important part in our economy. Originally, the role of government was to provide certain services such as the regulation of trade and national defense.

The government plays a greater part now, however. It watches over industries in order to protect workers and consumers. It even competes with some industries, such as the insurance industry. The government also takes an active part in guiding general economic trends.

Thus, even in the United States—the nation most dedicated to freedom from government controls—, the government has a great deal to do with the way you earn and spend your money. In fact, the government itself is one of the fastest-growing parts of the economy. It spends one-third of all the wealth produced by the nation each year.

I. How governments raise money: taxation
  A. Individual income tax
    1. The main tax
    2. A powerful tool
    3. Taxing and collecting
    4. Social Security tax
  B. Corporate income tax
  C. Excise tax
  D. Sales tax
  E. Property tax
  F. Taxpayer revolt

II. What government does for us
  A. Health and welfare
    1. Social Security
    2. Financing problems
  B. Education
  C. National defense
  D. Interest on debt
  E. Other government expenditures
III. Banking
  A. What banks do
    1. Banks as borrowers

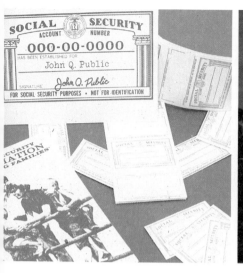

2. Banks as lenders
   3. The multiplier effect
   4. Other services
   B. The regulation of banks
      1. Regulating the money supply
      2. Government regulation
   C. Government banking
      1. Creating money
      2. Distributing money
IV. Insurance
   A. What insurance companies do
   B. Regulation of insurance companies
   C. Government insurance

gross income —— all the income earned before taxes and expenses are considered

taxable income —— gross income minus deductions

exemption —— a flat amount that you can subtract from your taxable income if you do not list any deductions

net income —— all the money that a business takes in from sales of goods or services minus costs and taxes; profits

gross national product —— the total amount of goods and services produced by a country in 1 year

Words to Know

tax —— money collected by a government so that the government can buy supplies and pay its public servants

progressive tax schedule —— tax rate in which the percentage of the income you pay in taxes rises as your income rises

deduction —— an amount subtracted from gross income to figure taxable income

How Governments Raise Money: Taxation

Since primitive people first set up governments to protect and rule themselves, governments have raised money by taxation. A **tax** is a sum of money that a person or a business must pay to a government. The government needs this money to pay public servants and to buy supplies.

"Taxes are the price we pay for civilization," Supreme Court Justice Oliver Wendell Holmes Jr. once said. But in recent years, the price has been very high. The average United States citizen turns over one-third of his or her earnings to the government in the form of taxes. That means that during 4 full months of the year, your family is working totally for the benefit of the government.

However, the first 4 months of your family's income is not collected as it is earned. This would leave you with nothing to live on. The different levels of government collect their taxes at different times and in different ways.

Individual Income Tax

If your parents are wage earners, as most are, part of each week's paycheck is withheld by their employers and turned over to the federal government. Depending

By preparing her income tax forms, this woman fulfills one of her yearly obligations to the government.

on where you live, part of the paycheck may also go to the state and local governments. This tax, the individual income tax, is based on the amount of money a person earns from all sources.

The Main Tax The individual income tax is the most important tax in the world today. It is the main source of money for most national governments among the world's industrialized countries—including the United States—and for many state governments in our country.

Why is this form of tax so widely used? One reason is that it is very easy to collect. It goes directly from the employer to the government.

Another reason for the widespread use of the individual income tax is that many people think it can be a very fair way of taxing people. This tax can be applied on a **progressive tax schedule**—that is, the people with the most income pay the largest percentage of their income in taxes.

A progressive tax schedule might have a tax rate of only 1 percent for a family with an income of $6,000 per year and a tax rate of 50 percent for a family with an income of $60,000. Why, you may ask, is it fair to ask for more tax money from wealthier people? It is fair because they can afford it. Suppose your family had a total income of $6,000. You would have a hard time paying for all your necessities. An income tax of 10 percent, or $600, would be an overwhelming loss to you. But that same 10 percent tax would not be at all difficult for someone earning $60,000 a year to pay.

A Powerful Tool There is a third reason why individual income taxes are a popular form of tax with national governments. These taxes give governments a good deal of control over the economy as a whole. The government can influence the kind of spending people do and the kind of investments they make through deductions. It can change the overall rate of taxation to stimulate or to slow general eco-

This family is one of millions that benefit from the deductions the government allows for every dependent child. The amount of the deduction may vary according to government tax requirements.

nomic activity. The government can also change the distribution of money in the country by making the tax more or less progressive. Let's look at each of these situations more closely.

A **deduction** is an amount that is subtracted from **gross income**—all the money you earn—to get **taxable income.** For example, the government allows people to subtract, or deduct, the interest on their mortgage from their income. It also allows people to subtract any interest earned from state or local bonds. The ability to take such deductions has a major effect on the way people spend and invest their money.

Suppose you earned $60,000 last year. Let's assume that, without deductions, you would have to pay $30,000 in federal income taxes. However, if you bought a house and had $6,000 in deductible expenses, your taxable income would be only $54,000. Now you might be paying only $25,000, instead of $30,000, in taxes. Since the government is willing to give a tax break to home owners, you—and many others—would be very likely to buy a house rather than rent an apartment. This benefits the construction industry a good deal. Thus, by allowing people to deduct certain kinds of spending from their taxable income, the government encourages the spending of money in those particular ways.

The government also encourages us to invest in certain government bonds by

The federal government allows the taxpayer many tax deductions. Among them are deductions on home mortgages. A deduction of this sort encourages citizens to buy homes.

making interest on them tax-free. At the same time, your state or local government will be receiving a low-interest loan to finance its highway or school construction.

But these deductions can also seem unfair. It is possible, for example, for one person to earn $30,000 a year and have a taxable income of $20,000 while another person earns $100,000 and has no taxable income at all. Deductions are, therefore, a very controversial part of every government's tax law.

Changes in the deductions that governments allow affect mainly those in higher tax brackets. Everyone else takes a flat, or set, deduction. This is called an **exemption.** Most governments have exemptions so that the poorest people will pay no tax at all. Thus, in 1978, United States citizens who earned less than $3,200 paid no income tax.

The government can influence the spending of people who use only this deduction by raising or lowering the overall tax rate. When the taxes are raised, people have less money and they spend less. When taxes are lowered, people spend more. Therefore, when the economy is sluggish, the government can give it a "boost" by lowering the taxes. However, the government cannot lower taxes too much. The government must be able to collect enough taxes for its own spending needs.

National governments also use individual income taxes to redistribute wealth. The more progressive the government makes the tax rate, the less of a difference there will be among the incomes of people. The money that is received is then used by the government to perform important services for everyone. However, a rate that is too progressive discourages people from working hard to earn more money since most of it is taken away. Our tax rate is designed to be fair to the less wealthy without taking away the incentive for people to work hard, accumulate wealth, and reinvest that wealth in the economy.

Social Security tax gives elderly people the assurance of a regular income on a monthly basis.

Taxing and Collecting When a government passes an income-tax law, it considers three points.

First, it decides how much money should be raised during the next year. Governments often raise or lower the tax rate depending on how much money will be needed.

Second, government considers how progressive the tax rate should be. If businesses are having trouble raising money and are therefore producing less, the government might make the tax laws less progressive. Then, wealthy people will be allowed to keep more of their money. Unlike people in the lower and middle classes, wealthy people do not usually spend extra income. They invest most of their money in the economy.

Third, the government decides what should be deducted from gross income in order to figure the taxable income.

At the end of the tax year, you figure out how much tax you should pay based on your income and the government's laws. Then you file a tax return, or form, and either pay to the government or receive from it the difference between the amount of tax due to the government and the amount withheld by your employer.

This is no simple process. The income-tax laws in the United States have become very complicated in recent years. Many taxpayers now question the fairness of these laws. But there is no agreement on any better way to raise money for the government. There is also no agreement on a fairer or simpler tax law.

The income tax is one of the great unresolved issues of democratic government. Until some agreement is reached, more and more taxpayers may simply stop paying their taxes. That is what is now happening in other countries.

Social Security Tax There is another part of the federal income tax that will be discussed at greater length later in this chapter. It is the Social Security and Medicaid tax, which is for pension, or retirement, and health insurance. This is a flat-rate tax on income up to a certain amount per year.

The Social Security tax is the federal government's second largest source of income. But the United States pays out about the same amount in Social Security benefits as it now receives in Social Security taxes.

Corporate Income Tax

The third most important source of income for the United States government—and a major source for state governments—is the corporate income tax.

Unlike the individual income tax, the corporate tax is usually a flat-rate tax on a corporation's **net income,** or profits. In recent years, the federal tax on large corporate profits—those over $50,000 a year—was over 40 percent. But few corporations pay that high a tax. They are allowed tax

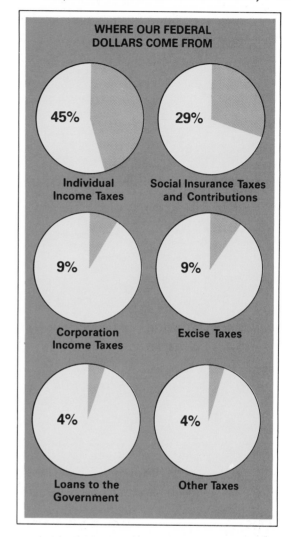

credits for reinvesting in their businesses, for employing the handicapped, and for training unemployed people for jobs. As with individual income taxes, the government balances the need to raise money and to be fair against other social needs.

Excise Tax

The excise tax is an important source of income for the federal government and for most state governments. It is a flat-rate tax paid by manufacturers of certain products that have been chosen for special taxation. These products include automobiles, gasoline, firearms, alcoholic beverages, and tobacco. The tax is not absorbed by the manufacturer, however. It is passed on to consumers, hidden in the prices they pay for the products.

Sales Tax

The sales tax is the single largest source of income for state governments. It is a flat-rate tax that is paid by purchasers of most products in most states. For example, when you buy something for $10 in an area with a 5 percent sales tax, you must pay the seller $10.50. The seller sends the extra 50 cents to the state government.

Some people feel that the sales tax is unfair. They say that it puts too great a burden on the poor, who must spend a greater part of their income on necessities. Many others feel that the sales tax is fair. After all, they argue, you pay taxes only on what you buy. In addition, most states do not tax food and rent, which are the major expenses of the poor.

Property Tax

The property tax is a flat-rate tax paid by owners of land, houses, and commercial property such as factories, office buildings, and stores. Not all property owners pay this tax, however. Many homes in blighted neighborhoods, factories in depressed areas, and nonprofit institutions such as churches and private schools are exempt.

Property tax is by far the most important source of income for local governments. It pays for those services that most closely affect our lives: public schools, police, fire protection, and sanitation.

As important as these services are to each of us, the property tax itself has become a controversial issue. This is partly because the cost of providing services has increased. Thus, the tax has also increased.

In some places, however, the tax is higher because more services are being provided—even more, perhaps, than most people in the community want. In other places, the tax has increased because huge areas of land have become tax-exempt. The thousands and thousands of dollars that this land used to bring in to the local government must now be paid by the property owners that are not exempt. As a result, some homeowners who earn no more than $8,000 to $10,000 are receiving property-tax bills for as much as $3,000.

They find this tax impossible to pay. What should be done? Should taxpayers simply not pay? Will local government take over people's homes? Will services be stopped? Will the tax structure be changed? These are questions that have not yet been answered.

Taxpayer Revolt

The **gross national product** is the total amount of goods and services produced by a country in 1 year. In 1976, the gross national product of the United States was about $2 trillion, or $2,000,000,000,000. In that same year, federal, state, and local governments collected $600 billion in taxes. That is 3 out of every 10 dollars produced by the people in the United States. Of that $600 billion, about $400 billion was collected by the federal government. The other $200 billion went to state and local governments. When taxes reach that level, people in the United States pay a good deal of attention to how their governments raise money and how they spend it.

At different periods in this country's history, taxpayer revolts have forced government to cut back on spending. In the late 1970s, taxpayers again began to question wasteful spending practices and the need for many government programs. The major targets on the national level are programs for national defense, social welfare,

WHAT HAPPENS TO YOUR PAYCHECK

This paycheck receipt shows the different deductions the government takes from each working man and woman. Aside from the deductions shown, money is also often taken out at the worker's request for health insurance, retirement benefits, or charities.

		STATEMENT OF EARNINGS - NOT NEGOTIABLE

```
REGULAR PAY   SALARY CONTINUATION   OVERTIME   OTHER PAY   AMOUNT   GROSS PAY
634.62                                                                634.62
HRS. PAID  HRS. NOT PD.  HRS. PAID  HRS. NOT PD.  HRS. PAID  HRS. WORKED      FOR PERIOD ENDING 092781
70.0

117.54    42.21   NY    29.79          STATE  DISAB./UNEMP.   NEW YORK CITY   11.29        TAXES
FED. WITHHOLDING  SOC. SECURITY  STATE  WITHHOLDING  STATE          CITY      WITHHOLDING

                                         7.93
MEDICAL   GROUP LIFE INS.   LONG TERM DISAB.   PENSION   CREDIT UNION   STOCK PURCHASE   BENEFIT PLANS

                                                                   OTHER DEDUCT  ****425.86
DESCRIPTION       AMOUNT        DESCRIPTION        AMOUNT                        NET PAY

SOCIAL SECURITY NO.   GROSS EARNINGS 11,333.57   FEDERAL WITHHOLDING TAX 2,024.43   BOND BALANCE   YEAR-TO-DATE
389917   SOC. SECURITY 730.06  STATE WITH. TAX 506.31  CITY WITH. TAX 194.85   PENSION SINCE 12-1 122.97
CHECK NUMBER
```

highways, and agriculture. But each program has vigorous and organized support in business, in Congress, and in other parts of the government.

In the meantime, many taxpayers have revolted against the burden of local and state taxes. The services that these governments offer are vital and most closely affect our lives. But these expenses are also the easiest for people to control. When taxes at all levels become too great, people can simply vote against the politicians who passed the tax laws.

— REVIEW —

1. What are the three reasons why individual income taxes are used by so many national governments?
2. Explain how deductions influence the ways in which people spend and invest.
3. What is the danger of a tax system that is too progressive?
4. What kinds of taxes do state governments use? Which taxes are their major sources of income?
5. What do you think should be done about the tax problem in areas where tax-exempt property has placed most of the tax burden on a smaller number of property owners?

Words to Know

interest——a fee that a borrower pays in return for the temporary use of the money use of the money

general-purpose debt —— borrowed money that may be spent on anything

special-purpose debt ——money that is borrowed to be spent for a specific purpose, such as for buying a house or building a highway.

What Government Does for Us

The Preamble to the Constitution gave the federal government the responsibility "to form a more perfect Union, establish justice, insure domestic tranquility, provide for the common defense, promote the general welfare, and secure the blessings of liberty."

At that time, no one had any idea that the expense of running the government would ever be 30 percent of the gross national product. As recently as 1955, federal-government expenses accounted for only 10 percent.

Why has there been such a sharp rise in expenses? The world has changed greatly in the last 20 to 30 years. There are now many more retired people. The number of school-age children has also risen sharply. Also, for the first time in its history, this nation has felt the need to maintain a world defense capability in peacetime. All these things have added to the level of public spending. To see how, we will have to examine just what government does.

Health and Welfare

If you lose your job, the government gives you unemployment insurance payments. If you are unable to work, the government gives you money for food, housing, clothing, and medical expenses. When you retire, you will receive Social Security benefits. These and other government health and social-welfare costs account for over $200 billion of the $600 billion in public spending. The largest single item is federal old-age benefits, better known as *Social Security.*

Social Security Social security benefits are monthly payments made to anyone at age 65 or over who has been in the work force for a certain number of years. You probably know someone who receives Social Security checks.

The federal government does not take the funds to pay old-age benefits from individual income taxes. This money comes from contributions made by working people. The amount that each person contributes depends on his or her income. When the first contributions were made in 1937, the Social Security tax was 1 percent of the first $3,000 earned in a year. By 1981, it was 6.65 percent of the first $29,700. The employer contributes an amount equal to the payment of the worker.

The money collected is not set aside for the worker's retirement. It pays for the benefits of the people who have already stopped working. When today's workers retire, their pension will be paid for by the next generation of workers.

In this way, inflation is taken into consideration. However, for the system to

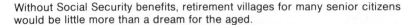

Without Social Security benefits, retirement villages for many senior citizens would be little more than a dream for the aged.

In recent years, American society has acknowledged that the handicapped can be useful, productive members of society. At the same time, increased amounts of our tax dollars have gone toward their education and vocational development.

work, there must be many more workers than retired people. People must work for more years than they spend on pension. And retired people should have other sources of income. Social Security was originally meant to be added to such things as savings, private pensions, and private insurance policies. It was to serve as a foundation for financial security in old age, not as the only means of support.

If any of the three conditions above is not met, the Social Security program will be in trouble. The cost of the benefits will be too much for the contributors to pay. Then, either the benefits will have to be reduced or the funds to pay for them will have to come from another source. If neither of these things happens, the Social Security program will simply go out of business.

Financing Problems In fact, Social Security is in a great deal of trouble. On the one hand, there are more retired people than ever before, and they are living longer.

In addition, many people are living on nothing but Social Security payments. As a result, the payments have become more and more generous in recent years. Some families can now receive $10,000 a year, tax free. Moreover, the Social Security program has been expanded to include Medicare. *Medicare* is health insurance for the elderly.

There is concern that open-ended pension payments—payments without a built-in limit—threaten the financial base of the federal government. Efforts are being made to see that Social Security payments do not grow as rapidly in the future.

Education

You have the right to a free education. Yet the costs of education are enormous. School costs and teachers' salaries come to more than $100 billion a year. State and local governments pay most of these costs.

The cost of education has risen sharply over the past 20 years. This is partly due to expensive new programs for the handicapped, for adults, and for preschool children. But most of the increase is due to the post-World War II "baby boom."

An enormous number of people were born between 1945 and 1950. All of them had to be educated, of course. Because so many children were going to school at once, new buildings were needed. New books, desks, equipment, and teachers—many teachers—were also needed.

Now that these students have passed through the educational system, spending on education should level off. However, it will probably not decrease. That is because the cost of teachers' salaries and fringe benefits—especially pensions—has increased much faster than inflation.

National Defense

National defense is one of the largest areas of expense for the government. The United States spends nearly $100 billion a year to support the armed forces and to provide other countries with military assistance.

National defense is a traditional function of government. The need for national defense is not questioned. However, the amount and the way in which these tax dollars are spent is the center of much argument.

Many people believe that too much money is spent on defense and that some of the money is wasted. They think that it could be better spent on social-welfare programs.

Even those who are in favor of large defense spending argue about how and where the money is spent. For example, if the Army closes a military base in South Carolina, it can mean that 5,000 civilian workers in the area lose their jobs. If the Air Force signs a contract with one company rather than with another company, many civilian jobs and large amounts of corporate profits are affected.

Since defense spending in a particular area directly affects the area's economy, there is constant political give-and-take over how national defense programs should be carried out. Many decisions are made for local economic reasons, not for national-defense reasons.

The need for modern weapons of war to protect us from attack is just one of many reasons why a significant chunk of our tax dollars is spent for defense.

The national-defense program shows why government continues to grow. Once a program is begun, many people come to depend upon it for jobs, income, or profits. It becomes harder to stop a program, even when it is no longer useful.

Interest on Debt

For many years, government spending has been growing faster than government income. In order to carry out its programs, the government does what you would do if your supply of cash was not enough to meet your needs. It borrows money.

The federal government owes a debt of $500 billion to people who buy government bonds or notes. State and local governments also have huge debts. In order to encourage people to lend money to the government, the government pays them **interest.** Interest is defined as a fee that a borrower pays in return for the temporary use of the money. This is another expense that government must pay, and it has increased sharply in recent years. The interest on federal, state, and local public debt is nearly $100 billion.

The federal government has a **general-purpose debt.** The money that it borrows may be spent on anything. Most state and local debt is **special-purpose debt.** The money borrowed is to be spent for a specific purpose, such as for a highway or a sewer system.

Other Government Expenditures

The other categories of government spending are the traditional ones, such as highways, sanitation, police, and fire protection. These expenses account for a comparatively small part of all government spending. They come to about $60 billion, which is 10 percent of the total. However, these expenses have also risen sharply.

Citizens have the greatest control over any spending done in the above ways because these services are supplied by local and state governments. As you read earlier, the latest tax revolt has been aimed at this kind of spending. It will be interesting to see whether this concern over high taxes will reduce federal spending as well. Remember that many people in the United States are now dependent on government programs.

———————— REVIEW ————————

1. What are four areas of government expense?
2. The success of the Social Security program is based on three conditions. What are they?
3. What is a special-purpose debt?
4. In your opinion, where should the government make major spending cuts?

Words to Know

credit —— access to money that you do not now have

spread —— the difference between the interest a bank charges and the interest a bank pays

mortgage —— a loan that is made to buy land, houses, real-estate developments, or commercial property

collateral —— security for a loan

multiplier effect —— the increase in wealth that results when money and credit move from person to person through the economy

check —— a demand for money

discount rate —— the interest that banks pay the government for their supply of money

reserve requirements —— the money that banks must keep in reserve instead of lending

inflation——a decrease in the value and buying power of money; a sharp, continuing rise in the prices of goods and services, usually caused by an abnormal increase in available currency and credit.

Banking

The Constitution gave the federal government alone the right to mint coins and print money. By centering the power of issuing money in the federal government, the Constitution gave the government a powerful tool for regulating the economy. The government can control the amount of money that is in circulation, which is the amount of money that you and other people have to spend. This, of course, has a ma-

jor effect on the economic activity of the nation.

The power to issue money put the government in the banking business, which had traditionally been the function of banks. It also gave the government the influence to regulate the activities of banks. Before we look at how the government acts as a banker and as a controller of banks, let's see exactly what part privately owned banks play in our economy.

What Banks Do

Banking is one of the most important industries in modern society. It exercises control over the one product that makes all other modern economic activities possible— money.

One of the primary functions of banks is to store their customers' money safely and securely in vaults such as the one in the photo below.

Banks gather and store money that is owned by individuals, business firms, and governments. They also lend that money to other individuals, business firms, and governments.

Banks as Borrowers Why do people leave their money with banks? For one thing, they leave it there so that it will be safe. Until recently, however, banks in many countries of the world were not as safe as they are today. The biggest problem was bank failure. If a bank closed, you simply lost all the savings you had deposited there. In other countries, people's long-time distrust of banks is still alive. Even in England, for example, many people still do not use banks.

However, safety is not the main reason for putting your money in a bank. Interest is. Banks pay people to deposit their money.

Until the 1930s, American banks did not encourage individuals to deposit small amounts of money. Instead, the federal government had a Postal Savings Plan, run by the post office, for small depositors. The post office sold interest-bearing notes that were guaranteed by the government. This savings plan was ended by the government in 1966. There was no longer any need for it in the United States. But similar plans exist in other countries.

Banks as Lenders Banks can afford to pay you for keeping your money with them because they do not simply keep it in their vaults. They keep only about 20 percent of the money there. The exact figure is set by the federal government, which bases its decision on current economic conditions. The rest of the money is lent to other people. Loans are a method by which banks expand their credit.

When you borrow money, you are receiving credit. **Credit** is access to money that you do not now have. Suppose you want to borrow money to buy a car. The bank might give you credit, but it will also

Granting mortgage loans to responsible citizens is another regular function of banks in some states.

charge you interest by the year for the use of that money. The bank received the money it is lending to you from its depositors. It pays those depositors interest on a yearly basis for the use of their money. The difference between the interest that a bank pays and the interest that a bank charges is the **spread.** Part of that money is profit. Part of it goes to maintain the bank's buildings and equipment and to pay all the people the bank employs.

Many bank loans are mortgages. A **mortgage** is a loan made to buy land, houses, real-estate developments, or commercial property such as factories and office buildings. Banks charge less interest for their mortgages than for any other kind of loan. That is because a mortgage is the safest kind of loan that a bank can make. The borrower uses her or his property as **collateral,** or security. If the loan payments are not made on time, the bank can take over the property.

People who take out other kinds of loans are charged higher interest. However, there is a maximum rate of interest that any bank can charge or pay its depositors. That rate is set by federal and state regulations.

The Multiplier Effect The bank is entitled to a profit because it is performing a vital service for society. It is creating wealth. By lending your money, it increases the possible number of transactions that take place in the economy. For instance, the $100 that you deposit in a bank might go to pay for someone else's home repairs. This pays a painter's salary, which in turn pays the store owner and the landlord. If they put that money in a bank, the money is lent once again to other people.

That $100 of yours has already been used four times, greatly increasing its value. If there had been no bank for you to deposit the money in, you probably would have just kept it in a safe place at home. Then none of that economic activity could have taken place.

As you can see, money and credit have a **multiplier effect.** They increase wealth as they move from person to person through the economy. Each new transaction gives more people the use of the money in circulation.

Without banks to give credit, borrowers would have to go to individuals for credit. But for individuals, lending is a very risky business. Most people could not afford a loss of money. It would ruin them financially. Therefore, if individuals were doing all the business of banking, most savings would be kept out of circulation. This would mean that business as we know it could not exist. Modern business has come to depend upon credit about as much as it depends upon money.

Other Services Holding money and lending money are the main functions of a bank. But banks also do other things. Some banks will offer experts to invest your money for you in stocks, bonds, and other money markets. Banks also make overseas transactions easier by making payments abroad in foreign currencies. Last, but not least, banks hold money for you to draw upon with a check. A **check** is a demand for money. Nearly three-fourths of the money that changes hands does so in the form of checks.

The Regulation of Banks

In a pure capitalist system, the law of supply and demand would be the only control on banks. In the United States, however, things work a little differently.

Regulating the Money Supply In the first place, the supply of money is affected by the federal government's power to issue money. You will learn how this money goes into and out of circulation later on in the chapter.

Banking activity is also indirectly controlled in two other ways. One way is the raising and lowering of the discount rate. The **discount rate** is the interest that banks pay the federal government for their supply of money. Raising the rate makes the money more expensive and harder to get. That limits the supply of money. Lowering the rate has the opposite effect.

The second indirect control is the raising or lowering of reserve requirements. The **reserve requirement** is the money that banks must keep in reserve instead of lending. This can strongly influence the amount of money in circulation. You would not want the reserve requirement to go too low, however. Then, the bank might not have enough money available to cash your paychecks, for example.

Government Regulation The more than 15,000 banks in the United States control more than $1 trillion. That is nearly one-fourth of all the wealth in the country.

In decaying areas such as this one, mortgage loans are less likely to be granted by banks, which see the loans as bad risks.

Of that amount, about $800 billion is on loan. More than $500 billion of the money on loan is in mortgages.

For the most part, the banks themselves are allowed to decide who gets credit and who does not. They determine who gets the money they need to stay in business. They decide whether to lend money for a house to be built in a new neighborhood or whether people repairing a house in an old neighborhood will receive the necessary money. However, because the industry's services are so important to the success of the economy, banking is heavily regulated.

The banking system is so regulated that there is frequent overlapping of authority. A national bank may be examined by a bank officer who controls its financial records, the Federal Reserve System, and the Federal Deposit Insurance Corporation (FDIC). The FDIC was created in 1933 to insure the accounts of depositors in member banks. A state bank may be examined by state officials, the Federal Reserve System,

and the FDIC. The government's regulatory system is set up to work in such a way that the different agencies involved take turns examining each bank.

Many states require banks to make a minimum percentage of their mortgages within the state. Banks have also been required to make mortgages in those neighborhoods that banks feel are not good risks.

The government also regulates the interest rates that banks pay and charge. Throughout our history, interest rates have caused much conflict. These rates were often high. But rapid changes in interest rates make borrowing and lending very risky.

What if you took out a 20-year mortgage at the unusually high rate of 15 percent last year, only to learn that the rate had gone down to 7 percent this year? You would be more than just angry if you lost your home because you could not pay this inflated rate.

To protect both borrowers and banks, the federal government and most state governments have laws setting maximum interest rates.

The government also regulates banks by requiring them to insure deposits. In that way, your savings are protected even if the bank should fail. A few years ago, Franklin National Bank—one of the nation's largest banks—did fail. It had made some unwise investments in foreign money. The shareholder-owners lost a great deal of money. But the depositors were paid back by the Federal Deposit Insurance Corporation, which has sold insurance to banks since 1934.

Government Banking

The government not only regulates banks but also performs many banking services itself. In fact, the government is in the banking business.

Creating Money The most important banking function performed by most governments today is the making and issuing of money. In the United States, this is done by the Federal Reserve System.

The government can print as much money as it chooses. You may wonder, then, why it doesn't print all the money it needs so there wouldn't be so much arguing over money in Congress. If the government printed that much money, the money would be worthless. The amount of money in circulation has to be based on real wealth for the economic system to work.

In the United States, the amount of money printed affects the economy directly. When there is more money than real wealth, the value of the dollar decreases and there is **inflation.** When there is too little money in circulation, credit is too tight. Then business activity suffers.

As you can see, the Federal Reserve Board has many things to consider when it wants to change the money supply.

Distributing Money When the government does choose to increase the

amount of money, it does not simply give some crisp new bills to a few lucky banks. It makes more money available for loans through the Federal Reserve Banks. When the government wants to decrease the money supply, it can recall outstanding loans that the Federal Reserve Banks have made.

The Federal Reserve Banks are bankers' banks. They lend money to banks and accept deposits from them. But the Federal Reserve Banks have other functions as well. One very important one is to serve as the government's banks. They hold government funds and issue all government checks.

―――――――――― REVIEW ――――――――――

1. What is the difference between interest and spread?
2. How does the multiplier effect work?
3. Why are the services that the banks provide to the community so important to the economy?
4. What are three ways in which the federal government controls the supply of money?
5. Do you think that either federal or state governments should allow banks to continue the practice of redlining? Why or why not?

Words to Know

insurance company —— a company that provides protection against unacceptable financial risks

insurance policy —— a contract between an insurance company and an individual or a business firm; states that the insurance company will pay should the risk being insured against occur

premium —— the price of an insurance policy

Insurance

What Insurance Companies Do

An **insurance company** protects you from an unacceptable financial risk by selling you a contract known as an **insurance policy.** The policy says that the company will pay you should the risk being insured against occur. The price you pay for the contract is called the **premium.**

Modern insurance started in England in the eighteenth century. The first two risks insured against were loss of life and loss of shipping. If, for example, you were sending out a ship and cargo worth $1 million, you might pay a premium of $10,000— or 1 percent—to buy a policy. That policy would provide for payment of up to $1 million if the ship or cargo were lost or damaged.

Insurance policies do not last forever. They have a fixed life span. Thus, your life might be insured for 1 year, or your ship might be insured for one voyage. More often, however, individual lives are insured for 5 years or longer. The insurance company can more easily determine and price the risks involved over this period of time.

That is, an insurance company has accurate figures on how many people out of every 1,000 of a certain age, health, and income will die during that period. Since insurance companies insure large numbers of people, they have a fairly good idea of how much they are going to have to pay in claims. Therefore, they make sure that the money they take in is equal to or more than the claims. This is how the financial risk is shared.

Insurance companies will not insure you against medical costs or property damage for a period of 5 years, as they would your life. To cover these risks, you have to take out a new policy each year. That is because the cost of health care, of repairing damaged cars and property, and of losses from damage suits have risen very sharply in recent years. As a result, insurance companies cannot predict more than 1 year in advance how much they will have to pay in claims.

The successful insurance companies know how to select and price risks accurately. Therefore, they take in more money than they pay in claims. The money that they accumulate is invested in the nation's economy. This means that the companies

Before buying an insurance policy, the couple in this photo are having the salesperson explain all its advantages and disadvantages. Whether they are buying life insurance or property-liability, they will have their choice among a number of different plans for each.

earn more money, which permits them to charge lower premium rates for insurance policies. That benefits everyone. In fact, most insurance companies break even on policies. They earn their profits from dividends, interest, and returns on their investments.

The modern insurance industry is divided into two main parts. The larger companies are *life-insurance companies*. These offer loss-of-life coverage, old-age benefits, and medical insurance. There is over $2 trillion in life-insurance coverage in the United States today. Prudential Insurance and Metropolitan Life are the two largest suppliers of this kind of insurance.

Most insurance companies also offer *property-liability insurance*. This protects people from damage to property as well as legal liability arising from damage to their property. For example, suppose that the roof of your house collapsed and injured a guest. Property-liability insurance would pay for your guest's medical expenses as well as for the cost of putting up a new roof. Many of the property-liability companies also insure automobiles.

Regulation of Insurance Companies

Unlike banks, insurance companies are regulated almost entirely by the states. State insurance commissions require companies to keep a certain percentage of their money available for the immediate payment of claims. They also require companies to prove the need for increases in premium rates. If the commission feels that the rates are not justifiable, it will reject a company's application for an increase. This happens often. However, the result may be that the insurance company will refuse to insure anyone in the state against the particular risk for which the rate increase was denied. That happens most often with automobile insurance.

Many states require drivers to carry insurance so that injured people can sue for injuries and damages. However, no company wants to insure drivers with bad driving records. For this reason, insurance commissions require automobile-insurance companies to organize a high-risk pool for the purpose of sharing the cost of insuring such drivers. Many states also require insurance companies to organize high-risk pools in other areas where insurance is legally required. For example, there might be pools for workers' compensation—payment for injuries that happen on the job. Without such pools, certain industries would not be allowed to operate in the state as a result of the fact that the industry was not able to get insurance.

Government Insurance

The federal government offers insurance directly in several areas. Sometimes it competes with insurance companies, and sometimes it provides new kinds of insurance that companies are not yet willing to offer. The government takes the lead in this area because insurance companies cannot insure a new risk at a low rate. They do not have the experience necessary to measure and price the risk. The government, on the other hand, can take a loss and pay for it with tax money.

The largest government insurance program is that of old-age pensions and health insurance for people over 65—Social Security and Medicare. However, the government is now seriously considering a complete program of health insurance for citizens of every age. But since doctors' bills and hospital bills have risen sharply in recent years, such a program would be very costly. It would also compete with existing private programs such as Blue Cross and Blue Shield. Therefore, the complete health-insurance program is a very controversial issue.

Due to government-sponsored health insurance for the elderly, the senior citizens in this picture are able to have their blood pressure checked at centers especially set up for them.

Less controversial is government insurance against risks that private insurance firms may not cover, or cover at rates too high for many citizens. These plans are not all available in every state. A few of the plans offered by the government are federal crime, fire, and flood insurance.

People in the United States are taking out more and more insurance as they measure the risks involved in driving, owning homes and businesses, and supporting their families during illness. Because of this, insurance is a rapidly growing industry. As people come to demand more types of insurance at rates they can afford, the government's role in insurance may grow. However, most people in this country agree that private companies should do the job of insuring whenever possible. Then the govern-

ment and our tax money are not involved. Also, private insurance companies reinvest premiums in the economy, thus benefiting the entire nation.

REVIEW

1. What is the purpose of insurance companies?

2. Where do insurance companies' profits actually come from?

3. What kinds of protection do property-liability companies offer?

4. How does a high-risk pool work?

5. Do you think that the government should provide complete medical insurance for citizens of all ages? Why or why not?

How the United States Works

Bank Tellers

There was a time when many people did not trust banks. They kept their savings in an old sock or hidden in a mattress. These days, however, most people cannot do without banks. That is because so many transactions are made by check or credit card. Your parents, for example, do not receive their pay in cash on payday. They are paid by check. To turn the check into money, they have to take it to a bank. They usually take only part of the check in cash. The rest is deposited in a checking or savings account.

Bank tellers handle all the deposits to and withdrawals from the different kinds of bank accounts. Before any withdrawals are made, the teller must make sure that the money is going to the right person. This is done by checking the signature of the person requesting the money against a sample signature that is kept on file. The teller also makes sure that there is enough money in the account to cover the withdrawal. Then, the money is counted carefully—twice. If the bank customer is making a deposit, all the money is counted and the checks are totaled. Once again, the teller must be certain of the amount. At the end of the day, the tellers go over their work to make sure that there were no errors.

Most banks have their own training program for new tellers. A high school degree is usually required for acceptance into the program. The training may take anywhere from 2 days to 3 weeks. When it is finished, the new tellers usually work with a more experienced person for a few days. Then, they start to work on their own.

Most bank tellers make between $5,500 and $9,500 a year. The number of jobs is growing because banks are now staying open for longer hours. Banks are also hiring part-time tellers to work during busy periods such as midday and Fridays. However, some jobs may become outdated as more machine tellers come into use.

Reading About . . .

Credit ———————————————————————

This chapter has been concerned with the government and its role in the economy. Now let's look into the question of credit and what it takes to get it.

As you read, ask yourself the following questions:

● Do you think that credit scoring is fair?
● Can you be a good citizen and still not receive credit?

Two people are standing side by side in a bank lobby filling out applications for a car loan. One is a lawyer, married, 35 years old, who makes $45,000 a year and owns a house. The other person is a mechanic, single, 25 years old, who makes $10,000 a year and lives in an apartment. Who gets turned down?

The answer in this case could easily be the lawyer. This kind of surprising verdict is being delivered increasingly by credit-scoring systems, which are mathematical methods for distinguishing the "goods" from the "bads," as they say in the credit industry. Credit scoring replaces the more or less intuitive judgment of a credit officer. Instead of being evaluated subjectively, the answers to questions on a credit application are scored on a carefully calculated point system, as is the data from credit bureaus. Depending on how many points you make, you either get the loan or you don't.

In the case of the lawyer and the mechanic, this particular bank does not give the lawyer extra points for belonging to a prestigious profession. The experience of some big lenders has taught them that among their customers, occupation has no bearing on credit worthiness. Well then, isn't $45,000 a year better than $10,000? It certainly is, but the bank's studies show that a 35-year-old with a family and a big income is likely to be on an acquisition binge, piling up possessions and debts. In fact, the bank has found out from a credit bureau that the lawyer recently missed a loan payment. His absentmindedness cuts his score.

The mechanic, on the other hand, has had a previous loan at the bank and paid it off early. Moreover, he has both checking and savings accounts at the bank, while the lawyer has only a checking account. The clincher is that the mechanic has worked in the same job and rented the same apartment for the past five years. The lawyer recently changed both job and house. Stability is greatly valued by lenders.

Credit scoring has grown rapidly in the 1970s, both in use and sophistication. Montgomery Ward, which is reputed to have the most sophisticated system in operation today, uses credit scoring in all its stores. Sears Roebuck began using credit scoring in 1968 and has extended it to more than a quarter of its stores. With 4.5 million credit-card holders and a half-million applicants per year, the Bank of America relies heavily on credit scoring. Without scoring, credit approval can be a pretty arbitrary affair. Oldtime credit officers operated with a bagful of dubious rules of thumb and a high regard for their own shrewdness.

Credit scoring selects from a mass of historical data the questions that most clearly separate good risks from bad for a particular lender and then determines the value given to each answer. However, the questionnaires generally focus on certain characteristics:

Stability. The most important thing for the lender to know is that the borrower has put down roots. Therefore, most scoring systems take into account the number of years since the lender changed jobs or residence. A favorite tip-off to stability is a home phone, on the assumption that deadbeats and transients don't have phones.

Occupation. Lenders usually assign a value to an applicant's job, if only to get a further measure of stability. The highest marks normally go to professionals and the lowest to unskilled workers. But Sears has discovered that occupation has no predictive value among its customers; theoretically a bartender can score at Sears as high as a company president.

Income. Though most lenders ask how much an applicant makes, it is more important for them to know how much income the applicant has to spare. "Someone earning $30,000 a year and spending $40,000 is not as good a risk as someone earning $700 a month who regularly puts $200 in a savings account," says Kenneth Larkin, a senior vice-president at the Bank of America.

Financial history. A person's past credit record is so important that in a few scoring systems—Penney's for one—a bad credit-bureau report can override an otherwise good score.

Age. As a person becomes older, his or her credit record usually becomes better; but often there is a dip in the 30s or 40s because those tend to be years of heavy spending. If any age discrimination is built into credit scoring, it works against the young. There doesn't seem to be much point in asking a 21-year-old how long he or she has held the same job or lived in the same place or whether she or he is a homeowner.

Fair, Isaac & Co., a California firm that develops scoring systems, believes lenders should use a special questionnaire for people under 30 or 35. Amendments to the federal Equal Credit Opportunity Act that take effect in March, 1977, forbid credit discrimination on such grounds as race, color, religion, national origin, and age. The Federal Reserve Board has ruled that people rejected for credit have a right to know not just that they scored low but specifically why.

Despite inhibitions imposed by federal law, scoring systems usually predict a borrower's behavior with great accuracy. Companies that use scoring systems find that for the first time they can predict their losses to within a fraction of a percentage point. They can't eliminate all bad loans, nor do they want to because they would turn down too many good risks at the same time. But they can either reduce their credit losses or approve more borrowers without increasing their losses.

In almost all scoring systems, a credit officer can veto the system's impersonal judgment and substitute her or his own. But Fair, Isaac wishes its clients would stop doing that; it considers human intuition no match for a good scoring system. Sears' experience seems to confirm this opinion. Sears keeps track of what happens after a credit manager says *yes* to a loan when the scoring system has said no: 95 percent of the loans are hard or impossible to collect.

Review

Fact Review

1. Name five kinds of taxes and discuss the importance of each one.
2. Which of the following are not involved with taxation?
   a. deduction
   b. interest
   c. exemption
   d. premium
   e. collateral
3. What are the four major areas of government concern?
4. What are the two major functions of banks? Explain.
5. How and by whom are insurance companies regulated?

Developing Your Vocabulary

What are the differences between the following pairs of words?
   a. exemption and deduction
   b. gross income and net income
   c. general-purpose debt and special-purpose debt
   d. interest and spread

Developing Your Reading Skills

Read the following paragraph and then answer the questions that follow:

Everyone grumbles about having to pay taxes, but very few people would argue against the value of taxes in our country. Without taxes there would be no unemployment benefits if you were laid off from your job or Social Security benefits when you retired. Without taxes there would also be no free public school education, meaning that only the economically advantaged could afford to be educated. Without taxes there would not even be a national defense program, police and fire protection, a decent highway system, or proper sanitation. No one would dispute the fact that large sums of government monies are mis-spent or mis-handled, but you would have to have an awfully good alternative before arguing that taxes were not necessary.

1. Which of the following do you think is the main idea, or point, of this paragraph?
   a. People pay taxes, but they don't like paying them.
   b. Without taxes no one would be able to get an education.
   c. Even though people don't like to pay taxes, taxes are necessary to the well-being of our society.
   d. The more tax dollars the government collects, the more money is poorly handled.

Developing Your Writing Skills— Forming and Supporting an Opinion

In this chapter, you have learned what insurance is and you have seen how it is used. Now consider the following question:

Forming an opinion
1. Do you think that the government should offer insurance against risks that private insurance firms will not cover?

Supporting an opinion
2. After thinking about this question, write a paragraph that answers it. Begin with a topic sentence that sums up your views. Continue with evidence or arguments to support your opinion.

YOUR GOVERNMENT & ITS HISTORY

The Creation of the Federal Reserve System

The central banking and monetary system of the United States is the Federal Reserve System. It is often referred to as "the Fed." The Federal Reserve System was established by an act of Congress. It was approved by President Woodrow Wilson in December 1913, and it began operations the following year.

In other countries, there is often a single national bank located in the capital city. This is the banking center of the country. In the United States, however, Congress created a system of twelve regional banks instead of a single national bank.

Before the Federal Reserve System was created, there were serious weaknesses in the American banking system. American monetary policy had long been *inelastic*. This means that the amount of money in circulation did not increase or decrease to meet the changing needs of business and agriculture.

After the Civil War, the American economy went through a series of ups and downs. The periods of economic decline were often accompanied by unemployment and business failures. One such "down" period took place in 1907. The Panic of 1907 brought with it bank failures. It resulted in new demands in Congress for reforms to strengthen the banking and monetary system.

In 1908, Congress created the National Monetary Commission to study banking problems and to recommend solutions. Members of the commission visited Europe to learn how banking systems operated in other nations. In 1912, the commission gave Congress its 38-volume report. The commission suggested that Congress pass a law favoring a central banking system under government control. With this law, the government would have the ability to increase or decrease the amount of money in circulation.

A bill was presented to Congress in 1913. It was the basis of the Federal Reserve System. For months, the debates in

Congress dragged on without action being taken. When members of Congress prepared to take a recess to avoid the hot summer weather in Washington, D.C., the President threatened to call them back in a special session if they did not complete work on the bill. Finally, after 6 months, the bill became law on December 23, 1913.

The basic aim of the Federal Reserve System is to control the nation's supply of money. The United States was divided into twelve Federal Reserve Districts. A Federal Reserve Bank was created in each district. Banks were established in Boston, New York, Philadelphia, Cleveland, Richmond, Atlanta, Chicago, St. Louis, Minneapolis, Kansas City, Dallas, and San Francisco. These banks are not open to the public. They offer special services to banks in their districts that are members of the Federal Reserve System.

Banks that become members of the System have to purchase stocks, or shares of ownership, in their District Reserve Bank. Member banks have to keep part of their funds on deposit in the District Reserve Bank. As members of the Federal Reserve System, these banks receive a number of important privileges. For example, they can borrow funds from their District Reserve Bank.

The most powerful tool given the Fed is the reserve requirement. The funds member banks have to keep on deposit in District Banks are known as reserves. If the Fed decides to increase the total reserves, member banks might have to call in loans. In other words, member banks can force their borrowers to pay what is owed. Member banks might have to cut back on the total funds available for making new loans in order to increase their reserves in the District Bank. By raising or lowering the reserve requirement, the Fed decreases or increases the amount of money member banks put in circulation. This controls the money supply.

Another important tool the Federal Reserve System has is the discount rate. If banks wish to raise additional money, they can borrow from the Federal Reserve District Bank. This is why District Banks are called "bankers' banks." They lend money to member banks in the same way that member banks make loans to the public. Federal Reserve Banks charge member banks a fee for loans. This fee is called the discount rate. Each District Bank can decide its own discount rate. If the rate is raised, member banks are likely to borrow less from the District Bank. If the fee is lowered, borrowing increases. In this way, the Fed also regulates the amount of money member banks can put into circulation. The reserve requirement and the discount rate are two important ways in which the Federal Reserve System is able to influence the amount of money in circulation.

1. Why was the Federal Reserve System established? When was it established?

2. What was the purpose of the System?

3. How does the Fed regulate the amount of money in circulation?

4. How many Federal Reserve Districts are there? In which district do you live?

5. Do you think that the Federal Reserve System plays an important role in the American economy? Tell why or why not.

SKILLS

Developing your basic civic education skills

(conflicting viewpoints)

Increasing the Number of People in the Social Security System

As you have learned in this chapter, Social Security is the federal government's second-largest source of income. Only the individual income tax is a larger source of government funds. Social Security is paid for by working peo-

ple. The amount of the tax depends upon an individual's income. The money collected is used by the government to give monthly payments to persons 65 years of age or older. The payments go to people who have retired after spending a certain number of years working.

For the Social Security system to work, there should be many more workers paying this tax than the number of

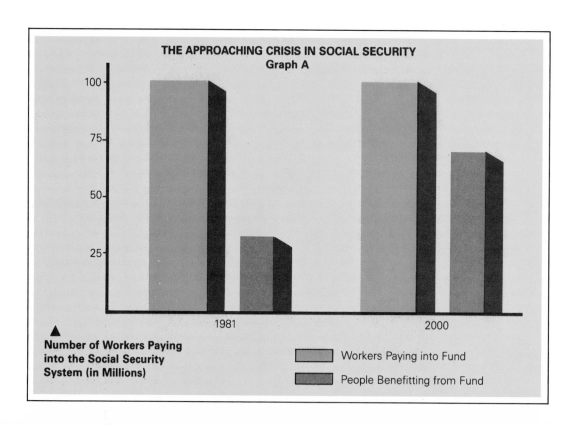

THE APPROACHING CRISIS IN SOCIAL SECURITY
Graph A

▲ Number of Workers Paying into the Social Security System (in Millions)

Workers Paying into Fund

People Benefitting from Fund

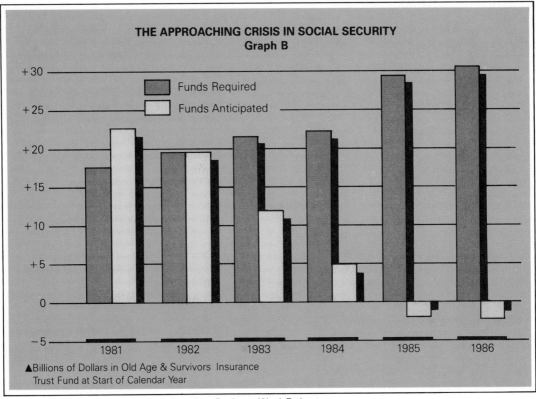

THE APPROACHING CRISIS IN SOCIAL SECURITY
Graph B

- Funds Required
- Funds Anticipated

▲Billions of Dollars in Old Age & Survivors Insurance
Trust Fund at Start of Calendar Year

DATA: Social Security Administration Based on *Business Week* Estimate

persons collecting retirement benefits from it. In recent years, though, the number of people receiving Social Security benefits has been increasing. In 1981, for every 100 workers paying into the Social Security system, there were 31 people receiving benefits. It is predicted that by the year 2000, for every 100 workers paying into the system, there will be 70 people receiving benefits. (See Graph A.) To afford this, an increase of as much as 40 percent in the Social Security tax would be needed.

If we look at the crisis in the Social Security system in a short-term way, we can see how serious a problem it is. Unless the government can find another way to raise money, more money will be needed than will be raised. (See Graph B.)

The Social Security program, as you can see, is in trouble. The cost of providing benefits is rapidly becoming greater than contributors can pay.

What is to be done? Many solutions have been suggested. One of these suggestions is to increase the number of taxpayers who contribute to Social Security. There are more than 2.9 million federal employees in government. These civil servants do not pay Social Security tax on their incomes. Should they be required to do so? Would bringing them under the Social Security program help to strengthen it? The following selection debates this issue.

Should Federal Employees Be Required to Pay Social Security Taxes?

Wilbur J. Cohen, former Secretary of the Department of Health, Education, and Welfare:

> Yes, this should be done by covering all members of Congress, members of the Cabinet, and newly hired federal employees. Employees in privately owned industry are covered by Social Security, and many have additional protection under private retirement plans, which have worked very well. As a former federal employee and a member of the National Association of Retired Federal Employees, I support this principle for federal employees, as do most employers and unions.

Steve Skardon, official of the National Association of Retired Federal Employees:

> Social Security has enough problems already. Each time Congress has expanded the number of people under Social Security, it eventually had to raise Social Security taxes to finance the resulting benefits. Adding federal employees could at first mean more revenue for Social Security. But it will certainly create greater long-term demands on the system when these folks start drawing monthly benefit checks after they retire. The real issue is Social Security. As long as the system remains a costly combination of insurance, welfare, and retirement protection, government

officials will always be looking for new ways to bail it out.

1. Which of the following statements are fact?

   a. Social Security benefits come from taxes paid by working people.

   b. Combining insurance, welfare, and retirement protection makes Social Security an expensive program.

   c. The Social Security tax is the federal government's second-largest source of income.

   d. Federal employees do not pay Social Security taxes.

   e. Social Security already has many problems.

   f. Adding people to the Social Security program will lead to higher taxes.

2. Briefly tell why you selected the statements you did in question 1.

3. In question 1, which statements are opinion?

4. Briefly tell why you selected the statements you did in question 3.

5. Match the main points in *a* to *e* below with the individual who made them.

   a. Requiring federal employees to pay Social Security taxes could at first mean more revenue for the program.

   b. Federal employees should be treated like employees in private industry.

   c. Social Security already has too many problems to think of increasing the number of people under the program.

   d. Most employers and unions favor requiring federal employees to pay Social Security taxes.

   e. Whenever the number of people covered by Social Security has been

The Social Security system is made up of the workers and employers who pay into the fund and the retired people who receive its benefits. As each generation of workers ages and retires, a new generation must take its place for the system to continue to operate.

increased, an increase in taxes has been necessary.

(1) Wilbur J. Cohen
(2) Steve Skardon

6. At this point, would you favor or oppose the proposal to require federal employees to pay Social Security taxes and, therefore, receive Social Security benefits when they retire? Briefly state your reasons. Would you consider your answer to be a hypothesis or a generalization? Why?

Should the Federal Government Limit the Earnings of People Receiving Social Security Benefits?

As you have learned, men and women who spend a certain number of years working and paying Social Security taxes can get monthly benefits after they retire at the age of 65. Many people 65 and older continue to live very active lives. Large numbers of them look for full-time or part-time jobs to earn income that will add to benefits from Social Security. But the federal government has placed a limit on the extra income these persons may earn. The limit is $6,000. This limit is enforced by a large federal tax placed on all income above that amount. Is this fair? Should people receiving Social Security checks be allowed to earn all the extra income they can? The following section debates this issue.

Should Congress Eliminate the Earnings Limit for Retired People Who Receive Social Security Benefits?

Senator Barry Goldwater, Republican, Arizona:

One of the major problems in the Social Security program is the discouragement of work by the earnings limit. Instead of encouraging older persons to remain productive workers benefiting themselves and the entire economy, Social Security penalizes work . . . by taxing 50-percent of any wages earned over $6,000. The major argument for doing away with the ceiling is fairness for older persons. The money they have paid into Social Security is theirs, not the government's. The government should have no say in how it is paid back.

Michael J. Romig, Director of the Human Resources Office, U.S. Chamber of Commerce:

The earnings limit follows Social Security's basic purpose of replacing income and protecting against dependency and hardships during retirement. An employed person earns income, and, therefore, is not retired. To do away with the ceiling would destroy sound policy. It would unfairly give scarce Social Security funds to employed persons who were without need of those benefits. It would force young workers to pay taxes in order to add to the incomes of older co-workers drawing Social Security benefits. It would raise costs and require a tax increase.

7. Which of the following statements are fact?

a. The earnings limit discourages work.

b. Doing away with the earnings ceiling will raise the cost of Social Security.

c. The government should have no say in how Social Security funds are paid back to retired persons.

d. People drawing Social Security benefits may have other sources of income.

e. The federal government places a 50 percent tax on wages over $6,000 earned by persons receiving Social Security benefits.

f. To do away with the ceiling would destroy Social Security policy.

g. Retired workers 65 or older may draw Social Security benefits.

8. Briefly, tell why you selected the statements you did in question 7.

9. In question 7, which statements are opinion?

10. Briefly tell why you selected the statements you did in question 9.

11. Match the main points that follow with the individual who made them.

a. Any employed person who earns an income should not be considered retired.

b. Doing away with the limit on earnings would be unfair to young workers.

c. The earnings limit is unfair to older persons.

d. Money paid into Social Security belongs to the taxpayers, not to the federal government.

(1) Barry Goldwater

(2) Michael J. Romig

UNIT 9 REVIEW

Fact Review

1. Name the two major material resources. Give examples of each.
2. What are the two major economic systems in the world today? How are they different?
3. What is the economy of scale? Why is it important?
4. Give three reasons why individual income taxes are a popular form of tax with the national government.
5. Name five areas in which the government provides funds.
6. Explain the role of the Federal Reserve Banks in our economy.
7. Which of the following are not associated with insurance:
   a. credit
   b. premium
   c. collateral
   d. high-risk pool

Developing Your Vocabulary

Give a definition for each of the following words. Then use the words in a paragraph about economic resources.

   a. capital formation
   b. human resources
   c. entrepreneurs
   d. material resources

Developing Your Reading Skills

Read the following passage and then answer the questions that follow:

Business, like government, is subject to different ways and means of operation. Just as there are two major economic systems of government, there are three basic forms of business.

A sole proprietorship—an individually owned business—is the most popular of the three forms because it is the simplest. It is also the system best suited to the person wanting to run her or his own business.

For people more concerned with capital expansion, a partnership is more advantageous to their needs. Under a partnership form of operation, two or more persons co-own, and often co-operate, a business. By doing this, they are able to combine both their economic resources and their individual talents and interests.

Finally, when the owners of sole proprietorships or partnerships feel the need to expand, they get their money by forming the third form of business—a corporation—and dividing the ownership of the business into shares, some of which are offered for sale. Of the three forms of business, the corporation has the most ability to combine economic resources and maintain growth.

1. Tell which of the questions below can be answered from the reading:
   a. What are the three basic forms of business?
   b. In what way is government like business?
   c. Which is the best form of business for a person who wants to open his or her own pest extermination business?
   d. What are the owners of stocks called?
2. Now give the answers to the questions above that can be found in the reading.

Glossary

Pronunciation Key

ă	pat	ng	thing	z	rose, size, xylophone, zebra
ā	aid, fey, pay	ŏ	horrible, pot	zh	garage, pleasure, vision
â	air, care, wear	ō	go, hoarse, row, toe	ə	about, silent, pencil, lemon, circus
ä	father	ô	alter, caught, for, paw	ər	butter
b	bib	oi	boy, noise, oil		
ch	church	ou	cow, out		
d	deed	ŏŏ	took		
ĕ	pet, pleasure	ōō	boot, fruit		
ē	be, bee, easy, leisure	p	pop	œ	*French* feu
f	fast, fife, off, phase, rough	r	roar	ü	*French* tu
		s	miss, sauce, see	KH	*Scottish* loch
g	gag	sh	dish, ship	N	*French* bon
h	hat	t	tight		
hw	which	th	path, thin		
ĭ	pit	th	bathe, this	Primary stress′	
ī	by, guy, pie	ŭ	cut, rough	bi·ol′o·gy bī ŏl′ə jē	
î	dear, deer, fierce, mere	û	circle, firm, heard, term, turn, urge, word	Secondary stress′	
j	judge	v	cave, valve, vine	bi′o·log′i·cal bī′ə lŏj′ ĭ kəl	
k	cat, kick, pique	w	with		
l	lid, needle	y	yes		
m	am, man, mum	yōō	abuse, use		
n	no, sudden				

© 1977 Houghton Mifflin Company. Reprinted by permission from *The American Heritage School Dictionary*.

Abridge (ə **brĭj′**): to limit or diminish. (p. 311)

Adjourn (ə **jûrn′**): to end a meeting or session. (p. 95)

Administrative Law (ăd mĭn′ĭ strā′tĭv lô): the law dealing with how the government is to be organized and what powers each part of the government will have. (p. 46)

Adolescence (ăd′l ĕs′əns): the period between childhood and adulthood, roughly the same as the teenage years. (p. 22)

Affirm (ə fûrm′): to uphold a lower court's decision. (p. 214)

Agribusiness (ăg′rĭ bĭz′nĭs): a company that processes and distributes food. (p. 488)

Alien (ā′lē ən) or (āl′yən): someone who lives in a country but is not a citizen. (p. 26)

Alimony (ăl′ə mōn′ē): support payments given by one spouse—husband or wife—to the other after a legal separation or divorce. (p. 455)

Ambassador (ăm băs′ə dər): the highest rank of diplomat. (p. 162)

Amendment (ə mĕnd′mənt): a formal change in a document, such as the Constitution. (p. 308)

Amnesty (ăm′nĭ stē): a pardon that is given to a group of people. (p. 163)

Anarchy (ăn′ər kē): a condition in which society has no laws nor government to make laws. (p. 41)

Annulment (ə nŭl′mənt): a court ruling that a marriage never legally existed at all. (p. 455)

Appellate Jurisdiction (ə pĕl′ĭt joor′ĭs dĭk′shən): the authority of a court to review a decision made by a lower court. (p. 212)

Arbitration (är′bĭ trā′shən): a method of settling disputes by submitting them to a person who is agreed upon by both parties to the dispute. (p. 458)

Arbitrator (är′bĭ trā′tər): a person who hears and decides arbitration cases. (p. 458)

Arraignment (ə rān′mənt): the court process during which an accused person enters a plea to the charges against him or her. (p.423)

Arson (är′sən): the crime of deliberately setting a fire with the intent to damage property. (p. 315)

Assault (ə sôlt′): threatening someone in such a way as to make that person fear that you are about to commit battery. (p. 453)

Attorney General (ə tûr′nē

jĕn′ər əl): head of the Department of Justice. (p. 183)

Bail (bāl): amount of money that an accused person puts up to guarantee that she or he will be present at a trial. (p. 240)

Bail-Bonding Agent (bāl **bŏnd′** ĭng **a′**jənt): a person who supplies bail so that accused persons may be freed before trial. (p. 422)

Battery (**băt′**ə rē): hitting or touching another person in an offensive way. (p. 453)

Bicameral Legislature (bī **kăm′**ər əl **lĕj′**ĭs lā′chər): a lawmaking body that has two parts—from the Latin for "two chambers." (p. 101)

Bill (bĭl): a plan or proposal for a law. (p. 120)

Bill of Rights (bĭl ûv) or (ŏv) or (əv rīts): the first ten amendments to the United States Constitution. (p. 81)

Binding Arbitration (**bīn′**dĭng är′bĭ **trā′**shən): an arbitration in which both sides accept the arbitrator's decision as final and binding. (p. 458)

Block Association (blŏk ə sō′ sē **a′**shən): a group of citizens who work together to improve their neighborhood. (p. 285)

Bonds (bŏndz): promises to repay given by businesses in exchange for loans. (p. 189)

Book (bo͝ok): to write the charges against a person into the police records. (p. 422)

Budget (**bŭj′**ĭt): a plan showing expected income and expenses. (p. 188)

Cabinet (**kăb′**ə nĭt): advisors to the President who serve as the heads of executive departments. (p. 68)

Candidate (**kăn′**dĭ dāt) or (-dĭt): a person who seeks to be elected to public office. (p. 358)

Capital (**kăp′**ĭ tl): the materials and equipment that are used to make and distribute goods and services; the money used to buy equipment, materials, and land. (p. 477)

Capital Formation (**kăp′**ĭ tl fôr **mā′**shən): the gathering and combining of economic resources in order to build up a nation's industrial capacity, which then increases productivity and produces wealth. (p. 477)

Capitalism (**kăp′**ĭ tl ĭz′əm): the economic system in which the means for producing goods and services are privately owned. (p.367)

Caucus (**kô′**kəs): a meeting of the Democratic members of the House of Representatives; a closed meeting of a political group. (p. 125)

Censure (**sĕn′**shər): to reprimand, or give a verbal spanking to, someone. (p. 243)

Charter (**chär′**tər): a written document, granted by the government, that defines the rights of a corporation. (p. 486)

Check (chĕk): a demand for money. (p. 518)

Checks and Balances (chĕks) and (**băl′**əns əs): part of the separation of powers, in which each branch of government can check, or block, the actions of the other branches so that all are in balance. (p. 80)

Child Abuse (chīld ə byo͞os′): the physical or mental mistreatment of a child. (p. 456)

Circuit (**sûr′**kĭt): region (the United States is divided into eleven circuits, each of which has a United States Courts of Appeals). (p. 268)

Civil Disobedience (**sĭ′**vəl dĭs ə bē′dē əns): concept according to which a person may—or should—break a law that he or she considers unjust, accepting arrest and even imprisonment without trying to escape punishment. (p. 334)

Civil Law (**sĭ′**vəl lô): the law dealing with disputes between private parties or between private parties and the government. (p. 45)

Civil-Law System (**sĭv′**əl lô **sĭs′**təm): a system, dating back to the code of Justinian, that is based upon laws arranged in codes, and in which precedents do not have the force of law. (p. 53)

Civil Rights (**sĭv′**əl rīts): the basic rights of an individual. (p. 46)

Civil Servant (**sĭv′**əl **sûr′**vənt): someone who works for the government in a nonmilitary job. (p. 191)

Civil Service System (**sĭv′**əl **sûr′**vĭs **sĭs′**təm): a merit system for government jobs. (p. 191)

Civilian (sĭ **vĭl′**yən): a person who is *not* serving in the armed forces. (p. 183)

Closed Primary (klōzd **prī′** mĕr ē): a primary election that is open only to members of a political party and closed to all others. (p. 369)

Cloture (**klō′**chər): a vote to end debate on a bill and stop a filibuster. (p. 132)

Coalition (kō′ə **lĭsh′**ən): an alliance of two or more parties. (p. 363)

Code (kōd): a listing of all laws that are in effect. (p. 48)

Collateral (kə **lăt′**ər əl): security for a loan. (p. 517)

Collective Bargaining (kə **lĕk′**tĭv **bär′**gĭn ĭng): the give-and-take discussions about wages and working conditions between an employer and union leaders, who speak on behalf of all workers. (p. 490)

Commission (kə **mĭsh′**ən): a group of officials—usually elected—who have duties and jobs that are described by law. (p. 288)

Commission (local government) (kə **mĭsh′**ən): a system of local government in which voters elect a small number of commissioners. (p. 288)

Committee (kə **mĭt′**e): a small group of lawmakers (Congress turns over much of its work to many types of committees). (p. 122)

Common Law (kŏm′ən lô): a system based both on laws and on judges' decisions, or precedents. (p. 52)

Communist Economy (kŏm′yə nĭst ĭ kŏn′ə mē): the form of socialism in which the government determines what will be produced and where people will work. (p. 481)

Community Property (kə myo͞o′nĭ tē prŏp′ər tē): property that belongs equally to wife and husband. (p. 455)

Complaint (kəm plānt′): written statement presented to a court to start a lawsuit. (p. 208)

Compulsory Schooling (kəm pŭl′sə rē sko͞o′lĭng): the policy of requiring children to attend school until they reach a certain age. (p. 339)

Concurrent Jurisdiction (kən kûr′ənt jo͝or′ĭs dĭk′shən): the authority over a case shared by both federal and state courts. (p. 212)

Concurrent Powers (kən kûr′ənt pou′ərz): powers that are shared by the federal and state government. (p. 48)

Conscientious Objector (kŏn′shē ĕn′shəs əb jĕkt′ər): a pacificist who refuses to be drafted as a military fighter. (p. 338)

Consideration (kən sĭd′ə rā′shən): something of value that is exchanged as the result of a contract. (p. 449)

Constitution (kŏn′stĭ to͞o′shən): a document that tells how a government is to be organized, and what powers each part of the government is to have. (p. 72)

Constitutional Amendment (kŏn′stĭ to͞o′shə nəl ə mĕnd′mənt): a formal change in the wording of a constitution. (p. 76)

Consumer (kən so͞o′mər): a person who buys goods and services. (p. 480)

Contract (kŏn′trăkt′): a form of agreement that binds people to do things (A contract must involve an offer, an acceptance, and a consideration). (p. 447)

Corporation (kôr′pə rā′shən): an artificial being—created by law and given the right to carry on a business. (p. 486)

Corrections Agency (kə rĕk′ shənz ā′jən sē): an agency, such as a prison, that deals with persons who have been convicted of crimes. (p. 426)

Council-Manager (local government) (koun′səl măn′ĭ jər): a system of local government in which voters elect a city council, which hires a city manager. (p. 288)

County (koun′tē): the largest unit of local government. (p. 289)

Court (kôrt) or (kōrt): a part of government that works to settle disputes by applying laws or precedents to specific cases. (p. 206)

Court-Martial (kôrt′) or (kōrt′ mär′shəl): a trial conducted by military officers under military law. (p. 215)

Credit (krĕd′ĭt): access to money that you do not now have. (p. 517)

Crime (krīm): any action that violates a law and for which the law provides punishment. (p. 45)

Criminal Justice System (krĭm′ə nəl jŭs′tĭs sĭs′təm): the part of society that deals with crimes and their effects; includes law-enforcement agencies, criminal courts, and corrections agencies. (p. 416)

Criminal Law (krĭm′ə nəl lô): law dealing with acts seen as harmful to a society. (p. 45)

Culture (kŭl′chər): the way of life in a society. (p. 15)

Damages (dăm′ĭj əz): payment of money ordered by a court to make up for a wrong. (p. 239)

Deduction (dĭ dŭk′shən): an amount subtracted from gross income to figure taxable income. (p. 507)

Defamation (dĕf′ə mā′shən): the spreading of false information that harms another person's reputation. (p. 454)

Defendant (dĭ fĕn′dənt): a person against whom a court case is brought. (p. 208)

Defense (dĭ fĕns′): the accused person's side in a criminal case. (p. 424)

Delegated Powers (dĕl′ə gāt ĕd pou′ərz): the powers of Congress that are listed in the Constitution. (p. 98)

Delinquent (dĭ lĭng′kwənt): a juvenile who is found by a court to have broken a law or committed a status offense. (p. 431)

Democracy (dĭ mŏk′rə sē): a government in which the people rule themselves. (p. 70)

Dictatorship (dĭk tā′tər shĭp): a government in which one person siezes and holds total power. (p. 69)

Diplomat (dĭp′lə măt): an official representative of one country in its dealings with another country. (p. 162)

Discharge (dĭs chärj′): to bring a bill out of committee, against the committee's will, by majority vote of the whole House. (p. 130)

Discount Rate (dĭs′kount rāt): the interest that banks pay the government for their supply of money. (p. 518)

Discrimination (dĭ skrĭm′ə nā′shən): the act of treating a person or group differently from other people. (p. 30)

Dissenting Opinion (dĭ sĕn′tĭng ō pĭn′yən): opinion issued by one or more justices to explain why they disagree with the majority opinion. (p. 218)

Divorce (dĭ vôrs′): a legal proceeding that ends a marriage. (p. 455)

Domestic (də mĕs′tĭk): relating to one's own home or country; opposite of *foreign*. (p. 146)

Due Process of Law (do͞o) or (dyo͞o prŏs′ĕs) of (lô): government action taken fairly and in line with procedures set down in the law. (p. 316)

Economic Resources (ē′kə nŏm′ĭk rē′sôrs′əz): the materials and the work that go into producing all things of value. (p. 476)

Economic System (ē′kə nŏm′ĭk sĭs′təm): the way in which goods and services are produced, distributed, and consumed. (p. 476)

Economics (ē′kə nŏm′ĭks): the study of how economic systems work. (p. 473)

Elastic Clause (ĭ lăs′tĭk klôz): the part of the United States Constitution that gives Congress its implied powers (it allows the power of Congress to expand to meet new problems). (p. 98)

Electoral College (ĭ lĕk′tər əl kŏl′ĭj): all the electors. (p. 150)

Electorate (ĭ lĕk′tər ĭt): all the people who are qualified to vote. (p. 358)

Electors (ĭ lĕk′tərz): people elected by voters in a presidential election. (They, rather than the voters, actually elect the president.) (p. 150)

Emancipated Minor (ĭ măn′cə pā′təd mī′nər): a minor who no longer has a legal duty to her or his parents and whose parents are freed of legal duties toward the minor. (p. 462)

Embassy (ĕm′bə sē): the most important government office of one country in a foreign country. (p. 181)

Entrepreneurs (än′trə prə nûrz′): the people who risk their money and time to start and run new businesses. (p. 478)

Ethnic Group (ĕth′nĭk groop): a group of people who have a common race, religion, or national origin. (p. 27)

Evidence (ĕv′ĭ dəns): facts or testimony given by one side or the other in a court case. (p. 208)

Executive Agreement (ĭg zĕk′yə tĭv ə grē′mənt): a written agreement between nations, usually dealing with routine matters. (p. 163)

Executive Branch (ĭg zĕk′yə tĭv branch): the part of the government that carries out the laws. (p. 79)

Executive Department (ĭg zĕk′yə tĭv dĭ pärt′mənt): a department of the federal government that is headed by a Cabinet member. (There are thirteen altogether.) (p. 180)

Executive Ordinance (ĭg zĕk′yə tĭv ôr′dn əns): a governor's orders that tell how a law will be carried out. (p. 266)

Exemption (ĭg zĕmp′shən): a flat amount that you can subtract from your taxable income if you do not list any deductions. (p. 508)

Expel (ĭk spĕl′): to throw out, remove. (p. 103)

Expense (ĭk spĕns′): the cost of producing a good or service. (p. 480)

Farmer's Cooperative (fär′mərz kō ŏp′ər ə tĭv): an association of independent farmers that shares equipment and means of distribution. (p. 488)

Favorite Son or Daughter (fā′vərĭt sŭn) or (dô′tər): an important person who is nominated for President by his or her delegation to a national convention. (Such a nomination is made primarily as a bargaining tactic.) (p. 371)

Federal Government (fĕd′ər əl gŭv′ərn mənt): the central government in a federation; the national government of the United States. (p. 77)

Felony (fĕl′ə nē): a serious crime, such as murder or robbery. (p. 416)

Feudal Law (fyood′l lô): guidelines set to make clear what peasant and lord could reasonably expect from one another. (p. 52)

Filibuster (fĭl′ə bŭs′tər): a drawn-out Senate speech that is aimed at killing a bill. (p. 132)

Fixed Sentence (fĭkst sĕn′təns): a prison sentence for a definite length of time. (p. 429)

Floor Leader (flôr lē′dər): a member of Congress chosen by a political party to help put the party's bills through Congress. (p. 125)

Free Enterprise (frē ĕn′tər prīz′): the form of capitalism that exists in the United States. (p. 48)

General Election (jĕn′ər əl ĭ lĕk′shən): the final election following the primaries. (p. 370)

General-Purpose Debt (jĕn′ər əl pûr′pəs dĕt): borrowed money that may be spent on anything. (p. 515)

G.O.P. (gē ō pē): "Grand Old Party," the Republican Party. (p. 361)

Government (gŭv′ərn mənt): an organization set up to make rules for a group of people and to see that the rules are carried out: a power that rules the people. (p. 64)

Grand Jury (grănd joo′rē): an investigating jury; decides whether there is enough evidence to hold a criminal trial. (p. 209)

Gross Income (grōs ĭn′kŭm): all the income earned before taxes and expenses are considered. (p. 507)

Gross National Product (grōs năsh′ə nəl prŏd′əkt): the total amount of goods and services produced by a country in one year. (p. 510)

Grounds for Divorce (groundz fôr dĭ vôrs′): the reasons that must be present before the state will grant a divorce. (p. 453)

Human Resources (hyoo′mən rĭ sôrs′əz): the labor of people. (p. 476)

Impeach (ĭm pēch′): formally accuse a government official of a serious crime. (p. 99)

Implied Powers (ĭm plīd′ pou′ərz): the powers of the Congress not listed in the Constitution but needed in order to put into effect the delegated powers. (p. 98)

Inauguration (ĭ nô′gyə rā′shən): ceremony at which a new president takes office. (p. 152)

Independent Agencies (ĭn′dĭ pĕn′dənt ā′jən sēz): parts of the executive branch that handle jobs that are not in either the executive departments or the executive office. (p. 188)

Indeterminate Sentence (ĭn′dĭ tûr′mə nĭt sĕn′təns): a prison sentence for an indefinite period of time, such as 2 to 8 years. (p. 429)

Indictment (ĭn dīt′mənt): a grand jury's written statement charging someone with a crime. (p. 316)

Inflation (ĭn flā′shən): a decrease in the value and buying power of money. (p. 520)

Infraction (ĭn frăk′shən): a minor law violation, punishable by a fine; sometimes not even considered to be a crime. (p. 417)

Initiative (ĭ nĭsh′ē ə tĭv): the right of voters to propose bills by collecting signatures on petitions. (p. 337)

Insurance Company (ĭn shŏŏr′ əns kŭm′pə nē): a company that provides protection against unacceptable financial risks. (p. 521)

Insurance Policy (ĭn shŏŏr′əns pŏl′ĭ sē): a contract between an insurance company and an individual or a business firm; states that the insurance company will pay should the risk being insured against occur. (p. 521)

Intelligence (ĭn tĕl′ə jəns): information that affects a nation's safety. (p. 146)

Interest (ĭn′trĭst): the percentage of a loan that a borrower pays in return for the temporary use of the money. (p. 515)

Interpret (ĭn tûr′prĭt): explain the meaning of a law; apply the law to a specific case. (p. 232)

Item Veto (ī′təm vē′tō): a governor's power to reject part of a bill and approve the rest of it. (p. 266)

Jail (jāl): a small prison run by a city or country. (p. 428)

Judge (jŭj): an official who presides over a trial. (p. 158)

Judicial Branch (jōō dĭsh′əl brănch): the part of the government that runs the courts and says what the law means. (p. 79)

Judicial Review (jōō dĭsh′əl rĭ vyōō′): the right of a court to review the actions and set aside the decisions of other branches of government. (p. 229)

Jurisdiction (jŏŏr′ĭs dĭk′shən): the authority of a court to consider a case. (p. 212)

Jurors (jŏŏr′ərz): members of a jury. (p. 209)

Jury (jŏŏr′ē): a group of citizens chosen to hear evidence in a court case and decide on questions of fact. (p. 209)

Jury Duty (jŏŏr′ē dōō′tē): the responsibility of serving on juries when ordered to do so. (p. 340)

Justice (jŭs′tĭs): member of the United States Supreme Court. (p. 217)

Juvenile (jōō′və nəl): someone who is not legally an adult; generally, someone under 18 years of age. (p. 430)

Keynote Speech (kē′nōt spēch): a kickoff speech at a political party convention. (p. 371)

Labor (lā′bər): the work that people do in organizations and in shaping material resources into goods and services. (p. 476)

Labor Union (lā′bər yōōn′yən): an association of employees that work for good wages and working conditions. (p. 299)

Land (lănd): resources including the soil, the mineral deposits under the soil, and timbers. (p. 477)

Law (lô): a binding rule of society that has been set up by the customs of the people and backed up by some kind of force. (p. 42)

Lawsuit (lô′sōōt′): court case. (p. 208)

Legal Separation (lē′gəl sĕp′ə rā′shən): a formal court-arranged separation of a married couple, generally granted when there are grounds for divorce. (p. 453)

Legislative Branch (lĕj′ĭs lā′tĭv brănch): the part of the government that makes the laws. (p. 79)

Liable (lī′ə bəl): legally responsible. (For example, if you are liable for damages, you are legally responsible for paying those damages.) (p. 452)

Limited Liability (lĭm′ĭ tĭd lī′ə bĭl′ĭ tē): a business owner's responsibility for losses that is only as great as his or her investment in the business. (p. 486)

Lobbyist (lŏb′ē ĭst): a person who acts as an agent for a pressure group in trying to influence the policies of government. (p. 396)

Majority Opinion (mə jôr′ĭ tē ō pĭn′yən): opinion issued by the majority in a court case; has legal force. (p. 218)

Majority Party (mə jôr′ĭ tē pär′tē): the political party with more members in Congress. (p. 124)

Mass Media (măs mē′dē ə): public channels of communication—such as newspapers, magazines, television, radio, books, and films. (p. 389)

Material Resources (mə tîr′ē əl rĭ sôrs′əz): all the material things that are used to create goods and services. (p. 476)

Mayor-Council (local government) (mā′ər koun′səl): a system of local government in which voters elect a mayor and a city council. (p. 286)

Military Draft (mĭl'ĭ tĕr ē drăft): a system for requiring people to enter the military service. (p. 338)

Militia (mĭ lĭsh'ə): an army of citizens. (p. 320)

Minor (mī'nər): a juvenile; someone who has not reached the legal age of adulthood. (p. 459)

Minority (mĭ nôr'ĭ tē): a group within a society that differs in important ways—appearance, subculture, values—from most members of that society and is therefore considered to be "different." (p. 30)

Minority Party (mĭ nôr'ĭ tē pär' tē): the political party with fewer members in Congress. (p. 124)

Misdemeanor (mĭs'dĭ mē'nər): a minor crime, for which the penalty is 1 year or less in prison. (p. 417)

Monarchy (mŏn'ər kē): a government in which power is passed down from one member of a family to another. (p. 69)-

Money (mŭn'ē): coins or paper that people accept as having a standard value. (p. 476)

Mortgage (môr'gĭj): a loan that is made to buy land, houses, real estate developments, or commercial property. (p. 517)

Multiplier Effect (mŭl'tə plī ər ĭ fĕkt'): the increase in wealth that results when money and credit move from person to person through the economy. (p. 518)

Municipality (myōō nĭs'ə păl'ĭ tē): a city, town, village, or borough that a state sets up as a unit of local government. (p. 282)

Natural Law (năch'ər əl lô): certain fundamental principles of justice that are believed to apply to all people. (p. 50)

Naturalization (năch'ər ə lĭ zā' shən): the process by which an alien becomes a citizen. (p. 26)

Negligent (nĕg'lĭ jənt): failing to take the care that a reasonable person would take. (p. 451)

Net Income (nĕt ĭn'kŭm): all the money that a business takes in from sales of goods or services minus costs and taxes; profits. (p. 509)

Night Watch (nīt wŏch): a volunteer force that watched the town or city streets at night before police forces came into being. (p. 422)

Nominating Convention (nŏm'ə nā tĭng ken vĕn'shən): a meeting of the members of a political party to choose their candidates for an election. (p. 369)

Nonbinding Arbitration (nŏn' bĭn dĭng är'bĭ trā'shən): an arbitration in which either side is free to reject the arbitrator's decision and take the case to court. (p. 459)

Norms (nôrmz): the rules of behavior of a society or a group. (p. 18)

Northwest Ordinance (nôrth wĕst' ôr'dn əns): a law, passed in 1787, that told how parts of the Northwest Territory—the land between the Ohio River and the Great Lakes—could become states. (p. 259)

Oath (ōth): sworn statement. (p. 242)

Offer (ô'fər): a promise to give something or to do something for someone else in exchange for something else. (p. 447)

Offerer (ô'fər ər): someone who makes an offer. (p. 447)

Open Primary (ō'pən prī'mĕr ē): a primary election that is open to all voters, regardless of what party they belong to. (p. 369)

Opinion (ō pĭn'yən): a judgment or a belief; something that someone thinks is true. A statement issued by a court to explain the reasoning behind a decision. (p. 218)

Oral Contract (ôr'əl kŏn'trăkt): a contract made by agreement, with nothing in writing. (p. 450)

Ordinances (ôr'dn əns əz): laws passed by a local government. (p. 287)

Original Jurisdiction (ə rĭj'ə nəl jōōr'ĭs dĭk'shən): the authority of a court to start a case. (p. 212)

Pacifist (păs'ə fĭst): someone who believes that taking part in war is wrong on religious or moral grounds. (p. 338)

Pardon (pär'dn): an official act that forgives an individual for a crime. (p. 163)

Parliamentary Democracy (pär' lə mĕn'tə rē dĭ mŏk'rə se): a democracy in which a single group of people makes the laws and carries them out. (p. 70)

Parole (pə rōl'): release from prison under official supervision and before completion of a sentence. (p. 184)

Partnership (pärt'nər shĭp): a business that is owned by two or more persons as co-owners. (p. 485)

Party Platform (pär'tē plăt' fôrm): a statement of principles and promises that is drawn up by a political party. (p. 371)

Passport (păs'pôrt): an official travel document. (p. 182)

Patronage (pā'trə nĭj): giving out government jobs as political rewards. (p. 191)

Peers (pîrz): one's equals in a society. (p. 21)

Petit Jury (pĕt'ē jōōr'ē): a trial jury; gives a verdict in a trial. (p. 209)

Pigeonhole (pĭj'ĭn hōl): kill a bill by holding it in committee and not returning it to the floor for debate and vote. (p. 129)

Plaintiff (plăn'tĭf): person who takes a case to court. (p. 208)

Plank (plăngk): a principle or a promise in a party platform. (p. 371)

Plea (plē): to answer a criminal charge. (p. 423)

Plea Bargaining (plē bär'gĭ nĭng): a deal between the prosecution and the defense in which the defense agrees to plead guilty to a reduced charge. (p. 424)

Pocket Veto (pŏk′ĭt **vē′**tō): the way a president may kill a bill by "pocketing" it for 10 days and not signing it; only possible if Congress adjourns during the 10 days. (p. 133)

Policing Power (pə **lē′**sĭng **pou′**ər): a state's right to pass laws to protect the health, safety, and welfare of its people. (p. 258)

Political Party (pə lĭt′ĭ kəl **pär′** tē): a group of people who have joined together to take part in elections with the goal of winning control of the government. (p. 124)

Poll Tax (pōl tăks): a tax on people who want to vote. (p. 318)

Polls (pōlz): voting places. (p. 359)

Pollster (pōl′stər): someone who takes polls. (p. 387)

Popular Vote (pŏp′yə lər vōt): the votes cast by citizens in an election. (p. 151)

Precedent (prĕs′ĭ dnt): something decided in an earlier court case. (p. 53)

Prejudice (prĕj′ə dĭs): an emotional belief that members of a certain group are unequal; a prejudgment. (p. 23)

Premium (prē′mē əm): the price of an insurance policy. (p. 521)

President-elect (prĕz′ĭ dənt ē lĕkt′): a person who has been elected President but has not yet taken office. (p. 151)

President of the Senate (prĕz′ĭ dənt) of the (sĕn′ ĭt): the Vice President of the United States, who serves as presiding officer of the Senate. (p. 106)

President Pro-tempore (prĕz′ĭ dənt prō tĕm′pə rē): officer who presides over the Senate when the Vice President is not there. (p. 106)

Presidential Democracy (prĕz′ĭ dĕn′shəl dĭ mŏk′rə sē): a democracy in which one group makes laws and another carries them out under the leadership of a president. (p. 71)

Presidential Succession (prĕz′ĭ dĕn′shəl sək sĕsh′ən): the replacement of a President by another person, according to a set order, whenever the office becomes empty. (p. 154)

Presidential Veto (prĕz ĭ dĕn′shəl vē′tō): The way a President kills a bill by returning it to Congress unsigned, with a list of reasons for not signing. (p. 160)

Pressure Group (prĕsh′ər grōōp): an organized group of people who share common goals and try to influence the policies of government. (p. 393)

Primary Election (prī′mē rē ĭ lĕk′shən): a preliminary election to choose a party's candidate. (p. 369)

Prison (prĭz′ən): a place operated by a state or federal government where people convicted of serious crimes are held. (p. 426)

Probation (prō bā′shən): a type of sentence that lets a convicted person go free, but requires the person to follow certain rules under supervision. (p. 426)

Probation Officer (prō ba′shən ô′fĭ sər): an official whose job is to study a convicted person's record and recommend whether or not the person should be placed on probation; also, an official who supervises persons on probation. (p. 426)

Productivity (prō dŭk tĭv′ĭ tē): the measure of the output of goods or services that a worker produces each hour. (p. 477)

Profit (prŏf′ĭt): the difference between the cost of producing a product and the price at which it is sold. (p. 480)

Program (prō′grăm): the laws and actions that a President recommends to Congress. (p. 160)

Progressive Tax Schedule prə grĕs′ĭv tăks skĕj′ōō əl): tax rate in which the percentage of the income you pay in taxes rises as your income rises. (p. 506)

Propaganda (prŏp′ə găn′də): the art of shaping other people's opinions for one's own purposes. (p. 399)

Prosecution (prŏs ĭ kyōō′shən): the government's side in a criminal case. (p. 423)

Public Opinion (pŭb′lĭk ō pĭn′ yən): judgments about any public matter that are shared by a large number of people. (p. 386)

Quorum (kwôr′əm): a majority of the members of a legislative body, which must be present in order to conduct official business. (p. 131)

Ratify (răt′ə fī′): to approve of an action; to confirm an appointment. (p. 309)

Recall (rē′kôl): an election in which voters can put an elected official out of office before the official's term ends. (p. 242)

Recognize (rĕk′əg nīz′): to formally deal with a nation or its government, usually by exchanging diplomats with it. (p. 162)

Referendum (rĕf ə rĕn′dəm): the right of voters to approve or reject bills that are passed by the legislature. (p. 264)

Register (rĕj′ĭ stər): to have one's name put on a list of qualified voters. (p. 358)

Regulatory Agencies (rĕg′yə lə tôr′ē ā′jən sēz): independent agencies that help to control the nation's economy. (p. 188)

Rehabilitation (rē′hə bĭl ĭ tā′ shən): preparing a convicted person for a life of useful activity. (p. 426)

Reprieve (rĭ prēv′): an official act that stops the carrying out of a criminal sentence. (p. 129)

Republic (rĭ pub′lĭk): a government in which people choose representatives to run the government for them. (p. 70)

Reserve Requirements (rĭ zûrv′ rĭ kwīr′məntz): the money that banks must keep in reserve instead of lending. (p. 518)

Reserved Powers (rĭ **zûrvd′ pou′**ərz): powers that are set aside by the Constitution for the states. (p. 78)

Retribution (rĕt rə **byōō′**shən): paying back someone for a wrong. (p. 425)

Reverse (rĭ **vûrs′**): overturn an earlier decision. (p. 231)

Rider (**rī′**dər): an addition to a bill that is unrelated to the subject of the bill. (p. 132)

Rob (rŏb): to take something from a person by force, against the person′s will. (p. 416)

Role (rōl): a special behavior expected from someone in a given position. (p. 19)

Rural Area (**rōōr′**əl **ar′**ē ə): an area with a town population of fewer than 2500. (p. 23)

Securities (sĭ **kyōōr′**ĭ tēz): stocks and bonds. (p. 189)

Seditious Libel (sĭ **dĭsh′**əs **lī′**bəl): stirring up opposition to a government by criticizing or making fun of it. (p. 314)

Segregated (**sĕg′**rĭ gāt əd): separated, or set apart. (p. 231)

Sentence (**sĕn′**təns): the punishment given to a person convicted of a crime. (p. 424)

Separation of Powers (sĕp′ə **rā′**shən) of (**pou′**ərz): the division of government into branches, each with its own powers. (p. 78)

Servitude (**sur′**vĭ tōōd): the condition of being a servant to another, like a slave. (p. 318)

Session (**sĕsh′**ən): a series of meetings. (One session of Congress lasts from January 3 until the session is adjourned.) (p. 95)

Share Holder (shâr **hōl′**dər): an owner of stock in a corporation. (p. 486)

Slander (**slăn′**dər): defamation by word of mouth. (p. 454)

Small-Claims Court (smôl klāmz kôrt): a court that handles civil cases involving small amounts of money, usually without the need for lawyers. (p. 457)

Socialism (**sō′**shə **līz′**əm): the economic system in which the means of producing goods and services are owned or controlled by the government. (p. 481)

Socialization (**sō′**shə lə **zā′**shən): the day-by-day process by which a person learns the skills, values, and norms of a society or a group. (p. 20)

Society (sə **sī′**ĭ tē): the largest group of people who share a common way of life. (p. 14)

Sole Proprietorship (sōl prə **prī′**ĭ tər shĭp): a business that is owned by one person. (p. 484)

Speaker of the House (**spē′**kər) of the (hous): presiding officer of the House of Representatives. (p. 105)

Special District (**spĕsh′**əl **dĭs′**trĭkt): a unit of local government that performs a specific public service. (p. 282)

Special-Interest Group (**spĕsh′**əl **in′**trĭst grōōp): a pressure group. (p. 393)

Special-Purpose Debt (**spĕsh′**əl **pûr′**pəs det): money that is borrowed to be spent for a specific purpose, such as for buying a house or building a byway. (p. 515)

Spread (sprĕd): the difference between the interest a bank charges and the interest a bank pays. (p. 517)

Status Offense (**stā′**təs) or (**stăt′**əs ə fens′): an offense that can be committed only by juveniles, not by adults—for example, running away from home. (p. 430)

Statutory Law (**stăch′**ōō tôr ē lô): laws, or statutes, passed by lawmaking bodies and regulations made by executive departments and agencies. (p. 209)

Stereotype (**stĕr′**ē ə tīp): an oversimplified picture of a group of people or of an idea. (p. 401)

Stock (stŏk): a share of ownership in a corporation. (p. 189)

Strict Liability (strĭkt lī′ə **bĭl′**ĭ tē): a legal responsibility that exists whether one is negligent or not. (p. 452)

Strike (strīk): an organized work stoppage, a labor union′s strongest way of trying to get a company to agree to favorable working terms. (p. 490)

Subculture (**sŭb′**kŭl chər): the way of life of a group within a larger society. (p. 19)

Subpoena (sə **pē′**nə): a court order instructing someone to appear in court or to produce a document. (p. 340)

Suburb (**sŭb′**ûrb): an urban area that is near a large city and largely dependent upon the city for jobs and services. (p. 25)

Suffrage (**sŭf′**rĭj): the right to vote. (p. 318)

Symbolic Speech (sĭm **bŏl′**ĭk spēch): an action that uses a sign or symbol, rather than actual words, to make a point. (p. 236)

Tax (tăks): money that a person or a business must pay to a government so that the government can buy supplies and pay its public servants. (p. 506)

Taxable Income (**tăk′**sə bəl **in′**kŭm): gross income minus deductions. (p. 506)

Technology (tĕk **nŏl′**ə jē): the methods and materials used to produce and distribute goods and services. (p. 477)

Term (tûrm): the period during which one set of elected officials serves; also, the length of time an elected official serves. (One term of Congress lasts two sessions, or 2 years.) (p. 95)

Third Party (thûrd **pär′**tē): a minor party, not one of the two major parties. (p. 363)

Tort (tôrt): a wrongful action that causes someone harm; sometimes called a *civil wrong*. (p. 451)

Town (toun): a unit of local government within a country. (p. 282)

Township (**toun′**shĭp): a division of a county found in some mid-

Atlantic and midwestern states. (p. 282)

Trademark (trād′märk′): a special word or symbol that stands for a product. (p. 185)

Treaty (trē′tē): a formal written agreement between nations. (p. 163)

Trial (trī′əl): formal court proceeding at which evidence is heard and a case is decided. (p. 208)

Unalienable Right (ūn ā′lē ən ə bəl rīt): a right that can neither be given up nor taken away. (p. 74)

Unconstitutional (ūn′kŏn stĭ tōō′shə nəl): in conflict with the Constitution and, therefore, illegal. (p. 230)

Unicameral Legislature (yōō′nĭ kăm′ər əl lĕj′ĭ slā chər): a legislature made up of one house. (p. 262)

Urban Area (ûr′bən âr′ē ə): an area with at least one city of 2500 or more. (p. 23)

Values (văl′yōōz): a group's beliefs about what is right or proper. (p. 18)

Verdict (vûr′dĭkt): a jury's decision. (p. 208)

Victimless Crime (vĭk′tĭm lĭss krīm): a crime, such as drunkenness or gambling, that affects mainly the lawbreaker. (p. 417)

Void (void): unenforceable; not legally binding. (p. 450)

Voting (vō′tĭng): the formal process by which people express their choice about the way government should be run. (p. 132)

Waive (wāv): to give up voluntarily. (p. 422)

Warrant (wôr′ənt): a search order granted by a judge. (p. 316)

Whip (hwĭp) or (wĭp): a person who helps the floor leader put bills through Congress. (p. 125)

White-Collar Crime (wĭt) or (hwĭt kŏl′ər krīm): a crime committed by someone of high social status, without the use of force—for example, price-fixing. (p. 417)

Declaration of Independence

When in the Course of human events, it becomes necessary for one people to dissolve the political bands which have connected them with another, and to assume among the Powers of the earth, the separate and equal station to which the Laws of Nature and of Nature's God entitle them, a decent respect to the opinions of mankind requires that they should declare the causes which impel them to the separation.

We hold these truths to be self-evident, that all men are created equal, that they are endowed by their Creator with certain unalienable Rights, that among these are Life, Liberty and the pursuit of Happiness. That to secure these rights, Governments are instituted among Men, deriving their just powers from the consent of the governed. That whenever any Form of Government becomes destructive of these ends, it is the Right of the People to alter or to abolish it, and to institute new Government, laying its foundation on such principles and organizing its powers in such form, as to them shall seem most likely to effect their Safety and Happiness. Prudence, indeed, will dictate that Governments long established should not be changed for light and transient causes; and accordingly all experience hath shown, that mankind are more disposed to suffer, while evils are sufferable, than to right themselves by abolishing the forms to which they are accustomed. But when a long train of abuses and usurpations, pursuing invariably the same Object evinces a design to reduce them under absolute Despotism, it is their right, it is their duty, to throw off such Government, and to provide new Guards for their future security. —Such has been the patient sufferance of these Colonies; and such is now the necessity which constrains them to alter their former Systems of Government. The history of the present King of Great Britain is a history of repeated injuries and usurpations, all having in direct object the establishment of an absolute Tyranny over these States. To prove this, let Facts be submitted to a candid world.

He has refused his Assent to Laws, the most wholesome and necessary for the public good.

He has forbidden his Governors to pass Laws of immediate and pressing importance, unless suspended in their operation till his Assent should be obtained; and when so suspended, he has utterly neglected to attend to them.

He has refused to pass other Laws for the accommodation of large districts of people, unless those people would relinquish the right of Representation in the Legislature, a right inestimable to them and formidable to tyrants only.

He has called together legislative bodies at places unusual, uncomfortable, and distant from the depository of their Public Records, for the sole purpose of fatiguing them into compliance with his measures.

He has dissolved Representative Houses repeatedly, for opposing with manly firmness his invasions on the rights of the people.

He has refused for a long time, after such dissolutions, to cause others to be elected; whereby the Legislative Powers, incapable of Annihilation, have returned to the People at large for their exercise; the State remaining in the mean time exposed to all the dangers of invasion from without, and convulsions within.

He has endeavoured to prevent the population of these States; for that purpose obstructing the Laws of Naturalization of Foreigners; refusing to pass others to encourage their migration hither, and raising the conditions of new Appropriations of Lands.

He has obstructed the Administration of Justice, by refusing his Assent to Laws for establishing Judiciary Powers.

He has made Judges dependent on his Will alone, for the tenure of their offices, and the amount and payment of their salaries.

He has erected a multitude of New Offices, and sent hither swarms of Officers to harass our People, and eat out their substance.

He has kept among us, in times of peace, Standing Armies without the Consent of our legislature.

He has affected to render the Military independent of and superior to the Civil Power.

He has combined with others to subject us to a jurisdiction foreign to our constitution, and unacknowledged by our laws; giving his Assent to their acts of pretended legislation:

For quartering large bodies of armed troops among us:

For protecting them, by a mock Trial, from Punishment for any Murders which they should commit on the Inhabitants of these States:

For cutting off our Trade with all parts of the world:

For imposing taxes on us without our Consent:

For depriving us in many cases, of the benefits of Trial by Jury:

For transporting us beyond Seas to be tried for pretended offences:

For abolishing the free System of English Laws in a neighbouring Province, establishing therein an Arbitrary government, and enlarging its Boundaries so as to render it at once an example and fit instrument for introducing the same absolute rule into these Colonies:

For taking away our Charters, abolishing our most valuable Laws, and altering fundamentally the Forms of our Governments:

For suspending our own Legislature, and declaring themselves invested with Power to legislate for us in all cases whatsoever.

He has abdicated Government here, by declaring us out of his Protection and waging War against us.

He has plundered our seas, ravaged our Coasts, burnt our towns, and destroyed the lives of our people.

He is at this time transporting large armies of foreign mercenaries to compleat the works of death, desolation and tyranny, already begun with circumstances of Cruelty & perfidy scarcely paralleled in the most barbarous ages, and totally unworthy the Head of a civilized nation.

He has constrained our fellow Citizens taken Captive on the high Seas to bear Arms against their Country, to become the executioners of their friends and Brethren, or to fall themselves by their Hands.

He has excited domestic insurrections amongst us, and has endeavoured to bring on the inhabitants of our frontiers, the merciless Indian Savages, whose known rule of warfare, is an undistinguished destruction of all ages, sexes and conditions.

In every stage of these Oppressions We have Petitioned for Redress in the most humble terms: Our repeated Petitions have been answered only by repeated injury. A Prince, whose character is thus marked by every act which may define a Tyrant, is unfit to be the ruler of a free People.

Nor have We been wanting in attention to our British brethren. We have warned them from time to time of attempts by their legislature to extend an unwarrantable jurisdiction over us. We have reminded them of the circumstances of our emigration and settlement here. We have appealed to their native justice and magnanimity, and we have conjured them by the ties of our common kindred to disavow these usurpations, which, would inevitably interrupt our connections and correspondence. They too have been deaf to the voice of justice and of consanguinity. We must, therefore, acquiesce in the necessity, which denounces our Separation, and hold them, as we hold the rest of mankind, Enemies in War, in Peace Friends.

We, therefore, the Representatives of the United States of America, in General Congress, Assembled, appealing to the Supreme Judge of the world for the rectitude of our intentions, do, in the Name, and by Authority of the good People of these Colonies, solemnly publish and declare, That these United Colonies are, and of Right out to be Free and Independent States; that they are Absolved from all Allegiance to the British Crown, and that all political connection between them and the State of Great Britain, is and ought to be totally dissolved; and that as Free and Independent States, they have full Power to levy War, conclude Peace, contract Alliances, establish Commerce, and to do all other Acts and Things which Independent States may of right do. And for the support of this Declaration, with a firm reliance on the Protection of Divine Providence, we mutually pledge to each other our Lives, our Fortunes and our sacred Honor.

Constitution of the United States

We the people of the United States, in Order to form a more perfect Union, establish Justice, insure domestic Tranquility, provide for the common defence, promote the general Welfare, and secure the Blessings of Liberty to ourselves and our Posterity, do ordain and establish this CONSTITUTION for the United States of America.

Article 1 *(Legislature)*

Section 1. All legislative Powers herein granted shall be vested in a Congress of the United States, which shall consist of a Senate and House of Representatives.

(House of Representatives)
Section 2. The House of Representatives shall be composed of Members chosen every second Year by the People of the several States, and the Electors in each State shall have the Qualifications requisite for Electors of the most numerous Branch of the State Legislature.

(Qualifications for Representatives)
No Person shall be a Representative who shall not have attained to the Age of twenty-five Years, and been seven Years a Citizen of the United States, and who shall not, when elected, be an Inhabitant of that State in which he shall be chosen.

(Method of Apportionment)
Representatives and direct Taxes shall be apportioned among the several States which may be included within this Union, according to their respective Numbers, which shall be determined by adding to the whole Number of free Persons, including those bound to Service for a Term of Years, and excluding Indians not taxed, three fifths of all other Persons. The actual Enumeration shall be made within three Years after the first Meeting of the Congress of the United States, and within every subsequent Term of ten Years, in such Manner as they shall by Law direct. The Number of Representatives shall not exceed one for every thirty Thousand, but each state shall have at Least one Representative; and until such enumeration shall be made, the State of New Hampshire shall be entitled to chuse three, Massachusetts eight, Rhode Island and Providence Plantations one, Connecticut five, New York six, New Jersey four, Pennsylvania eight, Delaware one, Maryland six, Virginia ten, North Carolina five, South Carolina five, and Georgia three.

(Vacancies)
When vacancies happen in the Representation from any State, the Executive Authority thereof shall issue Writs of Election to fill such Vacancies.

(Rules of the House, Impeachment)
The House of Representatives shall chuse their Speaker and other Officers; and shall have the sole Power of Impeachment.

(Senators)
Section 3. The Senate of the United States shall be composed of two Senators from each State, chosen by the Legislature thereof, for six Years; and each Senator shall have one Vote.

Immediately after they shall be assembled in Consequence of the first Election, they shall be divided as equally as may be into three Classes. The Seats of the Senators of the first Class shall be vacated at the Expiration of the second Year, of the second Class at the Expiration of the fourth Year, and of the third Class at the

Expiration of the sixth Year, so that one-third may be chosen every second Year; and if Vacancies happen by Resignation, or otherwise, during the Recess of the Legislature of any State, the Executive thereof may make temporary Appointments until the next Meeting of the Legislature, which shall then fill such Vacancies.

(Qualifications of Senators)

No person shall be a Senator who shall not have attained to the Age of thirty Years, and been nine Years a Citizen of the United States, and who shall not, when elected, be an Inhabitant of that State in which he shall be chosen.

(Vice President)

The Vice President of the United States shall be President of the Senate, but shall have no vote, unless they be equally divided.

The Senate shall chuse their other Officers, and also a President pro tempore, in the absence of the Vice President, or when he shall exercise the Office of the President of the United States.

(Impeachments)

The Senate shall have the sole Power to try all Impeachments. When sitting for that purpose, they shall be on Oath or Affirmation. When the President of the United States is tried, the Chief Justice shall preside: And no person shall be convicted without the Concurrence of two thirds of the Members present.

Judgment in Cases of Impeachment shall not extend further than to removal from Office, and disqualification to hold and enjoy any Office of honor, Trust, or Profit under the United States: but the Party convicted shall nevertheless be liable and subject to Indictment, Trial, Judgment, and Punishment, according to Law.

(Elections)

Section 4. The Times, Places and Manner of holding Elections for Senators and Representatives, shall be prescribed in each state by the Legislature thereof: but the Congress may at any time by Law make or alter such Regulations, except as to the Places of Chusing Senators.

(Sessions)

The Congress shall assemble at least once in every Year, and such Meeting shall be on the first Monday in December, unless they shall by Law appoint a different Day.

(Proceeding of the House and the Senate)

Section 5. Each House shall be the Judge of the Elections, Returns and Qualifications of its own Members, and a Majority of each shall constitute a Quorum to do Business; but a smaller number may adjourn from day to day, and may be authorized to compel the Attendance of absent Members, in such Manner, and under such Penalties, as each House may provide.

Each house may determine the Rules of its Proceedings, punish its Members for disorderly Behavior, and, with the Concurrence of two thirds, expel a Member.

Each House shall keep a Journal of its Proceedings, and from time to time publish the same, excepting such Parts as may in their Judgment require Secrecy; and the Yeas and Nays of the Members of either House on any question shall, at the Desire of one fifth of those Present, be entered on the Journal.

Neither House, during the Session of Congress, shall, without the Consent of the other, adjourn for more than three days, nor to any other Place than that in which the two Houses shall be sitting.

*(Members' Compensation
and Privileges)*

Section 6. The Senators and Representatives shall receive a Compensation for their Services, to be ascertained by Law, and paid out of the Treasury of the United States. They shall in all Cases, except Treason, Felony, and Breach of the Peace, be privileged from Arrest during their Attendance at the Session of their respective Houses, and in going to and returning from the same; and for any Speech or Debate in either House, they shall not be questioned in any other Place.

No Senator or Representative shall, during the Time for which he was elected, be appointed to any civil Office under the Authority of the United States, which shall have been created, or the Emoluments whereof shall have been increased, during such time; and no Person holding any Office under the United States shall be a Member of either House during his continuance in Office.

(Money Bills)

Section 7. All Bills for raising Revenue shall originate in the House of Representatives; but the Senate may propose or concur with Amendments as on other bills.

*(Presidential Veto and
Congressional Power
to Override)*

Every Bill which shall have passed the House of Representatives and the Senate, shall, before it become a Law, be presented to the President of the United States; If he approve he shall sign it, but if not he shall return it, with his Objections, to that House in which it shall have originated, who shall enter the Objections at large on their Journal, and proceed to reconsider it. If after such Reconsideration two thirds of that House shall agree to pass the bill, it shall be sent, together with the objections, to the other House, by which it shall likewise be reconsidered, and if approved by two thirds of that House, it shall become a Law. But in all such Cases the Votes of both Houses shall be determined by Yeas and Nays, and the Names of the Persons voting for and against the Bill shall be entered on the Journal of each House respectively. If any Bill shall not be returned by the President within ten Days (Sundays excepted) after it shall have been presented to him, the Same shall be a Law, in like Manner as if he had signed it, unless the Congress by their Adjournment prevent its Return, in which Case it shall not be a Law.

Every Order, Resolution, or Vote to which the Concurrence of the Senate and House of Representatives may be necessary (except on a question of Adjournment) shall be presented to the President of the United States; and before the Same shall take Effect, shall be approved by him, or being disapproved by him, shall be repassed by two thirds of the Senate and House of Representatives, according to the Rules and Limitations prescribed in the Case of a Bill.

*(Congressional
Powers)*

Section 8. The Congress shall have Power To lay and collect Taxes, Duties, Imposts and Excises, to pay the Debts and provide for the common Defence and general Welfare of the United States; but all Duties, Imposts and Excises shall be uniform throughout the United States;

To borrow money on the credit of the United States;

To regulate Commerce with foreign Nations, and among the several States, and with the Indian Tribes;

To establish an uniform Rule of Naturalization, and uniform Laws on the subject of Bankruptcies throughout the United States;

To coin Money, regulate the Value thereof, and of foreign Coin, and fix the Standard of Weights and Measures;

To provide for the Punishment of counterfeiting the Securities and current Coin of the United States;

To establish Post Offices and post Roads;

To promote the Progress of Science and useful Arts, by securing for limited Times to Authors and Inventors the exclusive Right to their respective Writings and Discoveries;

To constitute Tribunals inferior to the Supreme Court;

To define and punish Piracies and Felonies committed on the high Seas, and Offenses against the Law of Nations;

To declare War, grant Letters of Marque and Reprisal, and make Rules concerning Captures on Land and Water;

To raise and support Armies, but no Appropriation of Money to that Use shall be for a longer Term than two Years;

To provide and maintain a Navy;

To make Rules for the Government and Regulation of the land and naval forces;

To provide for calling forth the Militia to execute the Laws of the Union, suppress Insurrections and repel Invasions;

To provide for organizing, arming, and disciplining the Militia, and for governing such Part of them as may be employed in the Service of the United States, reserving to the States respectively, the Appointment of the Officers, and the Authority of training the Militia according to the discipline prescribed by Congress;

To exercise exclusive Legislation in all Cases whatsoever, over such District (not exceeding ten Miles square) as may, by Cession of particular States, and the acceptance of Congress, become the Seat of Government of the United States, and to exercise like Authority over all Places purchased by the Consent of the Legislature of the State in which the Same shall be, for the Erection of Forts, Magazines, Arsenals, dock-Yards, and other needful Buildings;—And

To make all Laws which shall be necessary and proper for carrying into Execution the foregoing Powers, and all other Powers vested by this Constitution in the Government of the United States, or in any Department or Officer thereof.

(Limits on Congressional Power)

Section 9. The Migration or Importation of such Persons as any of the States now existing shall think proper to admit, shall not be prohibited by the Congress prior to the Year one thousand eight hundred and eight, but a tax or duty may be imposed on such Importation, not exceeding ten dollars for each Person.

The privilege of the Writ of Habeas Corpus shall not be suspended, unless when in Cases of Rebellion or Invasion the public Safety may require it.

No Bill of Attainder or ex post facto Law shall be passed.

No capitation, or other direct, Tax shall be laid unless in Proportion to the Census or Enumeration herein before directed to be taken.

No Tax or Duty shall be laid on Articles exported from any State.

No Preference shall be given by any Regulation of Revenue to the Ports of one State over those of another: nor shall Vessels bound to, or from, one State, be obliged to enter, clear, or pay Duties in another.

No Money shall be drawn from the Treasury, but in Consequence of Appropriations made by Law; and a regular Statement and Account of the Receipts and Expenditures of all public Money shall be published from time to time.

No Title of Nobility shall be granted

by the United States: And no Person holding any Office of Profit or Trust under them, shall, without the Consent of the Congress, accept of any present, Emolument, Office, or Title, of any kind whatever, from any King, Prince, or foreign State.

(Limits on Powers of the States)

Section 10. No State shall enter into any Treaty, Alliance, or Confederation; grant Letters of Marque and Reprisal; coin Money; emit Bills of Credit; make any Thing but gold and silver Coin a Tender in Payment of Debts; pass any Bill of Attainder, ex post facto Law, or Law impairing the Obligation of Contracts, or grant any Title of Nobility.

No State shall, without the Consent of the Congress, lay any Imposts or Duties on Imports or Exports, except what may be absolutely necessary for executing its inspection Laws: and the net Produce of all Duties and Imposts, laid by any State on Imports or Exports, shall be for the Use of the Treasury of the United States; and all such Laws shall be subject to the Revision and Control of the Congress.

No State shall, without the Consent of Congress, lay any duty of Tonnage, keep Troops, or Ships of War in time of Peace, enter into any Agreement or Compact with another State, or with a foreign Power, or engage in War, unless actually invaded, or in such imminent Danger as will not admit of delay.

Article II   (EXECUTIVE)

(President)

Section 1. The executive Power shall be vested in a President of the United States of America. He shall hold his Office during the Term of four years, and, together with the Vice President, chosen for the same Term, be elected as follows:

(Election of President)

Each State shall appoint, in such Manner as the Legislature thereof may direct, a Number of Electors, equal to the whole Number of Senators and Representatives to which the State may be entitled in the Congress: but no Senator or Representative, or Person holding an Office of Trust or Profit under the United States, shall be appointed an Elector.

(Electors)

The Electors shall meet in their respective States, and vote by Ballot for two persons, of whom one at least shall not be an Inhabitant of the same State with themselves. And they shall make a List of all the Persons voted for, and of the Number of Votes for each; which List they shall sign and certify, and transmit sealed to the Seat of the Government of the United States, directed to the President of the Senate. The Pesident of the Senate shall, in the Presence of the Senate and House of Representatives, open all the Certificates, and the Votes shall then be counted. The Person having the greatest Number of Votes shall be the President, if such Number be a Majority of the whole Number of Electors appointed; and if there be more than one who have such Majority, and have an equal Number of Votes, then the House of Representatives shall immediately chuse by Ballot one of them for President; and if no Person have a Majority, then from the five highest on the List the said House shall in like Manner chuse the President. But in chusing the President, the Votes shall be taken by States, the Representation from each State having one Vote; a quorum for this Purpose shall consist of a Member or Members from two-thirds of the States, and a Majority of all the States shall be necessary to a Choice. In every Case, after the Choice of the President, the Person having the greatest Number of Votes of the Electors shall be the Vice President. But if there should remain two or more who have equal votes, the Senate shall chuse from them by Ballot the Vice President.

The Congress may determine the Time of chusing the Electors, and the Day on which they shall give their Votes; which Day shall be the same throughout the United States.

(Qualifications of President)

No person except a natural-born Citizen, or a Citizen of the United States, at the time of the Adoption of this Constitution, shall be eligible to the Office of President; neither shall any Person be eligible to that Office who shall not have attained to the Age of thirty-five years, and been fourteen Years a Resident within the United States.

(Succession to the Presidency)

In Case of the Removal of the President from Office, or of his Death, Resignation, or Inability to discharge the Powers and Duties of the said Office, the same shall devolve on the Vice President, and the Congress may be Law provide for the Case of Removal, Death, Resignation, or Inability, both of the President and Vice President, declaring what Officer shall then act as President, and such Officer shall act accordingly, until the disability be removed, or a President shall be elected.

(Compensation)

The President shall, at stated Times, receive for his Services a Compensation, which shall neither be increased nor diminished during the Period for which he shall have been elected, and he shall not receive within that Period any other Emolument from the United States, or any of them.

(Oath in Office)

Before he enters on the execution of his Office, he shall take the following Oath or Affirmation—"I do solemnly swear (or affirm) that I will faithfully execute the Office of President of the United States, and will, to the best of my Ability, preserve, protect, and defend the Constitution of the United States."

(Powers of the President)

Section 2. The President shall be Commander in Chief of the Army and Navy of the United States, and of the Militia of the several States, when called into the actual Service of the United States; he may require the Opinion, in writing, of the principal Officer in each of the executive Departments, upon any subject relating to the Duties of their respective Offices, and he shall have Power to Grant Reprieves and Pardons for Offenses against the United States, except in Cases of Impeachment.

(Making of Treaties)

He shall have Power, by and with the Advice and Consent of the Senate, to make Treaties, provided two thirds of the Senators present concur; and he shall nominate, and by and with the Advice and Consent of the Senate, shall appoint Ambassadors, other public Ministers and Consuls, Judges of the supreme Court, and all other Officers of the United States, whose Appointments are not herein otherwise provided for, and which shall be established by Law: but the Congress may by Law vest the Appointment of such inferior Officers, as they think proper, in the President alone, in the Courts of Law, or in the Heads of Departments.

(Vacancies)

The President shall have Power to fill up all Vacancies that may happen during the Recess of the Senate, by granting Commissions which shall expire at the End of their next Session.

(Additional Duties and Powers)

Section 3. He shall from time to time give to the Congress Information of the State of the Union, and recommend to their Consideration such Measures as he shall judge necessary and expedient; he may, on extraordinary occasions, convene both Houses, or either of them, and in Case of Disagreement between them, with respect to the Time of Adjournment, he may adjourn them to such Time as he shall think proper; he shall receive Ambassadors and other public Ministers; he shall take Care that the Laws be faithfully executed, and shall Commission all the Officers of the United States.

(Impeachment)

Section 4. The President, Vice President and all civil Officers of the United States, shall be removed from Office on Impeachment for, and Conviction of, Treason, Bribery, or other high Crimes and Misdemeanors.

Article III (JUDICIARY)

(Courts, Judges, Compensation)

Section 1. The judicial Power of the United States, shall be vested in one supreme Court, and in such inferior Courts as the Congress may from time to time ordain and establish. The Judges, both of the supreme and inferior Courts, shall hold their Offices during good Behaviour, and shall, at stated Times, receive for their Services, a Compensation, which shall not be diminished during their Continuance in Office.

(Jurisdiction)

Section 2. The judicial Power shall extend to all Cases, in Law and Equity, arising under this Constitution, the Laws of the United States, and treaties made, or which shall be made, under their Authority;—to all Cases affecting ambassadors, other public ministers and consuls;—to all cases of admiralty and maritime Jurisdiction;—to Controversies to which the United States shall be a Party;—to Controversies between two or more States;—between a State and Citizens of another State;—between Citizens of different States,—between Citizens of the same State claiming Lands under Grants of different States, and between a State, or the Citizens thereof, and foreign States, Citizens or Subjects.

In all Cases affecting Ambassadors, other public Ministers and Consuls, and those in which a State shall be Party, the supreme Court shall have original Jurisdiction. In all the other Cases before mentioned, the supreme Court shall have appellate Jurisdiction, both as to Law and Fact, with such Exceptions, and under such Regulations as the Congress shall make.

(Trial by Jury)

The trial of all Crimes, except in Cases of Impeachment, shall be by Jury; and such Trial shall be held in the State where the said Crimes shall have been committed; but when not committed within any State, the Trial shall be at such Place or Places as the Congress may by Law have directed.

(Treason)

Section 3. Treason against the United States, shall consist only in levying War against them, or in adhering to their Enemies, giving them Aid and Comfort. No Person shall be convicted of Treason unless on the Testimony of two Witnesses to the same overt Act, or on Confession in open Court.

The Congress shall have power to declare the Punishment of Treason, but no Attainder of Treason shall work Corruption of Blood, or Forfeiture except during the Life of the Person attainted.

Article IV (FEDERAL SYSTEM)

Section 1. Full Faith and Credit shall be given in each State to the public Acts, Records, and judicial Proceedings of every other State. And the Congress may by general Laws prescribe the Manner in which such Acts, Records, and Proceedings shall be proved, and the Effect thereof.

(Privileges and Immunities of Citizens)

Section 2. The Citizens of each State shall be entitled to all Privileges and Immunities of Citizens in the several states.

A Person charged in any State with Treason, Felony, or other Crime, who shall flee from Justice, and be found in another State, shall on demand of the executive Authority of the State from which he fled, be delivered up, to be removed to the State having Jurisdiction of the crime.

No Person held to Service or Labour in one State, under the Laws thereof, escaping into another, shall, in Consequence of any Law or Regulation therein, be discharged from such Service or Labour, but shall be delivered up on Claim of the Party to whom such Service or Labour may be due.

(Admission and Formation of New States; Governing of Territories)

Section 3. New States may be admitted by the Congress into this Union; but no new State shall be formed or erected within the Jurisdiction of any other State; nor any State be formed by the Junction of two or more States, or parts of States, without the Consent of the Legislatures of the States concerned as well as of the Congress.

The Congress shall have Power to dispose of and make all needful Rules and Regulations respecting the Territory or other Property belonging to the United States; and nothing in this Constitution shall be so construed as to Prejudice any Claims of the United States, or of any particular State.

(Federal Protection of the States)

Section 4. The United States shall guarantee to every State in this Union a Republican Form of Government, and shall protect each of them against Invasion; and on Application of the Legislature, or of the Executive (when the Legislature cannot be convened) against domestic Violence.

Article V (AMENDMENTS)

The Congress, whenever two-thirds of both Houses shall deem it necessary, shall propose Amendments to this Constitution, or, on the Application of the Legislatures of two-thirds of the several States, shall call a Convention for proposing Amendments, which, in either Case, shall be valid to all Intents and Purposes, as part of this Constitution, when ratified by the Legislatures of three-fourths of the several States, or by Conventions in three-fourths thereof, as the one or the other Mode of Ratification may be proposed by the Congress; Provided that no Amendment which may be made prior to the Year One thousand eight hundred and eight shall in any Manner affect the first and fourth Clauses in the Ninth Section of the first Article; and that no State, without its Consent, shall be deprived of its equal Suffrage in the Senate.

Article VI (CONSTITUTION AS SUPREME LAW)

All Debts contracted and Engagements entered into, before the Adoption of this Constitution, shall be as valid against the United States under this Constitution, as under the Confederation.

This Constitution, and the Laws of the United States which shall be made in Pursuance thereof; and all Treaties made, or which shall be made, under the Authority of the United States, shall be the supreme Law of the Land; and the Judges in every State shall be bound thereby, any Thing in the Constitution or Laws of any State to the Contrary notwithstanding.

The Senators and Representatives before mentioned, and the Members of the several State Legislatures, and all executive and judicial Officers, both of the United States and of the several States, shall be bound by Oath or Affirmation to support this Constitution; but no religious Test shall ever be required as a qualification to any Office or public Trust under the United States.

Article VII (RATIFICATION)

The Ratification of the Conventions of nine States shall be sufficient for the Establishment of this Constitution between the States so ratifying the same.

Done in Convention by the Unanimous Consent of the States present the Seventeenth Day of September in the Year of our Lord one thousand seven hundred and Eighty seven, and of the Independence of the United States of America the Twelfth. In Witness whereof We have hereunto subscribed our Names.

Articles in Addition to, and Amendment of, the Constitution of the United States of America, Proposed by Congress, and Ratified by the Legislatures of the Several States, Pursuant to the Fifth Article of the Original Constitution.

Amendment I [1791] (FREEDOMS)

(Speech, Press, Assembly, and Petition)
Congress shall make no law respecting an establishment of religion, or prohibiting the free exercise thereof; or abridging the freedom of speech, or of the press; or the right of the people peaceably to assemble, and to petition the Government for a redress of grievances.

Amendment II [1791] (RIGHT TO BEAR ARMS)

A well regulated Militia, being necessary to the security of a free State, the right of the people to keep and bear Arms shall not be infringed.

Amendment III [1791] (QUARTERING OF SOLDIERS)

No soldier shall, in time of peace, be quartered in any house, without the consent of the Owner, nor in time of war, but in a manner to be prescribed by law.

Amendment IV [1791] (FREEDOM OF PERSONS)

(Warrants, Searches, and Seizure)
The right of the people to be secure in their persons, houses, papers, and effects, against unreasonable searches and seizures, shall not be violated, and no War-

rants shall issue, but upon probable cause, supported by Oath or affirmation, and particularly describing the place to be searched, and the persons or things to be seized.

Amendment V
[1791]   (CAPITAL CRIMES)

(Protection of the Accused; Compensation)
No person shall be held to answer for a capital or otherwise infamous crime, unless on a presentment or indictment of a Grand Jury, except in cases arising in the land or naval forces, or in the Militia, when in actual service in time of War or public danger; nor shall any person be subject for the same offence to be twice put in jeopardy of life or limb; nor shall be compelled in any criminal case to be a witness against himself, nor be deprived of life, liberty, or property, without due process of law; nor shall private property be taken for public use, without just compensation.

Amendment VI
[1791]   (TRIAL BY JURY)

(Accusation, Witnesses, Counsel)
In all criminal prosecutions, the accused shall enjoy the right to a speedy and public trial, by an impartial jury of the State and district wherein the crime shall have been committed, which district shall have been previously ascertained by law, and to be informed of the nature and cause of the accusation; to be confronted with the witnesses against him; to have compulsory process for obtaining witnesses in his favor, and to have the Assistance of Counsel for his defence.

Amendment VII
[1791]   (CIVIL LAW)

In suits at common law, where the value in controversy shall exceed twenty dollars, the right of trial by jury shall be preserved, and no fact tried by a jury, shall be otherwise reexamined in any Court of the United States, than according to the rules of the common law.

Amendment VIII
[1791]   (BAILS, FINES, AND PUNISHMENTS)

Excessive bail shall not be required, nor excessive fines imposed, nor cruel and unusual punishments inflicted.

Amendment IX
[1791]   (RIGHTS RETAINED BY THE PEOPLE)

The enumeration in the Constitution, of certain rights, shall not be construed to deny or disparage others retained by the people.

Amendment X
[1791]   (RIGHTS RESERVED TO THE STATES)

The powers not delegated to the United States by the Constitution, nor prohibited by it to the States, are reserved to the States respectively, or to the people.

Amendment XI
[1798]   (JURISDICTIONAL LIMITS)

The Judicial power of the United States shall not be construed to extend to any suit in law or equity, commenced or prosecuted against one of the United States by Citizens of another State, or by Citizens or Subjects of any Foreign State.

Amendment XII [1804]   (ELECTORAL COLLEGE)

The Electors shall meet in their respective States and vote by ballot for President and Vice President, one of whom, at least, shall not be an inhabitant of the same State with themselves; they shall name in their ballots the person voted for as President, and in distinct ballots the person voted for as Vice President, and they shall make distinct lists of all persons voted for as President, and of all persons voted for as Vice President, and of the number of votes for each, which lists they shall sign and certify, and transmit sealed to the seat of the government of the United States, directed to the President of the Senate;—The President of the Senate shall, in the presence of the Senate and House of Representatives, open all the certificates and the votes shall then be counted;—The person having the greatest number of votes for President, shall be the President, if such number be a majority of the whole number of Electors appointed; and if no person have such majority, then from the persons having the highest numbers not exceeding three on the list of those voted for as President, the House of Representatives shall choose immediately, by ballot, the President. But in choosing the President, the votes shall be taken by states, the representation from each state having one vote; a quorum for this purpose shall consist of a member or members from two-thirds of the states, and a majority of all the states shall be necessary to a choice. And if the House of Representatives shall not choose a President whenever the right of choice shall devolve upon them, before the fourth day of March next following, then the Vice President shall act as President, as in the case of the death or other constitutional disability of the President.— The person having the greatest number of votes as Vice President, shall be the Vice President, if such number be a majority of the whole number of Electors appointed, and if no person have a majority, then from the two highest numbers on the list, the Senate shall choose the Vice President; a quorum for the purpose shall consist of two-thirds of the whole number of Senators, and a majority of the whole number shall be necessary to a choice. But no person constitutionally ineligible to the office of President shall be eligible to that of Vice President of the United States.

Amendment XIII [1865]   (ABOLITION OF SLAVERY)

Section 1. Neither slavery nor involuntary servitude, except as a punishment for crime whereof the party shall have been duly convicted, shall exist within the United States, or any place subject to their jurisdiction.

Section 2. Congress shall have power to enforce this article by appropriate legislation.

Amendment XIV [1868]   (CITIZENSHIP)

(Due Process of Law)

Section 1. All persons born or naturalized in the United States, and subject to the jurisdiction thereof, are citizens of the United States and of the State wherein they reside. No State shall make or enforce any law which shall abridge the privileges or immunities of citizens of the United States; nor shall any State deprive any person of life, liberty, or property, without due process of law; nor deny to any person within its jurisdiction the equal protection of the laws.

(Apportionment;
Right to Vote)

Section 2. Representatives shall be apportioned among the several States according to their respective numbers, counting the whole number of persons in each State, excluding Indians not taxed. But when the right to vote at any election for the choice of electors for President and Vice President of the United States, Representatives in Congress, the Executive and Judicial officers of a State, or the members of the Legislature thereof, is denied to any of the male inhabitants of such State, being twenty-one years of age, and citizens of the United States, or in any way abridged, except for participation in rebellion, or other crime, the basis of representation therein shall be reduced in the proportion which the number of such male citizens shall bear to the whole number of male citizens twenty-one years of age in such State.

(Disqualification
for Office)

Section 3. No person shall be a Senator or Representative in Congress, or elector of President and Vice President, or hold any office, civil or military, under the United States, or under any State, who, having previously taken an oath, as a member of Congress, or as an officer of the United States, or as a member of any State legislature, or as an executive or judicial officer of any State, to support the Constitution of the United States, shall have engaged in insurrection or rebellion against the same, or given aid or comfort to the enemies thereof. But Congress may by a vote of two-thirds of each House, remove such disability.

(Public Debt)

Section 4. The validity of the public debt of the United States, authorized by law, including debts incurred for payment of pensions and bounties for services in suppressing insurrection or rebellion, shall not be questioned. But neither the United States nor any State shall assume or pay any debt or obligation incurred in aid of insurrection or rebellion against the United States, or any claim for the loss or emancipation of any slave; but all such debts, obligations, and claims shall be held illegal and void.

Section 5. The Congress shall have the power to enforce, by appropriate legislation, the provisions of this article.

Amendment XV
[1870]

(RIGHT TO VOTE)

Section 1. The right of citizens of the United States to vote shall not be denied or abridged by the United States or by any State on account of race, color or previous condition of servitude.

Section 2. The Congress shall have power to enforce this article by appropriate legislation.

Amendment XVI
[1913]

(INCOME TAX)

The Congress shall have power to lay and collect taxes on incomes, from whatever source derived, without apportionment among the several States, and without regard to any census or enumeration.

Amendment XVII
[1913]

(SENATORS)

(Election)

The Senate of the United States shall be composed of two Senators from each State, elected by the people thereof, for six years; and each Senator shall have one vote. The electors in each State shall have the qualifications requisite for electors of the most numerous branch of the State legislatures.

(Vacancies)

When vacancies happen in the representation of any State in the Senate, the executive authority of such State shall issue writs of election to fill such vacancies: *Provided,* That the legislature of any State may empower the executive thereof to make temporary appointments until the people fill the vacancies by election as the legislature may direct.

This amendment shall not be so construed as to affect the election or term of any Senator chosen before it becomes valid as part of the Constitution.

Amendment XVIII
[1919] (PROHIBITION)

Section 1. After one year from the ratification of this article the manufacture, sale, or transportation of intoxicating liquors within, the importation thereof into, or the exportation thereof from the United States and all territory subject to the jurisdiction thereof for beverage purposes is hereby prohibited.

Section 2. The Congress and the several States shall have concurrent power to enforce this article by appropriate legislation.

Section 3. This article shall be inoperative unless it shall have been ratified as an amendment to the Constitution by the legislatures of the several States, as provided in the Constitution, within seven years from the date of the submission hereof to the States by the Congress.

Amendment XIX
[1920] (FEMALE SUFFRAGE)

The right of citizens of the United States to vote shall not be denied or abridged by the United States or by any State on account of sex.

Congress shall have power to enforce this article by appropriate legislation.

Amendment XX
[1933] (TERMS OF OFFICE)

Section 1. The terms of the President and Vice President shall end at noon on the 20th day of January, and the terms of Senators and Representatives at noon on the 3d day of January, of the years in which such terms would have ended if this article had not been ratified; and the terms of their successors shall then begin.

Section 2. The Congress shall assemble at least once in every year, and such meeting shall begin at noon on the 3d day of January, unless they shall by law appoint a different day.

(Succession)

Section 3. If, at the time fixed for the beginning of the term of the President, the President elect shall have died, the Vice President elect shall become President. If a President shall not have been chosen before the time fixed for the beginning of his term, or if the President elect shall have failed to qualify, then the Vice President elect shall act as President until a President shall have qualified; and the Congress may by law provide for the case wherein neither a President elect nor a Vice President elect shall have qualified, declaring who shall then act as President, or the manner in which one who is to act shall be selected, and such person shall act accordingly until a President or Vice President shall have qualified.

Section 4. The Congress may by law provide for the case of the death of any of the persons from whom the House of Representatives may choose a President whenever the right of choice shall have devolved upon them, and for the case of the death of any of the persons from whom the Senate may choose a Vice President whenever the right of choice shall have devolved upon them.

Section 5. Sections 1 and 2 shall take effect on the 15th day of October following the ratification of this article.

Section 6. This article shall be inoperative unless it shall have been ratified as an amendment to the Constitution by the legislatures of three-fourths of the several States within seven years from the date of its submission.

person who has held the office of President, or acted as President, for more than two years of a term to which some other person was elected President shall be elected to the office of the President more than once.

But this Article shall not apply to any person holding the office of President when this Article was proposed by the Congress, and shall not prevent any person who may be holding the office of President, or acting as President, during the term within which this Article becomes operative from holding the office of President or acting as President during the remainder of such term.

Amendment XXI [1933] (REPEAL OF PROHIBITION)

Section 1. The eighteenth article of amendment to the Constitution of the United States is hereby repealed.

Section 2. The transportation or importation into any State, Territory, or possession of the United States for delivery or use therein of intoxicating liquors, in violation of the laws thereof, is hereby prohibited.

Section 3. This article shall be inoperative unless it shall have been ratified as an amendment to the Constitution by conventions in the several States, as provided in the Constitution, within seven years from the date of the submission hereof to the States by the Congress.

Amendment XXII [1951] (TERM OF PRESIDENT)

No person shall be elected to the office of the President more than twice, and no

Amendment XXIII [1961] (WASHINGTON, D.C.)

(Enfranchisement of Voters in Federal Elections)

Section 1. The District constituting the seat of Government of the United States shall appoint in such manner as the Congress may direct:

A number of electors of President and Vice President equal to the whole number of Senators and Representatives in Congress to which the District would be entitled if it were a State, but in no event more than the least populous State; they shall be in addition to those appointed by the States, but they shall be considered, for the purposes of the election of President and Vice President, to be electors appointed by a State; and they shall meet in the District and perform such duties as provided by the twelfth article of amendment.

Section 2. The Congress shall have power to enforce this article by appropriate legislation.

Amendment XXIV
[1964]   (POLL TAX)

Section 1. The right of citizens of the United States to vote in any primary or other election for President or Vice President, for electors for President or Vice President, or for Senator or Representative in Congress, shall not be denied or abridged by the United States or any State by reason of failure to pay any poll tax or other tax.

Section 2. The Congress shall have the power to enforce this article by appropriate legislation.

Amendment XXV
[1967]   (SUCCESSION)

Section 1. In case of the removal of the President from office or his death or resignation, the Vice President shall become President.

Section 2. Whenever there is a vacancy in the office of the Vice President, the President shall nominate a Vice President who shall take the office upon confirmation by a majority vote of both houses of Congress.

Section 3. Whenever the President transmits to the President pro tempore of the Senate and the Speaker of the House of Representatives his written declaration that he is unable to discharge the powers and duties of his office, and until he transmits to them a written declaration to the contrary, such powers and duties shall be discharged by the Vice President as Acting President.

Section 4. Whenever the Vice President and a majority of either the principal officers of the executive departments, or of such other body as Congress may by law provide, transmit to the President pro tempore of the Senate and the Speaker of the House of Representatives their written declaration that the President is unable to discharge the powers and duties of his office, the Vice President shall immediately assume the powers and duties of the office as Acting President.

Thereafter, when the President transmits to the President pro tempore of the Senate and the Speaker of the House of Representatives his written declaration that no inability exists, he shall resume the powers and duties of his office unless the Vice President and a majority of either the principal officers of the executive departments, or of such other body as Congress may by law provide, transmit within four days to the President pro tempore of the Senate and the Speaker of the House of Representatives their written declaration that the President is unable to discharge the powers and duties of his office. Thereupon Congress shall decide the issue, assembling within 48 hours for that purpose if not in session. If the Congress, within 21 days after receipt of the latter written declaration, or, if Congress is not in session, within 21 days after Congress is required to assemble, determines by two-thirds vote of both houses that the President is unable to discharge the powers and duties of his office, the Vice President shall continue to discharge the same as Acting President; otherwise, the President shall resume the power and duties of his office.

Amendment XXVI   (VOTING AT
[1971]   AGE 18)

Section 1. The right of citizens of the United States, who are eighteen years of age or older, to vote shall not be denied or abridged by the United States or any State on account of age.

Section 2. The Congress shall have power to enforce this article by appropriate legislation.

ACKNOWLEDGMENTS

Page 32, From *Skipping Village* by Lois Lenski, Copyright © 1927, renewed 1955 by The Lois Lenski Covey Foundation, Inc. and reprinted by permission of the copyright owners; **32,** "Commuter" from *The Lady Is Cold* by E. B. White, Copyright 1925 by E. B. White, reprinted by permission of Harper & Row, Publishers, Inc.; **32,** Gerald Raftery, "Apartment House," Copyright © by Gerald Raftery, reprinted by permission; **34,** From *Letters From an American Farmer* by J. Hector St. John de Crevecoeur, pp. 35–40, Copyright © 1957 by Elsevier-Dutton Publishing Co., Inc., used by permission; **35,** From *A Nation of Immigrants* by John F. Kennedy, Copyright 1964, reprinted by permission of Harper & Row, Publishers, Inc.; **36,** "Changes in the Populations of Some Cities," from *Newsweek,* May 4, 1981, Copyright 1981 by Newsweek, Inc., all rights reserved, reprinted by permission; **37,** Both charts are reprinted from *U.S. News and World Report,* Copyright 1981 U.S. News & World Report, Inc.; **38,** From Lynda Falkenstein and Lynne Schwab, "Folk Law," *Update,* Fall, 1980, Volume IV, No. 3, p. 10, © 1980 American Bar Association, used by permission; **56,** "Technology Catches Pioneer Cabin Builder," reprinted by permission of the Associated Press; **60,** Reprinted with the permission of Henry Valdespino, Jr.; **83,** "Self-Government Experiment by Students in Scandal," reprinted by permission of the Associated Press; **86,** From *Thomas Jefferson, Champion of the People* by Clara Ingram Judson, Copyright © 1952 by Clara Ingram Judson, used by permission of Follett Publishing Company; **88,** Based on "What Are These Men Doing?" by Jack Harmon, *San Antonio Express-News,* April 20, 1975; **108,** "What a Congressman Must Do for the Folks Back Home," January 10, 1977, reprinted from *U.S. News and World Report,* Copyright 1977 U.S. News & World Report, Inc.; **112,** © 1975 American Heritage Publishing Co., Inc., reprinted by permission from *The American Heritage History of the Congress of the United States;* **116,** Reprint from *Family Weekly,* copyright 1977, 641 Lexington Ave., New York, N.Y. 10022; **136,** From "Obstacle Course on Capitol Hill," by Robert Bendiner, Copyright © 1965 McGraw-Hill Book Company, used with the permission of McGraw-Hill Book Company; **138,** From *Andrew Jackson: Frontier Statesman* by Clara Ingram Judson, Copyright © 1954 by Clara Ingram Judson, used by permission of Follett Publishing Company; **141,** From "Congress Does Not Mirror Population," *San Antonio Express-News,* November 28, 1980; **142,** From "Congressional Rating," *San Antonio Express-News,* April 30, 1981; **143,** Adapted from "Gonzales Has Sound Idea for Congress," *San Antonio Express-News,* May 24, 1981; **144,** From "Don't be Beastly to Congress," *Newsweek,* July 13, 1981, Copyright 1981 by Newsweek, Inc., all rights reserved, reprinted by permission; **144,** From "Automatic Savings," *San Antonio Express-News,* June 17, 1981; **160,** Adapted from *The Vantage Point* by Lyndon Baines Johnson, Copyright © 1971 by HEC Public Affairs Foundation, reprinted by permission of Holt, Rinehart and Winston, Publishers; **168,** Excerpt adapted from pp. 44–50 in *The Presidency* by Gerald W. Johnson, Copyright © 1962 by Gerald W. Johnson, by permission of William Morrow & Company; **170,** Adapted from *In and Out of the White House, from Washington to the Eisenhowers* by Ona Griffin Jeffries, © 1960 by Ona Griffin Jeffries, used with the permission of McIntosh & Otis, Inc., New York; **172,** From "Carter Would Limit Term to Six Years," April 29, 1979, © 1979 by The New York Times Company, reprinted by permission; **172,** Reprint by permission of *Family Weekly,* copyright 1978, 641 Lexington Ave., New York, N.Y. 10022; **172,** Reprint by permission of *Family Weekly,* copyright 1981, 641 Lexington Ave., New York, N.Y. 10022; **173,** From "Plan for 6-year Presidents," *San Antonio Express-News,* November 26, 1979; **174,** Reprint by permission of *Family Weekly,* copyright 1981, 641 Lexington Ave., New York, N.Y. 10022; **174,** Reprinted by permission of the Tribune Company Syndicate, Inc.; **174,** Adapted from "Plan for 6-year Presidents," *San Antonio Express-News,* November 26, 1979; **175,** Based on "It's Time We Had a Woman President," *San Antonio Express-News,* April 20, 1975; **177,** "Teens Back Equal Rights Amendment," *San Antonio Express-News,* August 17, 1978, used with the permission of the Gallup Poll; **194,** From "Power in the Wind," *Newsweek,* February 20, 1978, Copyright 1978 by Newsweek, Inc., all rights reserved, reprinted by permission; **197,** Excerpts taken from *The Writings of George Washington from the Original Manuscript Sources 1745–1799,* U.S. Government Printing Office; **197,** Adapted from pp. 286–292 of *American History Told by Contemporaries,* Vol. XXX, edited by Albert Bushnell Hart, Copyright © The Macmillan Company, New York, used with the permission of Macmillan, Inc.; **200,** From "A Matter of Title," *San Antonio Express-News,* June 16, 1981; **200,** From "Caught by Own People," *San Antonio Express-News,* May 14, 1981; **201,** From "Poll Finds Most Would Take Low-Paying Jobs," *San Antonio Express-News,* April 6, 1981, used with the permission of the Los Angeles Times Service; **202,** From "Loafers, Hondo Needs You" by Vickie Davidson, *San Antonio Express-News,* June 15, 1977; **220,** From "Powell: Justice's Life Lonely, Quiet," August 20, 1976, © 1976 by The New York Times Company, reprinted by permission; **222,** Adapted from *The American Republic* by Richard Hofstadter, William Miller, Daniel Aaron, published by Prentice-Hall, Inc., 1959, Copyright © 1959 by William Miller, used with permission; **224,** From Margaret Stimmann Branson, "Teaching Global Law," *Update,* Fall, 1980, Vol. IV, No. 3, pp. 25–26, © 1980 American Bar Association, used by permission; **226,** From "Female Judges Face Serious Problems," November 15, 1979, © 1979 by The New York Times Company, reprinted by permission; **238,** Adapted from *The Supreme Court of the United States,* U.S. Government Printing Office; **245,** From "Teaching the Judges," *Newsweek,* August 21, 1978, Copyright 1978 by Newsweek, Inc., all rights reserved, reprinted by permission; **250,** Reprint by permission of *Family Weekly,* copyright 1979, 641 Lexington Ave., New York, N.Y. 10022; **251,** Reprint by permission of *Family Weekly,* copyright 1977, 641 Lexington Ave., New York, N.Y. 10022; **252,** Reprint by permission of *Family Weekly,* copyright 1980, 641 Lexington Ave., New York, N.Y. 10022; **252,** Reprint by permission of *Family Weekly,* copyright 1977, 641 Lexington Ave., New York, N.Y. 10022; **253,** "Bad Judges—How to Get Rid of Them," reprinted by permission of the Associated Press; **271,** From "Deterioration of I-80 Is Typical of Interstate System's Problems," June 18, 1978, © 1978 by The New York Times Company, reprinted by permission; **276,** Adapted with permission from "One Day in the Life of a State Trooper" by Gerald Moore, *Reader's Digest,* February 1975; **277,** Adapted from "Answering Texas Welfare Questions," *The Northside Recorder,* San Antonio, Texas, October 16, 1980; **289,** Adapted from "Side Trips: The Women of Walthourville," *New Times,* January 10, 1975, Copyright 1975, reprinted by permission; **293,** Adapted from "Confessions of a Town Councilman" by Richard Lemon, *New York News,* October 21, 1976, Copyright 1976, New York News, Inc., reprinted by permission; **296,** From *The Good Old Days—They Were Terrible!* by Otto L. Bettmann, Copyright © 1974 by Otto L. Bettmann, published by Random House; **298,** From "Cisneros Has a Bash at Trash" by Jack Handley, *San Antonio Express-News,* June 1, 1975; **299,** Adapted with permission from "Policewomen on Patrol," by Virginia Armat, *Reader's Digest,* July 1975; **301,** From "EPA Order Ires Brady" by Joe Fohn, *San Antonio Express-News,* May 12, 1981; **302,** Adapted from "Bureaucrats Tackle Small Town of Brady," *San Antonio Express-News,* May 15, 1981; **302,** From "One Good Idea Merits One Other" by Roddy Stinson, *San Antonio Express-News,* May 17, 1981; **314,** From "The Man from T.R.A.S.H.," *Newsweek,* July 21, 1975, Copyright 1975 by Newsweek, Inc., all rights reserved, reprinted by permission; **324,** Excerpts from "Striking Back at the Super Snoops," *Time,* July 18, 1977, Copyright 1977 Time Inc., all rights reserved, reprinted by permission from TIME; **329,** "Court Protest Issue Battled," reprinted by permission from the Associated Press; **330,** Reprinted with the permission of Jeff Fothergill, Terri Hailey, Kenneth Kirkpatrick, and Herbert Stumberg; **331,** Reprint by permission of *Family Weekly,* copyright 1978, 641 Lexington Ave., New York, N.Y. 10022; **343,** "Your Right to Write" by Morris Udall, January 23, 1978, reprinted from *U.S. News and World Report,* Copyright 1978 U.S. News & World Report, Inc.; **348,** Reprinted with the permission of Jon Alworth; **350,** From "The Injustice of Jury Duty" by Bill Crane, *San Antonio Express-News,* July 22, 1979; **352,** Adapted from "'Rejects' from Jury Share Time, Service" by Edna McGaffey, *San Antonio Express-News,* August 5, 1979; **365,** Adapted from p. 46 in *Our American Government and How It Works,* new revised edition by Wright Patman, Copyright © 1974 by Wright Patman, reprinted by permission of Harper & Row, Publishers, Inc,; **375,** Excerpts from "Is Campaign Oratory a Waste of Breath?" by Paul Douglas, *New York Times Magazine,* October, 19, 1958, © 1958 by The New York Times Company, reprinted by permission; **378,** Adapted from David Crockett, *The Autobiography of David Crockett,* Copyright 1923 by Charles Scribner's Sons, New York, Copyright renewed; **381,** "Election Drew 30-year Low in Voter Percentage," reprinted by permission of the Associated Press; **381,** From "Right to Vote: Who Cares?" by James J. Kilpatrick, *San Antonio Express-News,* December 7, 1977, used by permission of James J. Kilpatrick; **382,** From "The Turned-Off Voter," *Newsweek,* September 13, 1976, Copyright 1976 by Newsweek, Inc., all rights reserved, reprinted by permission; **383,** "Gallup Youth Survey," *San Antonio Express,* October 19, 1977, used with the permission of The Gallup Poll; **402,** Adapted from pp. 23–30 in *The Lobbyists* by James Deakin, reprinted by permission of Public Affairs Press; **408,** Reprint by permission of *Family Weekly,* copyright 1980, 641 Lexington Ave., New York, N.Y. 10022; **409,** Adapted from "Your Role in Politics" by Lamar Smith, *San Antonio Express-News,* November 16, 1980; **410,** From "So You Want to Become a Candidate?" by Marcy Meffert, *San Antonio Light,* February 16, 1978, Northeast Supplement, used with the permission of the *San Antonio Light*; **434,** Adapted from "A Shock Treatment to Cut Youth Crime," May 26, 1978, reprinted by permission of *The Wall Street Journal,* © Dow Jones & Company, Inc., 1978, all rights reserved; **438,** Adapted from *Crisis in Corrections: The Prison Problem* by Janet Harris, copyright © 1973 by McGraw-Hill, used with the permission of McGraw-Hill Book Company; **440,** Adapted from "'Scared Straight' Success Overrated" by Walt Menninger, *San Antonio Express-News,* December 14, 1980, used with the permission of Universal Press Syndicate; **441,** From *Newsweek,* December 23, 1974, Copyright 1974 by Newsweek, Inc., all rights reserved, reprinted by permission, adapted from "Sentences with Sense," *Reader's Digest,* April, 1975; **442,** Example 4 is taken from "Fitting Punishment to Crime," *Reader's Digest,* © Copyrighted 1974, the *Courier-Journal,* reprinted with permission from the *Louisville Courier-Journal* and from the October, 1974, *Reader's Digest*; **442,** Example 5 is taken from "Judge Orders College 'Term'," reprinted by permission of the Associated Press; **442,** Example 6 is taken from "Judge Sets Punishments to Fit Crimes," reprinted by permission of the Associated Press; **443,** both charts are taken from "Americans Say Prison Life Not Harsh Enough," reprinted by permission of the Associated Press; **464,** From "A Father on Trial for What His Son Did," copyright © 1972, Time, Inc., reprinted with permission; **468,** From "Esquivel: Courtrooms Must Admit News Media" by Frank White, *San Antonio Express-News,* June 14, 1981; **469,** Excerpts taken from "Television Gets Foot in Door of Courts," January 30, 1981, © 1981 by The New York Times Company, reprinted by permission; **469,** From "Cameras Interfere with Court Decorum," *San Antonio Express-News,* March 6, 1981; **470,** From "Esquivel: Courtrooms Must Admit News Media" by Frank White, *San Antonio Express-News,* June 14, 1981; **470,** Adapted from "Court Cameras Get Endorsement" by Harry S. Lipsig, Letter to the Editor, *San Antonio Express-News,* April 1, 1981; **471,** From "Cameras in District Courtrooms Decision up to Supreme Court" by David Guarino, *San Antonio Express-News,* February 7, 1981; **494,** Excerpts from *Economic Features of Every Society* by Lawrence Abbott are reprinted by permission of Harcourt Brace Jovanovich, Inc., Copyright © 1960 by Harcourt Brace Jovanovich, Inc.; **496,** Adapted from *The Americans: A History of the United States* by the staff of the Social Studies Curriculum Center at Carnegie-Mellon University, Copyright © 1970, used with the permission of Holt, Rinehart, & Winston, Publishers; **497,** Adapted from Samuel Gompers, "The American Labor Movement, Its Makeup, Achievements, and Aspirations" as reprinted in *Free Government in the Making* by Alpheus Thomas Mason, published by Oxford University Press, New York, 1949; **499,** *The World Almanac & Book of Facts,* 1981 edition, Copyright © Newspaper Enterprise Association, 1980, New York, N.Y. 10166; **525,** Adapted from "A New Way to Score with Lenders" by Jeremy Main, *Money Magazine,* February 1977, by special permission, © 1977, Time Inc., all rights reserved; **532,** Reprint by permission of *Family Weekly,* copyright 1981, 641 Lexington Ave., New York, N.Y. 10022; **534,** Reprint by permission of *Family Weekly,* copyright 1981, 641 Lexington Ave., New York, N.Y. 10022.

Photo Credits

Title page: Whitney Museum; *Unit Opener 1:* 11: Sybil Shackman/Monkmeyer. *Chapter 1:* 12–13: (l to r) Sam Falk/Monkmeyer, David Strickler/Monkmeyer, Tim Eagan/Woodfin Camp; 15: Tim Eagan/Woodfin Camp; 17: Jeffrey Foxx/Woodfin Camp; 19: Arthur Grace/Sygma; 20: William Hubbell/Woodfin Camp; 21: Tim Eagan/Woodfin Camp; 22: William Hubbell/Woodfin Camp; 26: Sybil Shelton/Monkmeyer; 27: Albert Moldvay/Woodfin Camp; 28: Gerhard Gscheidle/The Image Bank; 29: Daniel Brody/Stock, Boston; 31: William Hubbell/Woodfin Camp; 34: Edward Hicks, "Residence of David Twining"/Abby Aldrich Rockefeller Collection, Williamsburg, Virginia. *Chapter 2:* 40–41: (l to r) Michael J. Pettypool/Uniphoto, Marc & Evelyn Bernheim/Woodfin Camp, Serge Lemoine/Sygma; 43, 44: The Bettmann Archive; 46: Arthur Grace/Stock, Boston; 47: (l) Freda Leinwand/Monkmeyer, (r) Arthur Grace/Sygma; 48, 50: Culver Pictures; 51: Scala; 52: Culver Pictures; 55: The Bettmann Archive; 58: Essex Institute, Salem, MA. *Chapter 3:* 64–64: (l to r) Mimi Forsyth/Monkmeyer, Arthur Grace/Sygma, Owen Franken/Sygma; 67: (tl) Owen Franken/Stock, Boston, (tr) Arthur Grace/Sygma, (b) Frank Wilcox/The Image Bank; 68: Sybil Shelton/Monkmeyer; 69, 73: Culver Pictures; 74: Joseph Martin/Scala; 75: Culver Pictures; 76: William S. Weems/Woodfin Camp; 78: Paul Conklin/Monkmeyer; 79: (t) Bill Fitz-Patrick/The White House, (b) Bill Fitz-Patrick/The White House; 81: The Bettmann Archive; 82: Werner Wolff/Black Star; 86: Yale University Art Gallery. *Unit Opener 2:* 93: Craig Aurness. *Chapter 4:* 94–95: (l to r) Wally McNamee/Woodfin Camp, Dennis Brack/Black Star, Robert Sherbow/Uniphoto; 98: Jason Laure/Woodfin Camp; 99: (t) Tony Karody/Sygma, (b) J. P. Laffont/Sygma; 100: UPI; 103: Shepard Sherbell/Echave & Associates; 105: Arthur Grace/Sygma; 107: (t) Shepard Sherbell/Echave & Associates, (b) UPI; 108: Tom Tracy/Black Star; 112: Corcoran Gallery, Washington, D.C. *Chapter 5:* 118–119: Wally McNamee/Woodfin Camp, 119 (r): Bert Miller/Black Star; 120: Wally McNamee/Woodfin Camp; 121: Arthur Grace/Sygma; 122: Wally McNamee/Woodfin Camp; 124: Donald Patterson/Stock, Boston; 125: (t) Shepard Sherbell/Echave & Associates, (b) UPI; 128: (t) Shepard Sherbell/Echave & Associates, (c) Divison of Tourism and Economic Development, State of Alaska—Juneau; 129: Sylvia Johnson/Woodfin Camp; 131: Shepard Sherbell/Echave & Associates; 133: David Hume Kennerly/Liaison; 135: Tom McHugh/Photo Researchers; 138: Chicago Historical Society; 143: by permission of Johnny Hart and Field Enterprises, Inc. *Unit Opener 3:* 147: Wally McNamee/Woodfin Camp. *Chapter 6:* 148: (l) J. P. Laffont/Sygma; 148–149: Wally McNamee/Woodfin Camp; 151: Wide World; 153: Bill Fitz-Patrick/The White House; 155: Black Star; 156: Cynthia Johnson/The White House; 157: Wally McNamee/Woodfin Camp; 158: Leif Skoogfors/Woodfin Camp; 160: Wally McNamee/Woodfin Camp; 161, 163: Wide World; 164: Wally McNamee/Woodfin Camp; 166: Wide World; 167: United Nations; 170: Smithsonian Institute. *Chapter 7:* 178–179: Wally McNamee/Woodfin Camp, Elizabeth Resnick/DPI, Hugh Rogers/Monkmeyer; 181: Jan Lukes/Photo Researchers; 182: Jason Laure/Woodfin Camp; 184: (t) Rhoda Sidney/Monkmeyer, (b) Sybil Shelton/Monkmeyer; 185: USDA; 187: David Valdez/HUD: 190: Marvin Newman/Woodfin Camp; 196: The Bettmann Archive; 199: GOOSEMYER by Parker & Wilder, © Field Enterprises, Inc., Courtesy of Field Newspaper Syndicate; 200: CROCK by Rechin and Parker, © Field Enterprises, Inc., Courtesy of Field Newspaper Syndicate; 201: "Reprinted by permission of the Chicago Tribune—New York News Syndicate, Inc." *Unit Opener 4:* 205: Shepard Sherbell/Echave & Associates. *Chapter 8:* 206–207: (l to r) Wally McNamee/Woodfin Camp, Craig Aurness/Woodfin Camp, Robin Forbes/The Image Bank; 208: Dennis Brack/Black Star; 210: Miriam Reinhard/Photo Researchers; 211: David Plowden/Photo Researchers; 212: Dennis Brack/Black Star; 213, 215: Wide World; 216: New York Times; 217: Wide World; 219 Larry Mulvehill/Photo Researchers; 222: The Bettmann Archive. *Chapter 9:* 228–229: (l to r) Robin Forbes/The Image Bank, William Hubbell/Woodfin Camp, Mimi Forsyth/Monkmeyer; 230: (l) Wide World, (r) Culver Pictures; 232, 233: Wide World; 235: Don Carl Steffen/Photo Researchers; 236: UPI; 237: Mimi Forsyth/Monkmeyer; 238: Wide World; 241: Culver Pictures; 243: Wide World; 244: Ted Streshinsky/The Image Bank; 248: National Portrait Gallery. *Unit Opener 5:* 255: Wally McNamee/Woodfin Camp. *Chapter 10:* 256–257: (l to r) Steven L. Borns/Black Star, Adam Woolfitt/Woodfin Camp, Cliff Fleurner/The Image Bank; 258: (l) Edward Lettau/Photo Researchers, (r) Jeff Lowenthal/Woodfin Camp; 259 Wide World; 260: Norman Skarewitz/Black Star; 264: Russ Kinne/Photo Researchers; 265: Jeff Lowenthal/Woodfin Camp; 266: Wide World; 267: Don Getsug/Photo Researchers; 208: Bruce Roberts/Photo Researchers; 274: The Bettmann Archive. *Chapter 11:* 280–281: (l to r) Hans Wendler/The Image Bank, Geoffrey Gove/Photo Researchers, Larry Mulvehill/Photo Researchers; 283: David Barnes/Photo Researchers; 284: Hugh Rogers/Monkmeyer; 285: Freda Leinwand; 288: Hugh Rogers/Monkmeyer; 291: (t) David Barnes/Photo Researchers, (b) Rod Hanna/Black Star; 293: Jame Theologos/Monkmeyer; 296: Culver Pictures. *Unit Opener 6:* 305: Geoffrey Gove/The Image Bank. *Chapter 12:* 306–307: (l to r) Owen Franken/Stock, Boston, Sam C. Pierson/Photo Researchers, Fred Maroon/Photo Researchers; 309: Frank Johnston/Black Star; 311: Wide World; 312: Martin A. Levick/Black Star; 313: John Running; 315: Jan Lukas; 317: Edward Lettau/Photo Researchers; 319: (l) Culver Pictures, (b) Bruce Roberts/Photo Researchers; 320: Dennis Brack/Black Star; 323: Freda Leinwand/Monkmeyer; 326: Culver Pictures. *Chapter 13:* 332–333: (l to r) Michael Manheim/Photo Researchers, Mimi Forsyth/Monkmeyer, Ted Spiegel; 335: (t) The Bettmann Archive, (b) Wide World; 336: (t) Christopher Springman/Black Star, (b) James Wilson/Woodfin Camp; 338: Jeffrey Foxx/Woodfin Camp; 339: John Launois/Black Star; 341: Rhode Galyn/Photo Researchers; 346: Southern Pacific Co.; 349: (t) GOOSEMYER by Parker & Wilder, © Field Enterprises, Inc., Courtesy of Field Newspaper Syndicate, (c) By permission of Johnny Hart and Field Enterprises, Inc., (b) "Reprinted by permission of the Chicago Tribune–New York News Syndicate, Inc." *Unit Opener 7:* 355: Jan Lukas/Photo Researchers. *Chapter 14:* 356–357: (l to r) Roger Clark, Jr./Photo Researchers, Peter Southwick/Stock, Boston, Dennis Brack/Black Star; 358: Will Blanche/DPI; 359: Owen Franken/Stock, Boston; 361: A. M. Wettach/Black Star; 364: (t) Culver Pictures, (b) Leif Skoogfors/Photo Researchers; 366: (c) Sam Pierson, Jr./Photo Researchers, (b) Wide World; 367: Wide World; 369: Olivier Rebbot/Woodfin Camp; 371: Sam Pierson, Jr./Photo Researchers; 372: Lester Sloan/Woodfin Camp; 373: Mimi Forsyth/Monkmeyer; 374: John Marmaras/Woodfin Camp; 378: Culver Pictures; 382: STRICTLY BUSINESS by Dale McFeatters, © Field Enterprises, Inc., Courtesy of Field Newspaper Syndicate; 383: Reprinted by permission of NEA, Inc.; *Chapter 15:* 384–385: (l to r) James Wilson/Woodfin Camp, Mike Mazzachi/Stock, Boston, Ken Hawkins/Sygma; 386: Wide World; 387: Charles Gatewood/Magnum; 389: David Hiser/The Image Bank; 391: Bill Apton/The Image Bank; 392: Shepard Sherbell/Echave & Associates; 394: (t) Chamber of Commerce of the United States, (b) Myron Wood/Photo Researchers; 395: Bill Mahan/Photo Researchers; 396: Penelope Breese/Liaison; 397: Dennis Brack/Black Star; 402: Mimi Forsyth/Monkmeyer; 406: UPI. *Unit Opener 8:* 413: Martin Levick/Black Star. *Chapter 16:* 414–415: (l to r) Ellis Herwig/Stock, Boston, Shepard Sherbell/Echave & Associates, Ken Lax/The Image Bank; 416: John Running/Black Star; 418: Sepp Seitz/Woodfin Camp; 419: (b) Josephus Daniels/Photo Researchers; 421: Lawrence Frank; 423: John Running/Black Star; 424: Susan McElhinney/Woodfin Camp; 426: (t) Stephen Feldman/Photo Researchers, (b) J. P. Laffont/Sygma; 428: David Plowden/Photo

INDEX

Italicized page numbers refer to illustrations. **Boldface** page numbers refer to charts of tables.